Communications
in Computer and Information Science 152

Gang Shen   Xiong Huang (Eds.)

Advanced Research on Computer Science and Information Engineering

International Conference, CSIE 2011
Zhengzhou, China, May 21-22, 2011
Proceedings, Part I

 Springer

Volume Editors

Gang Shen
International Science & Education Researcher Association
Wuhan Section, Wuhan, China
E-mail: 1073648534@qq.com

Xiong Huang
International Science & Education Researcher Association
Wuhan Section, Wuhan, China
E-mail: 499780828@qq.com

ISSN 1865-0929   e-ISSN 1865-0937
ISBN 978-3-642-21401-1   e-ISBN 978-3-642-21402-8
DOI 10.1007/978-3-642-21402-8
Springer Heidelberg Dordrecht London New York

Library of Congress Control Number: Applied for

CR Subject Classification (1998): C.2, I.2, H.4, H.3, D.2, I.4

Typesetting: Camera-ready by author, data conversion by Scientific Publishing Services, Chennai, India

Printed on acid-free paper

Springer is part of Springer Science+Business Media (www.springer.com)

Preface

The International Science & Education Researcher Association (ISER) puts its focus on the study and exchange of academic achievements of international researchers, and it also promotes educational reform in the world. In addition, it serves as academic discussion and communication platform, which is beneficial for education and for scientific research, aiming to stimulate researchers in their work.

The CSIE conference is an integrated event concentrating on computer science and information engineering. The goal of the conference is to provide researchers working in the field of computer science and information engineering based on modern information technology with a free forum to share new ideas, innovations, and solutions. CSIE 2011 was held during May 21-22, in Zhengzhou, China, and was co-sponsored by the ISER, Beijing Gireida Education Co. Ltd., the and Yellow River Conservancy Technical Institute, China. Renowned keynote speakers were invited to deliver talks, and all participants had the chance to discuss their work with the speakers face to face.

In these proceedings, you can learn more about the field of computer science and information engineering from the contributions of international researchers. The main role of the proceedings is to be used as a means of exchange of information for those working in this area. The Organizing Committee made great efforts to meet the high standard of Springer's *Communications in Computer and Information Science* series. Firstly, poor-quality papers were rejected after being reviewed by anonymous referees. Secondly, meetings were held periodically for reviewers to exchange opinions and suggestions. Finally, the organizing team held several preliminary sessions before the conference. Through the efforts of numerous individuals and departments, the conference was successful and fruitful.

During the organization, we received help from different people, departments, and institutions. Here, we would like to extend our sincere thanks to the publishers of CCIS, Springer, for their kind and enthusiastic assistance and support of our conference. Secondly, the authors should also be thanked for their submissions. Thirdly, the hard work of the Program Committee, the Program Chairs, and the reviewers is greatly appreciated.

In conclusion, it was the team effort of all these people that made our conference a success. We welcome any suggestions that may help improve the conference in the future and we look forward to seeing all of you at CSIE 2012.

March 2011   Gang Shen

Organization

Honorary Chairs

Chen Bin   Beijing Normal University, China
Hu Chen   Peking University, China
Chunhua Tan   Beijing Normal University, China
Helen Zhang   University of Munich, Germany

Program Committee Chairs

Xiong Huang   International Science & Education Researcher Association, China
Li Ding   International Science & Education Researcher Association, China
Zhihua Xu   International Science & Education Researcher Association, China

Organizing Chairs

ZongMing Tu   Beijing Gireida Education Co. Ltd., China
Jijun Wang   Beijing Spon Technology Research Institution, China
Quan Xiang   Beijing Prophet Science and Education Research Center, China

Publication Chair

Gang Shen   International Science & Education Researcher Association, China
Xiong Huang   International Science & Education Researcher Association, China

International Program Committee

Sally Wang   Beijing Normal University, China
Lin Chen   Yellow River Conservancy Technical Institute, China
Guangchao Du   Yellow River Conservancy Technical Institute, China
Jian Hu   Yellow River Conservancy Technical Institute, China
Kun Shang   Yellow River Conservancy Technical Institute, China
Xinfa Dong   Yellow River Conservancy Technical Institute, China
Jianhai Ye   Yellow River Conservancy Technical Institute, China
Aiping Ding   Yellow River Conservancy Technical Institute, China
Xiuchi Hu   Yellow River Conservancy Technical Institute, China

Jianling Tan	Yellow River Conservancy Technical Institute, China
Yongxia Tao	Yellow River Conservancy Technical Institute, China
Huili Yang	Yellow River Conservancy Technical Institute, China
Ge Wang	Yellow River Conservancy Technical Institute, China

Co-sponsored by

International Science & Education Researcher Association, China
Yellow River Conservancy Technical Institute, China
VIP Information Conference Center, China

Reviewers

Chunlin Xie	Wuhan University of Science and Technology, China
Lin Qi	Hubei University of Technology, China
Xiong Huang	International Science & Education Researcher Association, China
Gang Shen	International Science & Education Researcher Association, China
Xiangrong Jiang	Wuhan University of Technology, China
Li Hu	Linguistic and Linguistic Education Association, China
Moon Hyan	Sungkyunkwan University, Korea
Guangwen	South China University of Technology, China
Jack H. Li	George Mason University, USA
Marry Y. Feng	University of Technology Sydney, Australia
Feng Quan	Zhongnan University of Finance and Economics, China
Peng Ding	Hubei University, China
Song Lin	International Science & Education Researcher Association, China
XiaoLie Nan	International Science & Education Researcher Association, China
Zhi Yu	International Science & Education Researcher Association, China
Xue Jin	International Science & Education Researcher Association, China
Zhihua Xu	International Science & Education Researcher Association, China
Wu Yang	International Science & Education Researcher Association, China
Qin Xiao	International Science & Education Researcher Association, China

Weifeng Guo	International Science & Education Researcher Association, China
Li Hu	Wuhan University of Science and Technology, China
Zhong Yan	Wuhan University of Science and Technology, China
Haiquan Huang	Hubei University of Technology, China
Xiao Bing	Wuhan University, China
Brown Wu	Sun Yat-Sen University, China

Table of Contents – Part I

Table of Contents – Part II

The Existence of Analytic Solutions of a Functional Differential Equation with State Dependent Argument

Lingxia Liu

Department of Mathematics, Weifang University,
Weifang, Shandong 261061, P.R. China
llxmath@126.com

Abstract. In this paper the existence of analytic solutions of a functional differential equation with state dependent argument is studied. We obtain results of analytic solutions in the case of α at resonance, and the case of α near resonance under the Brjuno condition.

Keywords: analytic solution; *Schröder* transformation; resonance; Brjuno condition.

1 Introduction

In the last few years there has been a growing interest in functional differential equations with state dependent delay. Functional differential equation of the form $x'(t) = f(x(\sigma(t)))$ has been studied by many authors. In [1-3], analytic solutions of the state dependent functional equations $x'(z) = x(x(z))$, $x'(z) = x^{[m]}(z)$ and

$$x'(z) = x(az + bx(z)), \ a, b \in C, \ a \neq 1, b \neq 0 \tag{1}$$

are found. As in [3], let $y(z) = az + bx(z)$, then $x(z) = (y(z) - az)/b$, $x'(z) = (y'(z) - a)/b$, so Eq.(1) change into

$$y'(z) - a = y(y(z)) - ay(z), \tag{2}$$

Let $y(z) = g(\beta g^{-1}(z))$, then Eq.(2) is reduced to the auxiliary equation

$$\beta g'(\beta z) = g'(z) \left[g(\beta^2 z) - ag(\beta z) + a \right], z \in C, \tag{3}$$

where iteration of the unknown function is not involved but an indeterminate complex β needs to be discussed. In this paper, we need to find invertible analytic solutions of the Eq.(3) for possible choices of β. When the complex β in (3) is not on the unit circle in **C** or β lies on the unit circle in **C** but satisfies the Diophantine condition: $|\mu| = 1$, μ *is not a root of unity, and* $\log \dfrac{1}{|\mu^n - 1|} \leq T \log n$, $n = 2, 3, \cdots$, *for some positive constant* T. The existence of analytic solutions of (3) was given in [3]. Since then, we

G. Shen and X. Huang (Eds.): CSIE 2011, Part I, CCIS 152, pp. 1–7, 2011.
© Springer-Verlag Berlin Heidelberg 2011

have been striving to give a result of analytic solutions for chose β near a root of the unity, i.e., neither being roots of the unity nor satisfying the Diophantine condition. The Brjuno condition provides such a chance for us. In this paper, we consider the analytic solutions of Eq.(3) satisfying the condition

$$g(0) = (\beta - a)/(1 - a),\tag{4}$$

where the complex β satisfies the following hypotheses:

(H1) $\mu = e^{2\pi i\theta}$, where $\theta \in \mathbf{R}\backslash\mathbf{Q}$ is a Brjuno number [4, 5], i.e., $B(\theta) = \sum_{k=0}^{\infty} \frac{\log q_{k+1}}{q_k} < \infty$,

where $\{p_k / q_k\}$ denotes the sequence of partial fraction of the continued fraction expansion of θ, and is said to satisfy the Brjuno condition.

(H2) $\alpha = e^{2\pi i q/p}$ for some integers $p \in \mathbf{N}$ with $p \geq 2$ and $q \in \mathbf{Z}\backslash\{0\}$ and $\alpha \neq e^{2\pi i l/k}$ for all $1 \leq k \leq p - 1$ and $l \in \mathbf{Z}\backslash\{0\}$.

Observe that β is a p-th unit root (or called p-order resonance) in the case of (H2), while the case (H1) contains a part of α near resonance.

A change of variable further transforms (3) into the differential-difference equation

$$\phi'(w + \alpha) = \phi'(w)[\phi(w + 2\alpha) - a\phi(w + \alpha) + a],\tag{5}$$

where α is a complex constant. The solution of this equation has properties similar to those of (3). If Eq. (5) has invertible solution $\phi(w)$, then we can show that $x(z) = \frac{1}{b}\left[\phi(\phi^{-1}(z) + \alpha) - az\right]$ is an analytic solution of (1).

2   Analytic Solutions of Auxiliary Equation

When β is on the unit circle but not a root of unity, the analysis of the convergence of $g(z)$ is complicated. In [2] [3], the related questions as β satisfies Diophantine condition were discussed. In the section, we will consider the existence of analytic solution for the equation (3) under the Brjuno condition which is weaker than the Diophantine condition.

As stated in [6], for a real number θ we let θ denote its integer part and let $\{\theta\} = \theta - [\theta]$. Then every national number θ has a unique expression of the Gauss' continued fraction $\theta = a_0 + \theta_0 = a_0 + \frac{1}{a_1 + \theta_1} = \ldots$, denoted simply by $\theta = [a_0, a_1, \ldots, a_n, \ldots]$, where a_j's and θ_j's are calculated by the algorithm: (a) $a_0 = [\theta]$, $\theta_0 = \{\theta\}$ and (b) $a_n = \left[\frac{1}{\theta_{n-1}}\right]$, $\theta_n = \left\{\frac{1}{\theta_{n-1}}\right\}$ for all $n \geq 1$. Define the sequences $(p_n)_{n\in\mathbb{N}}$ and $(q_n)_{n\in\mathbb{N}}$ as follows $q_{-2} = 1, q_{-1} = 0, q_n = a_n q_{n-1} + q_{n-2}$; $p_{-2} = 0, p_{-1} = 1, p_n = a_n p_{n-1} + p_{n-2}$. It is easy to show that $p_n / q_n = [a_0, a_1, \ldots, a_n]$. Thus, for every $\theta \in \mathbf{R}\backslash\mathbf{Q}$ we associate, using its convergence, an arithmetical function $B(\theta) = \sum_{n \geq 0} \frac{\log q_{n+1}}{q_n}$. We say that θ is a Brjuno number or that it satisfies Brjuno condition if $B(\theta) < +\infty$. The Brjuno condition is weaker than the Diophantine condition. For example, if $a_{n+1} \leq ce^{a_n}$ for all $n \geq 0$, where $c > 0$ is a constant, then $\theta = [a_0, a_1, ..., a_n, ...]$ is a Brjuno number but is not a Diophantine number. So, the case (H1) contains both Diophantine condition and a part of μ ``near'' resonance.

Let $\theta \in \mathbf{R} \backslash \mathbf{Q}$ and $(q_n)_{n \in \mathbb{N}}$ be the sequence of partial denominators of the Gauss's continued fraction for θ. As in [6], let $A_k = \{n \geq 0 \mid \|n\theta\| \leq \frac{1}{8q_k}\}$, $E_k = \max(q_k, \frac{q_{k+1}}{4})$, $\eta_k = \frac{q_k}{E_k}$. Let A_k^* be the set of integers $j \geq 0$ such that either $j \in A_k$ or for some j_1 and j_2 in A_k, with $j_2 - j_1 < E_k$, one has $j_1 < j < j_2$ and q_k divide $j - j_1$. For any integer $n \geq 0$, define

$$l_k(n) = \max\left((1 + \eta_k)\frac{n}{q_k} - 2, \ (m_n \eta_k + n)\frac{1}{q_k} - 1\right), \quad \text{where} \quad m_n = \max\{j \mid 0 \leq j \leq n, j \in A_k^*\}. \text{ We then}$$

define function $h_k : \mathbf{N} \rightarrow \mathbf{R}_+$ as follows: $\begin{cases} \frac{m_n + \eta_k n}{q_k} - 1, & \text{if } m_n + q_k \in A_k^*, \\ l_k(n), & \text{if } m_n + q_k \notin A_k^*. \end{cases}$ Let

$g_k(n) := \max\left(h_k(n), [n/q_k]\right)$, and define $k(n)$ by the condition $q_{k(n)} \leq n \leq q_{k(n)+1}$. Clearly, $k(n)$ is non-decreasing. Then we are able to state the following result:

Lemma 1. (Davie's Lemma [7]) Let $K(n) = n \log 2 + \sum_{k=0}^{k(n)} g_k(n) \log(2q_{k+1})$. Then

(a) There is a universal constant $\gamma > 0$ (independent of n and θ) such that

$$K(n) \leq n\left(\sum_{k=0}^{k(n)} \frac{\log q_{k+1}}{q_k} + \gamma\right),$$

(b) $K(n_1) + K(n_2) \leq K(n_1 + n_2)$ for all n_1 and n_2, and (c) $-\log|\alpha^n| - 1 \leq K(n) - K(n-1)$.

Theorem 1. Suppose (H1) holds, then for any complex number $\eta \neq 0$, equation (3) has a solution of the form

$$g(z) = \frac{\beta - a}{1 - a} + \eta z + \sum_{n=2}^{\infty} b_n z^n, \tag{6}$$

which is analytic on a neighborhood of the origin.

Proof. We seek a solution of (3) in a power series of the form (6), substituting (6) into (3), we see that

$$\beta(\beta^n - 1)(n+1)b_{n+1} = \sum_{k=0}^{n-1} (k+1)(\beta^{2(n-k)} - a\beta^{n-k})b_{k+1}b_{n-k}, n \in \mathbf{Z}^+. \tag{7}$$

in a unique manner. Furthermore, since $0 \leq k \leq n-1$, we see that

$$\left|\frac{(\beta^{2(n-k)} - a\beta^{n-k})(k+1)}{\beta(n+1)}\right| \leq 1 + |a| := M, n \in \mathbf{Z}^+. \tag{8}$$

Then we have

$$|b_{n+1}| \leq \frac{M}{|\beta^n - 1|} \sum_{k=0}^{n-1} |b_{k+1}| \cdot |b_{n-k}|, n \in \mathbf{Z}^+. \tag{9}$$

Now we define a sequence $\{B_n\}_{n=0}^{\infty}$ by $B_0 = 0$, $B_1 = \eta$ and $B_{n+1} = M \sum_{k=0}^{n-1} B_{k+1} B_{n-k}$, $n = 1, 2, \cdots$. Now if we define

$$G(z) = \sum_{n=1}^{\infty} B_n z^n, \tag{10}$$

Then $G^2(z) = \sum_{n=2}^{\infty} (B_1 B_{n-1} + B_2 B_{n-2} + \cdots + B_{n-1} B_1) z^n = \sum_{n=1}^{\infty} (B_1 B_n + B_2 B_{n-1} + \cdots + B_n B_1) z^{n+1} = \frac{1}{M} \sum_{n=1}^{\infty} B_{n+1} z^{n+1}$

$= \frac{1}{M} (G(z) - |\eta| Z)$. So $G(z) = \frac{1}{2M} \left[1 \pm \sqrt{1 - 4M |\eta| z} \right]$. Because $G(0) = 0$, then

$$G(z) = \frac{1}{2M} \left[1 - \sqrt{1 - 4M |\eta| z} \right], \tag{11}$$

which converges for $|z| \leq \frac{1}{4M |\eta|}$, so the series (11) converges on a neighborhood of the origin. Hence there is a constant $T > 0$ such that $B_n \leq T^n$, $n = 1, 2, \cdots$.

Now, we can deduce, by induction, that $|b_n| \leq B_n e^{K(n-1)}$, $n \geq 1$, where $K : \mathbf{N} \to \mathbf{R}$ is defined in Lemma 1. In fact $|b_1| = |\eta| = B_1$. For inductive proof we assume that $|b_j| \leq B_j e^{K(j-1)}$, $j \leq n-1$. From (9) and Lemma 1 we know $|b_{n+1}| \leq \frac{M}{|\beta^n - 1|} \sum_{k=0}^{n-1} B_{k+1} e^{K(k)} \cdot B_{n-k} e^{K(n-k-1)}$

$\leq \frac{e^{K(n-1)}}{|\beta^n - 1|} B_{n+1}$. Note that $K(k) + K(n-k-1) \leq K(n-1) \leq K(n) + \log |\alpha^n - 1|$, then $|b_{n+1}| \leq B_{n+1} e^{K(n)}$ as required. Note that $k(n) \leq n(B(\theta) + \gamma)$ for some universal constant $\gamma > 0$. Then $|b_n| \leq T^n e^{(n-1)(B(\theta)+\gamma)}$, that is, $\limsup_{n \to \infty} (|b_n|)^{\frac{1}{n}} \leq \limsup_{n \to \infty} (T^n e^{(n-1)(B(\theta)+\gamma)})^{\frac{1}{n}} = T e^{B(\theta)+\gamma}$. This implies that the convergence radius of (6) is at least $(Te^{B(\theta)+\gamma})^{-1}$. This completes the proof.

In case (H$_2$) the constant β is not only on the unit circle in $\mathbf{C}$, but also resonant of the order p. In such a case Diophantine condition or Brjuno condition is not satisfied. Let $\{C_n\}_{n=1}^{\infty}$ be a sequence defined by $C_1 = |\eta|$,

$$C_{n+1} = \Gamma M \sum_{k=0}^{n-1} C_{k+1} C_{n-k}, n \in Z^+, \tag{12}$$

where $\Gamma = \max \left\{ 1, |\beta^n - 1|^{-1}, n = 1, 2, \cdots p-1 \right\}$, M is defined in Theorem 1.

Theorem 2. Suppose (H2) holds. Let $\{b_n\}_{n=0}^{\infty}$ be determined recursively by $b_0 = (\beta - a)(1 - a)$, $b_1 = \eta$, and

$$\beta(\beta^n - 1)(n+1) b_{n+1} = V(n, \beta), n \in \mathbf{Z}^+, \tag{13}$$

where $V(n, \beta) = \sum_{k=0}^{n-1}(k+1)(\beta^{2(n-k)} - a\beta^{n-k})b_{k+1}b_{n-k}$. If $V(sp, \beta) = 0$ for all $s = 1, 2, \cdots$, then Eq.(3) has an analytic solution $g(z)$ in a neighborhood of the origin such that $g(0) = (\beta - a)/(1 - a)$, $g'(0) = \eta$, and $g^{(sp+1)}(0) = (sp+1)!\eta_{sp+1}$, where all $\eta_{sp+1}'s$ are arbitrary constants satisfying the inequality $|\eta_{sp+1}| \leq C_{sp+1}$ and the sequence $\{C_n\}_{n=1}^{\infty}$ is defined in (12). Otherwise, if $V(sp, \beta) \neq 0$ for some $s = 1, 2, \cdots$, then the Eq.(3) has no analytic solutions in any neighborhood of the origin.

Proof. As in the proof of Theorem 1, we seek a power series solution of (3) of the form (6), where the equality in (7) is indispensable. If $V(sp, \beta) \neq 0$ for some natural numbers s, the equality in (7) does not hold for $n = sp$. This is because $\beta^{sp} - 1 = 0$, then such a circumstance Eq.(3) has no formal solutions. When $V(sp, \beta) = 0$ for all natural numbers s, for each s the corresponding b_{sp+1} in (7) has infinitely many choices in $\mathbf{C}$, that is, the series (6) define a family of solutions with infinitely many parameters. Choose $b_{sp+1} = \eta_{sp+1}$ arbitrary such that $|\eta_{sp+1}| = C_{sp+1}, s = 1, 2, \cdots$, where C_{sp+1} is defined by (12). Now we prove the power series solution (6) converges in a neighborhood of the origin. Note that $|\beta^n - 1|^{-1} \leq \Gamma$ for $n \neq sp$, then

$$|b_{n+1}| \leq \Gamma M \sum_{k=0}^{n-1}|b_{k+1}| \cdot |b_{n-k}|, \quad n \neq sp, s = 1, 2, \cdots. \tag{14}$$

Note that the equation

$$H^2(z) - \frac{1}{\Gamma M}H(z) + \frac{1}{\Gamma M}|\eta|z = 0 \tag{15}$$

has a solution $H(z) = \frac{1}{2\Gamma M}\left[1 - \sqrt{1 - 4\Gamma M |\eta| z}\right]$, which is analytic on $B(0; \frac{1}{4\Gamma M |\eta|})$, so $H(z)$ converges on a neighborhood of the origin. Let $w(z) = \sum_{n=1}^{\infty} C_n z^n$, then

$$w^2(z) = \sum_{n=2}^{\infty}(C_1 C_{n-1} + C_2 C_{n-2} + \cdots + C_{n-1}C_1)z^n = \sum_{n=1}^{\infty}(C_1 C_n + C_2 C_{n-1} + \cdots + C_n C_1)z^{n+1}$$

$$= \frac{1}{\Gamma M}\sum_{n=1}^{\infty} C_{n+1} z^{n+1} = \frac{1}{\Gamma M}(w(z) - |\eta| Z).$$

i.e.,

$$w^2(z) - \frac{1}{\Gamma M}w(z) + \frac{1}{\Gamma M}|\eta|z = 0. \tag{16}$$

From (15) and (16) we see that $w(z) = H(z) = \sum_{n=1}^{\infty} C_n z^n$, so $w(z)$ is converges on a neighborhood of the origin. Moreover, by induction we can easily prove $|b_n| \leq C_n, n = 1, 2, \cdots$. So the series (6) converges on a neighborhood of the origin.

3 Existence of Analytic Solutions

Theorem 3. Under the conditions of Theorem 1 or 2, the equation (1) has an analytic solution of the form

$$x(z) = \frac{1}{b} g(\beta g^{-1}(z)) - \frac{a}{b} z \tag{17}$$

on a neighborhood of the $(\beta - a)/(1 - a)$, where $g(z)$ is an analytic solution of Eq.(3).

Proof. By Theorem 1 or 2, we can find an analytic solution $g(z)$ of the auxiliary equation (3) in the form of (6) in a neighborhood of the origin. Since $g'(0) = \eta \neq 0$, the function $g^{-1}(z)$ is analytic in a neighborhood of the point $g(0) = (\beta - a)/(1 - a)$. If we now define $x(z)$ by means of (17), then from (3)

$$x'(z) = \frac{1}{b} \beta g'(\beta g^{-1}(z))(g^{-1})'(z) - \frac{a}{b} = \frac{\beta g'(\beta g^{-1}(z))}{b g'(g^{-1}(z))} - \frac{a}{b}$$

$$= \frac{1}{b} \Big[g(\beta^2 g^{-1}(z)) - a g(\beta g^{-1}(z)) + a \Big] - \frac{a}{b} = \frac{1}{b} \Big[g(\beta^2 g^{-1}(z)) - a g(\beta g^{-1}(z)) \Big],$$

and $x(az + bx(z)) = x(g(\beta g^{-1}(z)) = \frac{1}{b} \Big[g(\beta^2 g^{-1}(z)) - a g(\beta g^{-1}(z)) \Big]$ as required. So (17) is an analytic solution of Eq.(1).

Theorem 4. Suppose that $\beta = e^{\alpha}$ and one of the following conditions is fulfilled:

(A_1) $\Re \alpha = 0$, $\Im \alpha = 2\pi\theta$ and $\theta \in \mathbf{R} \backslash \mathbf{Q}$ is a Brjuno number;

(A_2) $\Re \alpha = 0$, $\Im \alpha = \dfrac{2\pi q}{p}$ and q, p satisfy the assumptions of (H_2).

Then equation (1) has a solution of the form

$$x(z) = \frac{1}{b} \Big[\phi(\phi^{-1}(z) + \alpha) - az \Big] \tag{18}$$

in a neighborhood of the origin, where $\phi(w)$ is an analytic solution of differential-difference equation (5) in the half-plane $\Omega_{\kappa} = \{ w : \Re w < \ln \kappa, -\infty < \Im w < +\infty \}$ for certain constant $\kappa > 0$.

Proof. First of all, we note that if α satisfies (A_1) or (A_2), then $\beta = e^{\alpha}$ satisfies the corresponding condition (H1) or (H2). From Theorem 1-2, we know that there is a positive κ such that Eq.(3) has an analytic solution $g(z)$ in a neighborhood of the origin $U_{\kappa} = \{ z : |z| < \kappa \}$. Let the variable $z = e^w$, then we have that $z \in U_{\kappa}$ if $w \in \Omega_{\kappa}$. Define an analytic function $\phi(w)$ for $w \in \Omega_{\kappa}$ by the equation $\phi(w) = g(e^w)$. We assert that $\phi(w)$ satisfies equation (5) when $e^{\alpha} = \beta$. In fact, $\phi'(w) = g'(e^w)e^w$,

$$\phi'(w + \alpha) = g'(e^{w+\alpha})e^{w+\alpha} = g'(\beta z)e^{w+\alpha} = \frac{1}{\beta} g'(z) \Big[g(\beta^2 z) - a g(\beta z) + a \Big] \cdot e^w \cdot e^{\alpha}$$

$$= g'(e^w)e^w\left[g(e^{2\alpha+w}) - ag(e^{\alpha+w}) + a\right] = \phi'(w)\left[\phi(w+2\alpha) - a\phi(w+\alpha) + a\right].$$

Since $g'(0) = \eta \neq 0$, the function g^{-1} is analytic in a neighborhood of the point $g(0) = (\beta - a)/(1 - a)$. Thus $\phi^{-1}(z) = \ln g^{-1}(z)$ is analytic in a neighborhood of the point $g(0) = (\beta - a)/(1 - a)$. Let $x(z) = \frac{1}{b}\left[\phi(\phi^{-1}(z) + \alpha) - az\right]$, then $x'(z) = \frac{1}{b}\left[\frac{\phi'(\phi^{-1}(z) + \alpha)}{\phi'(\phi^{-1}(z))} - a\right]$, from (5)

we have $x'(z) = \frac{1}{b}\left[\phi(\phi^{-1}(z) + 2\alpha) - a\phi(\phi^{-1}(z) + \alpha)\right]$, and

$$x(az + bx(z)) = x(\phi(\phi^{-1}(z) + \alpha)) = \frac{1}{b}\left[\phi(\phi^{-1}(z) + 2\alpha) - a\phi(\phi^{-1}(z) + \alpha)\right]$$

as required. Then (18) is an analytic solution of (1). This completes the proof.

References

1. Eder, E.: The functional differential equation x'(t)=x(x(t)). J. Differential Equations 54, 390–400 (1984)
2. Si, J.G., Li, W.R., Cheng, S.S.: Analytic solutions of an iterative functional differential equations. Comput. Math. Appl. 33(6), 47–51 (1997)
3. Si, J.G., Cheng, S.S.: Analytic solutions of an functional differential equations with state dependent argument. Taiwanese J. Math. 1, 471–480 (1997)
4. Bjuno, A.D.: Analytic form of differential equations. Trans. Moscow Math. Soc. 25, 131–288 (1971)
5. Marmi, S., Moussa, P., Yoccoz, J.C.: The Brjuno functions and their regularity properties. Comm. Math. Phys. 186(2), 265–293 (1997)
6. Carletti, T., Marmi, S.: Linearization of Analytic and Non-Analytic Germs of Diffeomorphisms. Bull. Soc. Math. 128, 69–85 (2000)
7. Davie, A.M.: The critical function for the semistandard map. Nonlinearity 7, 219–229 (1994)
8. Bessis, D., Marmi, S., Turchetti, G.: On the singularities of divergent majorant series arising from normal form theory. Rend. Mat. Appl. 9, 645–659 (1989)

Design and Analysis of a Sun Tracking System

Yaozhang Sai, Rujian Ma, and Xueyan Yang

School of Control Science and Engineering,
University of Jinan, 250022 Jinan, China
saiyaozhang@163.com, rjma.ujn@gmail.com

Abstract. A compound biaxial sun tracking system is designed to improve the efficiency of solar panels for power generation. The difference between sensor signals can be judged by the system and the stepper motor can be controlled to drive solar panels to track the sun. At the same time, the system can calculate the elevation angle and azimuth of the sun to drive solar panels to the best location by given information in cloudy circumstances. The advantages of the two track methods are complementary in different situations, thus the efficiency of solar panels for power generation is increased. The battery maintenance is taken into consideration when solar panels do not work normally. The motion characteristics of the system are analyzed to verify the feasibility of the design.

Keywords: Sun tracking; compound track; control system; AVR MCU.

1 Introduction

Many solar energy equipments have been widely used since the solar energy is a kind of clean energy. However, the low transfer efficiency of the equipments had not been solved. As far as the solar cells are concerned, they can be divided into four categories, i.e., the monocrystalline silicon solar cells, the polycrystalline silicon solar cells, the amorphous silicon solar cells and the thin-film silicon solar cells. Monocrystalline silicon solar cells have the highest rate of photoelectrical conversion. The theoretical conversion efficiency is 24% to 26%. But the current conversion efficiency of industrial-scale production is about 17%. However, Monocrystalline silicon solar cells have the high cost, complex process of production, and it is not easy to promote to use. Solar cells commonly used in commercial are thin-film solar cells and polycrystalline silicon solar cells. The theoretical conversion efficiency of polycrystalline silicon is about 20% and the actual efficiency of production is 12% to 14% [1]. The market share of the thin-film solar cells is increasing year by year because of its low costs. Although a thin-film solar cell with conversion efficiency of 24.2% was developed by Institute for Solar Energy Systems in Fraunhofer, Germany, which is the highest record in Europe [2], the conversion efficiency of commercial thin-film batteries is only about 6% to 8% [3]. It can be seen that the actual value of conversion efficiency is much lower than that of theoretical value. Therefore, new methods need to be developed to improve the conversion efficiency.

Most present used solar energy devices are fixed at an angle to the sky and designers must calculate the best angle to maximize solar energy collection [4]. As the sun position changes with time, it is necessary to adopt a solar tracking device to improve the utilization of solar energy. Previous studies show that the solar energy absorbed

G. Shen and X. Huang (Eds.): CSIE 2011, Part I, CCIS 152, pp. 8–14, 2011.

by the biaxial sun tracking system is 35% higher than that of the fixed system [5]. Therefore, the study of sun tracking control system is imperative.

2 System Design

Several aspects must be taken into consideration in sun tracking system design. The first is how to determine and respond to the sunny and cloudy. The second is how the solar panel moves to track sun in different states. The third is how to deal with the problem of battery overused in continuous cloudy days.

The main normally used methods of sun tracking are active tracking and passive tracking. There are controlled release tracking, clock-type tracking and elevation angle-azimuth tracking in active tracking. Passive tracking includes pressure-tracking and photoelectric tracking. Since the active tracking is not reversible, the tracking error will accumulate and the tracking accuracy is not high. Although the elevation angle – azimuth tracking has higher accuracy [6], it needs to keep running, this will result in the waste energy in cloudy days. Passive tracking has higher accuracy and low cost [7], but tracking system can do nothing and sometimes move the platform in the wrong state in cloudy days. A compound tracking system, a combination of active and passive tracking methods, is used to track sun in the study. It is composed of photoelectric tracking and elevation angle-azimuth tracking, and takes advantages of two methods in different weather conditions to make the system more accurate and stable.

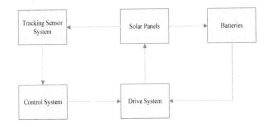

Fig. 1. Diagram of the system composition

The whole system is based on photosensitive sensors. According to the information measured by photosensitive, MCU can control the solar panels to track sun. The system includes tracking sensor system, control system, driving system, solar panels and batteries. The diagram of the system composition is shown in Fig. 1.

There are five photosensitive sensors in the tracking sensor system. A photosensitive sensor detects light intensity to judge the weather. The other photosensitive sensors are responsible for tracking sun. Four photosensitive sensors can detect the light intensity of four corners. Four sensors point to four directions, and tilted 45 degrees with the horizontal direction. Tracking sensor device is shown in Fig. 2. When the east-west light intensity received by the sensor is inconsistent, the system will get the value which voltage difference that sensors provide is converted to, and judge which direction has strong light. Then the system can control the motor to run to the direction. When sensors output voltage value is same, the motor is stopped. The method of judge which the running direction of solar panels is north or south is same.

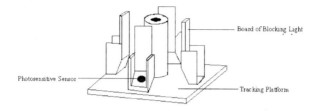

Fig. 2. Tracking sensor device

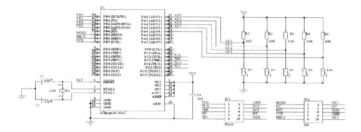

Fig. 3. Scheme of the tracking system

Control system is the core of the whole system, which is responsible for judging and processing the information obtained from the other parts. AVR MCU is used for the control system since it is high performance, low power consumption RISC structure, CMOS 8-bit microcontroller [8]. The AVR MCU used in the system is Atmega 16 produced by Atmel Corporation. The on-chip resources are rich and the confidentiality is good. It has the high speed, high performance and low power consumption. Its peripherals have 8-channel ADC which is 10-bit [9] and has A/D conversion function. Therefore, the information given by tracking sensor system can be used in the MCU. The scheme of the tracking system is shown in Fig. 3.

Two stepper motors are used for the dual-axis drive device. They can make solar panels turn along vertical and horizontal axes. Each axis has an absolute photoelectric rotary encoder. The main characteristics of it are zero fixed and the angle of per revolution is monotonic in 0-359°. Each location has a corresponding code. Encoder is mainly to assure system to turn to the specified angle. When the weather is cloudy, the system can automatically make solar panels point to the best location for this season at noon, which makes the sun tracking system into a fixed solar system. Thus, the method deals with the problem properly when the system can not find the best location in cloudy days, and not make system wrong movement [10]. The best location can be computed by MCU which uses the time, the date and latitude and longitude. The system uses DS12C887 as a clock chip, which has complete clock and calendar functions. MCU can output eight different signals by three ports to control motors. The system needs a decoder to encode, so it makes two stepper motors of the system running in different directions. The drive control system is shown in Fig. 4.

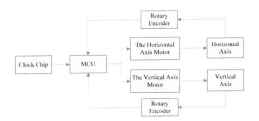

Fig. 4. Drive control system

Lead-acid battery is selected in the system since it has low price and easy maintenance. And the raw materials can be easily obtained. In the battery part, the battery
must be protected. When the system is in the case of continuous cloudy days, the battery can not be charged in time, and almost all the power of it is released. Because of
"memory" of the battery, the voltage can not reach the rated voltage after the battery
is charged. To prevent this from happening, there are two batteries in the system.

3   Software Design

When the certain intensity of light can not be detected by the photosensitive sensor,
the system can check the clock. If the time is more than 7 am, the system is set to
cloudy state. The system can calculate the azimuth angle and the height of sun at noon
by the time, the local latitude and longitude, etc., while the stepper motors will make
the solar panels turn to the location. Then the system continues to detect light intensity. When the weather is sunny, the state of the system will be changed. The system
will not aimlessly search for sunlight.

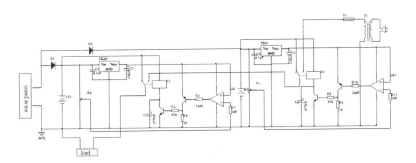

Fig. 5. The battery protection circuit

When the voltage of the main battery is below 10 volts, the battery will stop dis-
charging. At the same time, the spare battery will supply power. After the main battery
is charged by the solar panels, the main battery will supply power again. When the
system is in extreme circumstances and the voltage of the spare battery is below 10v,
the solar panels can not supply power for the main battery. The commercial electricity
will supply power for the device. The battery protection circuit is shown in Fig. 5.

The light intensity of four directions will be detected by four photosensitive sensors in the sunny day. When the light intensity of the corresponding direction is different, MCU will control device to turn to the suitable location where the light intensity of the four directions is same. When the battery is over-discharging, the system will automatically use a spare battery or the external power to supply power. The battery can be protected, and the system can continuously run in this way. Program flow chart is shown in Fig. 6.

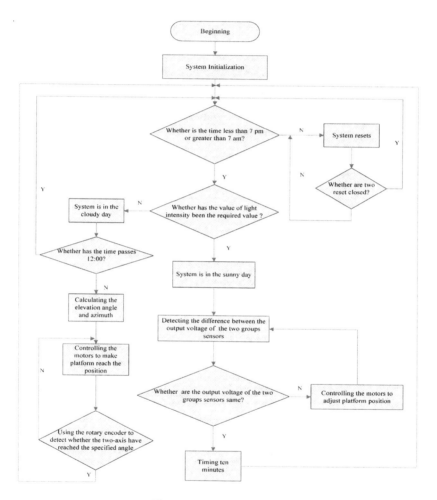

Fig. 6. Program flow chart

4 Motion Analysis

The motion characteristics of platform of the sun tracking system can be determined by the state of the system. The control of the system is different in the different states of the system. So the motion of the platform is also different.

When the weather is sunny, the tracking device of the system will provide the tracking information, and MCU will use this information to judge whether the device is in the best position. At the same time MCU can control the motors to make platform turn to the best position where sunlight is perpendicular to the solar panels.

The system has three reset switches, one depends on time and two depend on position. The platform resets automatically when the time is 7 pm. When the elevation angle is 90°, the platform will touch the reset switch, and the stepper motor of vertical axis will stop working. The resetting of elevation angle is end. When the azimuth angle of solar panels is -135°, the other reset switch will be touched, and the stepper motor of horizontal axis will stop working. At this time the system stops resetting.

When the system is in cloudy days, solar panels will turn to the position in which sunlight will vertically shine the solar panels at noon. At this time the system can use the local latitude and longitude, time and date to calculate the elevation angle and azimuth of sun. The platform will use the two values to run to the best position.

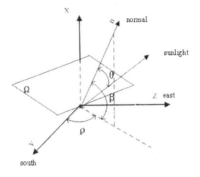

Fig. 7. Coordinate system of the platform

The coordinate system of the platform is coincident with the horizon coordinate system of position of sun. The coordinate system of the platform is shown in Fig. 7. The rotation angle of horizontal axis of tracking system is coincident with the elevation angle of sun. The rotation angle of horizontal axis, β, and the rotation angle of vertical axis, ρ, can be expressed as follows [11].

$$\beta = \arcsin(\sin \delta \sin \varphi + \cos \delta \cos \omega \cos \varphi) \tag{1}$$

$$\rho = \arcsin(\cos \delta \sin \omega / \cos \beta) \tag{2}$$

Where δ is the declination angle of the sun, n is the order number of date in a year, φ is the latitude angle, ω is the hour angle and L is the longitude of the location. The values can be gotten by the following equations.

$$\delta = 23.5 \sin[(284 + n) \times 360 / 365] \tag{3}$$

$$B = 360(n - 81) / 364 \tag{4}$$

$$E = 9.87 \sin 2B - 7.53 \cos B - 1.5 \sin B \tag{5}$$

$$t_n = t \pm (L - 120)/15 + E/60 \tag{6}$$

$$\omega = 15(t_n - 12) \tag{7}$$

The two rotation angles can be calculated by the above equations. When the system gets the angles, it can control the motors to make the platform to the corresponding position. The absolute photoelectric rotary encoder can detect whether the platform reaches the corresponding position.

5 Conclusions

A compound sun tracking system is designed where the Atmega 16 MCU is used as the control core. It can use photosensitive sensor to track sun. At the same time, it can also make platform to the best position by calculation in cloudy days. The system combines the advantages of two methods of active and passive tracking. The advantages of the system are simple in structure, low cost and easily for maintenance. The system can improve the photoelectric conversion effectively.

References

1. Li, Y.D.: Key technology of silicon solar cells. PhD Thesis of Heilongjiang University (2009)
2. Cheng, Z.X., Wang, X.L.: The expatiates of the solar energy photovoltaic cell. Information Recording Materials 2 (2007)
3. Ni, M., Leung, M.K., Sumathy, K.: Progress on solar cell research. Renewable Energy, 9–11 (2004)
4. Hartley, L.E., Martinez-Lorenzo, J.A., Utrillas, M.P., et al.: The optimization of the angle of inclination of a solar collector to maximize the incident solar radiation. Renew Energy 17, 291–309 (1999)
5. Chen, W., Li, J.H.: Research on the tracker controller methodologies in utilization of solar energy. Energy Engineering, 18–21 (2003)
6. Rubio, F.R., Ortegaa, M.G., Gordilloa, F., et al.: Application of new control strategy for sun tracking. Energy Conversion and Management 48, 2174–2184 (2007)
7. Sun, Y.Y.: Sun tracking platform for adaptive reprecision. PhD Thesis of Wuhan University (2005)
8. Luo, P., Pei, H.L.: A servo system based on AVR micro controller unit in unmanned aerial vehicle. Computer Engineering and Application 42, 210–213 (2006)
9. Zhang, C.F., Zou, X.J., Yu, Z.G.: Intelligent control instrument based on Atmega 16. Control & Automation 23, 124–125 (2007)
10. Wentzela, M., Pouris, A.: The development impact of solar cookers: A review of solar cooking impact research in South Africa. Energy Policy 35, 1909–1919 (2007)
11. Li, P., Liao, J.C., Cai, L.L., et al.: Study on motion control law of 2-axis sun tracking system. Machinery 48, 23–26 (2010)

Research and Understanding to Grid's Architecture

Ming-yuan Cui[1] and Lei Wang[1,2]

[1] NanChang Institute Of Technology Nanchang, China
cuimy1001@126.com
[2] School of Information Science & Technology
Southwest Jiaotong University,
Chengdu, China

Abstract. The basic concept of grid is introduced at the beginning of this paper, then Web services and how they benefit for grids are introduced. The architecture of grid is analyzed briefly based on above foundation. Grid's architecture is related to OGSA and OGSI. OGSA acts as a virtual standards which are used to build grid's services and applications which are services-oriented and OGSA provides an appropriate infrastructure for grid's application by using Web services' technology. OGSA can't come true correlative services been described by itself, so OGSI are put forward in order to implement the primary services of OGSA according to Web services. At last, an instance of grid's application is given to demonstrate the use of grid.

Keywords: Web services; grid; architecture; OGSA; OGSI.

1 Introduction

In 1999, Iran Foster gave grid a definition in his paper titled "The Grid: Blueprint for a New Computing Infrastructure"[1]: A computational grid is a hardware and software infrastructure that provides dependable, consistent, pervasive, and inexpensive access to high-end computational capabilities". This special definition comes from early grids which are used to interconnect the high-performance device between disparate labs and university in America.

Buyya defines the Grid as[2] "Grid is a type of parallel and distributed system that enables the sharing, selection, and aggregation of geographically distributed "autonomous" resources dynamically at runtime depending on their availability, capability, performance, cost, and users' quality-of-service requirements." The Grid is distinguished from conventional distributed computing by its focus on large-scale resource sharing, innovative applications, and in some cases, high performance orientation.

The Grid aims to be self-configuring, self-tuning, and self-healing, similar to those of autonomic computing. It aims to fulfill the vision of Corbato's Multics: like a utility company, a massive resource to which a user gives his or her computational or storage needs. The Grid's goal is to utilize the shared storage and cycles from the middle and edges of the Internet.It should also be noted that Grids aim at exploiting synergies that result from cooperation--ability to share and aggregate distributed computational capabilities and deliver them as service.

G. Shen and X. Huang (Eds.): CSIE 2011, Part I, CCIS 152, pp. 15–21, 2011.
© Springer-Verlag Berlin Heidelberg 2011

2 Architecture of the Grid

2.1 OGSA and Its Correlative Technologies

GT2 [3] and its early versions had been extensively used to build early grid. However, in those phrases, the Globus-based grid systems differ from each other and were difficult to interoperate as they were using different protocols. At the same time, owing to the push of IT companies such as IBM, Microsoft, Sun and so on, Web service becoming increasingly the computing platform by which we build distributed-business applications in disparate kinds of environment, so it gives birth to the specification on building the next architecture of grid systems in GGF4 meeting .This specification is OGSA . This event is a crucial step in history of grid.

The standard which is extensively authorized and received currently is OGSA (Open Grid Services Architecture) which is developed by GGF (Global Grid Forum). OGSA is a specification about information, and the objective of OGSA is to normalize all the grid's application services. For example, job and services for resource managed, communication and security. OGSA describe the Service-Oriented Architecture for grid and implement the sets of distributed computing based on Web Services.

OGSA is based on Web Services, it adopts standard protocols such as XML and HTTP and builds an oriented-service distributed systems. OGSA extend the concept of service in order to meet the special needs . OGSA has defined each aspect of the grid's service, those embody two aspects, one is that what characters the grid should own and another is management for grid's life cycle. But OGSA only define what interface the grid need have, and does not implement those interface. OGSI-WG put forward a technical specifications which are concerned with the implementation of grid service in the descriptive course of OGSA in Web services context .

Web services: Web Services act as a promising infrastructure of middleware . Web Services are published, discovered and used through the Web. Web services is based on Service-Oriented Architecture, in those kind of architecture, client act as a requester of service, and Server a provider of service .Web services is based on open standards such as XML and HTTP protocols, those open standards are industry-supported extensively, and they have probability to be applied porpularly. In essence, the Web services is a software application whose characters are loose-couple (Client/Server), enveloped, have no relation to platform and program design language and provide server-end with synthetical components which are capable of being described, discovered , issued and called in Intranet or Internet.

An explicit explanation will be given for above definition: loose-couple means that the change for implementation of Web services is free, there is no influence on the client-end of the service if the interface of the service keeps no change; the character of envelop means that the implementation of Web services is invisible to the client-end of the service. Having no relation to platform and program design language means Web services can be implemented by any kind of programming language; Description is used to describe the capability that a Web services can provide and based on XML interface. Issue: Web services may use service number of registration to register and can access in the Intranet and Internet by the service number of registration. Discovery means that the client of Web services can discover service by retrieving the registration of the service and matching their request of the service. Call means Client bind a service through a standard transport protocol such as HTTP and XML protocol.

Intranet or Internet means that a Web service is applicable only in an organization. Another case is it can provide access traversing the Fire-Wall.

How Web services benefit for grid: Web services is being represented as an open standards based on XML and can be used to build distributed-service in disparate kinds of computing environments. Web services can be described, issued, discovered and bind to WSDL by WSDL. WSDL is a rich language which is used to describe the interface. The technology which is related to Web services provides a promising platform which can integrate service that provided by different kinds of systems. The framework of Web services is help to build grid owing to followings advantage. First, grid need supports in dynamic discovery and the synthesis of the grid's services in different kinds of environment, this a necessary mechanism which is help to register and find definition of interfaces, description of port's implementation; grid need supports which is used to create agent dynamically by special bind of interface. WSDL meets those needs by providing a standard mechanism. It can define specification of interfaces respectively according to the actual case of their special binds. Web services are based on international standards accepted porpularly. Being adopted extensively means that the framework based on Web services can develop amount of tools and extended service. For example, can create bound WSDL processing program for different environment, such as WSIF (Web services Invocation Framework) [4], or a workflow system using WSDL ,The host's environment used to Web services.

2.2 The Architecture of OGSA

OGSA acts as a virtual standard which is used to build grid's system which are services-oriented and OGSA define the feature of grid's service on environment of Web services.

The objective of OGSA: The objectives of OGSA are aim to five aspects, and these are as followings: The first object is to manage resources across distributed heteroge-neous platforms. The second is to deliver seamless QoS (quality of service). The to-pology of grids is often complex. Interaction of grid resources is usually dynamic. It's important that the grid provide robust, behind-the-scenes services such as authoriza-tion, access control, and delegation. And the third is aims to provide a common base for autonomic management solutions. A grid can contain many resources, with nu-merous combinations of configurations, interactions, and changing state and failure modes. Some form of intelligent self regulation and autonomic management of these resources is necessary. The fourth is to define open, published interfaces. OGSA is an open standard managed by the GGF standards body. For interoperability of diverse resources, grids must be built on standard interfaces and protocols. And the last objec-tive is to exploit industry standard integration technologies. The authors of OGSA had foresight to leverage existing solutions where appropriate. The foundation of OGSA is Web services.

From the bottom is physical and logical resources layer, the physical resources is comprise of servers, storage and network. The logical resources provide additional function by virtualizing and aggregating the resources in the physical layer. General purpose middleware such as file systems, database managers, directories, and work-flow managers provide these abstract services on top of the physical grid.

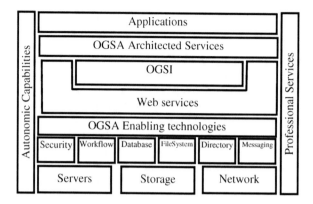

Fig. 1. The OGSA architecture

The second layer in the OGSA architecture is Web service. All grid resources-- both logical and physical -- are modeled as services.

The Open OGSI specification defines grid services and builds on top of standard Web services technology. OGSI exploits the mechanisms of Web services like XML and WSDL to specify standard interfaces, behaviors, and interaction for all grid resources. OGSI extends the definition of Web services to provide capabilities for dynamic, stateful, and manageable Web services that are required to model the resources of the grid.

The Web services layer, with its OGSI extensions, provide a base infrastructure for the next layer- architected grid services. The GGF is currently working to define many of these architected grid services in areas like program execution, data services, and core services. Some are already defined, and some implementations have already appeared. As implementations of these newly architected services begin to appear, OGSA will become a more useful SOA.

The top of the figure 1 is Grid applications layer. Over time, as a rich set of grid-architected services continues to be developed, new grid applications that use one or more grid architected services will appear. These applications comprise the fourth main layer of the OGSA architecture.

Extending Web services for grid: The GGF OGSA working group believed it was necessary to augment core Web services functionality to address grid services requirements. OGSI extends Web services by introducing interfaces and conventions in three main areas. Firstly, there's the dynamic and potentially transient nature of services in a grid. Therefore, grid services need interfaces to manage their creation, destruction, and life cycle management. Secondly, there's state. Grid services can have attributes and data associated with them, similar in concept to the traditional structure of objects. Objects have behavior and data. Likewise, Web services needed to be extended to support state data associated with grid services. Thirdly, the Client-end can subscribe their interesting services by a call-back's operation which destination is server and source is client-end.

Implementations of interfaces: OGSA has defined each aspect concerned with grid's services, such as feature of grid's services , which interface are need, but

OGSA does not specify the implementation of interfaces. So OGSI provides technical specifications which implement grid's services been defined in description of OGSA. Currently, the OGSI's implementations which are issued include GT3[2], MS.NET Grid , OGSI.NET and so on. The core services of GT3 is the crucial technology for implement of OGSI's specification.

Here is an interaction model provided by OGSI for Web services:OGSI introduces an interaction model for grid services. OGSI provides a uniform way for software developers to model and interact with grid services by providing interfaces for discovery, life cycle, state management, creation and destruction, event notification, and reference management.

Interfaces and conventions in OGSI: There are interfaces in OGSI as follows:

Factory: Grid services that implement this interface provide a way to create new grid services. Factories may create temporary instances of limited function, such as a scheduler creating a service to represent the execution of a particular job, or they may create longer-lived services. Not all grid services are created dynamically. For example, some might be created as the result of an instance of a physical resource in the grid such as a processor, storage, or network device.

Life cycle: Because grid services may be transient, grid service instances are created with a specified lifetime. The lifetime of any particular service instance can be negotiated and extended as required by components that are dependent on or manage that service. The life cycle mechanism was architected to prevent grid services from consuming resources indefinitely without requiring a large scale distributed "garbage collection" scavenger.

State management: Grid services can have state. OGSI specifies a framework for representing this state called Service Data and a mechanism for inspecting or modifying that state named Find/ Set ServiceData. Further, OGSI requires a minimal amount of state in Service Data Elements that every grid service must support, and requires that all services implement the Find/Set ServiceData portType.

Service groups: Service groups are collections of grid services that are indexed, using Service Data, for some particular purpose. For example, they might be used to collect all the services that represent the resources in a particular cluster-node within the grid.

Notification: The state information (Service Data) that is modeled for grid services changes as the system runs. Many interactions between grid services require dynamic monitoring of changing state. Notification applies a traditional publish/subscribe paradigm to this monitoring. Grid services support an interface (NotificationSource) to permit other grid services (NotificationSink) to subscribe to changes.

HandleMap: When factories are used to create a new instance of a grid service, the factory returns the identity of the newly instantiated service. This identity is composed of two parts, a Grid Service Handle (GSH) and a Grid Service Reference (GSR). A GSH is guaranteed to reference the grid service indefinitely, while a GSR can change within the grid services lifetime. The HandleMap interface provides a way to obtain a GSR given a GSH.

OGSA architected services:

Grid's application can be built by compatible services of OGSA. OGSA architected services are composed of grid core services, grid program execution services and grid data services. Here we introduce the grid core services and grid program execution services simply.

Grid core services include Service management, Service communication, Policy services and Security services.

Services management Provides functions that manage the services deployed in the distributed grid. Service management automates and assists with a variety of installation, maintenance, monitoring, and troubleshooting tasks within a grid system. It includes functions for provisioning and deploying the system components. It also includes functions for collecting and exchanging data about the operation of the grid. This data is used for both "online" and "offline" management operations, and includes information about faults, events, problem determination, auditing, metering, accounting, and billing.

Service communication includes a range of functions that support the basic methods for grid services to communicate with each other. They support several communication models that may be composed to permit effective inter-service communication, including queued messages, publish-subscribe event notification, and reliable distributed logging.

All those lead to such fact, that is the concept of "service" in grid is confusion, sometimes it is referred to protocol entities; in other times, interactions between grid a service user and the service provider.

As to Policy services, it Creates a general framework for creation, administration, and management of policies and agreements for system operation. Policies governing security, resource allocation, and performance as well as an infrastructure for "policy aware" services to use policies to govern their operation. Policy and agreement documents provide a mechanism for the representation and negotiation of terms between service providers and their clients (either user requests or other services).

The last core service of grid is Security services, its function is to support, integrate, and unify popular security models, mechanisms, protocols, and technologies in a way that enables a variety of systems to interoperate securely. These security services enable and extend core Web services security protocols and bindings, and provide service-oriented mechanisms for authentication, authorization, trust policy enforcement, credential transformation. The following narrative is the simple introduction for grid program execution services:While OGSI and grid core services are generally applicable to any distributed computing system, grid program execution class is unique to the grid model of distributed task execution that supports high-performance computing, parallelism, and distributed collaboration.

Principles of job scheduling and workload management implemented as part of this class of services are central to Grid computing and the ability to virtualize processing resources. We have already seen early specifications of interfaces in this category, such as the Community Scheduling Framework (CSF) announced at GGF 8 in Seattle.

Compute virtualization conventions specified by program execution services ; These interfaces support the concept of data virtualization and provide mechanisms related to distributed access to information of many types including databases, files, documents, content stores, and application-generated streams.

To exploit and virtualize data using placement methods like data replication, caching, and high-performance data movement to give applications required QoS (quality of service ,QoS) across the distributed grid. Methods for federating multiple disparate, distributed data sources may also provide integration of data stored under differing schemas such as files and relational databases.

3 E-Minerals Projects - An Application of Grid

Many environmental problems, such as transport of pollutants, development of remediation strategies, weathering, and containment of high-level radioactive waste, require an understanding of fundamental mechanisms and processes at a molecular level [5]. Computer simulations at a molecular level can give considerable progress in our understanding of these processes. The vision of the e-Minerals project is to combine developments in atomistic simulation tools with emerging grid computing technologies in order to stretch the potential for undertaking simulation studies under increasingly realistic conditions, and which can scan across a wide range of physical and chemical parameters. The e-Minerals project brings together simulation scientists, applications developers and computer scientists to develop UK e-science/grid capabilities for molecular simulations of environmental issues. A common set of simulation tools is being developed for a wide range of applications, and the integrated compute grid environment that is being established will lead to a significant leap in the capabilities of these powerful scientific tools. This work is supported by an effort to support the working of the e-Minerals project team as a fully functional virtual organization and collaborator.

4 Conclusions

The following conclusions can be drawn through the above analysis of grid's architecture and its correlative technologies:

OGSA is based on technology of Web services. OGSA act as virtual standards which is used to build grid's system which are services-oriented and OGSA define the feature of grid's service on environment of Web services. OGSI is a specification which implements primary interfaces of grid's service which are defined in the context of OGSA.

References

1. Foster, I., Kesselman, C. (eds.): The Grid:Bluepoint for a New Computing Infrastructure, 1st edn. Morgan Kaufmann Publishers, San Francisco (1998)
2. Sandholm, T., Gawor, J.: The Globus Toolkits 3 core –A grid Service Cont- ainer Framework (July 2003),
   http://wwwnix.globus.org/toolkit/3.0/ogsa/docs/gt3_core.pdf
3. Aozhenli, Baker, M.: The core technologies for computer network. TsingHua University Press, PeKing (2006)
4. Mukhi, N: .Web Service Invocation Sans SOAP,
   http://www.ibm.com/developerworks/library/ws-wsif.html
5. Grid Projects: E-Minerals-Environment from the Molecular Level,
   http://acet.rdg.ac.uk/research/grid/index.php

A Novel Compensation Strategy for Dynamic Sag Corrector

Xiaoying Zhang[1,2], Cunlu Dang[1,2], and Jun Yan[1,2]

[1] Lanzhou University of Technology, College of Electrical and Information Engineering,
Langongpingstr. 287, 730050 Lanzhou, P.R. China
[2] Key Laboratory of Gansu Advanced Control for Industrial Processes,
Langongpingstr. 287, 730050 Lanzhou, P.R. China
zhxy525@gmail.com

Abstract. Voltage sags constitute 80% of power quality problem, and Dynamic Sag Corrector (DySC) has been considered to be an effective custom power device which mitigates voltage sags. DySC has a concise structure compared with dynamic voltage restorer (DVR). DySC adopts different compensation strategies according to the loads' sensitivity to voltage amplitude and phase jump. This paper proposes a novel compensation strategy named integrated compensation strategy for DySC. The simulation test for single-phase voltage sag compensation verifies that the proposed strategy can mitigate the phase jump accompanied voltage sags and decrease the amplitude of injecting DySC voltage.

Keywords: power system; voltage sag; dynamic sag corrector (DySC); compensation strategy; software phase-locked loop (SPLL).

1 Introduction

Control of most of the advanced manufacturing systems is mainly based on semiconductor devices, with the development of modern science and technology. It causes such loads to be more sensitive against power system disturbances, such as voltage sags/swells, flicker, harmonic distortion, impulse transient and interruptions [1, 2]. Among the above-mentioned power quality issues, productivity loss due to deep voltage sags has been called "the most important concern affecting industrial and commercial customers," and voltage sags have become the dominant form of power quality problem [3]-[6]. Voltage sags originate from faults on the transmission and distribution systems that are caused by various events, such as animal contact, storms, equipment failure, and insulator failures (due to vandalism) [7]. Thus, it can be seen that voltage sags are inevitable in transmission and distribution systems.

However, voltage sags can cause huge losses. For example, an interrupted automotive assembly line cost one US manufacturer US$250000, and interruptions to semiconductor hatch processing cost US$30000-US$1 million per incident [8].Conventional solutions such as surge suppressors and voltage regulators do not solve the voltage sag problem. Uninterruptible power supply (UPS) systems can resolve the problem, while their high operational costs preclude applying them broadly for noncritical industrial and commercial processes. The dynamic voltage restorer (DVR) is known as a device to alleviate voltage sags, while DVR has a limit of

G. Shen and X. Huang (Eds.): CSIE 2011, Part I, CCIS 152, pp. 22–28, 2011.

injecting voltage dictated by the series transformer and converter rating. The limit of injecting voltage restricts the compensation capacity of DVR.

Dynamic sag corrector (DySC) has been considered to be another custom power device which alleviates voltage sags. DySC has a larger compensation capacity than DVR. It can protect against 98% of voltage sag events. During voltage sags, DySC injects a voltage to restore the load-side voltage and exchanges active/reactive power with the surrounding system. In order to control the active power exchange and overcome the shortcoming of conventional compensation strategies, a novel compensation strategy is proposed.

2 Dynamic Sag Corrector

The DySC was designed on the following principles.

- Cost of ownership should be reduced by providing statistically significant insurance.

- Size and weight should be minimized. The standard DySC products, up to 500-kVA modules, do not include a series transformer, and include little energy storage.

2.1 Single-Phase MiniDySC

The single–phase DySC (MiniDySC) is derived from a patented voltage boost circuit [9], [10] (see Fig. 1). The single-phase inverter is configurable to operate in voltage boost or bypass mode, and is capable of providing 100% boost to the incoming ac line voltage. This allows it to correct for deep voltage sags down to 50%. Further, the inverter dc bus provides the ability to also handle deeper voltage sags down to 0 V. The ride-through under these conditions is limited by the amount of stored energy.

Rather than depending on stored energy to compensate the missing voltage, the DySC draws power from the input line whenever the missing voltage magnitude is 50% or less. The smaller DySC units include sufficient energy storage to compensate for 100% missing voltage for 3 cycles. Optional additional storage, in the form of capacitors, can increase the ride-through time to 15 cycles or more. This latter feature will allow the MiniDySC to protect against the interruption of power up to the first utility reclose operation following a fault, a prevalent type of power quality event in high-lightning suburban areas.

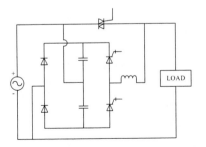

Fig. 1. Topology of single-phase MiniDySC

2.2 Three-Phase MegaDySC

For higher power levels up to 2 MVA, a series transformer coupled device provides a more favorable solution. This type dynamic sag corrector is called high power DySC unit (MegaDySC). The MegaDySC can handle deep voltage sags, and can provide ride-through if adequate energy storage is provided.

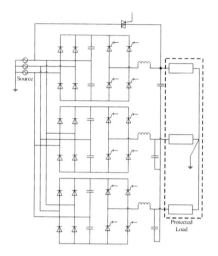

Fig. 2. Topology of three-phase MegaDySC

3 Compensation Strategy for Dynamic Sag Corrector

DySC operates to maintain the load supply voltage at its rated value and exchanges active/reactive power with the surrounding system. Hence, it is necessary to provide proper compensation strategies in order to reduce the active power exchange. Widely used in present DySC control are pre-sag compensation strategy and in-phase compensation strategy. The pre-sag compensation strategy tracks supply voltage continuously and restores load voltage to the pre-sag condition. Using this method, the load-side voltage can be restored ideally, but injected active power cannot be controlled. On the other hand, the in-phase compensation strategy tracks the phase angle of supply voltage continuously and the injecting voltage has low amplitude. However, if DySC adopts the in-phase compensation strategy, the injected active power cannot be controlled, and it could result in poor load ride-through capability for long-duration sags.

This paper proposes a novel compensation strategy named integrated compensation strategy. The novel strategy can overcome the disadvantages of conventional pre-sag compensation strategy and in-phase compensation strategy. DySC which adopts this method can maintain the amplitude of load-side voltage to normal value and mitigate the phase jump during the period of voltage sags. Fig. 3 shows the single-phase vector diagram of the proposed compensation strategy. $\dot{U}_{C(pre-sag)}$ represents the injecting DySC voltage of pre-sag compensation and $\dot{U}_{C(in-phase)}$ represents the injecting DySC voltage of in-phase compensation. In early stage of compensation, the load voltage is in phase with the pre-sag voltage, and in later stage of compensation, the load voltage is in phase with the supply voltage. That's to say, during the compensation, the injecting compensation voltage $\dot{U}_C$ varies form $\dot{U}_{C(pre-sag)}$ to $\dot{U}_{C(in-phase)}$.

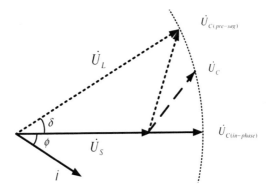

Fig. 3. Single phasor diagram of integrated compensation strategy

When DySC adopts compensation strategies to restore the load voltage during voltage sags, the phase angle information of supply voltage is required. However, when single-phase voltage sags take place in three-phase power system, they cause a voltage unbalance by generating negative-sequence and zero-sequence voltages. The voltage unbalance will cause an oscillation error in the measurement of the phase angle using compensation strategies. Software phase-locked loop [11] can solve this problem. It can alleviate the oscillation error caused by negative-sequence and zero-sequence voltages. The proposed integrated compensation strategy could be implemented based on software phase-locked loop.

When DySC adopts the proposed compensation strategy, the frequency of injecting voltage will fluctuate during the compensation. The frequency fluctuation is related to the parameters of software phase-locked loop. Fig. 4 presents the frequency fluctuation which ranges from 49.82 Hz to 50.18 Hz during the duration of voltage sag compensation, and this frequency fluctuation is allowed by GB/T 15945-2008 (Chinese national standard: Power quality – Frequency deviation for power system).

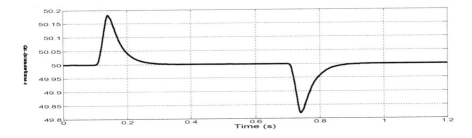

Fig. 4. Frequency fluctuate of load voltage

4 Simulation

This section gives the simulation results when using the proposed compensation strategy. Fig. 5 shows the waveform of phase-A. According to Fig. 5, the nominal value of foundational component voltage is 220 V (rms), and the initial angle is $0°$; from 0.1s to 0.25s, the rms value declined to 176 V, and the phase jump is $30°$.

Fig. 6 shows the waveform of load voltage, and Fig. 7 shows the angle between the load voltage and supply voltage. In Fig. 6 and Fig. 7, obviously, there is a phase jump when using the in-phase compensation strategy. It also shows that the proposed strategy can mitigate the phase jump accompanied voltage sags.

Fig. 8 illustrates the waveform of compensation voltages, and shows that the amplitude of injected UDVR voltage is highest when using the pre–sag compensation strategy.

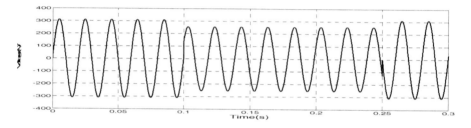

Fig. 5. Voltage waveform of phase A

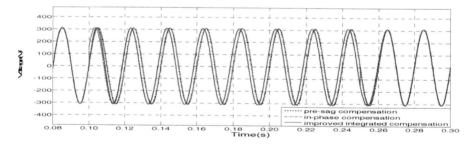

Fig. 6. Voltage waveforms of compensation results at load side

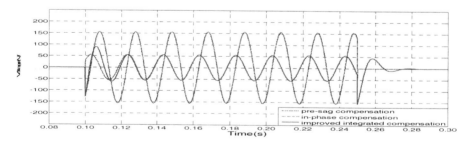

Fig. 7. Waveforms of injecting DySC voltage

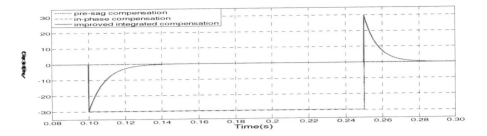

Fig. 8. Angle between the load voltage and supply voltages

5 Conclusion

The main purpose of a DySC is to protect sensitive loads from sags/swells and interruptions in the supply side. If the load is phase-shift sensitive, this protection must include compensation that guards from a sudden phase jump that accompanies a voltage sag.

This paper proposes an integrated compensation strategy. The simulation results verify that the proposed strategy can mitigate the phase jump and decrease the amplitude of injecting DySC voltage.

Acknowledgments. This work is supported by Excellent Youth Teacher Foundation of Lanzhou University of Technology (No. Q200814).

References

1. Kumar, G.V.N., Chowdary, D.D.: DVR with Sliding Mode Control to Alleviate Voltage Sags on a Distribution System for Three Phase Short Circuit Fault. In: 3rd IEEE International Conference on Industrial and Information Systems, pp. 1–4. IEEE Press, New York (2008)
2. Peng, C., Chen, Y., Sun, J.: Study of Dynamic Voltage Restorer and Its Detecting Method. Electric Power Automation Equipment 23(1), 68–71 (2003) (in Chinese)
3. Wang, T., Xue, Y., Choi, S.S.: Review of Dynamic Voltage Restorer. Automation of Electric Power Systems 31(9), 101–107 (2007) (in Chinese)
4. Hamzah, N., Muhamad, M.R., Arsad, P.M.: Investigation on the Effectiveness of Dynamic Voltage Restorer for Voltage Sag Mitigation. In: 5th Student Conference on Research and Development, pp. 1–6. IEEE Press, New York (2007)
5. Ge, C., Cheng, H., Wang, X., Zhong, M., Chen, G., Miao, Y., et al.: DVR Control Algorithm Based on Minimal Energy. Electric Power Automation Equipment 29(1), 70–74 (2009) (in Chinese)
6. Abi-Samra, N., Carnovale, D., Malcolm, W.: The Role of the Distribution System Dynamic Voltage Restorer in Enhancing the Power at Sensitive Facilities. In: Proceeding of WESCON 1996, Wescon, Los Angeles, pp. 167–181 (1996)
7. Brumsickle, W.E., Schneider, R.S., Luckjiff, G.A., Divan, D.M., McGranaghan, M.F.: Dynamic Sag Correctors: Cost-Effective Industrial Power Line Conditioning. IEEE Transactions on Industry Applications 37(1), 212–217 (2001)

8. Hunter, I.: Power Quality Issues-a Distribution Company Perspective. IEEE Power Engineer. 15(2), 75–80 (2001)
9. Divan, D.M.: Single Phase AC Power Conversion Apparatus. U.S. Patent 5 099 410 (March 1992)
10. Divan, D.M., Luckjiff, G., Schneider, R., Brumsickle, W., Kranz, W.: Dynamic Voltage Sag Correction. U.S. Patent 6 118 676 (September 2000)
11. Cai, L., Jing, P., Wu, S., Li, H.: Control Strategies of Dynamic Voltage Restorer. Electric Power Automation Equipment 27(11), 22–25 (2007) (in Chinese)

A Constructive Algorithm for Designing Biorthogonal Bivariate Wavelets with Finite Support[*]

Qingjiang Chen, Na Bai, and Yongmei Shang

School of Science, Xi'an University of Arch. and Technology, Xi'an 710055, P.R. China
qjchen66xytu@126.com, zxc123wer@126.com

Abstract. Wavelet analysis has been developed into a new branch for over twenty years. The notion of vector-valued binary wavelets with two-scale dilation factor associated with an orthogonal vector-valued scaling function is introduced. The existence of orthogonal vector-valued wavelets with multi-scale is discussed. A necessary and sufficient condition is presented by means of vector-valued multiresolution analysis and paraunitary vector filter bank theory. An algorithm for constructing a sort of orthogonal vector-valued wave-lets with compact support is proposed, and their properties are investigated.

Keywords: bivariate wavelets, time-frequency analysis, filter banks, orthogonal, para-unitary,vector-valued, oblique frames, wavelet analysis.

1 Introduction

Wavelet analysis is nowadays a widely used tool in applied mathematics. The advantages of wavelet wraps and their promising features in various application have attracted a lot of interest and effort in recent years. Aside from the traight forward construction of Daubechies' wavelets, only a few, specific construcion of multivariate orthonormal wavelet systems exist presently in the literature. The main advantage of wavelets is their time-frequency localization property. Already they have led to exciting applications in signal processing [1], fractals, image processing [2] and so on. Sampling theorems play a basic role in digital signal processing. They ensure that continuous signals can be processed by their discrete samples. Vector-valued wavelets are a sort of generalized multiwavelets [3]. Vector-valued wavelets and multiwavelets are different in the following sense. For example, prefiltering is usually required for discrete multiwavelet transforms but not necessary for discrete vector-valued wavelet trans-forms [4]. In real life, video images are vector-valued signals. Vector-valued wavelet transforms have been recently investigated for image processing by scholar W. Li. Chen and Cheng studied orthogonal compactly supported vector-valued wavelets with 2-scale. Inspired by [5,6], we are about to investigate the construction of a class of orthogonal compactly supported vector-valued wavelets with multi-scale. Similar to uni-wavelets, it is more complicated and meaningful to investigate biorthogonal vector-valued wavelets with 2-scale.

---

[*] Foundation item: The research is supported by National Natural Science Foundation of China (Grant No:10971160), and by Natural Science Foundation of Shaanxi Province (Grant No:2009J M1002).

G. Shen and X. Huang (Eds.): CSIE 2011, Part I, CCIS 152, pp. 29–35, 2011.
© Springer-Verlag Berlin Heidelberg 2011

2 Preliminaries and Multiresolution Analysis

By Z and Z_+ , we represent all integers and all non-negative integers, respectively. Set v, a be two constant numbers and $2 \leq a, v \in Z$. By $L^2(R^2, C^v)$, we denote the set of arbitrary vector-valued functions $H(t)$, i.e, $L^2(R^2, C^v) := \{H(t) = (h_1(t), h_2(t), \cdots, h_v(t))^T : h_l(t) \in L^2(R^2), \ l = 1, 2, \cdots, v\}$, where T means the transpose of a vector. For example, video images and digital films are examples of vector-valued functions where $h_l(t)$ denotes the pixel on the l-th column at time t. For any vector-valued function $H(t) \in L^2(R^2, C^v)$, $\|H\|$ denotes the norm of vector-valued function $H(t)$, i.e., $\|H\| := (\sum_{l=1}^{v} \int_{R^2} |h_l(t)|^2 \, dt)^{1/2}$, and its inte-gration is defined as $\int_{R^2} H(t)dt := (\int_{R^2} h_1(t)dt, \ \int_{R^2} h_2(t)dt, \ \cdots, \ \int_{R^2} h_v(t)dt)^T$ .The Fourier transform of $\Gamma(t)$ is defined by

$$\hat{\Gamma}(\xi) := \int_{R^2} \Gamma(t) \cdot e^{-it\xi} \, dt \ .$$

For two functions $\Gamma, H \in L^2(R^2, C^v)$, their *symbol inner product* is defined by

$$\langle \Gamma(\cdot), H(\cdot) \rangle := \int_{R^2} \Gamma(t) H(t)^* \, dt, \tag{1}$$

where $*$ means the transpose and the complex conjugate, and I_v denotes the $v \times v$ identity matrix. A sequence $\{\Upsilon_l(t)\}_{l \in Z^2} \subset U \subseteq L^2(R^2, C^v)$ is called an orthonormal set of the subspace U , if the following condition is satisfied

$$\langle \Upsilon_j(\cdot), \Upsilon_k(\cdot) \rangle = \delta_{j,k} I_v, \ j, k \in Z^2. \tag{2}$$

Definition 1. We say that $H(t) \in U \subseteq L^2(R^2, C^v)$ is an orthogonal vector-valued function of the subspace U if its translations $\{H(t-u)\}_{u \in Z^2}$ is an orthonormal col-lection of the subspace U , i.e.,

$$\langle H(\cdot - n), H(\cdot - k) \rangle = \delta_{n,k} I_v, \ n, k \in Z^2. \tag{3}$$

Definition 2 [5]. A sequence $\{G_v(t)\}_{v \in Z^2} \subset U \subseteq L^2(R^2, C^v)$ is called an orthonormal basis of U , if it satisfies (2), and for any $F(t) \in U$, there exists a unique sequence of $v \times v$ constant matrices $\{Q_k\}_{k \in Z^2}$ such that

$$F(t) = \sum_{u \in Z^2} Q_u G_u(t), \ t \in R^2. \tag{4}$$

Definition 3 [5]. A vector-valued multiresolution analysis of $L^2(R^2, C^v)$ is a nested sequence of closed subspaces $\{Y_l\}_{l \in Z}$ such that (i) $Y_l \subset Y_{l+1}, \forall l \in Z$; (ii) $\bigcap_{l \in Z} Y_l = \{0\}$; $\bigcup_{l \in Z} Y_l$ is dense in $L^2(R^2, C^v)$, where 0 is the zero vector of space

$L^2(R^2, C^v)$; (iii) $\phi(t) \in Y_0$ if and only if $\phi(a^l t) \in Y_l$, ; (iv) there is $F(t) \in Y_0$ such that the sequence $\{F(t-u), u \in z^2\}$ is an orthonormal basis of subspace Y_0.

By Definition 2 and Definition 3, we obtain $F(t)$ satisfies the below equation:

$$F(t) = \sum_{k \in Z^2} P_k F(at - k) \tag{5}$$

where $\{P_k\}_{k \in Z^2}$ is a finite supported sequence of $v \times v$ constant matrices, i.e., $\{P_k\}_{k \in Z^2}$ has only finite non-zero terms, and the others are zero matrices. By taking the Fouries transform for (5), and assuming $\hat{F}(\xi)$ is continuous at zero, we have

$$\hat{F}(a\xi) = \mathcal{P}(\xi)\hat{F}(\xi), \quad \xi \in R^2, \tag{6}$$

$$a^2 \mathcal{P}(\xi) = \sum_{k \in Z^2} P_k \cdot \exp\{-ik\xi\}. \tag{7}$$

Let W_j $(j \in Z)$ denote the orthocomplement subspace of Y_j in Y_{j+1} and there exist $a^2 - 1$ vector-valued functions $G_s(t) \in L^2(R^2, C^v)$, $s = 1, 2, \cdots, a^2 - 1$ such that their translations and dilations form a Riesz basis of W_j, i.e.,

$$W_j = clos_{L^2(R^2, C^v)}(\text{span}\{G_s(a^j t - u): s = 1, 2, \cdots, a^2 - 1, \ u \in Z^2\}), j \in Z. \tag{8}$$

Since $G_s(t) \in W_0 \subset Y_1$, $s = 1, 2, \cdots, a^2 - 1$ there exist three finitely supported sequences $\{B_k^{(s)}\}_{k \in z}$ of $v \times v$ constant matrices such that

$$G_s(t) = \sum_{u \in Z^2} B_u^{(s)} F(at - u), \quad s = 1, 2, \cdots, a^2 - 1. \tag{9}$$

$$a^2 \mathcal{B}^{(s)}(\xi) = \sum_{u \in Z^2} B_u^{(s)} \exp\{-iu\xi\}. \tag{10}$$

Then, the refinement equation (10) becomes the following equation

$$\hat{G}_s(a\xi) = \mathcal{B}^{(s)}(\xi)\hat{h}(\xi), \quad s = 1, 2, 3, \cdots, a^2 - 1, \ \xi \in R^2. \tag{11}$$

If $F(t) \in L^2(R^2, C^v)$ is an orthogonal vector one, then it follows from (3) that

$$\langle F(\cdot), F(\cdot - u) \rangle = \delta_{0,u} I_v, \quad u \in Z^2. \tag{12}$$

We say that $G_s(t) \in L^2(R^2, C^v)$, $s \in A = \{1, 2, \cdots, a^2 - 1\}$ are orthogonal vector-valued wavelet functions associated with the vector-valued scaling function $F(t)$, if

$$\langle F(\cdot - k), G_s(\cdot - u) \rangle = O, \quad s = 1, 2, \cdots, a^2 - 1, \ k, u \in Z^2, \tag{13}$$

and $\{G_s(t-u), s \in A, u \in Z^2\}$ is an orthonomal basis of W_0. Thus we have

$$\langle G_r(\cdot), G_s(\cdot - n) \rangle = \delta_{r,s} \delta_{0,n} I_u, \quad r, s = 1, 2, \cdots, a^2 - 1; \ n \in Z^2. \tag{14}$$

Lemma 1 [6]. Let $F(t) \in L^2(R^2, C^v)$. Then $F(t)$ is an orthogonal vector-valued function if and only if

$$\sum_{k \in Z^2} \hat{F}(\xi + 2k\pi) \hat{F}(\xi + 2k\pi)^* = I_v, \quad \xi \in R^2. \tag{15}$$

Lemma 2. If $F(t) \in L^2(R^2, C^v)$, defined by (5), is an orthogonal vector-valued scaling function, then for $a = 2$, $\forall u \in Z^2$, we have the following equalities,

$$\sum_{\sigma \in Z^2} P_\sigma (P_{\sigma+4u})^* = 4\delta_{0,u} I_v. \tag{16}$$

$$\sum_{t=0}^{3} P(\xi + \sigma_t \pi) P(\xi + \sigma_t \pi)^* = I_v, \quad \xi \in R^2, \ \sigma_t \in Z^2. \tag{17}$$

Proof. By substituting (5) into the relation (12), for $\forall k \in Z^2$, we obtain that

$$\delta_{0,k} I_v = \langle F(\cdot - k), F(\cdot) \rangle = \sum_{l \in Z^2} \sum_{u \in Z^2} \int_{R^2} P_l F(2t - 2k - l) F(2t - u)^* (P_u)^* dt$$

$$= \frac{1}{4} \cdot \sum_{l \in Z^2} \sum_{u \in Z^2} P_l \langle F(\cdot - 2k - l), F(\cdot - u) \rangle (P_u)^* = \frac{1}{4} \sum_{u \in Z^2} P_u (P_{u+4k})^*.$$

3 Construction of a Class of Vector-Valued Wavelets

In the following, we begin with considering the existence of a class of compaly supported orthogonal vector-valued wavelet functions for the case of $a = 2$.

Theorem 1. Let $F(t) \in L^2(R^2, C^v)$ defined by (5), be an orthogonal vector-valued scaling function. Assume $G_s(t) \in L^2(R^2, C^v)$, $s = 1, 2, 3$. Then $G_s(t)$ are orthogonal vector-valued wavelet functions associated with $F(t)$ if and only if

$$\sum_{t=0}^{3} P(\xi + \sigma_t \pi) B^{(s)}(\xi + \sigma_t \pi)^* = O, \quad \sigma_t \in Z^2, \tag{18}$$

$$\sum_{t=0}^{3} B^{(r)}(\xi + \sigma_t \pi) B^{(s)}(\xi + \sigma_t \pi)^* = \delta_{r,s} I_v, \quad \sigma_t \in Z^2, \tag{19}$$

where $r, s \in \{1, 2, 3\}$, $\xi \in R^2$, or equivalently,

$$\sum_{l \in Z^2} P_l (B^{(s)}_{l+2u})^* = O, \quad s = 1, 2, 3, \ u \in Z^2; \tag{20}$$

$$\sum_{l \in Z^2} B^{(r)}_l (B^{(s)}_{l+2u})^* = 4\delta_{r,s} \delta_{0,u} I_v, \ r, s = 1, 2, 3, \ u \in Z^2. \tag{21}$$

Proof. Firstly, we prove the necessity. By Lemma 1 and (6), (11) and (13), we have

$$O = \sum_{u \in Z^2} \hat{F}(2\xi + 2u\pi)\hat{G}_s(2\xi + 2u\pi)^*$$

$$= \sum_{u \in Z^2} \mathcal{P}(\xi + u\pi)\hat{F}(\xi + u\pi) \cdot \hat{F}(\xi + u\pi)^* B^{(s)}(\xi + u\pi)^*$$

$$= \sum_{t=0}^{3} \mathcal{P}(\xi + \sigma_t\pi)B^{(s)}(\xi + \sigma_t\pi)^*, \quad \sigma_t \in Z^2.$$

It follows from formula (14) and Lemma 1 that

$$\delta_{r,s}I_v = \sum_{u \in Z^2} \hat{G}_r(2\xi + 2u\pi)\hat{G}_s(2\xi + 2u\pi)^* = \sum_{t=0}^{3} B^{(r)}(\xi + \sigma_t\pi)B^{(s)}(\xi + \sigma_t\pi)^*, \sigma_t \in Z^2.$$

Next, the sufficiency will be proven. From the above calculation, we have

$$\sum_{u \in Z^2} \hat{F}(2\xi + u\pi)\hat{G}_s(2\xi + u\pi)^* = \sum_{\sigma=0}^{3} B^{(r)}(\omega + \sigma\pi/2)B^{(s)}(\omega + \sigma\pi/2)^* = \delta_{r,s}I_u.$$

$$\langle F(\cdot), G_s(\cdot - k) \rangle = \frac{1}{\pi^2}\int_{[0,\pi/2]^2} \sum_{u \in Z^2} \hat{h}(2\omega + 2u\pi)\hat{G}_s(2\xi + 2u\pi)^* e^{4ik\xi}d\xi = O,$$

$$\langle G_r(\cdot), G_s(\cdot - k) \rangle = \frac{1}{\pi^2}\int_{[0,\pi/2]^2} \sum_{u \in Z^2} \hat{G}_r(2\omega + 2u\pi)\hat{G}_s(2\xi + 2u\pi)^* \cdot e^{4ik\xi}d\xi = \delta_{0,k}\delta_{r,s}I_v.$$

Thus, it follows that $F(t)$ and $G_s(t), s = 1,2,3$ are mutually orthogonal ones, and $\{G_s(t),\ s = 1,2,3\}$ are a family of orthogonal vector-valued functions. This shows he orthogonality of $\{G_s(\cdot - u),\ s = 1,\ 2,3\}_{u \in z^2}$. Similar to [7,Proposition 1], we can prove its completeness in W_0.

Theorem 2. Let $F(t) \in L^2(R^2, C^v)$ be a 4-coefficient compactly supported orthogonal vector-valued scaling functions satisfying the following refinement equation:

$$F(t) = P_0F(2t - \mu_0) + P_1F(2t - \mu_1) + \cdots + P_3F(2t - \mu_3), \quad \mu_0, \cdots \mu_3 \in Z^2.$$

Assume there exists an integer ℓ, $0 \le \ell \le 3$, such that $(4I_v - P_\ell(P_\ell)^*)^{-1}P_\ell(P_\ell)^*$ is a positive definite matrix. Define $Q_s(s = 1,2,3)$ to be two essentially distinct Hermitian matrice, which are all invertible and satisfy

$$(Q_s)^2 = [4I_v - P_\ell(P_\ell)^*]^{-1}P_\ell(P_\ell)^*. \tag{22}$$

$$\begin{cases} B_j^{(s)} = Q_sP_j, & j \ne \mu_\ell, \\ B_j^{(s)} = -(Q_s)^{-1}P_j, & j = \mu_\ell, \end{cases} \quad s = 1,2,3, \ j \in \{\mu_0, \mu_1, \mu_2, \mu_3\}. \tag{23}$$

Then $G_s(t)$ $(s = 1, 2, 3)$, defined by (24), are orthogonal wavelets with $F(t)$:

$$G_s(t) = B_0^{(s)} F(2t) + B_1^{(s)} F(2t - 1) + \cdots + B_4^{(s)} F(2t - 4). \tag{24}$$

Example 1. Let $F(t) \in L^2(R^2, C^3)$ be 4-coefficient orthogonal vector-valued scaling function satisfy the following equation:

$$F(t) = P_0 F(2t - \mu_0) + P_1 F(2t - \mu_1) + \cdots + P_3 F(2t - \mu_3), \quad \mu_0, \cdots \mu_3 \in Z^2$$

where $P_3 = O$, $P_0(P_3)^* = O$, $P_0(P_0)^* + P_1(P_1)^* + P_2(P_2)^* + P_3(P_3)^* = 4I_3$.

$$P_0 = \begin{pmatrix} \dfrac{\sqrt{2}}{2} & \dfrac{\sqrt{2}}{2} & 0 \\ -\dfrac{1}{2} & \dfrac{\sqrt{2}}{3} & 1 \\ 0 & 0 & \dfrac{2\sqrt{3}}{3} \end{pmatrix}, \quad P_1 = \begin{pmatrix} 1 & 0 & 0 \\ 0 & \dfrac{\sqrt{2}}{6} & 0 \\ 0 & 0 & \dfrac{\sqrt{3}}{3} \end{pmatrix}, \quad P_2 = \begin{pmatrix} \dfrac{\sqrt{2}}{2} & -\dfrac{\sqrt{2}}{2} & 0 \\ \dfrac{1}{2} & \dfrac{\sqrt{2}}{3} & -1 \\ 0 & 0 & \dfrac{2\sqrt{3}}{3} \end{pmatrix},$$

Suppose $\ell = 1$. By using (22), we can choose

$$Q_1 = diag(\sqrt{2}/2, 1/\sqrt{53}, \sqrt{2}/4), \quad Q_2 = diag(\sqrt{2}/2, 1/\sqrt{53}, -\sqrt{2}/4).$$

By applying formula (23), we get that $B_3^{(1)} = B_3^{(2)} = O$,

$$B_0^{(1)} = \begin{pmatrix} \dfrac{1}{2} & \dfrac{1}{2} & 0 \\ -\dfrac{\sqrt{53}}{106} & \dfrac{\sqrt{106}}{159} & \dfrac{\sqrt{53}}{53} \\ 0 & 0 & \dfrac{\sqrt{6}}{6} \end{pmatrix}, \quad B_2^{(2)} = \begin{pmatrix} \dfrac{1}{2} & -\dfrac{1}{2} & 0 \\ \dfrac{\sqrt{53}}{106} & \dfrac{\sqrt{106}}{159} & -\dfrac{\sqrt{53}}{53} \\ 0 & 0 & -\dfrac{\sqrt{6}}{6} \end{pmatrix}$$

$$B_2^{(1)} = \begin{pmatrix} \dfrac{1}{2} & -\dfrac{1}{2} & 0 \\ -\dfrac{\sqrt{53}}{106} & \dfrac{\sqrt{106}}{159} & -\dfrac{\sqrt{53}}{53} \\ 0 & 0 & \dfrac{\sqrt{6}}{6} \end{pmatrix}, \quad B_0^{(2)} = \begin{pmatrix} \dfrac{1}{2} & \dfrac{1}{2} & 0 \\ -\dfrac{\sqrt{53}}{106} & \dfrac{\sqrt{106}}{159} & \dfrac{\sqrt{53}}{53} \\ 0 & 0 & -\dfrac{\sqrt{6}}{6} \end{pmatrix}.$$

$$B_1^{(1)} = -diag(\sqrt{2}, \sqrt{106}/6, 2\sqrt{6}/3), \quad B_1^{(2)} = diag(-\sqrt{2}, -\sqrt{106}/6, 2\sqrt{6}/3).$$

Applying Theorem 2, we obtain that $G_i(t) = B_0^{(t)} F(2t - \mu_0)$ $+ B_1^{(t)} F(2t - \mu_1) + \cdots$ $+ B_3^{(t)} F(2t - \mu_3), t = 1, 2, 3$ are orthogonal vector-valued wavelet functions associated with the orthogonal vector-valued scaling function.

4 Conclusion

A necessary and sufficient condition on the existence of a class of orthogonal vector-valued binary wavelets is presented. An algorithm is proposed.

References

[1] Zhang, N., Wu, X.: Lossless of color masaic images. IEEE Trans. Image Delivery 15(6), 1379–1388 (2006)
[2] Efromovich, S., et al.: Data-Diven and Optimal Denoising of a Signal and Recovery of its Derivation Using Multiwavelets. IEEE Trans. Signal Processing 52(3), 628–635 (2004)
[3] Shen, Z.: Nontensor product wavelet packets in L_2 (R^3). SIAM Math. Anal. 26(4), 1061–1074 (1995)
[4] Xia, X.G., Suter, B.W.: Vector-valued wavelets and vector filter banks. IEEE Trans. Signal Processing 44(3), 508–518 (1996)
[5] Chen, Q., Cheng, Z.: A study on compactly supported orthogonal vector-valued wavelets andwavelet packets. Chaos, Solitons & Fractals 31(4), 1024–1034 (2007)
[6] Yang, S., Cheng, Z., Wang, H.: Construction of biorthogonal multiwavelets. Math. Anal. Appl. 276(1), 1–12 (2002)
[7] Charina, M., Chui, C.K., He, W.: Tight frames of compactly supported multivariate multiwavelets. J. Comput. Appl. Math. 233, 2044–2061 (2010)

A Brief Study on Resource Management of Self-study Center Based on Web

Xianzhi Tian

Wuhan university of Science and Technology, Zhongnan Branch
Julia030712@163.com

Abstract. In the paper, the author has studied the resource management of self - study center based on web. In the paper, all of the studies are finished in self-study center. In the study, different methods of resource management have been proposed by the author Thus she thinks that scientific resource management is necessary and useful for development of students and some effective ways can be used in promoting teaching reform and improving teaching efficiency.

Keywords: resource management; autonomous learning; self-study center; web application.

1 Introduction

In English teaching in China, different teachers adopted different teaching modes. But all of them have one aim. That is, to improve teaching efficiency of teachers and learning efficiency of students. As for autonomous learning abilities, it covers many aspects, and it will be improved step by step with many different strategies. In all aspects, resource pool is very important for improving autonomous learning abilities of students. As for students, there are colorful resources on the web. But they don't know how to sort all resources out from each other. And they can not distinguish the effectiveness and applications of each one. Owning to the unclear understanding of learning materials, students learn by themselves with uncertain learning aims.

In the present days, the center of teaching reform lies on turning of roles of students. The resources pool is also used for improving learning autonomous abilities of students. As for autonomous learning , different names of autonomous learning have been used home and abroad, for example, Learner Autonomy, Self-directed Learning, Self-access, Self-instruction, Independence, Language Awareness etc. No matter how the expressions can be used , it has been a hot topic in modern society. It is connected with the development of our society closely. In modern society, individual development is the base for the individual existence. In order to have good existence abilities, the author must learn to be independent, thus it requires students to learn in autonomous ways. Secondly, students are near modern information, and many kinds of knowledges can be learned through web or other forms connecting with web such as self-study center. It also requires students to learn in autonomous ways outside classroom. Autonomous learning mode is closely connected with resource pool in learning course.

In the paper, the author has proposed different ways or methods to manage resource pool base on web. It is proposed from several aspects. The first one lies on

G. Shen and X. Huang (Eds.): CSIE 2011, Part I, CCIS 152, pp. 36–41, 2011.

management of contents, the second one lies on building of resources scientifically. The third one is the management of evaluation system for testing students. From the analysis and comparison of management of resource pool, the author wants to alert students to make full use of resource pool in autonomous learning center.

2 Brief Introduction of Resource Pool

Generally speaking, resource pool is the premise and foundation of network educa-tion. With the gradual expansion of network,teaching resources of the network is more and more abundant, teaching resources are effective to develop teaching reform. Thus ,the management of resource pool has become the key of network education and autonomous learning. Resource pool refers to all kinds of resources system to be used for complement class teaching.

In teaching reform of college English, different schools have different measures on improving teaching and learning efficiency. Reformers have tried many methods in their teaching course. The typical ones are listed in the following with good effectiveness.

Table 1. Basic contents of Resource Pool

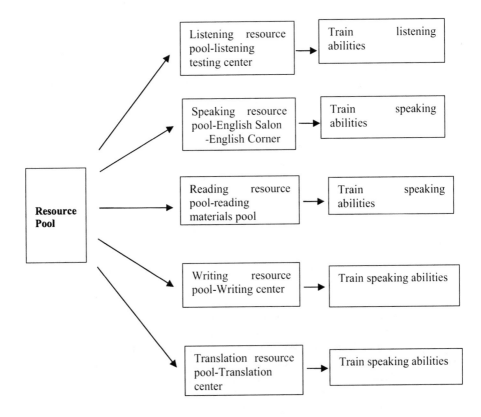

From the above table, we can see that resource pool in English teaching includes five aspects: Listening resource pool-listening testing center, Speaking resource pool-English Salon and English Corner, Reading resource pool-reading materials pool, Writing resource pool-Writing center, Translation resource pool-Translation center. The five aspects are applied to train five kinds of abilities, that is to say, listening ability, speaking ability, reading ability, writing ability and translation ability.

All those abilities can be realized by many elements including personal ones and environmental ones. Resources pool is included in environmental ones. Resources pool influences the development of students especially their linguistic abilities indirectly.

Nowadays, there are some problems about different kinds of resources to be used and searched. It is time for teachers to sort them out scientifically and necessary for learners to use them systematically. How can teachers sort them out and how can learners use them systematically, which become important topics for reformers in colleges. In the present, the problems existing in resources are listed in the following:

Table 2. Problems existing in resources

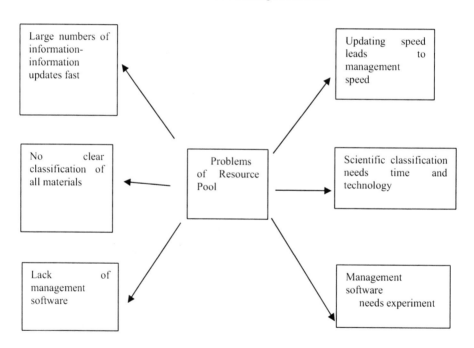

From the above table, we can see that the problems of resource pool mainly includes three aspects. The first one is on large numbers of information, and at the same time, information updates very fast, thus it leads to the difficulties of information being sorted out. Secondly, no clear classification of all materials has appeared in resource management, which leads to difficulties of learning courses for students because scientific classification needs time and technology. Learners should analyse learning materials firstly, and then decide to choose which kind of learning materials to learn. Finally, in present resource pool, it lacks of management software. At the same time, management software needs time to make experiments. When teachers use a certain kind of software, he must consider to make the software have experiment in students to test its efficiency and usefulness. All of the problems should be considered in the management of resource pool system. It is very necessary for teachers to build scientific and systematic resource pool in teaching course. It is beneficial for teaching course and learning results of students.

3 Resource Management of Self-study Center Based on Web

With the development of information technology, students put most of their spare time on web. As for learning course, students are trying their best on autonomous learning besides class learning. In order to train autonomous learning abilities and prolong the inside class learning onto outside learning, teachers have probed many measures concerning about learning resource.

When it comes to self-study center, some teachers think about learning center or game center. In fact, different colleges have different definitions. But the common one is on "self-study", which is equal to autonomous learning. In self-study center, the most important one is on resource. Colorful and rich resources are necessary for development of students. How can teachers manage those resources? The question is worth thinking. Systematic management is the base for effective learning. Therefore, the author has explored the effective and systematic management in this paper to improve teaching and learning efficiency.

Resource management mainly includes the following aspects. Each aspect has its own characteristics. It can be divided into classification of resource, resource refreshing, application of resources and management of resource software.

Table 3. Resource management table

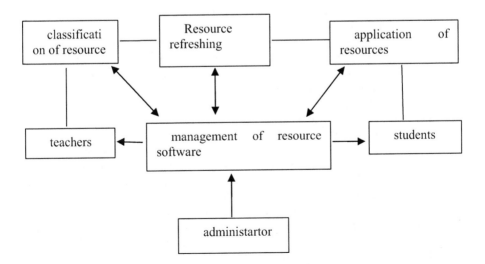

From the above table, it is easy to see that resource management mainly includes teachers, students and administrators with their proper coordination. Besides personal elements, it mainly includes classification of resource, Resource refreshing and application of resources. Each one is in very complex step to be finished. As for classification, teachers must know the contents and distinguish their differences among them very clearly. So teachers must discuss all materials in the resource pool in meeting or e-meeting at regular intervals based on a certain rule. Sometimes, classification must be evaluated by some experts in the field for its effectiveness. As for resource refreshing step, it is the main responsibilities of the administrator. But it is also concerned with teachers and students. The refreshing materials must be checked or evaluated by teachers. Therefore, resource refreshing course is also not very easy, which is deeply influenced by the base of students, the teaching mode of teachers. As for application of resource, it is the most complex one in resource management for its flexibilities during the course.

In order to manage the resource pool, teachers must spend a lot of time to think about it and practise it in learners. The complex steps are on classification of resources and evaluation of effectiveness of resource. The management is in a long way, which needs the efforts of many teachers and students. But in a short time, teachers and students need to do the following things:

◆ In order to manage the resource pool, teachers should divide his/her class into several groups. Each group is in the same level of learning base. To different group, teachers should distribute different learning materials to them. It is connected closely with classification of resources. At the same time, teachers should appoint a leader in each group, which will separate heavy task into each small group. After a period of learning, teachers will have meetings or e-meetings among each leaders. From each leader of each group, teachers know how to adjust their teaching plan and continue their teaching course.

◆ Besides group system, it is better for administrators to use management software to manage the resource pool. In management software, it can regulate learning plans, learning time, learning test and learning evaluation after a period of learning. It is very useful for learners and teachers. Sometimes, the management should have correction function for learners. That is to say, students can know their learning results after a period of learning and doing exercises. For example, SAP management software is very convenient for the management of the whole factory. The lesson is the same with management software for a learning resource pool for autonomous learners. Finally, learning evaluation system is also very important, which is beneficial for further learning of learners. Therefore, management software is required to include this function.

◆ In the course of management, task distribution should be clear and in step by step. Therefore, teachers should understand the bases of each students very clearly before distributing learning task. Only can they know the base of students does they distribute learning task scientifically.

◆ In fact, resource pool is closely connected with autonomous learning abilities if students. Teachers should know how to deal with learning efficiency of students in self-study center. Self-study center is hard to manage, and it needs the whole effort of teachers, students and administrators.

All in all, the management of resource pool is in a long course, and it needs the whole efforts of all participants. The application of it should also be considered scientifically.

3 Conclusion

In the paper, the author has briefly studied the resource management of resource pool in self-study center. It is based on web and modern information technology. It requires time to test. And ideal and scientific management needs the whole efforts of teachers, students , administrators and all participants. The author will explore it in her further study and tries her best to improve teaching efficiency.

References

1. Little, D.: Learner Autonomy and Human Interdependence: some Theoretical and Practical Consequences of A Social-interactive View of Cognition, Learning and Language. In: Sinclair, B.I. (ed.) Learner Autonomy, Teacher Autonomy: Future Directions, pp. 15–23. Longman/Pearson Education, Harlow (2000a)
2. Sheerin, S.: An Exploration of the Relationship Between Self-access and Independent Learning. In: Benson, P., Voller, P. (eds.) Autonomy and Independence in Language Learning, p. 63. Longman, London (1997)
3. Pierson, H.D.: Learner culture and learner autonomy in the Hong Kong Chinese context. In: Pemberton, R., Li, E.S., Or, W.F. (eds.) Taking Control: Autonomy in Language Learning. Hong Kong University Press, Hong Kong (1996)
4. Wang, D.Q.: Fostering learner autonomy in college English study. Foreign Languages World 5, 17–23 (2002)
5. Zhan, X.: An Investigation into the Characteristics of Chinese Non-English Majors' Autonomous English Learning. Unpublished master's dissertation Huazhong University of Science and Technology (2004)

Empirical Research on Yield Curve of China Bond Market

Yuxian Zheng

Zhejiang Water Conservancy and Hydropower College, Hangzhou, China
zhengyx@mail.zjwchc.com

Abstract. The yield curve of bonds is an instrument that gives us the necessary information for valuing deterministic financial cash flows, measuring the economic market expectations and testing the effectiveness of monetary policy decisions. In the present paper, we focus on fair price calculation and residual analytics of sample bond by different models to find most effective method for china bond interest rate modeling.

Keywords: yield curve; discount; sport rate; forward rate; least square method; residual.

1 Introduction

As a direct graphic description to the term structure of interest rate, yield curve represents the relations between rates and maturity times of different bonds. The empirical research shows that the yield curve plays a very important part in both macro-finance and micro-finance regions of developed finance markets. At macro level, the yield curve, which objectively reflects the changing situation of return rates of the bond market, is an indicator of monetary policy and the balance of monetary supply and demand. At micro level, basic functions of the yield curve in risk measurement, accounting, performance measurement, asset pricing, economic forecasting and many other aspects, are conducive to the development of bond market and market-oriented reform of interest rates [1]. Due to the importance of the yield curve, research and attention on it has increasingly become a hot spot issue of both theoretical and practical areas.

Since the development of China's bond market began late, the theoretical study for the yield curve is lagging behind, which started in the late 90's. The work worth mentioning in the recent years is that applying models widely used abroad to do empirical researches and comparison analysis on bond yield curves of our country. The research of Yuling Zhao [2] shows that, aimed at the current situation of China with the small amount of distribution of short-term bonds, less variety of long-term bonds, large proportion of medium-term bonds and unhealthy term structure, N-S model is applicable to construct the Treasury yield curve of China. Shiwu Zhu and Jianheng Chen [3] compared polynomial spline method with Svensson extended model, and they found that Svensson extended model had better fitting results at the near-end and was more stable at the far-end. Feng Zhu [4] applied Svensson extended

G. Shen and X. Huang (Eds.): CSIE 2011, Part I, CCIS 152, pp. 42–48, 2011.

model and cubic B spline function model to estimate the yield curve, and the result showed that yield curves fit by FNZ model and Svensson model got closer when the number of sample bonds increased. In this paper, by the perspective of calculating the sample bond price of yield curves and analyzing the residual, we use the data of Chinese bond market and focused on doing empirical research using several yield curve fitting models that are internationally accepted, to find fitting methods of yield curves that are suitable for Chinese bond market.

2 Models and Methods

At present, yield curve models that are widely used in the actual studies are all based on a continuous function assumption of discount factor from a static perspective. This method has the following two approaches: one is the segment fitting technique, using different spline functions as basis functions to estimate the segmental discount factor; Another idea is the whole fitting technique, which use a parameterized model to get yield curves, and the number of parameters to be estimated of this model is less than that of the spline function technique. Yield curves fitted by N-S model, Svensson extended model and FNZ model have more economic meanings and are more consistent with the interest rate expectation theory. According to a survey of Bank for International Settlements in 1999, without exception, major Western central banks use these three models in fitting the yield curve.

Table 1. Yield curve fitting methods of some central banks

Country	Yield curve fitting model
Belgium	N-SModel, Svensson Model
Canada	Svensson Model
Finland	N-S Model
France	N-S Model, Svensson Model
German	Svensson Model
Italy	N-S Model
Japan	Maximum smoothing spline，i.e. FNZ Model
Norway	Svensson Model
Spain	N-S Model (by 1995), Svensson Model
Sweden	Svensson Model
England	Svensson Model
U.S.A.	Maximum smoothing spline，i.e. FNZ Model

Data source: Official website of Bank for International Settlements http://www.bis.org/ [5]

2.1 N-S Model

Nelson & Siegel(1987) [5] use Laguerre function to construct models. They set instantaneous forward rate F(t) as a constant plus Laguerre function, and derived the implicit current yield curve R(t) and discount factor D(t):

$$F(t) = \alpha_0 + \alpha_1 \exp(-\frac{t}{\beta}) + \alpha_2 \cdot \frac{t}{\beta} \cdot \exp(-\frac{t}{\beta}) \tag{1}$$

$$R(t) = \alpha_0 + \alpha_1 \cdot \frac{\beta}{t} \cdot [1 - \exp(-\frac{t}{\beta})] + \alpha_2 \cdot \frac{\beta}{t} \cdot [1 - \exp(-\frac{t}{\beta})(\frac{t}{\beta} + 1)] \tag{2}$$

$$D(t) = \exp\{-\alpha_0 t - \alpha_1 \beta[1 - \exp(-\frac{t}{\beta})] - \alpha_2 \beta[1 - \exp(-\frac{t}{\beta})(\frac{t}{\beta} + 1)]\} \tag{3}$$

Where $\alpha_0 > 0$, $\alpha_0 + \alpha_1 > 0$, $\beta_1 > 0$.

2.2 Svensson Model

In order to enhance the fitting ability for different term structure of interest rate, Svensson(1994) [6] improved the N-S model by introducing two new parameters, to make the curve be capable to simulate shapes of double top and double U.

$$F(t) = \alpha_0 + \alpha_1 \exp(-\frac{t}{\beta_1}) + \alpha_2 \cdot \frac{t}{\beta_1} \cdot \exp(-\frac{t}{\beta_1}) + \alpha_3 \cdot \frac{t}{\beta_2} \cdot \exp(-\frac{t}{\beta_2}) \tag{4}$$

$$R(t) = \alpha_0 + (\alpha_1 + \alpha_2)\frac{\beta_1}{t}(1 - e^{-t/\beta_1}) - \alpha_2 e^{-t/\beta_1} + \alpha_3 \frac{\beta_2}{t} \cdot [1 - e^{-t/\beta_2}(\frac{t}{\beta_2} + 1)] \tag{5}$$

$$D(t) = \exp\{-\alpha_0 t - (\alpha_1 + \alpha_2)\beta_1(1 - e^{-t/\beta_1}) + \alpha_2 t e^{-t/\beta_1} - \alpha_3 \beta_2[1 - e^{-t/\beta_2}(\frac{t}{\beta_2} + 1)]\} \tag{6}$$

Where $\alpha_0 > 0$, $\alpha_0 + \alpha_1 > 0$, $\beta_1 > 0$, $\beta_2 > 0$.

2.3 FNZ Model

There are a variety of objectives we can use in index tracking, in which the most important one is tracking error. The objective of excess return is also used in many articles, to construct a portfolio that generates a larger return than the index. Since we discuss pure index tracking in this paper, we only deal with the objective of index tracking below.

In order to find balance between accuracy and smoothness, based on the assumption of cubic B spline of forward instantaneous rate, Fisher, Nychka and Zervos [7] first used smooth spline instead of regression spline to fit curves. They gave rise to FNZ model by adding a punishment item in the objective function to control the vibration of curves. The responding forward rate, instantaneous rate and discount factor function have forms as below.

$$F(t) = \sum_{i=1}^{n} a_i B_{i,k}(t), \quad D(t) = \exp[-\sum_{i=1}^{n} a_i \int_0 B_{i,k}(s)ds], \quad R(t) = (\sum_{i=1}^{n} a_i \int_0 B_{i,k}(s)ds)/t \tag{7}$$

Where $t_j, \cdots, t_{j+k}$ are B-spline functions of order k.

$$B_{j,k}(t) = \frac{t - t_j}{t_{j+k-1} - t_j} B_{j,k-1}(t) + \frac{t_{j+k} - t}{t_{j+k} - t_{j+1}} B_{j+1,k-1}(t), B_{j,1}(t) = \begin{cases} 1 & t \in [t_j, t_{j+1}) \\ 0 & t \notin [t_j, t_{j+1}) \end{cases} \tag{8}$$

3 Empirical Research on Chinese Bond Market

3.1 Estimating Parameters

Refer to methods in [7] and according to no-arbitrage principle, we do coupon stripping to bonds with fixed payment of interest, and get its risk neutral price:

$$P_0 = AA \times D \tag{9}$$

Where P_0 is the theoretical price of the bond, AA is the coupon matrix of the sample bond, D is the discount factor vector.

The purpose of estimating parameters is to make the difference between the theoretical price and the market price of the coupon bond be the smallest. Let X be the parameter to be estimated of N-S model and Svensson extended model, and let β and λ be the cubic B-spline coefficient and smoothing parameter of FNZ model. Using the least square method, we can turn parameter estimation into solving an optimization problem:

$$\min_{X}(P - AA \times D) \times (P - AA \times D)' \tag{10}$$

$$\min_{\lambda,\beta}[(P - AA \times D) \times (P - AA \times D)' + \lambda\beta'H\beta] \tag{11}$$

3.2 Selection and Processing of Sample Data

In this paper, the fixed-rate bonds of the bond market between Chinese banks are chosen as samples. Bonds issued in a way of discount or floating rate are removed. Taking liquidity of bonds into account, data of bonds that with neither close price nor purchase and sale prices is not used to fit the yield curve. The principle to determine the price of sample bonds is: if there are deals in a day, the price is the weighted average price of all deal price; if there are no deals but purchase and sale prices, the price is the arithmetic average of the mean price of purchase and sale prices.

3.3 Comparison between Different Models

Without loss of generality, we chose transaction data of fixed rate treasure in interbank bond market on Apr. 23, 2008 (Table 2) as sample data. We use it in the empirical research of the three most popular models, and compare with the yield curve fitted by Hermitt interpolation by Central Depository Trust & Clearing Co., Ltd.

(1) Discount factor
  Discount factor of these three models are very close, but after 15 years there is difference between the discount factor calculated by FNZ model and the other two models, which causes a difference between current rate and forward instantaneous rate.
(2) Current yield curve
  There is a large difference at the far-end (especially after 15 years) between the curves calculated by FNZ model and the other models. Considering the greatest

maturity of sample bonds is 14.86, this means that the fitting effect of long-term rate by FNZ model is bad with large fluctuations when there is few sample data. The long-term rates fitted by N-S model and Svensson model are more smooth and there is little difference between them and the yield curve of Central Depository Trust & Clearing Co., Ltd. It is noteworthy that, in the estimation of short-term interest rates, the results of FNZ model and N-S model are close, and the downward sloping of Hermitt interpolation is large, while the result of Svensson model is a U-turn curve. These results explain the increase of short-term interest rate caused by liquidity premium.

(3) Forward instantaneous rate
    At the far-end of the curve of forward instantaneous rate, FNZ model has a larger downward sloping, but N-S model and Svensson model are close and quite smooth. At the near-end of the curve forward instantaneous rate, FNZ model and N-S model are close, while a U-turn yield curve is fitted by Svensson model.

3.4 Residual Analysis of Theoretical Price of Sample Bonds

From equation (9), discount factor of different models can be used to calculate the corresponding theoretical price P_0 of sample bonds. In this paper, we use the sample data above to do in-sample test and out-of-sample test based on the three models and residual analysis of theoretical price.

(1) Price error P_0-P (In-sample error): We can see from Table 5 and Fig.4 that the discount factor curves of N-S model , Svensson model and FNZ model are similar, and the error of theoretical price of sample bonds calculated by these models are close. Furthermore, price errors of short-term and long-term bonds are small, but that of medium-term bond is larger.

(2) Residual analysis (Table 3): Both in-sample and out-sample tests of these three models have good effects. Respectively, the standard error of Svensson model in both in-sample and out-of-sample are the smallest.

Table 3. Root mean square error of both in-sample and out-of-sample bond prices

Root mean square error of N-S model		Root mean square error of Svensson model		Root mean square error of FNZ model	
In-sample	Out-of-sample	In-sample	Out-of-sample	In-sample	Out-of-sample
0.1243	0.2125	0.1184	0.2085	0.1244	0.5082

3.5 The Economic Implications of the Model Parameters

From equations (1) to (6), we have

$$\lim_{t \to \infty} F(t) = \lim_{t \to \infty} R(t) = \alpha_0 , \lim_{t \to 0} F(t) = \lim_{t \to 0} R(t) = \alpha_0 + \alpha_1 , \tag{12}$$

Hence α_0 represents the long-term interest rate level. The instantaneous rate is mainly determined by α_0 and α_1. The coefficient of α_2 is a function of maturity that starts from 0, increases and then decreases to 0 again, so the value of α_2 determines the curvature of curve. α_0 , α_1 , α_2 are called long-term factor, short-term factor and medium-term factor respectively.

Table 4. Adjustment of RMB benchmark rates and bank deposit reserve ratio

Date	Escalation of 1-year benchmark interest rates	Date	Escalation of bank deposit reserve ratio
2007.07.21	0.27	2007.8.15	0.5
2007.08.22	0.27	2007.9.25	0.5
2007.09.15	0.27	2007.10.25	0.5
2007.12.21	0.27	2007.11.26	0.5

Data source: Website of People's Bank of China

In the second half of 2007, China raised its benchmark interest rate and the bank deposit reserve ratio for four times (Table 4). We chose the bilateral trade data and quote data of fixed rate bonds in Chinese interbank bond market from July 2, 2007 to December 21, 2007 as samples, to estimate the dynamic changing process of long-term factor of Svensson model. And we also consider the affects of policies of interest rates to the yield curve. We find that

- The fluctuation range of long-term factor of Chinese fixed-rate bond is large.
- Long-term interest rate factor will be raised before the benchmark interest.
- The long-term factor will increase by the increase of the deposit reserve ratio.

4 Conclusions

In this paper, by the perspective of calculating the sample bond price of yield curves and analyzing the residual, we use the data of Chinese bond market and focused on doing empirical research using several yield curve fitting models that are internationally accepted. We find that when there are few samples, the performance of FNZ model on fitting the yield curve at the far-end is not good, while Svensson model has a more complicated structure than N-S model at the near-end of the yield curve. The tests of both in-sample and out-of-sample shows that the root mean square error of Svensson model is the smallest. We therefore suggest that Svensson be used in modeling yield curves of Chinese bond market. Besides, our research will focus on the predicting of yield curves based on these models.

References

1. Yu, J.: Yiming Review and development of yield curve theory and its application (2008)
2. Zhao, Y.: Comparison and analysis of the construction of Chinese bond yield curve. Shanghai Finance (9), 29–31 (2003)
3. Zhu, S., Chen, J.: Empirical research on the maturity structure of bond interest rate. Finance Research (10), 63–73 (2003)

4. Zhu, F.: Estimation of current yield curve of bonds. Securities Market Herald 4, 31–36 (2003)
5. Nelson, C.R., Siegel, A.F.: Parsimonious Modeling of Yield Curves. Journal of Business 60-4 (1987)
6. Svensson, L.E.O.: Estimating and Interpreting Forward Rates: Sweden 1992-4. National Bureau of Economic Research Working Paper #4871 (1994)
7. Fisher, M., Nychka, D., Zervos, D.: Fitting the Term Structure of Interest Rates with Smoothing Splines. Board of Governors of the Federal Reserve System (U.S.), Finance and Economics discussion Series 95-1 (1994)

Research of Digital Watermark Based on Arnold and DCT Technology

Cun Shang and Yan-li Li

Service Computer Technology and Graphics Lab
Department of Computer Science and Technology
Xinyang Agricultural College, Henan, 464000, China
shang10278@163.com

Abstract. Digital watermarking is one of the effective methods which can protect the copyright of multimedia data. This thesis presented a digital watermarking technology based on Arnold and DCT techniques. To improve the robustness of watermark, this thesis adopted the multi-embedded strategy. The DC coefficients in the block of the same location of each color components, are embedded the same robust watermark. The robust watermark is a binary copyright image being transformed by Arnold. The results show that, the proposed watermarking algorithm is an effective way to identify the copyright of image.

Keywords: Digital watermarking; HSI color space; DCT Transform; Robustness.

1 Introduction

With the rapid development of digital technique and Internet,Digital watermarking technique becomes more and more important in protecting the intellectual property rights of digital products. This paper puts forward the digital watermarking algorithm based on Arnold and DCT technique. To increase the difficulty of deciphering, improved Arnold transform is used to encrypt the binary watermark image. The application of DCT transform in watermarking technology has come to maturity, besides, DCT transform has small calculation, and is compatible with international popular compression and encoding standards, so this paper believes that watermark embedding is in DCT domain, and the energy of transformed DCT image centers on the middle and low frequency components of DC coefficients and AC coefficients. Good robustness will be obtained when digital watermark is embedded into these components. By experiment, this algorithm has a good robustness on common image processing and malicious attacks.

2 Selection of Color Space

Original image is a color image, as result, for a color image watermarking technology research, the most crucial point is how to choose color space for watermark

G. Shen and X. Huang (Eds.): CSIE 2011, Part I, CCIS 152, pp. 49–54, 2011.

embedding. Most of the color of color image is presented by RGB color space, but RGB and other similar color model can not suit people's color sensitivity well. HSI color space, which presents color more naturally and directivity, is more suitable for the characteristics of human being's vision, and can handle the luminance component in the image in the separation of color and brightness[1].

3 Pretreatment of Watermark Image

Watermark system should be pretreated before watermark embedding. This not only plays a key role in system robustness, but also has very important significance in the security of digital watermarking system. It increases the difficulty of guessing attack for attacker. In this paper, Arnold transform is used in the process of pretreatment because it is simple, easy to use, and cyclical.

Arnold transform is defined as follows: Suppose a point (x, y) is on a square unit; the point (x, y) is transformed to another point (x', y'); the transformation is in accordance with formula 1:

$$\begin{bmatrix} x' \\ y' \end{bmatrix} = \begin{bmatrix} 1 & 1 \\ 1 & 2 \end{bmatrix} \begin{bmatrix} x \\ y \end{bmatrix} \mathrm{mod}\, m \cdot \tag{1}$$

In the formula, (x, y) is the pixel coordinate of original image; (x', y') is the pixel coordinate of the new image after transformation; in (x, y) and $(x', y') \in \{0, 1 \ldots M\text{-}1\}$, M represents the exponent number of digital image matrix[2]. After the Arnold scrambling transformation of the original watermark image, Arnold, disordered images appear, as shown in Fig. 1 and 2:

Fig. 1. original watermark image before embedding

Fig. 2. watermark image after scrambling transformation

The spatial location of the watermark image and images has been changed after been treated with Arnold scrambling Transformation and scrambling respectively, but the pixel values and the size of image has not been changed.

4 Analysis and Selection of Position of Watermark Embedding

The choice of position of watermark embedding is very important for guaranteeing invisibility and robustness of the system. In order to take full advantage of the masking effect of human eyes on frequency, the image needs to be transformed from space domain to transform domain. This paper chooses discrete cosine transform as the transformation method.

4.1 Discrete Cosine Transform

When image being processed, two-dimensional DCT transform is operated by way of blocks of pixels. In this paper, the images are processed by block DCT transform because of the large amount of calculation if the images are transformed by two-dimensional DCT as a whole. After DCT transform, N is set 8, and images are divided into 8×8 blocks, for the frequency increases little but the complexity increases a lot if N is bigger than 8. After discrete cosine transform, on the upper left corner of the image is low frequency coefficient, whose value is large, and most of the energy concentrates on this part, where the color is bright white, while the low-energy part is black. This shows that human visual system is sensitive to the change of low-frequency DCT coefficients, but is difficult to detect that of high-frequency coefficients.

4.2 Selection of Watermark Embedding Coefficient

In the digital watermark algorithm of DCT domain,To ensure the watermark of good invisibility and robustness, the DCT coefficients which are often used to embed watermark can still be better retained after been processed and attacked by common images. This method can guarantee the robustness of the watermark; meanwhile, large amount of watermark can be embedded based on non-visibility.This algorithm chooses low-frequency coefficients, which has good robustness, as coefficient of the watermark that is about to be embedded.

5   Implementation of Digital Watermarking Based on Arnold and DCT

5.1 Pretreatment of the Watermark

Suppose original image is 24-bit true color image K, in the size of M×N. The copyright watermark embedded is the binary watermark image *WR*. When the watermark is about to be embedded, it needs to be pretreated, during which the image is transformed to binary sequence:

1) Binary watermark image *WR* is processed by Arnold scrambling transformation by M times, in order to remove the pixel spatial relativity in the watermark image, and enhance the robustness and security of the watermarking algorithm. M is set the key to the encrypted watermark image.
2) *WR* is transformed into sequence {0,1}; each element is defined as WR_k.
3) "0"in *WR* is transformed into "-1", in order to get WR_k {-1, 1}; the effect of rounding errors can be removed.

5.2 Algorithm Watermark Embedding

1) Conversion of Color Space
First, original color image *k* is converted from RGB mode HSI mode. Cylinder conversion is used in this paper.

2) Extract the Luminance Component *I* and Divide into Blocks

The luminance component *I*, whose image has been extracted, is divided into in 8×8blocks, and a cross block matrix is obtained. These sub-blocks are not covered by each other. Each block is expressed as f_k^I (*x, y*) (*x,y*=1,2,...8, *k*=1,2...); each sub-block f_k^I (*x, y*) corresponds to the corresponding watermark WR_k of the robust watermark *WR*.

3) DCT Transform and Coefficient Quantization

Each block f_k^I (*x, y*) of the image is transformed by DCT, in order to obtain DCT coefficient matrix F_k^I (*u, v*); (*u,v*=1,2...8,*k*=1,2,..). F_k^I (*u, v*) is the coefficient which needs to be quantifed.

4) Robust Watermark Embedding

Select DC coefficient C_k^I (1) of robust watermark that is about to be embedded in each block, and embed the watermark by way of additive embedding, according to formula 2. which, $c_k^{I'}$ (1) is the DC coefficient of the embedded watermark in the block. α is the embedding strength, whose value will directly affect the Effectiveness of the algorithm. Through experimenta, the appropriate value of α is 0.79, so that the invisibility and robustness of the watermark can be taken into account simultaneously.

$$C_k^{I'}(1)= C_k^I(1)+\alpha WR_k \qquad (2)$$

6   Experimental Results and Performance Testing

6.1 Performance Evaluation

Performance evaluations of image watermarking systems is used for quantitative evaluation to the carriers.

6.2 Test of Invisibility of the Watermark

The test of this algorithm is processed on Matlab 7.0 platform. According to the algorithm, a robust watermark is embedded in the original image. The embedding strength of the robust watermark is set at 0.79. The image with embed watermark is shown in Fig.4. By comparison, the image with embedded watermark has not degraded significantly through observation, and the visual system is not aware of any differences. It suggests that the digital watermarking technique proposed in this paper has good invisibility. Not having been attacked, the robust watermark is extracted from the image that has an embedded watermark, as shown in Fig.5.

6.3 Anti-attack Experiment

1) Median Filter

Fig. 6, 7 and 8 are the embedded watermarks and extracted watermarks with superposition of different noise. The effect of watermark extraction after the median

Fig. 3. Original Image   **Fig. 4.** Image with Embedded   **Fig. 5.** Extracted Copyright
Watermark   Watermark

Fig. 6. 1×3 Watermark Extracted being median   **Fig. 7.** 3×3 Watermark Extracted After being
filtered   median filtered

Fig. 8. 5×5 Watermark ExtractedAfter being median filtered

Table 1. Watermark Extraction Effect after the Image Median Filter is Embedded

Median Filter	1×3	3×3	5×5
NC	0.981	0.963	0.913

filter is embedded in the image is shown in Table 1. The experiment suggests that the copyright watermark has a good ability of resisting median filter.

2) JPEG Lossy Compression

JPEG compression with quality factor 90, 80, 70, 60 are used respectively. The compression effect is mainly expressed by quality factor. In the Fig.9, Fig.10, Fig.11, Fig.12, the bigger the quality factor is, the better the effect of the extracted watermark image will be. The effect of watermark extraction after JPEG compression of different quality factor is shown in Table 2.

Fig. 9. NC =90   **Fig. 10.** NC =80   **Fig. 11.** NC =70   **Fig. 12.** NC =60

Table 2. Effect of Watermark Extraction after JPEG Compression of Different Quality Factor

Median Filter	90	80	70
NC	0.973	0.956	0.922

In the experiment, the watermark is still effectively extracted after the image, which has embedded watermarks, has been compressed appropriately. This indicates that the algorithm has good robustness to JPEG compression.

7 The References Section

This paper has chosen the color images of 24-bit RGB as the original image, using HSI color space, which is closer to people's understanding and interpretation to color. And then, the effect of the algorithm based on DCT technique has been tested. The experiment has mainly assessed and analyzed the invisibility and robustness of the watermark algorithm. The comparison experiment shows that this method has good invisibility, and strong robustness under the condition that the watermark doesn't affect the quality of the original image.

References

1. Bender, W., Gruhl, D., Morimoto, N.: Technique for data hiding. IBM Systems Journal 35(3-4), 313–336 (1996)
2. Hsu, C.-T., Wu, J.L.: Hidden Signature in Image Processing. 8(1), 58–68 (1999)
3. Cox, I.J., Miller, M.L.: The First 50 years of Electronic watermarking. EURASIP J. of Applied Signal Proceessing 2, 126–132 (2002)
4. Neilson, G.M.: On Marching Cubes. IEEE Transactions on Visualization and Computer Graphics 9(3), 283–297 (2003)
5. Gao, J.G., Fowler, J.E., Younan, N.H.: An Image Adaptive Watermark Based on Redundant Wavelet Transform. In: Processing of the IEEE International Conference On Image processing, Thessaloniki (2001)
6. Niu, X., Lu, Z., Sun, S.: Digital watermarking of still images with graylevel ditigil watermarks. IEEE Trans. on Consumer Electronics 46 (2000)

Technology of Application System Integration Based on RIA

Caifeng Cao , Jianguo Luo, and Zhixin Qiu

School of Computer Wuyi University, Jiangmen 529020, China
cfcao@126.com

Abstract. Application system integration is an important aspect of industry informatization construction. For scattered, autonomous, heterogeneous application system, this paper puts forward a full set of solution of application system integration based on RIA technology and some open-source frameworks. The scheme realizes the integration of different tech. Web system, J2EE application system, .NET application system, FMS3 streaming media system, different type database systems and Web services. It provides an application platform with rich user experience and friendly user interface. At last, the scheme usability is proved by UPRS.

Keywords: RIA, application system integration, rich client, Adobe AIR.

1 Introduction

Application system integration is to combine different systems organically into a new system with integrative and stronger function according to application requirements. It has gone deep into user's specific business and application. On the most occasions, Application system integration is also called as the integration of industry information solution [1]. It includes several characteristics as follows.

1) System integration takes satisfying user needs as essential starting point, reflects user-centered thoughts.

2) System integration contains technology, management and business, and so on. It is a comprehensive system engineering. But it reflects more the design, debugging and development technologies.

3) The cost performance is a crucial reference factor on evaluating the rational design and successful implementation of system integration project[1].

The goal of application system integration is to construct loosely-coupled distributed application system on the basis of existing scattered, autonomous, heterogeneous application system. It not only provides users with global distribution application, but also never impacts on the use of original system [2]. In the aspect of technology, it must realize seamless system function integration and data integration in order to achieve resource sharing, interflow and interaction. In the aspect of application, it should provide comprehensive integrated information system platform with powerful function, amicable interface and rich user experience for industry or organization.

G. Shen and X. Huang (Eds.): CSIE 2011, Part I, CCIS 152, pp. 55–60, 2011.

In order to reach the aim as above, this paper adopts the newly developing RIA (Rich Internet Application) technology, and puts forward a complete set of the realization solution on system integration.

2 RIA and Application Integration

RIA integrates desktop application, Web application and interactive multimedia communication, which forms a new generation of network application development technology. RIA itself has good integration characteristic. Firstly, in system structure, RIA combines B/S with C/S, and integrates the both advantages into itself. It not only has characteristics of C/S personalized client and abundant function, but also uses popular HTTP protocol and Web server technology to deploy system conveniently. On the meanwhile, the client running manner and flexible online/offline mechanism largely lower the load on Web server and the dependence to network transmission. Secondly, on the aspect of realizing system function, it provides mark language, script language, object and component, Web service and database technology. It has strong expressive force to realize user interface with rich user experience, and provides the access to Web application system, J2EE application system, flow media application system and Web service. So, RIA can realize the function integration of heterogeneous application system. It provides the access to different kind remote or local database and XML file. So, RIA can realize the data integration of heterogeneous application system.

RIA has special advantages and broad technology inclusivity in the aspects of structure and client design, which makes it become effective application system integration technology.

3 Application Integration Realization Based on RIA

Currently, most information systems are developed in Web technology, in which ASP.NET, JSP and PHP have equal roles. J2EE technology is one of first choices to develope comprehensive application system. Flow media application system also has a wide application. There are many developing technologies in RIA, such as Adobe Flex/Flash, Microsoft Avalon and Java SWT, etc. This paper describes the integration method to above mainstream application system by Adobe RIA technology.

Flex provides MXML tag language and ActionScript script language, combines JavaScript/Ajax to realize rich client programme. Flex application programme can access Web service based on SOAP, access Web page based on HTTP, and call local application system. It realizes cross-platform running.

1) Integrating different kinds Web application system

The integration of Web application system adopts request/response mode of B/S system in essence. Flex application programme requests to invoke some web page programmes, then server runs it and returns the result. The both communication bases on HTTP. Flex application programme acts as the role of client, and realizes the interactive function among systems by HTTPService component. The key codes are as follows.

```
<mx: HTTPService id="Rq1"
//invoke web page
        url=http://192.202.12.11/Cl1.aspx   method="POST"
        result=lastResult.replyData   //result
        <mx:request> //define passed parameter
            <var1>10</var1>
            ...
        </mx:request>
        <mx:Button label="Execute Call"
click="Rq1.send()"/>
        //execute invoking
</mx: HTTPService >
```

As to web system itself, their programming is as before. For example, ASP.net uses Request component to get client data, and uses Response component to output data to client.

For Web system based on JSP or PHP, only url attribute of HTTPService needs to be modified. For example, url=http://192.202.12.18/Cl2.jsp, url=http://192.202.12.15/Cl3.php.

2) Integrating J2EE application system

Open-source software BlazeDS realizes AMF-RPC(Action Message Format and Romote Procedure Call). It is an agency gateway that runs on J2EE server. Flex application programme realizes the invocation to Java class and JavaBean by BlazeDS and self-contained RemoteObject component. The key codes are as follows.

```
//configure web.xml and service-config.xml
<mx: RemoteObject id="j2eeClass"
destination="computing">
//destination indicates remote Java class
<mx: method name="Computing_zz"//remote object method
        result= j2eeClass.Computing_zz>   //return result
</mx: RemoteObject>
```

3) Integrating .NET application system

Open-source software FluorineFx realizes AMF-RPC. It is a agency gateway that runs on .NET server. Flex application programme can invoke .NET class and component by FluorineFx and self-included RemoteObject component. The key codes are as follows.

```
//configure web.xml and service-config.xml
<mx: RemoteObject id="netClass"
destination="processing">
Endpoint="http:// 192.202.12.19/Fluorine/gateway.aspx"
  <mx: method name="processing_dd"
        result="netClass.processing_dd">
  </mx: RemoteObject>
```

4) Integrating flow media application system

FMS3(Flash Media Server 3) is a new generation of flow media server. It has not only Flash multi-media interactivity, but also has new characteristics of realtime voice and video, and synchronized sharing. Its client runs on Flash Player. Flex application programme just runs on Flash Player plugin. So, it can communicate with FMS3 efficiently and timely.

Flex Builder provides some components for programming, such as NetConnection, NetStream, Camera. For example:

```
//Action Script code
l1=new NetConnection()•
//connect server
l1.connect("rtmp://192.202.12.20/video")•
p1= new NetStream()•
p1.play("video1")•  //play video
```

5) Accessing different kinds of database system

There are two ways to access database system. First, Flex appliction can access different databases indirectly by other application system, such as Web system, J2EE application system. Second, it can access remote database by BlazeDS and DataService components. The realization process is as Fig. 1.

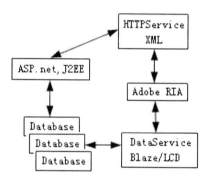

Fig. 1. Access database

6) Accessing Web service

Web service is a kind of software component with independent function, which has many advantages, such as unrelated with platform, Loosely coupled and integratability, etc. It is important technology to construct distributed system. Adobe/Flex supports SOAP protocol, and realizes interaction with Web service by WebService components. The key codes are as follows.

```
<mx: WebService id="Ser1"
  Wsdl=http://192.202.12.18/Service1.wsdl
  <mx:operation name="doMultiply"> //executing method
      <mx:request> //define passed parameters
          p1=10
          ...
      </mx:request>
  </mx:operation>
   result="Ser1.doMultiply.send( )" //execute and invoke
   </mx: WebService>
```

In sum, the solution of application system integration based on RIA is as Fig. 2.

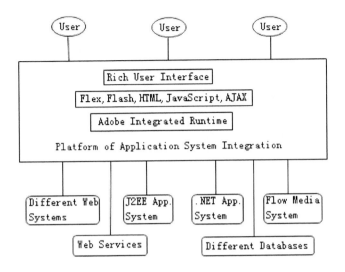

Fig. 2. Scheme of application system integration

4   Design Instance

Universal Patient Record System (UPRS) is a set of software system ,which makes doctors consult and knows related information about patient promptly and convinently. URPS provides a mobile work platform, which can connect medical record management systems of different hospitals at random time for doctors. With some permissions, doctors can extract patient information from different information management systems in many hospitals.

With the technology of above system integration, UPRS can access patient record databases in different hospitals, invoke different format documents, play doctors' realtime treatment videos, and reappear different format medical images. It fully meets the needs of users.

5   Conclusion

RIA technology develops rapidly. Its maturer development tools, running environment,especially related components, make it not only be an important client software technology,but also the effective means of application system integration. This paper deeply discussed Adobe RIA technology in system integration, elaborated technique realization of integrating different application system, and put forward the whole solution of system integration. While integrating function and data, the original system independence is assured. This scheme was used in UPRS, and obtained the recognition of user and expert.

References

1. System Integration, http://baike.baidu.com/view/43762.htm
2. Liu, W.-D., Song, J.-X., Fang, X.-T.: An Approach to Intergrate Infirmation System. J. Computer Science 32(5), 67–70 (2005) (in Chinese)
3. Zhang, Y.-f.: Proficient in Technology of Flex Network Development. Publishing House of Electronics Industry, Beijing (2009) (in Chinese)
4. Cao, C.-f.: Agile Manufacturing Resource Integration Based on RIA and Service Grid. In: 2010 International Conference on Mechanic Automation and Control Engineering, pp. 6058–6061. IEEE Computer Society, Piscataway (2010) (in Chinese)
5. Cao, C.-f.: The Research on Developing Technologies of C/S System Based on HTTP. J. Computer Engineering and Design 28(5), 1239–1241 (2007) (in Chinese)
6. Gourdol, A.: Desktop Integration in Adobe AIR 2, http://tv.adobe.com/watch/adc-presents/
7. David, M.: Inside HTML5: The Browser becomes a first class RIA citizen, http://www.insideria.com/

A New Multi-scale Texture Analysis with Structural Texel

Qiang Song

College of Mechanical and Transportation Engineering,
China University of Petroleum,
Beijing, China
songqiang@cup.edu.cn

Abstract. This paper presents a new methodology for multi-scale texture analysis. The basic idea is that an image texture is viewed as a tessellation of square texels of different sizes and pixel levels. A textural image is decomposed into a set of scale images and each scale image consists of square texels of the same size. The texels in a scale image may have different pixel values. The degree of presence of a texel in a textural image can be measured by the image area occupied by the texel in terms of pixel. The histogram of texel area is shown to be a useful texture feature, and a dominant texture scale derived from the histogram provides a good reference parameter for computing gray-level co-occurrence matrix.

Keywords: texture analysis, multi-scale, structural texel, histogram, dominant texture scale.

1   Introduction

Texture analysis plays an important role in computer vision and pattern recognition, and is useful in a variety of applications such as industrial automation, biomedical image processing, and remote sensing [1], [2], [3], [4]. There have been two main approaches to texture analysis: the statistical approach and the structural approach [5], [6]. The structure approach considers a texture to be composed of texels. The texels are regions with similar pixel and region properties. An image texture can be described by the number, types and spatial layout of texels. Texture can be quantitatively evaluated as having properties of fineness, coarseness, smoothness, irregular, or randomness. Each of these qualities is related to some properties of texels and their spatial interaction [7]. When the texels are small in size and the spatial interaction is constrained to a local neighborhood, the resulting texture is a micro-texture. When the texels begin to have their own distinct shape and regular organization, the texture becomes a macro-texture. This shows scale is an important aspect of texture. Textural scale relates to such parameters as the size of the texel, or the size of local neighborhood used for texture analysis. When the scale goes from

G. Shen and X. Huang (Eds.): CSIE 2011, Part I, CCIS 152, pp. 61–66, 2011.
© Springer-Verlag Berlin Heidelberg 2011

small to large, a texture is examined from a micro-level to a macro-level. This multi-scale processing, which humans obviously apply successfully to texture perception [8], is a strong motivation for texture analysis. It seems to be a logical observation that a given image has a textural scale around which the textural characteristics are most prevailing and distinct. This scale may be defined as the dominant texture scale.

2 Multi-scale Texture Analysis

2.1 Theoretical Background

Two factors contribute to the property of texel. One is the shape of the neighborhood domain, and the other is the topological function of the texel over the domain. Since images are always digitized into a grid, square is chosen as the texel shape in this paper. The basic idea of the multi-scale texture analysis is that an image texture is viewed as a tessellation of square texels of different sizes and pixel levels. A textural image can be decomposed into a set of scale images and each scale image consists of square texels of the same size. The texels in a scale image may have different pixel values. For two different textual images, some of their scale images may be similar or the same, other scale images may be very different and contribute to the overall differences. Such analysis provides the multi-scale information of a textural image.

For a textural image of $H \times W$ pixels (H and W are the numbers of rows and columns of the image, respectively), the sizes of texels vary from 1 pixel to min (H, W) pixels. $I(x, y)$ indicates the pixel value at the location of (x, y). The variance of pixel values within the d-scale texel region is no greater than a specified value ε:

$$\frac{1}{d^2} \sum_{(i,j)\in(d\times d)} |I(i,j) - M| \le \varepsilon .$$ (1)

This is called the error condition and

$$M = \frac{1}{d^2} \sum_{(i,j)\in(d\times d)} I(i,j) .$$ (2)

If the error tolerance ε is big enough, then the whole image can be represented by only one texel, all pixel value are the same as the mean pixel value of the whole image. If the error tolerance ε is small enough, for example, $\varepsilon = 0$, then the highest number of texels will be used.

2.2 Computer Realization

All texels should be sorted according to size (scale), large texels prior to small ones. First the largest texel is applied. If in a square region, the error condition is satisfied, this region will represented by this texel with pixel value M. If the error condition is not satisfied, the texel is moved by one pixel in the order of left to right, top to bottom. The error condition is checked for each move. Then the second largest texel goes through the same steps. This procedure is repeated until the smallest texel of one pixel is applied. Fig. 1 shows the multi-scale analysis of a textural image with square texels and the error tolerance ε is set to 6. The analysis results in many scale images, and each scale image contains areas represented by texels of the same properties in terms of size.

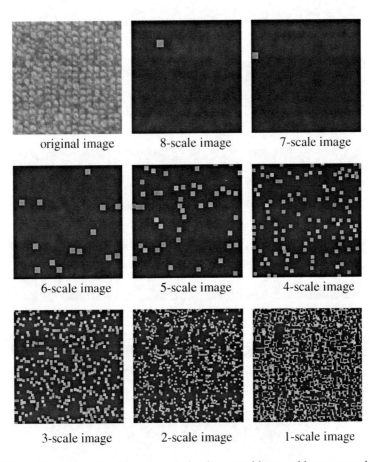

original image	8-scale image	7-scale image
6-scale image	5-scale image	4-scale image
3-scale image	2-scale image	1-scale image

Fig. 1. Illustration of multi-scale analysis of a textural image with square texels

Real texture images are more complicated. Fig. 2 shows the multi-scale analysis of a real textural image from hot-rolled plate surface, and the error tolerance ε is set to 10.

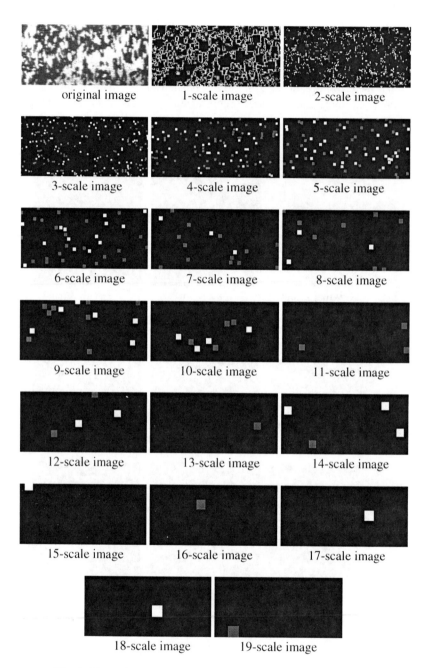

Fig. 2. Illustration of multi-scale analysis of a real textural image

2.3 Scale-Area Histogram

Once a textural image is analyzed, we have available a list of scale images, each relating to a specific texel or scale. Various texture features can be derived from the scale images to characterize image texture. The degree of presence of a texel in a textural image can be measured by the image area occupied by the texel in terms of pixel, which is the total object area in each scale image. The histogram of texel area shows the composition of a textural image in terms of texel. Fig. 3 shows scale-area histograms for three test images, and the error tolerance ε is set to 6. The horizontal axis indicates the size of texel, and the vertical axis indicates the texel areas in terms of pixels. Texel sizes vary from 1 pixel to 31 pixels. The dominant texel may be defined as the texel that occupies the most of the image area. Visually, the dominant texels are most prominent. The size of the dominant texel may indicate some sort of dominant scale factor. Quantification of a texture based on such a dimension would probably show the prevailing characteristic of the texture. For example, the largest texel area occurs at location for texel scale of 15 pixels for test image A. Therefore, the texel of 15 pixels can be considered as the dominant texel for this image.

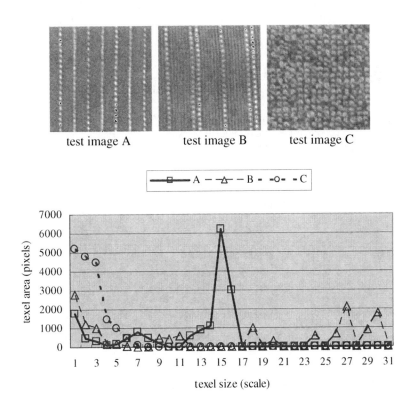

Fig. 3. Scale-area histograms for three test textural images

3 Conclusions

In this paper, we propose a new methodology for multi-scale texture analysis. A textural image is decomposed into a set of scale images and each scale image consists of square texels of the same size. The scale-area histogram of texel is shown to be a useful texture feature. The proposed multi-scale analysis could capture the underlying pattern. It provides useful texture information for image classification, such as, the dominant scale, area and counts of texels. However, it is a search and needs to be further improved, such as the spatial relationship of texel within scale images.

References

1. Wal, D., Herman, D.P.M.J., Dool, A.W.: Characterisation of surface roughness and sediment texture of intertidal flats using ERS SAR imagery. Remote Sens. Environ. 98, 96–109 (2005)
2. Mäenpaä, T., Turtinen, M., Pietikäinen, M.: Real-time surface inspection by texture. Real-Time Imaging, 289–296 (2003)
3. Chen, W.M., Chang, R.F., Kuo, S.J.: 3-D ultrasound texture classification using run difference matrix. Ultrasound in Med. & Biol. 31(6), 763–770 (2005)
4. Verma, B., Kulkarni, S.: A fuzzy-neural approach for interpretation and fusion of colour and texture features for CBIR systems. Appl. Soft Comput. 5, 119–130 (2004)
5. Ojala, T., Pietikäinen, M., Mäenpaä, T.: Multiresolution gray-scale and rotation invariant texture classification with local binary patterns. IEEE Trans. Pattern Anal. Machine Intell. 24(7), 971–987 (2002)
6. Chen, J.L., Kundu, A.: Rotation and gray scale transform invariant texture identification using wavelet decomposition and hidden markov model. IEEE Trans. Pattern Anal. Machine Intell. 16, 208–214 (1994)
7. Haralick, R.M., Shapiro, L.: Computer and Robot Vision, vol. 2. Addison-Wesley Publishing, New York (1993)
8. Daugman, J.G.: An information-theoretic view of analog representation in striate cortex. Comp. Neurose., 403–424 (1990)

Illumination Invariant Texture Classification with Pattern Co-occurrence Matrix

Qiang Song

College of Mechanical and Transportation Engineering,
China University of Petroleum, Beijing, China
songqiang@cup.edu.cn

Abstract. A new illumination invariant feature extraction method for texture classification is proposed. In order to capture the local image texture, texture pattern transform (TPT) in a local neighborhood of a monochrome texture image is introduced. The TPT is robust against any monotonic transformation of the gray scale. The joint distributions of two different TPT, which can be characterized using a pattern co-occurrence matrix (PCM), can be used for texture classification. The PCM technique only requires comparison and counting operations, and thus is highly computationally efficient. The properties of PCM include translation and illuminant invariance, which is highly desirable in real-world applications. Illumination invariant texture classification experimental results show that the texture features derived from PCM achieve good discrimination.

Keywords: illumination invariant, texture classification, pattern co-occurrence matrix.

1   Introduction

Image texture, defined as a function of the spatial variation in pixel intensities, is useful in a variety of applications and has been a subject of intense study by many researchers [1], [2], [3], [4]. One immediate application of image texture is the classification of image regions using texture properties. Texture classification involves deciding what texture category an observed image belongs to. In order to accomplish this, one needs to have an a priori knowledge of the classes to be recognized. Once this knowledge is available and the texture features are extracted, one then uses pattern classification techniques in order to do the classification.

Texture classification is an important and useful area of study in machine vision. Most natural surfaces exhibit texture and a successful vision system must be able to deal with the textured world surrounding it. However, real-world textures may be subjected to varying illumination conditions, and a major problem of texture classification is that textures in the real world are often not uniform due to uneven illumination. This has inspired a collection of studies which generally incorporate invariance with respect to illumination.

This paper focuses on illumination invariant texture classification, and the study approaches illumination invariance by assuming that the gray-scale transformation in

G. Shen and X. Huang (Eds.): CSIE 2011, Part I, CCIS 152, pp. 67–72, 2011.
© Springer-Verlag Berlin Heidelberg 2011

local region is a linear function [5]. Some applications realized illumination invariance by global normalization of the input image using histogram equalization [6]. However, this is not a general solution, as global histogram equalization cannot correct local gray-scale variations.

2 Texture Pattern Transform

We start the derivation of illumination invariant texture operator by defining texture pattern transform *TPT* in a local neighborhood of a monochrome texture image as

$$TPT = f(n_p - n_c) = \begin{cases} 1, & n_p \geq n_c \\ 0, & n_p < n_c \end{cases}. \tag{1}$$

where n_c corresponds to the gray value of the center pixel and n_p corresponds to the gray value of its neighboring pixel for a displacement vector $d = (dx, dy)$.

Signed difference $n_p - n_c$ is not affected by changes in mean luminance; hence, texture pattern transform in Eq. 1 is invariant against gray-scale shifts. We can transform a texture image into a binary image with a displacement vector d (Fig. 1).

65	71	48	61	22
62	44	65	69	91
71	63	61	95	94
76	57	75	52	67
54	48	68	43	65

0	1	0	1	
1	0	0	0	
1	1	0	1	
1	0	1	0	
1	0	1	0	

Fig. 1. Example of transforming a texture image (left) into a binary image (right) using TPT with $d = (1, 0)$

By assigning a binomial factor 2^p for each pixel value in a 2×2 neighborhood, we transform the binary image into a monochrome image (called pattern image) with sixteen gray scale levels, which is shown in Fig. 2. Fig. 3 shows some pattern images corresponding different displacement vector d.

p_3	p_0
p_2	p_1

$$\text{Pixel Value} = p_0 \times 2^0 + p_1 \times 2^1 + p_2 \times 2^2 + p_3 \times 2^3$$

Fig. 2. Illustration to obtain pixel values of pattern image

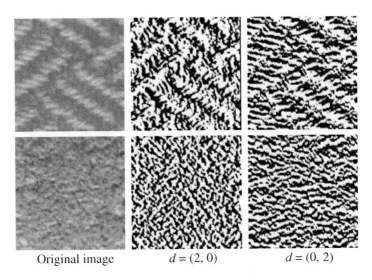

| Original image | $d = (2, 0)$ | $d = (0, 2)$ |

Fig. 3. Original texture image and pattern images corresponding different displacement vector

3 Pattern Co-occurrence Matrix

The pattern co-occurrence matrix $P_{d1, d2}$ for two displacement vectors is defined as follows. The entry (i, j) of $P_{d1, d2}$ is the number of occurrences of the pair of gray levels i and j which come from the same position in two pattern images I_{d1} and I_{d2}, respectively. Formally, it is given as

$$P_{d1,d2}(i, j) = \forall\{(x, y) \in (H \times W) \mid I_{d1}(x, y) = i, I_{d2}(x, y) = j\} \; . \qquad (2)$$

where I_{d1} and I_{d2} are pattern images with different displacement vectors $d1$ and $d2$, H and W are the height and width of two pattern images.

The pattern co-occurrence matrix (PCM) is normalized by dividing all entries of the matrix as

$$p_{d1,d2}(i, j) = \frac{P_{d1,d2}(i, j)}{\sum_i \sum_j P_{d1,d2}(i, j)} \; . \qquad (3)$$

An example of obtaining PCM is shown in Fig. 4, using displacement vectors $d = (1, 0)$ and $(1, 1)$. The PCM reveals certain properties about the spatial distribution of the texture patterns in the texture image.

4 Experiments

We evaluate the capability of the PCM for illumination invariant texture classification. The image data including 24 texture classes from the Outex [7] is

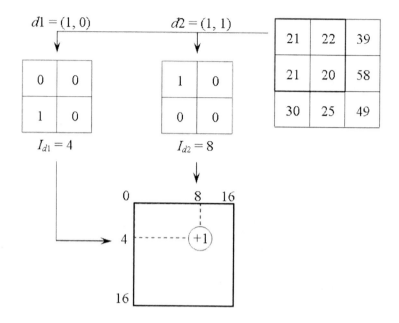

Fig. 4. Example of obtaining the pattern co-occurrence matrix

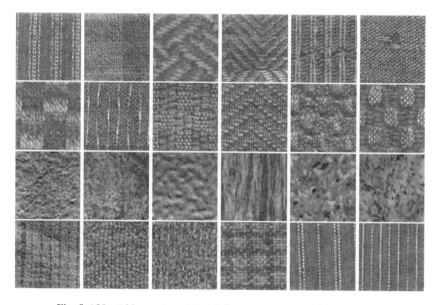

Fig. 5. 128 × 128 samples of the 24 Outex textures used in experiment

shown in Fig. 5. Each texture available is captured using three different simulated illuminants provided in the light source: 2300K horizon sunlight denoted as "horizon", 2856K incandescent CIE A denoted as "inca", and 4000K fluorescent tl84 denoted as "tl84". For each texture class, image samples of size 128 × 128 are used. They are extracted from original 538 × 746 images by centering the 5 × 4 sampling grid and are non-overlapping with each other.

For measuring the distance between feature vectors, several distance measures can be employed. The city block distance dominates in both recognition accuracy and computational efficiency in our experiments. Thus the city-block distance will be used here. Let $P(i)$ and $Q(i)$ represent the K-dimensional feature vectors of two images, where $i = 0, 1, ..., K - 1$. The city block metric is defined as

$$d(P,Q) = \sum_{i=0}^{K-1} |P(i) - Q(i)| . \tag{4}$$

In forthcoming experiment, the classifier is trained with the reference textures (20 samples of illuminant "inca" in each texture class) and tested with all samples captured using illuminant "tl84" and "horizon" (Hence, there are 24 × 20 × 2 = 960 validation samples in total). During the experiments, the nearest neighbor classification rule is used. The texture classification results are given in Table 1, where each entry in the middle is the probability (in percentage) that a texture sample is classified correctly.

Table 1. Percentages of correct classification for PCM in illumination invariant texture classification

d	tl84	horizon
(1,0) & (0,1)	81.3	79.6
(1,-1) & (1,1)	81.7	80.0
(2,0) & (2,1)	87.5	83.3
(2,-2) & (2,2)	88.3	84.2

5 Conclusions

In this paper, a theoretically and computationally simple approach which is robust in terms of illumination variations is proposed. A texture image can be transformed into a binary image using texture pattern transform, and the result is not affected by changes in mean luminance. The pattern co-occurrence matrix is derived from two different texture pattern transforms. Excellent experimental results obtained in illumination invariant texture classification where the classifier is trained in "inca" illuminant and tested with samples from other illuminants ("tl84" and "horizon"), demonstrate that good discrimination can be achieved with texture features derived from PCM.

References

1. Wal, D., Herman, D.P.M.J., Dool, A.W.: Characterisation of surface roughness and sediment texture of intertidal flats using ERS SAR imagery. Remote Sens. Environ. 98, 96–109 (2005)
2. Mäenpää, T., Turtinen, M., Pietikäinen, M.: Real-time surface inspection by texture. Real-Time Imaging, 289–296 (2003)
3. Chen, W.M., Chang, R.F., Kuo, S.J.: 3-D ultrasound texture classification using run difference matrix. Ultrasound in Med. & Biol. 31(6), 763–770 (2005)
4. Verma, B., Kulkarni, S.: A fuzzy-neural approach for interpretation and fusion of colour and texture features for CBIR systems. Appl. Soft Comput. 5, 119–130 (2004)
5. Ojala, T., Pietikäinen, M., Mäenpää, T.: Multiresolution gray-scale and rotation invariant texture classification with local binary patterns. IEEE Trans. Pattern Anal. Machine Intell. 24(7), 971–987 (2002)
6. Chen, J.L., Kundu, A.: Rotation and gray scale transform invariant texture identification using wavelet decomposition and hidden markov model. IEEE Trans. Pattern Anal. Machine Intell. 16, 208–214 (1994)
7. Ojala, T., Mäenpää, T., Pietikäinen, M.: Outex–a new framework for empirical evaluation of texture analysis algorithms. In: Proceedings of the 16th International Conference on Pattern Recognition, Quebec City, Canada, pp. 701–706 (2002)

Research on Algorithm of Image Segmentation Based on Color Features[*]

Jie-yun Bai and Hong-e Ren

College of Information and Computer Engineering
Northeast Forestry University
Harbin 150040, China
bai_jieyun@126.com,
rhe1962@yeah.net

Abstract. Green index of tree leaves is an important parameter for leaf image segmentation. An innovative method based on color features was presented to automatically extract and split tree leaves from digital image analyses. Based on the features of leaves and its background components, an algorithm was designed to extract the leaves contour, and the corresponding program was developed. This method was simple, and it have a high degree of accuracy as well as a clearly distinguish degree and many other advantages such as good consistency with human visual system. It completely meets the effectiveness and clarity requirements of image segmentation.

Keywords: Color features, machine vision, Image processing, Image segmentation.

1 Introduction

With the world's industrial economic development, the rapid increase in population, the unlimited human desire and the production life of the uncontrolled rise, low-carbon living and low-carbon economy are advocated today, how to accurately measure the amount of oxygen emissions and carbon sequestration of trees to serve for carbon sinks, carbon sequestration trading, carbon sequestration projects in species selection and energy saving measures has always been a problem. However, oxygen emissions and carbon sequestration of the trees can be reflected by the color of tree to some extent. The plant world is considered to be the green kingdom of nature, this green color of plants is given by particular organism chlorophyll. Leaf color is an important characteristic index of tree groups, which directly reflects changes in chlorophyll content, and is used to indicate the photosynthesis process of growing trees, nutritional status and other attributes of trees. Therefore, the degree in green color of a leaf can reflect the degree of the amount of chlorophyll, in other words, it can reflect the capacity in carbon and oxygen fixation of trees [1]. So, how to access to accurate color information of leaves becomes the crux of the problem.

[*] Research was supported by Northeast Forestry University Graduate Thesis Grant (STIP10).

G. Shen and X. Huang (Eds.): CSIE 2011, Part I, CCIS 152, pp. 73–78, 2011.
© Springer-Verlag Berlin Heidelberg 2011

Image is an extension of human vision, and we can immediately and accurately measure the leaf color through the image. Image representation Based on color features became one of the image segmentation technologies with very extensive and in-depth application. In recent years, many researchers carried out a series of work in this field, and got a lot of valuable research results. As early as 1995, Woebbecke et al segment crop and soil background on the use of color, and the results found using rgb chromaticity coordinates of plants and soil and residue background color coordinate difference vary greatly, the use of (R-G), (G-B), (2B-R-B), (G-B) / | R-G | other factors to distinguish between plants and non-plant background is very effective in which(2G-R-B)is the most effective factor for plant testing[2]. Meyer et al further improved on this basis, who used the super-green (2G-RB) and ultra-red (1.4RG), obtained a good image with the background segmentation and found that HIS space could well inhibit the light and humidity, which is because the transformed image of the color information and brightness information are separated. Light to the object color is the brightness of the direct impact (I) component, so the computer can automatically segment image according to different lighting conditions change in the pattern recognition [3]. In 2007, Mao converted the color feature and threshold value into a split plane of the RGB space, using segmentation error evaluation of Bayes theory, optimized segmentation features and threshold, and improved the accuracy of weed image segmentation [4]. In 2008, Zhao Jinhui used color features (2G-RB and 2R-GB) to extract non-green plants and disease lesions [5].

However, as the technical difficulty of identifying the color difference between leaves based on machine vision, there still exists some distance away from the practical. In the HSI, two-dimensional color space used to represent the color of light, the third dimension expresses the intensity of color, and the color space can adapt to changes in light intensity of the occasion than RGB model [6]. Therefore, in this study image is preprocessed by using the 2G-RB model, and was successfully segmented based on pixels similarity distance in the H component which applied improved HSI model, and good results have achieved in the experiment.

2   Color Model

RGB color model is a color of industry standards and the most widely used one color system. The RGB color model is an additive color model in which red, green, and blue light are added together in various ways to reproduce a broad array of colors. In the RGB model, the so-called RGB color table is provided by CIE 700nm (red), 546.1nm (green), 435.8nm (blue) the three primary colors, of which R, G, and B respectively represent the red, green and blue.

2.1   2G-RB Model

Through the image pixel value statistical analysis, we found that green channel sub-pixel value is generally greater than the red and blue channel component value in the same kind of green plants, and the image of each pixel R, G and B sub-values are also different under different light conditions. The green component of the leaves is obvious, so increasing the weight of the green component and highlighting the green features can be used to separate leaves from the background.

RGB model to 2G-RB model transformation formula is:

$$\begin{cases} R(i, j) = R(i, j) \\ G(i, j) = G(i, j) \quad if\ (B(i, j) > G(i, j)orR(i, j) > G(i, j)) \\ B(i, j) = B(i, j) \end{cases} \tag{1}$$

$$\begin{cases} R(i, j) = R(i, j) \\ G(i, j) = 2G(i, j) \quad (otherwise) \\ B(i, j) = B(i, j) \end{cases} \tag{2}$$

" i ": the horizontal coordinates of pixels, " j ": the vertical coordinates of pixels " $R(i, j), G(i, j), B(i, j)$ ": is the value of red, green and blue components of the coordinate (i, j) .

2.2 Improved HSI Model

HSI model, which is similar with the human eye visual model of color perception, is the color model and has three characteristics. Firstly, the model can eliminate the impact of I component, which can develop image processing methods based on color features; Secondly, this model is in good agreement with the human eye's visual description; Third, H(hue) component can define a color without any deviation. HSI and RGB color table can be interchangeable. Set pixel $f(i, j)$ RGB components are $R(i, j)$, $G(i, j)$, $B(i, j)$, and $I(i, j)$, $H(i, j)$, $S(i, j)$ are the various components in the improved HSI model. RGB to the improved HIS color model transformation formula is:

$$I(i, j) = \max(R(i, j), G(i, j), B(i, j)) \tag{3}$$

$$S(i, j) = \frac{\min(R(i, j), G(i, j), B(i, j))}{\max(R(i, j), G(i, j), B(i, j))} \tag{4}$$

$$H(i, j) = \begin{cases} H_0(i, j), \quad (B(i, j) \le G(i, j)) \\ 2\pi - H_0(i, j), (B(i, j) > G(i, j)) \end{cases} \tag{5}$$

This is the conversion formula to HSI model, and formula to obtain $H_0(i, j)$ is:

$$H_0(i, j) = acr\cos \frac{R(i, j) - G(i, j) + \frac{1}{2}(R(i, j) - B(i, j))}{\sqrt{(R(i, j) - G(i, j))^2 + (R(i, j) - B(i, j)) \times (G(i, j) - B(i, j))}} \times \frac{180}{\pi}$$

"$H(i, j), I(i, j), S(i, j)$": is the value of hue, intensity and saturation components of the coordinate $f(i, j)$.

3 Color Extraction and Image Segmentation Algorithm

Although the threshold segmentation algorithm has a short processing time and is simple in form, its corresponding segmentation error can not meet the requirements of the development of practical devices. In addition, as the same object with different light intensity and angle, the resulting image and the extracted image features will have substantial differences. Whether the segmented image meets the needs of the human visual system should also be considered. Therefore, the algorithm chosen HSI model, and eliminated the luminance component, according to similarity distance of H component in the green range as the basis for division with good results.

The following is the image segmentation steps:

1. Turn-by-pixel $(f_1, f_2, ... f_n)$ scan the input RGB image, and if $R(i, j) > G(i, j)$ or $B(i, j) > G(i, j)$ use the formula (1) for processing; otherwise, use the formula (2) for processing.
2. According to the formula (4), calculate the value of the corresponding pixel's hue $H(i, j)$, if $120° \leq H(i, j) \leq 150°$, put the point (A) as a reference point (T) for green zone, because the green color changes between $120°$ and $150°$.
3. Normalize the reference point(T) ,and convert to rgb, conversion formula is:

$$r = \frac{R(i, j)}{255}, g = \frac{G(i, j)}{255}, b = \frac{B(i, j)}{255} \tag{6}$$

4. According to the formula (3), (4) and (5), make the reference point (T) transform from RGB to HSI model.
5. Continue to scan the next pixel (B), and calculate the values of hue (H), intensity (I) and saturation(S) components follow the steps (3) and (4).
6. Gong YH et al found that in the human perceptual HVC color space, color similarity distance is less than 1.5, which is considered that human vision is almost the same, when the similarity distance is greater than 6.0,which is considered to have a significant difference[7]. Therefore, the similarity of HSI color model can also be measured by the similarity distance [8]. Set the similarity distance between point ($B(i, j)$) and the reference point ($T(i, j)$) is $E_{NBS}(B, T)$, and the pair of colors $B = (H_B, I_B, S_B)$ and $T = (H_T, I_T, S_T)$.

$H_B = H_B - 120 / \pi$, $H_T = H_T - 120 / \pi$, represent that they are in the green zone.

$$\Delta V_1 = | I_B(1 - S_B) - I_T(1 - S_T) | \tag{7}$$

$$\Delta V_2 = \left| I_B \left(1 + \frac{S_B \cos H_B}{\cos\left(\frac{60}{\pi} - H_B\right)} \right) - I_T \left(1 + \frac{S_T \cos H_T}{\cos\left(\frac{60}{\pi} - H_T\right)} \right) \right| \quad (8)$$

$$\Delta V_3 = \left| I_B - I_T \right| \quad (9)$$

$$E_{NBS}(B,T) = \sqrt{2(\Delta V_1)^2 + 2(\Delta V_2)^2 + 9(\Delta V_3)^2 + \Delta V_1 \Delta V_2 + 3\Delta V_1 \Delta V_3 + 3\Delta V_2 \Delta V_3} \quad (10)$$

7. When the similarity $E_{NBS}(B,T)$ is less than 0.1, which is considered to be similar to the reference point (T), the point (B) can be preserved as green area, and put the point (B) as the new reference point (T) at the same time. Otherwise, the reference point (T) does not change, and the pixel value of the point (B) is set to (0, 0, 0) as the black background. Continue to scan following steps 2 to 7.
8. The final image will have some interference noise. We filter the noise and output the final image.

4 Experimental Results and Analysis

To test the performance of the algorithm, simulation experiments were conducted in MATLAB7.0 environment. Experimental conditions are the Pentium 4, 2.8 GHz, 1 GB RAM and Windows XP operating system. In the RGB color space, we use 2128×1886 24-bit true color image as the test image, Fig. 1 was extracted by 2G-RB model green component, HSI model extraction H component, as well as the results of the algorithm.

2G-RB   HIS   the paper

Fig. 1. Lists several ways to segment the leaves based on color features and shows the segmentation results. Their running time are: 3.3133s, 49.953s, 65.750s.

The results show that: 2G-RB algorithm is simple and faster with processing time for 3.3133 seconds, but this method can not accurately extract the leaf image, which has been completely ineffective and invaluable. In HIS model, the processing effect of H component algorithm is better than 2G-BR for extracting green features, but still do not reach the applications. However, using the proposed image segmentation method obtains a more satisfactory result, and is better in line with the human visual system; meanwhile the operation speed is similar to the H component algorithm in

HIS model. Therefore, the algorithm is an effective and practical method for leaves image segmentation.

5 Conclusion

In this paper, we make color features of leaf and background as a starting point, and process leaves image by using digital imaging technology as well as a new method of leaves image segmentation. It has a high degree of accuracy and a certain degree of feasibility, but processing speed is slow and the algorithm is yet to be improved. If we can establish correspondence between green characteristic parameters of leaves image and indicators of leaves carbon fixation and oxygen emissions, we can accurately measure the capacity of trees' oxygen emissions and carbon sequestration by using digital image technology.

References

1. Wang, F.-Y., Li, S.-K.: Obtaining Information of Cotton Population Chlorophyll by Using Machine Vision Technology. J. Acta Agronomica Sinica 33(12), 2041–2046 (2007)
2. Woebbecke, D.M., Meyer, G.E., Bargen, K.V., Mortensen, D.A.: Shap features for identifying young weeds using image analysis. Transactions of the ASAE 38(1), 271–281 (1995)
3. Meyer, G.E., Neto, J.C.: Verification of color vegetation indices for automated crop imaging applications. Computers and Electronics in Agriculture 63(2), 282–293 (2008)
4. Mao, H.-p., Hu, B., Zhang, Y.-c., et al.: Optimization of color index and threshold segmentation in weed recognition. J. Transactions of the CSAE 23(9), 154–158 (2007)
5. Zhao, J.-h., Luo, X.-w., Zhou, Z.-y.: Image Segmentation Method for Sugarcane Diseases Based on Color and Shape Feature. J. Transactions of the Chinese Society for Agricultural Machinery 39(9), 100–103 (2008)
6. Lv, X.-l., et al.: Study on the Machine Vision Recognition of Field Mature Tomatoes. Journal of Anhui Agri. Sci. 36, 1322–1323 (2008)
7. Gong, Y.H., Proietti, G.: Image indexing and retrieval based on human perceptual color clustering. In: The International Conference on Computer Vision, Mumbai (1998)
8. Li, Y.-f., Zhou, D.-x., et al.: Watershed Algorithm Based on Morphological Segmentation of adhesion of rice grain. J. Computer& Information Technology, 42–47 (2010)

A New Web Services Filtrating Mechanism with Latent Semantic Analysis*

Guangjun Huang and Xiaoguo Zhang

School of Electrical and Information Engineering,
Henan University of Science and Technology
Luoyang, Henan, 471003, China
guangjunhuang@126.com

Abstract. This paper analyzes some existing web services description models and services matching methods, puts forward a Web services filtrating mechanism based on latent semantic analysis to solve lower matching efficiency and precision of the available services discovery mechanisms that is short of services filtrating mechanism and matched with keywords. Firstly, this filtrating algorithm describes basic attributes and QoS attributes of Web services using tree structure attributes template. Secondly, the paper builds latent semantic analysis space using certain terms-frequency statistic method and weights method. And then, the paper builds advertising services index database, and filtrates the Web services according to the service request. Experiments results show that this algorithm has higher precision and recall ratio, can improve services matching efficiency largely.

Keywords: latent semantic analysis; Web services; services filtrating; weight.

1 Introduction

At present, most Web services description languages follow the model {S, C, P}, such as WSDL, SCDL, OWL-S and so on, as in [1]. In this model, owing to lacking QoS description in this model, HU Jianqiang put forward a QoS-based Web services description language, uses basic description, keynote description and QoS description to describe Web services, as in [2]. Many researchers extend OWL-S by introducing services quality ontology, such as YE Hongjuan from Shanghai University, as in [3].

Thus it can be seen, most services-matching algorithms lack a service filtrating technology, have bigger services-matching work and having lower matching efficiency. Moreover, most service-matching methods matching the services basic attributes, QoS attributes by keywords, such as StarWSDS system based on QWSDL and so on, as in [2]. So, this paper puts forward a Web services filtrating mechanism based on Latent Semantic Analysis, this method filtrates the services that basic description and QoS description satisfy request firstly before the services-matching, then matches the services functions and actions.

---

* The Henan Natural Science Fund Committee, award #102102210159.

G. Shen and X. Huang (Eds.): CSIE 2011, Part I, CCIS 152, pp. 79–85, 2011.
© Springer-Verlag Berlin Heidelberg 2011

2 Related Works

2.1 LSA

LSA, Latent Semantic Analysis, points out that some words arising in a document or a passage context is not completely random, it is affected by a latent semantic structure. If we distill this semantic structure and build a semantic relation about these words, we can avoid searching deviations that result from words usage variety and random, as in [4].

2.2 Service Attributes Analyze

This paper describes service basic attributes and QoS attributes as service attributes tree by using tree structure attributes moulding board, as in Fig.1, then make the service attributes tree regard as service document to build word-service matrix and preprocess. So, our algorithm make services filtrating process translate into the filtrating process based on service attributes tree. This tree structure attributes moulding board can increase or reduce information branch conveniently according to different instance, and it can display information hiberarchy intuitively.

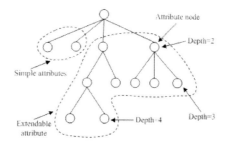

Fig. 1. Tree structure attributes moulding board

In Fig.1, simple attribute is the attributes that only one simple text can denote, such as service name and so on. Extendable attribute is the attributes denoted by several different layers texts, every extendable attribute is made up of several different layers simple attributes. Moreover, the words in the texts appear only once generally. In the tree structure, the importance of a word is generally affected by its layer. Higher layer generally contains the main information, it has bigger weight. Lower layer generally explains the main information further, it has smaller weight. Thus it can be seen that we can not denote the word importance well by using primal word frequency directly. Therefore, according to the particularity of service basic descriptions and QoS descriptions, this paper uses two methods to calculate word frequency, they are named primitive word frequency statistic and equivalence word frequency statistic, and we compared the services filtrating efficiency of these two methods by experiments. Now we will define several statistic variables as below.

tf_{ij} —primal frequency for word i of service attributes tree j, tf_{ikj} —primal frequency for word i in layer k of service attributes tree j, tf'_{ij} —equivalence frequency for word i in service attributes tree j, tf'_{ikj} —equivalence frequency for word i in layer k of service attributes tree j, T_{depth} —the depth of service attributes tree j, $Nodeik_{depth}$ —the depth of word i in layer k.

In the primitive word frequency statistic, if the depth of service attributes tree is n, we can directly statistic primal frequency of word i in layer k, then plus them using (1).

$$tf_{ij} = \sum_{k=1}^{n} tf_{ikj} \tag{1}$$

In the equivalence word frequency statistic, first we calculate word i equivalence frequency in each layer of service attributes tree j, then plus word i equivalence frequency of all layers and integer the equivalence frequency of word i in service attributes tree j. The calculating formula is (2) and (3).

$$tf'_{ikj} = tf_{ikj} \times (1 + \log_2 [T_{depth} - (Nodeik_{depth} - 1)]) \tag{2}$$

$$tf'_{ij} = \left\lceil \sum_{k=1}^{n} tf'_{ikj} \right\rceil \tag{3}$$

This paper builds two word-service matrix by using these two word frequency statistic methods, then designs services filtrating method based on them to compare their efficiency. Besides word frequency statistic method, the approaches of the service filtrating method are uniform.

3 Web Services Filtrating

In fact, Web services discover is the matching process between services requests and advertising services. Services matching should ensure higher precision, better agility and higher efficiency. Therefore, this paper puts forward a Web services filtrating algorithm based on latent semantic analysis, this algorithm has higher precision and higher recall ratio and improves services matching efficiency largely. This paper makes basic descriptions and QoS descriptions of Web services store as tree structure, then mapped into LSA space and produce semantics multi-vector, ultimately filtrates the services according to services similarity.

3.1 Web Services Filtrating Flow

Firstly, collect training services set to build LSA space. Secondly, make basic descriptions and QoS descriptions of advertising services map into LSA space and spawn advertising index vectors, then build a database with these vectors. Meanwhile, make basic descriptions and QoS descriptions of the service request map into LSA space and spawn request index vector. Finally, calculate similarity between request index vector and advertising index vectors, then insert the services that the similarity bigger or equal the similarity threshold into result list until having matched all the advertising services and return result list ordered by similarity.

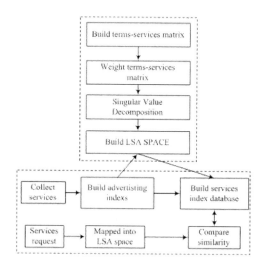

Fig. 2. Services filtrating flow chart based on LSA.

3.2   Web Services Filtrating Step

The Web services filtrating algorithm of this paper mainly contains three steps.

1   Build LSA Space

In the process of building LSA space, we should firstly collect Web services examples, distill the words that can denote service attributes from service basic descriptions and QoS descriptions, and then build the word-service matrix. The matrix is as follows.

$X_{m \times n} = [X_{ij}] = (\text{service}1, \text{service}2, ..., \text{service}n) = (\text{term}1, \text{term}2, ..., \text{term}m)^{T}$, the value of X_{ij} is the word frequency of word i in the service j. This paper uses primitive word frequency and equivalence word frequency from II.B section of the paper to calculate word frequency. At the same time, we should have statistics of the services number that have word i, the sum of word i in all the services and the number of valid words in service j. Prepare for weighting the word-service matrix, the element of the weighted word-service matrix is closer to the relation of word and services in natural language. The weight function of the paper is (4) as follows.

$$W(i, j) = LW(i, j) \times GWT(i) \times GWD(j) \tag{4}$$

$LW(i, j)$ is the local word weight, $GWT(i)$ is the global word weight, $GWD(j)$ is the global weight of the service document. Now we will define several statistics variables as follows.

gf_i —the frequency sum of word i in one service attributes tree, sgf —the frequency sum of all the words in whole set of service attributes tree, dl_j —the length of service attributes tree j, namely, the sum of words in service attributes tree j.

This paper employs logarithm word frequency as local word weight, so as to reduce this effect of high frequency words toward LSA space. The logarithm weight function is (5) as follows.

$$LW(i, j) = \log_2 (tf_{ij} + 1) \tag{5}$$

Entropy is generally recognized that the information that some word provides for services documents set is larger, the word distinguish ability toward service document is stronger, its global weight should be higher. So, the word global weight function of the paper is (6) as follows.

$$GWT(i) = 1 + \frac{\sum_j P(docj \mid termi) \log_2 P(docj \mid termi)}{\log_2 n} \tag{6}$$

$P(docj \mid termi) = \dfrac{tf_{ij}}{gf_i}$ is the appearing probability of document j when word i appears.

Similarly, we can define service document global weight as (7) with entropy theories.

$$GWD(j) = 1 - \frac{\sum_{i=1}^{m} \frac{gf_i}{sgf} \cdot \log_2 \frac{gf_i}{sgf}}{\sum_i \frac{tf_{ij}}{dl_j} \cdot \log_2 \frac{tf_{ij}}{dl_j}} \tag{7}$$

We uses MATLAB do SVD transform and gains matrix T, S, D, and reserves several maximal singular value, the reserved amount of singular value is k. Then we gain the front k columns of T, D separately, do contrary SVD operation and can gain an approximate matrix of primitive matrix as follows.

$\hat{X}_k = T_k S_k D_k^T$, $T_k = (t_1, t_2,..., t_k)$, $S_k = diag(\sigma_1, \sigma_2,...,\sigma_k)$, $D_k = (d_1, d_2,...,d_k)$. Thereby, we can gain a LSA space that built with span$\{t_1, t_2,..., t_k\}$ and span$\{d_1, d_2,..., d_k\}$.

2 Build Advertising Vector Index Database

After the TSVD, we can regard the rows of $D_k S_k$ as services vector that can denote the services when we filtrate the services. Because S_k is a constant toward different documents, we can use the rows of matrix D_k to denote documents. We can regard doc$_i$ $=(\sigma_1 d_{1i}, \sigma_2 d_{2i}, ... , \sigma_k d_{ki})^T$ as the denotation of service i in k dimensions vectors space. However, the services that can denote like this are services that have done TSVD, if a service that is denoted as frequency vector does not contain in $X_{m \times n}$, we need make it map into LSA space. We can use (8) to calculate equivalent vector like the row vector of D_k for the service.

$$doc^* = doc^T T_k S_k^{-1} \tag{8}$$

In order to making the important dimensions play an important role, we need weight the dimensions, the dimension weight can equal its singular value. After weighting the dimension, we can use (9) to calculate equivalent service vector.

$$doc^* = doc^T T_k \tag{9}$$

Because the $GWT(i)$ not only affects the semantic structure but also affects services document similarity, the final equivalent vector of service is calculated by (10).

$$\text{doc}^* = \text{doc}^T W_t T_k \tag{10}$$

The W_t of the (10) is a diagonal matrix as (11), the diagonal elements are the global weight of the corresponding words.

$$W_t = \begin{pmatrix} GWT(1) & & \\ & \cdots & \\ & & GWT(m) \end{pmatrix} \tag{11}$$

It can be seen, the services index database mainly contains two parts. One is the advertising services having attended TSVD, we can take $\text{doc}_i = (\sigma_1 d_{1i}, \sigma_2 d_{2i}, \ldots, \sigma_k d_{ki})^T$ as the denotation of service i in the LSA space. The other is the newly collecting advertising services, we can use (10) to make them map into LSA space and build advertising index vectors.

3 Services Similarity Calculation

We suppose LSA low dimension vectors of two services as follows, $\text{Ser}_i^* = (\text{Ser}_{i,1}^*, \ldots, \text{Ser}_{i,k}^*)^T$, $\text{Ser}_j^* = (\text{Ser}_{j,1}^*, \ldots, \text{Ser}_{j,k}^*)^T$. We uses the vector cosine algorithm (12) to calculate the similarity between request service and advertising services.

$$\text{Sim}(\text{Ser}_i^*, \text{Ser}_j^*) = \frac{\sum_{h=1}^{k} \text{Ser}_{i,h}^* . \text{Ser}_{j,h}^*}{\sqrt{\sum_{h=1}^{k} (\text{Ser}_{i,h}^*)^T} . \sqrt{\sum_{h=1}^{k} (\text{Ser}_{j,h}^*)^T}} \tag{12}$$

4 Emulation Test

Now, we will define filtrating precision and filtrating recall ratio referencing existing the definition of precision and recall ratio. The definition is the (13) and (14) as follows. A_r is the set of the services that should filtrate out. A is the set of the return services that filtrated out actually. The filtrating precision and recall is higher, the algorithm is better, as in [5]. We can write filtrating precision as $P_{filtrate}$ for short, and we can write filtrating recall as $R_{filtrate}$ for short.

$$P_{filtrate} = \frac{|A \cap A_r|}{|A|} \tag{13}$$

$$R_{filtrate} = \frac{|A \cap A_r|}{|A_r|} \tag{14}$$

We design one prototype WSFS based on primitive word frequency and another prototype WSFS based on equivalent word frequency separately. We build a test set WSFS-TC that uses OWLS-TC V2 in [6] and adds QoS descriptions. We test the filtrating algorithm based on Keywords combination and StarWSDS QWSDL-based, as in [2]. We set the similarity threshold value is 0.6. The emulation test statistics of this paper is showed in TABLE I as follows.

Table 1. Emulation Test Statistic

Filtrating algorithm	$P_{filtrate}$	$R_{filtrate}$
Keywords combination	32%	91%
StarWSDS QWSDL-based	65%	93%
WSFS based on primitive word frequency	71%	94%
WSFS based on equivalent word frequency	76%	95%

5 Conclusion

This paper uses the newly researches of academia for reference, analyses the newly Web services description model and most services matching algorithm and puts forward a Web service filtrating method based on LSA. Then we build a prototype system and test the validity by emulation experiments. The experiments show that this services filtrating algorithm has higher precision and recall ratio, can filtrate the irrelative services, save the services matching time and improve services matching efficiency.

References

1. Gao, X., Yang, J., Papazoglou Midke, P.: The capability matching of Web services. In: Proceedings of the IEEE Four International Symposium on Multimedia Software Engineering (MSE 2002), California, USA, pp. 56–63 (2002)
2. Hu, J.-q., Zou, P., Wang, H.-m., et al.: Research on Web Service Description Language QWSDL and Service Matching Model. Chinese Journal of Computers 28(4), 505–513 (2005)
3. Ye, H.-j., Ye, F.-y., Li, X.,et al.: Central technology of Web service discovery based on semantic. Computer Application 26(11), 2661–2662 (2006)
4. Yu, Z.-t., Fan, X.-z., Guo, J.-y., et al.: Answer Extracting for Chinese Question-Answering System Based on Latent Semantic Analysis. Chinese Journal of Computers 29(10), 1889–1891 (2006)
5. Wu, J., Wu, Z.-h., Li, Y.,et al.: Web Service Discovery Based on Ontology and Similarity of Word. Chinese Journal of Computers 28(4), 595–601 (2005)
6. http://projects.semWebcentral.org/frs/download.php/255/owls-tc2.zip[EB/OL]

Ant Colony Optimization to Improve Precision of Complex Assembly

M. Victor Raj[1], S. Saravana Sankar[2], and S.G. Ponnambalam[3]

[1] Department of Mechanical Engineering,
Dr. Sivanthi Aditanar College of Engineering, Tiruchendur, India
mvictor_raj@yahoo.com
[2] Department of Mechanical Engineering, Kalasalingam University,
Krishnankoil, India
ssaravanasankar@yahoo.co.in
[3] School of Engineering, Monash University Sunway Campus,
46150 Bandar Sunway, Malaysia
sgponnambalam@eng.monash.edu.my

Abstract. An assembly consists of two or more mating parts. The quality of the assembly is mainly based on the quality of mating parts. The mating parts may be manufactured using different machines and processes with different standard deviations. Therefore, the dimensional distributions of the mating parts are not similar. This results in clearance between the mating parts. To obtain high precision assemblies, clearance variation has to be reduced. Selective assembly helps to reduce this clearance variation. In this paper, appropriate selective group combination for assembling the mating parts is obtained using an ant colony optimization (ACO). The combination obtained has resulted in an appreciable reduction in clearance variations.

Keywords: Selective assembly, Quality, Ant Colony Optimization, Interchangeable assembly.

1 Introduction

In the present day of competitive world, the most important performance measure of a product is its quality. Quality of every product produced has direct impact on the profit. In a manufacturing system, production of poor quality that does not have precision leads to more rejection and higher cost of production. Hence the major goal of any manufacturing system remains to achieve minimum rejection of products of final assembly on account of poor quality. As a key to quality, tolerance is the most important factor. When two or more components are assembled together to form an assembly, the clearance of the assembly depends on the tolerance of the individual components that are assembled. A quality assembly demands for a closer clearance variation which in turn may demand production of individual components with close tolerance. Production of individual components with closer tolerance will require sophisticated technology and incur higher production cost. However, high precision assembly can be made using relatively low precision components by means of

G. Shen and X. Huang (Eds.): CSIE 2011, Part I, CCIS 152, pp. 86–93, 2011.

selective assembly procedure. In selective assembly, the mating parts are manufactured with wide tolerances. The mating part population is then partitioned to form selective groups, and the appropriate selective groups are assembled interchangeably.

Much of research work has been done in the past to address the issues associated with selective assembly methodology. Kannan and Jayabalan [1] proposed a uniform grouping method and an equal probability method for selective assembly problems. The authors analysed above method with the case example of a hole and shaft assembly. Kannan and Jayabalan [2] proposed a new grouping method for complex assembly with three mating parts (as in a ball bearing: inner race, balls and outer race). Here, a new method was proposed for partitioning the lots to form selective groups. Kannan, Jayabalan and Jeevanantham [3] described a method to find the selective groups to minimize the assembly variation when the parts are assembled linearly. A genetic algorithm was used to find the best combination of selective groups to minimize the assembly variation. Asha, Kannan and Jayabalan [4] applied non-dominated sorting genetic algorithm to the selective assembly problem. The authors made different combinations of selective groups instead of corresponding selective groups. The combination obtained has reduced assembly variation. Mease, Nair and Sudjianto [5] defined selective assembly as a cost effective approach for reducing the overall variation and thus improving the quality of an assembled product. Shun Matsuura and Nobuo Shinozaki [6] analysed a piston and cylinder assembly. The authors derived an optimal manufacturing mean design that minimises the number of surplus components.

In recent times, attempts have been made to solve the combinatorial optimization problems by making use of ant colony optimization algorithm. The pioneering work was done by Dorigo [7], and an introduction to the ACO algorithms was dealt with in Dorigo et al. [8]. In this paper, an ant colony optimization algorithm is proposed to select best combination of selective groups the result is compared with Non-dominated Sorting Genetic Algorithm (NSGA) found in the literature.

2   Problem Background

The clearance depends upon the tolerance of the mating parts, which is based on the manufacturing process. In order to obtain precision assemblies, the clearance variation has to be reduced. To achieve minimum clearance variation, the mating parts have to be manufactured with close tolerance. It requires sophisticated manufacturing system. It may not be possible under economic consideration. Selective assembly helps to make high precision assemblies from relatively low precision mating parts. In this paper the main aim is to minimize the clearance variations of a complex assembly.

3   The Problem

Table 1 shows the quality characteristics of a piston-cylinder assembly shown in Fig. 1. By considering all the above quality characteristics of piston and cylinder

Table 1. Representation of characteristics of the piston and cylinder assembly

Sl. No.	Component	Characteristic	Representation	Tolerance
1	Piston	Piston groove diameter	A	18 μm
2	Piston	Piston diameter	B	12 μm
3	Piston	Piston groove thickness	C	12 μm
4	Piston ring	Piston ring width	D	18 μm
5	Piston ring	Piston ring thickness	E	6 μm
6	Piston ring	Piston ring outer diameter	F	24 μm
7	Cylinder	Cylinder inner diameter	G	24 μm

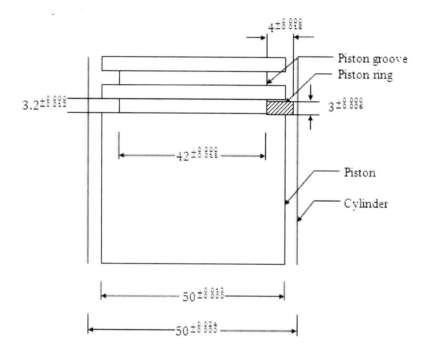

Fig. 1. Piston and cylinder assembly

assembly, the following are the four possible combinations contributing the assembly clearance.

i) Clearance 1 (C_1=A+D+G):
   Piston groove diameter (A)
   Piston ring width   (D)
   Cylinder inner diameter (G)

ii) Clearance 2 (C_2=C+E):
   Piston groove thickness (C)
   Piston ring thickness (E)

iii) Clearance 3 (C_3=B+G):
Piston diameter (B)
Cylinder inner diameter (G)

iv) Clearance 4 (C_4=F+G):
Piston ring outer diameter (F)
Cylinder inner diameter (G)

All the four possible combinations (C_1, C_2, C_3 and C_4), which contribute for the clearance variation in the assembly, are considered as different objective functions. The dimensional distributions of all the characteristics are as shown in Fig. 2. They are divided into six selective groups. The selective group tolerance value for characteristic A is 3 µm, B is 2 µm, C is 2 µm, D is 3 µm, E is 1 µm, F is 4 µm and G is 4 µm. The clearance variation is calculated by using equations (1),(2) and (3)

$$Clearance\ variation = Maximum\ clearance - minimum\ clearance \qquad (1)$$

$$Maximum\ clearance = Selective\ group\ number \times Group\ tolerance\ value \qquad (2)$$

$$Minimum\ clearance = (Selective\ group\ number - 1) \times Group\ tolerance\ value \qquad (3)$$

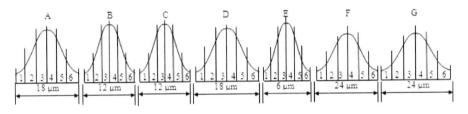

Fig. 2. Dimensional distributions of the characteristics

In traditional selective assembly method, the corresponding selective groups are assembled. If the corresponding selective groups are assembled, the assembly clearance variations for the population are very high. The calculation for clearance variation 1 is shown in Table 2. The objective is to find the best combination of selective groups, which helps to minimize clearance variation in all the four clearances.

Table 2. Calculation of CV_1 while corresponding selective groups are assembled

Characteristic A			Characteristic D			Characteristic G			Clearance		Clearance
SG	Min	Max	SG	Min	Max	SG	Min	Max	Min	Max	variation CV_1
1	0	3	1	0	3	1	0	4	0	10	
2	3	6	2	3	6	2	4	8	10	20	
3	6	9	3	6	9	3	8	12	20	30	60-0=60
4	9	12	4	9	12	4	12	16	30	40	
5	12	15	5	12	15	5	16	20	40	50	
6	15	18	6	15	18	6	20	24	50	60	

Note:- SG-Selective Group

3.1 Objective Function

The components considered here have more than one quality characteristics. When assembled, the clearances obtained between different quality characteristics is also more than one. So it is a multi-objective problem. The multi-objective functions are combined into one combined objective function, Z, as shown in equation (4).

$$Z = \sum_{i=1}^{N} w_i C_i \tag{4}$$

Where, N = Number of objective functions
  w = Weights
  C = Clearance variation
Weights are fractional numbers ($0 \leq w_i \leq 1$), and all weights are summed up to one.

$$\sum_{i=1}^{N} w_i = 1$$

Mathematically, equal weights to all objectives offer best solutions. Hence it is taken as $w_1 = w_2 = w_3 = w_4 = 0.25$.

4 Ant Colony Optimization

The ACO algorithm makes use of simple agents called ants that iteratively construct solutions to combinatorial optimization problems. The generation (or construction) of solutions by ants is guided by (artificial) pheromone trails and problem-specific heuristic information. After the construction of a random solution, every ant gives feedback on the solution by depositing pheromone (i.e., updating trail intensity) on each solution component. Typically, solution components which are part of better solutions or used by ants over many iterations will receive a higher amount of pheromone, and hence, such solution components are more likely to be used by the ants in future iterations of the ACO algorithm. This is achieved by making use of "evaporation factor" in updating trail intensities. The basic modules of the ACO are presented below.

Initialization module:
  Initialize the pheromone trails and parameters.
Evaluation module:
  While (termination condition is not met) do the following:
  – Construct a solution.
  – Improve the solution by local search.
  – Update the pheromone trail or trail intensity, denoted τ_{pt}, where $\tau_{max} \leq \tau_{pt} \leq \tau_{min}$.
Output module:
  Return the best solution found.

In the context of application of the ACO algorithm to selective assembly problems, τ_{pt} denotes the trail intensity (or desire) of selective group i in position p of a sequence. It is to be noted that for every selective group i for any possible position p, a pheromone value is stored and updated in each iteration. In order to ensure that the trail intensities do not go beyond certain limits during the process of updating the trail, the ACO introduces the maximum and minimum values for τ_{pt}, denoted by τ_{max} and τ_{min}, respectively.

4.1 Initialization Module

Initially, all τ_{pt} are set equal to τ_{max}, where τ_{max} is set equal to $1/((1-\rho)\times M_{best})$, and τ_{min} is set equal to $\tau_{max}/6$. Note that ρ denotes the persistence of the trail and is set to 0.75. It is also to be noted that $\tau_{max}\geq\tau_{pt}\geq\tau_{min}$ is always maintained in the search process of the ACO. The term "M_{best}" refers to the best value of objective function that has been obtained so far. The solution is improved by the local search.

4.2 Evaluation Module

In this evaluation module, the objective criterion is to find out the clearance variation for the ant sequence. The evaluation module has the following three steps:

  i)   Construction of a solution
  ii)   Improving the solution by local search
  iii)   Updating the pheromone trail

4.2.1 Construction of Solution

An ant starts constructing a sequence by choosing a random combination of selective groups for all the seven quality characteristics. The length of sequence is equal to the number of groups multiplied by number of quality characteristics [6×7=42). The randomly generated sequence is 542163,365412,164235,245631,214635,264531,526341.

4.2.2 Improving the Solution by Local Search

The local search procedure used in this work is explained with a numerical example. Suppose we have {6–5–4–3–2–1} as the seed sequence for a quality characteristics. Call it the current seed sequence. Initialize a set of n distinct selective groups of a characteristic, say, {1,2,3,4,5,6} denoted by Ω. Randomly choose a selective group i, say, selective group 3 from Ω. Insert it in all possible positions of the current seed sequence, thereby getting sequence {3–6–5–4–2–1},{6–3–5–4–2–1}, {6–5–3–4–2–1}, {6–5–4–2–3–1}, and {6–5–4–2–1–3}. Choose the best sequence with respect to the objective under consideration; say, sequence {6–5–4–2–1–3} is chosen. If it is better than the current seed sequence {6–5–4–3–2–1}, then update the current seed sequence as {6–5–4–2–3– 1}; else {6–5–4–3–2–1} is retained as the current seed sequence. Assume that the {6–5–4–2–3–1} is chosen. Remove the chosen selective group (i.e., selective group 3) from Ω. Randomly choose another selective group j from Ω and proceed with all possible insertions in the current seed sequence. Compare the best among these sequences with the current seed sequence, and update the current seed sequence, if necessary. Remove selective group j from Ω. Likewise, proceed until all n selective groups are checked.

4.2.3 Updating of Trail Intensities

An ant sequence is subjected to the local search procedure to enhance the quality of solution. Let the objective function of the improved sequence be denoted by $M_{current}$. Subsequently, trail intensities are updated.

4.3 Output Module

The best combination of selective groups obtained by ACO is given as the output.

5 Results

The proposed ACO algorithm is coded in MATLAB. The solutions obtained are compared with the solution obtained by non-dominated sorting genetic algorithm NSGA [4]. From Table 3, it is clear that, ACO outperforms the assembly of corresponding selective groups and the best combination of selective groups obtained by NSGA.

Table 3. Best combination of selective groups obtained using ACO

Method	Characteristic A - B - C - D - E - F - G							Clearance variation			
								CV_1	CV_2	CV_3	CV_4
TM	123456-123456-123456-123456-123456-123456-123456							60	18	36	48
NSGA	132645-365412-146325-256314-615243-142635-634251							19	12	28	16
ACO	652314-432615-431625-213645-345162-431625-346152							18	9	18	8

Note:- TM-Traditional Method

6 Conclusion

In this work, an ant colony optimization (ACO) algorithm is proposed and applied to a complex assembly to improve its precision by minimizing the four possible clearance variations of that assembly. With the assembly of corresponding selective groups, the population assembly clearance variation is not appreciable for all the four clearances i.e., [18+18+24 = 60 µm], [12+6 = 18 µm], [12+24 = 36 µm], [24+24 = 48 µm]. The proposed algorithm has produced best combination of selective groups. Clearance variation achieved for the population is 19 µm for clearance 1, 12 µm for clearance 2, 24 µm for clearance 3 and 16 µm for clearance 4. The mating part population is partitioned to form selective groups after measurement by advanced dimension measuring devices. The components from selective groups are assembled as per combinations obtained in this paper.

References

1. Kannan, S.M., Jayabalan, V.: A new grouping method for minimizing the surplus parts in selective assembly. Qual. Eng. 14(1), 67–75 (2001a)
2. Kannan, S.M., Jayabalan, V.: A new grouping method to minimize surplus parts in selective assembly for complex assemblies. Int. J. Prod. Res. 39(9), 1851–1864 (2001b)

3. Kannan, S.M., Jayabalan, V., Jeevanantham, K.: Genetic algorithm for minimizing assembly variation in selective assembly. Int. J. Prod. Res. 41, 3301–3313 (2003)
4. Asha, A., Kannan, S.M., Jayabalan, V.: Optimization of clearance variation in selective assembly for components with multiple characteristics. Int. J. of Adv. Manuf. Technol. 38, 1026–1044 (2008)
5. Mease, D., Nair, V.N., Sudjianto, A.: Selective assembly in manufacturing: statistical issues and optimal binning strategies. Technometrics 46(2), 165–175 (2004)
6. Matsuura, S., Shinozaki, N.: Optimal process design in selective assembly when components with smaller variance are manufactured at three shifted means. Int. J. Prod. Res., 1–14 (2010) iFirst
7. Dorigo, M.: Optimization, learning and natural algorithms (in Italian). Ph.D. thesis, Department di Elettronica, Politecnico di Milano, Italy (1992)
8. Dorigo, M., Maniezzo, V., Colorni, A.: The ant system: optimization by a colony of cooperating agents. IEEE Trans. Syst. Man. Cybern. Part B 26, 29–41 (1996)

Empirical Study for Explicit Knowledge Evaluation in the Enterprise R&D Process

Zhou Wen-Yong, Wang Jing, and Hu Jing-Jing

School of Economics & Management Tongji University,
Shanghai 200092, China
zhouwyk@126.com, seuwj@yahoo.cn, jj09320501@163.com

Abstract. Explicit knowledge affects the efficiency and effectiveness of the management in the Enterprise R & D Process (ERDP) directly, yet the classification, evaluation and application of explicit knowledge in this process remain to be studied further. Based on the relevant literature study, the explicit knowledge is classified and the Evaluation System of Explicit Knowledge (ESEK) is constructed in this paper. The empirical study is built on the information from 50 valid questionnaires filled out by the R&D personnel. Empirical analyses have taught us that 6 dimensions (knowledge operation, R&D investment, R&D innovation, R&D accomplishment, R&D potential) of the ESEK are proposed by using Exploratory Factor Analysis (EFA) method. The study suggest that enterprises can evaluate and improve the efficiency and effectiveness of explicit knowledge management through the above 6 dimensions and comes to some new ideas about the classification, evaluation and improvements of explicit knowledge in ERDP.

Keywords: R&D process, Explicit knowledge, Knowledge evaluation.

1 Introduction

How to manage knowledge has become an important issue in the past few decades, and the Knowledge Management (KM) community has developed a wide range of technologies and applications for both academic research and practical applications [1]. Most study on KM evaluation in the ERDP has been developed theoretically and conceptually. ESEK is rarely mentioned and the index system hasn't yet formed into a consistent one. Therefore, the explicit knowledge evaluation has become a difficult point in ERDP.

Currently, KM evaluation has two patterns: process-oriented evaluation and result-oriented evaluation. Study on KM evaluation will be out of academic limits and develop to a perspective of comprehensive evaluation [2]. However, whatever the way of thinking is and methods used are in the development of KM evaluation, the key problem still lies in the explicit classification and index system construction.

The objective of the study is to enrich the theoretical and practical research on KM and to provide a new approach for the explicit knowledge evaluation. For this purpose,

G. Shen and X. Huang (Eds.): CSIE 2011, Part I, CCIS 152, pp. 94–99, 2011.

the author classifies the explicit knowledge and constructs the evaluation system on the basis of relevant literature.

2 Structure for Evaluation System

2.1 Classification of Explicit Knowledge

According from the literature [1][4][5][6], the explicit knowledge in ERDP can be classified by 3 dimensions, the source, shared level and application scope combining as in table 1.

Table 1. The classification of explicit knowledge in EERP

dimension	classification	implication
Source	Individual explicit knowledge	Individual processed, can be articulated and transferred to others
	Group explicit knowledge	Group shared, can be understood and exchanged
Shared level	Private explicit knowledge	Possessed by one but not shared with others.
	Shared explicit knowledge	Possessed by both the parties in cooperation
Application scope	Internal explicit knowledge	Explicit knowledge exist inside the organization
	External explicit knowledge	Explicit knowledge exist outside the organization

2.2 Factor Structure

R&D process can be divided into the following five stages: demand identification, R&D conceptualization, program design, program implementation, result completion [3][7][8]. The level of KM depends on these factors such as enterprises' infrastructure, core technologies, number of R&D institutions, as well as their knowledge sharing, management system and innovative atmosphere and so on. Moreover, enterprises itself is a dynamic complex system. Only the multi-dimensional system can reflect the comprehensive level of the management correctly. Based on the general, scientific, practical and operational principles, the ESEK is constructed as in table 2.

3 Empirical Study

3.1 Sample Selection and Data Collection

A total of 30 R&D-based enterprises covering a wide range of industry sectors are involved in the study. The personnel in R&D department are required to grade the

Table 2. Primary index system of explicit knowledge evaluation

Dimension	item
Quality of the personnel	a_1 average education level
	a_2 percent of the knowledgeable workers
	a_3 R&D and innovation capabilities
Technologies & facilities	a_4 function of facilities' standard
	a_5 number of R&D institutions
	a_6 core technology
	a_7 advanced R&D facilities
Corporate culture	a_8 leaders' attitude
	a_9 R&D collaboration
	a_{10} innovative environment
	a_{11} training opportunities
	a_{12} cooperation with outside R&D agencies
Knowledge operation	a_{13} knowledge sharing
	a_{14} knowledge acquisition and transformation
	a_{15} sophistication of knowledge database
	a_{16} utilization degree of knowledge
	a_{17} knowledge maintenance
R&D result	a_{18} total R&D funding
	a_{19} number of R&D achievement
	a_{20} number of valid patents

items' importance on the questionnaires based on their work experiences and the actual situation of their enterprises. A sample of 50 respondents is obtained finally. The sample consists of 24% of women and 76% of men; 56% of workers and 44% of managers; 36% of age 25 or below, 46% of age 26 to 35, 18% of age 36 or above; 18% of associates or below, 38% of undergraduates, 44% of postgraduates or above ; 18% of less than a year of work experience, 28% of 2 to 5 years of work experience, 46% of 6 to 9 years of work experience, 26% of more than 10 years of work experience.

3.2 Methods and Tools

Data processing software SPSS13.0 was employed in the study. Specific methods include: (1) Principal component analysis to obtain the initial component matrix; (2)

Varimax rotation method to derive the component matrix if the components are not significant; (3) Regression analysis to obtain component score coefficient matrix.

3.3 Data Processing Results

(1) Results of descriptive statistics

Preliminary results of the sample are as follows: The average scores of the 20 items are all above 12 points; the standard deviations of the items are all less than 4.8. They both demonstrate that most of the respondents believe all the 20 items listed in the evaluation system are rather important. Meanwhile, the respondents with a bachelor degree or above takes up more than 80% of the total and the respondents with five years or more of work experiences takes up more than 70% of the total. They both indicate that the majority of respondents have higher educational background and years of R&D experience. The results of descriptive statistics show the validity and reliability of the collected data.

(2) Results of EFA

KMO and Bartlett's test indicate that KMO= 0.792> 0.5, Bartlett=602.697, and P= 0.000<0.01. So the sampling varieties are relative and the data areappropriate for factor analysis. Then the author extracts the component factors on the principal of that the eigenvalue is more than 1.Then we get the data processing results: f_1 is defined as knowledge operation, which mainly reflects the activities of the explicit knowledge and consists of 7 items (a_{10}, a_{11}, a_{12}, a_{13}, a_{15}, a_{16}, a_{17}); f_2 is defined as R&D investment, which mainly reflects emprises' investment in R&D and consists of 4items(a_6, a_8, a_9, a_{18}); f_3 is defined as R&D innovation, which mainly reflects the innovation capability of the enterprise and consist of 3 items(a_3, a_7, a_{14}); f_4 is defined as R&D result, which mainly reflect the compliment achieved in ERDP and consist of 3 items(a_5, a_{19}, a_{20});f_5 is defined as R&D potential, which mainly reflects the potential of the enterprise in the future development and consists of 3 items(a_1, a_2, a_4). Finally, the modified explicit knowledge evaluation is constructed as in table 3.

4 Implications

The Data in table 3 show that: (1) The knowledge operation (f1), R & D investment (f2) and R & D innovation (f3) are ranked top 3 among all the dimensions; (2) Enterprises should attach great importance to the application and sharing of the knowledge in R&D process; (3) R & D investment determines the R& D output to some extent; (4) Innovation is the source and power of the output which plays an important role in the process..

To improve the management of explicit knowledge in ERDE, 3 viewpoints are proposed in this study: (1) Creating a favorable atmosphere for knowledge sharing; encouraging the externalization and socialization of tacit knowledge such as establishing knowledge database by coding the knowledge, carrying out academic exchanges and discussions between R & D institutions, enhancing the qualification of

Table 3. Evaluation index system of explicit knowledge

dimension	item	Eigenvalue	variance	Cumulative	rate
Knowledge operation(f_1)	$a_{10}, a_{11}, a_{12}, a_{13},$ a_{15}, a_{16}, a_{17}	4.39	21.951	21.951	1
R&D investment(f_2)	a_6, a_8, a_9, a_{18}	2.763	13.815	35.766	2
R&D innovation(f_3)	a_3, a_7, a_{14}	2.533	12.667	48.433	3
R&D output(f_4)	a_5, a_{19}, a_{20}	2.497	12.485	60.981	4
R&D potential(f_5)	a_1, a_2, a_4	2.037	10.186	71.103	5

the personnel and offering more staff training. (2) Increasing more tangible (e.g. research funding, core technologies) and intangible (e.g. personnel introduction and cultivation, leaders' attention, team collaboration) investment. (3) Encouraging the establishment of innovation mechanism. Enterprises should improve the innovative capacity of the staff and introduce advanced equipment and technology from outside in terms of technological mechanism. And they should also transform previous R&D pattern of separate projects to a whole innovative establishment, as well as formerly single subject and department oriented pattern to a multi-disciplinary and cross-departmental R&D pattern.

5   Summary and Outlook

The main devotion of the study is as followings. Firstly, the explicit knowledge in ERDP is classified into personal explicit knowledge and group explicit knowledge, private explicit knowledge and shared explicit knowledge, internal explicit knowledge and external explicit knowledge. Secondly, the evaluation system which consists of 6 dimensions (knowledge operation, R&G investment, R&G innovation, R&G output and R&D potential) is constructed. Thirdly, enterprises in the sample are evaluated and ranked comprehensively.

The study also puts forward some suggestions in order to improve the enterprises' management. First, create a favorable atmosphere for knowledge sharing; second, increase more tangible and intangible investment; third, encourage the establishment of innovation mechanism.

Nevertheless, there are still some limitations in this study. Firstly, we recognize the sample of the study is not enough with just 50. Secondly the empirical study neglected the differences between R&D institutions in enterprises of different types. Therefore, quantitative indicators can be introduced to avoid results inconsistency and improvement-oriented evaluation on the basis of process-oriented and result-oriented can be added in the future study.

References

1. Liao, S.-h.: Knowledge Management Technologies and Applications- Literature Review from 1995 to 2002. Expert Systems with Applications 25, 155–164 (2003)
2. Ye, C.-s., Wang, C.-l., Wang, C.J., Liu, H.-w.: A Study on Knowledge Management Evaluation Model at Home and Abroad. Information Studies: Theory &Application 31(5), 684–686 (2008)
3. Zhou, W.-y., Yuan, C.: A Review of Knowledge Management in the Enterprise R&D Process. Science & Technology and Economy 22(128), 13–16 (2009)
4. Rodgers, P.A., Clarkson, J.P.: Knowledge Usage in New Product Development. In: IDATER 1998 Conference (1998)
5. Collins, H.M.: The Structure of Knowledge. Social Research 60, 95–116 (1993)
6. Zhou, Y.-s., Zhang, Y.-f., Zhou, P.-x.: Knowledge Management in the Enterprises' Project-Developing. Information Science 22(12), 1507–1510 (2004)
7. Tian, Q.-f., Zeng, Y.-q.: A Study on the Frame Work of Knowledge Management System of Product R&D. Journal at Intelligence 3, 50–52 (2007)
8. Bao, C.-y.: A study on Knowledge Management of Products' R&D. Technological Development of Enterprise 26(2), 65–67 (2007)

Comparison of Two-Stage Supply Chain Performance in Four Types: Based on Different Dominant Advantages Perspective

Zhou Wen-Yong and Xu Ying

School of Economics & Management, Tongji University, Shanghai, 200092, China
zhouwyk@126.com, filwcy2003@sina.com

Abstract. Different dominant advantages affect supply chain performance. This paper discusses four types of two-stage supply chain model under Stackelberg game by revenue sharing contract, considers a new parameter and enriches supply chain models in theory. Comparisons of reorder quantity, game process, different enterprises' interests and total profit of supply chain are made, based on the equilibrium and each member's profit. The result shows that whether the leading enterprise is supplier or retailer, as long as having absolute advantage, can the leader maximize its own profit, while achieving global optimization of the supply chain.

Keywords: Retailers, Suppliers, Supply Chain Performance, Leading Advantage of Corporation.

1 Introduction

A stackelberg game is existed in two-stage supply chain with single supplier and single retailer. Since the non-cooperation of this game, [1] there are "first-mover advantage" and "late-mover advantage". [2] Dominant firms develop different contracts, such as the wholesale price contract [3], buy back contract [4], revenue sharing contract [5], quantity flexibility contract [6], etc. to achieve the desired objectives. When the leading enterprise (either supplier [7] or retailer [8]) dominants advantage completely, the dominant position can be used to force the following enterprise just obtain its retained profit, while the leading enterprise itself gets all the remaining profit, and supply chain performance achieving optimal level. However, once the leading supplier dominants advantage partly, supply chain performance reduced. [9]

According to different leading enterprises and dominant advantages, the two-stage supply chain is classified into four types in this paper. Using revenue sharing contract as the way of coordinating supply chain, four Stackelberg game models are constructed and solved by adverse induction. Then compare and analyze supply chain performance in the perspective of objective function, the game process, equilibrium, and different corporate profits in four types.

Based on the similar studies, we combine four types of supply chain and make a comparative analysis innovatively in different leading firms and different dominant

G. Shen and X. Huang (Eds.): CSIE 2011, Part I, CCIS 152, pp. 100–106, 2011.

advantages considering shortage cost. Then, in theory, the model of leading supplier with comparative advantage is added. This paper further verifies the conclusion that stackelberg game can make the supply chain coordinate. Moreover, whether the supplier or the retailer as leading enterprise, if it can not dominant advantage completely, not only its own interest will be damaged, but also the level of overall supply chain performance is reduced.

2 Classification of Two-Stage Supply Chain and Hypotheses

2.1 Classification of Two-Stage Supply Chain

According to different leading enterprise, the two-stage supply chain is divided into the supply chain of leading supplier and the supply chain of leading retailer. Suppliers are the traditional core enterprises of supply chain in industrial age. However, the position of retailers is raised by the customer-centric sales model and the important role of information resources. [10] And, according to different dominant advantages, the two-stage supply chain belongs to the supply chain of leading enterprise with absolute advantage and comparative advantage. The dominant enterprises not just takes the lead to achieve their interest target, they also give priority to developing a strategy. In accordance with the decision-making order, we in this paper consider the leading enterprise with absolute advantage only when it can have priority completely, or it has comparative advantage. Thus four types of two-stage supply chain model are constructed.

2.2 Parameter Definition

The cost per unit of product is C. Supplier sells the products to retailer by transfer price: W_b after increasing adding price: δ. At the beginning of each demand cycle, retailer orders the products in quantities of Q, then sells to consumers with market price: $P(P \geq W_b)$. Shortage cost during the sales period is h, and the products remained at the end of sales period will be sold with salvage value: V. The profit of supplier, retailer and the supply chain is C_s, C_r and $C_{s,r}$ respectively. The proportion of revenue sharing which retailer gets is R ($R \in [0, 1]$).

2.3 Research Hypothesis

We suppose that retailer faces stochastic demand with probability density function $f(x)$ and distribution function $F(x)$. Revenue sharing proportion R is decided by leading enterprise, and supplier decides transfer price W_b. Each product sold by price P brings RP to retailer and $(1-R)P$ to supplier.

When the leading company makes decision, we suppose the following one will choose to participate in supply chain if the profit is not less than its retained profit. Suppose the retained profit of supplier and retailer is C_s^0 and C_r^0.

In the game process, variable quantities need to be decided are: proportion of revenue sharing R, transfer price W_b and reorder quantity Q. In this paper, we mark off absolute and comparative advantage according to this decision-making order (Table 1).

Table 1. Hypothesis of different leading advantages by decision-making order

Leading enterprise	Leading advantage	decision-making order		
Supplier	Absolute	①S: W_b	②S: R	③R: Q
	Comparative	①S: W_b (R)	②R: Q	③S: R
Retailer	Absolute	①R: R(W_b)	②R: Q(W_b)	③S: W_b
	Comparative	①R: R(W_b)	②S: W_b	③R: Q

Note: S for supplier; R for retailer; W_b (R) represents that W_b is a function of R.

For short, we donate S-A the type of leading supplier with absolute advantage, and S-C, R-A, R-C the other three types in the following paper.

3   Setting Up and Solution

3.1   Reference Model

Taking newsboy model [11] as basic reference, we get the optimal reorder quantity: $Q = F^{-1}(\dfrac{P+h-C}{P+h-V})$. In the contract of revenue sharing, a new parameter: revenue sharing proportion: R is included. For supply chain operation, we suppose: $RV \leqq W_b$ $\leqq RP$, that is to say, $\dfrac{W_b}{P} \leq R \leq \dfrac{W_b}{V}$ [12]. Thus we extend newsboy model as:

The objective function of retailer is

$$C_r(Q) = RP\int_0^\infty \min(Q,x)f(x)dx - W_bQ + RV\int_0^Q (Q-x)f(x)dx - Rh\int_Q^\infty (x-Q)f(x)dx =$$

$$(RP+h-W_b)Q - R(P-V)\int_0^Q F(x)dx - Rh\int_Q^\infty xf(x)dx - RhQ\int_0^Q f(x)dx, \qquad (1)$$

The solution is

$$Q^* = F^{-1}[\frac{RP-W_b+Rh}{R(P-V+h)}], \quad W_b = RC \qquad (2)$$

With the revenue sharing contract, the supplier can choose the appropriate combination of transfer price and revenue sharing proportion to distribute the total profit to the supplier and the retailer in any division, while realizing the supply chain coordination. [13].

In order to make both retailer and supplier to collaborate, their each profit can not be less than the retained profit, and the sum of their retained profit should be lower than the maximum profitability of the supply chain, which is denoted as $C_{s,r}^{max} = \max C_{s,r}(W_b, R, Q)$.

So, the following constraint conditions should be met:

$$C_r(Q) \geq C_r^0, \quad C_s(W_b, R) \geq C_s^0, \quad C_{s,r}^{max} \geq C_r^0 + C_s^0 \tag{3}$$

3.2 Model Setting-Up

Three types of supply chain models are set up in the conditions of S-A, R-A and R-C. [14] This paper develops these models and adds a new parameter: shortage cost, h, then discusses a forth model which has a leading supplier with comparative advantage theoretically. Four types of models are built and their objective functions are listed as the following (Constraint conditions are the same as formula 3):

Type S-A: $C_s = \max\{(P-C)Q - (P-V)\int_0^Q F(x)dx - h\int_Q^\infty (x-Q)f(x)dx - C_r\}$

$C_r(Q) = \max\{RP\int_0^\infty \min(Q,x)f(x)dx - W_b Q + RV\int_0^Q (Q-x)f(x)dx - Rh\int_Q^\infty (x-Q)f(x)dx\}$

Type S-C:

$C_s = \max\{[(1-R)(P+h) + W_b - C]Q^* - (1-R)[(P-V)\int_0^{Q^*} F(x)dx + h\int_{Q^*}^\infty xf(x)dx + hQ^* F(Q^*)]\}$

Note: Q*stands for Q*(W$_b$), coming from the first objective function of this type; W$_b$= W$_b$(R).

Type R-A: $C_r = \max\{(P-C)Q - (P-V)\int_0^Q F(x)dx - h\int_Q^\infty (x-Q)f(x)dx] - C_s^0\}$

Type R-C: $C_r(Q) = \max\{RP\int_0^\infty \min(Q,x)f(x)dx - W_b Q + RV\int_0^Q (Q-x)f(x)dx - Rh\int_Q^\infty (x-Q)f(x)dx\}$

$C_s(R,W_b) = \max[(1-R)(P+h) + W_b - C]Q^* - (1-R)[(P-V)\int_0^{Q^*} F(x)dx + h\int_{Q^*}^\infty xf(x)dx + hQ^* F(Q^*)]$

3.3 Computing Results

We get four sets of Nash equilibrium by adverse induction showing as the following table:

Table 2. Nash equilibriums of four types of supply chain

SC types	Q	R	W_b
L-A	$F^{-1}\left[\dfrac{RP-W_b+Rh}{R(P-V+h)}\right]$	$\dfrac{C_r^0}{(P-V)[Q-\int_0^Q F(x)dx]+VQ-h\int_Q^\circ (x-Q)f(x)dx-}$	$W_b = RC$
L-C	$F^{-1}\left[\dfrac{RP-W_b+Rh}{R(P-V+h)}\right]$	$\max\{\arg\max C_s(R\vert W_b^*(R),Q^{**}),$ $root[C_r(W_b^*(R)\vert R,Q^{**})=C_r^0]\}$	$W_b = root\{W_b$ $=R[C-Q\dfrac{\partial W_b}{\partial Q}]\}$
R-A	$F^{-1}\left[\dfrac{RP-W_b+Rh}{R(P-V+h)}\right]$	$1-\dfrac{C_s^0-\delta Q}{(P-V)[Q-\int_0^Q F(x)dx]+VQ-h\int_Q^\circ (x-Q)f(x)}$	$W_b^* = C+\delta$ $(\delta \geq 0)$
R-C	$F^{-1}\left[\dfrac{RP-W_b+Rh}{R(P-V+h)}\right]$	$\min\{\arg\max C_r(R\vert W_b^*,Q^*),$ $root[C_s(W_b^*\vert R,Q^*)=C_s^0]\}$	$W_b(R)=root\{W_b(R)$ $=R[C-Q\dfrac{\partial W_b(R)}{\partial Q}]\}$

4   Discussion of the Results

Based on the results of four models and the each member's profit, the comparison is listed as table 3.

Table 3. Comparison of game process and each member's profit

SC types	Action order	Decision order	Each member's profit		
			Supplier	Retailer	Supply chain
L-A	$S \to S \to R$	(R^*,W_b^*,Q^*)	$> C_s^0$	$= C_r^0$	$= C_{s,r}^{max}$
L-C	$S \to R \to S$	(W_b^*,Q^*,R^*)	$\geq C_s^0$	$\geq C_r^0$	$\leq C_{s,r}^{max}$
R-A	$R \to R \to S$	(R^*,Q^*,W_b^*)	$= C_s^0$	$> C_r^*$	$= C_{s,r}^{max}$
R-C	$R \to S \to R$	(R^*,W_b^*,Q^*)	$\geq C_s^0$	$\geq C_r^0$	$\leq C_{s,r}^{max}$

Note: in the line of "Action order", S stands for supplier and R stands for retailer.

4.1   Analysis of Reorder Quantity

Newsboy model shows supply chain would be coordinative only when the reorder quantity meets: $Q^* = F^{-1}(\dfrac{P+h-C}{P+h-V})$. Thus, no matter which enterprise is the leader and how to distribute the profits in supply chain, so long as meeting the reordering level, supply chain's overall profit will not be affected. However, in the case of comparative advantage, the reorder quantity is not determined at last which will be affected by the following decision. Then the final expression might not be in conformity with the above one, so the supply chain is uncoordinated.

4.2 Analysis of Game Order

In theory, there are two kinds of game processes in different dominant models: absolute and comparative advantage. The result comparison shows, the leading enterprise will try to have absolute advantage if having options. But it is worth noticing that the "$R \rightarrow R \rightarrow S$" game order need a retailer having enough power advantage, as the revenue sharing proportion and expected reorder quantity included in the first decision are both the functions of transfer price, which will be decided by the supplier. However, the "$S \rightarrow S \rightarrow R$" game order only need a supplier who has the advantage of drawing the contract.

4.3 Analysis of Different Enterprises' Profits

In general, the following enterprise can only have retained profit, at the same time, the leading one using its advantage will obtain more than the retained profits, even all the profits remained in the supply chain. And, it is crucial to the leading enterprise, not only to master the right to contract drawing, but more importantly, to have the priority of taking action.

4.4 Analysis of Total Profit of Supply Chain

To the supply chain's total profit, the two types of dominant model can both achieve the global optimum. That is to say, the leading enterprise not only achieves its own profit maximization, but also facilitates the supply chain coordination by revenue-sharing contract. 3.2 also shows, in the conditions of comparative advantage, total profit is declined for having to consider more objective functions. Thus, giving up the dominant advantage will not only bring the reduction of the leader's interest, but also affect the supply chain performance.

5 Summary and Outlook

In this paper, four types of supply chain model in different dominant cases are presented. Then comparisons of stackelberg game results and supply chain performance are made and analyzed. The study shows: whether the leading enterprise is supplier or retailer, as long as the leader has absolute advantage, its own profit will be maximal, as well as achieving global optimization, which is in agreement with reference [14]. We also consider an adding parameter: shortage cost, though which has

no effects on the final conclusion. Furthermore, the model of supplier as leading
enterprise with comparative advantage is added in theory and we make a
comprehensive comparison of four types of supply chain. The results show that
whether the leading enterprise is supplier or retailer, once giving up its first-mover
advantage, that is to say, absolute advantage turning into comparative, it will make its
own interest reduced and supply chain uncoordinated.

Nevertheless, there are still some shortcomings in this study. We have only analysis
these supply chain models in theory, so how to put it into practice need to be explored.
What's more, breaking the restriction of risk-neutral decision-makers and information
symmetry to research the way to coordinating supply chain in case of risk-averse
members or information asymmetry still needs further discussion.

References

1. Meng, Q.: Comparison of Profit Distribution in Two Different Supply Chain Cooperation Forms. Modern Management Science 4, 43–44 (2008)
2. Liu, Z., Huang, Z.: Survey on Stackekberg Game. Journal of Southwest Institute of Technology 14(2), 5–12 (1999)
3. Lariviere, M., Porteus, E.: Selling to the Newsvendor: an Analysis of Price-Only Contracts. Manufacturing and Service Operations Management 3(4), 293–305 (2001)
4. Padmanabhan, V., Png, I.P.L.: Returns Policies: Make Money by Making Good. Sloan Management Review, 65–72 (Fall 1995)
5. Sijie, L., Zhanbei, Z.: Supply Chain Coordination and Decision Making under Consignment Contract with Revenue Sharing. International Journal of Production Economics 1(120), 88–97 (2009)
6. Barnes-Schuster, D., Bassok, Y., Anupindi, R.: Coordination and Flexibility in Supply Contracts with Options. Manufacturing and Service Operations Management 4(3), 171–207 (2009)
7. Pang, Q.-h.: Research on Profit Division in Supply Chains Based on Stackelberg Game with Buyback Contract. Science Technology and Engineering 9(16), 4873–4876 (2009)
8. Jiang, M.X., Yan, L.L., Jin, S.S., Feng, D.Z.: Coordinating Price Model for Retailer Dominant in a Two-echelon Supply Chain. In: 2009 IEEE 16th International Conference on Industrial Engineering and Engineering Management. IEEE Press, New York (2009)
9. Li, P.-q.: A Stackelberg Model in Private Electronic Markets with Supplier's Weaker Dominant Position. Industrial Engineering and Management 14(4), 18–24 (2009)
10. Li, Y.-j.: Analysis of a Supply Chain Game Dominated by Retailers. Journal of Huaiyin Teachers College Social Science 30(6), 756–758 (2008)
11. Gallegog, G., Moon, I.: The distribution free newsboy problem: review and extensions. The Journal of the Operational Research Society 44(8), 825–834 (1993)
12. Cai, J.-h., Zhou, G.-g.: Influence of revenue sharing contracts on the performance of a two-echelon supply chain. Computer Integrated Manufacturing Systems 14(8), 1636–1645 (2008)
13. Chen, H.-y.: The Supply Chain Coordination of Short-Life-Cycle Products. Tsinghua University, Beijing (2003)
14. Zhang, G.-l., Liu, Z.-x.: Stackelberg Game of Profit Division in Supply Chains with Dominant Firms. Systems Engineering 24(10), 19–23 (2006)

Particle Filters for Visual Tracking

Fasheng Wang

Department of Computer Science & Technology,
Dalian Neusoft Institute of Information
116023 Dalian, China
wangfasheng@neusoft.edu.cn

Abstract. Particle filter has grown to be a standard tool for solving visual tracking problems in real world applications. This paper discusses in detail the application of particle filter in visual tracking, including single object and multiple objects tracking. Choosing a good proposal distribution for the tracking algorithm in particle filtering framework is the main focus of this paper. We also discussed the contributions related to dealing with occlusion, interaction, illumination change using improved particle filters. A conclusion is drawn in section 4.

Keywords: visual tracking, particle filter, proposal distribution.

1 Introduction

Visual Tracking is one of the most important problems in computer vision field. Generally speaking, there are two approaches for handling visual tracking problems, that is the bottom-up and the up-bottom [1]. The former approach tries to consider the visual tracking problem as an inference problem under Bayesian framework. In this approach, state space models about object state transition and observation models are constructed, and the posterior probability density of object states can be recursively estimated using the prior probability and observations available. According to this point of view, Kalman filter is firstly used in solving visual tracking problems [2]. But Kalman filter can only valid for linear, Gaussian tracking models. When the system models are non-linear, unscented Kalman filter (UKF) [3] can be used. In the real world applications, visual object tracking is usually affected by background clutter, camera motion and object occlusions, which lead to nonlinearity and multi-mode represented through the system and measurement models. In that case, both the Kalman filter and the UKF can not work efficiently. Particle filter, also known as sequential Monte Carlo method [4], has become a standard tool for non-parametric estimation in visual tracking applications, which can handle nonlinear, non-Gaussian systems in real world applications.

In recent years, particle filter has been successfully applied into many fields such as computer vision, robotics, signal processing, economics, etc.. In 1998, M. Isard firstly proposed CONDENSATION (another name of particle filter) algorithm in visual tracking applications. He successfully proved that, particle filter outperformed the Kalman filter in the same tracking circumstances. Following his work, many

G. Shen and X. Huang (Eds.): CSIE 2011, Part I, CCIS 152, pp. 107–112, 2011.
© Springer-Verlag Berlin Heidelberg 2011

researchers paid special attentions to particle filter. In particle filtering framework, the awkward circumstances such as object occlusions, background clutters, multi-object tracking, etc., can be handled effective so long as appropriate proposal distributions are chosen.

2 Particle filter

According to the Bayesian theorem, estimating the object states is equivalent to determining the posterior probabilistic density $p(x_k \mid y_{1:k})$ of the object state variable. Where $x_k \in R^{n_x}$ is state vector, y_k is system observations (such as sensor information), and k is discrete time. The basic idea of particle filter is to represent $p(x_k \mid y_{1:k})$ using a set of weighed particles (samples) $\{x_k^{(i)}, w_k^i\}_{i=1}^N$, where N is the number of particles used, w_k^i is particle weight to evaluate the importance of a particle [5]. The main steps of particle filter are: prediction and update. In prediction process, each particle is propagated through the system state transition model, in which stochastic noises are added to simulate system state noise. In update process, update each particle using the most recent observations such as object information in the next frame. At last, the resampling scheme is used to remove the updated particles with very little weight, and duplicate the large weight particles. At each time step, the particles are drawn from a distribution called proposal distribution. The detailed algorithm can be found in the literature.

A key issue in particle filtering algorithm is proposal distribution selection. Selecting a good distribution can reduce the effect of degeneration and improve the tracking performance greatly in real world applications. Gordon [4] firstly propounded to use the transition prior $p(x_k \mid x_{k-1})$ as the proposal distribution which has been widely adopted by researchers for tracking. However, the transition prior has an evident drawback that it does not consider the recent observations y_k which contains much valuable information of the object. Merwe [7] et al. gave an alternative choice, in which the proposal distribution was approximated as a Gaussian distribution, and the mean and covariance of the distribution were propagated and updated by the UKF, through which the effect of the recent observations were considered. The algorithm was named as the unscented particle filter (UPF). Yuan [8] proposed to use Guass-Hermite filter to generate the proposal distribution. Wang [9] proposed a mixed proposal distribution. In real world tracking applications, it is important to design appropriate proposal distribution, which make fully use of the useful information and obtain better tracking result.

Another important issue of particle filtering algorithm is the selection of resampling scheme. The main purpose of introducing resampling is to restrain the effect of degeneration and improve the diversity of particles. But it can lead to sample impoverishment problem [7].

The two issues mentioned above are still the important research direction in particle filter and corresponding applications.

3   Recent Advances of Visual Tracking Applications

Early in 1998, Isard [6] firstly proposed to use CONDENSATION algorithm for visual tracking. The CONDENSATION (CONditional DENSity propagATION) algorithm is the earliest name in visual tracking world. After his work, many researchers proposed a lot of improved particle filtering algorithm and considered the CONDENSATION algorithm to be a comparison target. The CONDENSATION adopts the transition prior [4] as the proposal distribution. And it was proved to outperform the Kalman filter in object contour tracking. But as proclaimed in the former part, the CONDENSATION algorithm does not take into account the most recent observations, that is, the object contour in the current frame or at the current moment. It estimates the object's state at time k according to the state of the previous moment $k-1$ which can not adapt to the changing tracking environment.

Yong Rui proposed to use the UPF algorithm for face tracking and obtained improved performance compared to the CONDENSATION algorithm. Peihua Li [11] used the UPF algorithm in visual contour tracking. In his experiments, real time tracking of the contour using the UPF was much better than that using the CONDENSATION algorithm.

Many researchers have been working hard to improve the tracking accuracy and robustness of the particle filter in visual tracking applications. Most of them considered to fuse useful object features into the particle filtering framework. Katja [12] proposed to use the color histogram distribution for the proposal distribution, while the Bhattacharyya coefficient as the similarity measure between tow distributions. Because the color distribution is robust to partial occlusion, are rotation and scale invariant and computationally efficient. The proposed method can give improved performance compared to the Mean Shift and CONDENSATION algorithm. However, due to the sensitivity of the color information to the illumination in the tracking environment, the robustness of the proposed algorithm is bad.

Shaohua Zhou [13] proposed an improved particle filtering algorithm for simultaneous tracking and recognition of human faces from video. In his work, he introduced an adaptive appearance model and an adaptive-velocity motion mode to describe the inter-frame appearance change and embed them in the particle filtering framework. Compared to the CONDENSATION algorithm, the improved algorithm can achieve a stabilized tracker and accurate recognizer when confronted by pose and illumination variations. Jaco Vermaak [14] gives a mixture Gaussian proposal distribution for the sake of tracking multiple moving objects. To capture multi-modality this paper formulates the filtering distribution as a M-component mixture model, that is, $p(x_k | y_{1:k}) = \sum_{m-1}^{M} \pi_{m,k} p_m(x_k | y_{1:k})$, with $\sum_{m=1}^{M} \pi_{m,k} = 1$. Note that no parametric model is assumed for the individual mixture components. Each component corresponds to an individual object. This mixture particle filter is able to maintain the multi-modality inherent in tracking problems where the standard particle filter fails, as was illustrated on a synthetic and a real world tracking problem.

On the basis of Jaco Vermaak's work [14], Kenji Okuma [15] proposed a Boosted particle filter (BPF) aim at solving varying number of object tracking problems in hokey games. The problem of tracking a varying number of non-rigid objects has two major difficulties. First, the observation models and target distributions can be highly non-linear and non-Gaussian. Second, the presence of a large, varying number of objects creates complex interactions with overlap and ambiguities. Kenji Okuma constructed the proposal distribution using a mixture model that incorporated information from the dynamic models of each player and the detection hypotheses generated by Adaboost. The learned Adaboost proposal distribution allows us to quickly detect players entering the scene, while the filtering process enables us to keep track of the individual players. However, the BPF algorithm did not have explicit mechanisms to model mutual occlusions between the objects, thus it loses the identities of the targets after occlusions. In order to solve the problem, Yizheng Cai [16] proposed anther improved tracking framework based on particle filter, in which, the rectification technique is employed to find the correspondence between the video frame coordinates and the standard hockey rink coordinates so that the system can compensate for camera motion and improve the dynamics of the players. At the same time, a global nearest neighbor data association algorithm is introduced to assign boosting detections to the existing tracks for the proposal distribution in particle filters. And the mean-shift algorithm is embedded into the particle filter framework to stabilize the trajectories of the targets for robust tracking during mutual occlusion. The system designed using the proposed algorithm can automatically and robustly track a variable number of targets and correctly maintain their identities regardless of background clutter, camera motion and frequent mutual occlusion between targets.

Xuan Song [17] proposed probabilistic detection-based particle filter (PDPF) for multiple objects tracking. The contributions in [15, 16] are name as Deterministic detection-based particle filter (DDPF) in Xuan Song's work. He points out the drawbacks of DDPF algorithm, that is, lose the information of interactions among detections; non-detection or false alarms influence tracking performance greatly. The PDPF algorithm incorporates possible probabilistic detections and information from dynamic model to construct a mixed proposal for particle filter, which quite effectively models interactions and occlusions among targets. The PDPF can not only obtains a better approximation of posterior than previous method in the condition of interactions and occlusions, but also minimize the influence of uncertain detections. However, this work also has some limitations: With the increasing number of the interactions, the complexity of our method grows exponentially. Some important parameters should be adjusted manually.

When the tracking systems are affected by small system noise or the covariance of observation noise is very small, the standard particle filter is easy to degenerate. The kernel particle filter (KPF) proposed by Cheng Chang [18] can solve this problem successfully. The KPF invokes kernels to form a continuous estimate of the posterior density function. Particles are allocated based on the gradient information estimated from the kernel density estimate of the posterior. Results from simulations and experiments with real video data show the improved performance of the KPF algorithm when compared with that of the standard particle filter. The superior performance is evident in scenarios of small system noise or weak dynamic models where the standard particle filter usually fails. The KPF is also successfully applied into multiple objects tracking problem [19].

Changjiang Yang [20] proposed a hierarchical particle filter (HPF) which is special for fast multiple objects tracking problem. The HPF characterizes the tracked objects using color and edge orientation histogram features. While the use of more features and samples can improve the robustness, the computational load required by the particle filter increases. To accelerate the algorithm while retaining robustness, the authors adopt several enhancements in the algorithm. The first is the use of integral images for efficiently computing the color features and edge orientation histograms, which allows a large amount of particles and a better description of the targets. Next, the observation likelihood based on multiple features is computed in a coarse-to-fine manner, which allows the computation to quickly focus on the more promising regions. Quasi-random sampling of the particles allows the filter to achieve a higher convergence rate. The resulting tracking algorithm maintains multiple hypotheses and offers robustness against clutter or short period occlusions. In 2007, Yonggang Jin [21] proposed another improved particle filter for multi-object tracking, that is, variational particle filter (VPF). The VPF is efficient in dealing with object occlusions and interactions. The proposal distribution designed for VPF is constructed using variational inference method. Object is modeled by a mixture of a non-parametric contour model and a non-parametric edge model using kernel density estimation. With the VPF, the number of particles needed for multi-object tracking can be significantly reduced.

When multiple objects features are considered in visual tracking, the dimension of the object states can increase drastically. In order to overcome this problem, Stefan Duffner et al. [22] proposed an improved particle filter which is characterized by the use of a dynamic partitioned sampling (DPS). The DPS strategy divides the high dimensional state space into several subspaces, with each corresponds to an individual object feature. During sampling process, the samples are drawn using a hierarchical sampling method, while the sampling sequence is determined by the reliability of the object features. The reliability of each feature is measured in terms of its ability to discriminate the object with respect to the background, where the background is not described by a fixed model or by random patches but is represented by a set of informative "background particles" which are tracked in order to be as similar as possible to the object. The robustness of the improved algorithm in several challenging video sequences is very good.

4 Conclusion

This paper gives a comprehensive review of the recent advances of particle filter applied in visual tracking applications. Researchers have been working hard to improve the performance of particle filter based tracking algorithms. In theoretical aspect, a lot of new contributions have been published, especially optimal algorithm based particle filter, which can greatly enhance the advance of visual tracking applications.

References

1. Yilmaz, A., Javed, O., Shah, M.: Object Tracking: A Survey. ACM Computing Surveys 38(4) Article No.13, 45 pages (2006)
2. Lee, J., Kim, M., Kweon, I.: A Kalman filter based visual tracking algorithm for an object moving in 3D. In: IEEE/RSJ International Conference on Intelligent Robots and Systems, vol. 1, pp. 342–347 (1995)

3. Li, P., Zhang, T., Ma, B.: Unscented Kalman Filter for Visual Curve Tracking. Image and Vision Computing 22(2), 157–164 (2004)
4. Gordon, N.J., Salmond, D.J., Smith, A.F.: Novel approach to nonlinear/non-Gaussian Bayesian state estimation. IEE Proc.-F. 140(2), 107–113 (1994)
5. Doucet, A., Gordon, N.: Sequential Monte Carlo methods in practice. Springer, New York (2001)
6. Isard, M., Blake, A.: CONDENSATION- conditional density propagation for visual tacking. International Journal of Computer Vision 29(1), 5–28 (1998)
7. Merwe, R., Doucet, A., Freitas, N., Wan, E.: The Unscented Particle Filter. Technical report CUED/F-INFENG/TR-380, Cambridge University, England (2000)
8. Yuan, Z., Zheng, N., Jia, X.: The Gauss-Hermite Particle Filter. Acta Electronica Sinica 31(7), 970–973 (2003)
9. Wang, F., Zhao, Q.: A New Particle Filter for nonlinear filtering problems. Chinese Journal of Computers 31(2), 346–352 (2008)
10. Rui, Y., Chen, Y.: Better Proposal Distributions: Object Tracking Using Unscented Particle Filter. In: IEEE International Conf. on Computer Vision and Pattern Recognition (2001)
11. Li, P., Zhang, T., Arthur, E.C.: Visual contour tracking based on particle filters. Image and Vision Computing 21(1), 111–123 (2003)
12. Nummiaro, K., Koller-Meier, E., Gol, L.V.: An Adaptive Color-based Particle Filter. Image and Vision Computing 21(1), 99–110 (2003)
13. Zhou, S., Chellappa, R., Moghaddam, B.: Adaptive Visual Tracking and Recognition Using Particle Filters. In: IEEE Int'l Conf. on Multimedia & Expo., pp. 349–352 (July 2003)
14. Vermaak, J., Doucet, A., Perez, P.: Maintaining Multi-Modality through Mixture Tracking. In: International Conference on Computer Vision (2003)
15. Okuma, K., Taleghani, A., de Freitas, N., Little, J.J., Lowe, D.G.: A Boosted Particle Filter: Multitarget Detection and Tracking. In: Pajdla, T., Matas, J(G.) (eds.) ECCV 2004. LNCS, vol. 3021, pp. 28–39. Springer, Heidelberg (2004)
16. Cai, Y., Freitas, N., Little, J.J.: Robust Visual Tracking for Multiple Targets. In: Leonardis, A., Bischof, H., Pinz, A. (eds.) ECCV 2006. LNCS, vol. 3954, pp. 107–118. Springer, Heidelberg (2006)
17. Song, X., Cui, J., Zha, H., et al.: Probabilistic Detection-based Particle Filter for Multi-target Tracking. In: British Machine Vision Conference (2008)
18. Chang, C., Ansari, R.: Kernel Particle Filter for Visual Tracking. IEEE Signal Processing Letters 12(3), 242–245 (2005)
19. Chang, C., Ansari, R., et al.: Multiple object tracking with kernel particle filter. In: International Conference on Computer Vision and Pattern Recognition, vol. 1, pp. 566–573 (2005)
20. Yang, C., Duraiswami, R., Davis, L.: Fast Multiple Object Tracking via a Hierarchical Particle Filter. In: International Conference on Computer Vision (2005)
21. Jin, Y., Mokhtarian, F.: Variational Particle Filter for Multi-Object Tracking. In: International Conference on Computer Vision (2007)
22. Duffner, S., Odobez, J.M.: Dynamic Partitioned Sampling for Tracking with Discriminative Features. In: British Machine Vision Conference (2009)

A Scalable Mobile Live Video Streaming System Based on RTMP and HTTP Transmissions

Qian Chang, Zehong Yang, and Yixu Song

Dept. of Computer Science and Technology, Tsinghua Univ., Beijing, China
Tsinghua National Laboratory for Information Science and Technology
State Key Laboratory of Intelligent Technology and Systems
changqian9@gmail.com, yangzehong@sina.com, songyixu@163.com

Abstract. In this paper we introduce a scalable 3G live streaming system. It has a mobile client which captures and publishes video streams to a media server. Then the server broadcasts and archives received streams simultaneously. Our system uses flash technology in the end-user development and thus we get very wide device support. By applying self-adaptive HTTP and RTMP transmissions, our system can keep working well under mobile network environment with limited time delay. Our experiments showed that even on 3G mobile phones the live streaming time delay was no more than 5 seconds when RTMP transmission was used. As videos contents are very private and sensitive to users, we also built an authorization service in our system to ensure the security of transferred contents.

Keywords: live streaming; RTMP streaming; HTTP streaming; mobile computing; 3G networks; flash player; streaming security.

1 Introduction

Mobile live video streaming is a new kind of wireless network application. It can capture videos from a mobile device, and then uploads the videos to media server that publishes video streams to all clients immediately. The mobile device can be deployed to many different infrastructures easily and people can get rich on-line information about its environment even from quit a long distance. It's very useful and powerful for civil and military purpose. With the fast development in 3G networks, mobile live video streaming is becoming more and more feasible and low-cost. We believe that the application will be more and more popular and play an important part in our future life.

The system we built contains the following three components: a capturing & uploading client, a live streaming & storage server and a flash player based receiver. The capturing & uploading mobile client was built on a mobile computer, running a compact Linux system and applications for video capturing, video encoding and content transmission. The computer connects to a 3G module, by which it can upload streams to media server through wireless broadband network. The live streaming & storage server hosts rtmp and http services to receive and publish videos over rtmp

G. Shen and X. Huang (Eds.): CSIE 2011, Part I, CCIS 152, pp. 113–118, 2011.

and http layers. The server also runs an authority service to protect users' privacy. As our published contents are all encoded in adobe FLV format, our streams can be watched in flash player based web browsers or applications directly. Below is a brief work-flow chart of our system:

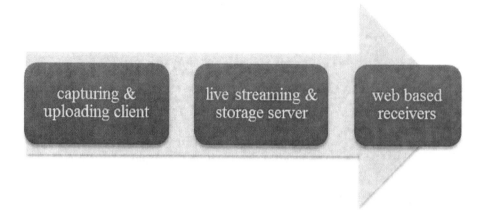

Fig. 1. The brief work flow of video streaming system

2   Video Encoding

As we mentioned before, we used flash player based web pages and Adobe AIR based applications to play videos. They can be both developed in Actionscript language and supported by a large scale of devices. Therefore our end-user service could be very scalable and need very low development cost. The flash video format has quickly established itself as the format of choice for embedded streaming on the web. Notable users of the Flash Video format include YouTube, Hulu, Google Video, Yahoo! Video, metacafe, Reuters.com, and many other news providers [2]. We will further talk about its performance and actual user experience based on our experiment results in Chapter 4. He is a list of supported flash video formats based on our investigations ([1][4]):

Table 1. Supported optimized media formats for different flash players

Player version	Supported Optimized Media Formats
PC 6	Sorenson Spark
PC 7	Sorenson Spark
PC 8	On2 VP6, Sorenson Spark
PC 9.0.115 AIR and above	On2 VP6, Sorenson Spark, H.264 Baseline, H.264 High Profile
Mobile 10.1	On2 VP6, Sorenson Spark, H.264 Baseline

We also test videos encoded in various flash video formats and here are there comparisons:

Table 2. Performance of different flash video on mobile

Video Format	Compression Level	Decoding on mobile
Sorenson Spark	Poor	Fast
On2 VP6	Good	Fast
H.264 Baseline	Better than On2 VP6	Good
H.264 High Profile	Much better than H.264 Baseline	Very bad

Our system is designed to support various computers and mobile devices so that users can access the service and start watching live content anywhere. Base on the above investigation, we decide to use On2VP6 and H.264 Baseline to support all PCs and Flash Support mobile devices. We gave up Sorenson Spark according to Adobe's official recommendation for its low compression performance. Based on our experiments, On2 VP6 and H.264 Baseline showed better encoding/decoding performance against H.264 High Profile and much better quality against Sorenson Spark.

3   Live Video Publishing

Good live video publishing requires fast video encoding and low-delay content transport. Since video uploading and transmission technology is the key to good and smooth streaming experience, we put many efforts on the design and optimization in our uploading client and live streaming server. Here we will introduce and discuss our implementations and considerations.

3.1   Real-Time Messaging Protocol (RTMP) and Transport Protocols

The RTMP was designed for high-performance transmission of audio, video, and data between Adobe Flash Platform technologies, including Adobe Flash Player and Adobe AIR. The raw TCP-based RTMP maintains a single persistent connection and allows real-time communication. n. To guarantee smooth delivery of video and audio streams, while still maintaining the ability to transmit bigger chunks of information, the protocol may split video and data into fragments. The size of the fragments used can be negotiated dynamically between the client and server. Therefore the video transmission is more instantaneous and the more adaptive to network condition. We choose this as our live streaming protocol to get better experience and less delay. Although our RTMP is more flexible for live streaming, it cannot work well when network is very bad (e.g. <10kB/s). For this case, we give up RTMP streaming and upload (or download) recorded segments piece by piece through HTTP channel, which does not require persistent connection and user can get better streaming experience under bad network conditions.

3.2   Video Recording and Uploading

Our uploading client is built on an Atom powered Linux computer. The client is connected to a 3G network card for wireless transport and a web-cam for video recording. We chose Linux as our system for it's easy to handle video encoding and Internet transmission using various protocols. Linux also has a wide range of driver supports in 3G network Cards and web-cams, which can reduce the cost of our system and bring much more hardware choices. To implement RTMP live uploading, we use Flazr, a Java RTMP streaming implementation, as the framework of our uploading application. Since Flazr lacks of video capturing and encoding functions, we develop a native application with libffmpeg and libv4l. This native application will handle web-cam by using Video4Linux API and encode the raw video to On2 VP6 or H.264 Baseline format by using FFMpeg lib. Then it will pass encoded video segments to a Flazr based application for RTMP uploading.

The length of the video segment has great impacts on bandwidth usage and streaming delay. Longer segment will make less RTMP requests and therefore consume less bandwidth, and the streaming sever load will be lighter at the same time. However, the time-delay will be longer. Therefore the length of each segment is a trade-off between the time-delay and system efficiency. We recommend setting the length of a single video segment to 0.5s-2s. The following is a chart of the work flow:

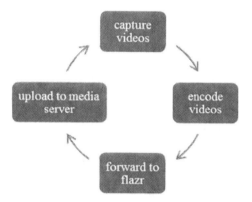

Fig. 2. The work flow of our uploading client

3.3   Video Streaming Server

Our live streaming server are designed to support different uploading and downloading users concurrently, our server needs to identify each session and have related authentication functions to ensure content security. Besides, because we use both RTMP and HTTP protocols for streaming, we need to implement content protection separately and RTMP and HTTP handlers at server side should be able to share authentication information so that both uploading and downloading users don't need to re-login after changing transmission protocol.

3.3.1   HTTP Server

We use HTTP server to our session validation service for HTTP transmission don't require persistent connection and we can handle more session validation requests.

Because many RTMP servers cannot make SQL queries or read/write external data from memory, HTTP server have to share information with RTMP server through disk files. HTTP server will write session information to specific files after each user login action and clear related session information after each user logout action. The RTMP server checks the authentication files periodically so that it can keep up with HTTP server.

3.3.2 RTMP Server

The official distribution of RTMP server is Adobe Flash Media Server. There are also lots of other full implementation RTMP servers, including commercial and free distributions. For example, Helix Universal Server from Real Networks streams live and on-demand RTMP, RTMPS, RTMPE contents. Red5 Open Source Media Server is a reverse-engineered open source project which aims to produce a complete implementation written in Java. A C++ implementation called crtmpserver is also available. As most of RTMP servers can make remote procedure calls besides streaming media contents, we do some authorization chats in RTMP channel before start streaming. RTMP connections will be rejected if token provided is not valid. Therefore we can ensure that videos can only be accessed by its owner. Below is the chart of our media server's authentication work flow:

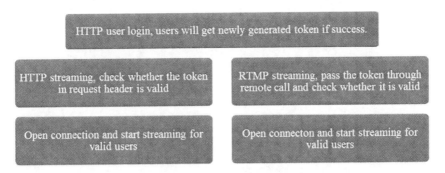

Fig. 3. Our media server's authentication work flow

4 Experiments and Conclusions

To evaluate the performance and user experience of our system, we did some experiments on different devices and under various network environments. Here are results of our experiments.

The above results show that our live streaming service can work smoothly on all PCs and most popular android phones. Network bandwidth is the determinant of streaming FPS. When the video resolution increases to 640×480 and the bandwidth is sufficient, mobile phones drop a few frames (<10%) but the regression is not very noticeable.

Table 3. Live streaming frame rates under different environments[1]

	320X240 FPS	640x480 FPS
PC Wi-Fi	24	24
Motorola Droid Wi-Fi	24	22
PC CDMA2000 3G	24	24
Motorola Droid CDMA2000 3G	24	22
PC CDMA2000 1x	8-10	2-3
Motorola Droid CDMA 1x	8-10	2-3

Acknowledgments. This work is supported by The National High Technology Research and Development Program of China. (Program Number: 2007AA11Z241)

References

1. Adobe Systems Incorporate: List of codecs supported by Adobe Flash Player: Adobe Developer Center
2. Wikipedia Flash Video, http://en.wikipedia.org/wiki/Flash_Video
3. Adobe Systems Incorporated: Real Time Messaging Chunk Stream Protocol (2009)
4. Edmond Au.: Delivering video for Flash Player 10.1 on mobile devices: Adobe Mobile and Devices Developer Center

---

[1] Test Environments:
Adobe Flash Player 10.1, Video Encoding: On2 VP6, Mobile OS: Android 2.2
Mobile CPU: Cortex A8 600MHz, PC OS: Windows 7, Mac OS X, and Linux.

Study on Design Method of Crop Structural Growth System Based on Object-Based[*]

Ping Zheng, ZhongBin Su, JiCheng Zhang, and XiangQin Liu

Engineering college, Northeast Agricultural University, Harbin 150030, China

Abstract. The paper tried to use visualization and object-based technology to design crop growth system. The method could present the flexibility, easy to manage, code reuse features of object-based technology. The system designed by this method could provide function-expanded interface for the simulation system, also lay the foundation for simulation soybean mass growth state. There would be a great significance in visualization research of virtual crops.

Keywords: Virtual plant; Object-oriented; Soybean structure; Growth system.

1 Introduction

Along with the computer technology and graphics becomes mature, virtual crop has been developing rapidly and become the new important research methods and means in agricultural field. It has been received widespread concern. At twenty years of development process, the virtual crops research include soybean, cotton and rice etc involving crop's function and structure, the relationship between simulation and yielding crops design form, field optimizing cultivation measures, and achieved significant research progress. The crop morphological structure of virtual simulation is one of the important crop simulation based on crops among them. It is the premise of further study. Therefore, analysis of crop morphological structure and simulation crops growth process become a virtual crop researcher's key research problem.

Generally, the construction method of crop form is designed by agronomy experts through a lot of experiments and measured crop growth data. Then the model is built by experience principle according to some experimental data. Computer developers understand these models and convert it into computer software module. In the past simulation study, the same crop is simulated by the same or similar method. However the same method will be done by different development process, different management space, unfavorable to the user intuitive operation. This situation would not display computer efficient and flexible technical characteristics to make software and hardware material waste.

In view of the above question, this paper takes soybean structural simulation as an example. It built crop growth simulation system based on the development of object-oriented modeling ideas, and designed the simulation process by visual and object-oriented modeling method, which reflected of the flexible, easy management, the

---

[*] The paper is sponsored by Heilongjiang Education Important Project(1154z1011), and by Northeast Agricultural University Doctor Fund(2009RC54).

G. Shen and X. Huang (Eds.): CSIE 2011, Part I, CCIS 152, pp. 119–123, 2011.
© Springer-Verlag Berlin Heidelberg 2011

characteristics of code reuse of object-oriented technology. This method could increase extended interface for simulation system and provide large simulation scale.

2 Object-Oriented Modeling Thoughts

In object-oriented data model, the entity is expressed as a class including attribute set and behavior set. In the object's interior, the class attributes with special values to distinguish among each customer. All objects are belonging to the same class, with sharing the same class patterns of behavior. Object-oriented database maintains contact by logic contain (logical containment).

Object-oriented database data is related with object code encapsulation into a single component. Therefore object-oriented data model emphasis that object (including by the data and the code component) rather than individual data. This is mainly from object-oriented programming language by inheritance. In an object-oriented programming language, programmers can define its internal structure, characteristics and behavior of the new type or object class. So, that can't think the data is independent existence. This design method highly emphasizes software reusability and interoperability which could shorten the development cycle and provide the system stability and reliability of the system. Generally objects should have the basic feature to follow certain standard, provide services. Application components in development system should get reusability, easy to modify and convenient operation and easy management maintenance etc.

3 Growth System Object-Oriented Design

3.1 Crop Growth Characteristics

Before soybean organs are designed by object-oriented, it should analyze the characteristics of soybean form firstly. Soybean is an annual herb leguminous. And its structure is relatively simple with the main characteristics of legumes. Its flower is composed by five petals of wing flowers; Fruit is pods with two full of nutrient cotyledons. The first pair really leaves is oval univalent. After those, the true leaf is composed by three leaflets with long alternate hilt. Although the soybean plant form varied, but generally plant height is 90-120 centimeters. All above ground organs bears many small pastels.

3.2 Object-Oriented Designs

Considering the soybean each organ relatively independent, soybean plant is divided into different organs components, establish their own form object module, such as the stalk of components, leaf components, pod objects, etc, according to the connection relations between the preset component indirect mouth, facilitating implementation overall plant assembly.

For example, the paper takes soybean blade as an example to introduce organ the form of objects. In the past the length of soybean leaf blade, it is in accordance with the Logistic function along with time. As the same principle, the growth of leaf profile could be simulated by second interpolation method. And leaf vein grew according to L-system derivation rule. So it will input the amount of length and width into pre-designed program, by using least-square method get length growth equations parameter value and contour growth equations parameter values, which can gain this breed soybean leaf profile's growth model. By extracting the veins of the initial string and iterative rule, according to leaf growth time calculation iterations, can obtain the veins of the form as shown in Fig.1.

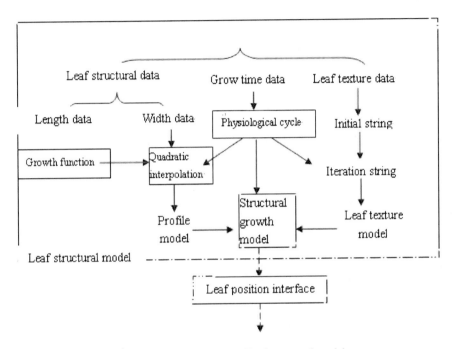

Fig. 1. The design process of leaf structural model

According to above summary of leaf structural design features as follows:

class leaves
{attributes:
Initial growth time; Growth period; End growth time, Bears the position;
Length array, Width array; Iterations; Growth cycle;
The veins of the string; The veins of the initial string array; Iterative string array;
... Actions:
Length growth equations parameters extraction (length arrays);
Outline growth equations parameters extraction (length array, width arrays);
Length array = length growth (length growth equations, time),
Outline-growth (length arrays, time);
Growth period = Initial growth time - End growth time; Iteration = Growth period/growth cycle,

The veins of the string = the veins of the initial string array + iterative string array * iterations;

... Interface:

Three leaf relative positions interface ();

Environmental component interfaces, Expert system component interfaces, Visual component interfaces,

Data interaction component interfaces, Model validation interface;

...

}

4 Simulation System Design

4.1 Function Modules

The structural object is the core part in system design. Then set expert system analysis module, environmental interface module and visual display module, etc. It will extend the structural models to function model. And it could realize the interactive between users and whole model.

4.2 Simulation Advantage

1) Reusability.

Once the establishment of soybean's some certain organ's visualization model, its corresponding organ modeling method has been confirmed. If users want to simulate various soybean breeding, it only modifies the component parameters by collection data. Reusability components could avoid repetition of writing code and save time. But it need to make sure that the system organ components are written with highly generalization and universality.

Such as leaf structural component has established (as shown in Fig.1). Users input the soybean's leaf images. The system could adjust the parameters of different blades to obtain different kinds of blade configuration.

2) Closure.

Each composition of the soybean plant organs has its own distinct component characteristics. It can adopt different models by its established methods. Leaf components application of computer graphics method to set up, ovate contour model, etc. Such different components according to their own advantages write personnel can select simulate object, not interfere with each other, the relative independence. In modification, add and remove a component, other components will not be affected. But these components in writing before you decide relevant interface standards and organs, ensure the growth of plants created scales of integrity and continuity.

3) Expansibility.

In soybean plant visualization simulation process, can be various organs   as component intelligently. Also can be visualized as a whole plant components, the simulation analysis of data from the front, expert system design and the plant type design etc after as corresponding modules, using different personnel and the method to carry on the management, increase plant simulation and authenticity of the practicability, outstanding computer simulation of flexibility.

4) Group simulation.

For soybean form model function expansion, may establish the specific requirements of the function model. Will be a single tree soybean plant morphology model and function model as a component design, according to the design of field plant distribution, through repeated calls this component adjustment parameters, can obtain within DTW group plant form the visualization simulation effect, increase system simulation display space and effects.

4 Conclusions

The paper takes the visualization simulation soybean plant as the example. It introduces the component technology crop form based on the method of simulation system. It is not just a crop plants form can indivisible whole, and as function expandable individuals. Method can fully embody the computer software programming advantage, fast and effective for plant model visualization of expression, improved software programming speed, save manpower and material resources and component based development method to crop function expansion and group form simulation. In the later system design should notice to rationally divided organ components, define the component function, to improve the development of the system efficiency and quality.

References

1. Cao, W.-x.: Agricultural Information Science. China Agriculture Publishing, Beijing (2004) (in Chinese)
2. Barthelemy, D.: Botanical Background for Plant Architecture Analysis and Modeling. In: Proceedings of Plant Growth Modeling and Applications, pp. 1–20. Tsinghua University Press, Beijing (2003)
3. Guo, X., Zhao, C., Xiao, B., et al.: Design and implementation of three-dimensional geometric morphological modeling and visualization system formaize. Journal of Agricultural Engineering 4, 144–149 (2007) (in Chinese)
4. Kang, L., Su, Z.-b., Zheng, P., et al.: Research on Modeling Leaf Based on L-system. Agricultural Machinery Research 7, 180–182 (2006) (in Chinese)
5. Song, Y., Guo, Y., Li, B., et al.: Virtual maize model Ⅱ.plant morphological constructing based on Organ biomass accumulation. Ecological Journal 23(12), 2579–2586 (2003)
6. Su, Z., Meng, F., Kang, L., et al.: Virtual plant modeling based on Agent technology. Agricultural Engineering 21(8), 114–116 (2005) (in Chinese)
7. Su, Z., Zheng, P., Sun, H., Zhang, J., Li, X.: Study on Establishment Soybean Controllable Strucutural Model. In: CCTA 2007, vol. 1, pp. 685–693 (2007) ISTP
8. Zheng, P., Su, Z., Kang, L.: Modeling of Virtual Soybean Topology Based on Growth Function. Agricultural Machinery Research 7, 193–194 (2006) (in Chinese)
9. Su, Z., Zheng, P., Sun, H., Zhang, J.: Study on Method of Modeling and Visualization of Soybean. In: PMA 2006 (2006)

The Study on the Method of Face Detection

Jie Mu, Wei Liu, and ShiJie Jiang

Kaifeng Institute of Education, Kaifeng, Henan, China
Mj9435@163.com

Abstract. For the last few years, face recognition has attracted much attention. As a part of face recognition, the face detection is significant to computer vision and feature detection. This article is based on massive literature; it has carried on the research summary of face detection methods and classification from pattern recognition's processing stage. It also a certain supplement to the former classification of face detection methods.

Keywords: Face Detection, Feature Detection, Classification.

1 Introduction

The face detection belongs to the scope of feature detection, and it is synthesized the computer vision, digital image processing and multi-disciplinary contents. The research on face feature detection has a vital significance regarding to the artificial intelligence, security, finance and so on. The face detection carries on the analysis extraction and face recognition through human face's biological features. There are many researches related to the face detection engineering, and some successfully used in status appraisal, security, and information extraction and so on.

2 Classifications Based on Method Features

The ways to classify method characters: This classification method can be roughly divided as elasticity template, geometry, and algebra, the Principal Component Analysis (PCA) (feature face or Eigenface), Fisher face, statistical property: Eigenface method and Hidden Markov Model (HMM), connectionism, neural network (NN), Dynamic Link Architecture (DLA).

The main feature and application of methods has been revealed through these categories, and, it contributes others for further research to learn more. Besides, there are thirteen cases of classification method in some literature which is summarized.

2.1 Based on Geometry Characteristic Method

The basic ideas of Geometrical characteristics can be divided into: ① Manual defining feature point. ② Auto extraction feature point. This method is used for representing feature vector by using geometry relation, face detection is finally considered as the distance match between characteristic vectors.

The typical algorithm of Geometrical characteristics is divided into two aspects which are the outline of the models and deformable template model according to

G. Shen and X. Huang (Eds.): CSIE 2011, Part I, CCIS 152, pp. 124–128, 2011.

literature, but Multi-Template Matching should belong to Geometrical characteristics. Besides, face detection is divided into three categories which are based on Geometrical relationship.

2.1.1 The Method Based on Prior Knowledge

It can be made a series of criteria according to prior knowledge. It is detected as human face while the image of the test region meets the standards.

2.1.2 The Method Based on Feature Invariant

The method based on feature invariant is focused on detecting invariable character of human face, such as using a bandpass filter to choose a segment of frequency, and then setting a series of thresholds to find eyes and mouth area according to the knowledge of morphologic, furthermore, the method of any map match is purposed to describe correctly the geometric distribution of facial features.

2.1.3 The Method Based on Template

The method based on template can be classified into two categories: reservation template and transformation template. First of all, transformation template defines a template parameter, and then modifies the parameter based on the detection zone in order to detect one of the locations of human face organs. Active Shape Models (ASM) and Active Appearance Models (AAM) are the typical methods.

2.2 The Face Recognition Based on Template Matching

The simplest way is considered human face template as an ellipse. Face detection means the ellipse in the image. Another method is represented human face with a group of independent small template, such as eyes template, mouth template, nose template, eyebrow template and chin template and so on. Moreover, elasticity template is defined by programmable parameters which are based on a group of prior

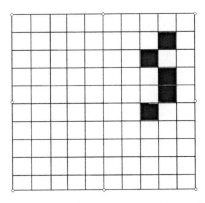

Fig. 1. Sample of template matching

knowledge. In order to find out the parameter, it needs the edge, peak value, and valley value and intensity information in the image as well as the prior knowledge of shape feature which the energy function is designed appropriately.

2.3 The Method Based on Elastic Graph Matching

The method of elastic graph matching represents human face with spares graph, according to the distance between the points to the edge. Firstly searching most likely original graph, then it process each node with best matching method to obtain another graph, the location of the node approximately corresponds to the oriental graph. The typical algorithm is a method based on Dynamic Link Architecture.

2.4 The Method Based on Neural Network

The method of neural network has applied in face recognition in a long history. This method is used to solve the recognition of human face in complex system composed by many simple processing units, and at early used to recognize the human face which is renovate dirty and damaged. Different neural network describes different sides of biologic network on the different levels. The method based on neural network used the ability of studying and classify to process human facial feature extraction and recognition.

2.5 The Method Based on Subspace Methods

The subspace methods is classified in algebraic characteristic methods, it searches out a spatial switching linearly and nonlinearly maps the oriental image to the subspace, so obtaining the compact data in the subspace. PCA, LDA, ICA are typical in this method.

PCA preserves principal components for obtaining the Lower Dimensional space of human face.

LDA finds a direction has minimum between-class scatter and maximum within-class scatter when a training sample is projected to this direction.

ICA hunts a group of Independent Component switch used to express sample data.ICA remove correlation at the whole statistics, so can be used by the signal statistics higher and lower.

Above three methods nonlinearly subspace methods is using kernel method, by nonlinearly mapping make the sample in kernel space linear separable, or approximately linear separable, then classified in kernel space using linear methods.

2.6 Face Recognition Based on HMM Model

Hidden Markov Model (HMM) consists of two parts, the first one is limited Markov chains, and the second one is sequential observation. According to this model, different person can be represented by different HMM parameter, and the same person can produce a sequence of observations due to the change of posture and expression, and it can be represented by the same HMM model.

Nefian divides human face into five overlapping areas (hair, brow, eyes and mouth). In accordance with this division, it contains five states of sequential HMM to represent human face. And then it processes each part with KL transformation, finally, each part of the greatest characteristic vector will be used as observation for HMM training.

2.7 Face Recognition Based on Wavelet Feature

After the wavelet changed the image through the filter, each human face will be represented by the image which is composed with wavelet coefficients. The main factor of wavelet is to provide an image of multi-resolution analysis method. At the same time, the wavelet also provides a spatial and frequency method. Some others are based on skin model, visual feature, machine learning, mechanism, and statistics method and so on.

This method is useful for grasping method; however, the classification repeats redundancy, so it is necessary to build a unified reflection method.

3 Classification Based on the Processing of Feature Recognition

It is necessary to discuss the processing procedure classification from the aspects of feature recognition, processing procedure is divided into preprocessing, feature extraction, feature recognition. Feature extraction and feature recognition are essential.

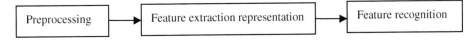

Fig. 2. Stages of Pattern Recognition

Such as PCA method can be used in feature extraction as well as feature recognition. PCA method adopts KL transformation, and then giving up the minor contents of the results of KL transformation, furthermore, PCA method will be called Eigenface if PCA method is used for face recognition. So feature extraction method can be represented as feature representation or feature extraction determinant.

There is a table below that shows some face detection methods:

Table 1. Classify of Human facial detection methods

Preprocessing	Feature extraction representation	Feature recognition
Skin color, Blocks, Electrograph blocks	Nerve network, LNMF, Fisher Discrimination, PCA, Wavelet, CCA, LLE, AAM, ASM, Contourlet transformation, Grayscale, Genetic Algorithm, Brightness, DCT transformation, Curvature, Adaboost, Fractal Theory,3DLBP	PCA, Nerve network, Nearest classifier, k- neighbor classifier , LDA, Fisher

4 Conclusion

Face recognition has a wide application prospect, the development of the methods has a vital significance to man-machine interaction, feature detection, image recognition, biometric feature, military, economy, information gathering. The main aspect of face recognition is developing the existing method to the development of a three-dimension. The method is still being developed.

References

1. Nle, X.: A Review of Face Recognition. Journal of ChongQing There Gorges University 117, 14–18 (2009)
2. Liu, C.: On the Techniques of Face Recognition. Journal of ANHUI Electrical Engineering Professional Technique College 13(3), 87–90 (2008)
3. Liu, Y., Li, L., Bayaritu: A Survey of Human Face Recognition. Journal of Inner Mongolia University 40(4), 493–498 (2009)

Research on Network Curriculum Construction and Applications

Jinquan Wang, Fuchun Fan, Wei Zu, and Dongdong Wang

Academic Administration
Huaiyin Institute of Technology
Huai'an Jiangsu, China
wjq203@163.com

Abstract. In order to resolve the problems about network curriculum construction and application, this paper gives some advices, such as enhancing publicity of network, training the ability of teacher to drive network technology, guiding teacher to construct network curriculum, strengthening construction of university software and hardware, guiding student to use network curriculum correctly and efficiently, strengthening system construction and regularizing management. Huaiyin Institute of Technology has done as the given advices and got good result about network curriculum construction and application.

Keywords: Network Curriculum, Construction, Application.

1 Introduction

Recently, most university successively construct network curriculum in different model and way. In comparison to traditional curriculum (teaching and learning), network curriculum has some advantages, for example, module miniaturization, diversification, flexible automation, in favor of student independent study, network curriculum construction is popular in most university. But in the process of network curriculum construction and application, there exist some problems, for example, construct but less use, use but not more, use more but no interaction, interact but not be frequent, so the value of network curriculum can not be truly reflected.

2 Existing Problems of Network Curriculum Construction

2.1 The Concept of Network Curriculum and Courseware Is Not Clear

The concept of network curriculum and network courseware is not clear at present, they are considered as one concept sometimes, someone comprehend network curriculum as simple enumeration of curriculum content. For example, there are 440 network curriculums register in the network platform of Huaiyin Institute of Technology, about 150 network curriculums just simply enumerate curriculum brief introduction, teaching program, teaching plan, PPT and upload to the network platform.

G. Shen and X. Huang (Eds.): CSIE 2011, Part I, CCIS 152, pp. 129–133, 2011.

Courseware is a kind of computer software that design specially for teaching action. Network courseware is a kind of courseware that apply network environment. Network curriculum is teaching action summation which shows some subject content of course and implementation. The starting point between curriculum and courseware is different, the starting point of courseware is teaching action, curriculum is social needing.

2.2   Engineering Level of Network Curriculum Developer Is Not Advanced

The important reason of restricting network curriculum teaching quality improvement is that part of teacher is not familiar with network curriculum technology or not accustomed to operate network technology to teach.[1-2] In every kind of university, some staff members for teaching main curriculum is good at teaching and scientific research but not network media technology.

2.3   Network Curriculum Construction Pay Attention to the Appearance of Teaching Content, Look Down on Academic Environment Design

Network education is the fundamental model of media education in 21st Century, but network construction is not meaning to quality of teaching improve. [3] Network curriculum not only provides information, but also impacts students to make them to be their own teacher. At present, most network curriculum still emphasize teaching and knowledge impartation, there is knowledge teaching and learning at the first sight of the interface of network curriculum, but no guide for instructional design and situation.

2.4   Form of Teaching Content Expression Is Monotonous

At present, most network curriculum presenting in the way of webpage corresponds the character of web-based instruction and is the trend of web-based instruction development. But most webpage present in state static at present, organization way of webpage is linear, webpage update is less. At present, there are three kind of way of teaching content presenting: text and still image, PowerPoint lecture, staff members for teaching main curriculum videotape and lecture presenting at the same time.

2.5   Network Curriculum Evaluation Is Difficult

Because of the character of network curriculum and the course independence of learner studying, the result evaluation is the main mode of network curriculum evaluation, test and assignment is the main form. The process evaluation is difficult and is not incompatible with the new evaluation idea which not only care about studying result, but also studying process and emotion, manner, action change. The result evaluation emphasizes the concept of mark, neglect the process evaluation, encourage mechanical memorizing and weaken the subject consciousness of learner.

3 Problems of Network Curriculum Application

3.1 Equipment of Software and Hardware Is Not Enough

Enhancing the availability factor of network curriculum and realizing the teaching effect of network curriculum depend on web-based instruction platform which operate steadily and fast. Now most university has established their own campus local area network, but there still exist some problem about network, for example, low network running speed, unsteadied property; expensive cost for asking network, exchange visits obstacle between China Educational and Research Network and China telecommunication network; network curriculum terminal system — lower computer popularizing rate, the number of student computer ownership is less that restrict the network utilization factor and extent. [4]

3.2 The Ability of Teacher Utilizing Network Is Not Strong

Application level of computer network technology is unevenness which is the important factor of influencing network curriculum teaching and application efficiency. Some part of teacher is not familiar with network curriculum technology or not used to use network technology to teach. In fact, network technology of some backbone teacher, academic pacesetter and some staff members for teaching main curriculum in university is not fit to their education and research level, however, this part of teaching resource is most supposed to be shared by university network platform.

3.3 Management System and Operation Mechanism Is Not Efficient Enough

Improving service efficiency of network curriculum needs impeccable management system and operation mechanism of network curriculum. At present, it does not form the orderly development system environment which support and guarantee network curriculum construction and application, for example, no good outlay investment mechanism, undefined duty and task among different level and department, lacking scientific reasonable efficient quality standard and monitoring system. All of those result in few application of network curriculum in real teaching, less replacing classroom teaching.

3.4 Independent Study Ability of Student Is Not Strong

It lacks good circumstance for student independent study. The form of network curriculum study often finds expression in man-machine conversation in a narrow and small room. It has no any learning situation to lead that knowledge learning run through overall learning process. It does not benefit student to utilize original knowledge and learning experience to study new knowledge, also not benefit turning external academic motivation to internal academic motivation, driving the curiosity of student, arousing the exploring and discovering interest.

4 Advice of Network Curriculum Construction and Application Promotion

4.1 Enhancing Publicity and Training, Improving Teacher to Understand the Concept of Network Curriculum and the Ability of Driving Network Technology

To resolve teachers mistake understanding about network curriculum construction, the most important thing is that every university should enhance training teacher to construct network curriculum, especially enhance some backbone teacher and academic pacesetter to grasp network curriculum knowledge and improve network technology, encourage them pay more attention to network curriculum and take part in construct network curriculum.

In the beginning period of network curriculum construction in Huaiyin Institute of Technology (HYIT), HYIT vigorously publicize the knowledge about network curriculum and promote network curriculum construction by administrative method, train some teacher of every department and form a group of network curriculum construction backbone teacher. This group of network curriculum construction backbone teacher set a good example and guides the department to construct network curriculum.

4.2 Guiding Teacher to Construct Network Curriculum which Content Form of Expression Is Abundant and Strong Interactive

It needs guide teacher to pay more attention to arouse student learning enthusiasm when they design and construct network curriculum rather than simply enumerate curriculum brief introduction、 teaching program、 teaching plan、 power point lecture in curriculum website, therefore it need network curriculum teaching content form of expression be abundant, besides using written language and picture to illuminate curriculum teaching content, adopting cartoon or video to narrate discipline emphasis and difficult point. HYIT has enhanced the whole level of network curriculum construction by encouraging teacher to innovate network curriculum construction.

4.3 Strengthening University Software and Hardware Construction

University should guarantee the network curriculum visited quality by improving network running speed and enhancing network stability. University could dissolve the interflow obstacle between university China Education and Research Network and China telecom of students' dormitory, convenient for student free using the resource of network curriculum. University could increase the investment of computer hardware and construct more computer room for student study. Wireless network has covered all studying place of HYIT, student can study by network at any time in campus.

4.4 Guiding Student to Use Network Curriculum Correctly and Efficiently

Students need more autorhythmicity and autonomy to study network curriculum, also have communicative competence, ability of participation, network etiquette and skill of operating computer as they study by network. As university lay down personnel training project, it should pay more attention to set up the curriculum which improve student ability of network studying, network communication, network etiquette. Teacher of network curriculum need pay attention to train student the ability of network studying, network communication, network etiquette and guide student scientific, efficient using network curriculum as they teach and construct network curriculum. After HYIT guides student using network curriculum, the gross of visiting network curriculum is already two hundred thousands.

4.5 Strengthening System Construction and Regularizing Management

Impeccable operation mechanism and management system is powerful guarantee for promoting network curriculum construction and healthful development. Firstly, network curriculum construction needs uniform technology standard and construction criterion to guide network curriculum construction and application. Secondly, it needs impeccable management rules and regulations, measures for implementation of network curriculum, for example, strict qualification examination system, project approval, invite bids, quality monitoring.

5 Conclusion

In the process of modern education engineering construction, hardware construction is base, resource construction is emphasis, teaching is objective. The present problem of modern education engineering construction could be resolved for a long time. But, as the first priority and core of resource construction, network curriculum quality enhancing is important to promote network curriculum application, come into being good auxiliary effect to entire teaching link. Efficient and proficient application of network can promote network curriculum construction.

Acknowledgement

This paper is fully supported by the High Education Research Project of Education Department of Jiangsu Province, China (Grant Number : SuJiaoGao [2009]27-151).

References

1. Zhang, M., Han, Y., Pan, F.: University Network Curriculum Construction Discussion and Analysis. J. Science Information 4, 54 (2007)
2. Zu, W.: Problem about Network Curriculum Construction Application in Teaching Application. J. Vocational Education Research 11, 138–139 (2007)
3. Wu, T., Ma, J.: The Implementation of Network Teaching Platform in Colleges and Universities. J. Journal of Hebei Polytechnic University 4, 74–76 (2009)
4. Feng, N.: Discussion of Network Curriculum Back-stage Management. J. Distance Education in China 11, 65–68 (2006)

An Enhanced Power Saving Mechanism in Ad Hoc Network at MAC Layer

Shaoping Jiang, Shaoxian Tang, Yueqi Liao, and Wang Li

School of Information Science and Technology, Hunan Agricultural University,
Changsha 410128, China

Abstract. Nodes in Ad Hoc network are typically powered by batteries, so how to improve energy efficiency, save energy and prolong the life span of networks are critical problems at all layers of the protocol stack. IEEE802 11 specifies power saving mechanism (PSM) under distributed coordination function (DCF) for energy efficiency. On the basis of an analysis and comparison IEEE802 11PSM, this work proposes an adaptive power saving mechanism (EPSM) EPSM improves PSM model that could only send one package in one BI, dramatically reduces transfer delay, and prolongs the life span of central nodes to save energy using central nodes alternant wake- up The results of simulation show that EPSM has better performance than PSM in decreasing transportation delays, saving energy, and prolonging life span of nodes.

Keywords: Ad Hoc network, 802 11PSM, transmission delay, power management.

1 Introduction

With the development of portable computers and wireless technology, a new wireless network-the mobile ad hoc network will be widely used in military, commercial, residential field. The ad hoc network is a kind of wireless network which can provide nodes without any base station. It, as an unconstrained dynamic reconfigurable multi-hop wireless network, offers temporary communications in some special circumstances, This network consists of a large number of independent nodes which all such two functions as hosts and routers. The communication between nodes is realized by the cooperation between multiple nodes through wireless channel. The mobile ad hoc network, which is quite different from traditional wireless network, is completely self-organized instead of depending on any fixed network or central control, It has some prominent characteristics: the self-construction of network, the dynamic topology, limited wireless bandwidth, network security and energy limitations of mobile terminals and so on. Unlike the case of most fixed devices with a fixed power supply, we should be very cautious to the energy use of mobile devices. Energy-saving is very important for the mobile ad hoc network. he mobile ad hoc network is powered by portable batteries, whose technological development is far slower than computer technology, which prompts us to pay more attention to energy issues and to make energy-saving strategies in the protocol layer. Current researches in this area are mainly about energy-saving in different levels of network protocols, such as the media access layer, the network layer and the transport layer.

G. Shen and X. Huang (Eds.): CSIE 2011, Part I, CCIS 152, pp. 134–141, 2011.

2   The Status of Ad Hoc Energy Research

2.1   The MAC Layer of Power Control Strategy for Energy Saving at Ad Hoc Network

To save energy by power control has long been the concern of researchers. The main idea of MAC layer power control is to obtain the minimum power required through the process of power detection and then transmit with minimal power. When sending messages with same length, different modulation methods are adopted. Different rates of data transmission require different transmit power. Suppose that the modulation way is i, transmission rate is Ri bit/s, transmission power is PiW, so the energy consumed when transmit 1bit information is W=(Pi / Ri)J. The smaller W is, the higher the energy efficiency is.

Monks proposed a PCMA protocol based on power control, which is to achieve the maximum reuse of the channel space and the MAC protocol of CSMA/CA has been improved. On the one hand, PCMA protocol increases a feedback dialogue on sending energy / receiving the energy transmission based on the traditional handshake of 802.11, making nodes be able to send data using less power, the dialogue appears in the data channel before sending; on the other hand, by radio the receiver sends a maximum noise power capacity limits that he can tolerate after getting the current power level of signal noise, and periodically sends the capacity limit and busy audio signal in the busy audio channels through the pulse. The strength of the busy pulse signal reflects the maximum noise of the nodes in the upper limit.

Yu-chee Tseng and others proposed the multi-channel power-control protocol taking the channel assignment, multiple access and power control problem into account, in which the control packets and broadcast packets are sent in the control channel with the greatest power but the data packet and ACK are sent in the data channel with minimal power. SKandukuri and others put forward a multiple access power control strategy based on constraint test, which designs three kinds of optimized modes: using low-power when channel is poor but greater delay is allowable; using higher power when channel and delay is general; using the maximum power when the delay constraints is high.

Energy-efficient strategy, based on power control, use the minimum power transmission at the time of data transmission, which makes the problem of the hidden node more prominent.

2.2   The MAC Layer of the Adaptive Power Strategy for Energy Saving at Ad Hoc Network

802.11 power management is currently popular on the market with reference to the main criteria for the wireless network card, is also an agreement with the greatest reference in the power management research of the MAC layer, whose power-saving mode is generally 802.11PSM (Power Saving Mode), and the foundation of many power management protocols.

The literature presents an adaptive mechanism which adjust the size of ATIM window according to the dynamic changes in network load. When the network load is larger, it uses the larger ATIM window, so that all of the sites have enough time to notice they have to send the packet. When the network load is small it uses a smaller ATIM window in order to save energy.

The LISP protocol brought forward by Chunyu Hu and other is an adaptive mechanism, which adjusts the node based on the forecast within the period of the BI data transfer to wake up automatically. First of all, the node in the ATIM window corkscrews the surrounding nodes and learn according to the status of the nodes, and then predicts when it should wake up to transmit data. If the prediction fails, the node go into sleep state, and adjust the learning state.

3   EPSM New Basic Idea of Energy-Saving Mechanism

Generally speaking, a wireless network card has 4 modes of operation: sending, receiving, idle and sleep. Table 1 shows that the power consumption of sending, receiving and idle state is almost the same, but differently much less power is needed in sleep mode. On the other hand, experiments and observation has proved that the energy consumption in the existing mobile ad hoc networks is not in proportional to the amount of active communication in the network, which shows the energy consumption of idle equipment in the total energy consumption plays a large proportion. So how to change the corresponding equipment in idle mode into sleep mode in appropriate methods can greatly save energy. Table 1 shows the measured results of the wireless card in a variety of operating modes.

Table 1. Shows the measured results of the wireless card in a variety of operating modes

Card type	Power supply / V	Transmit mode/mA	Receive mode/ m A	Idle mode/ m A	Sleep mode/ mA
WaveLAN(11M bit/ s)	4. 74	284	190	156	10
WaveLAN(2 M bit/ s)	4. 74	280	204	178	14
Proxim RangeL AN2- 7410	5	265	130	N/ A	2
Smart Spread	5	150	80	N/ A	5

In 802.11PSM, time is divided into a series of BI (beacon interval). Each site wakes up periodically at the beginning of each BI stays awake at the serial time of a ATIM (Ad Hoc Traffic Indication Message). When a node has some packets to be sent to another one, it must send the ATM frames to the destination site in the ATIM window, informing the destination site to keep sober to accept the packets after the end of the ATIM window. The transmission of ATIM frames is also based on DCF mechanism. After sending the ATIM frames, the site must be sober in the remaining time of BI. When a site receives the ATIM frames, it must respond to an ACK, and remains sober afterwards. The site that has sent ATIM frames and received the ACK bases on the normal DCF competition to send a packet after the end of the TIM window. If the sending site sends the ATIM frame in the ATIM window but does not

receive the ACK, it should continue in the next ATIM window and tries to send another ATIM frame, it can sleep at the end of ATIM window before the next BI.

3.1   The Description of a New Energy-Saving Mechanism EPSM

At the beginning of the first ATIM window of the early BS (when all nodes remain active), each ATIM frame carries the number of packets to send the other node and a counter as well. Each node pluses one when pass a counter. So, each node can know the current number of the data packet that BI will send and receive. ATIM receives its frame, judge itself and its neighboring nodes to check whether each node needs to transfer data. If the node itself needs to transmit data, then it determines the current hop to wake up in the corresponding period time. If the node needs to transmit data to neighboring nodes, then judge whether the adjacent nodes have finished data transmission at the beginning of the next BI. If it has ended, then it wakes up at the beginning of the next BI; if not, it maintains sleep instead and notifies neighbors within the ATIM time. In order to save energy better, we allow the node send data automatically enter sleep mode after determining that they have completed all the data to be sent and received and in the current cycle of the BI. If the node itself needs to send data, then it wakes up in the cycle of the next BI; if not, it keeps waiting until the second cycle of BI to re-awake. This mechanism allows data packets to pass multiple relay nodes in a BI cycle and a node likewise can send and receive multiple data packets. Compared with the 802.11psm, this can greatly reduce the packet transmission delay. At the same time, each node must also maintain a table to record the BS value of all the status of neighbor nodes.

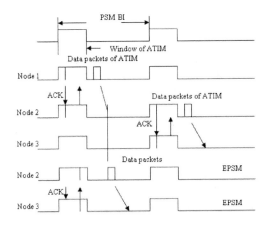

Fig. 1. The description of a new energy-saving mechanism EPSM

When one node needs to send ATIM frame to another node, it firstly should check the state of the other party to determine whether it is in the ATIM window. If not, it should not send and wait until the next sync going into the ATI M window. This mechanism of competition cycle by staggering nodes reduces energy consumption in the same BI cycle for more nodes' competition and makes the central node alternately awake to reach the purpose that prevents causing paralysis of the entire network due to the excessive frequent transfer of data. In Figure 1, we can see the difference between the 802.11PSM with the new mechanism EPSM. In the PSM Nodes can only transmit data to the next hop node in a BI, but in EPSM they can transmit data to a few hop nodes. This will significantly reduce the delay of the data transmission.

4 Performance Analysis

We assume that there is an H hop link in an ad hoc network: $n_0 \rightarrow n_1 \rightarrow n_2 \rightarrow ... \rightarrow n_H$. The node n_0 sends packets to the network at a speed of λ. In M AC layer for each hop the packet processing time requires an average of Δp (including RT S, CTS, the data packet and the transmission time and interval time of ACK frame).

4.1 IEEE802 11 noPSM

In the normal mode of 802.11 protocol, any node can send data at anytime when it wants to as long as there is no conflict. Therefore, we can draw to-end delay is:

$$d_{nopsm} = \overline{D}_{nopsm} = H\Delta_P \tag{1}$$

Because 802.11 requires the node to stay awake in the normal mode, idle power consumption is very large in light load and moderate load, which makes the survival time of nodes greatly shortened and thus energy efficiency is very bad.

4.2 IEEE802 11 PSM

In 802.11PSM mode, each node in a BI cycle can only receive or send a packet. Therefore, the source node (destination node) needs a BI cycle to send (receive) a packet, while the relay node needs two BI cycles to send (receive) a packet. Suppose a node needs to send data in time t_g, the t_g is possible within the ATIM period but also may be absent. If $t_g < T_{atim}$, an packet is sent in the current time slot; if $t_g > T_{atim}$, it must wait until the next time slot to be sent. According to the average distribution rate, available to the average of t1:

$$E(t_1) = \frac{1}{2}BI_{PSM} + \Delta_p + T_{atim}(1 - \frac{t_{atim}}{BI_{psm}}) \tag{2}$$

After the first jump, when the data reach the node $n_{i-1}(i>1)$, it must wait until the beginning of the next BI to send to the next hop n_i, Therefore:

$$t_i = BI_{psm} - (T_{atim} + \Delta_p) + (T_{atim} + \Delta_p) = BI_{PSM} \ (i > 1) \tag{3}$$

So the end-to-end delay is:

$$D = \sum_{i=1}^{H} t_i = t_1 + (H-1)BI_{psm} \tag{4}$$

So the average delay is:

$$\overline{D}_{psm} = (H - \frac{1}{2})BI_{psm} + \Delta_p + T_{atim}(1 - \frac{T_{atim}}{BI_{psm}}) \tag{5}$$

4.3 EPSM (Enhanced Power Saving Mechanism)

EPSM's delay at the first jump is the same as the PSM's, however, after the first jump data can be transmitted to the next hop in the current BI, so we can get the delay of the EPSM:

$$D_{epsm} = t_1 + H\Delta_p + T_{atim} \tag{6}$$

So the average delay is:

$$\overline{D}_{epsm} = \frac{1}{2}BI + H\Delta_p + T_{atim}(1 = \frac{T_{atim}}{BI_{psm}}) \tag{7}$$

4.4 Comparative Analysis

By IEEE802.11, 802.11PSM and EPSM contrast, we know $\overline{D}_{nopsm} > \overline{D}_{epsm} > \overline{D}_{psm}$. In the data transmission process, if H is relatively large, $\overline{D}_{nopsm}$ is approximately equal to $\overline{D}_{epsm}$ and $\overline{D}_{epsm}$ is much larger than $\overline{D}_{psm}$.

5 Simulation Results and Analysis

5.1 Simulation Model and Performance Parameters

The simulation tools used in this article is NS2.28 developed by the Berkeley. Simulation environment settings are as follows: the nodes are randomly distributed within the 1000m # 1000m; the node's reception range is 200m and its moving speed is 10m/s; the node's initial energy is 40J; the power consumption of nodes when sending and receiving data, staying idle and asleep in set to 1.4W, 1.3W, 0.83W and 0.13W respectively, and the energy consumed when converting between sleep and awake state will not be taken into account; BI cycle and the length of time of the ATIM window are set to 1000ms and 20ms; It uses the DSR protocol for routing protocols; the simulation results is the average of 10 times. Due to energy saving effect of PSM is almost not able to embody under heavy load, so here we only discuss the case of light load.

5.2 Simulation Results and Evaluation

The end to end delay comparison of noPSM, PSM, and EPSM are shown in Figure 2(a), from which we can see that the delay of the PSM and the EPSM is the same when there is only one hop between the source node and destination node. As the number of hops of the source node and destination node increases, the end-to-end delay of the PSM increases in a multiple way, while the increase of the EPSM is very relative flat. This is because the PSM can only transmit a packet in a BI cycle, but for EPSM packet can pass through many intermediate nodes in a BI cycle, and a node can send multiple packets. Therefore, EP and SM greatly reduce the end-to-end delay of the transmission.

Performances are compared in terms of the survival time on noPSM PSM and EPSM. The survival time refers to the time of the first node in network which runs out of energy. With the increased number of nodes, we can see that the survival time of the 3 kinds of agreements all has increased because central node increases correspondingly with the increasing of the total number of nodes and thus contributes to the increase of the network lifetime by reducing the excessive use of the central node. It can be seen from the Figure 2(b) that the EPSM further avoids an early depletion of the energy of the central node because it makes the nodes which just finishes data transmission into sleep mode and thus staggers competition cycle of the node to reduces retransmission caused by channel contention and makes the data are distributed, by which the network lifetime is increased by about 10% compared with PSM.

Through simulation experiment we can see that EPSM performances much better than the PSM in terms of reducing the transmission delay and improving the network lifetime.

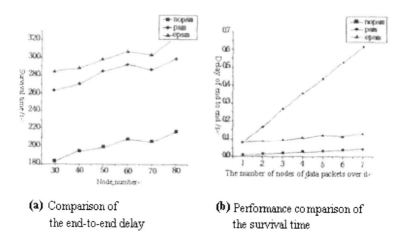

(a) Comparison of
the end-to-end delay

(b) Performance comparison of
the survival time

Fig. 2. Samples of Performance comparison

6   Conclusion

Because most of the nodes in Ad Hoc networks are powered by limited batteries, energy-saving strategy is becoming a research hotspot in the field. This article focuses on the energy mechanism in Ad Hoc Networks with IEEE802.11PSM mode, and proposes a new EPSM saving mechanism. Simulation was carried out to prove that it can play a good energy saving effect because it is able to greatly decrease the transmission delay in the case of light and moderate load when compared with the PSM model.

References

1. Yu, H.: Wireless mobile self-organizing mesh. Posts & Telecom Press, Beijing (2005)
2. Jeffrey, P.M., Vaduvur, B., Wen- Mei, W.: A power controlled multrple access protocol for wireless packet network. In: Proceedings of IEEE INFOCO, pp. 219–228 (2001)
3. Tseng, Y.C., Lin, S., et al.: A multi- channel MAC protocol with power control for multi-hop mobile ad hoc network. In: Computing System Workshops, pp. 419–424 (2001)
4. Kandukuri, S., Bambos, N.: Power control multiple access in wireless communication networks. In: Proceedings IEEE INFOCOM, pp. 386–395 (2000)
5. Jung, E.S., Vaidya, N.H.: An energy efficient MAC protocol for wireless LANs. In: Proc. of IEEE INFOCOM, pp. 1103–1344 (2002)
6. Hu, C.Y., Hou, J.C.: A link – indexed statistical traffic prediction approach to improving IEEE 802 11 PSM. Ad Hoc Network 3, 529–545 (2005)

Naive Bayesian Classifier Based on the Improved Feature Weighting Algorithm

Tao Dong[1], Wenqian Shang[1], and Haibin Zhu[2]

[1] School of Computer, Communication University of China,
Beijing, 100024, China
victor666.ok@163.com
[2] Senior Member, IEEE, Dept. of Computer Science,
Nipissing University,
North Bay, ON P1B 8L7, Canada
haibinz@nipissingu.ca

Abstract. Text categorization is a fundamental methodology of text mining and it is also a hot topic of the research of data mining and web mining in recent years. It plays an important role in building traditional information retrieval, web indexing architecture, Web information retrieval, and so on. This paper presents an improved algorithm of text categorization which combines a feature weighting technique with Naïve Bayesian classification. Experimental results show that using the improved Gini index algorithm to feature weight can improve the performance of Naïve Bayesian classifiers and increase the practical values of the sensitive information system.

Keywords: text categorization; Gini index; feature weighting; Naïve Bayes.

1 Introduction

With the rapid development of network technologies, the network data grow exponentially. How to effectively organize and manage information and quickly, accurately and completely find useful information for users is a major challenge for information sciences and technologies. As a key technique to process and organize large amount of texts, text categorization can solve the problem of information clutters to a large extent, and make users locate the information they need rapidly and accurately. Therefore, text categorization has become a fundamental technology with great practical values and is well-accepted and has made great progresses [1][2].

There are some commonly used algorithms of text categorization: kNN, Naïve Bayes, SVM, neural networks, maximum entropy and so on. Among them, naive Bayesian classifiers get the extensive attentions and universal applications with their unique advantages of high speed, small error rate and implementations online.

Therefore, this paper presents a Naive Bayesian classifier based on an improved feature weight algorithm of Gini index. Experimental results show that our method is effective and feasible.

G. Shen and X. Huang (Eds.): CSIE 2011, Part I, CCIS 152, pp. 142–147, 2011.

2   Classical Naïve Bayesian Classifier

Naive Bayesian classifiers assume that the value of each feature has an independent influence on a given class, and this assumption is called class conditional independence that is used to simplify the computation, and in this sense, we call it "Naive".

There are mainly two kinds of naive Bayesian models for different implementations. One is the multivariate Bernoulli model that only considers whether the feature item appears in the text, if the feature item appears, denoted as 1, otherwise as 0. The other is the multinomial model that considers the characteristics' number of occurrences in the text.

In the multinomial model,

$$P(x_t|c_j) = \frac{1+c_{jt}}{2+N_{c_j}} \tag{1}$$

where C_{jt} is the number of texts in C_j that contains feature x_t, and N_{cj} the number of all texts in C_j. In the multinomial model,

$$P(d|c_j) = \prod_{t=1}^{n} \frac{P(x_t|c_j)^{N_{it}}}{N_{xt}!} \tag{2}$$

where N_{xt} represents the number of occurrences in the text of feature x_t.

$$P(x_t|c_j) = \frac{1+\sum_{t=1}^{n} N_{it}P(c_j|d_i)}{|V|+\sum_{t=1}^{|V|}\sum_{t=1}^{n} N_{it}P(c_j|d_i)} \tag{3}$$

where $|V|$ represents the number of occurrences in the text d_i of feature x_t.

For the no-label text in the test texts, we can use the trained classifiers to find the posteriori probability of text d which belongs to class c_j. We use x_t to represent t^{th} characteristic entry in text d, and the formula as follows:

$$P(c_j|d) \infty P(c_j) \prod_{t=1}^{n} P(x_t|c_j) \tag{4}$$

In this paper, we choose the multinomial model.

3   Improved Naïve Bayesian Classifier

3.1   Traditional Gini Index Algorithm

Gini index is a non-purity method to split properties for classes, binary, discrete and other types of fields. It is proposed by Breiman et al. in 1984 [3] and has been widely used in the CART algorithm, SLIQ algorithm, SPRINT algorithm and the decision tree algorithm of the Intelligent Miner algorithm. The algorithm is described as follows:

We assume that Q is a set of data samples of s, its class labels have m different values which define m different classes (c_i, i=1…m). |C| is the total number of classes, and we divide Q into m sub-sets according to class labels (Q_i, i=1…m). We assume that Q_i is a set of samples belonging to class c_i, s_i is the number of samples in Q_i. Then the Gini index of Q is:

$$Gini(Q) = 1 - \sum_{i=1}^{|C|} P_i^2 \qquad (5)$$

Where P_i is the probability of any sample belonging to c_i, and is estimated by s_i/s. When Gini(Q) is the minimum 0, namely, all the samples in the set belong to the same class and we can get the maximum useful information at this time; when all samples in the set have a uniform distribution for the classes, the Gini (Q) get the maximum value and we get the minimum useful information at this time.

3.2   Improved Gini Index Algorithm

The initial form of Gini index is to measure a "hybrid degree", i.e., the property for categorization, namely, the smaller "hybrid degree" the better property. If we use the following form [4]:

$$Gini(W) = \sum_{i=1}^{|C|} P_i^2 \qquad (6)$$

It is to measure a "purity" that is the property for categorization, namely, the larger "purity" the better property. In literature [5], they also use the "purity" measured form of Gini. This form helps to reflect the impact of feature selection for categorization, hence we also use this measurement to conduct the feature selection of texts.

This "purity" form of the Gini index can be further changed as follows:

$$Gini(W) = \sum_{i=1}^{|C|} \sqrt{P(W|C_i)} \qquad (7)$$

3.3   Feature Weighting Technique

Weight adjustment aims to highlight important features and inhibit the secondary ones. TF-IDF is a commonly used function of feature weight adjustment, but the IDF function in the TF-IDF function can not reflect the feature's importance well. Therefore, we use a feature evaluation function to replace the IDF function and construct a new feature weight function, TF-TWF function. TWF represents a feature evaluation function, the TF-TWF weighting formula is as follows:

$$W_t = TF - TWF(x_t) = TF(x_t) \times TWF(x_t) \qquad (8)$$

Among them, $TF(x_t)$ means the word frequency of feature t in text d. $TWF(x_t)$ is a common evaluation function that is used to mark each feature and reflects the correlation between features and various types.

After the weight adjustment based on TF-TWF, the feature's importance in the classifier has changed with the change of weight. According to the adjusted feature's weight, modifying the feature's importance in the classifier, then we can calculate the $P(c_j|d)$ as follows:

$$P(c_j|d) = \log[P(c_j)] + \sum_{t=1}^{n} TF - TWF(x_t) \times \log[P(x_t|c_j)] \qquad (9)$$

Where TF-TWF(x_t) is a new weight function of feature x_t. The feature that has a higher weight plays a greater role in the naive Bayesian classifier; and the feature with a smaller TF-TWF(x_t)   plays a smaller role in the naive Bayesian classifier[6][7].

3.4   The New Bayesian Decision Model

Through the description above, we can get the new Bayesian decision model as follows:

$$P(c_j|d) = \log[P(c_j)] + \sum_{t=1}^{n} TF - Gini(x_t) \times \log[P(x_t|c_j)] \qquad (10)$$

Then the new decision rule of our Naive Bayesian classifier is: assigning d to the class of the maximum probability $P(c_j|d)$, namely, getting the $\arg\max P(c_j|d)$.

4   Experimental Results and Analysis

Experimental data comes from the articles in a large number of Chinese websites. These data include two classes of sensitive information and non-sensitive information. Experiment 1 uses a total of 1500 texts. The set of training samples has 1000 texts which consist of 500 texts about sensitive information and 500 texts about non-sensitive information; the set of test samples has 500 texts which consist of 250 texts about sensitive information and 250 texts about non-sensitive. There is no overlap between the training samples and the test samples. The feature selection for reservations is 2000.

The experimental results are as follows:

Classifiers	Precision(%)	Recall(%)	F-score(%)
kNN	96.76	55.41	70.44
Naïve Bayes	96.60	96.60	96.60
Improved Naïve Bayes	83.61	100	91.08

Fig. 1. Comparison of categorization performance

Experiment 2 uses a total of 1000 texts. The set of training samples has 900 texts which consist of 450 texts about sensitive information and 450 texts about non-sensitive information; the set of test samples has 100 texts which consist of 50 texts about information and 50 texts about non-sensitive information. There is no overlap between the training samples and the test samples. The feature selection for reservation is 2000.

The experimental results are as follows:

Classifiers	Precision(%)	Recall(%)	F-score(%)
kNN	69.20	72.00	70.60
Naïve Bayes	80.77	84.00	82.35
Improved Naïve Bayes	71.88	92.00	80.70

Fig. 2. Comparison of categorization performance

From Table 1 and Table 2, we can see that the improved Naive Bayesian classifier has shown better results on the different sensitive information data sets. It increases 10 to 20 percent on the categorization performance compared to the kNN classifier. This improvement is obvious. Although slightly inferior to the Naive Bayesian classifier on the accuracy of categorization, the recall has been increased 4 to 8 percent. As we know, in an identification system for sensitive information, the most important performance indicator is identifying the sensitive information as much as possible and not missing sensitive information. In other words, this kind of system's value is mostly determined by the recall. In this regard, the improved algorithm has achieved a great success.

5   Conclusion

This paper introduces a new algorithm of text categorization--- Naïve Bayesian classifier based on the improved feature weighting algorithm of Gini index. The algorithm takes into account that different features have different usefulness for categorization, integrates the Gini index to feature weighting techniques effectively and gives the feature different weights. At last, we combine it with the Naive Bayesian classifier. Experimental results prove that this algorithm has a good performance on the accuracy and practical value in an identification of sensitive information system, therefore this improvement is successful.

Acknowledgment

This research is partly supported by the project "Digital New Media Content Production, Integration, Operation and monitoring (2009)" of Beijing Municipal Special Fund for Cultural and Creative Industries and partly supported by the project "Engineering planning project" of Communication University of China (XNG1030).

References

1. Sebastiani, F.: Machine learning in automated text categorization. ACM Computing Surveys 34(1), 1–47 (2002)
2. Carbonell, J., Cohen, W.W., Yang, Y.: Guest Editorial for the Special Issue on Text Categorization. Machine Learning (2000)
3. Breiman, L., Friedman, J., Olshen, R., et al.: Classification and Regression Trees. Wadsworth Internatinoal Group, Monterey (1984)
4. Shang, W.Q., Huang, H.K., Liu, Y.L., Lin, Y.M., Qu, Y.L., Dong, H.B.: Research on the Algorithm of Feature Selection Based on Gini Index for Text Categorization. Computer Research and Development 43(10), 1688–1694 (2006)
5. Gupta, S.K., Somayajulu, D.V., Arora, J.K., Vasudha, B.: Scalable Classifiers with Dynamic Pruning. In: Proc. of the 9th International Workshop on Database and Expert Systems Applications. IEEE Computer Society, Los Alamitos (1998)
6. Tang, H.L., Sun, J.T., Lu, Y.C.: Text categorization and evaluation function in combination with TEF-WA weight adjustment technique. Computer Research and Development 42(1), 47–53 (2005)
7. Wang, D.Y., Wang, J.: Improved Feature Weighting Algorithm for Text Categorization. Computer Engineering 36(9), 197–199 (2010)

Automation Control of Powerpoint in C + + Builder

Xiaokui Liu and Baoqing Gu

Computer Center, Anyang Normal University, Henan, China
liuxiaokui11@163.com

Abstract. With the popularization of Microsoft Office series, it has become one of the compulsory courses for undergraduates of all majors nowadays. Besides, the importance of Office calling and automation has been shown clearly, especially in the computer examination system. This paper provides a good method to achieve Powerpoint calling and automation, the method uses the technology of OLE in development of software with C + + Builder.

Keywords: C + + Builder; OLE; PPT; Powerpoint; Office Automation.

1 Introduction

The automatic control of scoring to Office, such as word, excel and powerpoint files has become increasingly important in the realization of electronic and automated computer examination. There're plentiful materials or papers concerning about the automatic control of word and excel, but the papers about controlling of powerpoint scoring has been rare. The writer of this paper tends to offer two ways of calling and automatic controlling of Powerpoint 2000 (called PPT for short as below) through OLE technology in C + + Builder6.0.

2 Introduction to OLE Principle

OLE (Object Linking and Embedding) technology can be accessed by any programming tool or macro language that supports automation, such as Visual Basic, Delphi, C + + Builder, Visual C + + and so on. Even scripting languages such as VBScript and J scrip also support automation. Everyone can choose a programming tool according to their own needs. Here we use the C + + Builder6.0.

All the Office document editing process and results are recorded in the file. the format, symbols, styles, are all saved through the objects and attributes of a file. Through OLE Automation we can get the value of these objects and attributes, [1] through which the operating conditions of the candidates are informed.

3 Two Methods to Call PPT through OLE

3.1 The First Way Is to Start the PPT and Generate an OLE Object by Using CreatOleObject Function [2]

This method employs OLE Automation mechanism. OLE Automation is one specification of OLE 2. 0 that allows other applications to call the software through the way

G. Shen and X. Huang (Eds.): CSIE 2011, Part I, CCIS 152, pp. 148–151, 2011.

of object [3]. OLE Basically automation actions require two roles: one is server (OLE Server), the other is the control side (OLEController). OLE Server program defines a set of attributes and commands, and describe their functions through the description of the type. OLE Server program exports its methods and properties through the IDispatch interface, through which OLE Controller program can call OLE Server procedures. As long as the software itself has the function of OLE Server, you can write an application to call OLEController software. In the automation process of PPT through C + + Builder, PPT acts as OLE Server, and the applications developed by C + + Builder serve as OLE Controller.

The function of this way is very powerful, which can completely control PPT file, use all the properties of PPT, and even including VBA macro code written by one.

But this method also has shortcomings, for instance it has no C + + Builder code hinting, exceptional handling needs to be written by your own. Especially for beginners who do not have much experience, it's not easy to debug and it's error-prone. It requires a lot of information or help of VBA or MSDN.

Several important objects such as Application, Slides, Shapes, Presentations, Selection are mainly involved when PPT is accessed through OLE automation. Objects SlideShowWindow can be obtained by function OlePropertyGet, and then the attributes of each specified slide can be analyzed one by one of (that is, to examine the knowledge points) or the slide can be controlled.

To control the PPT in application, you have to call CreateOLEObject () to create an instance of OLE Automation objects, and CreateOLEObject () is declared in ComObj. Hpp, so the beginning of the program must include ComObj. Hpp file. The main program code is listed as below.

```
// - - - - - - - - - - - - - - - - - - - - - -
# Include <ComObj. Hpp>
// We put the following code inside a button event, the main code is as followings:
void __fastcall TForm1:: Button1Click (TObject * Sender)
{
    Variant vPowerPoint;
    try
    {
    // Start the PPT, and get a handle, its assigned vPowerPoint
        vPowerPoint = CreateOleObject ("PowerPoint.Application");
    }
  catch (...)
      {
    ShowMessage ("Error starting PPT! May not be installed PPT");
      }
// Visual interface to Powerpoint
vPowerPoint.OlePropertySet ("Visible", true);
// Clip to open a PPT file, here "D: / example. Ppt" file
vPowerPoint.OlePropertyGet ("Presentations"). OleFunction ("Open", "D: / example.
ppt", false, false, true);
// Draw the total number of slides, and assigned to the variable nSlidesCount
int    nSlidesCount    =    vPowerPoint.OlePropertyGet    ("ActivePresentation").
OlePropertyGet ("Slides"). OlePropertyGet ("Count");
```

```
// Show this clip
vPowerPoint.OlePropertyGet        ("ActivePresentation").        OlePropertyGet
("SlideShowSettings"). OleFunction ("Run");
// Show the next slide
Variant  vSlideShowWin  =  vPowerPoint.OlePropertyGet  ("ActivePresentation").
OlePropertyGet ("SlideShowWindow");
vSlideShowWin.OlePropertyGet ("View"). OleFunction ("Next");
// Jump to the second page
vSlideShowWin.OlePropertyGet ("View"). OleFunction ("GoToSlide", 2);
// Back
vSlideShowWin.OlePropertyGet ("View"). OleFunction ("Previous");
// Skip to the last page
vSlideShowWin.OlePropertyGet ("View"). OleFunction ("Last");
// Run a Macro
vPowerPoint.OleFunction ("Run", "'1. ppt '! Macro1");
// Close Powerpoint
vPowerPoint.OleProcedure ("Quit");
// Free memory variable
vPowerPoint = Unassigned;
}
```

3.2 The Second Way Is Realized through the Control of the Components

The PPT is embedd through component ToleContainer, and then through the control of which to fulfill this method. The greatest advantage of this method is convenient debugging, with timely or prompt syntax error help.

The following components can be directly seen in the Office2k page in C + + Builder6.0:

TPowerPointApplication components: PPT application components can complete the calling for PPT application, and it is the core components of the PPT calling.

TPowerPointPresentation components: can present processing components and process the specific content of the presentation.

TPowerPointSlide components: can process a certain slide in PPT presentation.

We continue to put all the code inside a button event, as followings:

```
void __fastcall TForm1:: Button2Click (TObject * Sender)
{
// Start the PPT
TPowerPointApplication1-> Connect ();
// Open "D: / example. Ppt" presentation
TPowerPointApplication1-> Presentations-> Open ((WideString) "D: / example.
Ppt", (MsoTriState) 0, (MsoTriState) 0, (MsoTriState) 0);
// Will open the PPT file the first component embedded TpowerPointPresentation
TPowerPointPresentation1->        ConnectTo        (TPowerPointApplication1->
Presentations-> Item (Variant (1)));
// Set visible PPT presentation
TPowerPointApplication1-> set_Visible (true);
// Set the window height and width
```

```
    TPowerPointApplication1-> ActiveWindow-> View-> Application-> set_Height
(200);
    TPowerPointApplication1-> ActiveWindow-> View-> Application-> set_Width
(250);
    // Remove the number of slides
    int nSlidesCount = TPowerPointApplication1-> ActivePresentation-> Slides->
Count;
    // Will open the PPT slide presentation of the first two components embedded in
TPowerPointSlide1
    TPowerPointSlide1->          ConnectTo          (TPowerPointApplication1->
ActivePresentation-> Slides-> Item (Variant (2)));
    // Get the layout of slide 2 of the code corresponding to
    int nLayout = TPowerPointSlide1-> get_Layout ();
    // Get the first two slides in the sound of the name of the title animation
    AnsiString s = TPowerPointSlide1-> Shapes-> Title-> AnimationSettings->
SoundEffect-> get_Name ();
    // Get the first two slides in the order of the title animation player
    int nOrder = TPowerPointSlide1-> Shapes-> Title-> AnimationSettings->
get_AnimationOrder ();
    // The following individual components in order to cancel the connection and
embedding
    TPowerPointSlide1-> Disconnect ();
    TPowerPointPresentation1-> Disconnect ();
    TPowerPointApplication1-> Quit ();
    }
```

4 Conclusion

The two methods of calling PPT through OLE technology in C + + Builder have been tested and run well. The second way is used in the examination system of basic computer developed by our own department and have been functioning well for four consecutive semesters. Here are just parts of the main codes. These codes are used for accessing or controlling of the properties of the existing PPT. More automated controlling, such as the creation of PPT file, insertion of objects and the setting or change functions of their attributes will be presented one after another in future studies.

References

1. Li, Y., Gan, Z.: C + + Builder Advanced Application Programming Guide. Tsinghua University Press, Beijing (2002)
2. Wang, X.: C + + Builder programming skills, experience and examples of, vol. 313. People's Posts and Telecommunications Press, Beijing (2004)
3. Chen, Z., Chen, H.: Proficient in C + + Builder 5 Programming Advanced Tutorial. China Youth Press, Beijing (2001)

Analytic Solutions of a Class of Iterative Functional Differential Equation Near Resonance

LingXia Liu

Department of Mathematics, Weifang University,
Weifang, Shandong 261061, P.R. China
llxmath@126.com

Abstract. This paper is concerned with a functional differential equation. By reducing the equation with the *Schröder* transformation to another functional differential equation, an existence theorem is established for analytic solutions of the original equation. For the constant α given in the *Schröder* transformation, we discuss α near resonance under the Brjuno condition. Furthermore, we discuss analytic solutions of the differential-difference equation.

Keywords: iterative differential equation; analytic solutions; *Schröder* transformation; Brjuno condition; resonance.

1 Introduction

Iterative differential equations as a special type of functional differential equations, attracted the attention of researcher recently [1-6]. In [5], analytic solutions of the following iterative functional differential equations $x'(z) = \sum_{s=1}^{m} c_s x^{[s]}(z)$ are found. More general form

$$x'(z) = f\left(\sum_{s=0}^{m} c_s x^{[s]}(z)\right) \tag{1}$$

are discussed in [6], where m is nonnegative integers, $c_0, c_1, \cdots c_m$ are complex constants, $x^{[s]}(z) = x(x^{[s-1]}(z))$ and f is given complex-valued functions of α complex variable. As well as in [6], we reduce this problem with the *Schröder* transformation

$$x(z) = y(\alpha y^{-1}(z)) \tag{2}$$

to the auxiliary equation

$$\alpha y'(\alpha z) = y'(z) f\left(\sum_{s=0}^{m} c_s y(\alpha^s z)\right), \ z \in C, \tag{3}$$

where iteration of the unknown function is not involved but an indeterminate complex α needs to be discussed. We need to find invertible analytic solutions of the equation (3) for possible choices of α. When the complex α in (2) is not on the unit circle in **C** ($0 < |\alpha| < 1$) or α lies on the unit circle in **C** but satisfies the Diophantine condition:

G. Shen and X. Huang (Eds.): CSIE 2011, Part I, CCIS 152, pp. 152–158, 2011.
© Springer-Verlag Berlin Heidelberg 2011

$|\mu|=1$, μ *is not a root of unity, and* $\log\dfrac{1}{|\mu^n-1|}\leq T\log n$, or α is a p-th unit root, the existence of analytic solutions of (3) was given in [6]. Since then, we have been striving to give a result of analytic solutions for those α near a root of the unity, i.e., neither being roots of the unity nor satisfying the Diophantine condition. The Brjuno condition provides such a chance for us. In this paper, the complex α in [2] satisfies $f(0)=\alpha$ and the following hypotheses:

(H) $\mu = e^{2\pi i \theta}$, where $\theta \in$ **R\Q** is a Brjuno number ([7, 8]), i.e., $B(\theta) = \displaystyle\sum_{k=0}^{\infty} \dfrac{\log q_{k+1}}{q_k} < \infty$,

where $\{p_k / q_k\}$ denotes the sequence of partial fraction of the continued fraction expansion of θ, and is said to satisfy the Brjuno condition.

A change of variable further transforms (3) into the differential-difference equation

$$g'(w+\beta) = g'(w)f(\sum_{s=0}^{m} c_s g(w+s\beta)), \qquad (4)$$

where β is a complex constant. The solution of the equation has properties similar to those of (3). If (4) has an invertible solution $g(w)$, then we can show that $x(w) = g(g^{-1}(w)+\beta)$ is an analytic solution of (1).

2 Analytic Solutions of the Auxiliary Equation

We now discuss the existence of analytic solution of (3) in the initial condition

$$y(0) = 0, \, y'(0) = \eta \neq 0. \qquad (5)$$

To do this, we now recall briefly the definition of Brjuno numbers and some basic facts. As state in [9], for a for a real number θ we let θ denote its integer part and let $\{\theta\} = \theta - [\theta]$. Then every national number θ has a unique expression of the Gauss' continued fraction $\theta = a_0 + \theta_0 = a_0 + \dfrac{1}{a_1+\theta_1} = ...$, denoted simply by $\theta = [a_0, a_1, ..., a_n, ...]$, where a_j's and θ_j's are calculated by the algorithm: (a) $a_0 = [\theta]$, $\theta_0 = \{\theta\}$ and (b) $a_n = \left[\dfrac{1}{\theta_{n-1}}\right]$, $\theta_n = \left\{\dfrac{1}{\theta_{n-1}}\right\}$ for all $n \geq 1$. Define the sequences $(p_n)_{n\in N}$ and $(q_n)_{n\in N}$ as follows

$$q_{-2} = 1, q_{-1} = 0, q_n = a_n q_{n-1} + q_{n-2}; \ p_{-2} = 0, p_{-1} = 1, p_n = a_n p_{n-1} + p_{n-2}.$$

It is easy to show that $p_n / q_n = [a_0, a_1, ..., a_n]$. Thus, for every $\theta \in$ **R\Q** we associate, using its convergence, an arithmetical function $B(\theta) = \displaystyle\sum_{n\geq 0} \dfrac{\log q_{n+1}}{q_n}$. We say that θ is a Brjuno number or that it satisfies Brjuno condition if $B(\theta) < +\infty$. The Brjuno condition is weaker than the Diophantine condition. For example, if $a_{n+1} \leq ce^{a_n}$ for all $n \geq 0$, where $c > 0$ is a constant, then $\theta = [a_0, a_1, ..., a_n, ...]$ is a Brjuno number but is not a

Diophantine number. So, the case (H1) contains both Diophantine condition and a part of μ ``near'' resonance.

In order to discuss analytic solutions of the auxiliary equation (3) under (H), we need to introduce Davie's Lemma. First, we recall some facts in [10] briefly. Let $\theta \in \mathbf{R}\backslash\mathbf{Q}$ and $(q_n)_{n\in\mathbb{N}}$ be the sequence of partial denominators of the Gauss's continued fraction for θ as in the Introduction. As in [9], let $A_k = \{n \geq 0 \mid \|n\theta\| \leq \dfrac{1}{8q_k}\}$,

$E_k = \max(q_k, \dfrac{q_{k+1}}{4})$, $\eta_k = \dfrac{q_k}{E_k}$. Let A_k^* be the set of integers $j \geq 0$ such that either $j \in A_k$ or for some j_1 and j_2 in A_k, with $j_2 - j_1 < E_k$, one has $j_1 < j < j_2$ and q_k divide $j - j_1$.

For any integer $n \geq 0$, define $l_k(n) = \max\left((1+\eta_k)\dfrac{n}{q_k} - 2, \ (m_n\eta_k + n)\dfrac{1}{q_k} - 1\right)$, where

$m_n = \max\{j \mid 0 \leq j \leq n, j \in A_k^*\}$. We then define function $h_k : \mathbf{N} \to \mathbf{R}_+$ as follows:

$$
\begin{cases}
\dfrac{m_n + \eta_k n}{q_k} - 1, & \text{if} \quad m_n + q_k \in A_k^*, \\[2mm]
l_k(n), & \text{if} \quad m_n + q_k \notin A_k^*.
\end{cases}
$$

Let $g_k(n) := \max\left(h_k(n), \left[\dfrac{n}{q_k}\right]\right)$, and define $k(n)$ by the condition $q_{k(n)} \leq n \leq q_{k(n)+1}$. Clearly, $k(n)$ is non-decreasing. Then we are able to state the following result:

Lemma 1. (Davie's Lemma [10]) Let $K(n) = n\log 2 + \sum_{k=0}^{k(n)} g_k(n)\log(2q_{k+1})$. Then

(a) There is a universal constant $\gamma > 0$ (independent of n and θ) such that
$K(n) \leq n\left(\sum_{k=0}^{k(n)} \dfrac{\log q_{k+1}}{q_k} + \gamma\right)$,

(b) $K(n_1) + K(n_2) \leq K(n_1 + n_2)$ for all n_1 and n_2, and

(c) $-\log|\alpha^n - 1| \leq K(n) - K(n-1)$.

Now we state and prove the following theorem under Brjuno condition. The idea of our proof is acquired from [10].

Theorem 1. Suppose that (H) holds, then for any $\eta \neq 0$, the equation (3) has an analytic solution $y(z)$ in a neighborhood of the origin such that $y(0) = 0, y'(0) = \eta$.

Proof. Let

$$f(z) = \sum_{n=0}^{\infty} a_n z^n, a_0 = \alpha. \tag{6}$$

We seek a power series solution of (3) of the form

$$y(z) = \sum_{n=1}^{\infty} b_n z^n, b_1 = \eta. \tag{7}$$

Substituting (6) and (7) of f, y in (3) and comparing coefficients, we have

$$(\alpha - a_0)b_1 = 0 \tag{8}$$

$$(\alpha^{n+1} - a_0)(n+1)b_{n+1} = \sum_{k=0}^{n-1} \sum_{\substack{l_1+l_2+\cdots+l_t=n-k \\ t=1,2,\cdots n-k}} (k+1)a_t b_{k+1} \prod_{j=1}^{t}(\sum_{s=0}^{m} c_s \alpha^{sl_j} b_{l_j}) \tag{9}$$

Note that $a_0 = \alpha$, so we can choose $b_1 = \eta \neq 0$ and by (9) we have

$$b_{n+1} = \frac{1}{(\alpha^{n+1} - \alpha)(n+1)} \sum_{k=0}^{n-1} \sum_{\substack{l_1+l_2+\cdots+l_t=n-k \\ t=1,2,\cdots n-k}} (k+1)a_t b_{k+1} \prod_{j=1}^{t}(\sum_{s=0}^{m} c_s \alpha^{sl_j} b_{l_j}), n=1, 2, \cdots. \tag{10}$$

then the sequence $\{b_n\}_{n=2}^{\infty}$ is successively determined by (10) in a unique manner.

In what follows we need to prove to prove the series (7) is convergent in a neighborhood of the origin. Since $f(z)$ is analytic in a neighborhood of the origin, there exists a positive δ such that $|z| < \delta$, i.e., $f(z)$ is analytic in $|z| < \delta$. So for any $r \in (0, \delta)$, there exists a positive constant M such that

$$|a_n| \le \frac{M}{r^n}, n = 0, 1, 2, \cdots. \tag{11}$$

So, when $|\alpha| = 1$, then

$$|b_{n+1}| \le \frac{M}{|\alpha^n - 1|} \sum_{k=0}^{n-1} \sum_{\substack{l_1+l_2+\cdots+l_t=n-k \\ t=1,2,\cdots n-k}} \frac{1}{r^t}(\sum_{s=0}^{m}|c_s|)^t |b_{k+1}| \|b_{l_1}\| \|b_{l_2}| \cdots |b_{l_t}|. \tag{12}$$

As in [6], we construct a governing series of (7). First, we consider the implicit functional equation

$$w(z) = |\eta| z + M \frac{\frac{1}{r} \sum_{s=0}^{m}|c_s| w^2(z)}{1 - \frac{1}{r} \sum_{s=0}^{m}|c_s| w(z)}. \tag{13}$$

Define the function

$$G(z, w) = w - |\eta| z - M \frac{\frac{1}{r} \sum_{s=0}^{m}|c_s| w^2}{1 - \frac{1}{r} \sum_{s=0}^{m}|c_s| w}$$

for (z, w) in a neighborhood of $(0,0)$. Then $G(0,0) = 0$, $G'_w(0,0) = 1 \neq 0$. Thus, there exists a unique function $w(z)$, analytic in a neighborhood of zero, such that $w(0) = 0$, $w'(0) = |\eta|$ and $G(z, w(z)) = 0$, so $w(z)$ can be expanded into a convergent power series

$$w(z) = \sum_{m=1}^{\infty} B_n z^n, B_1 = |\eta|. \tag{14}$$

Substituting (14) into (13) and comparing coefficients, we have $B_1 = |\eta|$,

$$B_{n+1} = M \sum_{k=0}^{n-1} \sum_{\substack{l_1+l_2+\cdots+l_t=n-k \\ t=1,2,\cdots,n-k}} \frac{1}{r^t} (\sum_{s=0}^{m} |c_s|)^t B_{k+1} B_{l_1} B_{l_2} B_{l_t}. \tag{15}$$

Note that the series (14) converges in a neighborhood of the origin, then there is a constant $T > 0$ such that $|b_n| < T^n$, $n = 1, 2, \cdots$.

Now we prove $|b_n| \leq B_n e^{K(n-1)}$, $n = 1, 2, \cdots$, where $K : \mathbf{N} \to \mathbf{R}$ is defined in Lemma 1. In fact, $b_1 = |\eta| = B_1$. We assume that $|b_j| \leq B_j e^{K(j-1)}$, $j \leq n$. From Lemma 1 and (12) we have

$$|b_{n+1}| \leq \frac{M}{|\alpha^n - 1|} \sum_{k=0}^{n-1} \sum_{\substack{l_1+l_2+\cdots+l_t=n-k \\ t=1,2,\cdots,n-k}} \frac{1}{r^t} (\sum_{s=0}^{m} |c_s|)^t B_{k+1} B_{l_1} B_{l_2} \cdots B_{l_t} e^{K(k)+K(l_1-1)+K(l_2-1)+\cdots+K(l_t-1)}$$

$$\leq \frac{e^{K(n-1)}}{|\alpha^n - 1|} M \sum_{k=0}^{n-1} \sum_{\substack{l_1+l_2+\cdots+l_t=n-k \\ t=1,2,\cdots,n-k}} \frac{1}{r^t} (\sum_{s=0}^{m} |c_s|)^t B_{k+1} B_{l_1} B_{l_2} \cdots B_{l_t} = \frac{e^{K(n-1)}}{|\alpha^n - 1|} B_{n+1}.$$

Note that $K(l_1-1) + K(l_2-1) + \cdots + K(l_t-1) \leq K(n-2) \leq K(n-1) \leq K(n) + \log|\alpha^n - 1|$, then

$$|b_{n+1}| \leq B_{n+1} e^{K(n)} \leq T^{n+1} e^{K(n)}.$$

Note that $K(n) \leq n(B(Q) + \gamma)$ for some universal constant $\gamma > 0$, then $|b_{n+1}| \leq T^{n+1} e^{n(B(Q)+\gamma)}$, that is, $\limsup_{n \to \infty} (|b_{n+1}|^{\frac{1}{n}}) = \limsup_{n \to \infty} (T^{\frac{n+1}{n}} e^{B(Q)+\gamma}) = T e^{B(Q)+\gamma}$. This implies that the convergence radius of the series (7) is at least $(Te^{B(\theta)+\gamma})^{-1}$.

Theorem 2. Suppose that $\Re\beta = 0, \Im\beta = 2\pi\theta$ and $\theta \in \mathbf{R} \setminus \mathbf{Q}$ is a Brjuno number. Then there exists a positive number κ such that Eq. (4) has an analytic solution $g(w)$ in the half-plane $\Omega_\kappa = \{w : \Re w < \ln K, -\infty < \Im w < +\infty\}$, and satisfies $\lim_{\Re w \to -\infty} g(w) = 0$.

Proof. If $\Re\beta = 0, \Im\beta = 2\pi\theta$ and $\theta \in \mathbf{R} \setminus \mathbf{Q}$ is a Brjuno number, then $\alpha = e^\beta$ satisfies the corresponding condition (H). From Theorem 1, therefore, we know that there is a positive κ such that Eq. (3) has an analytic solution $y(z)$ in a neighborhood of the origin $U_\kappa = \{z : |z| < \kappa\}$. Write $w = u + iv$, where u and v are real numbers. Let the variable z be connected with w by the equation $z = e^w = e^{u+iv} = e^u(\cos v + i\sin v)$. Then $|z| = e^u$. Furthermore, it is easy to see that $|z|$ tends to 0 when u tends to $-\infty$. This shows that there exists a positive number κ such that $z \in U_\kappa$ if $w \in \Omega_\kappa$. Define an analytic function $g(w)$ for $w \in \Omega_\kappa$ by the equation $g(w) = y(e^w)$. We assert that $g(w)$ satisfies Eq. (4) when $e^\beta = \alpha$. In fact, $g'(w) = y'(e^w)e^w$, then

$$g'(w+\beta) = y'(e^{w+\beta})e^{w+\beta} = y'(e^w\alpha) \cdot \alpha e^w = e^w \cdot y'(e^w) f(\sum_{s=0}^{m} c_s y(e^{s\beta} \cdot e^w))$$

$$= e^w \cdot y'(e^w) f(\sum_{s=0}^{m} c_s y(e^{w+s\beta})) = g'(w) f(\sum_{s=0}^{m} c_s g(w+s\beta)),$$

and $\lim_{\Re w \to -\infty} g(w) = \lim_{\Re w \to -\infty} y(e^w) = y(0) = 0$. This completes the proof.

3   Analytic Solutions of (1)

Having knowledges about the auxiliary equation (3) and (4), we are ready to give analytic solutions of (1).

Theorem 3. Suppose that Theorem 1 holds. Then equation (1) has an analytic solution of the form $x(z) = y(\alpha y^{-1}(z))$ in a neighborhood of the origin such that $x(0) = 0$, $x'(0) = \alpha$, where $y(z)$ is an analytic solution of Eq. (3).

Proof. In view of Theorem 1, we may find an analytic solution $y(z)$ of form (7) in a neighborhood of the origin. Since $y'(0) = \eta \neq 0$, the function $y^{-1}(z)$ is analytic in a neighborhood of the origin. Let $x(z) = y(\alpha y^{-1}(z))$, then

$$x^{[i]}(z) = y(\alpha^i y^{-1}(z)), \quad x'(z) = \frac{\alpha y'(\alpha y^{-1}(z))}{y'(y^{-1}(z))},$$

so from (3) we have

$$x'(z) = \frac{\alpha y'(\alpha y^{-1}(z))}{y'(y^{-1}(z))} = f(\sum_{s=0}^{m} c_s y(\alpha^s y^{-1}(z))) = f(\sum_{s=0}^{m} c_s x^{[s]}(z)),$$

and

$$x(0) = y(\alpha y^{-1}(0)) = y(0) = 0, \quad x'(0) = \frac{\alpha y'(\alpha y^{-1}(0))}{y'(y^{-1}(0))} = \frac{\alpha y'(0)}{y'(0)} = \alpha.$$

Theorem 4. Suppose that conditions in Theorem 2 hold. Then Eq. (1) has an analytic solution $x(z)$ of the form $x(z) = g(g^{-1}(z) + \beta)$ in a neighborhood of the origin, where $g(z)$ is an analytic solution of Eq. (4) such that $x(0) = 0$.

Proof. In view of Theorem 2, we may find an analytic solution $g(z)$ of Eq. (4) in the half-plane $\Omega_\kappa = \{w : \Re w < \ln \kappa, -\infty < \Im w < +\infty\}$, and the function $g^{-1}(z)$ is analytic in a neighborhood of the origin. If we now define $x(z)$ by $g(g^{-1}(z) + \beta)$, then

$$x^{[i]}(z) = g(g^{-1}(z) + i\beta), \quad x'(z) = \frac{g'(g^{-1}(z) + \beta)}{g'(g^{-1}(z))},$$

so from (4) we have

$$x'(z) = \frac{g'(g^{-1}(z) + \beta)}{g'(g^{-1}(z))} = f(\sum_{s=0}^{m} c_s g(g^{-1}(z) + s\beta)) = f(\sum_{s=0}^{m} c_s x^{[s]}(z)),$$

and $x(0) = g(g^{-1}(0) + \beta) = \lim_{\Re z \to -\infty} g(z) = 0$. The proof is complete.

References

1. Eder, E.: The functional differential equation x'(t)=x(x(t)). J. Differential Equations 54, 390–400 (1984)
2. Wang, K.: On the equation x'(t)=f(x(x(t)). Funkcial. Ekvac. 33, 405–425 (1990)
3. Stanek, S.: On global properties of solutions of functional differential equations x'(t)=x(x(t))+x(t). Dynam. Systems Appl. 4, 263–278 (1995)
4. Si, J.G., Li, W.R., Cheng, S.S.: Analytic solutions of an iterative functional differential equations. Comput. Math. Appl. 33(6), 47–51 (1997)
5. Si, J.G., Cheng, S.S.: Note on an iterative functional-differential equations. Demonstratio Math. 31(3), 609–614 (1998)
6. Xu, B., Zhang, W.N., Si, J.G.: Analytic solutions of an iterative functional differential equations which violate the Diophantine condition. J. Difference Equ. Appl. 10(2), 201–211 (2004)
7. Bjuno, A.D.: Analytic form of differential equations. Trans. Moscow Math. Soc. 25, 131–288 (1971)
8. Marmi, S., Moussa, P., Yoccoz, J.C.: The Brjuno functions and their regularity properties. Comm. Math. Phys. 186(2), 265–293 (1997)
9. Carletti, T., Marmi, S.: Linearization of Analytic and Non-Analytic Germs of Diffeomorphisms of (C, 0). Bull. Soc. Math. 128, 69–85 (2000)
10. Davie, A.M.: The critical function for the semistandard map. Nonlinearity 7, 219–229 (1994)

An LMI Approach to Guaranteed Cost Control of Stochastic Linear Time-Delay Systems

ZiJun Guo and WeiHua Mao

Institute of Applied Mathematics,
South China Agriculture University,
Guangzhou 510640, People's Republic of China
zijunguo@126.com

Abstract. For stochastic linear time-delay systems with a given quadratic cost function, the guaranteed cost control problem, by state feedback controllers, was studied by introducing Lyapunov functional, using Ito lemma, Schur complement lemma and stochastic analysis methods. Sufficient conditions for the existence of guaranteed cost controllers are given in terms of linear matrix inequalities. And then the optimal guaranteed cost control law which minimizes the guaranteed cost of the stochastic linear closed-loop time-delay systems is also formulated.

Keywords: Stochastic linear time-delay systems, Guaranteed cost control, Schur complement lemma, Ito lemma, Linear matrix inequalities.

1 Introduction

The problem of guaranteed cost control was first studied by Chang and Peng in 1972[1], it has been extensively studied, much effort has been directed towards finding a controller in order to guarantee stability and to guarantee an adequate level of performance[2-6]. There are two principal approaches to guaranteed cost control problem: Matrix Riccati Equation method, and the Linear Matrix Inequalities (in short LMI) approach [7-11].

Stochastic modelling has come to play an important role in many branches of science, industry and agriculture, such as the control of stochastic systems. In this paper, we discuss the guaranteed cost control problem for a class of stochastic linear time-delay systems based on the LMI approach. A sufficient condition for the existence of guaranteed cost controllers is derived. Furthermore, it is shown that the sufficient condition is equal to the solvability of a system of LMI, and its solutions provide a representation of guaranteed cost controllers.

2 Problem Formulation

Throughout this paper, unless otherwise specified, we let $(\Omega, \mathcal{F}, \{\mathcal{F}_t\}_{t \geq 0}, P)$ be a complete probability space with a filtration $\{\mathcal{F}_t\}_{t \geq 0}$ satisfying the usual conditions (i.e. it is

G. Shen and X. Huang (Eds.): CSIE 2011, Part I, CCIS 152, pp. 159–164, 2011.
© Springer-Verlag Berlin Heidelberg 2011

right continuous and $\mathcal{F}_0$ contains all P-null sets). Let $w(t)$ denote one-dimensional Brownian motion defined on this probability space. If A is a vector or matrix, its transpose is denoted by A^T, and $A > 0$ means A is positive-define matrix. We also introduce the notation $\mathbb{R}_+^n = \{x \in \mathbb{R}^n : x_i > 0, 1 \le i \le n\}$. Let $C^{2,1}$ $(\mathbb{R}_+ \times \mathbb{R}^n, \mathbb{R}_+)$ denote the family of all functions $V(t,x)$ from $\mathbb{R}_+ \times \mathbb{R}^n$ to $\mathbb{R}_+$ which are continuously twice differentiable in x and once in t. Let $d > 0$ and $p > 0$, denote by $L_{\mathcal{F}_0}^p([-d,0];\mathbb{R}^n)$ the family of $\mathbb{R}^n$-valued stochastic processes $\xi(s,\omega)$, $-d \le s \le 0$ such that $\xi(s,\omega)$ is $\mathcal{B}([-d,0]) \times \mathcal{F}_0$-measurable (i.e. jointly measurable in s and ω) and $\int_{-d}^0 E|\xi(s,\omega)|^p ds < \infty$.

Consider a class of stochastic linear time-delay systems with n interacting components described by the following state-space equation:

$$\begin{cases} dx(t) = [Ax(t) + A_1 x(t-d)]dt + Bu(t)dt + Cx(t)dw(t) \\ x(t) = \varphi(t), t \in [-d,0]. \end{cases} \tag{1}$$

Where $x(t) \in \mathbb{R}^n$ is the state vector, $u(t) \in \mathbb{R}^m$ is the control input vector, A, A_1, B and C are known constant real matrices of appropriate dimensions, $\varphi(t) \in L_{\mathcal{F}_0}^p([-d,0];\mathbb{R}^n)$ is a given initial state vector-value.

Associated with systems (1), the quadratic cost function is

$$J = E\int_0^\infty [x^T(t)Qx(t) + u^T(t)Ru(t)]dt. \tag{2}$$

Where $Q \in \mathbb{R}^{n \times n}$ and $R \in \mathbb{R}^{m \times m}$ are given positive-define symmetric matrices.

Definition 1. Consider the stochastic linear time-delay systems (1), if there exists a control law $u(t)$ and a positive scalar J^* such that the closed-loop time-delay systems are asymptotical stable and the closed-loop value of the cost function (2) satisfies $J \le J^*$, then J^* is said to be a guaranteed cost and $u(t)$ is said to be a guaranteed cost control law for the systems (1).

Our objective is to develop a procedure to designing a state feedback guaranteed cost control law $u(t) = Kx(t)$ for the stochastic linear time-delay systems (1). Let $u(t) = Kx(t)$, then the closed-systems become to the following stochastic linear time-delay differential equations

$$\begin{cases} dx(t) = ([A + BK]x(t) + A_1 x(t-d))dt + Cx(t)dw(t) \\ x(0) = \varphi(t), t \in [-d,0] \end{cases} \tag{3}$$

3 Main Results

We first present a sufficient condition for the existence of state feedback guaranteed cost control laws for the stochastic linear time-delay systems (1). For convenience, let us define the diffusion operator $\mathcal{L}$ acting on any function $V(t,x) \in C^{2,1}(\mathbb{R}_+ \times \mathbb{R}^n, \mathbb{R}_+)$ by $\mathcal{L}V(t,x(t)) = V_t + V_x[(A+BK)x(t) + A_1x(t-d)] + trace(x(t)^T C^T V_{xx} Cx(t))/2$.

Where $V_x = (V_{x_1},...,V_{x_n})_{1 \times n}$, and $V_{xx} = (V_{x_i x_j})_{n \times n}$.

Theorem 1. If there exist a symmetric positive-define matrices $P \in \mathbb{R}^{n \times n}$, $S \in \mathbb{R}^{n \times n}$, and a matrix $K \in \mathbb{R}^{n \times n}$, $\Sigma = Q + S + K^T RK + P(A+BK) + (A+BK)^T P + C^T PC$, such that

$$\begin{pmatrix} \Sigma & PA_1 \\ A_1^T P & -S \end{pmatrix} < 0, \tag{4}$$

then $J \le E[\varphi(0)^T P\varphi(0) + \int_{-d}^{0} \varphi(\tau)^T S\varphi(\tau)d\tau]$, and $u(t) = Kx(t)$ is a guaranteed cost controller.

Proof. Suppose now there exist symmetric matrices $P > 0, S > 0$ such that the matrix inequality (4) holds. Define a $C^{2,1}$-function $V : \mathbb{R}^n \times \mathbb{R}_+ \to \mathbb{R}_+$ by

$$V(t,x(t)) = x^T(t)Px(t) + \int_{-d}^{t} x^T(u)Sx(u)du. \tag{5}$$

It is not difficult to show that

$$\mathcal{L}V = 2x(t)^T P(A+BK)x(t) + 2x(t)^T PA_1x(t-d) + x(t)^T Sx(t) - x(t-d)^T Sx(t-d) + x(t)^T C^T PCx(t)$$

$$= \left(x(t)^T \quad x(t-d)^T\right)\begin{pmatrix} \Sigma - Q - S - K^T RK & PA_1 \\ A_1^T P & -S \end{pmatrix}\begin{pmatrix} x(t) \\ x(t-d) \end{pmatrix} < x(t)^T(-Q - S - K^T RK)x(t) < 0.$$

Therefore, the closed-loop system (3) is asymptotically stable. Furthermore, the Itô formula shows that

$$dV(t,x(t)) = \mathcal{L}Vdt + x(t)^T(C^T P + PC)x(t)dw(t),$$

$$EV(t,x(t)) = EV(0,x(0)) + E\int_0^t \mathcal{L}Vds < EV(0,x(0)) - E\int_0^t x(u)^T(Q+S+K^T RK)x(u)du,$$

$$E\int_0^t x(u)^T(Q+S+K^T RK)x(u)du < EV(0,x(0)) - EV(t,x(t)).$$

As the closed-loop system (3) is asymptotically stable, when $t \to \infty, x^T(t)Px(t) \to 0$, $\int_{-d}^{t} x^T(u)Sx(u)du \to 0 \ a.s$. Hence, we get by dominated convergence theorem

$$J = E \int_0^\infty [x^T(t)Qx(t) + u^T(t)Ru(t)]dt = E \int_0^\infty x^T(t)(Q + K^TRK)x(t)dt$$
$$\leq EV(0, x(0)) = E[\varphi(0)^T P\varphi(0) + \int_{-d}^0 \varphi(\tau)^T S\varphi(\tau)d\tau].$$

It follows from the definition that the result of the theorem is true. This completes the proof.

We now prove that the above sufficient condition for the existence of guaranteed cost controllers is equivalent to the solvability of a system of LMIs, later we study the optimal guaranteed cost control law which minimizes the value of the guaranteed cost for the closed-loop stochastic system.

Theorem 2. For stochastic linear time-delay system (1), there exist a symmetric positive define matrix $P \in \mathbb{R}^{n \times n}, S \in \mathbb{R}^{n \times n}$, and a matrix $K \in \mathbb{R}^{m \times n}$ such that (4) holds if and only if there exist a symmetric positive define matrix $X \in \mathbb{R}^{n \times n}, V \in \mathbb{R}^{n \times n}$, and a matrix $W \in \mathbb{R}^{m \times n}$ such that the following linear matrix inequality is satisfied.

$$\begin{pmatrix} (AX + BW) + (AX + BW)^T & A_1V & X & W^T & (CX)^T & X \\ VA_1^T & -V & 0 & 0 & 0 & 0 \\ X & 0 & -Q^{-1} & 0 & 0 & 0 \\ W & 0 & 0 & -R^{-1} & 0 & 0 \\ CX & 0 & 0 & 0 & -P^{-1} & 0 \\ X & 0 & 0 & 0 & 0 & -V \end{pmatrix} < 0. \qquad (6)$$

Furthermore, if linear matrix inequality (6) has a feasible solution $X \in \mathbb{R}^{n \times n}, V \in \mathbb{R}^{n \times n}, W \in \mathbb{R}^{m \times n}$, then the feedback control law $u(t) = Kx(t) = WX^{-1}x(t)$ is a guaranteed cost law and $J^* \leq E[\varphi(0)^T X^{-1}\varphi(0) + \int_{-d}^0 \varphi(u)^T V^{-1}\varphi(u)du]$ is a guaranteed cost for the stochastic linear time-delay system.

Proof. By applying Schur complement lemma, the matrix inequality (4) holds if and only if

$$\begin{pmatrix} P(A + BK) + (A + BK)^T P & PA_1 & I & K^T & C^T & I \\ A_1^T P & -S & 0 & 0 & 0 & 0 \\ I & 0 & -Q^{-1} & 0 & 0 & 0 \\ K & 0 & 0 & -R^{-1} & 0 & 0 \\ C & 0 & 0 & 0 & -P^{-1} & 0 \\ I & 0 & 0 & 0 & 0 & -S \end{pmatrix} < 0, \qquad (7)$$

Pre-and post-multiplying both sides of inequality (7) by

$$\begin{pmatrix} P^{-1} & 0 & 0 & 0 & 0 & 0 \\ 0 & S^{-1} & 0 & 0 & 0 & 0 \\ 0 & 0 & I & 0 & 0 & 0 \\ 0 & 0 & 0 & I & 0 & 0 \\ 0 & 0 & 0 & 0 & I & 0 \\ 0 & 0 & 0 & 0 & 0 & I \end{pmatrix},$$

we have

$$\begin{pmatrix} (A+BK)P^{-1}+P^{-1}(A+BK)^{\mathrm{T}}P & A_1S^{-1} & P^{-1} & (KP^{-1})^{\mathrm{T}} & (CP^{-1})^{\mathrm{T}} & P^{-1} \\ S^{-1}A_1^{\mathrm{T}} & -S^{-1} & 0 & 0 & 0 & 0 \\ P^{-1} & 0 & -Q^{-1} & 0 & 0 & 0 \\ KP^{-1} & 0 & 0 & -R^{-1} & 0 & 0 \\ CP^{-1} & 0 & 0 & 0 & -P^{-1} & 0 \\ P^{-1} & 0 & 0 & 0 & 0 & -S^{-1} \end{pmatrix} < 0,$$

and denoting $X = P^{-1}, V = S^{-1}, W = KP^{-1} = KX$ yield the matrix inequality (6). Accordingly theorem 3.1, the remainder of this theorem is true. This completes the proof.

We introduce the notation $\Pi = \{(X,V,W) : X \in \mathbb{R}^{n\times n}, V \in \mathbb{R}^{n\times n}, W \in \mathbb{R}^{m\times n}\}$ such that (6) holds. If there exist a symmetric positive define matrix $X \in \mathbb{R}^{n\times n}, V \in \mathbb{R}^{n\times n}$, and a matrix $W \in \mathbb{R}^{m\times n}$ such that the linear matrix inequality (6) is satisfied, then $\Pi \neq \phi$. It is clear that Π is a convex solution set of the linear matrix inequality (6), therefore many efficient convex optimization algorithms can be used to design the optimal guaranteed cost controller, which minimizes the value of the guaranteed cost for the closed-loop stochastic linear system by solving a certain optimization problem. It is stated as the following theorem.

Theorem 3. For system (1) with guaranteed cost control function (2), if the following optimization problem

$$\min_{X,V,W,M_1,M_2} \mathrm{tr}(M_1 + M_2) \text{ Subject to}$$

(1) $(X,V,W) \in \Pi$, (2) $\begin{pmatrix} -M_1 & N_1^{\mathrm{T}} \\ N_1 & -X \end{pmatrix} < 0$, (3) $\begin{pmatrix} -M_2 & N_2^{\mathrm{T}} \\ N_2 & -V \end{pmatrix} < 0$

has a solution $X^*, V^*, W^*, M_1^*, M_2^*$, where $\mathrm{tr}(\cdot)$ denotes the trace of the matrix $(\cdot)$. Then the control law $u(t) = W^* X^{*-1} x(t)$ is an optimal state feedback guaranteed cost controller which ensures the minimization of the guaranteed cost J^* for the stochastic time-delay systems, where $\mathrm{E}\varphi(0)\varphi(0)^{\mathrm{T}} = N_1 N_1^{\mathrm{T}}$, $\mathrm{E}\int_{-d}^{0}\varphi(u)\varphi(u)^{\mathrm{T}}\,du = N_2 N_2^{\mathrm{T}}$.

Proof. By Schur complement lemma, (2) is equivalent to $-M_1 + N_1^{\mathrm{T}}X^{-1}N_1 < 0$, we have

$$\mathrm{E}[\varphi(0)^{\mathrm{T}}X^{-1}\varphi(0)] = \mathrm{tr}\{\mathrm{E}[\varphi(0)^{\mathrm{T}}X^{-1}\varphi(0)]\} = \mathrm{E}\{\mathrm{tr}[\varphi(0)^{\mathrm{T}}X^{-1}\varphi(0)]\} = \mathrm{E}\{\mathrm{tr}[X^{-1}\varphi(0)\varphi(0)^{\mathrm{T}}]\}$$
$$= \mathrm{tr}\{\mathrm{E}[X^{-1}\varphi(0)\varphi(0)^{\mathrm{T}}]\} = \mathrm{tr}\{X^{-1}\mathrm{E}[\varphi(0)\varphi(0)^{\mathrm{T}}]\} = \mathrm{tr}\{X^{-1}N_1 N_1^{\mathrm{T}}\} = \mathrm{tr}\{N_1^{\mathrm{T}}X^{-1}N_1\} < \mathrm{tr}\{M_1\}.$$

(3) is equivalent to $-M_2 + N_2^{\mathrm{T}}V^{-1}N_2 < 0$, we have $\mathrm{E}\int_{-d}^{0}\varphi(u)\varphi(u)^{\mathrm{T}}\,du < \mathrm{tr}(M_2)$, and $J^* \leq \mathrm{E}[\varphi(0)^{\mathrm{T}}X^{-1}\varphi(0) + \int_{-d}^{0}\varphi(u)^{\mathrm{T}}V^{-1}\varphi(u)\,du] < \mathrm{tr}(M_1 + M_2)$. If the optimization problem

has a solution $X^*, V^*, W^*, M_1^*, M_2^*$, then $J^* < \mathrm{tr}(M_1^* + M_2^*)$ and $\mathrm{tr}(M_1^* + M_2^*)$ is the optimal guaranteed cost (under minimum sense), $u(t) = W^* X^{*-1} x(t)$ is an optimal state feedback guaranteed cost law. This completes the proof.

Acknowledgments. The work described in this paper was supported by Science and technology projects in Guangdong Province (2007A020300009-9).

References

1. Chang, S.S.L., Peng, T.K.: Adaptive Guaranteed Cost Control Systems with Uncertain Parameters. IEEE Trans. Automat. Control 17, 473–483 (1972)
2. Yu, L.: Design of Stabilizing Controllers for Uncertain Linear Time-delay Systems. Control Theory Appl. 8, 68–73 (1991) (in chinese)
3. Phoojaruenchai, S., Furuta, K.: Memoryless Stabilization of Uncertain Linear Systems Including Time-varying State Delay. IEEE Trans. Automat. Control 37, 1022–1026 (1992)
4. Lee, J.H., Kim, S.W., Kwon, W.H.: Memoryless H∞ Controllers for Time-delayed Systems. IEEE Tran. Automat. Control 39, 159–162 (1994)
5. Petersen, I.R.: Guaranteed Cost LQG Control of A Class of Uncertain Linear Systems. IEEE Proc. Control Theory Appl. 142, 95–102 (1995)
6. Fischman, A., Dion, J.M., Dugard, L.: A Linear Matrix Inequality Approach for Guaranteed Cost Control. In: Proc. 13th IFAC World Congress, San Franciso, USA, vol. 4, pp. 197–202 (1996)
7. Petersen, I.R., McFarlane, D.C.: Optimal Guaranteed Cost LQG Control and Filtering for Uncertain Linear Systems. IEEE Trans. Automat. Control 39, 1971–1977 (1995)
8. Yu, L., Chu, J.: LMI Approach to Guaranteed Cost Control of Linear Uncertain Time-delay Systems. Automatica 35, 1155–1159 (1999)
9. Chen, G.D., Yu, L.: Decentralized Stabilization of Interconnected Dynamical Time-delay Systems. Control and Decision 15, 92–94 (2001) (in chinese)
10. Zhai, D., Zhang, Q.L.: Decentralized Control for Composite Systems with Input Saturation. Control Theory and Appl. 20, 280–282 (2003) (in chinese)
11. Gu, Z.Q., Liao, F.C., Zhai, D.: The Decentralized Guaranteed Cost Control of Descriptor Systems. Journal of Basic Science and Engnerring 12, 322–327 (2004) (in chinese)

Research on a Kind of Nuclear and Chemical Reconnaissance Robot

Qiang Yin[1], QuanJie Gao[1], HaoMing Liao[2], YanHong Zeng[2], JiuLin Zuo[2], GongFa Li[1], and JianGuo Zhu[3]

[1] College of Mechanical Automation, Wuhan University of Science and Technology, Wuhan 430081, China
[2] Honglin Factory, Xiaogan 432000, China
[3] Intelligent Robot Lab, Beijing Institute of Technology, Beijing 100081, China
{ydqking1210,rainy__yy}@sina.com
{gaoqj6328,hlxbrobt,lgfa2004}@126.com
{syqlyy2006,zhujianguo0301}@163.com

Abstract. The nuclear and chemical reconnaissance robot, a kind of remote robot, can realize various functions such as nuclear radiation detection, toxic gas detection, solid sampling, and so on. This paper analyzes the functional requirements of the robot, and puts forward the main technical indicators for the robot system. A small-sized nuclear and chemical reconnaissance robot is manufactured according to the requirements, and the overall structure and control system design of the robot is described. Experiment shows that whole system of the robot is reliable to meet the design requirements, and can conduct reconnaissance and detection task in dangerous conditions instead of manual operation.

Keywords: nuclear and chemical reconnaissance, robot, structure design, control system.

1 Introduction

Under the condition of the nuclear war or in terroristic incidents of the nuclear radiation, presently the available reconnaissance devices are mainly handheld, portable, vehicle-mounted and fixed equipment. There is always someone prepared to operate the equipment, so it has its limitations. For example, when leak happened in a chemical plant, the dangerous area, which staff cannot go into, is an unknown environment. Therefore, it is necessary to develop a nuclear and chemical reconnaissance robot, which could be used to identify sources of pollution as soon as possible, taking samples and dealing with danger at the scene of the accident, etc. Moreover, the robot could transmit information to the command centre in real time and provide reliable information for emergency response and rescue [1, 2].

This paper introduces a robot system which used for performance of nuclear and chemical reconnaissance. The robot with friendly human-computer interaction is operated by remote control to fulfil tasks instead of artificiality, such as moving, obtaining environmental information and on-site sampling under dangerous environment.

G. Shen and X. Huang (Eds.): CSIE 2011, Part I, CCIS 152, pp. 165–170, 2011.
© Springer-Verlag Berlin Heidelberg 2011

2 Functional Requirement

Since the working environment for the nuclear and chemical reconnaissance robot is harsh, in order to ensure that there is a safer operating environment for the operators, the robot should be controlled remotely control to perform operations far away from the dangerous zone. It is also demanded that the robot should be small, light, with easy assembly-disassembly for key components, and should possess a compact structure and a unique delivery system to facilitate the robot can reach the destination quickly and work in a short time. Also, the robot is required to adapt to a variety of ground environment, such as the Gobi Desert, the sand, the soft land, the meadow, the gravel road, the cement. The most important application of the robot is to carry out tasks of reconnoitering the chemical contamination or nuclear leakage at the scene of the accident, and to avoid the staff directly being exposed to the accident environment with poison or nuclear radiation [3, 4].

According to the functional requirements above, the main technical indicators which the robot systems need to meet are as follows:

(1) The volume size (length × width × height) is not more than 800mm × 500mm × 500mm; mass ≤ 70 kg; maximum travel speed ≥ 3km / h; continuous working time ≥ 3 hours.

(2) The working way is the wireless remote control. The maximum distance of remote control is not less than 1.5km.

(3) The arm performance: DOF ≥ 3; arm end can sample solid, liquid or gas.

(4) Scalability: the task modules are replaceable and can be equipped with a variety of detecting instruments or devices.

3 Structural Design

The nuclear and chemical reconnaissance robot is divided into the bodywork and remote terminal according to its function. The bodywork includes the delivery system, task module, power system, driving system, control system, vision system and communication systems, etc. The bodywork of the nuclear and chemical reconnaissance robot is shown in Fig.1. The robot can work by voluntary movement or by remote

Fig. 1. Bodywork of nuclear and chemical reconnaissance robot

control to performing the intended functions. The robot is equipped with a mechanical arm of 4 DOF. The arm end with replaceable interface has good flexibility and expandability, and can not only sample the solid and turn off the leaking valve, but also sample the liquid or gas.

3.1 Delivery System

The delivery system is the foundation for the robot to perform tasks, and is the supporting body of the robot. Its pedrail type possesses many advantages, such as high stability, small pressure on ground, excellent manoeuvrability and good climbing capacity,. The dual DC motor drive is adopted and each DC motor power is 100W. Meanwhile, in order to increase the ability of obstacle surmounting, the angle between the front pedrail and the support end is designed to 60 °.

3.2 Task Module

According to the required task, different task modules, such as mechanical arm, camera, small bucket, sampling pipe are both replaceable. The joint transmission systems adopt the mode of "DC + harmonic gear drive". The DC motor with the brake device could achieve self-locking protection to avoid the accidental power loss of mechanical arm.

In addition, other task modules can be loaded to achieve the corresponding functions according to the actual demand, for example portable explosives inspection equipment and portable radiation detector could detect suspicious objects remotely.

3.3 Remote Terminal

The remote terminal is the remote operation control part of the robot system, and its main configurations are the PC, monitor and touch screen, as shown in Fig.2. The remote terminal equipped with the embedded computer connects with the communication systems and receives data and images from bodywork of the robot. The movements of bodywork and mechanical arm are controlled by commands through the joystick or touch screen. The video display system can realize two display modes: the four-screen display and single-screen display, and easily switch between the two display modes. The human-machine interface of the remote terminal is friendly, and has two input modes: the touch screen and control panel. It is convenient for operators to control robots remotely and reliably.

Fig. 2. Remote terminal

4 Control System Design of the Robot

The upper-lower computer mode is adopted in the control system of the robot. The control mode is shown in Fig.3. The upper computer and lower computer both use PC104. They communicate through a wireless communication system. The main function of the upper computer located in the remote terminal is to pick the manipulation signal of the human-machine interface, take charge of computing the control algorithm, and then send commands to the lower computer and receive information through the wireless communication. The lower computer in the bodywork of the robot is mainly responsible for the information exchange and receiving control commands from the upper computer to manipulate the robot.

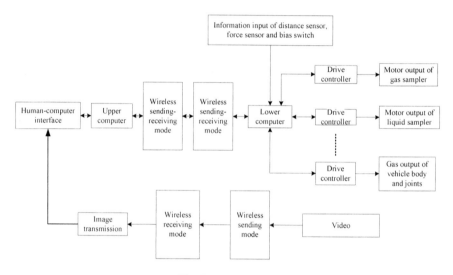

Fig. 3. Control mode

The upper computer is linked to the buttons, switches and touch screens on the operator panel of the remote terminal. In order to receive the operator's information, the keyboard values corresponding to the buttons, joysticks or switches are input into the upper computer through the keyboard interface board. These operational information and data are transmitted to the lower computer through communication systems between the upper computer and lower computer. Meanwhile, the upper computer receives the state information from the lower computer, such as speed, position and angle. After computing, the information is output to the monitor. The main function of drive controllers is to complete the serial communication with the lower computer and control the motor.

In addition, information picking can also be achieved through the touch-screen control interface. The main function of the control interface is to pick command information of the operator and send the command information to the lower computer via wireless data transmission device through the upper computer's serial port. Because the VC++ visual software not only can provide the good interface design capability, but also possesses the powerful function in the serial port communication, such as offering the communication control, the VC ++ is chosen to complete the development of the control interface.

5 Experimental Validation

The relevant validating test, including unit performance test and system performance test, is implemented to assess whether the function and index parameters of the robot and its unit components are consistent with design requirements. The unit performance test mainly inspects individual performances, such as the robot communication, motion and mechanical arm. The system performance test is to carry out the entire inspection of the robot on the premise of the reliable units. The mechanical arm and walking experiment are shown in Fig.4, and the experimental results are shown in Table 1.

Fig. 4. Experiments of the robot

Table 1. The experimental results of the robot

Test Name	Experimental Results	Design Requirements
Mass	52kg(Except tester mass)	≤70 kg
Volume	750mm×480mm×500mm	≤800mm×500mm×500mm
Maximum Travel Speed	3.6km/h	≥3km/h
Continuous Working Time	3.8h	≥3h
Remote Control Distance	3km(Open Area)	≥1.5km
Arm Performance	The 3-DOF mechanical arm is equipped with miniature buckets and pipes for sampling solid, liquid or gas; it can turn off leaking valves.	DOF≥3 ; The arm end can sample solid, liquid or gas。
Scalability	The task modules are replaceable and can carry portable explosives testers, portable radiation detectors or X-ray machines for nuclear and chemical reconnaissance.	The task modules are replaceable and can be equipped with a variety of detecting instruments or devices.

6 Conclusion

This paper introduces a robot system for nuclear and chemical reconnaissance, and describes its overall structure and control system design. The test verification shows that the nuclear and chemical reconnaissance robot system operates reliably and meets the technical requirements. The robot can be applied to identifying sources of pollution as soon as possible, taking samples and dealing with danger at the scene of the accident, etc. Moreover, the robot can transmit information to the command center in real time. The subsequent study is focused on these problems, such as how to improve the general compatibility of the robot control system, how to develop the modular and compact design to enhance its portability, and how to improve its self-control.

References

1. Jiang, Y., Wang, H.-g., et al.: A Climbing Robot System for Anti-terrorism Reconnaissance. Robot. 28(5), 530–535 (2006)
2. Li, B., Chen, H.-b., et al.: Current development and key techniques of mobile robot for scout and exploder-clearing. Mechatronics 10(4), 12–14 (2004)
3. Yang, J., Guo, Y., et al.: General design of tele-control reconnaissance robot for nuclear radiation. Chinese Journal of Scientific Instrument 28(4), 264–268 (2007)
4. Zheng, C.-e., Huang, Q., et al.: Design of a miniature autonomous surveillance robot. Science & Technology Review 25(21), 23–26 (2007)

LS-SVM Financial Achievement Prediction Based on Targets Optimization of Neighborhood Rough Sets

Guanhua Zhao, Wenwen Yan, and Yue Li

School of Accounting, Shandong University of Finance,
Jinan, China

Abstract. In order to improve the accuracy of financial achievement prediction and make the prediction effect better, this paper applies neighbourhood rough sets targets optimization in least square support vector machines (LS-SVM) and proposes a LS–SVM financial achievement prediction model which is based on neighborhood rough sets targets optimization. Meanwhile, it gives the algorithm realization procedures of the prediction model. After compared with factor analysis method, classical rough sets targets pretreatment method, this paper verifies that LS–SVM financial achievement prediction model based on neighborhood rough sets targets optimization can improve the model's prediction accuracy significantly.

Keywords: neighbourhood rough sets; classical rough sets; factor analysis; least square support vector machines; financial achievement prediction.

1 Introduction

Along with kinds of financial achievement prediction methods' statement, the research results of related financial prediction enrich day after day. In order to improve the accuracy of financial achievement prediction and make the prediction effect better, literature [1-8] conducted a series of studies to the problem.

This paper applies neighbourhood rough sets in the optimization of pre-selection target variables based on the above researches, and compares with classical rough sets and factor analysis method. In addition, this article chooses the change scope of corporate finance achievement as explanatory variable in forecasting model, but nearly all scholars before chose the variable that whether a company to be special treated or not. In fact, to forecast that the company's future financial achievement will whether rise or drop has more practical significance.

2 LS-SVM

The general description of LS-SVM is as follows: Given a collection of l training samples $\{(x_i, y_i), i = 1, 2, \cdots, l\}$, the i input data is $x_i \in R^n$, the i output data is $y_i \in \{+1, -1\}$, which is a dichotomous variable. LS-SVM is to construct a classification function:

G. Shen and X. Huang (Eds.): CSIE 2011, Part I, CCIS 152, pp. 171–178, 2011.

$$f(x) = \text{sgn}\left(w^T \varphi(x) + b\right) \tag{1}$$

In order that sample x can be classified exactly by $f(x)$, that is to solve the following optimization question:

$$\min \quad \frac{1}{2}\|w\|^2 + \frac{1}{2}C\sum_{i=1}^{l}\xi_i^2 \tag{2}$$

$$s.t \quad y_i(w^T \varphi(x_i) + b) = 1 - \xi_i \tag{3}$$

Here, $w = (w_1, w_2, \cdots, w_l)^T$ is a weight vector, which is a vector vertical to separating hyperplane, C is penalty factor, ξ_i is a slack variable that is bigger than zero, $\varphi(x_i)$ is named mapping function. The antithesis question of equation (2), (3) is Lagrange multinomial:

$$L(w,b,\xi,\alpha) = \frac{1}{2}\|w\|^2 + \frac{1}{2}C\sum_{i=1}^{l}\xi_i^2 - \sum_{i=1}^{l}\alpha_i\left[y_i(w^T\varphi(x_i)+b)+\xi_i-1\right] \tag{4}$$

Here, α_i is Lagrange multiplier, we takes the partial derivative by w, b, ξ_i, α_i separately with equation (4), and makes them to be equal to zero, and consider simultaneously $y_i \in \{+1,-1\}$, we have:

$$\begin{cases} w = \sum_{i=1}^{l}\alpha_i y_i \varphi(x_i) \\ \sum_{i=1}^{l}\alpha_i y_i = 0 \\ \alpha_i = C\xi_i \\ y_i\left[w^T\varphi(x_i)+b\right]+\xi_i-1=0 \end{cases} \tag{5}$$

Equation (5) can be written as the following equations:

$$\begin{bmatrix} I & 0 & 0 & -Z^T \\ 0 & 0 & 0 & -Y^T \\ 0 & 0 & CI & -I \\ Z & Y & I & 0 \end{bmatrix}\begin{bmatrix} w \\ b \\ \xi \\ \alpha \end{bmatrix} = \begin{bmatrix} 0 \\ 0 \\ 0 \\ \bar{1} \end{bmatrix} \tag{6}$$

Here, $Z = \left[\varphi(x_1) y_1, \varphi(x_2) y_2, \cdots, \varphi(x_l) y_l \right]^T$, $Y = \left(y_1, y_2, \cdots, y_l \right)^T$,
$\xi = \left(\xi_1, \xi_2, \cdots, \xi_l \right)^T$, $\alpha = \left(\alpha_1, \alpha_2, \cdots, \alpha_l \right)^T$, $\bar{1} = \left(1,1, \cdots, 1 \right)^T$, I is unit matrix.

Eliminates ξ and w, and then uses Mercer condition:

$$\Omega_{ij} = y_i y_j K \left(x_i, x_j \right) \tag{7}$$

After reorganization, equation (6) transforms to:

$$\begin{bmatrix} b \\ \alpha \end{bmatrix} = \begin{bmatrix} 0 & -Y^T \\ Y & \Omega + I/C \end{bmatrix}^{-1} \begin{bmatrix} 0 \\ \bar{1} \end{bmatrix} \tag{8}$$

Makes that $A = \Omega + I/C$, it is a symmetrical positive semidefinite matrices, whose inverse matrix A^{-1} exists. After solving linear equation (8), we can attain:

$$b = \frac{Y^T A^{-1} \bar{1}}{Y^T A^{-1} Y} \qquad \alpha = A^{-1} \left(\bar{1} - Yb \right) \tag{9}$$

So, the classification function solved is:

$$f(x) = \mathrm{sgn} \left(\sum_{i=1}^{l} \alpha_i y_i K \left(x_i, x \right) + b \right) \tag{10}$$

In equation (10), b and α is gotten by equation(10), y_i is determined by the character of training sample. When earnings per share of sample increases compared with last year's, $y_i = 1$, otherwise, $y_i = -1$. $K(x_i, x)$ is a kernel function, this article adopts Gaussian Kernel, its expression is $K(x_i, x) = \exp\left(-|x_i - x|^2 / 2\sigma^2 \right)$, σ^2 is Gaussian Kernel parameter.

3   Attribute Reduction of Neighborhood Rough Sets

T.Y. Lin put forward the concept of neighbourhood model firstly, which used the neighbourhood of spatial point to granulated universe space. It interpreted neighbourhood as basic information particles, which is used to describe other concepts of space.Hu Qinghua used neighborhood model to improve model based on classical rough set theory, and proposed the concept of neighbourhood rough sets. In this model, each real space point formed a δ neighbourhood, and δ neighbourhood family constituted basic information particles which can describe any concept of space.

For information systems IS= $\langle$U,A,V,f$\rangle$, here U={x1, x2,...,xn} means non-empty finite set which is named universe. In terms of financial results forecasts, universe is made up by a collection of the sample space, A is a collection of attribute, V is range. $f : U \times \overline{A}V$ is a information function, which indicates mapping relations between samples and their value of attribute. If $A=C \cup D$, here, C is condition attribute sets, D is decision attribute sets ,and $C \cap D = \emptyset$,then IS= $\langle U,A,V,f \rangle$ is a decision table.Given $xi \in U$ and $B \subseteq C$, then the neighbourhood of xi attribute set B can be defined as :

$\delta B(xi)=\{xj|xj \in U, \Delta B(x1, x2) \leq \delta\}$,here, Δ is distance function, for $\forall$ x1, x2, x3 $\in$ U, Δ meet the following conditions:

(1) $\Delta(x1, x2) \geq 0$, $\Delta(x1,x2)=0$,if and only if x1=x2 ;
(2) $\Delta(x1, x2)=\Delta(x2, x1)$;
(3) $\Delta(x1, x3) \leq \Delta(x1, x2)+\Delta(x2, x3)$。

For a sample set whose has N attributes, distance can be expressed by P norm: $\Delta_p(x_1,x_2) =(\sum_{i=1}^{N} |f(x_1,a_i) - f(x_2,a_i)|^P)^{1/P}$,here $f(x_i,a_i)$ is the value of sample x_i on attribute a_i. $\Delta_p(x_1,x_2)$ is in terms of numeric attribute set, but neighbourhood model extends distance calculation to those data which contain symbols and number, for symbolized attribute a_i, we can define:

(1) $f(x_1,a_i) - f(x_2,a_i) = 0$,when x_1, x_2 have the same value on a_i ;
(2) $f(x_1,a_i) - f(x_2,a_i) = 1$,when x_1, x_2 have different value on a_i.

Therefore, the lower approximation and upper approximation of neighbourhood rough set can be defined as:, $\underline{N}X = \{x_i|\delta(x_i) \subseteq X, x_i \in U\}$, $\overline{N}X = \{x_i|\delta(x_i) \cap X \neq \emptyset, x_i \in U\}$, then the approximate boundaries which is corresponding with X is $BN(X) = \overline{N}X - \underline{N}X$.

For a neighbourhood decision system NDT $=< U, C \cup D, V, f >$,U divides D into N equivalent class: $X_1, X_2, \ldots, X_N$, $\forall B \subseteq C$,the lower approximation, upper approximation and decision boundaries of D on B can be defined as: $\underline{N_B}D = \bigcup_{i=1}^{N} \underline{N_B}X_i$, $\overline{N_B}D = \bigcup_{i=1}^{N} \overline{N_B}X_i$, $BN(D) = \overline{N_B}D - \underline{N_B}D$ .The lower approximation of decision D is also called positive region, which is expressed as $POS_B(D)$.The size of positive region reflects separable degree of classification in a given attribute space, the greater the positive region, the less the boundaries which is to say the overlap region.

$$\gamma_B(D)= \frac{|POS_B(D)|}{|U|} \tag{11}$$

Equation(11) expresses the ratio of samples included in a certain type of decision to all samples in sample set according to the description of condition attribute.

Because there are dozens of targets which influence corporate financial performance, and between them there exist a wealth of information overlap and conflict, they can not only influence the generalization ability of support vector machines, but also make the structure of support vector machines more complicated. Therefore, it is necessary to use neighbourhood rough set theory to carry attribute reduction on the alternative indicators (condition attributes). That is to say, In the premise of maintaining the same classification ability, removes redundant attributes, reduce noise as well as reduce the cost of financial performance prediction, and improve forecasting effect. This paper proposes a attribute reduction operation which uses a fast reduction algorithm and uses condition attributes to measure the dependence of decision attributes and weighted progresses each attribute. Algorithm steps achieve by MATLAB R2007.

4 Experiment and Its Result Analysis

4.1 Pretreatment of the Indicator Data

Traditional factor analysis and the neighborhood rough sets reduction method are used in pre-treating the indicators so that we can compare the effects of financial performance by these tow methods.

First, do significant difference test of the 31 sample indicators using Wilcoxon signed rank method; second, do factor analysis of these variables which have significant difference to eliminate the existing multicollinearity between the variables. Treated by factor analysis, we identified eight factors which contain 16 original indicators ultimately and these eight factors are the model input variables. Table 1 shows these 8 factors and their indicators.

Table 1. Common factors and its including financial indicators after factor analysis treatment

Common Factors	Indicators Included in Common Factors
F_1	Net operating income rate (X_{11}) 、 Return on assets (X_{12}) 、 Total assets net profit margin (X_{13}) 、 Net profit margin of fixed assets (X_{14}) 、 ROE (X_{15})
F_2	Current ratio (X_1) 、 Ratio of working capital to total assets (X_3) 、 Asset-liability ratio (X_4)
F_3	Total assets turnover (X_{10}) 、 Growth of main business revenue (X_{16})
F_4	Cash ratio of main business income (X_{20}) 、 Net cash flow from operating activities per share (X_{21})
F_5	Sales cash ratio (X_{23})
F_6	The proportion of state-owned shares (X_{25})
F_7	Accounts receivable turnover (X_7)
F_8	Net profit growth rate (X_{19})

Based on standardization of the 31 candidate indicators, we use reduction based on neighborhood rough set for indicator selecting. For the comparison with the classical rough set method, CART classification learning algorithms was introduced in the experiment, the specific steps are: reduction on the classical rough set attribute, first use Equal frequency binning algorithm in Rosetta software for data discretization, then use Johnsonreducer algorithm to reduce the discrete data; for neighborhood rough set attribute reduction, we reach the results by the proposed algorithm using programming in MATLAB R2007. As the number of attributes reduction was impacted by algorithm by the impact of neighborhood size δ, δ take steps of 0.1 in this article and it ranges from 0.1 to 1, results show that when $\delta = 0.9$, classification accuracy come to the best (gets the best classification accuracy in the least number) Table 2 shows the attribute reduction under these two methods.

Table 2. The comparison of index reduction method between classical rough set and neighborhood rough set

Methods of pretreatment indicators	Indicators after reduction
Classical rough set reduction	Current ratio (X_1) 、 Quick ratio (X_2) 、 Asset-liability ratio (X_4) 、 Accounts receivable turnover (X_7) 、 Inventory turnover (X_8) 、 Net operating income rate (X_{11}) 、 Growth of main business revenue (X_{16}) 、 Growth rate of total assets (X_{18}) 、 Growth rate of net profit (X_{19}) 、 Cash ratio of main business income (X_{20}) 、 Net cash flow from operating activities per share (X_{21}) 、 Number of executives (X_{29})
Neighborhood rough set reduction	Accounts receivable turnover (X_7) 、 Growth of main business revenue (X_{16}) 、 Growth rate of net profit (X_{19}) 、 Net cash flow from operating activities per share (X_{21}) 、 Net cash flow per share (X_{22})

Consolidated Table 1 and Table 2, we can get that factor analysis extracted a total of 8 common factor, which contains16 indicators; classical rough set theory extracted 12 indicators, while the reduction of rough neighborhood rule extracted five indicators which extracted the least number of indicators.

4.2 Analysis of Experimental Results

Accuracy of the model under different indicators prediction pretreatment are shown in Table 3, we can see, no matter what kind of indicators pretreatment, LS-SVM model are better than SVM in predictive effect, which shows the quadratic programming for solving in SVM was changed into linear equations for solving in LS-SVM model, which not only reduces the difficulty of solving, but also improve the accuracy of model prediction; and then in the view of pretreatment method of the index, of the two models, neighborhood rough set Attribute reduction method is the best which followed by the classical rough set, and the worst is the factor analysis.

Table 3. Comparison table of model prediction accuracy after different indicators pretreatment prediction

Model name	Methods of pretreatment indicators	Penalty factor	Gaussian kernel parameter	Prediction accuracy
SVM model	Factor Analysis	×	0.47	84.0%
	indicators reduction of Classical rough set	×	0.47	88.4%
	indicators reduction of Neighborhood rough set	×	0.47	92.2%
LS-SVM model	Factor Analysis	5	1	88.0%
	indicators reduction of Classical rough set	5	1	90.6%
	indicators reduction of Neighborhood rough set	5	1	94.0%

5 Conclusions

From the analysis of the above experimental results, we can see, (1) A neighborhood rough set attribute reduction extracted a small number of indicators, the volume of effective information is big and can significantly improve the prediction accuracy; (2) LS-SVM model is better than SVM model in the overall forecast, and the efficiency of solving is better-than-SVM model; (3) Take the rate of change of company's financial performance rather than whether the company is ST as a variable in the model, use LS-SVM base on neighborhood rough set Reduction in this paper, the correct rate of the model's prediction can reach as high as 94%, which indicates that it is successful in using this improved model to predict financial performance of the company.

References

1. Yang, S., Li, H.: Financial crisis warning model based on BP neural network. Systems Engineering Theory & Practice 1, 12–18 (2005)
2. Li, B.: Empirical study on forecasting firms financial distress by nonlinear combining. Systems Engineering Theory & Practice 6, 222–225 (2004)
3. Fan, A., Palaniswami, M.: Selecting bankruptcy predictors using a support vector machine approach. In: Proceeding of the International Joint Conference on Neural Network, vol. (6), pp. 354–359 (2000)
4. Min, J.H., Lee, Y.-C.: Bankruptcy prediction using support vector machine with optimal choice of kernel function parameters. Expert Systems with Applications 28(4), 603–614 (2005)
5. Li, H., Feng, T.: A multivariate corporate financial early-warning model based on SVM. Communication and Computer 2(8) (2005)

6. Van Gestel, T., Baesens, B., Suykens, J., et al.: Bankruptcy prediction with least squares support vector machine classifiers, computational intelligence for financial engineering. In: Proceeding of IEEE International Conference, pp. 1–8 (2003)
7. Lin, H.: The research of least squares support vector machine method of listed company financial crisis forecasting. Market Modernization (10) (2006)
8. Hu, Q., Zhao, H., Yu, D.: Quick Reduction Method of Signal and Number Characters Based on Rough Sets. In: Xi, S., Yuan, T. (eds.) The Seventh China Rough Set and Computing Study Meeting (2007)

Interval Programming Model for the Journal Selection Problem

Yueyi Zhou

Library of Hangzhou Dianzi University , Hangzhouzhou, 310018, China
yueyizhou@126.com

Abstract. The problem of choosing a set of journals to order or to cancel is significant in applications of operations research to library decision making. This paper describes a zero-one interval linear programming approach that can consider all coefficients varied in some interval, and provide a satisficing solution.

Keywords: journal selection problem; Interval programming; satisficing solution.

1 Introduction

The journal selection problem, as discussed by Downs, R. B [1], has received considerable attention for its significance in applications of operations research to library decision making. Fundamentally, the model seeks to determine the optimal allocation of present and future (expected) funds to purchase scientific journals, using an objective function based on expected usage as a measure of journal worth. The importance of this problem in library management is examined in [2] and [3], and an review of this literature appear in Kraft and Hill [4].

All models described in the above papers are based on traditional mathematics programmings. Namely, the coefficients used in the model are real numbers. In reality however, these coefficients may vary in some interval. The purpose of this paper is to extend the model to establish an interval programming model for journal selection problem and to specify new solution methods which is capable of solving the extended models as well as the original model.

2 Problem Formulation

Let x_{jpq} $(q \geq p)$ be a binary-valued variable which assumes the value one if the library has acquired as of period q the issues of journal j published in period p (hence, holds them at a time $q - p$ units after their publication and continues to hold them for all subsequent periods), and zero if the library has not acquired these issues. It is assumed that all variables relate to an action as of the end of a specific acquisition period, $q = 0, 1, 2, \cdots, r$, and that the acquisition can apply to a journal published in any period p ranging over $p = 0, 1, 2, \cdots, q$. Furthermore, the index j denotes a specific journal from a set of s journals (that is, $j = 1, 2, \cdots s$) which contains all journals that are being considered by the library. Defining w_{jpq} as the

G. Shen and X. Huang (Eds.): CSIE 2011, Part I, CCIS 152, pp. 179–183, 2011.
© Springer-Verlag Berlin Heidelberg 2011

worth of acquiring as of period q the issues of journal j published in period p, the objective becomes that of maximizing

$$z = \sum_{j=1}^{s} \sum_{q=0}^{r} \sum_{p=0}^{q} x_{jpq} w_{jpq} \tag{1}$$

To represent the fact that a particular issue of a journal can be "first acquired" only once, it is then possible to write

$$\sum_{q \geq p} x_{jpq} \leq 1 \ , \ j = 1, \cdots s, \ p = 0, 1, \cdots q - 1. \tag{2}$$

The assumption that a particular issue, once obtained, is maintained thereafter (over the planning horizon) can be accommodated by introducing the budget constraints,

$$\sum_{\substack{j, p, q \\ p \leq q \leq h}} a_{jpq}^{h} x_{jpq} \leq b_{h} \tag{3}$$

for each period h, where the coefficient a_{jph}^{h} represents the cost of acquiring the "issue jp" in period h, and is thus given by

$$a_{jph}^{h} = C_1 + C_2 + C_3 \lambda_{jpq}^{h} \tag{4}$$

and where the coefficient a_{jpq}^{h} for $q < h$ represents the cost of maintaining "issue jp" in period h, after having acquired it in period q, and is given by

$$a_{jpq}^{h} = C_2 + C_3 \lambda_{jpq}^{h} \tag{5}$$

Where

b_q is the budget for period q for use in the acquisition of new journals and maintenance of the collection of journals;

C_1 is the cost of initially adding the issues of a journal to the collection, excluding subscription cost;

C_2 is the periodic storage and recurring costs, including some allotment for expected replacement of lost or defaced items;

C_3 is the cost per expected use of an item for circulation;

λ_{jpq}^{h} is the expected use in period q of journal j published in period p;

K_{jpq}^{h} is the subscription cost to acquire the issues of journal j published in period p if acquired in period q.

In reality, the coefficient C_1, C_2, C_3 may be fluctuate in some interval and thus a_{jpq}^{h} varies accordingly. Also, the budget for period q, b_q may be changed in an interval. Thus, we establish the following intervalprogramming model for journal selection problem

$$z = \sum_{j=1}^{s} \sum_{q=0}^{r} \sum_{p=0}^{q} x_{jpq} w_{jpq}$$

$$s.t. \sum_{q \geq p} x_{jpq} \leq 1, \; j = 1, \cdots s, \; p = 0, 1, \cdots q - 1,$$

$$\sum_{\substack{j, p, q \\ p \leq q \leq h}} a_{jpq}^{h} x_{jpq} \leq b_h^{I},$$

$$x_{jpq} = 0, 1.$$

(6)

where

$$a_{jph}^{h} = C_1^{I} + C_2^{I} + C_3^{I} \lambda_{jpq}^{h}$$

(7)

$$a_{jpq}^{h} = C_2^{I} + C_3^{I} \lambda_{jpq}^{h}$$

(8)

and $D^{I} = [\underline{D}, \overline{D}]$ is an interval number. For example, $D^{I} = [-1, 4]$,then $\underline{D} = -1, \overline{D} = 4$.

3 Solution Methods

The model of the Journal Selec-on Problem that we propose in the last section is an interval 0-1 linear programming problem. Thus, the solution may also varies in some interval. Consider the following two models generated by model (6) with conditions (7) and (8)

$$z = \sum_{j=1}^{s} \sum_{q=0}^{r} \sum_{p=0}^{q} x_{jpq} w_{jpq}$$

$$s.t. \sum_{q \geq p} x_{jpq} \leq 1, \; j = 1, \cdots s, \; p = 0, 1, \cdots q - 1,$$

$$\sum_{\substack{j, p, q \\ p \leq q \leq h}} \underline{a}_{jpq}^{h} x_{jpq} \leq \overline{b}_h^{I},$$

$$x_{jpq} = 0, 1.$$

(9)

and

$$z = \sum_{j=1}^{s} \sum_{q=0}^{r} \sum_{p=0}^{q} x_{jpq} w_{jpq}$$

$$s.t. \sum_{q \geq p} x_{jpq} \leq 1, \; j = 1, \cdots s, \; p = 0, 1, \cdots q - 1,$$

$$\sum_{\substack{j,p,q \\ p \leq q \leq h}} \overline{a}_{jpq}^{h} x_{jpq} \leq \underline{b}_{h}^{l},$$

$$x_{jpq} = 0,1.$$

(10)

It is easy to see that

$$\sum_{\substack{j,p,q \\ p \leq q \leq h}} a_{jpq}^{h} x_{jpq} \leq \overline{b}_{h}^{l}$$

(11)

is the largest feasible region defined by the interval inequality constraint $\sum_{\substack{j,p,q \\ p \leq q \leq h}} a_{jpq}^{h} x_{jpq} \leq b_{h}^{l}$, and

$$\sum_{\substack{j,p,q \\ p \leq q \leq h}} \overline{a}_{jpq}^{h} x_{jpq} \leq \underline{b}_{h}^{l}$$

(12)

is the smallest feasible region defined by the same interval inequality constraint. The models (9) and (10) are called the *optimistic optimum* model and the *pessimistic optimum model* respectively for problem (6).

Note that models (9) and (10) are traditional zero-one linear programming problem, they can be easily solved by simplex algorighm or interior point algorithm [5].

Denote the optimistic optimum solution by x^{L} and the pessimistic optimum solution by x^{R}, and the according optimistic optimum value and the pessimistic optimum value by z^{L} and z^{R}, respectively. Thus, the optimal value interval is given by $[z^{L}, z^{R}]$, for any $z \in [z^{L}, z^{R}]$, the corresponding solution is a satisficing solution.

4 Conclusion

This paper presents a interval zero-one linear programming approach to solve the problem of selecting or canceling appropriate journals. In doing so, this paper has extended the original research to include interval coefficients. Also, the optimal solution is a set of satisficing solution. The result is very flexible. So, it provide the decision maker a qiuck method to reach a conclusion according to the conditions changes.

Acknowledgments. This work was partially supported by Youth Foundation of China 61003194.

References

1. Downs, R.B.: The Implementation of Book Selection Policy in University and Research Libraries. In: Goldkor, H., Champaign (eds.) Selection and Acquisition Procedures in Medium-sized and Large Libraries, Illini-Union Bookstore (1963)
2. Broadus, R.N.: A proposed method for eliminating titles from periodical subscriptions. College & Res. Libraries 46, 30–35 (1985)
3. White, H.S.: Factors in the decision by individuals and libraries to place or cancel subscriptions to scholarly and research journals. Library Q 50, 287–309 (1980)
4. Kraft, D.H., Hill, T.W.: The Joumal selection problem in a University Library System. Mgmt. Sci. 19, 613–626 (1973)
5. Vanderbei, R.J.: Linear programming: Foundations and extensions. Kluwer Academic Publishes, Boston (1996)

A Cluster-Based MAC Scheme for Multimedia Support in Wireless Sensor Networks

LiYong Bao, DongFeng Zhao, and YiFan Zhao

School of Information Science and Engineering,
Yunnan University Kunming, 650091, P.R. China
lybao@ynu.edu.cn, zhaodf123@263.net,
shipzhaoyifan@yahoo.com.cn

Abstract. Based on the ideas of conflict-free transmission, priority-based service and dynamic load adaptation, this article proposes a scheduling strategy fit for the MAC scheme of WSNs, which has made possible the polling service capable of differentiating the clusters of different priority levels under two kinds of service policy. The scheme has improved the system's energy efficiency and the instantaneity of multimedia transmissions in wireless system via adjustment of the times of the gated services along with input load change. The theoretical model of this scheme is established through Markov chain and probability generating function. Mathematical analysis is made on the mean queue length and the mean inquiry cyclic time of the common nodes and the key node. It turns out that the findings from theoretical analysis correspond well with those from simulated experiments.

Keywords: WSNs; priority-based polling system; load adaptation; mean queue length; mean cyclic time.

1 Introduction

With the rapid development of chip, communication and sensing technologies, sensing technology are entering a new era of wireless sensor network [1]. The tiny sensing nodes, which consist of sensing, data processing and wireless communication components in WSNs, are deployed densely and randomly in large numbers [2]. The tiny nodes form the netwok in a self-organization manner. Based on the diverse onboard sensors, the WSNs can sense the field and communicate the information to the remote sink in an efficient and timely manner. The sensing performance and reliability have been improved significantly in WSNs. So the WSNs can be widely used in military sensing, security, environmental monitoring, traffic surveillance, medical treatment, building and structures monitoring, even anti-terrorism, etc [3-4].

However, since the sensor nodes are battery driven and it is impractical to recharge the battery for so many nodes after deployment, energy efficiency has been a key concern in the research work of WSNs. In many WSNs applications, the data gathering has the Quality of Services (QoS) requirements in terms of BER performance, end-to-end timeliness and reliability,etc. Therefore, to design the scheme with low energy consumption and flexible QoS provisioning is the guarantee for the efficient information gathering in WSN [5]. According to the analysis of sensor nodes, the main sources

G. Shen and X. Huang (Eds.): CSIE 2011, Part I, CCIS 152, pp. 184–190, 2011.

of energy consumption are sensing, wireless transmission and data processing. And the energy consumption caused by wireless transmission is much more than sensing and data processing. On the other hand, since most technologies in WSNs, such as data routing, distributed information processing, have the requirements for the wireless transmission. Wireless transmission technologies have been identified as the key technologies determining the energy consumption and QoS, which are also the basis for other technologies [6]. Therefore, in this thesis, the author carried out a deep and systematic research work on the energy efficiency and QoS guaranteeing by establishing Cluster-based MAC Scheme in WSNs.

Based on queuing theory [7-8], this research established the two-class priority node gated polling system. The system is made up of one Cluster Head (CH), one key node h at the first level, and N common nodes at the second level. The higher-priority key node applies an exhaustive-service policy with less time delay, which fits for the highly real-time performances. Meanwhile, the lower-priority common nodes use the gated policy with two-times services, which is based on the dynamically adjustable input load, to facilitate non-real-time transmissions. When the network load increases, service quality can be maintained with the increase of service times, which also fulfills the requirements of the non-real-time performances for fairness and time delay. The first and the second nodes receive alternatively the polling connection service from CH.

2 The Theoretical Model of the Scheme

2.1 The Operational Mechanism and Variable Definition of the System Model

The system operates on the FCFS rule. There is enough capacity of the memory at each node so that information grouping will not get lost. Polling services at each node include the following processes:

1)   The CH polls at the common node of i ($i = 1, 2, \cdots, N$) at the time of t_n. The lower priority business information packets number of queuing waiting for transmission in the buffer at the i node is $\xi_i(n)$, when the high priority business information packets number of queuing waiting for transmission in the memory at the key node is $\xi_h(n)$. The CH provides transmission service for the i node where the information packets in its queue is completed at the time of t_{n1}. Then, if there is new information packets coming into the memory of the i node within the service time, the lower priority business information packets number of queuing waiting transmission in the memory at the i node is $\xi_i(n1)$, and the higher priority business information packets number of queuing waiting for transmission in the buffer at the key node is $\xi_h(n1)$. According to the service regulations, the server continues to work for the i node, completing information packets within its queue via gated service for the second time in the i node at the time of t_{n2}. The overall time of the CH's service of the i lower priority queue is $v_i(n)$, with the information packets number of $\eta_j(v_i)$ when entering the j node ($j = 1, 2, \cdots N, h$) at the time of $\eta_j(v_i)$.

2) After the two-times gated service and via the transformational time of $u_{i1}(n)$,the inquiry starts for the information packets queue waiting to be transmitted at the key node h , with the information packets number of $\mu_j(u_{i1})$ when entering the j node $(j=1,2,\cdots N,h)$ at the time of u_{i1} .

3) The key node h receives service at the time of $t_{\bar{n}}$, when the higher priority business information packets number of queuing waiting for transmission in the buffer at the key node is $\xi_{ih}(\bar{n})$. After the completion of information grouping transmission within the key node via exhaustive service policy, the time of the server's service of the higher priority queue at the key node h is $v_h(n)$, with the information packets number of $\eta_j(v_h)$ when entering the j node $(j=1,2,\cdots N,h)$ at the time of v_h .

4) After the service of the key queue, there is a transformational time of $u_{i2}(n)$. Transmission service comes to the $i+1$ common node at the time of t_{n+1} , with the information packets number of $\mu_j(u_{i2})$ when entering the j node $(j=1,2,\cdots N,h)$ at the time of u_{i2} . Likewise, the lower priority business information packets number of queuing waiting for transmission in the buffer at the i $(i=1,2,\cdots,N)$ node is $\xi_i(n+1)$ at the time of t_{n+1} .

2.2 The Operational Conditions for the System

According to the operational process of the system, the operational conditions are defined as follows:

1) The information packets entering each common node follow the independent and identical distribution of probability, with the distributional probability generating function and mean value respectively as $A(z)$ and $A'(1)=\lambda$, and with the probability generating function and mean value of the information packets arriving at the key node h respectively as $A_h(z)$ and $A_h'(1)=\lambda_h$;

2) The time used by an information packet in the buffer of the common node when the CH transmits services follows an independent and identical distribution of probability, with the distributional probability generating function and mean value respectively as $B(z)$ and $B'(1)=\beta$, and with the distributional probability generating function and mean value of the transmission service time at the key node h respectively as $B_h(z)$ and $\beta_h=B_h'(1)$;

3) The static variable of the inquiry transformation time when polling from the i common node to the key node h follows an independent and identical distribution of probability, with the distributional probability generating function and mean value respectively as $R_{i1}(z)$ and $R_{i1}'(1)=\gamma_{i1}$. The static variable of the inquiry transformation

time when polling from the $i + 1$ common node to the key node h follows an independent and identical distribution of probability, with the distributional probability generating function and mean value respectively as $R_{i2}(z)$ and $R'_{i2}(1) = \gamma_{i2}$;

4)   The static variable of the time for the exhaustive service of information grouping arriving at the key node at any time slot follows an independent and identical distribution of probability, with the distributional probability generating function as $F_c(z)$;

2.3 Probability Generating Function of the System Status Variable

The system status can be described with the Markov chain which is non-periodic and ergodic. According to the operating process of the system, the probability generating function of the system status variable is shown as follows:

At the time of t_{n2}, the probability generating function of system status is illustrated as:

$$G_{i2}(z_1, z_2, \cdots, z_N, z_h) = \lim_{t \to \infty} E\left[\prod_{i=1}^{N} z_i^{\xi_{n2}} z_h^{\xi_{n2}}\right]$$

$$= G_{i1}\left(z_1, z_2, \cdots, B_i\left(A_h(z_h)\prod_{j=1}^{N} A_j(z_j)\right), z_{i+1}, \cdots, z_N, z_h\right) \quad (1)$$

at the time of $t_{\bar{n}}$, the probability generating function of system status is illustrated as:

$$G_{ih}(z_1, z_2, \cdots, z_N, z_h) = \lim_{t \to \infty} E\left[\prod_{i=1}^{N} z_i^{\xi_i(\bar{n})} z_h^{\xi_h(\bar{n})}\right]$$

$$= R_{i1}\left(A_h(z_h)\prod_{j=1}^{N} A_j(z_j)\right) G_{i2}\left(z_1, z_2, \cdots, B_{i2}\left(A_h(z_h)\prod_{j=1}^{N} A_j(z_j)\right), z_{i+1}, \cdots, z_N, z_h\right) \quad (2)$$

at the time of t_{n+1}, the probability generating function of system status is illustrated as:

$$G_{(i+1)1}(z_1, z_2, \cdots, z_N, z_h) = \lim_{t \to \infty} E\left[\prod_{i=1}^{N} z_i^{\xi_i(n+1)} z_h^{\xi_h(n+1)}\right]$$

$$= R_{i2}\left(A_h(z_h)\prod_{j=1}^{N} A_j(z_j)\right) G_{ih}\left(z_1, z_2, \cdots, z_N, B_h\left(\prod_{j=1}^{N} A_j(z_j) F_c\left(\prod_{j=1}^{N} A_j(z_j)\right)\right)\right) \quad (3)$$

2.4 The Analysis of Mean Queue Length

According to the definition of queue length, the mean queue length of the common node is drawn via derived function algorithm as:

$$g_{j1}(j) = \lim_{z_1 \cdots z_N, z_h \to 1} \frac{\partial G_j(z_1, z_2, \cdots, z_N, z_h)}{\partial z_j} = \frac{\lambda_j \sum_{i=1}^{N}(\gamma_{i1} + \gamma_{i2})}{(1 + \rho_j)\left(1 - \rho_h - \sum_{i=1}^{N} \rho_i\right)} \quad (5)$$

and the mean queue length at the key node is:

$$g_{ih}(h) = \lim_{z_1 \cdots z_N, z_h \to 1} \frac{\partial G_h(z_1, z_2, \cdots, z_N, z_h)}{\partial z_h} = \lambda_h(\gamma_{i1} + \gamma_{i2}) + \frac{\lambda_h \rho_i \sum_{i=1}^{N}(\gamma_{i1} + \gamma_{i2})}{1 - \rho_h - \sum_{i=1}^{N} \rho_i} \quad (6)$$

2.5 The Analysis of the Mean Inquiry Cycle

Based on the operational mechanism of the system and the theory of queuing, the mean inquiry cycle can be derived as:

$$E[\theta_i] = \frac{\sum_{j=1}^{N}(\gamma_{j1} + \gamma_{j2})}{1 - \rho_h - \sum_{j=1}^{N} \rho_j} \quad (7)$$

3 Theoretical Calculation, Simulated Experiment and Analysis

Both theoretical and simulated models are set in identical symmetrical conditions under which each node's information packets arrival follows the Poisson distribution with λ as the parameter, and all the node parameters follow the distribution of identical laws. The time slot width is taken as $10 \, \mu s$. With $N = 5$, $\beta_h = \beta_i = 10$, $\lambda_h = \lambda_i = \lambda$, $\gamma_{i1} = \gamma_{i2} = 2$, the system meets the stable condition of $\sum_{i=1}^{N} \rho_i + \rho_h < 1$ in which M stands for the number of service times of the controlled gated service at common nodes. The data in the following charts show that the theoretical value of the system model in this research correspond well with that of the experiment and it can represent the first order feature of the system.

1)   From the system stability condition of $\sum_{i=1}^{N} \rho_i + \rho_h < 1$, $0 < \rho_i < 1$ is inferred, signifying that when the gated service at common nodes becomes frequent, the mean queue length diminishes and gated policy service or that with two-times services exert influences on the mean queue length at the common nodes. The change of the mean queue length along with the arrival rate of information packets is illustrated in Fig.1. In case of the change with loading, stability and fairness as well as adaptability and flexibility of the system can be maintained via dynamic adjustment of gated policy service at common nodes.

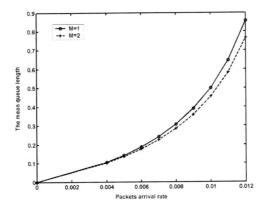

Fig. 1. The mean queue length at the common nodes

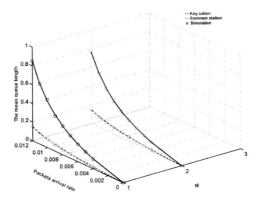

Fig. 2. A contrast between the mean queue length of key node and that of the common nodes

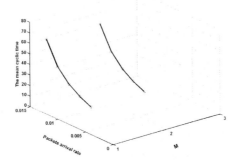

Fig. 3. The mean cyclic time of the system

2)   The results from the calculations via Formulae (6) and (7) and the simulated experiments (Fig.2 and 3) all reveal that in the models of the two-class priority node gated polling system, the change in the times of service M will not influence the mean queue length of key node and the system's mean cyclic time of the model.

3)   Fig. 2 shows that the mean queue length of key node and that of the common nodes are clearly differentiated. Even when the arrival rate is high, the mean queue length of key node is smaller than that of the common nodes. Meanwhile, when the gated policy service at the common nodes increases, it still maintains a smaller value. The priority of the key node is thus preserved.

4   Conclusion

In this paper, a research work on MAC scheme for multimedia support in WSNs has been done with focus on energy efficiency and QoS guaranteeing. This efficient scheme embodies the advantages of exhaustive and two-times gated policy service, and it classifies the system nodes by priority at two levels, based on which the dynamic adjustment of the comprehensive function of the system is made possible via the change of access connection so as to achieve the dynamic priority service along with the change in network loading and to enhance the fairness and flexibility of the service system. It concludes that this scheme enables WSNs to take on the features of good utility, good function.

Acknowledgments. The authors would like to give their sincere thanks to the financial support by the Nation Natural Science Foundation of China (No.61072079).

References

1. Demirkol, I., Ersoy, C., Alagoz, F.: MAC protocols for wireless sensor networks: a survey. IEEE Communications 44, 115–121 (2006)
2. Akyildz, I.F., Melodia, T., Chowdhury, K.R.: A survey on wireless multimedia sensor networks. The International Journal of Computer and Telecommunications Networking 51, 921–960 (2007)
3. Xiaohui, L., Kwok, Y., Hui, W.: Cross-layer design for energy efficient communication in wireless sensor networks. Wireless Communications and Mobile Computing 9, 251–268 (2009)
4. Gilbert, J.M., Balouchi, F.: Comparison of energy harvesting systems for Wireless Sensor Networks. International Journal of Automation and Computing 5, 334–347 (2008)
5. Shwe, H.Y., Jiang, X., Horiguchi, S.: Energy saving in wireless sensor networks. Journal of Communication and Computer 6, 20–27 (2009)
6. Rubin, I., De Moraes, L.F.: Message Delay Analysis for Polling and Token Multiple-Access Schemes for Local Communication Networks. IEEE J. Select. Areas Commun., 935–947 (1983)
7. Takagi, H.: Analysis of Polling Systems. The MIT Press, Cambridge (1986)
8. Zhao, D., Zheng, S.: Message Waiting Time Analysis for a Polling System with Gated Service. Journal of China Institute of Communications 15, 18–23 (1994)

Research on Knowledge Transfer in Software Engineering by Concept Lattice Isomorphic

ShengWei Li[1], DaoJun Han[1,2], PeiYan Jia[1], and XiaJiong Shen[1,2]

[1] School of Computer and Information Engineering, Henan University
KaiFeng, 475004, China
[2] Institute of Data and Knowledge Engineering, Henan University,
KaiFeng, 475004, China
{lisw,hdj,jpy,shenxj}@henu.edu.cn

Abstract. Concept lattice has many applications, e.g., software engineering, knowledge discovery. And isomorphic judgment of concept lattice is important in various fields, for instance, ontology similarity measure. In this paper, we apply the isomorphic judgment algorithm of concept lattice in software engineering to transfer knowledge in different domains after analyzed the foundation of transfer learning. Followed, an example of transfer knowledge in software engineering was introduced, and it shows the efficiency of our method.

Keywords: Concept Lattice; Isomorphism; Knowledge Transfer; Software Engineering.

1 Introduction

In recent years, transfer learning has emerged as a new learning framework to address the problem that how to transfer knowledge [1]. Concept lattice, the core data structure of formal concept analysis theory, has many applications, such as software engineering [2-3], knowledge engineering, data mining, etc [4-6]. In software engineering, a bulk of activities can be analyzed by concept lattice model [7], e.g., class-hierarchy design, reverse engineering, and requirement validation [8-9]. Concept lattice can also represent complex objects, especially in ontology representation and concept structure. Obviously, complex object and their relation are representation styles of a kind of knowledge, i.e. they are included in the extension of knowledge. Therefore, concept lattice is a kind of knowledge and can be transferred by isomorphic judging because isomorphism represents the similarity of structure in two objects, and the objects are refer to graph, lattice, table etc..

The isomorphism of concept lattice and the isomorphism of graph are similar, and researchers have developed many algorithms to solve the problem of graph isomorphism. e.g., classic approaches [10-11], genetic-based algorithms [12], neural network approaches [13], and DNA computing model [14], etc.. Meanwhile, The isomorphism of concept lattice is important and worthwhile to be further explored since there are many applications, such as scaling the similarity of complex examples in machine

G. Shen and X. Huang (Eds.): CSIE 2011, Part I, CCIS 152, pp. 191–197, 2011.

learning, generating structure mapping from source domain and target domain in transfer learning; Y. Zhao et al.[15] give an approach to measuring the similarity of ontologies by rough concept lattice. In [16], Han et al. build an algorithm to judge the isomorphism between two concept lattices.

In software engineering domain, there is much knowledge of old software systems could be reused or transferred to new systems to reduce the cost. Then, we could transfer the existing knowledge from source domain which we have mastered to target domain which we haven't grasped and need to use. During developing systems, a critical process is to design the table structure and their relations in database. In this paper, we use the isomorphic judgment algorithm to compare two given concept lattices generated from respective context that extracted from two ER graphs of different domains, and make a mapping between two concept lattice's nodes. Followed, we transferred some hiding knowledge from source domain to target domain.

The rest of this paper is organized as follows. Background knowledge will be introduced in Section 2. Then we describe the details of applying isomorphic judgment algorithm to transfer knowledge in two different domains. Finally, we draw a conclusion in Section 4.

2 Preliminary and Background

To introduce the knowledge transfer in software engineering, we give some basic background knowledge in this section, that is, concept lattice[8] and isomorphic judgment algorithm of concept lattices.

2.1 Concept Lattice

A formal context is a triple sets $K:=(G, M, I)$, where G is called a set of objects, M is called a set of attributes, I is a relation between G and M, also, $I \subseteq G \times M$. For $A \subseteq G$ and $B \subseteq M$, we can definite a ' operator, representation as: $A' = \{m \in M \mid \forall g \in A (gIm)\}$, $B' = \{g \in G \mid \forall m \in B (gIm)\}$, where ' is a closure operator, i.e., it is monotone, extensive, and idempotent. A formal concept of a formal context K is a pair (A, B), where $A \subseteq G, B \subseteq M$. And it has two limited conditions, that is $A' = B$ and $B' = A$. The set A is called the extension and B is called the intension of the concept (A, B). According to concept set and partial order set, we could easily give its hasse graph.

2.2 Isomorphic Judgment Algorithm of Concept Lattice

The framework of isomorphic judgment algorithm described as follows. Let L_s and L_t be two concept lattices, and L_s and L_t are source and target concept lattices respectively.

1. Computing the layer number of nodes by an equation for L_s and L_t.
2. Getting the *indegree*, *outdegree*, type of nodes for L_s and L_t.
3. Create equivalence classes for the nodes L_s and L_t.

4. Generate the sub-lattice of type b nodes as heuristic information for L_s and L_t.

5. For every equivalence class E_{si} of every layer of L_s, call the equivalence class algorithm ECA. If equivalence class algorithm for E_{si} is successful, then select next equivalence class, and repeat this whole procedure until total equivalence classes been processed. Else, return false.

The algorithm ECA is clear explained in [16]. Meanwhile, the paper [16] has introduced the experimental results and analysis process.

3 Applying Isomorphic Judgment Algorithm of Concept Lattice to Knowledge Transfer in Software Engineering

3.1 Introduction of Knowledge Transfer in Software Engineering

Software developers will encounter some different domains when dealing with their work. Despite the different domain knowledge (terms, concepts) and business process, there is some knowledge still could be reused to reduce the cost due to its similarity to some fields. Nowadays, the process of reusing was determined by the developers themselves, which was trivial and time-consuming.

Some documents, like word, table, and graph will be saved while generating the software, and which contain the requirements and design information. Obviously, database is a necessary component for most software systems. The traditional method to design the structure of tables and their relations is using the ER graph of respective domain requirement; the cost is high because it is depending on the ability of the developers. Then we could get the database design information by concept lattice isomorphic judging to transfer knowledge, so it could reduce the cost. The process of knowledge transfer describe as follow steps.

Step 1: Select two ER graphs of different domains d_1, d_2, denote as E_1, E_2 correspondingly.

Step 2: Convert E_1, E_2 to contexts respectively, denote as C_{E1}, C_{E2}.

Step 3: Apply concept lattice generating algorithm to get $CS(C_{E1})$, $CS(C_{E2})$.

Step 4: Use isomorphic judgment algorithm of concept lattice to operate $CS(C_{E1})$ and $CS(C_{E2})$.

Step 5: Transfer knowledge between d_1 and d_2 domains.

Note: In step 5, if there is no knowledge to transfer between two domains, then return null.

3.2 Case Analysis

To show the process of knowledge transfer by isomorphic judgment algorithm of concept lattice, we select an experiment case which extracted from software developing to analyze. For simplicity, the common MIS, student manage system and enterprise information manage system are selected as example to explain the applying process of isomorphic judgment algorithm of concept lattice. Fig. 1 shows the part of ER graph of student manage system.

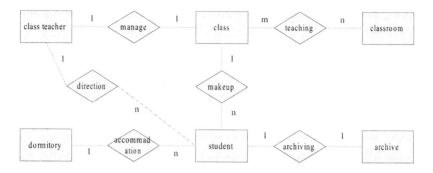

Fig. 1. The part of ER graph of student manage system

The corresponding table structure as follows.

(1) student:{student ID, name, sex, birth date, class ID, dormitory ID, archive ID, class teacher ID, ...}

(2) class teacher: {teacher ID, name, sex, excellent class teacher, professional qualification, course ID, ...}

(3) classroom: {classroom ID, address, capacity, ...}

(4) class: {class ID, student count, class teacher ID,......}

(5) dormitory: {dormitory ID,address,capacity,......}

(6) archive: {archive ID, type, ...}

(7) class classroom: {class ID, classroom ID,......}

We could obtain the part of ER graph in enterprise manage information system, illustrated by Fig. 2.

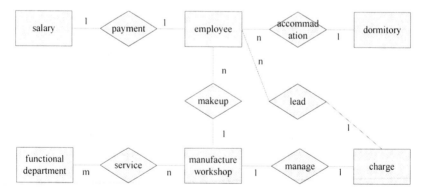

Fig. 2. The part of ER graph in enterprise manage information system

The common graph isomorphic judgment algorithm can't fit into isomorphic judging of ER graph. In this paper, we transform the ER graph into formal context, then construct the concept lattice and transfer the hiding knowledge after judging the isomorphic relation of two concept lattices.

ER graph represent the entities and their relations, we could regard entities as objects, and regard relations of entities as attributes, describing the Fig.1 as table 1.

Table 1. A relation table extracted from ER graph

| | 1 : 1 | | 1 : n | | | m : n |
	archiving	manage	accommodation	direction	makeup	teaching
dormitory			√			
student	√		√	√	√	
archive	√					
class teacher		√		√		
class		√			√	√
classroom						√

The three types of relations, 1:1, 1:n, and m:n have different meanings, therefore, we could extract the context from Table 1 by means of classify the types of relations. The context is described by Table 2.

Table 2. A context generated by Table 2

	archiving(a)	manage(b)	accommodation(c)	direction(d)	makeup(e)	makeup_n(f)	accommodation_n(g)(h)	teaching_n(h)	direction_n(i)
dormitory(1)			√						
student(2)	√					√	√		√
archive(3)	√								
class teacher(4)		√		√					
class(5)		√			√			√	
classroom(6)								√	

Similarly, we could get the context of Fig.2, described as Table 3.

Table 3. A Context that describing the enterprise manage information system

	serve_n(manA)	manage(B)	makeup(C)	Lead(D)	payment(E)	makeup_r(F)	accommodation_n(G)	lead_n(H)	accommodation(I)
functional department(1)	√								
manufacture workshop(2)	√	√	√						
charge(3)		√		√					
salary(4)					√				
employee(5)					√	√	√	√	
dormitory(6)									√

Selecting the Table 2, 3 as input, applying the concept generating algorithm, we could get two concept lattices described as Fig.3, Fig.4.

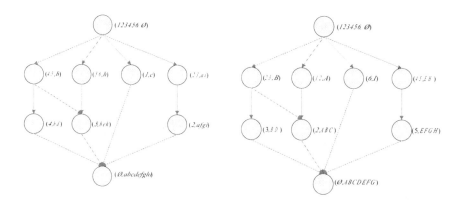

Fig. 3. Concept lattice generated by Table 4   **Fig. 4.** Concept lattice generated by Table 5

Using isomorphic judgment algorithm, we could get the result easily, and giving the mapping of nodes. So the knowledge of source domain, such as the table structure and the completely constrain of data are transferred to the knowledge of target domain and reduced the cost of develop and design. Here, knowledge can be transferred as:

(1) The structure of key table transferring, we should aim at the data column of source table.

- student • employee;
- class • manufacture workshop.

(2) The structure of added table transferring.

- class classroom • manufacture function workshop.

(3) The foreign key constraint of respective table.

Note: Side-effect of knowledge transferring is omitted. According to the definition of education-psychology [17], knowledge transferring is one study affects other studies. In this paper, we don't make a discussion on the effects of knowledge transferring because knowledge transferred using our algorithm, and whether or not of which is sufficient is determined by the users themselves.

4   Conclusion and Future Work

At first, we introduce a novel algorithm to judge isomorphism of two concept lattices; followed, our algorithm is used in software engineering to transfer the respective knowledge between two different domains. During the periods of software developing, there is much knowledge can be reused. We choose the necessary knowledge that database design to transfer knowledge by isomorphic judging, and the usefulness has been improved. In the future, we can utilize the isomorphic judgment algorithm to resolve the similarity measurement of two knowledge systems.

Acknowledgments. This work is supported by Natural Science Foundation of The Education Department of Henan Province, China under Grant No. 2009A520004.

References

1. Pan, S.J., Yang, Q.: A Survey on Transfer Learning. IEEE Transactions on Knowledge and Data Engineering 22(10), 1345–1359 (2010)
2. Hesse, W., Tilley, T.: Formal Concept Analysis Used for Software Analysis and Modelling. In: Ganter, B., Stumme, G., Wille, R. (eds.) Formal Concept Analysis. LNCS (LNAI), vol. 3626, pp. 288–303. Springer, Heidelberg (2005)
3. Xu, J.-q., Peng, X., Zhao, W.-y.: An Evolution Analysis Method Based on Fuzzy Concept Lattice and Source Code Analysis. Chinese Journal Of Computers 32(9), 1832–1844 (2009)
4. Li, L.-f., Zhang, D.-x.: The Application of Concept Lattice Theory in the Reduction of the Proposition Set in Two-Valued Propositional Logic. Acta Electronica Sinica 35(8), 1538–1542 (2007)
5. Valtchev, P., Missaoui, R., Godin, R.: Formal Concept Analysis for Knowledge Discovery and Data Mining: The New Challenges. In: Eklund, P. (ed.) ICFCA 2004. LNCS (LNAI), vol. 2961, pp. 352–371. Springer, Heidelberg (2004)
6. du Patrick, B.-R., Bridge, D.: Collaborative Recommending using Formal Concept Analysis. Knowledge-Based Systems 19(5), 309–315 (2006)
7. Tilley, T., Cole, R., Becker, P., Eklund, P.: A Survey of Formal Concept Analysis Support for software engineering activities. In: Proceedings of the First International Conference on Formal Concept Analysis - ICFCA 2003. Springer, Heidelberg (2003)
8. Ganter, B., Wille, R.: Formal Concept Analysis. Mathematical Foundations. Springer, Heidelberg (1999)
9. Ng, P.: A Concept Lattice Approach for Requirements Validation with UML State Machine Model. In: Fifth International Conference on Software Engineering Research, Management and Applications, pp. 393–400 (2007)
10. Li, F., Li, X.: Isomorphism Testing Algorithm for Graphs: Incidence Degree Sequence Method and Applications. Journal of Fudan University (Natural Science) 40(3), 318–325 (2001)
11. Zou, X.-x., Dai, Q.: A Vertex Refinement Method for Graph Isomorphism. Journal of Software (02), 213–219 (2007)
12. Wang, Y.K., Fan, K.C., Horng, J.T.: Genetic-Based Search for Error-Correcting Graph Isomorphism. IEEE Trans. Systems, Man, and Cybernetics 27(5), 588–597 (1997)
13. Nan, J.-H., Qi, H.: The decision-making neural networks model for solving the graph isomorphism problem. Chinese Journal of Computers 33(2), 300–304 (2010)
14. Liu, G.W., Yin, Z.X., Xu, J.: Algorithm of graph isomorphism with three dimensional DNA graph structures. Progress in Natural Science 15(2), 181–184 (2005)
15. Zhao, Y., Halang, W.A.: Rough concept lattice based ontology similarity measure. In: Proceedings of the First International Conference on Scalable Information Systems, Hong Kong (2006)
16. Han, D.-J., Li, L., Shen, X.-J.: Research on the Algorithm of Concept Lattice Isomorphic Judgment Based on Mapping of Equivalence Class. In: 2009 International Conference on Information Engineering and Computer Science, China, pp. 975–978 (December 2009)

Simulation Based Energy Potential Evaluation of Air Conditioners

Jian Yao and Chengwen Yan

Faculty of Architectural, Civil Engineering and Environment,
Ningbo University, Ningbo, China
yaojian@nbu.edu.cn

Abstract. The objective of this paper is to investigate the energy saving potentials of increasing the EER of air conditioners. A representative residential
building was modelled for building energy simulation with different EERs. The
results show that EER increase has a energy saving potential range of 4%-44%
depending on the EER ratings, and the heating energy savings is higher than the
total and cooling ones. A commonly availabe air conditioner with a 3.16 EER
may achieve a total energy savings of about 25%.

Keywords: Energy savings; Air conditioners; Energy Efficiency Ratio;
Simulation.

1 Introduction

In China, the building sector accounts for about 46.7% of the total energy consumption [1]. Improving the energy performance of building envelope is always be
considered firstly in building designs. For example, the adoption of wall [2] and roof
insulating materials [3], energy efficient windows [4] and shading devices [5] etc. In
addition to the performance improvement of building envelope, the energy performance of air conditioners greatly influence building energy efficiency [6]. The efficiency of air conditioners is often rated by the Energy Efficiency Ratio (EER) [7],
which is a measure of an air conditioner's efficiency and energy consumption. Commonly the higher the rating, the more efficient the unit and the less power consumed.
In China's design standard for building energy efficiency in hot summer and cold winter zone, it sets a 50% energy saving target for buildings compared with those built in
1980s, with 25% savings from energy efficiency measures on building envelope and
the other 25% from Energy Efficiency Ratio enhancement of air conditioners. Therefore increasing air conditioners' EER should be considered as a very significant measure in building designs. This standard requires the EER of an air conditioner adopted
should no less than 2.3 for cooling and 1.9 for heating. As the lack of research on the
EER improvement on building energy consumption in hot summer and cold winter
zone, this paper conducted a survey on the EER of currently used air conditioners,
evaluated the energy saving potentials based on simulations and gave suggestions on
air conditioner selection for building owners.

G. Shen and X. Huang (Eds.): CSIE 2011, Part I, CCIS 152, pp. 198–201, 2011.
© Springer-Verlag Berlin Heidelberg 2011

2   Methodology

2.1   The Base Residential Building

A representative six-floor and three-unit building in Ningbo city with the total area of 3544.56m^2 was modelled in building simulation software DeST-h. The height of each floor is 2.8m as well as the area of each household is 100m^2. The thermal design for the building envelope of this model is set to comply with the standard "hot summer and cold winter region residential building energy efficiency design standards". The air conditioners for the base residential building model are configured as continues system single zone heat pump, whose EER is 2.3 when cooling, and 1.9 when heating. Fig. 1 shows the base residential building.

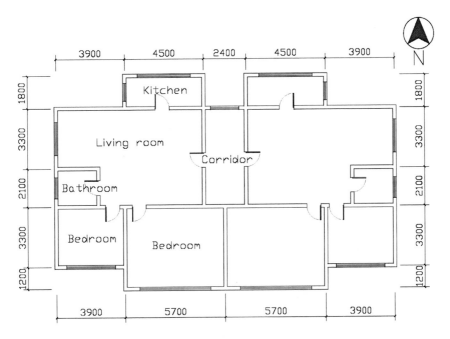

Fig. 1. One unit of the base residential building

2.2   EER Variation

According to our survey, a total of 294 air conditioners which belong to 18 different kinds were selected for comparison. The results are shown in table 1, in which the type represents the name of air conditioners with letters, the number means how many air conditioners were considered in this survey, and the EER for cooling and heating means the average results of each type. It can be seen that the EER is mainly between 2.8-3.8 with an average of 3.16 for cooling and 3.32 for heating, thus we consider that the increase of EER for air conditioners from 0.1-1.5 with a 0.1 interval.

Table 1. The EER for different air conditioners

Type	Number	EER for cooling	EER for heating
GLS	13	2.89	3.37
DJ	15	4.76	3.27
KL	17	2.97	3.09
CL	6	3.12	3.11
CH	14	2.93	3.12
HE	25	3.01	3.28
SX	17	3.06	3.72
RL	10	2.97	3.44
SX	20	2.91	3.1
SY	2	3.9	4.11
HEP	4	2.8	3.01
GL	36	3	3.33
MD	13	3	3.4
SL	9	3.6	3.64
HX	32	2.93	2.84
ZG	21	2.96	3.24
AKS	36	2.88	3.13
SLZG	4	3.16	3.6
Total/ Average	294	3.16	3.32

3 Results and Discussion

The energy saving performance as a function of EER increase was shown in Fig. 2. It shows that EER increase has a energy saving potential of 4%-44% depending on the EER ratings and it a bigger energy savings on heating than on cooling or total energy consumption. The cooling energy saving potential is relatively small compared to the total one. In addition, they all have an almost linearly relationship with the increase of EER and the biggest saving potentials are about 45%, 42% and 38%, respectively, for heating, total and cooling energy compared with the base residential building. If a person select an air conditioner with a 3.16 EER as mentioned above, he may achieve a total energy savings of about 25%. Therefore building owners should undoubtedly buy a air conditioner with higher EER if he wants a bigger energy savings.

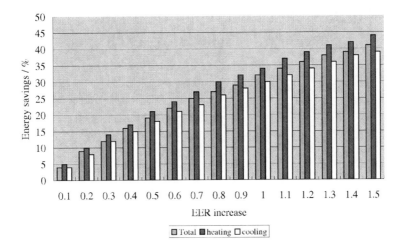

Fig. 2. Energy savings as a function of EER increase

4 Conclusions

In this paper the energy saving potentials of increasing the EER of air conditioners were simulated on a representative residential building. The results show that EER increase has a energy saving potential range of 4%-44% depending on the EER ratings, and the heating energy savings is higher than total ones for different EER increases and the cooling ones is least compared with the other two. A commonly availabe air conditioner with a 3.16 EER may achieve a total energy savings of about 25%.

References

1. Li, Z.Y., Zhang, C.: Prediction and Analysis of the Energy Saving Tendency in China's Building. Economist. 3, 20–22 (2010)
2. Zhou, Y., Ding, Y., Yao, J.: Preferable Rebuilding Energy Efficiency Measures of Existing Residential Building in Ningbo. Journal of Ningbo University (Natural science & engineering edition) 22, 285–287 (2009)
3. Niachou, A., Papakonstantinou, K., Santamouris, M., Tsangrassoulis, A., Mihalakakou, G.: Analysis of the green roof thermal properties and investigation of its energy performance. Energy and Buildings 33, 719–729 (2001)
4. Lee, E.S., Tavil, A.: Energy and visual comfort performance of electrochromic windows with overhangs. Build. Environ. 42, 2439–2449 (2007)
5. Yao, J., Xu, J.: Effects of different shading devices on building energy saving in hot summer and cold winter zone. In: 2010 International Conference on Mechanic Automation and Control Engineering, MACE 2010, Wuhan, China, pp. 5017–5020 (2010)
6. Yao, Yuan, Z.: Study on Residential Buildings with Energy Saving by 65% in Ningbo. Journal of Ningbo University (Natural science & engineering edition) 23, 84–87 (2010)
7. ANSI/AHRI 210/240-2008: 2008 Standard for Performance Rating of Unitary Air-Conditioning & Air-Source Heat Pump Equipment. Air Conditioning, Heating and Refrigeration Institute (2008)

Population-Based Learning Algorithm to Solving Permutation Scheduling Problems

Caichang Ding, Wenxiu Peng, Lu Lu, and Yuanchao Liu

School of Computer Science, Yangtze University,
Jingzhou, Hubei Province, China
hamigua_ping@hotmail.com

Abstract. Population-based methods are optimization techniques inspired by natural evolution processes. They handle a population of individuals that evolves with the help of information exchange procedures. Each individual may also evolve independently. Periods of cooperation alternatewith periods of self-adaptation. Population-based Learning Algorithm (PBLA), is another population-based method, which can be applied to solve combinatorial optimization problems. PBLA has been inspired by analogies to a social phenomenon rather than to evolutionary processes.Whereas evolutionary algorithms emulate basic features of natural evolution including natural selection, hereditary variations, the survival of the fittest, and production of far more offspring than are necessary to replace current generation.

Keywords: optimization techniques, self-adaptation, information exchange, social phenomenon.

1 Introduction

Among best-known population-based method are evolutionary algorithms. These can be perceived as a generalization of genetic algorithms, which operate on fixed-length binary strings. Evolutionary algorithms are stochastic search methods that mimic the metaphor of natural biological evolution. Evolutionary algorithms operate on a population of potential solutions applying the principle of survival of the fittest to produce better and better approximations to a solution.

Evolutionary algorithms model natural processes, such as selection, recombination, mutation, migration, locality, and neighborhood. Evolutionary algorithms work on populations of individuals instead of single solutions. At the beginning of the computation, a number of individuals are randomly initialized. The objective function is then evaluated for these individuals. The initial generation is produced. If the optimization criteria are not met the creation of a new generation starts. Individuals are selected according to their fitness for the production of offspring. Parents are recombined to produce offspring. All offspring will be mutated with a certain probability. The fitness of the offspring is then computed. The offspring are inserted into the population replacing the parents, producing a new generation. This cycle is performed until the optimization criteria are reached.

G. Shen and X. Huang (Eds.): CSIE 2011, Part I, CCIS 152, pp. 202–207, 2011.

Such a single population evolutionary algorithm is powerful and performs well on a broad class of problems. However, better results can be obtained by introducing many populations, called islands. Every island evolves for a number of generations isolated before one or more individuals are exchanged between the islands. The island-based evolutionary algorithm models the evolution of a species in a way more similar to nature than the single population evolutionary algorithm.

Development and proliferation of evolutionary algorithms have been initiated by and advanced in seminal works of Holland[1], Goldberg[2]. Despite the fact that evolutionary algorithms, in general, lack a strong theoretical background, the application results were more than encouraging. This success has led to emergence of numerous techniques, algorithms, and their respective clones that are now considered as belonging to the population-based class[3], and which differ in some respects from "classic" evolutionary algorithms.

2   Population-Based Learning Algorithm

Population-based Learning Algorithm (PBLA), is another population-based method, which can be applied to solve combinatorial optimization problems. PBLA has been inspired by analogies to a social phenomenon rather than to evolutionary processes.Whereas evolutionary algorithms emulate basic features of natural evolution including natural selection, hereditary variations, the survival of the fittest, and production of far more offspring than are necessary to replace current generation, PBLA takes advantage of features that are common to social education systems:

1)   A generation of individuals enters the system.
2)   Individuals learn through organized tuition, interaction, self-study, and self-improvement.
3)   Learning process is divided into stages.
4)   At higher stages, more advanced education techniques are used.
5)   The final stage can be reached by only a fraction of the initial population.

In PBLA, an individual represents a coded solution of the considered problem. Initially, a number of individuals, known as the initial population is randomly generated. Once the initial population has been generated, individuals enter the first learning stage. It involves applying some, possibly basic and elementary, improvement schemes. These can be based, for example, on some simple local search procedures. The improved individuals are then evaluated and better ones pass to a subsequent stage. A strategy of selecting better or more promising individuals must be defined and duly applied. In the following stages the whole cycle is repeated. Individuals are subject to improvement and learning, either individually or through information exchange, and the selected ones are again promoted to a higher stage with the remaining ones dropped-out from the process. At the final stage, the remaining individuals are reviewed and the best represents a solution to the problem at hand.

For a parallel PBLA the following features need to be defined:

1) A set of rules controlling how individuals are grouped into concurrent populations at various stages.
2) The respective rules for running learning and improvement algorithms in parallel at various stages.
3) Rules for information exchange and coordination between concurrent processes.

3 Designing Principles

Designing population learning algorithm intended for solving a particular problem type allows the designer a lot of freedom. Moreover, an effective PBLA would certainly require a lot of fine-tuning and experimenting. This could be considered as a disadvantage, at least as long as the process of setting different parameters of the population learning algorithm is rather based on heuristics instead of some theoretical or statistical rules, which, unfortunately, are not yet appropriately developed. Although PBLA shares many features with other population-based approaches, it clearly has its own distinctive characteristics.

In the following section a example implementation of the PBLA applied to solving a computationally difficult problem is discussed. The PBLA is seen here as a general framework for constructing hybrid solutions to difficult computational problems. From such a perspective the PBLA role is to structure, organize, sequence, and eventually help to apply in a parallel environment variety of techniques. Strength of the PBLA stems from combining in an "intelligent" manner the power of population-based algorithms using some random mechanism for diversity assurance, with efficiency of various local search algorithms. The later may include, for example, reactive search, tabu search, simulated annealing as well as the described earlier population based approaches.

Computational intelligence embedded into the population learning algorithm scheme is based on using the following heuristic rules:

1) To solve difficult computational problems apply a cocktail of methods and techniques including random and local search techniques, greedy and construction algorithms, etc., building upon their strengths and masking weaknesses.
2) To escape getting trapped into a local optimum[4][5] generate or construct an initial population of solutions called individuals, which in the following stages will be improved, thus increasing chances for reaching a global optimum.
3) Another means of avoiding getting trapped into local optima is to apply at various stages of search for a global optimum some random diversification algorithms.
4) To increase effectiveness of searching for a global optimum divide the process into stages retaining after each stage only a part of the population consisting of "better" or"more promising" individuals.

5)   Another means of increasing effectiveness is to use at early stages of search, improvement algorithms with lower computational complexity as compared to those used at final stages.

4   Application of the PBLA to Solving Permutation Scheduling Problems

This section contains a review of example PBLA implementation applied to solving combinatorial optimization problems[6][7]. Permutation scheduling problems are defined as scheduling problems where the solution is a permutation of tasks or jobs to be processed on one or more machines (processors). In the review, four permutation scheduling problems are considered, such as common due date, permutation flow shop, a single machine weighted tardiness, and multiprocessor task scheduling in multistage hybrid flowshops.

In a common due date problem there is a set of n non-preemptable tasks available at time zero. Tasks are to be processed on a single machine. Processing times of the tasks p_i, $i = 1, \ldots, n$ are known. There is also a common due date d. Earliness and tardiness of tasks are defined as $E_i = \max\{d - C_i, 0\}$ and $T_i = \max(C_i - d, 0)$, respectively ($i = 1, \ldots, n$) where C_i is the completion time of job i. Penalties per time unit of the task i being early or tardy are ai and bi, respectively. The objective is to minimize the sum of earliness and tardiness penalties:

$$\sum_i a_i E_i + \sum_i b_i T_i \to \min, i = 1, \ldots, n \tag{1}$$

It should be also noted that the due date is called unrestrictive if the optimal sequence of tasks can be constructed without considering the value of the due date. Otherwise the common due date is called restrictive. Obviously a common due date for which $d \geq \sum_i p_i$ holds is unrestrictive.

In a permutation flow shop there is a set of n jobs. Each of n jobs has to be processed on m machines $1, \ldots, m$ in this order. The processing time of job i on machine j is p_{ij}, where p_{ij} is fixed and nonnegative. At any time, each job can be processed on at most one machine, and each machine can process at most one job. The jobs are available at time 0 and the processing of a job may not be interrupted. In permutation flow shop problem (PFSP) the job order is the same on every machine. The objective is to find a job sequence minimizing schedule makespan (i.e., completion time of the last job).

In a single machine weighted tardiness problem there is a set of n jobs. Each of n jobs (numbered $1, \ldots, n$) is to be processed without interruption on a single machine that can handle no more than one job at a time. Job j ($j = 1, \ldots, n$) becomes available for processing at time zero, requires an uninterrupted positive processing time

p_j on the machine, has a positive weight w_j, and has a due date d_j by which it should ideally be finished. For a given processing order of the jobs, the earliest completion time C_j and the tardiness $T_j = \max(C_j - d_j, 0)$ of job j ($j = 1, \ldots, n$) can readily be computed. The problem is to find a processing order of the jobs with minimum total weighted tardiness $\sum_j w_j T_j$.

Finally, a multiprocessor task scheduling [8] in multi-stage hybrid flow shops is considered. The discussed problem involves scheduling of n jobs composed of tasks in a hybrid flow shop with m stages. All jobs have the same processing order through the machines, that is, a job is composed of an ordered list of multiprocessor tasks where the i-th task of each job is processed at the i-th flow shop stage (the number of tasks within a job corresponds exactly to the number of flow shop stages). Processing order of tasks flowing through stages is the same for all jobs. At each stage i, $i = 1, \ldots, m$, there are available m_i identical parallel processors. For the processing at stage i, task i being a part of the job j, $j = 1, \ldots, n$, requires $size_{i,j}$ processors simultaneously. That is, $size_{i,j}$ processors assigned to task i at stage i start processing the task simultaneously and continue doing so for a period of time equal to the processing time requirement of this task, denoted $p_{i,j}$. Each subset of available processors can process only the task assigned to them at a time. The processors do not break down. All jobs are ready at the beginning of the scheduling period. Preemption of tasks is not allowed. The objective is to minimize makespan, that is the completion of the lastly scheduled task in the last stage.

5   The Limitations of Population-Based Learning Algorithm

The Population-based approach provides a rich source of inspiration and its principles are directly applicable to computer systems. However, although it emphasizes auto-configuration, auto-organization, and adaptability capabilities, the population-based type remains useful for non-time-critical applications involving numerous repetitions of the same activity over a relatively large area, such as finding the shortest path or collecting rock samples onMars. Indeed, the approach deals with the cooperation of large numbers of homogeneous agents. Such approache usually relys on mathematical convergence results that reach the desired outcome over a sufficiently long period of time [9]. Notice that, in addition, the agents involved are homogeneous.

6   Conclusion

The proposed and provisionally validated simple, PBLA heuristic instance reduction algorithms, can be used to increase efficiency of the supervised learning. Computational experiment results support the claim that reducing training set size still preserves basic features of the analyzed data and can be even beneficial to a classifier accuracy. The approach extends a range of available instance reduction algorithms. Moreover, it is shown that the proposed algorithm can be, for some problems, competitive in comparison with the existing techniques. Possible extension of the approach could focus on establishing decision rules for finding a representation level suitable for each cluster thus allowing a variable representation level for different clusters.

References

1. Holland: Adaptation in Natural and Artificial Systems. The University of Michigan Press, Ann Arbor (1975)
2. Goldberg: Genetic Algorithms in Search, Optimization, and Machine Learning. Addison-Wesley, Reading (1989)
3. White, T.: Swarm intelligence and problem solving in telecommunications. Canadian Artificial Intelligence Magazine (1997)
4. Merz, P., Freisleben, B.: A Genetic Local Search Approach to the Quadratic Assignment Problem. In: Proc. of the 7th Int. Conf. on GA (ICGA 1997), pp. 465–472. Morgan Kaufmann, San Francisco (1997)
5. Aarts, P.E., Lenstra, J.K.: Local Search in Combinatorial Optimization. John Wiley & Sons, Chichester (1997)
6. Wu, C.S., Li, D.C., Tsai, T.I.: Applying the fuzzy ranking method to the shifting bottleneck procedure to solve scheduling problems of uncertainty. The International Journal of Advanced Manufacturing Technology 31(1), 98–106 (2006)
7. Zhang, W., Dietterich, T.: High Performance Job-Shop Scheduling with a Time-delay TD Network. In: Proc. of Advances in Neural Information Processing Systems, pp. 1024–1030. MIT Press, Cambridge (1996)
8. Rajakumar, S., Arunachalam, V.P., Selladurai, V.: Workflow balancing strategies in parallel machine scheduling. The International Journal of Advanced Manufacturing Technology 23(5), 366–374 (2004)
9. Parker, L.E.: ALLIANCE: An architecture for fault tolerant multi-robot cooperation. IEEE Transactions on Robotics and Automation 14, 220–240 (1998)

The Realization of Custom Extending Attribute Information of AutoCAD

Xiaosheng Liu, Feihui Hu, and Xiaoyu Zhang

School of Architectural and Surveying Engineering,
Jiangxi University of Science and Technology, Ganzhou, 341000, China
lxs9103@163.com

Abstract. In order to add custom attribute information to AutoCAD graphic data more flexibly and conveniently, we study the problem of custom extending CAD attribute information which exists in AutoCAD, and implement the custom extending function of AutoCAD attribute information by ObjectARX components in .NET development environment. Respectively, we adopt the XData way and database dictionary way for extending. Finally, we extend GIS attribute data in CAD graphic file and apply to practice. The application results show that this method is convenient, flexible and is worthy to be popularized.

Keywords: ObjectARX, XData, Database Dictionary, Attribute Information.

1 Introduction

Usually, we find that the graphic entities which have been drawn have already contained various basic properties of graphic, such as line type, layer, color and visibility when we draw graphics using AutoCAD software [1].Those properties are defined by AutoCAD software. However, these attributes did not include non-graphical attribute which were independent of graphic features of entity object. Because AutoCAD software did not provide the functions that user enters custom non-graphical attribute data, therefore, CAD users achieve adding custom attributes only by the text annotation if they want to add custom attributes in their own CAD drawing. However, when we add too much attribute data, we have to give up some of the secondary attribute data and only keep some important attribute data in order to ensure a clear and beautiful graphic file. It is impossible that CAD users defined the attributes in text annotation and try to hide these attributes [2, 3].

In order to solve the problem that adding non-graphical information (for example, the entity material, the price of an entity, the processing method of entity, the author's name and the rendering time) to graphic object, at last the author successfully achieved a "custom extending attribute data of CAD" function in AutoCAD software with the help of .NET environment and ObjectARX developing components.

2 AutoCAD and ObjectARX Information

AutoCAD software has some powerful graphics rendering and editing functions. In order to let user develop custom function, AutoDesk Company provided different development ways for different users. With the .NET technology progressed, starting from

G. Shen and X. Huang (Eds.): CSIE 2011, Part I, CCIS 152, pp. 208–214, 2011.
© Springer-Verlag Berlin Heidelberg 2011

AutoCAD 2006, AutoCAD added .NET API [4], so developers can use any language which supports .NET for AutoCAD second development in .NET environment [5].

ObjectARX is a software development package. It is launched by AutoDesk Company for the second development on AutoCAD platform. Actually, it is a Windows dynamic link library (DLL) procedure [6]. Using the library provided by ObjectARX, Developers can direct and quickly access to the AutoCAD drawing database [7], and can real-time extend the functions of AutoCAD during the operation. As ObjectARX class library uses the standard C++ class library packaging way, so developers can develop fast, efficient, simple AutoCAD second development.

3 Realization Method

We have two ways to extend attribute information of AutoCAD graphic object: the one is using extending data (Xdata) to add a certain amount of custom data for AutoCAD; the other is using dictionary to expand the non-graphical attribute of AutoCAD graphic object. The following are the implementation processes of two methods.

3.1 Using XData Way

In order to conveniently add a certain number of custom data to the AutoCAD graphic objects, ObjectARX provided XData to set or get data extended of graphic objects for developers [8]. These data can be defined and explained by developers, while AutoCAD only maintain these data regardless of their specific meaning. Extended data are appended to graphic entity basing on the form of results cache [9, 10]. Results cache express with ResultBuffer type. We need provide a double -data which contains a data description (TypedValue.TypeCode) and a data value (TypedValue.Value) when we use ResultBuffer object.

Using XData can add one or more extending data to graphic entity. These data maybe are String, Real, Integer, Entity Handle and other types of information. At the same time, their data are not more than 218K [11]. Supported by XData, DXF group code can only take the group code value which is between 1000 and 1071. Different group codes correspond to different information of types. Group code introduce which extended data used is shown in table 1.

Table 1. Codes used by Xdata

DXF Group Code values	Data contents extended of DXF Group Code values	DXF Group Code values	Data contents extended of DXF Group Code values
1000~1009	String （no more than 255 chars）	1010~1059	Floating-point
1001	Application Name of Xdata	1040	Floating-point in Xdata
1002	Control String of Xdata	1041	Distance value in Xdata
1003	Layer Name	1042	Scale Coefficients in Xdata
1004	Binary Data	1060~1070	16 Integer
1005	Database Object Handle	1071	32 Integer

The process which using XData implement extending Attribute Information of graphic object is: firstly, getting graphic entity we need add attributes; secondly, getting application name which entity login; thirdly, adding defined attribute value to ResultBuffer double-data; finally, deliver the defined attribute values to XData attributes which are from selected graphic object. The realization of the main code is as follows:

```
public void ExtentionByXData()
{
    ResultBuffer pResultBuffer = new ResultBuffer();
    for (int i = 0; i < dataGridView2.ColumnCount; i++)
    {
        string strField = dataGridView2
            .Rows[0].Cells[i].Value.ToString();
        string strTableName =
            dataGridView2.Columns[i].Name;
        pResultBuffer.Add(new TypedValue
            (1000, strTableName + " : " + strField));
    }
    pEntity.XData = pResultBuffer;
}
```

3.2 Using Databases Dictionary Way

ObjectARX also provides the class which type is DBDictionary for accessing dictionary from the database of AutoCAD. Dictionary is an object container which store non-graphical object in AutoCAD. AutoCAD Dictionary include named object dictionary and object extension dictionary [12]. Named object dictionary exists in each AutoCAD database, it holds the data of program level and is the root directory of all dictionaries; while object extension dictionary is a dictionary that it store various additional attribute information defined by user.

When we extend attribute information of graphic object by this way, we usually use the XRecord to define various types of data. Data items of XRecord are defined by ResultBuffer. DXF group code value of definition are shown in table 2:

Table 2. Codes used by XRecord

Group Code value	Type of Data	Group Code value	Type of Data
1~4、6~9、102、300~309	Text	310~319	Binary Data
10~17	Point or Vector	320~329	Handle
38~59、140~149	Floating-point	330~339	Soft Pointer ID
280~289	8-bit Integer	340~349	Hard Pointer ID
60~79、170~179、270~279	16-bit Integer	350~359	Soft Owner ID
90~99、210~219	32-bit Integer	360~369	Hard Owner ID

The process which using AutoCAD Dictionary implement extending Attribute Information of graphic object is: firstly, getting named object dictionary of the graphic object what we want to add attribute information; secondly, extending object dictionary in named object dictionary; thirdly, adding defined attribute information to XRecord by ResultBuffer; finally, implementing the extension of graphic object attribute by the method (SetAt()) of Extension dictionary. The main codes are as follows:

```
public void ExtentionByDictionary()
{
    DBDictionary pExtensionDic =(DBDictionary)
        trans.GetObject(pBlockRef.ExtensionDictionary,
        OpenMode.ForWrite, false);
    Xrecord pXrecord = new Xrecord();
    ResultBuffer pResultBuffer = new ResultBuffer();
    for (int i = 0; i < dataGridView2.ColumnCount; i++)
    {
        string strField = dataGridView2
            .Rows[0].Cells[i].Value.ToString();
        string strTableName =
            dataGridView2.Columns[i].Name;
        pResultBuffer.Add(new TypedValue(1000,
            strTableName   + "•" + strField));
    }
    pXrecord.Data = pResultBuffer;
    pExtensionDic.SetAt(strDirctionaryName,pXrecord);
    trans.AddNewlyCreatedDBObject(pXrecord,true);
}
```

4 Application and Effect

We need add GIS attribute data to CAD graphic data when we use CAD data in GIS system. Because GIS data is large and data classification is complex [13], so GIS attribute data which are added to CAD file are invisible. These data can not fully show spatial query and spatial analysis capabilities of GIS if users directly add text annotation to CAD file [14]. Therefore, we add GIS attribute data to XData or Extension Dictionary of CAD graphic object and achieved adding invisible GIS attribute data to CAD file. The specific operation of the function is shown in Figure 1. The first

Fig. 1. Operation process of custom extending attribute

thing is setting attribute field we will add; then add defined field to the table of attribute information and complete the information; and then select the extension way and perform the attribute extended command; lastly ,check the case of attribute information extended. The interfaces of functions are shown in Figure 2, 3, 4.

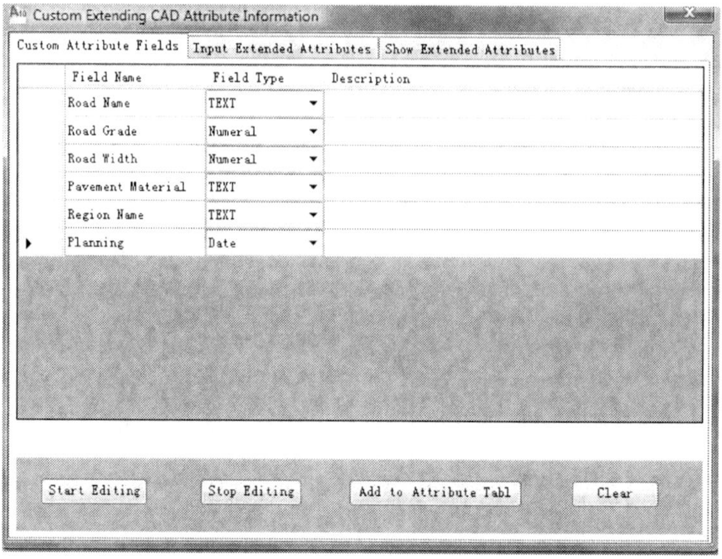

Fig. 2. Custom attributes field TAB

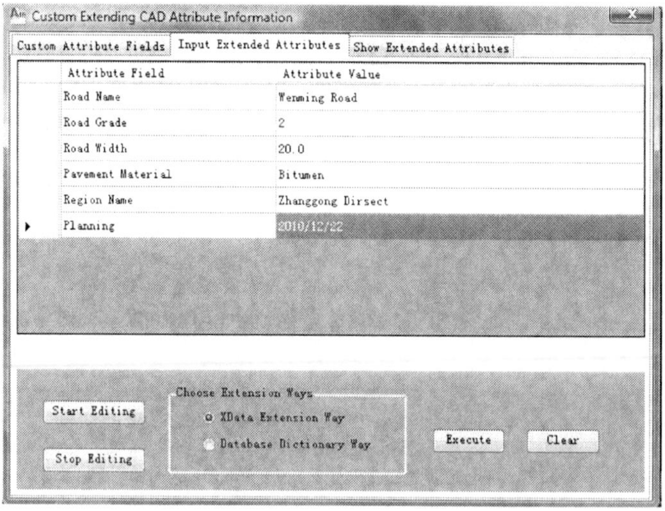

Fig. 3. Extended attribute entry TAB

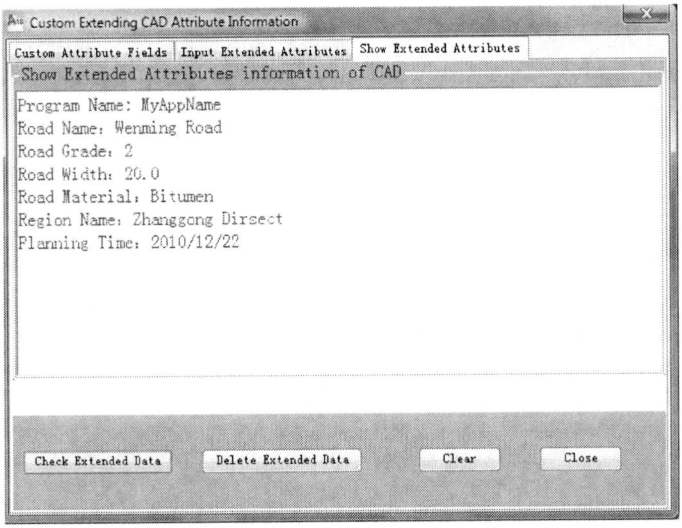

Fig. 4. Display extending attribute TAB

5   Conclusion

Aiming at the problem that CAD users extend custom attribute information of CAD in AutoCAD software, this thesis put forward two solutions: XData extension mode and Dictionary extension mode. Then, basing on the specific example, this thesis explained the applying processes of function and showed the effects of application. The effect fully reflects that the functions really solve the current problem what users encounter when they define extending attribute of CAD. The functions can bring convenience for the input work of CAD attribute information and has popularization value.

References

1. Qin, H., Cui, H., Sun, J.: Autodesk Series Product Development Training Course. Beijing Chemical Industry Press (2008)
2. Harada, L.: Pattern Matching over Multi-attribute Data Streams. Computer Science, Processing and Information Retrieval, 413–419 (2002)
3. Maher, M.L., Rutherford, J.H.: A model for synchronous collaborative design using CAD and database management. Research in Engineering Design, 85–98 (1997)
4. Grabowski, H., Anderl, R.: CAD-systems and their interface with CAM. Computer Science, Methods and Tools for Computer Integrated Manufacturing, 481–490 (1984)
5. Li, C.: AutoCAD ObjectARX Application Development Technology. National Defence Industry Press, Beijing (2005)
6. Weiler, K.J.: Boundary Graph Operators for Nonmanifold Geometric Modeling Topology Representations. In: Geometric Modeling for CAD Applications. Elsevier Science, Amsterdam (1988)

7. Liu, M., Katragadda, S.: DrawCAD:Using Deductive Object-Relational Databases in CAD. Computer Science, Database and Expert Systems Aplications, 481–490 (2001)
8. Kalta, M., Davies, B.J.: Guidelines for building 2D CAD models of turned components in CAD-CAPP integration. The International Journal of Advanced Manufacturing Technology, 285–296 (1993)
9. Andersen, O., Vasilakis, G.: Building an Ontology of CAD Model Information. Geometric Modelling. Numerical Simulation, and Optimization, 11–40 (2007)
10. Pairel, E., Hernandez, P., Giordano, M.: Virtual Gauge Representation for Geometric Tolerances in CAD-CAM Systems. Models for Computer Aided Tolerancing in Design and Manufacturing, 3–12 (2007)
11. Zhang, X., Zhang, Y., Deng, M.: GIS Data Organization Method in AutoCAD Environment. Journal of Surveying and Mapping 11, 45–48 (2003)
12. Robinson, D., McGregor, G., Lysaght, P.: New CAD Framework Extends Simulation of Dynamically Reconfigurable Logic. Computer Science, Field-Programmable Logic and Applications from FPGAs to Computing Paradigm, 1–8 (1998)
13. Yang, Y., Zhao, S.: GIS Data Collection Method Based on AutoCAD. Journal of Surveying and Mapping 5, 176–178 (2007)
14. Tse, R.O.C., Gold, C.M.: TIN meets CAD - extending the TIN concept in GIS. In: Sloot, P.M.A., Tan, C.J.K., Dongarra, J., Hoekstra, A.G. (eds.) ICCS-ComputSci 2002. LNCS, vol. 2331, p. 135. Springer, Heidelberg (2002)

Speech Emotion Recognition Using Support Vector Machines

Caiming Yu, Qingxi Tian, Fang Cheng, and Shiqing Zhang[*]

School of Physics and Electronic Engineering, Taizhou University
318000 Taizhou, China
tzczsq @163.com

Abstract. Speech emotion recognition is a new and challenging subject in artificial intelligence field. This paper explores the issues involved in applying support vector machines (SVM) classifier to emotion recognition in speech signals. The performance of SVM on speech emotion recognition task is compared with linear discriminant classifiers (LDC), K-nearest-neighbor (KNN), and radial basis function neutral network (RBFNN). The experimental results on emotional Chinese speech corpus demonstrate that SVM obtains the highest accuracy of 85%, outperforming the other used classification methods.

Keywords: Emotion recognition, Feature extraction, Support vector machines.

1 Introduction

Research on understanding and modeling human emotions, i.e., affective computing [1], is currently a very active topic within the engineering community. Speech is a main vehicle of human emotion expressions, since speech is one of the most powerful, natural and immediate means for human beings to communicate their emotions. Recognizing human emotions from speech signals, called speech emotion recognition, has increasing attracted much attention within artificial intelligence field due to its important applications to intelligent human-computer interaction [2], call centers [3], etc.

The basic speech emotion recognition system consists of two parts: feature extraction and emotion classification. Feature extraction is concerned with extracting relevant features from speech signals with respect to emotions. Emotion classification maps feature vectors onto emotion classes through a classifier's learning by data examples. After feature extraction, the accuracy of emotion recognition relies heavily on the use of a good pattern classifier. At present, the representative emotion classification methods, such as linear discriminant classifiers (LDC), K-nearest-neighbor (KNN), artificial neural network (ANN), have been widely used for speech emotion recognition [4, 5, 6]. Support vector machines (SVM) [7] became a popular classification tool due to its strong discriminating capability, which was successfully employed in various real-world applications. However, there is little attention to explore the

---

[*] Corresponding author.

G. Shen and X. Huang (Eds.): CSIE 2011, Part I, CCIS 152, pp. 215–220, 2011.
© Springer-Verlag Berlin Heidelberg 2011

performance of SVM on speech emotion recognition task. In the present study we employ an SVM-based classifier for emotion recognition in Chinese speech.

This paper is structured as follows. In Section 2, support vector machines (SVM) for classification is described. The emotional speech corpus and feature extraction are detailed in Section 3. Section 4 introduces the experiment study. Finally, in Section 5, the conclusions are presented.

2 Support Vector Machines (SVM) for Classification

Support vector machines (SVM)[7] is based on the statistical learning theory of structural risk management which aims to limit the empirical risk on the training data and on the capacity of the decision function. The basic concept of SVM is to transform the input vectors to a higher dimensional space by a nonlinear transform, and then an optimal hyperplane which separates the data can be found.

Given training data set $(x_1, y_1),...,(x_l, y_l), y_i \in \{-1,1\}$, to find the optimal hyperplane, a nonlinear transform, $Z = \Phi(x)$, is used to make training data become linearly dividable. A weight w and offset b satisfying the following criteria will be found:

$$\begin{cases} w^T z_i + b \geq 1, & y_i = 1 \\ w^T z_i + b \leq -1, & y_i = -1 \end{cases} \tag{1}$$

We can summarize the above procedure to the following:

$$\min_{w,b} \Phi(w) = \frac{1}{2}(w^T w) \tag{2}$$

Subject to $y_i(w^T z_i + b) \geq 1, \quad i = 1, 2,..., n$.

If the sample data is not linearly dividable, the following function should be minimized.

$$\Phi(w) = \frac{1}{2} w^T w + C \sum_{i=1}^{l} \xi_i \tag{3}$$

whereas ξ can be understood as the error of the classification and C is the penalty parameter for this term.

By using Lagrange method, the decision function of $w_0 = \sum_{i=1}^{l} \lambda_i y_i z_i$ will be

$$f = \text{sgn}[\sum_{i=0}^{l} \lambda_i y_i (z^T z_i) + b] \tag{4}$$

From the functional theory, a non-negative symmetrical function $K(u,v)$ uniquely defines a Hilbert space H, where K is the rebuild kernel in the space H:

$$K(u,v) = \sum_{i} \alpha \varphi_i(u) \varphi_i(v) \tag{5}$$

This stands for an internal product of a characteristic space:

$$z_i^T z = \Phi(x_i)^T \Phi(x) = K(x_i, x) \tag{6}$$

Then the decision function can be written as:

$$f = \text{sgn}[\sum_{i=1}^{l} \lambda_i y_i K(x_i, x) + b] \tag{7}$$

The development of a SVM emotion classification model depends on the selection of kernel function. There are several kernels that can be used in SVM models. These include linear, polynomial, radial basis function (RBF) and sigmoid function.

$$K(x_i, x_j) = \begin{cases} x_i^T x_j & Linear \\ (\gamma x_i^T x_j + coefficient)^{degree} & Polynomial \\ \exp(-\gamma | x_i - x_j |^2 & RBF \\ \tanh(\gamma x_i^T x_j + coefficient) & Sigmoid \end{cases} \tag{8}$$

3 Speech Corpus and Feature Extraction

3.1 Emotional Speech Corpus

The emotional speech Chinese corpus reported in our present study [8] was used for experiments. The Chinese corpus was collected from 20 different Chinese dialogue episodes from a talk-show on TV. In each talk-show, two or three persons discuss the problems such as social typical issues, family conflict, inspiring deeds, etc. Due to the spontaneous and unscripted manner of the episodes, the emotional expressions can be considered authentic. Because of the limited topics, the speech corpus consists of four kinds of common emotion including angry, happy, sad and neutral. This corpus collected in total contains 800 emotional utterances from 53 different speakers (16 male /37 female), speaker-independent, each of four emotion for about 200 utterances. All utterances recorded at a sample rate of 16 kHz and 16 bits resolution with mono-phonic Windows WAV format stored in computer.

3.2 Feature Extraction

It has been found speech prosody and voice quality are closely related to the expression of human emotion in speech [3, 8]. The popular prosody features contain pitch, intensity and duration. And the representative voice quality features include the first three formants (F1, F2, F3), spectral energy distribution, harmonics-to-noise-ratio (HNR), pitch irregularity (jitter) and amplitude irregularity (shimmer). The popular prosody and voice quality features are extracted for each utterance from the Berlin emotional speech database. Some typical statistical parameters such as mean, standard derivations (std), median, quartiles, and so on, are computed for each extracted feature. These extracted acoustic features, 48 in total, are presented as follows.

◆ Prosody features:

(1-10)Pitch: maximum, minimum, range, mean, std (standard deviation), first quartile, median, third quartile, inter-quartile range, mean-absolute-slope.

(11-19)Intensity: maximum, minimum, range, mean, std, first quartile, median, third quartile, inter-quartile range.

(20-25)Duration: total-frames, voiced-frames, unvoiced-frames, ratio of voiced to unvoiced frames, ratio of voiced-frames to total-frames, ratio of unvoiced-frames to total-frames (20ms/ frame).

◆ Voice quality features:

(26-37)First three formants F1-F3: mean of F1, std of F1, median of F1, bandwidth of median of F1, mean of F2, std of F2, median of F2, bandwidth of median of F2, mean of F3, std of F3, median of F3, bandwidth of median of F3.

(38-41)Spectral energy distribution in 4 different frequency bands: band energy from 0 Hz to 500 Hz, band energy from 500 Hz to 1000 Hz, band energy from 2500 Hz to 4000 Hz, band energy from 4000 Hz to 5000 Hz.

(42-46)Harmonics-to-noise-ratio: maximum, minimum, range, mean, std.

(47)Jitter: pitch perturbation in vocal chords vibration.

Jitter is calculated with the following equation (9), in which T_i is the i-th peak-to-peak interval and N is the number of intervals:

$$Jitter(\%) = \sum_{i=2}^{N-1}(2T_i - T_{i-1} - T_{i+1}) \bigg/ \sum_{i=2}^{N-1} T_i \qquad (9)$$

(48)Shimmer: perturbation cycle to cycle of the energy

Shimmer is calculated similarly to Jitter as shown in equation (10), in which E_i is the i-th peak-to-peak energy values and N is the number of intervals:

$$Shimmer(\%) = \sum_{i=2}^{N-1}(2E_i - E_{i-1} - E_{i+1}) \bigg/ \sum_{i=2}^{N-1} E_i \qquad (10)$$

4 Experiment Study

4.1 Experiment Setup

All extracted different acoustic features were normalized by a mapping to [0, 1] before anything else. To verify the performance of SVM on speech emotion recognition task, three typical methods, i.e., linear discriminant classifiers (LDC), K-nearest-neighbor (KNN) and artificial neural network (ANN) were used to compare with SVM. For KNN method, K is set to 1 for its best performance. For ANN method, we use the popular radial basis function neutral network (RBFNN) to perform ANN algorithm. We use the LIBSVM package [9] to implement SVM algorithm with RBF kernel, kernel parameter optimization, one-versus-one strategy for multi-class classification problem. The RBF kernel was used for its better performance compared with other kernels.

For all emotion classification experiments, we used LIBSVM to employed 10-fold stratified cross validations over the data sets so as to achieve more reliable experiment results. In other words, each classification model is trained on nine tenths of the total data and tested on the remaining tenth. This process is repeated ten times, each with a different partitioning seed, in order to account for variance between the partitions.

4.2 Experimental Results and Analysis

The different emotion recognition results of four classification methods, including LDC, KNN, RBFNN as well as SVM, is given in Table 1. As shown in Table 1, we can see that SVM obtains the highest accuracy of 85%, followed by RBFNN, KNN and LDC. This indicates that SVM has the strongest discriminating ability among all used four classification methods. Note that LDC and KNN get an accuracy of about 75%, demonstrating that LDC is highly close to KNN on classification task. In addition, RBFNN outperforms LDC and KNN, and achieves an accuracy of 83.34%.

To further explore the recognition results of different kinds of emotions when using SVM classifier, the confusion matrix of emotion recognition results obtained with SVM is given in Table 2. The confusion matrix of the results in Table 2 indicates that angry and neutral could be discriminated well. In detail, the recognition accuracy of angry and neutral is 87% and 93%, respectively. While other two emotions, happy and sad, only could be classified with relatively lower accuracies, in detail 82.5% for happy and 77.5% for sad. The main reason is that happy has a high confusion to angry and sad for each other because the three emotional utterances have confused speech parameters to a great extent.

Table 1. Emotion Recognition Results of Four Classification Methods

Methods	LDC	KNN	RBFNN	SVM
Accuracy (%)	75.21	75.13	83.34	85.00

Table 2. Confusion matrix of Emotion Recognition Results Obtained with SVM

	Angry	Happy	Sad	Neutral
Angry	174	19	7	0
Happy	24	165	10	1
Sad	8	24	155	13
Neutral	0	12	2	186

5 Conclusions

This paper presents a comparative study of four different used classification methods, i.e., LDC, KNN, RBFNN and SVM, for emotion recognition from emotional Chinese speech corpus. From the obtained results, we can conclude that SVM performs best and obtains the best performance with an accuracy of 85%, owing to its good discriminating ability. It's noted that in this study only four emotions including angry, happy, sad and neutral are classified. In the future, we aim to extend our emotional speech Chinese corpus and identify more other different emotion categories such as disgust, afraid, surprise and so on.

References

1. Picard, R.: Affective computing. MIT Press, Cambridge (1997)
2. Cowie, R., Douglas-Cowie, E., Tsapatsoulis, N., Votsis, G., Kollias, S., Fellenz, W., Taylor, J.G.: Emotion Recognition in Human-Computer Interaction. IEEE Signal Processing Magazine 18(01), 32–80 (2001)
3. Lee, C.M., Narayanan, S.S.: Toward Detecting Emotions in Spoken Dialogs. IEEE Transactions on Speech and Audio Processing 13(2), 293–303 (2005)
4. Dellaert, F., Polzin, T., Waibel, A.: Recognizing emotion in speech. In: Proceedings of 4th International Conference on Spoken Language Processing, Philadelphia, PA, USA, pp. 1970–1973 (1996)
5. Petrushin, V.: Emotion in speech: recognition and application to call centers. In: Proceedings of 1999 Artificial Neural Networks in Engineering, New York, pp. 7–10 (1999)
6. Nicholson, J., Takahashi, K., Nakatsu, R.: Emotion recognition in speech using neural networks. Neural Computing & Applications 9(4), 290–296 (2000)
7. Vapnik, V.: The nature of statistical learning theory. Springer, New York (2000)
8. Zhang, S.: Emotion Recognition in Chinese Natural Speech by Combining Prosody and Voice Quality Features. In: Sun, F., Zhang, J., Tan, Y., Cao, J., Yu, W. (eds.) ISNN 2008, Part II. LNCS, vol. 5264, pp. 457–464. Springer, Heidelberg (2008)
9. Chang, C., Lin, C.: LIBSVM: a library for support vector machines (2001) Software available at, http://www.csie.ntu.edu.tw/cjlin/libsvm

Research of Cities' Gas Load Predicting Model Based on Wavelet Neural Network

Jian Li and Xiaole Liu

Depart. of Computer Science and Engineering
Henan Institute of Engineering
Zhengzhou 451191, China
l.j2006@163.com

Abstract. Wavelet Neural Network (WNN) is a new neural network model based on wavelet analysis theory, which takes advantage of good localization of wavelet transform nature, and combines with neural networks' self-learning function, thereby, it has strong approximation ability and can approach any nonlinear function. This paper using wavelet neural network constructing the city gas load forecasting of mathematical model, and the model parameters determination, and impact load forecasting of various factors of the in-depth analysis and discussion.

Keywords: Wavelet Neural Network (WNN), gas, forecast, model.

As the expansion of cities in China, more and more gas was consumed. Therefore, it's required that gas pipeline network in cities need more scientific plan and management. As a result, mastering the size of gas consumption, characteristics, and variation, and forecasting the future load and characteristics of dynamic system of gas load are significant to realize the efficient operation, optimal operation and scientific management, to ensure gas pipeline network investment returns and protect the security of transmission and distribution system, reliable operation, and reasonable arrangements for post-project maintenance arrangements for equipment updates.

The so-called city gas consumption forecast is a way to estimate the gas load which based on historical data combined with meteorological data and other data and information. At present, the major gas companies in China mainly used the traditional load forecasting methods. For example, Industrial users forecasted gas load according to the day's actual consumption, and civil and business users forecasted gas load on the basis of sampling combined with the actual situation at that time. The disadvantage of this way was that the method can only be master by experienced engineer and accuracy was not high, which is difficult to adapt to the growing demand of gas pipeline network.

Wavelet Neural Network (WNN) is a new neural network model based on wavelet analysis theory, which takes advantage of good localization of wavelet transform nature, and combines with neural networks' self-learning function, thereby, it has strong approximation ability and can approach any nonlinear function. To the same learning task, wavelet network structure is more simple and faster, and can extract

G. Shen and X. Huang (Eds.): CSIE 2011, Part I, CCIS 152, pp. 221–225, 2011.

details of the gas load. By using wavelet analysis, it can analyze gas load at any level, and deal with the signal and extract them. This article will use wavelet neural network to construct mathematical model of city gas consumption to achieve more accurate load forecasting.

1   Wavelet Neural Network (WNN)

Wavelet neural network is a multi-input single-output feed forward neural network. Just like picture 1, it is composed of input layer, hidden layer and output layer. Hidden layer radial basis function as activation function, performs a fixed nonlinear transformation, the input space is mapped to a new space, the input layer in the implementation of the new space in linear combination, and adjustable parameter is the linear combination weights.

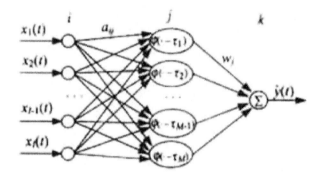

Fig. 1. Wavelet Neural Network (WNN)

I set the input layer nodes, the input vector X = [x1, x2, ..., xI], the hidden layer has M nodes (M = 2K +1), aij for the i-node input layer to hidden layer j, Wavelet basis between the nodes scale parameter, τj for the hidden layer node j, the displacement parameters of wavelet bases, wj is the first hidden layer nodes to the output node j the weight parameters, the following relationship:

$$\hat{y}(t) = \sum_{i=1}^{M} w_j \varphi(\sum_{i=1}^{t} a_{ij} x_i(t) - \tau_j)$$

Hidden nodes to determine the number of J and wavelet network parameter initialization is very important, just make sure the J, can be determined K, J's choice and (x) the precision of approximation, J greater the higher the approximation accuracy, but

The number of hidden layer neurons more parameters required to identify the more, therefore, approximation accuracy and structure need to be made between complexity and balance of the network model is usually defined number of hidden units so that identification error is less than When a certain minimum threshold number of neurons.

Wavelet network parameters include the scale parameter initialization aij, displacement parameters and weights wj τj initialization. The initialization of wj is the same with general neural network. aij, τj directly affect the initialization of the convergence of the entire network, but their initialization is currently no systematic approach, mainly based on the actual situation and experience. τj consider the main function to initialize the time-domain boundaries, domain boundaries can take two time values evenly between the displacement parameters as initial values; aij initialization handler will have to take into account the extreme, if the direct Series of the function extreme value scale parameter initialization, the convergence speed.

2 Model Parameters

The key of designing a network model focuses on the model structure and learning algorithm choice. According to the effect factors and variation of short-term load, the key of application of wavelet neural network is to determine the parameters and structure of learning samples of effective neural network model. In order to provide exact and original parameters for predicting outcomes, sample parameters must objectively describe the characteristics of the changing nature of gas consumption. Therefore, it must consider many factors such as the structure and habits of users and weather when choosing sample parameters. Gas consumption of one day is short-term forecast, and number and structure of users changes a little. Thereby, in constructing load model, input layer only consider the factors of weather and date. There are five factors in input layer maximum temperature, minimum temperature, average temperature, weather patterns (snow, rain, overcast, clouds, sunny), the date type (working day, rest day), and output layer is gas consumption.

In this paper, the structure of wavelet neural network is 5-14-1, the input layer nodes 5, 14 hidden layer nodes, 1 output layer node. Initial weights of the network is set to [-1,1] random number between, the network's input on the grounds Gauss function uniform distribution generated pseudo-random number.

3 Simulation and Error Analysis

In this paper, we put the gas consumption in a certain period of gas company of Z city as samples, and using the company's dispatch center live statistics and MATLAB programming language computer program for training the neural network. Maximum squared error of the sample under the premise of 0.0001, after 1000 steps operations, the training sample output after the completion of the comparison with the actual values in Table 1.

Table 1. Comparison of sample result and actual data after training

No.	Actual	Forecast	Differenc	No.	Actual	Forecast	Differenc
1	1534014	1532520	-0.10%	9	1529450	1542467	0.85%
2	1525975	1522103	-0.25%	10	1531265	1532798	0.10%
3	1528003	1542001	0.92%	11	1529821	1524325	-0.36%
4	1539965	1549440	0.62%	12	1522065	1532656	0.70%
5	1552093	1543556	-0.55%	13	1530120	1524979	-0.34%
6	1549230	1545001	-0.27%	14	1528779	1564652	2.35%
7	1510010	1534009	1.59%	15	1532110	1556543	1.59%
8	1518203	1541032	1.50%				

According to the model after training, we collected a group of 10 test samples for testing, comparing predicted and actual values shown in Table 2.

Table 2. Comparing predicted and actual values shown

No.	Actual	Forecast	Difference	No.	Actual	Forecast	Difference
1	1556465	1579885	1.50%	6	1569878	1566204	-0.23%
2	1549582	1552341	0.18%	7	1553220	1532468	-1.34%
3	1558987	1537024	-1.41%	8	1554882	1589751	2.24%
4	1552313	1578420	1.68%	9	1562328	1578140	1.01%
5	1544010	1578220	2.22%	10	1564220	1615480	3.28%

In the whole process of network training, the network shows a linear speed of convergence. The initial neural network training convergence speed is faster, is basically linear. But in the late training, the network error decreases more slowly, and the oscillation will be errors, easily falling into local minima. Wavelet network is also found that initial selection of the wavelet coefficients of scale factor a particularly sensitive. Wavelet parameter initialization is still lack of rigorous theoretical guidance, the general experience is the first high-scale training, lack of precision, and then to low-scale training, how to choose the appropriate initialization parameters is a key issue for WNN. Currently, we only compared by many experiments to choose from the better performance of a set of data.

There are some errors in the model. Reasons are flowing:

① There is arbitrariness in Short-term gas consumption which are related with the habits of users.

② Structure and quantity of gas consumption is changing.

③ There are other uncertainties such as sudden weather change and pipe network maintenance.

4 Conclusion

Although the mechanism of wavelet network is the same as neural network that hidden layer extracts feature of input samples and output layer classifies the input sample. But because of the localization of wavelet activation function, more different the function is, more powerful the approximation ability is. This feature is ideal for power unit such as data input and output data for non-uniformity of the approximation of the mathematical model. Short-term gas load predicting based on WNN integrates wavelet transform and neural network signal analysis and pattern recognition, which effectively improves the network efficiency and speed of training samples, and enhances robustness of network. Of course, the wavelet network are also some problems which need further research, such as the choice of wavelet functions, the determination of hidden nodes of wavelet network and the initialization of wavelet network parameters.

References

1. Huang, H.: RBF neural network in gas load forecasting, Guangdong building materials, 5th edn., pp. 182–184 (2005)
2. Peng, S., Su, X., Huang, Q.: Gas Load Forecasting and Analysis in Cities, magazine of Chongqing Architecture University, 4th edn., pp. 137–141 (2005)
3. Wen, L., Yan, M., Lian, L.: City Gas Load Forecasting. Gas and Heating 21(5), 387–389 (2001)
4. Yang, F.: Analysis and Application of Wavelet Engineering. Science Press, Beijing (1999)
5. Jiao, W., Zhan, C., Yan, M.: Short-term Gas Load Forecasting in Cities. Gas and Heating 21(6), 483–486 (2001)
6. Xiao, W., Liu, Y., Wang, S.: Hour Load of Fuzzy Neural Network. Gas and Heating 22(1), 16–18 (2002)

Consistency Degrees of Theories in n-Valued Gödel Logical System

Jun Li and Haiya Li

School of Science, Lanzhou University of Technology, Lanzhou, 730050, China
lj99120@yahoo.com.cn

Abstract. Based on the truth degrees of formulas and the deviations of theories defined by Hausdorff metric, the present paper introduced a new concept of consistency degrees of theories in n-valued Gödel logical system. Sufficient and necessary conditions for theories being consistent or inconsistent are given. The new index provided in the present paper can also be used to grade the consistency degrees of general theories in fuzzy logic systems.

Keywords: Truth degree; Hausdorff metric; Consistency degree; Polar index.

1 Introduction

Whether a theory we are dealing with is consistent or not is one of the crucial questions in any logical system. Moreover, the question that to what extent a theory is consistent or inconsistent is also one of the crucial questions in logic systems. In order to grade the extent of consistency degree of different theories, the concept of inconsistency degree of a fuzzy theory Γ has been introduced in [1,2] ,and different types of concepts of consistency degree which depend on the divergence degree of a fuzzy theory Γ are proposed in fuzzy propositional logics in [3]and[4]. In addition, based on the deduction theorems, completeness theorems and the integrated truth degree of formulas, Zhou and Wang introduced a new consistency index in four different types of fuzzy logic systems, i.e. Łukasiewicz fuzzy logic system Łuk, Gödel fuzzy logic system Göd, product fuzzy logic system Π and R_0 fuzzy logic system L^* [5].

What about the consistency degree of theories in the finite-valued propositional logic systems corresponding to the above fuzzy logic systems? Based on the truth degrees of formulas and deviations defined by Hausdorff metric, the present paper introduced the concept of consistency degrees of theories in n-valued Gödel logical system. Sufficient and necessary conditions for theories being consistent or inconsistent are given. The new index provided in the present paper can also be used to grade the consistency degrees of general theories in fuzzy logic systems.

2 Preliminaries

Suppose that $S = \{p_1, p_2, \ldots\}$ is a countable set, and $F(S)$ is the free algebra of type $(\neg, \&, \rightarrow)$ generated by S , where $\neg, \&, and \rightarrow$ are unary, binary and binary operators, respectively. Members of $F(S)$ are formulas and those of S are atomic formulas.

G. Shen and X. Huang (Eds.): CSIE 2011, Part I, CCIS 152, pp. 226–230, 2011.

Let $I_n = \{0, \frac{1}{n-1}, \frac{2}{n-1}, \cdots, \frac{n-1}{n-1}, 1\}$, define on I_n one unary operators and two binary operators as follows:

$$\forall x, y \in I_n, \quad \neg x = R_G(x,0), \quad x \& y = x \otimes_G y, \quad x \to y = R_G(x,y).$$

Where R_G and $\otimes_G$ are defined as follows:

$$R_G(x, y) = \begin{cases} 1, & x \le y, \\ y, & x > y. \end{cases} \qquad x \otimes_G y = x \wedge y,$$

then I_n becomes an algebra of type $(\neg, \&, \to)$. The tuple $(F(S), I_n, \neg, \&, R_G)$ are called n-valued Gödel logical system, denoted by G_n. R_G and $\otimes_G$ are called Gödel implication operator and Gödel t-norm respectively.

For any $A \in F(S), a \in I_n$, we introduce two simplified notations as follows:

$$A^n := \underbrace{A \& A \& \cdots \& A}_{n \ times}, \quad a^n := \underbrace{a \otimes_G a \otimes_G \cdots \otimes_G a}_{n \ times}$$

Definition 1. (Wang[6]) (i) A homomorphism $v : F(S) \to I_n$ of type $(\neg, \&, \to)$ from $F(S)$ into valuation lattice I_n, i.e.,

$$v(\neg A) = \neg v(A), v(A \& B) = v(A) \otimes_G v(B), v(A \to B) = R_G(A,B),$$

is called a valuation of $F(S)$. The set of all valuations will be denoted by Ω_0.

(ii) A formula $A \in F(S)$ is called a tautology if $\forall v \in \Omega_0, v(A) = 1$ holds.

A formula $A \in F(S)$ is called a contradiction if $\forall v \in \Omega_0, v(A) = 0$ holds.

(iii) Let $A, B \in F(S)$, if $v(A) = v(B)$ for each $v \in \Omega_0$, we call A and B are logically equivalent.

A subset Γ of $F(S)$ is called a theory. We say the formula A is a conclusion of Γ, denoted by $\Gamma \vdash A$, if A is deduced from Γ and the set of axioms by using Modus Ponens. The set of all conclusion of Γ is denoted by $D(\Gamma)$. A theory $\Gamma \subset F(S)$ is called inconsistent if $\Gamma \vdash \overline{0}$, otherwise, consistent, where $\overline{0}$ is a contradiction.

Deduction theorem is one of the most important theorems in two-valued logical system, it is still valid in Gödel logic systems.

Theorem 1 [6]. (Deduction theorem) Suppose that Γ is a theory, $A, B \in F(S)$, then

$$\Gamma \cup \{A\} \vdash B \text{ if and only if } \Gamma \vdash A \to B.$$

3   Truth Degrees of Formulas and Deviations of Theories

In this section, we will give the definition of truth degrees of formulas in G_n. Assume that $A = A(p_1, \cdots, p_m)$ is a formula generated by atomic formulas

$p_1, \cdots, p_m$ through connectives $\neg, \&, and \rightarrow$. Substitute x_i for p_i in $A(i = 1, \cdots, m)$ and keep the logic connectives unchanged but explain them as the corresponding operators defined on the valuation lattice I_n. Then we get a function

$\overline{A} : I_n^m \rightarrow I_n$ and call $\overline{A}(x_1, \cdots, x_m)$ the function induced by the formula A.

Definition 2 [6]. Suppose that $A = A(p_1, \cdots, p_m)$, the truth degree $\tau(A)$ of A is defined as follows:

$$\tau(A) = \frac{1}{n^m} \sum_{i=0}^{n-1} \frac{i}{n-1} \left| \overline{A}^{-1} (\frac{i}{n-1}) \right|$$

Where $\left| \overline{A}^{-1}_{(\frac{i}{n-1})} \right|$ is the cardinality of the set $\overline{A}^{-1} (\frac{i}{n-1})$.

Definition 3 [6]. Assume that $A, B \in F(S)$, let

$$\xi(A, B) = \tau((A \rightarrow B) \wedge (B \rightarrow A))$$

then $\xi(A, B)$ is called the similarity between A and B. $\rho(A, B) = 1 - \xi(A, B)$ is called the pseudo metric between A and B.

Theorem 2 [6]. Let $A \in F(S)$, then $\tau(A) = 1$ if and only if A is a tautology; $\tau(A) = 0$ if and only if A is a contradiction.

Definition 4. Suppose that Γ, Σ are non-empty subsets of $F(S)$. Define

$$H^*(\Gamma, \Sigma) = \sup\{\rho(\gamma, \Sigma) \mid \gamma \in \Gamma\}, \quad H(\Gamma, \Sigma) = \max\{H^*(\Gamma, \Sigma), H^*(\Sigma, \Gamma)\}$$

then $H : F(S) \times F(S) \rightarrow [0,1]$ is a pseudo metric in $F(S)$, $H(\Gamma, \Sigma)$ is called the hausdorff metric between Γ and Σ.

Definition 5. Suppose that $\Sigma, \Gamma \subset F(S)$, let

$$Dev(\Gamma, \Sigma) = H(D(\Sigma), D(\Gamma)),$$

$Dev(\Gamma, \Sigma)$ is called the relative deviation of Γ and Σ, if $\Sigma = \phi$, i.e., Σ is the empty set, then $Dev(\Gamma, \Sigma)$ is called the deviation of Γ, briefly denoted by $Dev(\Gamma)$.

Theorem 3. Suppose that $\Gamma \subset F(S)$, then $Dev(\Gamma) = \sup\{1 - \tau(A) \mid A \in D(\Gamma)\}$.

Proof. $Dev(\Gamma) = H(D(\Gamma), D(\phi)) = H^*(D(\Gamma), D(\phi)) \vee H^*(D(\phi), D(\Gamma))$

$= H^*(D(\Gamma), D(\phi)) = \sup\{\rho(A, D(\phi)) \mid A \in D(\Gamma)\} = \sup\{1 - \tau(A) \mid A \in D(\Gamma)\}$.

Theorem 4. Suppose that $\Gamma \subset F(S)$, then

(i) If Γ is inconsistent, then $Dev(\Gamma) = 1$, but not vice versa.

(ii) If Γ is completely consistent, i.e., all members of Γ are tautologies, then $Dev(\Gamma) = 0$.

Proof. It is obvious that (i) holds, we only prove (ii).If Γ is completely consistent, then it follows from the soundness theorem and the fact that the inference rule MP preserves tautologies that all members of $D(\Gamma)$ are tautologies, thus we can get from Theorem 2 that $\tau(A) = 1$ for every $A \in D(\Gamma)$, by Theorem 3,we have $\text{Dev}(\Gamma) = 0$.

4 Consistency Degrees of Theories

Definition 6. Suppose that $\Gamma \subset F(S)$, let $i(\Gamma) = \min\{\lceil \tau(A) \rceil \mid A \in D(\Gamma)\}$, $i(\Gamma)$ is called the polar index of Γ,where

$$\lceil x \rceil = \begin{cases} 1, & \text{if } 0 < x \leq 1. \\ 0, & \text{if } x = 0. \end{cases}$$

Theorem 5. Suppose that $\Gamma \subset F(S)$, then

    (i) Γ is inconsistent if and only if $i(\Gamma) = 0$.

    (ii) Γ is consistent if and only if $i(\Gamma) = 1$.

Proof. (i) If Γ is inconsistent, then $\bar{0} \in D(\Gamma)$, from Definition 6 and Theorem 2 we can easily get that $i(\Gamma) = 0$.Conversely, if $i(\Gamma) = 0$,then there exists $A \in D(\Gamma)$ such that $\lceil \tau(A) \rceil = 0$, since $\lceil \tau(A) \rceil = 0$ if and only if $\tau(A) = 0$,it follows from Theorem 2 that A is a contradiction and therefore Γ is inconsistent.

    (ii) If Γ is consistent,i.e., $\bar{0} \notin D(\Gamma)$,then by Theorem 2 we have that $\tau(A) > 0$ holds for all $A \in D(\Gamma)$,so $\lceil \tau(A) \rceil = 1$ holds for all $A \in D(\Gamma)$ and therefore $i(\Gamma) = 1$. Conversely, if $i(\Gamma) = 1$, it follows from Definition 6 that $\lceil \tau(A) \rceil = 1$ holds for all $A \in D(\Gamma)$, i.e., $\tau(A) > 0$ for all $A \in D(\Gamma)$,therefore A is not a contradiction for every $A \in D(\Gamma)$ and thus Γ is consistent.

The concept of polar index of a given theory can be used together with the concept of deviation to construct a new definition of consistency degree which reflects to what extent a theory is consistent as follows:

Definition 7. Suppose that $\Gamma \subset F(S)$, let

$$\eta(\Gamma) = 1 - \frac{1}{2}\text{Dev}(\Gamma)(2 - i(\Gamma))$$

$\eta(\Gamma)$ is called the consistency degree of Γ.

Theorem 6. Suppose that Γ is a theory in G_n, then

    (i) Γ is completely consistent if and only if $\eta(\Gamma) = 1$.

    (ii) Γ is consistent if and only if $\frac{1}{2} \leq \eta(\Gamma) \leq 1$;

(iii) Γ is consistent and $\mathrm{Dev}(\Gamma) = 1$ if and only if $\eta(\Gamma) = \dfrac{1}{2}$.

(iv) Γ is inconsistent if and only if $\eta(\Gamma) = 0$.

Proof. (i) If Γ is completely consistent ,i.e., all members of Γ are tautologies, it follows from Theorem 4 that $\mathrm{Dev}(\Gamma) = 0$,then by Definition 7 we can get that $\eta(\Gamma) = 1$ holds. Conversely, if $\eta(\Gamma) = 1$, it follows by Definition 7 that $\mathrm{Dev}(\Gamma)(2 - i(\Gamma)) = 0$, this means that $\mathrm{Dev}(\Gamma) = 0$ holds, and therefore Γ is completely consistent.

(ii) If Γ is consistent, then by Theorem 5, we have $i(\Gamma) = 1$, it is easy to see from Definition 7 that $\dfrac{1}{2} \leq \eta(\Gamma) \leq 1$ holds. Conversely, suppose that $\dfrac{1}{2} \leq \eta(\Gamma) \leq 1$, but Γ is inconsistent, then it follows from Theorem 4 and Theorem 5 that $\mathrm{Dev}(\Gamma) = 1$ and $i(\Gamma) = 0$, thus $\eta(\Gamma) = 0$ holds, a contradiction! Therefore Γ is consistent.

(iii) If Γ is consistent and $\mathrm{Dev}(\Gamma) = 1$,then $i(\Gamma) = 1$ and therefore $\eta(\Gamma) = \dfrac{1}{2}$.Conversely, if $\eta(\Gamma) = \dfrac{1}{2}$,then by (ii) we conclude that Γ is consistent and so $i(\Gamma) = 1$,and by Definition 7 we have $\mathrm{Dev}(\Gamma)(2 - i(\Gamma)) = 1$, it follows that $\mathrm{Dev}(\Gamma) = 1$, as desired.

(iv) If Γ is inconsistent, then $\mathrm{Dev}(\Gamma) = 1$ and $i(\Gamma) = 0$, it is easy to see that $\eta(\Gamma) = 0$ .Conversely, assume that $\eta(\Gamma) = 0$, we have by Definition 7 that $\mathrm{Dev}(\Gamma)(2 - i(\Gamma)) = 2$ .Since $0 \leq \mathrm{Dev}(\Gamma) \leq 1$ and $1 \leq 2 - i(\Gamma) \leq 2$, then it must be that $\mathrm{Dev}(\Gamma) = 1$ and $2 - i(\Gamma) = 2$,therefore $i(\Gamma) = 0$,i.e., Γ is inconsistent.

Acknowledgments. This work was Supported by the National Natural Science Foundation of China (No.10771129) and the Doctoral Foundation of Lanzhou University of Technology.

References

1. Gottwald, S., Novak, V.: On the consistency of fuzzy theories. In: Proceedings of 7th IFSA world congress, pp. 168–171. Academia, Prague (1997)
2. Novak, V., Perfilieva, I.: Mathematical Principles of Fuzzy Logic. Kluwer Academic Publishers, Boston (1999)
3. Wang, G.J., Zhang, W.X.: Consistency degrees of finite theories in Lukasiewicz propositional fuzzy logic. Fuzzy Sets and Systems 149, 275–284 (2005)
4. Zhou, X.N., Wang, G.J.: Consistency degrees of theories in some systems of propositional fuzzy logic. Fuzzy Sets and Systems 152, 321–331 (2005)
5. Zhou, H.J., Wang, G.J.: A new theory consistency index based on deduction theorems in several logic systems. Fuzzy Sets and Systems 157, 427–443 (2006)
6. Wang, G.J.: Introduction to Mathematical Logic and Resolution Principle. Science in China Press, Beijing (2000)

Design for Fuzzy Decoupling Control System
of Temperature and Humidity

Xi-Wen Liu and Tie-Feng Dai

School of Mechanical Engineering,
Xiangtan University,
411105 Xiangtan, Hunan, PRC
liuxiwen1111@163.com, beyond4302@163.com

Abstract. Grain drying process is a complicatedly hysteretic system with multivariate, nonlinearity, time-varying. Traditional control method is difficult to get ideal control effect since there's coupled relation between temperature and humidity, and it's difficult to build accurate mathematical models. Therefore, this thesis inducts decoupling ideas as well as fuzzy control method, realizing decoupling control of temperature and humidity of the system, and uses MATLAB to the corresponding simulation analysis, by comparing with the simulation results of PID control algorithm, it indicates that the system with more superior control effect and greatly improve control precision.

Keywords: temperature; humidity; fuzzy control; decoupling; MATLAB.

0 Foreword

Recently, fuzzy control is extensively researched and applied to solve non-linear and uncertain model in complicated system. In grain drying process, two main factors will influence the drying process: temperature and humidity. The temperature will directly influence the drying speed and also the quality of dried grain; High humidity makes against long-term storage, low temperature will influence the quality and performance rate, decreasing economic income [1]. Therefore, it must be controlled automatically. Nevertheless, drying process has the properties of multivariate, nonlinearity, time-varying, high delay, it's quite difficult to build accurate model during actual design, based on precise model of classic control method [2,3], modern control method [4] is difficult to reach desired effect. And fuzzy control [5,6] is based on fuzzy analects, fuzzy linguistic variables, fuzzy logical deduction, but not intelligent control method which based on precise models. Thus on basis of analyze main aspects of drying process, this thesis put forward fuzzy decoupling control system toward temperature, humidity in drying system, and achieve excellent control effect [7].

1 Fuzzy Control Scheme

In this thesis, temperature and humidity control of drain drying is divided into two parts: normal fuzzy control and fuzzy decoupling control. As shown in figure 1, it's a

G. Shen and X. Huang (Eds.): CSIE 2011, Part I, CCIS 152, pp. 231–236, 2011.

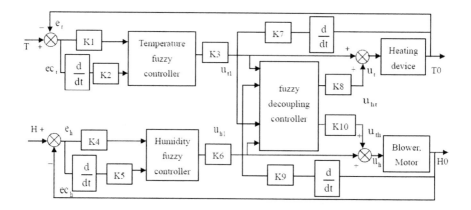

Fig. 1. Fuzzy decoupling control system structure

fuzzy control scheme. The fuzzy decoupling controller is a multi-input and multi-output one, and can be broke down into two-input & single tap fuzzy controller.

As shown, T,H each is the settled value of temperature and humidity in drying system, e_t, e_h each is the deviation of settled value and actual measured value. ec_t, ec_h is the variance ratio accompany with time. First against controlled value T0 and H0, without consider the coupling influence between them, it designs fuzzy temperature controller (F1) and fuzzy humidity controller (F2), U_{fl}, U_{hl} are the output values respectively. Then according to output of fuzzy controller F1 and F2, also the coupling relationship between T0 and H0, designs fuzzy decoupling temperature controller and fuzzy decoupling humidity controller, and designs fuzzy compensation item F21 of T0, fuzzy compensation item F12 of H0 respectively. Their output value should be U_{ht}, U_{th}. And it takes the sum of F1 and fuzzy compensation item F21 U_t ($U_t = U_{tl} + U_{ht}$) to control temperature, as the sum of F2 and fuzzy compensation item F12 $U_h (U_h = U_{hl} + U_{th})$ to control humidity [8,9].

Output value of temperature control and humidity control acts on each actuating mechanism. In this thesis, the temperature controller connects with heater, and by control the power of heater it controls the temperature; humidity controller connect with air blower, motor which used to expel grain. By control air blower, it through adjusting air flow of cold air to control humidity (When the humidity of grain is higher than set value, reduce cold air flow, grain will be dried under high temperature persistently; while the humidity of grain is lower than set value, increase cold air flow, the steam bring in by it will avoid over-dry of grain.). When humidity reach set value, through adjusting the speed of expelling motor, the speed of expel grain will be controlled.

2   Design of Fuzzy Logic Controller

Take temperature as an illustration, set E as temperature error, it's divided into 7 grading variables{NB(Negative Big), NM(Negative Medium), NS(Negative Small),

Z(Zero), PS(Positive Small), PM(Positive Medium), PB(Positive Big)}, EC is variance ratio of temperature error, U is output, and also can be divided into 7 grading
variables. Then quantizing them in fuzzy domain [-6, +6], total 13 grades, that's {-6, -
5 -4, -3, -2, -1, 0, +1, +2, +3, +4, +5, +6}. Membership functions all adopts triangle-
shape grade of membership [10]. Through experience get from temperature control of
grain drying, the control regulation is:

if E=NB then U=PB
if E=NS and EC=Z then U=PS

And so forth, if the fuzzy value of temperature deviation and temperature deviation
variance ratio is known at some point, we can get fuzzy control value according to
experience got from grain drying process. Then after experimental analysis and induction, we can get the temperature control rules as table 1. It's similar with fuzzy temperature controller and fuzzy humidity controller.

Table 1. Fuzzy control rules table of control variable U

U		E						
		NB	NM	NS	Z	PS	PM	PB
	NB	PB	PB	PB	PM	PS	NS	NB
	NM	PB	PB	PM	PM	PS	Z	NB
	NS	PB	PM	PM	PS	Z	NS	NB
EC	Z	PB	PM	PS	Z	NS	NM	NB
	PS	PB	PS	Z	NS	NM	NM	NB
	PM	PB	Z	NS	NM	NM	NB	NB
	PB	PB	PS	NS	NM	NB	NB	NB

3   Design of the Fuzzy Decoupling Controller

As has been noted, there are strong coupling phenomena between temperature control
and humidity control. If without consideration of this, the control effect will be bad,
even there maybe agitation. Therefore, this thesis leads into fuzzy compensation
decoupling control method of temperature and humidity. Take coupling which humidity acts on temperature as an illustration, below will introduce fuzzy decoupling
controller.

Set U_n as temperature normal fuzzy control output value, $\dot{H}0$ is variance ratio of
humidity H0, U_{ht} is fuzzy compensating output of humidity vs. temperature. They're
divided into 5 grading variables{NB, NS, Z, PS, PB}, then quantizing them in fuzzy
domain [-6, +6], a total of 13 ranks. According to experimental experiences [11]:
while heating affects little of humidity, the compensation to humidity is small, and
cooling has great influence to humidity, thus the compensation is big; similarly, hu-
midifying affect little of temperature, then compensation is small, but dehumidifying
has great influence to temperature, thus compensation is big. Therefore, get fuzzy
decoupling control rules as below table 2, it's similar to the decoupling compensation
control rules table which temperature acts on humidity.

Table 2. Fuzzy control rules table of control variable U_{ht}

U_{ht}		U_{rl}				
		NB	NS	Z	PS	PB
	NB	PB	PB	PS	PS	NB
	NS	PB	PS	PS	Z	NB
$\dot{H}0$	ZO	PB	PS	Z	NS	NB
	PS	PB	Z	NS	NS	NB
	PB	PB	NS	NS	NB	NB

From the control rules table, apply synthetic deduction algorithm, and according to weighted average judgment to calculate fuzzy decoupling compensation control enquiry form, as table 3 shows.

Table 3. Fuzzy decoupling compensation control query table

U_{ht}		U_{rl}											
	-6	-5	-4	-3	-2	-1	0	1	2	3	4	5	6
-6	5	4	4	4	4	3	3	3	3	3	1	1	-5
-5	5	4	4	4	4	3	3	2	2	2	0	0	-5
-4	5	4	3	3	3	3	3	2	1	1	0	-1	-5
-3	5	4	3	3	3	3	3	2	1	0	-1	-3	-5
-2	5	4	3	3	2	2	2	1	0	-1	-1	-3	-5
-1	5	4	3	3	2	1	1	0	-1	-2	-2	-3	-5
$\dot{H}0$ 0	5	4	3	3	2	1	0	-1	-2	-3	-3	-4	-5
1	5	3	2	2	1	0	-1	-1	-2	-3	-3	-4	-5
2	5	3	1	1	0	-1	-2	-2	-2	-3	-3	-4	-5
3	5	3	1	0	-1	-2	-3	-3	-3	-3	-3	-4	-5
4	5	1	0	-1	-1	-2	-3	-3	-3	-3	-3	-4	-5
5	5	1	0	-2	-2	-2	-3	-3	-3	-3	-3	-4	-5
6	5	1	-1	-3	-3	-3	-3	-3	-3	-3	-3	-4	-5

4 System Modeling and Simulation

The main problem while drying grain is the control of temperature and humidity in drying bin, the admissibility linear of its controlled object can be similar to large delay section of second order differential, such as $G(s)=\dfrac{Ke^{-\delta}}{(T_1S+1)(T_2S+1)}$. The delay of humidity and temperature is different since the delay time of temperature is longer [11]. With practical experiences, by theoretical deduction, can get the delivery function matrix: temperature object and humidity object while drying grain, see below formula (1) shows.

$$G(s)=\begin{bmatrix} G_{11}(s),G_{12}(s) \\ G_{21}(s),G_{22}(s) \end{bmatrix}=\begin{bmatrix} \dfrac{20e^{-0.02s}}{(0.5s+1)(s+1)}, & \dfrac{10e^{-0.02s}}{(3s+1)(2s+1)} \\ \dfrac{10e^{-0.02s}}{(s+1)(5s+1)}, & \dfrac{20e^{-0.02s}}{(1.5s+1)(s+1)} \end{bmatrix} \qquad (1)$$

Adopting fuzzy control algorithm in this thesis, compared with traditional PID control algorithm, it conducts MATLAB simulation, then get control response curve as figure 2 shows.

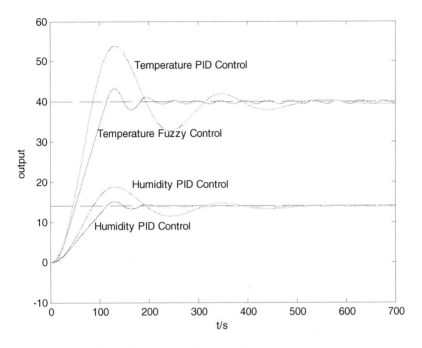

Fig. 2. Fuzzy decoupling control system structure

From simulation figure, by this control method, control effect overstrike a little, and with a quick response, thus it can reach control output in a short time; while traditional PID control method overtake more, and with a longer response period.

5 Closing Words

The research is focus on temperature, humidity and their coupled relation during grain drying process. It adopts fuzzy control method, analyzing temperature control and humidity control and also makes MATLAB simulation for them. After simulative comparison with traditional PID control, it's approved that this control method with strengthened accuracy and steadiness since its control effect overstrikes a little, and with a quick response.

References

1. Ye, Y.-Y.: Rice Dry Technology Development Tendency in Our Country. Grain Processing 33(3), 34–38 (2008) (in Chinese)
2. Marchant, J.A.: Control of High Temperature Continuous Flow Grain Dryers. Agricultural Engineer. 40(4), 145–149 (1985)

3. Courtois, F., Nouafo, J.L., Trystram, G.: Control Strategies for Corn Mixed-flow Dryers. Journal of Drying Technology 13(1-2), 147–164 (1995)
4. Liu, Q., Bakker-Arkema, F.W.: A Model-predictive Controller for Grain Drying. Journal of Food Engineering 49(4), 321–326 (2001)
5. Cai, L., Rad, A.B., Chan, W.-L.: A Genetic Fuzzy Controller for Vehicle Automatic Steering Control. IEEE Transactions on Vehicular Technology, 529–543 (2007)
6. Andujar, J.M., Barragan, A.J.: A Methodology to Design Stable Nonlinear Fuzzy Control Systems. Fuzzy Sets and Systems 154, 157–181 (2005)
7. Liu, C.-Y., Li, K., Song, Z.-Y., et al.: Decoupling Control and Simulation for Variable Flow Heating Systems. In: 2007 International Conference on Machine Learning and Cybernetic, pp. 419–424. IEEE Xplore Digital Library, New York (2007)
8. Omid, M., Lashgari, M., Mobli, H., et al.: Design of Fuzzy Logic Control System Incorporating Human Expert Knowledge for Combine Harvester. Expert Systems with Applications 37, 7080–7085 (2010)
9. Xiang, B.-X., Yu, S.-Y.: Computer Decoupling Control System Equipment Used in Laboratory. Microcomputer Information 21(1), 25–26 (2005) (in Chinese)
10. Shi, X.-M.: Fuzzy Control and its MATLAB Simulation. Tsinghua University Press, Beijing (2008) (in Chinese)
11. Peng, Y.-G., Wei, W.: Fuzzy Control over Temperature and Humidity of Artificial Climate Chest. Transactions of the Chinese Society of Agricultural Engineering 22(8), 166–169 (2006) (in Chinese)

Image Forward Motion Compensation Method for Some Aerial Reconnaissance Camera Based on Neural Network Predictive Control

Chongliang Zhong[1,2], Yalin Ding[1], and Jinbao Fu[1,2]

[1] Changchun Institute of Optics, Fine Mechanics and Physics,
Chinese Academy of Sciences, Changchun, 130033, China
[2] Graduate University of Chinese Academy of Sciences, Beijing, 100039, China

Abstract. In this paper, neural network predictive control method is used to compensate the image forward motion of a certain aerial reconnaissance camera and we have solved several problems that traditional control methods have. Firstly, according to the principle of imaging, we analyzed the reasons for the existence of image forward motion and established the mathematical model. Secondly, we analyzed the theoretically feasibility of the method. At last, simulation, experiments and test are used to validate the practical feasibility. Through what we have done, we conclude that neural network predictive control method can be used to compensate image forward motion for this certain camera and can make a perfect performance.

Keywords: aerial camera, image forward motion, image motion compensation, neural network, predictive control.

1 Introduction

When photographing, it need some exposure time for the recording medium to obtain enough optical energy. But there will be relative motion between the photographic medium and the object during exposure, because of high speed moving and posture changing of the airborne platform, swinging and vibration of the camera, etc. The result is that the image we got will be fuzzy. We call this phenomenon image motion. The magnitude and direction of the image motion will be different, for the working principles (framing type, fissure type, panoramic type, etc) and installation mode (roll, horizontal, vertical, etc) are various for different cameras [1 2 3]. The image quality has been affected seriously because of the existence of the image motion. In order to get clear and high quality images, we must compensate the motion of the image. Though there are several kinds of image motion, experiments show that image forward motion has the most serious affection [4]. So it has significance to do research on image forward motion compensation.

The methods for image motion compensation can be divided into three kinds, namely beforehand compensation, afterwards compensation and comprehensive compensation. Beforehand compensation can also be called active compensation and it compensates the motion before it occurred according to the causes that produce image

G. Shen and X. Huang (Eds.): CSIE 2011, Part I, CCIS 152, pp. 237–244, 2011.

motion, such as optical compensation and mechanical compensation [5]. The after-wards compensation can also be called passive compensation and it treats the fuzzy images with techniques such as image enhancement, image restoration to acquire clear and actual images. When there are high requirements for image quality and precision, beforehand and afterwards compensation can be used together, but domi-nated by beforehand compensation as possible.

In this paper, neural network predictive control method is used to compensate im-age forward motion. Analyze of the theoretical feasibility and experiments show that this method can be used to compensate image forward motion in the camera. It has stronger adaptability, higher control precision and faster operation speed than tradi-tional control method, such as PID algorithm.

2   Image Forward Motion in the Camera

2.1   Imaging Principle

Imaging principle of the camera is shown below.

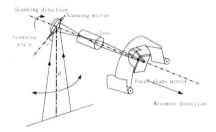

Fig. 1. Principle for imaging

The camera is installed in the airborne platform horizontally. The ray emitted by the ground scenery propagates to the scanning mirror and has been reflected to the objective mirror. Because the scanning mirror is 45°with horizontal, the angle be-tween the input and output ray is 90°. Through the objective mirror, the ray has been focused to the focal-plane reflector. The angle between the input and output ray is 90°, for the focal-plane reflector is also 45°with horizontal. At last, the image of the ground scenery can be formed at the focal-plane after the ray has come through the exposure slit that installed in the shutter mechanism near the focal-plane.

2.2   Production of Image Forward Motion and Optical Compensation

The principle of the image forward motion production is shown in Fig.2. When there is no compensation, the image of a point will become a line at the film, which makes the final image fuzzy.

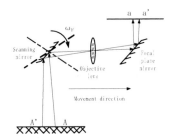

Fig. 2. Image forward motion

Through control, we can make the scanning mirror to rotate when exposure to make as possible aa'=0. If it is assumed that the airborne platform is static, then point A is moving backward by velocity V. The angular velocity for point A will be ω_c relative to the scanning mirror and

$$\omega_c = V(\sin\theta_S) / H \tag{1}$$

According to law of reflection, the compensation angular velocity ω_F can be expressed below

$$\omega_F = \omega_c / 2 = V(\sin\theta_S) / (2H) \tag{2}$$

Formula (2) is the ideal formula and the control equation for completely image forward motion compensation. There are there variables that affects the value of ω_F, so the expected angular velocity may change at the exposure time. For good explanation, see Fig. 3.

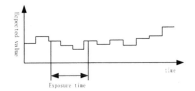

Fig. 3. The relationship between the expected angular velocity and time

The angular velocity should have good tracking ability with the expected value. Neural network predictive control method is used for image motion compensation in this paper.

3   Image Motion Compensation with Neural Network Predictive Control

3.1   Goal and Characteristics for Controlling

From what we have discussed, we can summarize the goal and characteristics of the issue. We hope the angular velocity of the scanning nirror can track the expected value as fast and accurate as possible. The most outstanding characteristic of the problem is that the expected angular velocity is varied and the value can be anyone in a certain range.

3.2 Theoretically Feasibility of the Method

There are three reasons that make neural network predictive control suitable for this issue. Firstly, this method use previous input and output data to predict current output, and then adjusts its control signal with optimal algorithm to make a fast and accurate control. Secondly, the generalization capacity of the neural network can use a certain amount of data to learn, so you don't need to list all the possible conditions and also you can't. Finally, offline training can be used in this method, so when photographing, the calculating speed will be faster. To sum up, neural network predictive control method is quit suitable for image forward motion compensation in this caitain camera.

3.3 Image Motion Compensation with Neural Network Predictive Control

Neural network has been widely used in all kinds of fields for its many advantages [6-11]. The schematic diagram for neural network predictive control is shown below.

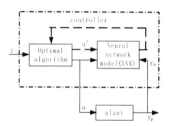

Fig. 4. Schematic diagram for neural network predictive control

The plant includes motor, retarding mechanism and scanning mirror, see Fig. 5.

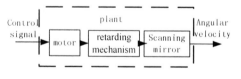

Fig. 5. Plant

The input $r = \omega_F$ is the expected angular velocity of the scanning mirror. As variables θ_S, V and H are measured by sensors, the value of ω_F can be calculated. The time domain response model of the plant can be expressed as

$$y_P(k+1) = f[y_P(k), y_P(k-1), \cdots, y_P(k-n),$$
$$u(k), u(k-1), \cdots\cdots, u(k-m)] \qquad (3)$$

Where $y_P(k)$ is the current angular velocity.

$u(k)$ is the currernt control signal for the plant.

$f(\bullet)$ is the system nonliner time domain response function.

The input for NNM

$$P = f[y_P(k), y_P(k-1), \cdots, y_P(k-n),$$
$$u(k), u(k-1), \cdots, u(k-m)] \tag{4}$$

Then the estimate model of NNM will be

$$y_m(k+1) = f_m[y_P(k), y_P(k-1), \cdots, y_P(k-n),$$
$$u(k), u(k-1), \cdots, u(k-m)] \tag{5}$$

Where $y_m(k+1)$ is the predictive angular velocity.

$f_m(\bullet)$ is the nonliner time domain response function of the plant.

The predictive precision of NNM can be expressed with $e_i(k)$, and

$$e_i(k) = y_m(k) - y_p(k) \tag{6}$$

It is obviously that the angular velocity that after compensation can be expressed as

$$y_p(k+1) = y_m(k+1) + e_i(k) \tag{7}$$

This method is based on receding horizon technique [12]. NNM predicts the current angular velocity of the scanning mirror with some special time horizon, and then the controller adjusts the control signal according to the predicted value and the optimization index J.

$$J = \sum_{j=N_1}^{N_2} [r(t+j) - y_p(t+j)]^2$$
$$+\rho \sum_{j=1}^{N_u} [u'(t+j-1) - u'(t+j-2)]^2 \tag{8}$$

Where N_1 and N_2 define the time window of the tracking error.

N_u defines the time window of the control increments.

u' is the tentative control signal.

r is the desired response.

y_m is the NNM response.

ρ determines the contribution that the sum of the squares of the control increments has on the performance index.

The schematic diagram of recognition with NNM is shown below.

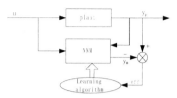

Fig. 6. Schematic diagram of recognition with NNM

The controller includes NNM and the optimization block, the latter one chooses u' according to the rule that J reaches the minimum. Then the optimization control signal u will be inputed to the plant to make the tracking performance optimal.

4   Simulation and Test

Plant recognization with NNM, results that after trainning are shown below

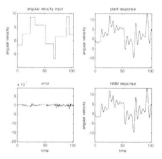

Fig. 7. NNM training result

We can include from Fig.7 that it has achieved the recognition with error magnitude 10^{-5}. Control the scanning mirror with the controller, the results have been shown in Fig.8, and contrast with PID algorithm is shown by Fig.9 .

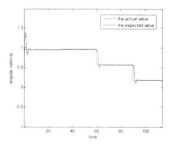

Fig. 8. Compensation result with neural network predictive control method

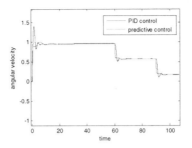

Fig. 9. Contrast between PID and neural network predictive control

We can see from Fig.9 that this method has an obvious advantage when compared with PID algorithm.

5   Conclusions

In this paper, neural network predictive control method is used for image forward motion compensation of a certain camera. This method has high precision, high reliability, high flexibility and fast response. Theoretical analysis, simulation and test show that neural network predictive control method is suitable and can be used to compensate image forward motion of this certain camera.

References

1. Xu, S.Y., Yu, T., Han, C.S., et al.: One batch type real-time adjusting of drift angle of space camera. J. Optics and Precision Engineering 17(8), 1908–1914 (2009)
2. Li, S., Zhang, B., Sun, H.: A real-time restoration algorithm for aerial side-oblique images with different rates of image motion. J. Optics and Precision Engineering 17(4), 895–900 (2009)
3. Xu, Y.C., Ding, Y.L., Tian, H.Y., et al.: The analysis of image motion compensation accuracy for Aerial Pushbroom Sensor. J. Optics and Precision Engineering 17(2), 453–459 (2009)
4. Liu, G.J., Jia, P.: Image motion compensation using image restoration based on wavelet and Wiener filtering. J. Micro. Computer Information 25(6-3), 296–297 (2009)
5. Li, X.H.: study on motion compensating control system in high-resolution space camera. D. Changchun Institute of Optics, Fine Mechanics and Physics (CIOMP), Chinese Academy of Sciences, CAS (2000)
6. Geng, J., Liu, X.D., Chen, Z., et al.: Realization of sorting & taxis of Preisach inverse hysteresis model using neural network. J. Optics and Precision Engineering 18(4), 855–862 (2010)
7. Chen, H., Zhu, J., Liu, Y.Y., et al.: Image fusion based on pulse coupled neural network. J. Optics and Precision Engineering 18(4), 995–1001 (2010)
8. Wu, Z.G., Wang, Y.J.: Multi-focus Image Fusion Algorithm Based On Adaptive PCNN And Wavelet Transform. J. Optics and Precision Engineering 18(3), 708–715 (2010)

9. Lou, S., Ding, Z.L., Yuan, F., et al.: Image Restoration Based on Hopfield Neural Network and Wavelet Domain HMT Model. J. Optics and Precision Engineering 17(11), 2828–2834 (2009)
10. Sheng, C.W., Wang, Z.Q., Liu, C., et al.: The Application of BP Neural Network on the Multi-position Strap-down North Seeking System. J. Optics and Precision Engineering 17(8), 1890–1895 (2009)
11. Zhao, Z.R.: Sliding mode control based on neural network for giant magnetostrictive smart component. J. Optics and Precision Engineering 17(4), 778–786 (2009)
12. Soloway, D., Haley, P.J.: Neural Generalized Predictive Control. In: Proceedings of the 1996 IEEE International Symposium on Intelligent Control, pp. 277–281 (1996)

Application of Multi-hierarchy Grey Relational Analysis to Evaluating Natural Gas Pipeline Operation Schemes

Wenlong Jia, Changjun Li, and Xia Wu

School of Petroleum Engineering, Southwest Petroleum University, Chengdu, China
Jiawenlong08@126.com

Abstract. In the condition of satisfying process requirement, determining the optimum operation schemes of natural gas pipeline network is essential to improve the overall efficiency of network operation. According to the operation parameters of natural gas network, the multi-hierarchy comprehensive evaluation index system is illustrated. This paper presents a multi-hierarchy grey relational analysis method which is suitable for evaluating the multi-hierarchy index system with combining the AHP and grey relational analysis. The comprehensive evaluating mathematic model for natural gas network operation schemes is built based on the method. Ultimately, the practical application shows that multi hierarchy grey relational analysis is effective to evaluate the nature gas pipeline network operation schemes.

Keywords: Natural gas pipeline; Operation schemes; Multi-Hierarchy; Grey relational analysis; Comprehensive evaluation.

1 Introduction

Gas transmission and distribution pipelines play an important role in the development and utilization of natural gas. The network operators can formulate different schemes in the condition of satisfying process requirement. However, the overall goal of operators is quality, quantity and timely supply of gas and best economic as well as the social benefit. Thus, select the optimum scheme from many reasonable options to improve the economic returns and social benefits of pipeline operation is a problem deserving of study [1].

The operation scheme of natural gas pipeline network is close related to the flow rate, temperature, and pressure at each node in the network [2]. It is almost impossible to list all the relevant and determine the relationship among them. However, grey relational analysis is proposed to solve uncertainty problems with incomplete information. This analysis method establishes an overall comparative mechanism, overcomes the limitation of pair-wise comparison [3]. This method has been widely used in the area of oil and gas pipeline optimum designing and comprehensive evaluation [4,5] since professor Wang Yuchun introduced this method into the optimum designing of natural gas pipeline in 1993 [6]. But the index system of objects evaluated is only one layer.

This paper builds the multi-hierarchy comprehensive evaluation index system for natural gas network and calculates their weights firstly. Then the multi-hierarchy grey

G. Shen and X. Huang (Eds.): CSIE 2011, Part I, CCIS 152, pp. 245–251, 2011.

relational analysis method is presented by the combining of the method of AHP and grey relational analysis. Ultimately, this paper evaluates seven different operation schemes of a natural gas network using the method presented.

2   Evaluation Index System and Weights Calculation

2.1   Index System

The index system is the evaluating criterion of the scheme. A natural gas pipeline operation scheme evaluating index system which contains 1 target index, 4 criterion indexes, 8 first grade indexes and 9 second grade indexes is built. The 4 criterion indexes are expressed as: (1) Flow rate in pipelines; (2) Operating income; (3) Operating risk; (4) Gas storage capacity. The first grade indexes are the details contained in criterion indexes. The second grade indexes involving the pipeline's running parameters which can be obtained through pipeline simulation, pipeline running database and formula calculation [2].

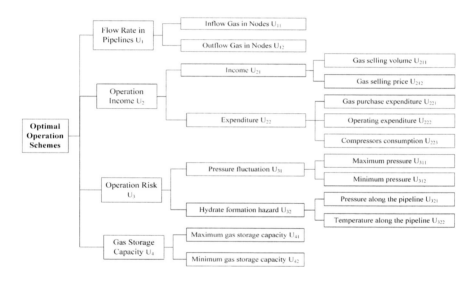

Fig. 1. Multi-hierarchy evaluation index system

2.2   Weights Calculation

Weights, which reflect the relative importance among the indexes, have direct influences on the grey relational grade and grey relational coefficient calculation. Analytic Hierarchy Process (AHP) can overcome the inconsistent problem of expert evaluation method by adjusting the pair wise comparison matrix[8]. However, the adjustment method much depends on personal experiences. Liangliang and Sheng Zhaohan [9] introduced the conception of optimum transmit matrix into AHP and presented an improved AHP through which weights can be obtained directly and without consistency checking. This paper adopts this method to calculate the weights.

3 Multi-hierarchy Grey Relational Analysis Method

We present a multi-hierarchy grey relational analysis method by introducing AHP into traditional grey relational analysis method.

3.1 Procedures of Traditional Grey Relational Analysis Method

The procedures of traditional grey relational analysis are summarized as follow [3]:

(1) Establish the index system of the objective evaluated as shown in Figure1.
(2) Calculate the weights of each index using the improved AHP.
(3) Build the basic database involving bottom indexes as following.
(4) Determine the optimum index sequences and build reference scheme according to up-forward optimum indexes and down-forward optimum indexes.
(5) Normalize indexes according to extreme difference normalization method
(6) Calculate the grey relational coefficient and build grey relational coefficient matrix
(7) Calculate the grey relational grade of each scheme according to weights method.

3.2 Procedures of Multi Hierarchy Grey Relational Analysis Method

Step1: Calculate the grey relational coefficient of each second grade index through step (1) – (6) of traditional grey relational analysis method.

Step2: On the basis of step (1) of traditional grey relational analysis, calculate the grey relational grade of the second grade indexes by (1):

$$R_{ik} = W_{ik}\xi_{ik}^{T} = [w_{ik1} \quad w_{ik2} \quad \cdots \quad w_{ikn}] \begin{bmatrix} \xi_{1ik1} & \xi_{1ik2} & \cdots & \xi_{1ikn} \\ \xi_{2ik1} & \xi_{2ik2} & \cdots & \xi_{2ikn} \\ \cdots\cdots\cdots\cdots\cdots \\ \xi_{mik1} & \xi_{mik2} & \cdots & \xi_{mikn} \end{bmatrix}^{T} \tag{1}$$

Where W_{ik} is the weight matrix of the second grade indexes; ξ_{ik} is the grey relation coefficient matrix of the second grade indexes; m is the total number of schemes; n is total number of the second grade indexes belonging to the same first grade index. ξ_{mikj} denotes the relational coefficient of the index ikj in scheme m, i is the serial number of criterion index layer, k is the serial number of the first grade index belonging to criterion index layer i, j is the serial number of second grade index belonging to the first grade index k; for example, ξ_{1211} indicates the grey relational coefficient of gas selling volume. $R_{ik}=[r_{1ik}, r_{2ik},...,r_{mik}]$ is the grey relational grade matrix of the n second grade indexes belonging to k^{th} first grade index.

Step3: Calculate the grey relational grade of the first indexes by (2):

$$
R_i = W_i \xi_i = W_i \begin{bmatrix} R_{i1} \\ R_{i2} \\ \cdots \\ R_{ih} \end{bmatrix} = \begin{bmatrix} w_{i1} & w_{i2} & \cdots & w_{ih} \end{bmatrix} \begin{bmatrix} r_{1i1} & r_{2i1} & \cdots & r_{mi1} \\ r_{1i2} & r_{2i2} & \cdots & r_{mi2} \\ \cdots\cdots\cdots\cdots\cdots \\ r_{1ih} & r_{2ih} & \cdots & r_{mih} \end{bmatrix} \tag{2}
$$

Where W_i is weight matrix of first grade indexes; w_{ik} is weight of the kth first grade index belonging to i^{th} criterion index. ξ_i is the grey relation coefficient matrix of the first grade indexes; h is the total number of the first indexes belonging to the same criterion layer; R_{ik} is the grey relational coefficient matrix of kth first grade index belonging to the ith criterion index; r_{mik} is the grey relational coefficient of the first grade index ik in scheme m. R_i is the grey relational grade matrix of first grade index belonging to i^{th} criterion index.

Step4: Calculate the comprehensive grey relational grade of criterion layer by (3).

$$
R = W\xi = W \begin{bmatrix} R_1 \\ R_2 \\ \cdots \\ R_p \end{bmatrix} = \begin{bmatrix} w_1 & w_2 & \cdots & w_p \end{bmatrix} \begin{bmatrix} r_{11} & r_{21} & \cdots & r_{m1} \\ r_{12} & r_{22} & \cdots & r_{m2} \\ \cdots\cdots\cdots\cdots\cdots \\ r_{1h} & r_{2h} & \cdots & r_{mh} \end{bmatrix} = \begin{bmatrix} r_1 & r_2 & \cdots & r_p \end{bmatrix} \tag{3}
$$

Where, p is the total number of criterion layer index; W is the weight matrix of criterion index; w_i is weight of the ith criterion index; ξ is the grey relation coefficient matrix of the criterion indexes; r_{mi} is the grey relational grade of first grade index belonging to i^{th} criterion indexes in scheme m; r_m is the comprehensive grey relational grade of mth scheme.

Finally, the superior or inferior of each scheme can be judged based on the values of comprehensive grey relational grade [r_1 r_2 ... r_p] of criterion layer indexes. The larger the value of r_i is, the greater the extent comparative scheme i tallies with reference scheme is. So is the better the comparative scheme.

4 Practical Application

China National Petroleum Corporation (CNPC) Sebei-Ningxia-Lanzhou gas transmission pipeline is 920 km in length, 660mm of inside diameter. There are 4 compressor stations and 26 inflow and distribution nodes along the pipeline. We got 7 operation schemes of the pipeline through simulation.

The weights calculated by improved AHP method of all the indexes are $W=(0.1644, 0.3557, 0.2848, 0.1951)$; $W_1=(0.5633, 0.4367)$; $W_2=(0.6000, 0.4000)$; $W_3=(0.7675, 0.2325)$; $W_4=(0.6667, 0.3333)$; $W_{31}=(0.6667, 0.3333)$; $W_{32}=(0.5000, 0.5000)$.

As shown in Figure 1, two first grade indexes incomeU_{21} and expenditureU_{22} can be obtained by formula calculation of corresponding second indexes. But there are not quantitative formulas to express the relationship among indexes pressure fluctuationU_{31}, hydrate formation hazardsU_{32} and corresponding second grade indexes. The relationships can be explained by multi-hierarchy grey relational analysis.

Table 1. Values of the second grade indexes

Second grade indexes	U_{311}(MPa)	U_{312}(MPa)	U_{321}(MPa)	U_{322}(K)
Scheme 1	5.51	2.00	4.03	263.4
Scheme 2	5.47	2.00	4.00	263.2
Scheme 3	5.89	2.00	4.26	265.7
Scheme 4	5.67	2.00	4.13	277.3
Scheme 5	5.79	2.00	4.20	273.8
Scheme 6	5.87	2.00	4.25	268.4
Scheme 7	6.05	2.00	4.36	269.9

Table 2. Grey relational coefficients of the second grade indexes

Second grade indexes	U_{311}	U_{312}	U_{321}	U_{322}
Scheme 1	0.9310	1.0000	0.9167	0.0142
Scheme 2	1.0000	1.0000	1.0000	0.0000
Scheme 3	0.2759	1.0000	0.2778	0.1773
Scheme 4	0.6552	1.0000	0.6389	1.0000
Scheme 5	0.4483	1.0000	0.4444	0.7518
Scheme 6	0.3103	1.0000	0.3056	0.3688
Scheme 7	0.0000	1.0000	0.0000	0.4752

Table 3. Values of the first grade indexes

First grade indexes	U_{11}	U_{12}	U_{21}	U_{22}	U_{31}	U_{32}	U_{41}	U_{42}
Scheme 1	973.8	905.7	1399.6	810.0	0.931	0.401	326.7	319.4
Scheme 2	889.3	878.0	1305.3	737.9	1.000	0.460	356.5	351.5
Scheme 3	545.7	517.8	846.3	395.6	0.275	0.000	328.0	325.3
Scheme 4	627.0	577.4	951.8	508.6	0.655	1.000	316.2	312.3
Scheme 5	398.8	354.2	556.2	320.1	0.448	0.598	334.3	331.9
Scheme 6	578.1	528.4	857.0	466.5	0.310	0.337	292.3	286.9
Scheme 7	789.9	744.4	1240.4	655.4	0.000	0.237	296.7	279.9

Table 4. Grey relational coefficient of the first grade indexes

First grade indexes	U_{11}	U_{12}	U_{21}	U_{22}	U_{31}	U_{32}	U_{41}	U_{42}
Scheme 1	1.0000	1.0000	1.0000	0.0000	0.9310	0.4019	0.5357	0.5514
Scheme 2	0.8531	0.9497	0.8881	0.1472	1.0000	0.4603	1.0000	1.0000
Scheme 3	0.2556	0.2965	0.3439	0.8458	0.2759	0.0000	0.5562	0.6345
Scheme 4	0.3969	0.4046	0.4691	0.6152	0.6552	1.0000	0.3717	0.4528
Scheme 5	0.0000	0.0000	0.0000	1.0000	0.4483	0.5981	0.6535	0.7265
Scheme 6	0.3118	0.3157	0.3566	0.7011	0.3103	0.3372	0.0000	0.0973
Scheme 7	0.6802	0.7075	0.8113	0.3155	0.0000	0.2376	0.0691	0.0000

Table 5. Grey relational grade of the first grade indexes

Criterion layer	U_1	U_2	U_3	U_{14}
Scheme 1	1.0000	0.9391	0.9188	0.5255
Scheme 2	0.8953	0.9003	1.0000	1.0000
Scheme 3	0.2735	0.6792	0.1910	0.5683
Scheme 4	0.4003	0.5998	0.8302	0.3786
Scheme 5	0.0000	0.0000	0.5223	0.6670
Scheme 6	0.3135	0.4432	0.3190	0.0000
Scheme 7	0.6921	1.0000	0.0000	0.0141

Table 6. Comprehensive grey relational grade of criterion layer and prior order of schemes

Scheme No.	Comprehensive grey relational grade	Prior order
Scheme 1	0.8733	2
Scheme 2	1.0000	1
Scheme 3	0.2587	5
Scheme 4	0.4646	3
Scheme 5	0.0000	7
Scheme 6	0.0316	6
Scheme 7	0.2893	4

Table 1 lists the original values of the second grade indexes U_{311}, U_{312}, U_{321} and U_{322}. The grey relational coefficients of the second grade indexes listed in Table 3 are calculated from step (1)-(6) based on Table 1. In other words, values of first grade indexes (U_{31}; U_{32}) in Table 4 are grey relational grade of second grade indexes (U_{311}, U_{312}; U_{321}, U_{322}) and the grey relational grades are calculated from equation (1). Table 5 lists grey relational coefficient of the first grade indexes. They are calculated as the same way as coefficients in Table 2. On the basis of Table 4, Table 5 is calculated with using of equation (2). Table 6 lists the comprehensive evaluation results which obtained based on the grey relational coefficients of the criterion layer indexes. The procedures ensure the information contained in lower index layers can be fully utilized when we evaluate the upper index layers.

In Table 6 are listed the evaluation results obtained. As can be seen, scheme 2 is the optimum scheme. But notice that not all the criterion indexes of scheme 2 are the optimum ones. Even though scheme 7 has the optimum operation income, its operation risk value is 0.0000 which means the scheme is the most unsafe one. Considering the factors above, scheme 7 is ranked 4th. Similar to scheme 7, scheme 1 has the best flow rate but is ranked 2nd. The results illustrate that the comprehensive prior order of the schemes are not depend on the prior order of any single one certain index, but depend on all the indexes' prior order. The analysis is consistent with practical conditions.

5 Conclusion

(1) Based on the natural gas pipeline network operation parameters, a multi-hierarchy index system used to evaluate the operation scheme is built. The system covers four evaluation criterions: flow rate in pipeline, operation income, operation risk and gas

storage capacity. Then this paper introduces an improved AHP to calculate the weights of each index.

(2) In order to evaluate the multi-hierarchy index system, a multi-hierarchy grey relational method is presented with combining AHP and grey relational analysis. The method can make full use of the information contained in lower layer to evaluate the upper layer indexes.

(3) Seven different operation schemes of Se-Ning-Lan gas pipeline are evaluated by the multi-hierarchy grey relational analysis method. The practical application shows that it is reasonable to evaluate the gas pipeline operation schemes by this method.

Acknowledgments. This paper is a project supported by sub-project of National science and technology major project of China (No.2008ZX05054) and China National Petroleum Corporation（CNPC） tackling key subject : Research and Application of Ground Key Technical for CO2 flooding, JW10-W18-J2-11-20.

References

1. Li, C.J., Zhao, J.Z.: Optimized Operation of Gas Transmission Pipelines. Natural Gas Industry 25(10), 106–109 (2004) (in Chinese)
2. Li, C.L.: Natural Gas Pipeline Transmission, 2nd edn. Petroleum Industry Press, Beijing (2008) (in Chinese)
3. Deng, J.L.: A Course on Grey System Theory. Huazhong Univ. of Sci. & Tech. Press, Wuhan (1990)
4. Liang, G.C., Zheng, Y.P.: Grey Correlation Analysis of Optimized Design for Underground Gas Storage. Natural Gas Industry 24(9), 142–144 (2004) (in Chinese)
5. Yang, D.W., Zhao, X.M.: Application of grey relation analysis method to efficiency evaluation of stations and tank farms in oil and gas gathering and transportation system. Journal of China University of Petroleum 31(4), 98–104 (2007) (in Chinese)
6. Wang, Y.C.: A New Method of Optimally Designing Transmission Line. Natural Gas Industry 13(6), 64–69 (1993) (in Chinese)
7. Jia, W.L., Li, C.J.: Comprehensive Evaluation on Regulation Schemes of Gas Transmission Pipelines. In: 1st ASCE International Conference on Pipeline and Trenchless Technology, pp. 581–590. ASCE Press, Shanghai (2009)
8. Bhushan, N., Kanwal, R.: Strategic Decision Making: Apply the Strategic Decision Making: Applying the Analytic Hierarchy Process. Springer, London (2004)
9. Liang, L., Sheng, Z.H.: An improved Analytic Hierarchy Process. System Engineering 7(3), 5–7 (1989) (in Chinese)

3D Garment Prototyping from 2D Drawings

Yueqi Zhong[1, 2], JuanFen Jiang[2], Zhaoli Wang[2], and Hongyan Liu[2]

[1] Key Laboratory of Ministry of Education on Textile Fabric Technology,
Donghua University, 201620 Shanghai, China
[2] College of Textiles, Donghua University,
201620 Shanghai, China
zhyq@dhu.edu.cn

Abstract. In this paper, we propose a novel approach to transfer the designer's 2D drawings into 3D virtual garment. The designer is required to provide minimum two silhouettes for the front view and the back view of the original design. The silhouettes are triangulated to form a mass-spring system. The virtual sewing of the silhouettes generates the initial shell of the 3D garment. The following drape simulation finalizes the 3D configuration of the original design. Euler integration and Verlet integration are employed for sewing and draping respectively. Various experimental results validate that this method is an effective approach in fast prototyping 3D counterpart of the original design.

Keywords: 2D drawing, triangulation, physically-based modeling, 3D garment.

1 Introduction

Sketching is the initial tool for garment design. The designer can express his/her ideal garment on the paint board with few strokes. Recent advances in "sketch-based interface & modeling" (SBIM) have made it possible to transfer the 2D sketches into 3D counterpart. The major concern in sketch-based interfaces for modeling (SBIM) [1] is to automate or assist the translation procedure from 2D sketches to 3D models. This technique makes computers understand and interpret sketches in three dimensions.

Takeo Igarashi et al. [2] first built the famous Teddy's sketching interface for 3D free form design. An inflation algorithm was proposed to create primitive 3D models with editing tools such as extrusion, cutting, and smoothing algorithms. The Smooth Teddy system [3] added advanced algorithms to reach mesh beautification, refinement and to organize the shapes hierarchically. Schmidt et al. [4] introduced the Shape-Shop, which was in the style of Teddy, the system not only optimized the user sketch interface, but also implemented direct 3D animation relied on hierarchical implicit volume modeling. Similar systems were extended in SmoothSketch [5] and Fiber-Mesh [6] for a better output.

To interpreting designers' sketches to 3D virtual garments, Turquin et al. [12] firstly introduced a sketch-based garment designing method. They used distances filed between the 2D garment silhouette and the character model to infer distance variations in 3D space, and constructed a primitive 3D garment template. For each fold stroke, two parameters, radius and amplitude, were linear interpolated to shape 3D fold. Hadap et al. [13] presented a geometric wrinkling algorithm to simulate cloth

G. Shen and X. Huang (Eds.): CSIE 2011, Part I, CCIS 152, pp. 252–257, 2011.

wrinkles. In their practice, modulation factors were adopted to conserve area. In the famous cartoon film "Shrek", the developers defined wrinkles deformation coefficients to approximate the wrinkles shape, and the initial wrinkles were smoothed by anti-aliasing [14].

In this paper, we propose a quite different approach in transferring the original design drawings into 3D garment. The enclosed shapes of the drawings are regarded as patterns that can be physically sewn together. The final 3D configuration is obtained by draping the sewn garment along the avatar. The organization of this paper follows. In section 1, we briefly review the related work in SBIM. In section 2, we introduce our methods in shape triangulation, sewing and draping. In section 3, we provide various results to verify our proposed method, and in section 4, we conclude our work.

2 Algorithms

The major steps involved in our proposed method are:

(1) Transfer the original drawings into a mass-spring system.
(2) Use two-stage integration to fulfill the virtual sewing and draping respectively.

2.1 Constructing a Mass-Spring System for the Original Drawings

At the beginning, the user is required to draw the designed garment to form a closed shape, as shown in Fig.1. After which, It is recommended to separate the sleeves and/or legs area to ensure that these parts can be rotated along the limbs of a given avatar. This is actually a preprocessing to promise a better pose synchronization between the patterns of the garment and the avatar when the pose of the avatar alters.

Fig. 1. Original design and the separated panels

Once the segmentation of the original drawing has been finished, each pattern will be meshed by Delaunay triangulation. The mesh density is adjustable to mimic different fabric style. Usually, sparse mesh indicates a less flexible style, such as the winter coat, while intense mesh implies a silk-like style, such as the evening dress. The sewing relationship is appointed manually, as shown in Fig.2. Each sewing pair must point to the same direction to ensure the correct sewing manner (see the arrow lines in Fig.2).

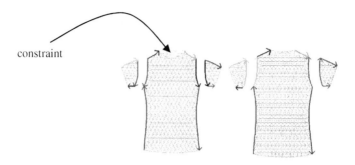

constraint

Fig. 2. Original patterns after Delaunay triangulation with constraints and arrowed seam-lines

The triangulated pattern is now transferred into a mass spring system. The vertices are regarded as masses, and the edges of each triangle are regarded as stretch springs. There is no shear springs since the triangular element is a stable configuration. The bending spring is added for every paired triangle that shares the same edge. The connection between two vertices that is not on the shared edge is regarded as the bending spring.

For collar area, a so-called constraint spring is added, as shown in Fig.2. These constraint springs are designed to maintain the shape of the collar to reach a reliable visual effect. When the constrained area is under heavily stretching, these constraints can hold the two ends close to its rest length. For this reason, the Hook constant of these springs is set the same as that of the stretch springs.

2.2 Two-Stage Integration for Virtual Sewing and Draping

After transferring from the 2D drawings to the physically-based fabric pieces, i.e., the patterns for virtual sewing, affine transformation will be performed to position these patterns around the avatar in terms of the pose of the limbs. For example, the sleeves are aligned with the axis (or bones) of the arms. Pants should be aligned with the legs. The affine transformation includes either the combined translation, rotation and scaling to fit the entire patterns against the avatar in the same manner or the singular treatment on a select pattern. In this way, the patterns can be placed and scaled with the best perception before the sewing should be initiated. Although our previous work provided the way to position the patterns automatically [15], the positioning can also be performed by the user manually to reach the maximum flexibility of manipulation. Fig.4 demonstrates the patterns after positioning.

In our practice, the sewing force is designed as the function of distance, air resistance, and damping, as detailed in our previous work [15]. The sewing is actually an area increasing procedure since the original design does not possess enough area to cover the curved surface of human body. Based on this limitation, the integration of virtual sewing is solved by Euler integration. The elongation of the springs is not limited. This is to ensure the area increasing can be engaged successfully. Once the sewing has been fulfilled, the draping is solved by Verlet integration where the strain control is strictly enforced as the constraint of computation.

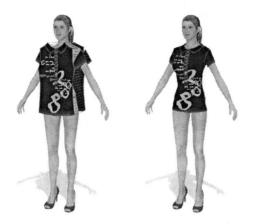

Fig. 3. Positioning the patterns and the finalized 3D model after sewing and draping

A straight-forward approach of Euler method is given by:

$$\begin{cases} \mathbf{v}_{n+1} = \mathbf{v}_n + h\mathbf{a}_n \\ \mathbf{x}_{n+1} = \mathbf{x}_n + h\mathbf{v}_{n+1} \end{cases} \tag{1}$$

Where $\mathbf{x}_{n+1}$, $\mathbf{v}_{n+1}$ denotes vector of position and velocity respectively at the end of the time step h. $\mathbf{x}_n$, $\mathbf{v}_n$ are initial vectors of position and velocity of the time step. $\mathbf{a}_n$ represents vector of acceleration at the beginning of the time step. The Verlet integration is in the style of

$$\mathbf{x}_{n+1} = 2\mathbf{x}_n - \mathbf{x}_{n-1} + h^2 \mathbf{a}_n . \tag{2}$$

where $\mathbf{x}_{n-1}$ is the position at the end of the previous time step.

The benefit of the two-stage integration is that the original pattern can be enlarged enough to cover the human body as an initial shell, and the model can be draped along the avatar without superficial artifact such as over elongation. Technically, Verlet integration is a stable scheme since the velocity is implicitly given and consequently, the velocity and position are always synchronized.

The collision happened in the first stage is solved by following the momentum conservation law to change the velocity of each mass after colliding, as detailed in our previous work [15]. For the collision happened in the second stage, the collision is handled by projecting the colliding elements out of the colliding surface. The moving direction is selected as the normal of the colliding surface. No self-intersection detection and response is involved in this approach to speed up the prototyping of 3D garment.

3 Results and Conclusion

We generated several garment models from 2D drawings to validate our proposed method, as shown in Fig.3. The visual effects indicate that this method is an effective approach in prototyping the original design in three dimensional views. The viewer can evaluate the design without making the real garment from scratch. Compared with the traditional 3D CAD system, it is no necessary to draft the original design into real patterns, which may save a huge cost in human labor and effort. We believe this is the major contribution of this work.

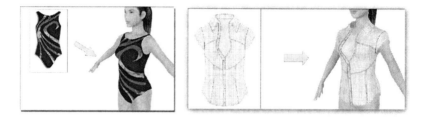

Fig. 3. More results of fast garment prototyping based our proposed method

To conclude our work, we provide an effective way in prototyping the 2D drawings of garment design. This method is to sew and drape the 2D drawings in a physical way. Delaunay triangulation is employed to transfer the drawings into a mass-spring system. A two-stage integration procedure is engaged for sewing and draping respectively to reach the final 3D configuration. The proposed method has been proved to be a novel and efficient approach by various examples for sketch based 3D garment reconstruction.

Acknowledgments. This work is supported by Natural Science Foundation of China (No. 60973072).

References

1. Olsen, L., Samavati, F.F., Sousa, M.C., Jorge, J.A.: Sketch-based Modeling: A Survey. Computer & Graphics 33, 85–103 (2009)
2. Igarashi, T., Matsuoka, S.: Teddy: A Sketching Interface for 3d Freeform Design. In: Proceedings of the SIGGRAPH 1999, New York, pp. 409–416 (1999)
3. Igarashi, T., Hughes, J.F.: Smooth Meshes for Sketch-based Freeform Modeling. In: International Conference on Computer Graphics and Interactive Techniques: ACM SIGGRAPH 2007 courses, San Diego, California (2007)
4. Schmidt, R., Wyvill, M.C., Sousa, M.C., Jorge, J.: ShapeShop: Sketch-Based Solid Modeling with BlobTrees. In: 2nd EUROGRAPHICS Workshop on Sketch-Based Interfaces and Modeling, Dublin, Ireland, pp. 53–62 (2005)

5. Karpenko, O.A., Hughes, J.F.: SmoothSketch: 3D Freeform Shapes from Complex Sketches. In: Proceedings of SIGGRAPH 2006 ACM Transactions on Graphics. ACM Press, New York (2006)
6. Nealen, A., Igarashi, T., Sorkine, O., Alexa, M.: FiberMesh: Designing Freeform Surface with 3D Curves. In: Proceedings of the SIGGRAPH 2007 ACM Transactions on Graphics. ACM Press, New York (2007)
7. Nealen, A., Sorkine, O., Alexa, M., Cohen-or, D.A.: Sketch-Based Interface for Detail-Preserving Mesh Editing. ACM Transactions on Graphics 24, 1142–1147 (2005)
8. Zimmermann, J., Nealen, A., Alexa, M.: SilSketch: Automated Sketch-Based Editing of Surface Meshes. In: EUROGRAPHICS Workshop on Sketch-Based Interfaces and Modeling (SBIM 2007) (2007)
9. Kara, L., Stahovich, T.: An Image-Based Trainable Symbol Recognizer for Hand Drawn Sketches. Computer & Graphics 29(4), 501–517 (2005)
10. Kara, L., Shimada, K.: Construction and Modification of 3D Geometry Using a Sketch-Based Interface. In: Proceedings of EUROGRAPHICS Workshop on Sketch-Based Interfaces and Modeling, SBIM 2006 (2006)
11. Kraevoy, V., Sheffer, A., Panne, M.: Modeling from Contour Drawing. In: EUROGRAPHICS Symposium on Sketch-Based Interfaces and Modeling, New Orleans, LA, pp. 37–44 (2009)
12. Turquin, E., Wither, J., Boissieux, L., Cani, M.P.: A Sketch-Based Interface for Clothing Virtual Characters. IEEE Computer Graphics and Applications, 72–81 (January/February 2007)
13. Hadap, S., Bangerter, E., Volino, P., Magnenat-Thalmann, N.: Animating Wrinkles on Clothes. In: Proceedings of the Conference on Visualization (1999)
14. Cutler, L.D., Gershbein, R., Wang, X.C., Crutis, C., Maigret, E., Prasso, L., Farson, P.: An Art-Directed Wrinkles System for CG Character Clothing and Skin. Graphical Models 69, 219–230 (2005)
15. Zhong, Y., Xu, B.: Three-dimensional Garment Dressing Simulation. Textile Research Journal 79, 792–803 (2009)

A Chaos-Based Image Encryption Scheme with Confusion- Diffusion Architecture

Zhi-xian Zhang and Ting Cao

College of Electronics Information Engineering,
Shenyang Aerospace University,
Shenyang, 110136, P.R. China
ct198636@163.com

Abstract. This paper proposes an efficient chaos-based image encryption scheme, in which shuffling the positions and changing the grey values of image pixels are combined to confuse the relationship between the cipher-image and the plain-image. Firstly, the Arnold Cat map is employed to shuffle the positions of the image pixels in the spatial domain. Then the discrete output signal of the Lorenz chaotic system is preprocessed to be suitable for the grayscale image encryption, and the shuffled image is encrypted by the preprocessed signal pixel by pixel. The experimental results demonstrate that the key space is large enough to resist the brute force attack and the distribution of grey values of the encrypted image has a random like behavior.

Keywords: Chaos, Image encryption; Arnold Cat map; Lorenz chaotic system.

1 Introduction

The fascinating developments in digital image processing and network communications during the past decade have created a great demand for real-time secure image transmission over the Internet and through wireless networks. Due to some intrinsic features of images, such as bulk data capacity and high correlation among pixels, traditional encryption algorithms such as DES, AES and RSA are not suitable for practical image encryption, especially under the scenario of on-line communications. To meet this challenge, a variety of encryption schemes have been proposed. Among them, chaos-based algorithms have shown some exceptionally good properties in many concerned aspects regarding security, complexity, speed, computing power and computational overhead, etc [1-4]. It has been proved that in many aspects chaotic maps have analogous but different characteristics as compared with conventional encryption algorithms [5-10].

A new scheme is suggested in this paper for secure image encryption. Shuffling the positions and changing the grey values of image pixels are performed simultaneously in the proposed method. The rest of this paper is organized as follows. Section 2 describes the proposed method. Section 3 presents the experimental results. Security analyses are given in Section 4, and finally this paper is concluded in Section 5.

G. Shen and X. Huang (Eds.): CSIE 2011, Part I, CCIS 152, pp. 258–263, 2011.
© Springer-Verlag Berlin Heidelberg 2011

2 The Proposed Cryptosystem

The image encryption algorithm includes two steps: Firstly, the positions of the pixels of the original image are shuffled by Arnold Cat map. Then the pixel values of the shuffled image are encrypted by Lorenz chaotic system.

2.1 Confusion by Arnold Cat Map

Image data have strong correlations among adjacent pixels. Statistical analysis on large amounts of images shows that averagely adjacent 8 to 16 pixels are correlative in horizontal, vertical, and also diagonal directions for both natural and computer-graphical images. In order to disturb the high correlation among pixels, we employ Arnold Cat map to shuffle the pixel positions of the plain-image. Without loss of generality, we assume the dimension of the original grayscale image I is $N \times N$. The co-ordinates of the pixels are $S = \{(x, y) \mid x, y = 0,1,2,...,N-1\}$. Arnold Cat map is described as

$$\begin{bmatrix} x' \\ y' \end{bmatrix} = A \begin{bmatrix} x \\ y \end{bmatrix} (\mod N) = \begin{bmatrix} 1 & p \\ q & pq+1 \end{bmatrix} \begin{bmatrix} x \\ y \end{bmatrix} (\mod N) \qquad (1)$$

where p and q are positive integers, $\det(A) = 1$. The map is area-preserving since the determinant of its linear transformation matrix equals (1). The (x', y') is the new position of the original pixel position (x, y) when Arnold Cat map is performed once. Iterated actions of A on a pixel $r_0 \in S$ form a dynamical system

$$r_{n+1} = A^n r_0 (\mod N) \text{ or } r_{n+1} = A r_n (\mod N) \qquad (2)$$

where $n = 0, 1, 2, \ldots$ The set of points $\{r_0, r_1, r_2, \ldots\}$ is an orbit of the system with a period, i.e., there exist positive integers T and n_0, such that $r_{n+T} = r_n$, $n = n_0, n_0 + 1, n_0 + 2, \ldots$ The period T depends on the parameters p, q and the size N of the original image. Thus the parameters p, q and the number of iterations M all can be used as the secret keys. Since there only exists a linear transformation and mod function, it is very efficient to shuffle the pixel positions using the Arnold Cat map. After several iterations, the correlation among the adjacent pixels can be disturbed completely. Some experiments are given in Section 3 to demonstrate the efficiency of Arnold Cat map. However, the periodicity of Arnold Cat map should degrade the security the encryption, because the possible opponents may iterate the Arnold Cat map continuously to reappear the original plain-image. As a remedy, we employ Lorenz chaotic system to change the pixel values next to improve the security.

2.2 Diffusion by Lorenz Chaotic System

Lorenz chaotic system is described as follows,

$$\begin{cases} \dfrac{dx}{dt} = \sigma(y - x) \\[2mm] \dfrac{dy}{dt} = rx - xz - y \\[2mm] \dfrac{dz}{dt} = xy - bz \end{cases} \qquad (3)$$

where σ, b and r are parameters. If one chooses $\sigma = 10$, $b = 8/3$, $c > 24.74$, the system is chaotic. The chaotic behavior of Lorenz chaotic system using fourth order Runge–Kutta algorithm is shown in Fig. 1. The step of the Runge–Kutta is chosen as 0.001.

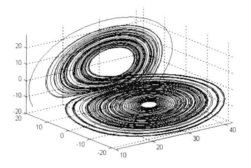

Fig. 1. Chaotic behavior of Lorenz system

In the proposed scheme, three discrete variables of the Lorenz chaotic system are employed to encrypt the shuffled image. The encryption process consists of three steps of operations.

(1) The pixels of the shuffled image are arranged by the order from left to right and then top to bottom and we can get a set $S = \{S_1, S_2, \ldots, S_{N \times N}\}$, in which each element is the decimal grey value of the pixel. Convert decimal pixel values to binary numbers and we can get a new set $B = \{B_1, B_2, \ldots, B_{N \times N}\}$.

(2) Iterate the Lorenz chaotic for N_0 times.

(3) The Lorenz chaotic system is iterated continuously. For each iteration, we can get three values x_i, y_i and z_i. These decimal values are preprocessed first as follows

$$B_{xi} = dec2bin(\mathrm{mod}((Abs(x_i - Floor(Abs(x_i))) \times 10^{14}, 256)), \qquad (4)$$

where $Abs(x)$ returns the absolute value of x. $Floor(x)$ rounds the elements of x to the nearest integers less than or equal to x. $\mathrm{mod}(x, y)$ returns the remainder after division. The function $dec2bin(x)$ converts decimal number x to binary value. Because in the proposed cryptosystem all the variables declared as type *double* which has a bit-length of 64 bits, all the variables have a 15-digit precision when expressed in scientific notation. The decimal fractions of the variables are multiplied by 10^{14}. Moreover, in $\mathrm{mod}(x, y)$ function the variable y is chosen as 256 because the grayscale image with 256 grey levels is used in the proposed scheme. The shuffled image is encrypted as

$$C_{3\times(i-1)+1} = B_{3\times(i-1)+1} \oplus B_{xi} \oplus C_{3\times(i-2)+1}$$

$$C_{3\times(i-1)+2} = B_{3\times(i-1)+2} \oplus B_{yi} \oplus C_{3\times(i-2)+2} \qquad (5)$$

$$C_{3\times(i-1)+3} = B_{3\times(i-1)+3} \oplus B_{zi} \oplus C_{3\times(i-2)+3}$$

where $i = 1, 2, \ldots$ represents the ith iteration of the Lorenz chaotic system. The symbol $\oplus$ represents the exclusive OR operation bit-by-bit. The Lorenz chaotic system is iterated until all the elements in the set $B = \{B_1, B_2, \ldots, B_{N\times N}\}$ is encrypted. Then every element in the encrypted set $C = \{C_1, C_2, \ldots, C_{N\times N}\}$ is converted into decimal numbers and we can obtain the cipher-image.

3 Experimental Results

Some experimental results are given in this section to demonstrate the efficiency of the proposed scheme. In all experiments, the precision is 10^{-14}, which is easy to be implemented on today's personal computer. The plain-image with size 256×256 is shown in Fig. 2(a) and the 3D histogram of the plain-image is shown in Fig. 2(b).

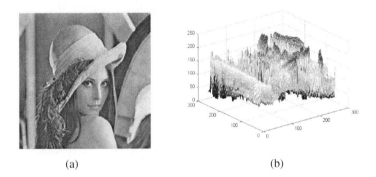

(a)   (b)

Fig. 2. Plain-image and its histogram: (a) plain-image; (b) 3D histogram of the plain-image

Fig. 3(a) is the shuffled image and Fig. 3(b) is the 3D histogram of the shuffled image. The secret keys are chosen as $p = 1$, $q = 1$ and $M = 5$. As can be seen that, Arnold Cat map only shuffle the pixel positions of the image since the histogram of the plain-image is the same as the shuffled image.

Fig. 4(a) illustrates the cipher-image and Fig. 4(b) is the corresponding 3D histogram. The secret keys to change the pixel values of the shuffled image are $x_0 = 1.3604$, $y_0 = 1.2052$, $z_0 = 1.5026$. As we can see, the 3D histogram of the ciphered image is fairly uniform and is significantly different from that of the original image. The encryption procedure complicates the dependence of the statistics of the output on the statistics of the input.

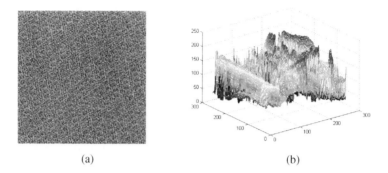

(a)   (b)

Fig. 3. Encryption by using Arnold Cat map: (a) shuffled image; (b) histogram of the shuffled image

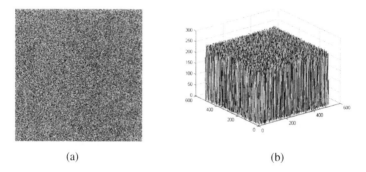

(a)   (b)

Fig. 4. Encryption by Lorenz chaotic system: (a) cipher-image; (b) histogram of the cipher-image

4   Security Analyses

A good encryption scheme should be sensitive to the secret keys, and the key space should be large enough to make brute-force attacks infeasible. In the proposed encryption algorithm, the initial values of Lorenz chaotic system are used as secret keys. If the precision is 10^{-14}, the key space size is 10^{42}. Moreover, the parameters p, q and M of Arnold Cat map are also used as the secret keys. The key space is large enough to resist all kinds of brute-force attacks. The experimental results also demonstrate that the proposed scheme is very sensitive to the secret key mismatch (10^{-14}).

Fig. 5 illustrates the key sensitivity capacity of the proposed scheme. The cipher-image is shown in Fig. 4(a), which is decrypted using $x_0 = 1.3604000001$, $y_0 = 1.2052$, $z_0 = 1.5026$, $p = 1$, $q = 1$ and $M = 5$. As can be seen that, even the secret key x_0 is changed a little (10^{-14}), the decrypted image is absolutely different from the plain-image. As we can see, the decrypted image with wrong keys has a histogram with random behavior. The sensitivity to initial conditions which is the main characterization of chaos guarantees the security of the proposed scheme. Undoubtedly, the secret keys are secure enough even a chosen plain-text/cipher-text attack is employed.

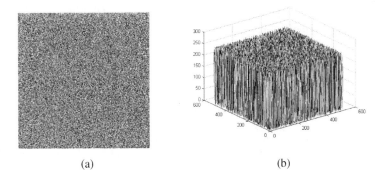

(a)   (b)

Fig. 5. The sensitivity to the secret key: (a) decrypted image (x_0 =1.3604000001, y_0 = 1.2052, z_0 = 1.5026); (b) histogram of the decrypted image

5 Conclusions

In this paper, a new image encryption scheme is presented. Shuffling the positions and changing the grey values of image pixels are combined simultaneously to ensure the security of the proposed method. The proposed algorithm has three advantages: (1) the algorithm has a large enough key space to resist all kinds of brute force attacks; (2) the cipher-image has a good statistical property; (3) the encryption algorithm is very sensitive to the secret keys.

References

1. Scharinger, J.: Fast encryption of image data using chaotic Kolmogorov flows. Journal of Electronic Imaging 7(2), 318–325 (1998)
2. Fridrich, J.: Symmetric ciphers based on two-dimensional chaotic maps. International Journal of Bifurcation and Chaos 8(6), 1259–1284 (1998)
3. Chen, G.R., Mao, Y.B., Chui, C.: A symmetric image encryption scheme based on 3D chaotic cat maps. Chaos Solitons & Fractals 21(3), 749–761 (2004)
4. Belkhouche, F., Gokcen, I., Qidwai, U.: Chaotic gray-level image transformation. Journal of Electronic Imaging 14(4), 043001 (2005)
5. Gao, H.J., Zhang, Y.S., Liang, S.Y., et al.: A new chaotic algorithm for image encryption. Chaos Solitons & Fractals 29(2), 393–399 (2006)
6. Pareek, N.K., Patidar, V., Sud, K.: Image encryption using chaotic logistic map. Image and Vision Computing 24(9), 926–934 (2006)
7. Kwok, H.S., Tang, W.K.S.: A fast image encryption system based on chaotic maps with finite precision representation. Chaos Solitons & Fractals 32(4), 1518–1529 (2007)
8. Behnia, S., Akhshani, A., Ahadpour, S., et al.: A fast chaotic encryption scheme based on piecewise nonlinear chaotic maps. Physics Letters A 366(4-5), 391–396 (2007)
9. Gao, T.G., Chen, Z.: A new image encryption algorithm based on hyper-chaos. Physics Letters A 372(4), 394–400 (2008)
10. Patidar, V., Pareek, N.K., Sud, K.K.: A new substitution-diffusion based image cipher using chaotic standard and logistic maps. Communications in Nonlinear Science and Numerical Simulation 14(7), 3056–3075 (2009)

Experimental Study on Diesel Vehicle's Fuel Consumption Feature While Coasting on Level Road

Hongliang Lin[1,2], Xuanmeng Cui[2], Qiang Yu[1], and Songpan Yang[3]

[1] Automobile School, Chang'an University, Xi'an, 710064, China
[2] Department of Automobile Engineering,
Shaanxi College of Communication Technology, Xi'an, 710018, China
[3] Xi'an Cummins Engine Company Limited
lin_hong_liang@163.com

Abstract. Coasting is frequently used by drivers on level road. So analyzing vehicle's fuel consumption feature during sliding process has practical significance on realizing reasonable driving and lowering fuel consumption. Taking some light-duty diesel vehicle as experimental object, this paper discussed the fuel economy variation discipline and curves based on various coasting tests, especially analyzed the fuel consumption difference between sliding in neutral and sliding in different gears. The result shows that vehicle's average fuel consumption rate while sliding in different gears is similar, which is about to 1/50 of sliding in neutral'. While sliding, the vehicle's fuel consumption rate basically maintains at a low level. But once the coasting speed is too low, the fuel consumption rate increases dramatically. Therefore, aiming at lowing fuel consumption and reducing emission discharge, vehicle sliding in gear should have priority to sliding in neutral and choosing a reasonable coasting speed range is important.

Keywords: diesel vehicle; energy saving; fuel consumption feature; coasting; polynomial fitting; linear regression analysis; driving behavior.

1 Introduction

By the oil crisis, automotive energy-saving work has been concerned around the world. At present, countries in the world dedicated to the research about vehicle emission reduction and energy conservation. Generally, factors that affect vehicle's fuel economy can be summarized into four main categories which include vehicle performance, road traffic situation, environmental condition and driver operating behavior. In other words, vehicle's fuel consumption was depended upon not only vehicle's design, manufacturing and assembly, but also road condition and driver's operation [1] [2]. Among those factors, driver is the principal and therefore driving behavior has a great influence on vehicle's actual running fuel consumption. Many studies about vehicle's fuel consumption had been carried on by scholars from Institute of Highway Ministry of Transport in the 9th five-year plan period. Surveys showed that difference of actual fuel consumption reached up to 2.34 L/100km to 6.81L/100km while different professional drivers drove the same vehicle and 7.46% to 22.35% difference existed in fuel consumption state. The above data indicated that driving technique had significant

G. Shen and X. Huang (Eds.): CSIE 2011, Part I, CCIS 152, pp. 264–270, 2011.
© Springer-Verlag Berlin Heidelberg 2011

impact on vehicle's fuel consumption [3]. Gao Jidong from Southeast University, sponsored by Natural Science Foundation, had studied vehicle's fuel consumption in urban road traffic system and established macroscopic model and microscopic model to analyze different driving behaviors' impact on vehicle's fuel consumption in city transport system [4]. Many studies showed that selecting proper operation mode was one effective way to improve the vehicle's running fuel economy. However, most related research home and abroad stayed at the qualitative evaluation level of driving technique, and deeper tests or quantitative evaluation about specific driving behaviors' impact on vehicle's fuel economy are inadequate seriously. So this paper, based on experiment, studied the light-duty diesel vehicle's fuel consumption discipline while it is coasting in different ways on the level road, so as to achieve vehicle driving economical and reasonably.

2 Experiment

According to Chinese National Standard, sliding experiment should be conducted on clean, dry, flat and straight road paved with concrete or asphalt [5]. The environmental information about test was shown in Table 1.

Table 1. Environmental information about test

Item	Content	Unit
Test time	29, November, 2008	/
Test site	comprehensive performance proving ground of Chang'an University	/
Environmental temperature	53.6	°F
Atmospheric pressure	0.970×10^5	Pa
Wind speed	2.0	m/s

2.1 Vehicle and Instruments

The information about experimental vehicle and instruments was listed in Table 2, and their pictures were shown in Fig. 1.

Table 2. Information about testing vehicle and instruments

No.	Name	Model	Origin
1	vehicle	JMC Transit JX6541D-H	China
2	32 access data collection system	DEWETRON-3010	Austria
3	satellite velometer	DEWETRON VGPS-200	Austria
4	fuel flow meter	ONO SOKKI FP-2240H	Japan

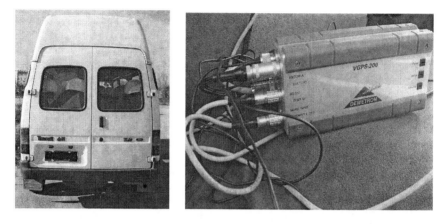

(a)   (b)

(c)   (d)

Fig. 1. Pictures of testing vehicle and instruments. The JMC Transit, light-duty diesel passenger vehicle, was selected for experiment which was shown in Fig. 1 a). The data collection system was used to collect and process dynamic data and signals about vehicle, shown in Fig. 1 b). Satellite velometer was used to measure the speed of the vehicle contactless, which was shown in Fig. 1 c). While fuel flow meter, shown as Fig. 1 d), was installed on the fuel supply system to measure the instantaneous fuel consumption during vehicle running process.

2.2   Experimental Scheme

The fuel consumption experiment while sliding in neutral. The vehicle accelerates to a certain speed and keeps it stable, and then transmission is placed in neutral when the vehicle starts to slide freely. During the sliding process, vehicle speed, fuel consumption rate and time data are collected by testing instruments.

The fuel consumption experiment while sliding in gears. The vehicle speeds up to a higher velocity while transmission is put into a certain gear position need to test, then release the acceleration pedal and make vehicle slide to a lower velocity. During the process, data about vehicle speed, fuel consumption rate and time are acquired by same instruments. While vehicle testing, sliding in neutral and sliding in different gears are conducted at the same section by turn, then by compared of the test data, vehicle's fuel consumption discipline of sliding in different ways and in different gears was discussed and analyzed.

Determination of sliding speed range. From the vehicle longitudinal dynamics, we know

$$v_a = 0.377 * \frac{r \cdot n^\sim}{i_g \cdot i_0}$$

(1)

Where, v_a is the vehicle velocity (km/h). r is the wheel rolling radius (m). n is engine speed(r/min). i_g is the transmission ratio, and i_0 is the final drive gear ratio [6]. By (1), we can determine the reasonable speed range while transmission is put in different position. The transmission ratio and corresponding speed range of testing vehicle are displayed in Table. 3.

Table 3. Transmission ratio and vehicle speed range

Transmission position	1	2	3	4	5
Gear ratio	4.17	2.24	1.47	1.00	0.82
Speed range (km/h)	9.0–23.2	16.8–43.2	25.6–65.9	37.7–96.8	45.9–110

Because of its lower speed range, 1st gear of transmission was not selected for sliding experiment. The initial sliding speed was selected at 75% to 80% of maximum speed and the end speed was selected as the minimum speed correspondingly. As to sliding in neutral, 30% to 80% of maximum velocity, that is medium speed range, was selected to test [7] [8].

Experimental data. The collected data are shown in Table. 4.

Table 4. Collected data of fuel consumption tests

Shift level position	Initial velocity (km/h)	Final velocity (km/h)	Sliding time (s)	Average fuel consumption rate (L/h)
Neutral	80.0737	38.035	41.5	0.7331L/h
2	32.0345	17.0956	6.6	0.01565L/h
3	50.7431	26.0155	13.0	0.01482L/h
4	76.0667	38.0249	22.3	0.01327L/h
5	88.1367	46.0525	25.7	0.01437L/h

3   Results and Analysis

3.1   Fitting Curves

According to test data, the fuel consumption rate curves about test vehicle fitted by the polynomial fitting are shown in Fig. 2 and Fig. 3.

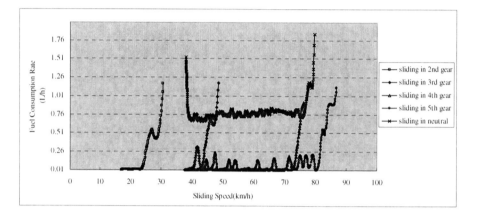

Fig. 2. Fitting curves about fuel consumption rate and sliding speed. Different mark on curves was used to distinguish fuel consumption rate of different transmission position.

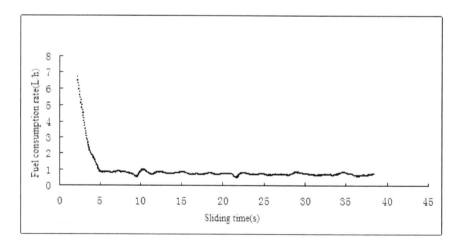

Fig. 3. The variation curve about fuel consumption rate and sliding time of vehicle when transmission is placed in neutral.

3.2   Discussions

Variation of fuel consumption rate with sliding speed. When the vehicle starts to slide, due to vehicle inertia, the engine injectors continue to inject fuel and injectors' action has lag time, so fuel consumption rate is very high at beginning time of sliding. But soon there would be a rapid decline in fuel consumption rate which would stabilize and fluctuate at a low level after a few seconds where fuel consumption rate is the true level, as shown in Fig.3.

Fuel consumption variation sliding in neutral. The fig. 2 shows, the fuel consumption rate while sliding in neutral is much higher than what while sliding in gears. After calculation, the average fuel consumption rate while sliding in neutral is 0.7331L/h, which almost is the engine idle fuel consumption. Moreover, when sliding speed decreases to a certain value, fuel consumption rate would increase rapidly whereas the speed still decreases.

Fuel consumption variation sliding in gears. The average fuel consumption rate while sliding in different gears is generally lower than what while sliding in neutral. Among those gears, the average fuel consumption rate while sliding in 2nd gear is the highest and the average fuel consumption rate while sliding in 3rd gear is the lowest, which difference up to 26.1%. Moreover, the time and distance while sliding in gears are much less than what sliding in neutral.

3.3 Regression Analysis

By linear regression analysis, equations for fuel consumption rate (q) and time (t) when transmission is placed in neutral and 2nd, 3rd, 4th and 5th gear are obtained successively as following (2), (3), (4), (5) and (6).

$$q_0 = 0.0079t + 0.7137, R^2 = 0.019\tilde{3} \tag{2}$$

$$q_2 = -0.0006t + 0.0204, R^2 = 0.011\tilde{9} \tag{3}$$

$$q_3 = 0.0009t + 0.0198, R^2 = 0.023\hat{1} \tag{4}$$

$$q_4 = -0.0043t + 0.0305, R^2 = 0.319\tilde{2} \tag{5}$$

$$q_5 = 0.0013t - 0.0011, R^2 = 0.0267\tilde{.} \tag{6}$$

4 Conclusions

By sliding fuel consumption tests on level road, this paper studies the fuel consumption discipline of light-duty diesel passenger vehicle while sliding in different ways. And the following conclusions are achieved.

Firstly, to light-duty diesel passenger vehicle, the average fuel consumption rate while sliding in neutral is much higher than what sliding in gears, and the former is about

50 times to the latter. The reason as following: while vehicle slides in gear, the engine is at high idling operation state because of low inertia drag. And the regulator actuates, so that the supply gear lever moves from the idle position to the direction of further reducing the fuel supply quantity, thus the fuel consumption rate is very low. Therefore, when the diesel vehicle slides, drivers can consider sliding in gear, which would attain lower fuel consumption and help to save energy and reduce exhaust emissions.

Secondly, when vehicle slides in neutral, the engine does not consume vehicle's kinetic energy. On the other hand, the engine will consume kinetic energy of the vehicle while sliding in gear. Thus, although fuel consumption rate while sliding in neutral is high, the sliding time and sliding distance is much higher than what sliding in gear, which benefits for the vehicle running.

Finally, when light-duty diesel passenger vehicle slides on level road, the fuel consumption rate maintains and fluctuates at low level and the average fuel consumption rate is low overall. But when the sliding speed decreases to a certain value, the fuel consumption rate will increase rapidly. Therefore, it is very important for drivers to choose reasonable sliding speed rang in order to reduce fuel consumption.

References

1. Felix, V.K., Michael, H., Falk, H., Andre, M., Hans-Joachim, W.: Driving with Tentacles: Integral Structures for Sensing and Motion. Journal of Robotic Systems 25(9), 640–673 (2008)
2. Li, L., Wang, F.: Advanced Motion Control and Sensing for Intelligent Vehicles, p. 48. Springer, Berlin (2007)
3. Behringer, R., Sundareswaran, S., Gregory, B., Elsley, R., Addison, B., Guthmiller, W., Daily, R., Bevly, D.: The DARPA grand challenge-development of an autonomous vehicle. In: Proc. 2004 IEEE Intelligent Vehicles Symposium, pp. 226–231. IEEE Press, New York (2004)
4. Gao, J., Li, M., Wang, J., et al.: Correlativity Study on Fuel Consumption Measurement Methods for Light Vehicles. Automotive Engineering 27, 395 (2005)
5. China State Administration of Quality Supervision: Vehicle Sliding Test Methods (GB/T12536-1990). Standards Press of China, Beijing (1990)
6. Chen, Y., Yu, Q.: Automobile Dynamics, 4th edn., pp. 36–48. Tsinghua University Press, Beijing (2009)
7. Liao, X., Dai, Q., Hu, X., Sun, H.: Fuel Economy Simulation of Automobile in Various Driving Operations Mode. Transactions of CSICE 21, 62–64 (2003)
8. Yu, Q., Chen, Y., Ma, J., Guo, R., Zhang, Q.: Study of Non-continuous Linear Control System of Combining Action with Engine Brake, Exhaust Brake and Retarder. China Journal of Highway and Transport 18, 117 (2005)

On Delaying CODP to Distribution Center in Mass Customization

Yanhong Qin

School of Management of Chongqing Jiaotong University,
Chongqing 400074, China
qinyanhong24@163.com

Abstract. The total assembly work is often implemented at the manufacture, and we propose that the total assembly work and some customization of parts at manufacture should be outsourced to distribution center of 3PL (third party logistics) company to reduce the level of inventory and cost of the whole supply chain, i.e. moving the CODP (customer order decoupling point) to distribution center in the downstream, and then, the advantage and condition of this strategy will be analyzed.

Keywords: CODP, 3PL, Distribution center, Customization.

1 Introduction

In order to achieve the scope and scale economy in mass customization, most enterprises are often implementing the same production process as long as possible and postponing the customized production process as much as possible to meet various and different customer requirement, and this is famous postponement manufacture strategy in mass customization. By the point changing the common semi-products production to the process of customized products production is known as customer order decoupling point (CODP). CODP divided the supply chain into two phases. Before CODP, the production stage is pushed by forecast requirement information and in this stage, many universal and modular semi-finished products are manufactured at the efficiency and cost of mass production, and after CODP, the production stage is pulled by realistic customer requirement information, small lot batch and customized products are manufactured based on flexible production line to meet certain customer requirement. That is to say, the CODP means the manufacturing strategy planned based on the forecast started to customized production driven by customer order, i.e. CODP is related to manufacturing strategy with a distinction is necessary between pre-CODP and post-CODP operations, since these have fundamentally different characteristics. Many researchers have classified the postponement strategy as time postponement (TP), place postponement (PP) and form postponement (FP). TP means the material flow is delayed until the customer requirement is certain, and PP means the finished product or semi-finished product inventory is located in the manufacture center or logistic center in the upstream of supply chain to delay the flow, by doing this, the total inventory level of supply chain can be reduced by inventory integration in upstream and inventory concentration in downstream so as to achieve benefits of scale inventory. FP is referred

G. Shen and X. Huang (Eds.): CSIE 2011, Part I, CCIS 152, pp. 271–276, 2011.
© Springer-Verlag Berlin Heidelberg 2011

to the manufacture, assembly, even design activities are delayed so that these activities are closer to the customer demand, its essence is to defer physical characteristics of product differentiation as much as possible. In FP, different positions of the CODP can form different mass customization strategy, such as MTS (make to stock), ATO (assemble to order), MTO (make to order) and ETO (engineer to order), and all of them are related to the ability of the manufacturing operations to accommodate customization or a wide product range, which can be selected depending on how far the customer request penetrates up the value chain. By far, most enterprise implemented the MTO strategy.

Currently, most companies are implementing strategies MTO by delaying the CODP prior to total assembly process at manufacture, that is to say, many various parts and modules are supplied to manufacture, and then, some of them are revised according to customer requirement and assembled with other general modules to form the finished product. Finally, the finished final product are transported to the distribution center (as shown in fig.1). In this mode, there exist many inventories in manufacture and distribution center. So in this paper, we propose that the total assembly work at manufacture should outsourced to distribution center of 3PL company to reduce the level of inventory and cost, i.e. moving the CODP to distribution center in the downstream, and we will discuss the advantage, difficulty or condition of this strategy.

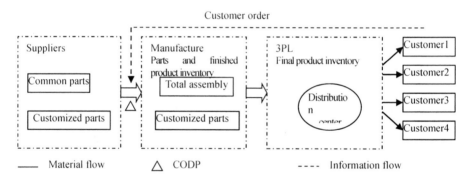

Fig. 1. Description of CODP at manufacture

2   The Advantage of CODP in Distribution Center

Some empirical studies have indicated that the manufacture can reduce cost by outsourcing some simple production activities to the 3PL (third party logistics) company by their additional function. When the customer orders are received in the distribution center, the 3PL will choose the appropriate way to conduct a series of customized logistics services, additional services process to reduce costs, short lead times and increase the degree of customization, i.e. the postponement manufacture at distribution center. And in this mode, what the manufacture do is to produce the modular common parts and customized parts, once the requirement is accepted, all the parts will be transport to the distribution center in JIT mode. The manufacture can realize the mass production at scale economy to strengthen its core competition and it can make full use of the additional production service and logistic function of 3PL to expand profit source of 3PL. When the final assembly or customized finished production happened in the stage of distribution center (as shown in fig.2), the differentiation activities of product or parts customization started from 3PL receiving order requirement, such as final product assembly, ingredient material, additional function to basic product, adjusting the appearance of product, and so on. For the mode of ingredient to order, 3PLs hold the high concentrated liquid stock, and they can achieve the different diluted concentrate product by mixing with water, in order to meet customer needs for different uses. For the mode of assembly to order, the 3PLs often hold some modular parts to assembly to order by obtaining the standard module or semi-finished product in advance and then revising or producing the customized parts.

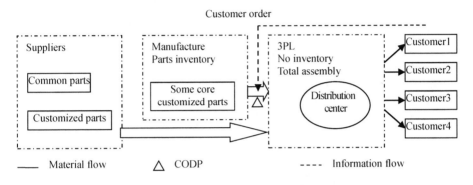

Fig. 2. Description of CODP at distribution center

When the CODP is at distribution center, both manufacture and logistic company will benefit. The product are revised and assembled based on customer requirement at the place closer to customer, so the response speed will improved obviously and efficiently. For manufacture, they can produce the common parts or generic basic product at the efficiency of mass production by adopting the special production line, and pre-digest the relative design, management, organization structure, etc. to improve its ability of producing core parts. Besides, the inventory will be reduced by eliminating the finished inventory and reducing the quantity and variety of parts inventory at manufacture, even in the whole supply chain. For 3PLs, when the CODP is at distribution center, the traditional operation relative with basic function, e.g. transportation, storage, transportation and handling, packaging, etc. which can be substituted by other competitors, because other logistics company can provide the very similar basic logistics activities in an easy way, the relationship between customers and logistics company is very unstable, and the price will become the most important attraction to customer. This is why the profit of logistics company providing only basic logistics function is very low and limited, subjecting to price competition but not service competition. When logistics company starts to engage in certain customization production and assembly manufacture, the status of logistics company will upgrade. In this condition, the 3PLs can provide the customization production service which is different from the other logistics company, because the production and relative logistics process is driven by customer, the competition between different logistics company is based on differentiated service but not logistics price. The relationship between customer and each 3PLs will be relatively stable, and the customer will be more relay on the customized service and relative logistic service of logistic company, so they will be less sensitive the price of service price.

3   The Condition of Delaying CODP at Distribution Center

However, the limited manufacturing capacity makes 3PL often only can bear part of the raw materials or parts of the manufacturing activities, most of the manufacturing and assembly activities still take place at the manufacturer.

The postponed manufacture activities happened at distribution center include two types: one is the popular business for most customers, which is closely relative to the storage, transport function, such as packaging, labeling. The advantage of this mode is less investment and easier operation, but the disadvantage is not strong value-added features, low level of customization, and low agility. The other one is the specialized business, that is, for a few special clients but with higher complexity of operations, such as assembly, additional functionality and so on. The advantage of this mode is that the strong dependence and loyalty of customer, and disadvantage is the need to invest in dedicated equipment, strong dependence on the manufacturer with high investment risk, which requires logistics providers and manufacturers must establish cooperative relations of mutual trust. With the integration of supply chain management and information technology, the mode of competition of supply chain enterprises are changing to cooperation between enterprises, and the trend is increasingly strengthened, which create a good business environment for moving the CODP at distribution center of 3PL.

For 3PL, they must estimate the benefits and costs when they implement the postponement strategy, and at the same time, the whole production of product can be broken down into generic process and customization process and these two processes must be completely separated in time and space fully, which is necessary to delay the CODP from manufacture to distribution center. In addition, the 3PL need to coordinate with manufactures and other partners in the supply chain to achieve successful postponement strategy.

Because the production process is not the core function of 3PL at distribution center, so the final assembly work or customization production can't be complex, for example, the final product can be finished by "plug and play" approach, and parts manufacturers can achieve the standardization, large scale of production to reduce product costs, while respond to the various needs of individual customers quickly. The condition where the CODP can be moved to distribution center is also relative with the standardization degree of accessories and packaging and the varieties of final products. The higher the degree of customer requirements are, the more easy the customization is implemented at distribution center. But, when the market channels are more decentralized and the scale of retailer is smaller, it will become more difficult for the 3PL to bear the delay manufacturing activities at distribution center. For the number of customers of customization requirements is few for the 3PLs, even if the 3PLs can bear some customization production, the effect of delaying the customized production and final assembly work will be reduced for the high cost per unit of product.

To obtain more profit or to reduce more cost by sharing the logistics facility, the 3PL at distribution center must possess the ability of certain production and manufacture customized parts to improve the customized degree of product or service and the flexible ability of their own logistics service. If the 3PL only serve for only few manufactures, then the production cost will be high, so the 3PL should serve for many manufactures in many production life stages to share the cost of production facility, reducing cost and investment risk. When the 3PLs start to implement postponed assembly, they must invest and construct some techniques as following:

(1)   Information

Increasingly, a key element of any manufacture and logistics system is the information system, which supports it. The information must be shared fully between manufacture, 3PLs and customers, so that the 3PLs can provide the right product in the right time and place for right customer, avoiding the frustrated service.

(2)   Financing

For the assembly facility is expensive, so the 3PLs must make great efforts to convince the manufacture to invest some capital in the manufacture facility to share the cost and invest risk by make contract with manufacture for long time period. At the same time, the 3PLs should return some profit from customized production to manufacture to fetch up some loss of transferring the production function.

(3)   Human resource

For the core competitive ability of 3PLs is the relative logistics activities, such as transportation, warehousing, distribution, packaging and so on, it is necessary for the manufacture to provide some technique training and consultation to 3PLs, such as special assembly technique, specific material, the drawing of some customized parts, etc., so as to improve the manufacture ability and efficiency of 3PLs.

(4)   Standardization and modularization

It means the modular and standardized logistics functions. As well known to us logistics service includes transportation, storage, transportation and handling, packaging, distribution, information processing, and each of them can be seen as a module to be standardized. They can be combined to maximize the total benefits of logistics services according to the specific needs of logistics customer. At the same time, standardization and modularization means modularize the logistics components, such as pallet, warehouse, transport vehicles, information format, and so on to aid the sharing logistics facility greatly.

(5)   Contract

To insure the interests of manufacture and logistics company, the contract must be bargained and observed by manufacture and logistics company. The contract must make sure the manufacture provide technique, necessary information, training, special drawing, etc. to logistics company, and the logistics company provide right customization and assembly production process for manufacture to serve its customer efficiently.

4 Conclusion

In this paper, we have discussed the shortness of CODP located at the manufacture, i.e. high level of parts and finished inventories and high cost, and then we delayed the CODP to the distribution center in the downstream of supply chain to reduce the inventory and respond to various customers quickly, that is to say, the total assembly work and some customization of parts at manufacture should outsourced to distribution center of 3PL company.

Acknowledgement

The research is supported by Chongqing Education Commission under Grant Number KJ100412.

References

1. Battezzati, L.G.: Cooperative Logistic Postponement. In: The 7th International Meeting for Research in Logistics, vol. 9, pp. 24–26 (2008)
2. Mason, R., Lalwani, C.: Mass customized distribution. International Journal of Production Economics 114, 71–83 (2008)
3. Alford, D., Sackett, P., Nedler, G.: Mass Customization—An Automotive Perspective. International Journal of Production Economics 65, 99–110 (2000)
4. Yang, J., Zhao, S.G.: Study on Postponement in Customization Supply Chain. Industrial Engineering and Management 4, 35–41 (2005)
5. Bukh, P.N., Johansen, J.: Multiple Integrated Performance Management Systems: IC and BSC in a Software Company. Singapore Management Review 24(3), 21–33 (2002)
6. Mason, R., Lalwani, C.: Mass customized distribution. International Journal of Production Economics 114, 71–83 (2008)

Structural Similarity Based Authentication Watermarking Algorithm

Fan Zhang[1,3], Gang Zheng[2], Yuli Xu[3], and Pengcheng Song[3]

[1] Institute of Image Processing and Pattern Recognition, Henan University,
Kaifeng, 475001, China
zhangfan@henu.edu.cn
[2] Kaifeng Electric Power Company, Kaifeng 475001, China
[3] College of Computer and Information Engineering, Henan University,
Kaifeng, 475001, China

Abstract. According to the structural similarity theory, the primary function of human visual system (HVS) is to extract the structural information from the view of human being. Therefore the structural information can be taken as an approximation measure of image quality. In this paper, a structural similarity based image authentication watermarking is proposed. The proposed algorithm can chooses the positions in original image where the pixels can be changed but cannot be perceived by human eyes. Experimental results show that the proposed algorithm meets the human visual effectively.

Keywords: Watermarking, Structural similarity, Authentication.

1 Introduction

With the rapidly development of Internet and digital technology, digital images are more easy to store, publish, copy, tamper, and so they are more easy to be attacked. When the digital image modified, it is difficult to notice by human eyes. This makes it difficult to determine the authenticity of image content. In some applications, we need to judge the authenticity and integrity of images. In court, people must ensure the integrity of the photos as evidence, as long as they can be notarized in the judgments. Therefore, the certification of image is necessary.

There are usually two image authentication methods, one method based on digital watermarking and another one method based on digital signature [1-3]. The digital watermarking based image authentication method is to embed a watermark into the original image as authentication information. The digital signatures based image authentication method is to separate the certification information with original image.

Digital images usually subject to a wide variety of distortions during acquisition, processing, compression, storage, transmission and reproduction. Any of which may result in a degradation of visual quality. The simplest and most widely used full-reference quality metric is the mean squared error (MSE), computed by averaging the squared intensity differences of distorted and reference image pixels, along with the related quantity of peak signal-to-noise ratio (PSNR). These are appealing because they are simple to calculate, have clear physical meanings, and are mathematically convenient in the context of optimization. But they are not very well matched to

G. Shen and X. Huang (Eds.): CSIE 2011, Part I, CCIS 152, pp. 277–282, 2011.

perceived visual quality. The structural similarity theory and structural similarity (SSIM) is proposed by Zhou Wang et al. [4, 5]. They construct a specific example of a structural similarity quality measure from the perspective of image formation.

In this paper, according to the characteristics of the human visual system, a structural similarity based image authentication watermarking is proposed. The proposed algorithm can mark the positions in the original image where the pixels can be changed, and in these specific locations, watermark is embedded. Experimental results show that the proposed algorithm meet the human visual effects, watermark information is not easily detected.

2   Structural Similarity Theory and SSIM

2.1   Limitations of Human Visual System

Human visual model is a simple approximation of the human visual system. The error sensitivity evaluation method simulates the initial stage of the human visual system function, and has been confirmed by the psychology and physiology experiments. HVS is a highly complex nonlinear system, and most of the primary visual models are linear or nearly linear, so they must form their own system by large numbers of assumptions and limits.

It is well known that visual processing of cognitive understanding and interaction will affect the perceived image quality. As an observer will give a different quality marks to same image in different circumstances. Image content and the observer area of interest, are also likely affect the image quality assessment. The method of error sensitivity is convenience when we directly measure the digital images. But when human observe an image, it is not a digital image, but a continuous display transformation of digital image. There are strong structures in images, not only there are strong correlation exists between their pixel, and those correlation associate with important information about image structure.

2.2   Structural Similarity Theory

Natural image signals are highly structured: Their pixels exhibit strong dependencies, especially when they are spatially proximate, and these dependencies carry important information about the structure of the objects in the visual scene. Although most quality measures based on error sensitivity decompose image signals using linear transformations, these do not remove the strong dependencies. Therefore, a new idea is: the human visual system is highly adapted to extract structural information from the viewing field. It follows that a measure of structural information change can provide a good approximation to perceived image distortion.

The structural similarity theory is different from previous approach, which simulating the function of relevant early-stage components in the HVS. Their greatest difference is top-down and bottom-up. This new philosophy can be best understood through comparison with the error sensitivity philosophy. First, the error sensitivity approach estimates perceived errors to quantify image degradations, while the new philosophy considers image degradations as perceived changes in structural information. Second, the error-sensitivity paradigm is a bottom-up approach, simulating the function of relevant early-stage components in the HVS. The new paradigm is a top-down approach, mimicking the hypothesized functionality of the overall HVS [6]. Third, the problems of natural image complexity and de-correlation are also avoided to some extent because the new philosophy does not attempt to predict image quality by accumulating the errors associated with psychophysically understood simple patterns. Instead, the new philosophy proposes to evaluate the structural changes between two complex-structured signals directly.

2.3 Structural Similarity Index

The structure Information of the concept of the different interpretations and the structure of the distortion of the different quantization can make the structure similarity theory has a difference implementation. SSIM interprets the structural information from image composed point view.

The luminance of the surface of an object being observed is the product of the illumination and the reflectance, but the structures of the objects in the scene are independent of the illumination. Consequently, to explore the structural information in an image, we wish to separate the influence of the illumination. Zhou Wang *et al.* define the structural information in an image as those attributes that represent the structure of objects in the scene, independent of the average luminance and contrast. Thus, the distortion modeling for three different factor combinations: luminance (L), contrast (C) and structure (S). The luminance is estimated as the mean intensity (μ_x, μ_y); use the standard deviation (σ_x, σ_y) as an estimate of the signal contrast; use the covariance (σ_{xy}) as a measure of the structural similarity. Finally, the three components are combined to yield an overall similarity measure the structural similarity (SSIM) index between signals x and y:

$$SSIM(x, y) = [l(x, y)]^\alpha \cdot [c(x, y)]^\beta \cdot [s(x, y)]^\gamma, \tag{1}$$

where $\alpha > 0$, $\beta > 0$ and $\gamma > 0$ are parameters used to adjust the relative importance of the three components.

$$l(x, y) = \frac{2\mu_x\mu_y + C_1}{\mu_x^2 + \mu_y^2 + C_1}, \tag{2}$$

$$c(x, y) = \frac{2\sigma_x\sigma_y + C_2}{\sigma_x^2 + \sigma_y^2 + C_2}, \tag{3}$$

$$s(x, y) = \frac{\sigma_{xy} + C_3}{\sigma_x\sigma_y + C_3}, \tag{4}$$

where the constant C_1 is included to avoid instability when $\mu_x^2 + \mu_y^2$ is very close to zero. Specifically, we choose:

$$C_1 = (K_1 L)^2, \tag{5}$$

where L is the dynamic range of the pixel values (255 for 8-bit grayscale images), and $K_1 \ll 1$ is a small constant.

$$C_2 = (K_2 L)^2, \tag{6}$$

where $K_2 << 1$. This definition again satisfies the three properties listed above.

When set $\alpha = \beta = \gamma = 1$ and $C_3 = C_2/2$, the SSIM index can be expressed in a specific form:

$$SSIM(x, y) = \frac{(2\mu_x\mu_y + C_1)(2\sigma_{xy} + C_2)}{(\mu_x^2 + \mu_y^2 + C_1)(\sigma_x^2 + \sigma_y^2 + C_2)}. \tag{7}$$

3   Watermark Algorithm Based on Structural Similarity

3.1   Watermark Embedding

Watermark embedding steps are as follows:

1) Given an original image a, without taking into account the case of HVS, the original image is embedding a watermark, and get a watermarked image b.

2) Using sliding window operation, the two images are separated in non-overlapping blocks within the same size window.

3) Calculating the mean, variance and covariance of each window in image a, b, and then use formula (7) calculating the structure similarity of corresponding block in two images.

4) If the structural similarity of corresponding block in two images is greater than a threshold value T, then mark the location of the block in the original image, and make the location information as a key.

According to the human visual characteristics, the threshold T is designed as follows:

$$T = JND(x, y) = J_1 + J_2(x, y). \tag{8}$$

5) In the original image a, embedding watermark in the marked blocks as the same way, and then the new watermarked image c is acquired.

3.2   Watermark Detection

Watermark detection is to extract the watermark from the watermarked image. If the watermark information can be extracted properly, it means that the image has not been tampered with, if the watermark information can not be extracted properly, it means that the original image has been tampered.

1) Will be certified and key images (watermark embedding location information) According to the watermark extraction algorithm proposed watermark

2) The extracted watermark and original watermark information to compare, if the same, then that image is true, otherwise, that the image is changed.

4   Experimental Results

In this section, some experimental results are introduced. In order to verify that the invisibility and the robustness of proposed algorithm, simulation experiments of image authentication watermarking algorithm based on the structural similarity are taken using standard images (Cameraman and Lena).

In the proposed algorithm, the invisibility performance is excellent. The invisibility comparison of digital watermarking algorithm between the proposed algorithm and the algorithm without considering the human visual effects are shown in Fig. 1.

Fig. 1. Invisibility comparison between the proposed algorithm and the algorithm without considering the human visual effects. (a) Lena original image. (b) Experimental result of the algorithm without considering the human visual effects. (c) Experimental result of the proposed algorithm.

According to the chosen threshold of this paper, we can mark the location in the original image where can be embedded watermark. The black spots as shown in Figure 2 represent the position where we will embed watermark information.

Fig. 2. This is the display of position where we will embed watermark information. (a) The position will be changed in Cameraman. (b) The position will be changed in Lena.

PSNR is usually used to judge a visual quality of images. If the value of PSNR is higher, it means the better image quality. On the contrary, it means the worse image quality. The comparison of visual quality of experimental result images has been made using PSNR. Table 1 shows the comparison of visual effect in different watermarking algorithms. The algorithms includes the proposed watermarking algorithm in this paper, the watermarking algorithm does not consider the HVS, and the experimental results of Reference [7].

Table 1. This is PSNR value comparison between the different algorithms on the same image

Images	The proposed algorithm	The algorithm does not consider the HVS	Reference [7]
Peppers	40.1243	32.7615	41.0682
Lena	42.7689	33.2252	44.1413
Cameraman	42.8645	33.7737	44.1659

5 Conclusions

An image authentication watermarking algorithm is proposed based on the structural similarity theory and SSIM. According to the structural similarity theory, the primary function of human visual system (HVS) is to extract the structural information from view of human being, and therefore the structural information can be taken as the approximation measure of an image perceived quality. The proposed algorithm can mark the positions in the original image where the pixels can be changed, and in these specific locations, watermark is embedded. Experimental results show that the proposed algorithm meets the human visual effects; watermark information is not easily to detect. After experimental verification, the proposed algorithm is a fragile digital watermarking algorithm and can be used as image authentication.

References

1. Barni, M., Bartolini, F.: Data hiding for ˉghting piracy. IEEE Signal Processing Magazine 21(2), 28–39 (2004)
2. Do, M., Vetterli, M.: The Contourlet transform: an efficient directional multiresolution image representation with bandlets. IEEE Transactions on Image Processing 14(4), 423–438 (2005)
3. Lou, O., Wang, X., Wang, Z.: Adaptive Image Watermarking Algorithm Based on the Characteristics of Important Coe±cients on Contourlet Domain. Computer Science 36(3), 237–240 (2009)
4. Wang, Z., Bovik, A.: A universal image quality index. IEEE Signal Processing Letters 9(3), 81–84 (2002)
5. Wang, Z., Bovik, A., Sheikh, H., Simoncelli, E.: Image quality assessment from error visibility to structural similarity. IEEE Transactions on Image Processing 13(4), 600–612 (2004)
6. Yang, W., Zhao, Y., Xu, D.: Method of image quality assessment based on human visual system and structural similarity. Journal of Beijing University of Aeronautics and Astronautics 34, 1–5 (2008)
7. Huang, L.: Research of image authentication based on digital watermarking, Ph.D Thesis, Hunan University (December 2008)

Image Denoising Based on Improved Non-local Algorithm

Feng Xue[1], Wei-hong Fan[2], and Quan-sheng Liu[3]

[1] School of Computer and Information engineering,
Peking University Shenzhen Graduate School, Shenzhen 518040, China
[2] School of Electronic Science and Engineering,
National University of Defense Technology, Changsha 410000, China
[3] LMAM, Universite de Bretagne SUD, Centre Y. Coppens, campus de Tohannic,
56017 VANNES, France

Abstract. An improved image denoising technique based on the nonlocal means (NL-means) algorithm is investigated in this research. The proposed method not only considers a non-local similarity of the intensity gray level of all pixels in the image, the gradient of pixels in small local windows are also computed to obtain the local structure information for each patch. The proposed algorithm is demonstrated on images corrupted by white Gaussian noise (WGN). The comparative experimental results show that the improved NL-means filter achieves better denoising performance.

Keywords: image denoising, nonlocal means, intensity gray level, gradient.

1 Introduction

All digital images contain some degree of noise. Often times this noise is introduced by the camera when a picture is taken. Image denoising is one of the classical problems in digital image processing, and has been studied for nearly half a century. Several denoising methods have been proposed such as neighborhood filtering, total variation minimization, Wiener filtering, Gaussian scalar mixture, etc.

Most denoising algorithms make two assumptions about the noisy image. The first assumption is that the noise contained in the image is white noise and the second assumption is that the true image (image without the noise) is smooth or piecewise smooth. These assumptions can cause blurring and loss of detail in the resulting denoised images. The non-local means algorithm does not make the same assumptions about the image. It exploits spatial correlation in the entire image for noise removal and adjusts each pixel value with a weighted average of other pixels in image. Since image pixels are highly correlated while noise is typically independently and identically distributed (i.i.d.), averaging of these pixels results in noise cancellation and yields a pixel that is similar to its original value [1][2]. The Figure 1 shows three pixels p, q1, and q2 and their respective neighborhoods. The neighborhoods of pixels p and q1 are similar, but the neighborhoods of pixels p and q2 are not similar. Adjacent pixels tend to have similar neighborhoods, but non-adjacent pixels will also have similar neighborhoods when there is structure in the image. The recently proposed nonlocal means algorithm (NL-means) has offered remarkably promising results [3][4].

G. Shen and X. Huang (Eds.): CSIE 2011, Part I, CCIS 152, pp. 283–289, 2011.

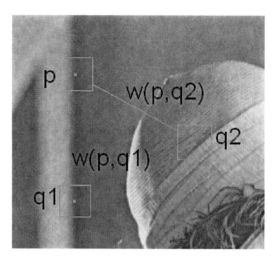

Fig. 1. Example of self-similarity in an image. Pixels p and q1 have similar neighborhoods, but pixels p and q2 do not have similar neighborhoods.

In this work, we propose an improved NL-means algorithm that adjusts the similarity matching process not only based on the similarity of the gray level of a pixel and also considered the similarity of gradient of pixels in non-local windows. The proposed modifications significantly improve the NL filter, both in PSNR as in computation time. It is shown that this algorithm has a significant performance gain over the traditional NL-means algorithm for various test images.

2   Proposed Method

Consider the following image model

$$v(i) = u(i) + n(i) \tag{1}$$

where $v(i)$ is the observed value of image, $u(i)$ would be the "true" value and $n(i)$ is the noise perturbation at a pixel i. The best simple way to model the effect of noise on a digital image is to add gaussian white noise. In that case, $n(i)$ are i.i.d. gaussian values with zero mean and variance σ^2.

Given a discrete noisy image $v = \{v(i) \mid i \in I\}$, the estimated value $NL(v)(i)$ is computed as a weighted average of all the pixels in the image,

$$NL(v)(i) = \sum_{j \in I} w_h(i, j) w_g(i, j) v(j) \tag{2}$$

where the family of weights $\{w_h(i, j)\}$, depends on the intensity similarity between the pixels i and j, satisfy the usual condition $0 \leq w_h(i, j) \leq 1$ and

$\sum_j w_h(i, j) = 1$; the family of weights $\{w_g(i, j)\}$, depends on the gradient similarity between the the pixels i and j, satisfy the condition $0 \le w_g(i, j) \le 1$ and $\sum_j w_g(i, j) = 1$ respectively the standard deviations of the intensity and gradient components which control the amount of averaging. One of the key elements for designing a high performance NL filter, is the selection of the similarity weights. Clearly, the similarity weights should be adapted to the image in order to achieve maximal improvement.

2.1 The Intensity Similarity Weight $w_h(i, j)$

In order to compute the intensity and gradient similarity between the image pixels, we define a similarity window Δ_i around the pixel i.

Definition 2.1. *A similarity window Δ_i is fixed square window of $n \times n$ pixels deprived of its center i. $\widetilde{N}_i = N_i \setminus \{i\}$ denotes a vector of the gray value of $k = p^2 - 1$ elements where the pixels are concatenated along a fixed lexicographic ordering.*

In order to compute the similarity of the intensity grey level $v(\widetilde{N}_i)$ and $v(\widetilde{N}_j)$, one can compute a Gaussian weighted Euclidean distance $\left\| v(\widetilde{N}_i) - v(\widetilde{N}_j) \right\|_{2,a}^2$.

Definition 2.2. *Let $\widetilde{N}_i$ be an square window deprived of its center i; $\widetilde{N}_j$ be an square window deprived of its center j; Let $p(x, y)$ be a pixel in the square window with the coordinate (x, y), $v(p)$ be the observed value of p, (x_{center}, y_{center}) be the center coordinate of window; let $D(x, y)$ be the spatial distance from (x, y) to (x_{center}, y_{center}) which is defined by*

$$D(x, y) = \sqrt{\left| x - x_{center} \right|^2 - \left| y - y_{center} \right|^2} \tag{3}$$

n be the size of window; then the gaussian weight Euclidean distance

$$\left\| v(\widetilde{N}_i) - v(\widetilde{N}_j) \right\|_{2,a}^2 = C \sum_{1 \le x, y \le n} \left| v(\widetilde{N}_i(x, y)) - v(\widetilde{N}_j(x, y)) \right|^2 \exp- \frac{D^2(x, y)}{a}$$

where

$$C = 1 \bigg/ \sum_{1 \le x, y \le n} \exp- \frac{D^2(x, y)}{a} \tag{4}$$

a be the deviations of spatial components.

The intensity similarity weight is defined by

$$w_h(i, j) = \frac{1}{Z(i)} \exp-\frac{\left\| v(\widetilde{N}_i) - v(\widetilde{N}_j) \right\|_{2,a}^2}{h} \tag{5}$$

where $Z(i)$ is the normalizing factor $Z(i) = \sum_j \exp-\frac{\left\| v(\widetilde{N}_i) - v(\widetilde{N}_j) \right\|_{2,a}^2}{h}$.

2.2 The Gradient Similarity Weight $w_g(i, j)$

Let $p(x, y)$ be a pixel in the $\widetilde{N}_i$, the gradient of p is defined by

$$G_x(\widetilde{N}_i(x, y)) = v(\widetilde{N}_i(x+1, y)) - v(\widetilde{N}_i(x, y)) \tag{6}$$

$$G_y(\widetilde{N}_i(x, y)) = v(\widetilde{N}_i(x, y+1)) - v(\widetilde{N}_i(x, y)) \tag{7}$$

In order to compute the gradient similarity of $v(\widetilde{N}_i)$ and $v(\widetilde{N}_j)$, we compute the gradient distance.

Definition 2.3. *Let $\widetilde{N}_i$ and $\widetilde{N}_j$ be two windows have same size, and the gradient at point (x, y) is defined by*

$$G(\widetilde{N}_i(x, y)) = (G_x(\widetilde{N}_i(x, y)), G_y(\widetilde{N}_i(x, y)))^T , \tag{8}$$

then the gradient distance $Dist_G(i, j)$ of $\widetilde{N}_i$ and $\widetilde{N}_j$ is computed by

$$Dist_G(i, j) = \sum_{1 \le x, y \le n} \left\| G(\widetilde{N}_i(x, y)) - G(\widetilde{N}_j(x, y)) \right\|_2^2 \tag{9}$$

where n is the window size.

The gradient similarity weight is defined by

$$w_g(i, j) = \frac{1}{Z(i)} \exp-\frac{Dist_G(i, j)}{g} \tag{10}$$

where $Z(i)$ is the normalizing factor $w_g(i, j) = \sum_j \exp-\frac{Dist_G(i, j)}{g}$.

3 Algorithm

Let I be image; For pixel x in I, $v(i)$ be the observed value.

Algorithm 3.1. *Initial: m(learning window size), n(neighborhood window size), h(intensity weight deviation), g(gradient weight deviation), a(spatial gaussian deviation)*

step0: for each pixel $x \in I$;
step1: take a window F centered in x and size m ;
step2: take a window S centered in x and size n ;
step3: for each pixel $y \in F$ and $y \neq x$;

step4: compute the intensity similarity weight $w_h(y,x)$;

step5: compute the gradient similarity weight $w_g(y,x)$;

step6: add the intensity weight $W_h += w_h(y,x)$;

step7: add the gradient weight $W_g += w_g(y,x)$;

step8: compute the de-noised value of pixel x , $NLv(x) += w_h(y,x)w_g(y,x)v(y)$;

step9: $NLv(x) = NLv(x)\big/W_h * W_g$;

step11: end of step0

4 Experimental Results

To compare performance of the traditional NL-algorithm and the proposed NL-algorithms, we apply them to 4 representative test images which are corrupted by various additive white Gaussian noise (AWGN) with zero mean and standard deviation σ = 20. For each case, three Gaussian noise patterns are generated and the averaged PSNR results of these three denoised images are reported in Table 1.

Table 1. PSNR performance comparison of denoised images

Image	NL-Algorithm	Improved NL-Algorithm
Lena	29.72	30.37
Peppers	30.85	31.57
Barbara	30.43	31.11
Airplain	29.87	30.59

In our experiments, we take the size of learning window $21*21$ and take similarity window $7*7$. Example denoised images are shown in Figure 2. As compared with the traditional NL-algorithm [2], this method has an average PSNR performance gain of 0.65 dB for σ = 20.

Original Image   Noisy image with the standard
                                  deviation 20

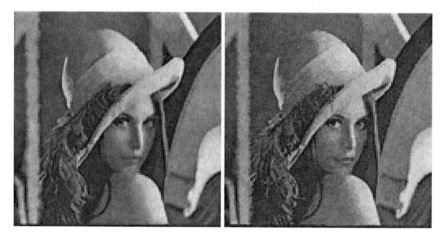

Restored image by Morel NL method   Restored image by proposed method
PSNR = 29.7188   PSNR = 30.3639

Fig. 2. Denoising example of Lena

5 Conclusions

After the analysis of the test results the non-local means algorithm proved to be a better algorithm for image. As expected, this algorithm did a better job of preserving edges than the other methods. It accomplished its goals of removing noise and preserving detail.

References

1. Buades, A., Coll, B., Morel, J.: On image denoising methods. Technical Report 2004-15, CMLA (2004)
2. Buades, A., Coll, B., Morel, J.: A non-local algorithm for image denoising. In: IEEE International Conference on Computer Vision and Pattern Recognition (2005)
3. Coupe, P., Yger, P., Barillot, C.: Fast non local means denoising for 3D MR images. In: Larsen, R., Nielsen, M., Sporring, J. (eds.) MICCAI 2006. LNCS, vol. 4191, pp. 33–40. Springer, Heidelberg (2006)
4. Karnati, V., Uliyar, M., Dey, S.: Fast non-local algorithm for image denoising. In: Proc. of IEEE ICIP, Cairo, Egypt (2009)

Research of Backward Congestion Control Mechanism[*]

Weihua Hu and Liping Tang

Computer Science, Hangzhou Dianzi University,
Zhejiang province, China

Abstract. This paper first analyzes the current network congestion control technology and presents a new mechanism named backward congestion control mechanism to solve the weakness of current explicit congestion notification mechanism. Finally, we use NS to simulate this mechanism in order to compare with the traditional TCP [1] congestion control mechanism. Experimental results show that the new mechanism has low latency and high congestion notification accuracy of congestion notification, further more the new mechanism can also distinguish between the reasons for the network packet loss and thus can be applied to a hybrid network.

Keywords: TCP, ECN, Congestion Control.

1 Introduction

The current network congestion is the most common problem, so the network congestion control algorithm will directly impact the network bandwidth utilization and network fluency. Traditional TCP congestion control mechanism use timeout and fast retransmit mechanism to detect the generation of network packet losing, that means packet losing was estimated accorded to RTT (Round-trip Time). Because of the weakness of traditional TCP congestion control mechanism there comes out many explicit congestion control mechanisms, such as ECN [2][7]+RED (Random Early Detection, Random Early Detection), VCP [3], XCP [4]. These explicit congestion control mechanisms will let the routers explicitly sending a message to the TCP device while there was a packet losing in the router, but these explicit congestion notification mechanisms have inherent weaknesses: ECN+RED got a large feedback delay while XCP protocol's change is too large for the rapid deployment of large-scale. VCP is based on the ECN therefore there also exists a large latency. What's more, these mechanisms are unable to accurately distinguish the reasons for the network packet losing. As we know, packet losing is not only caused by the overloaded network but also caused by the unstable link statue such as the unstable signal exited in the wireless network. With the rapid growing of wireless data we urgently need a congestion notification mechanism that compatible wireless network and wired network.

---

[*] Foundation: Zhejiang Natural Science Foundation (Y1090718).

G. Shen and X. Huang (Eds.): CSIE 2011, Part I, CCIS 152, pp. 290–296, 2011.
© Springer-Verlag Berlin Heidelberg 2011

2   Analysis of Common Congestion Control Techniques

2.1   Conventional Congestion Control Techniques

The current TCP version used a large number of open-loop congestion control, such as the retransmission policy, fast retransmit policy, etc.; also use closed-loop congestion control, such as implicit notice. All the congestion policy is called Additive Increase Multiplicative Decrease (AIMD)[5]. AIMD is the base of TCP congestion control framework many other congestion control mechanism extend out from the AIMD. The window changing of AIMD is shown in Fig1. In Fig1, cwnd is the current congestion window, while ssthresh is the threshold of the congestion window. As shown in Fig1, ssthresh1 is first value of ssthresh, ssthresh2 is the second, ssthresh2_new is the updated value of ssthresh, ssthresh3 is the third. Range A in Fig1 shown the slow start phase of AIMD, Range B corresponds to congestion avoidance phase of AIMD. TCP congestion is always based on three phases: first one is slow start, the second is congestion avoidance, the last one is congestion treatment. In the slow start phase the sender sends data in a single window, and soon began to increase the window to reach the threshold. When the window reached threshold, the slow start phase is over and entering congestion avoidance phase. Window in Congestion avoidance phase will be increased linearly in order to slow down the window increasing. Finally, if congestion is detected, the sender will return to slow start phase or the congestion avoidance phase which is determined by the algorithm of the sender using.

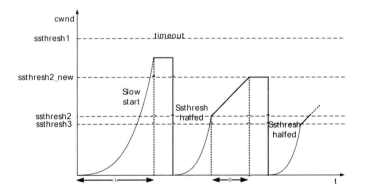

Fig. 1. AIMD Mechanism of TCP-Tahoe、TCP-Reno、TCP-NewReno

2.2   XCP and VCP Mechanism

XCP is a new explicit congestion protocol proposed by the Dina Katabi. An extra 20 bytes head was added beyond the IP header in XCP protocol[6]. This head is used for the exchanging of information with routers. When a packet leaves the sender, the sender will fill in RTT (Round-Trip Time) value, throughput value and network throughput value. Router will also recalculate the feedback value. After an ACK (ACKnowledge Character, TCP acknowledgment packet) was received, the sender will receive the feedback value and the sender will update its window accord to feedback window.

The full name of VCP is Variable-Structure Congestion Control Protocol which is proposed by xia in year 2005. VCP based on ECN while VCP redefine the bit used to marking the network stat. Like ENC, VCP use two bits to record the network stat. Two bits can represent four kinds of load levels. 00,01,10,11 representing ECN invalid, low load, high load, overload. The VCP based sender will adjust its window with MI (product-type increase), AI (and type added), MD (product type decrease) based on the load level.

3 Backward Explicit Congestion Notofication Mechanism

The most common ECN, VCP, XCP are all Forward Congestion Notification of implementation of TCP congestion control version. Backward Congestion Notification will have a direct dialogue with the TCP sender, which is different from Forward Congestion Notification. In Fig2, there are two TCP links. The first link contains S1 and R1 while the second link contains S2 and R2.

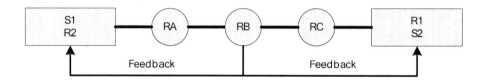

Fig. 2. Backward Notification

From Fig2 we know that congestion occured in Router B and Router B will generate a forward congestion notification that will be directly sent to S1 and S2. Router will not send notification to R1 or R2.

3.1 Tag Processing Strategy of TCP Receiver

The TCP link has two types of link status: one-way link and two-way link. Each end of a two-way link is both a sender and receiver, while one-way link contains only one sender or one receiver in each end.

For the receiver of one-way link, there must be a possibility of receiving a backward congestion notification generated by router. In fact, in one-way link, the receiver needn't process this congestion notification because the receiver will not send out any data and needn't manage its window, so in one-way link, the receiver must ignore the backward congestion notification. The implementation of this paper will choose to discard such a notification directly.

For two-way link, the receiver is also a sender, so the backward congestion notification must not be discarded.

3.2 Tag Adjustment of TCP Sender

For the backward congestion control mechanism, when the TCP receiver got a TCP packet, the TOS bits of IP header will be checked by the TCP receiver. If the TOS bits were set, it means this packet contains congestion notification, otherwise this packet is a normal TCP packet.

We used two bits of the TOS bits, which means there are four class marked by the two bits and different class need different treatment strategy.

Class one, coding is 00: This means the backward congestion control notification is not active, so the TCP receiver will treat is as a normal TCP packet.

Class two, coding 10: This means this packet is generated by the router. There is no TCP data except congestion notification in this packet. The sequence number in this packet indicates the location of this sequence in the TCP sender's window, so the TCP receiver can calculate the maxim sequence number in the window. We calculate the maxim sequence number to prevent the congestion notification in same window to change the TCP sender's window over and over again. Once the TCP sender finish the processing of this packet, the TCP sender will discard this packet and never sending to its upper layer.

Class three, coding 10: This processing of this class is like the class two except one thing, that is after the processing of the congestion notification, the TCP sender choosing to sending the packet to its upper layer, because this packet got TCP data and should not be discarded before the processing TCP task.

Class four, coding 11: This coding type is not used yet.

3.3 Timeout Adjustment of TCP Sender

The meaning of timeout in backward congestion control mechanism is different from the traditional versions such as TCP-Tahoe, TCP-Reno, TCP-NewReno. It is more precise and have no ambiguity.

In the backward congestion control mechanism, packets are dropped during transmission for two reasons: First, the router discarded the packet due to lack of processing resources, and the router will send a congestion notification to the TCP sender; the other is caused by unstable link (such as signal instability, broken links and so on), which was reflected in packet timeout.

In None Explicit Congestion Control Mechanism, the above two factors can result in timeout. Therefore, this kind version of the TCP sender cannot distinguish the exact cause of packet drops and TCP window adjustment will adopt a unified strategy. For TCP-NewReno, its threshold is reduced to half and the current window is set to 1.

Because the backward congestion control mechanism can distinguish the reasons for discarding packets, so the backward congestion control mechanism will not consider the network congestion occurred while timeout came out and will not reduce the window threshold, but only half the value of the current window.

4 Experiment

In the real network, the network data flow is irregular. Congestion can occurred at anywhere in anytime. This section will analyze the effect of backward congestion control mechanism in multi-bottleneck link environment. This section corresponding to the experimental test topology shown in Fig3:

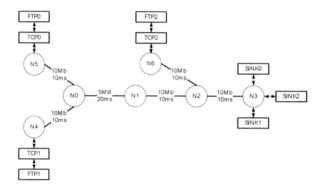

Fig. 3. Topology of Multi-Bottleneck Link

In Fig3, there are seven nodes of routers and have three group of TCP link. Group 0 of TCP sender is bounded to node N5, group 1 of TCP sender is bounded to node N4 and group 2 of TCP sender is bounded to N6 while all the groups of receiver is bounded to node N3. In group 0, there are 80 TCP links existed, in group 1 there are 60 while 50 in group 2. As stated above, there are two bottleneck links in Fig3, which are node N0 to node N1 of link, node N2 to node N3 of link.

We are in the NS simulator for the TCP value of the total window which is shown in Fig4. The left sides of Fig4 shown the window value of the total in version of TCP-NewReno while the right sides shown the window value of the total in version of Backward Congestion Control Notification Mechanism.

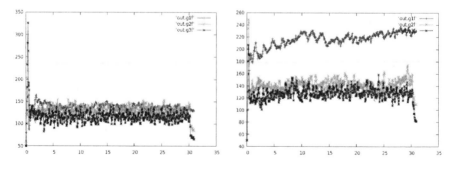

Fig. 4. Total value of TCP window for Multi-Bottleneck Link

In Fig 4, line out.g1 stands for the 0 group of TCP, line out.g2f stands for the 1group of TCP and line out.g3f stands for the 2 group of TCP. We know from Fig3 that the TCP links in group 2 contains one bottleneck link while the others contain two bottleneck links.

The left sides of Fig4, has shown the total window of TCP value with the version of TCP-NewReno and it shown that the TCP links in group 0 still have a low total window although there are 80 links in the 0 group. Rapid growing RTT is caused by the serious congestion which makes the total window in 0 group closed to that in group of 1 and this means the TCP agents in group 0 cannot get a fair sharing of bandwidth under serious network congestion.

It is different from the left sides of Fig4 that the 0 group of TCP has a highest value of total TCP window and the value of 1 group is a little higher than that of 2 group which means the fair of TCP in Backward Congestion Control Notification Mechanism is more effective than that in TCP-NewReno. For further analysis of TCP global synchronization, we compared the average of the two versions of TCP data window which shown in Fig5.

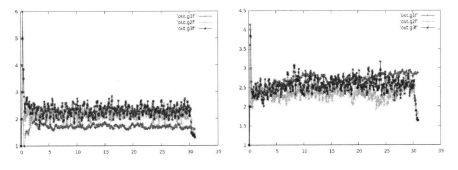

Fig. 5. Average value of TCP window for Multi-Bottleneck Link

Like Fig4, the left sides of Fig5 shown the value with the version of TCP-NewReno while the right sides of Fig5 shown the value with the version of Backward Congestion Control Mechanism. As is shown in the left sides, the value is more stable than that in the right sides, but the 0 group which contains the most TCP links has the lowest value. We analyzed in group 1 and group 2 shows the curve of distribution at the left sides which shows curve group 1 and group 2 have the high degree of coincidence. In the right sides of Fig5, the value of each group is close to each other and all they curve have a low degree of coincidence which is to say, in the TCP global synchronization problem, backward congestion control mechanism is better than TCP-NewReno.

5 Conclusion

In summary, Backward Congestion Control Mechanism can accurately feedback network congestion information and have a good TCP fairness. In the hybrid network it can accurately distinguish the reasons for packet loss and can adjust different strategy accord to different reasons which can increase the network bandwidth utilization.

References

[1] Postel, J.: Transmission Control Protocol. RFC793. 1981-9. 1-2
[2] ECN in TCP/IP Network(ECN) (October 10, 2010),
    http://bbs.exam8.com/thread-127937-1-1.html
[3] Feng, G.: Dynamical analysis for fairness onvergence of VCP protocol, pp. 1–2. Polytechnical University, Xi'an Sanxi province (2010)
[4] XCP eXplicit Control Protocol (November 8, 2010),
    http://research.cnnic.cn/html/index_74.html
[5] Forouzan, B.A.: TCP/IP Protocal Suite, 3rd edn. McGraw-Hill Education (Asia) Co & Tsinghua University Press
[6] Wang, K.: Research of Congestion Control Algorithm Based on XCP Protocol, pp. 2–3. Southeast Jiaotong University, Mianyang Sichuan Province (2008)
[7] Zhen, Y., Wei, D.: Flow control algorithm based on ECN probabilistic marking, pp. 2–2. School of Telecommunication and Network Technology, Beijing (2005)
[8] Floyd, S., Fall, K.: Promotion the use of end-to-end congestion control in the internet. IEEE/ACM Transaction on Networking (August 1999)

Development of AC Servo Control Simulation Model and Application in Undergraduates Education

Guo-qiang Chen[1] and Jian-li Kang[2]

[1] School of Mechanical and Power Engineering, He'nan Polytechnic University,
Jiaozuo 454003, He'nan Province, China
[2] School of Architectural and Artistic Design, He'nan Polytechnic University,
Jiaozuo 454003, He'nan Province, China
jz97cgq@sina.com, kangjl@hpu.edu.cn

Abstract. The servo control is widely used in many kinds of fields, and is also a typical teaching case for several engineering disciplines. The aim of the paper is to discuss how to demonstrate the fundamental and detail for the student. After introducing the structure of the servo system, the paper analyzed the correlative curricula. The modeling methods to the key subsystems were discussed. Finally the application level of the simulation was also presented.

Keywords: servo control, simulation model, education, computer simulation.

1 Introduction

The servo control is widely used in many kinds of fields [1], such as robots, numerical control machines, and instruments and meters. Among all the servo systems, the one based on PMSM (Permanent Magnet Synchronous Motor) has found more and more applications because of many advantages, such as high reliability, small moment of inertia and small volume [2,3]. The servo control system is a typical teaching case for several engineering disciplines. The teaching material is extensive, but the computer simulation is a powerful tool for the instructor and student. The simulation method and model have been presented and discussed in the published literature [4-8]. Since this field of research has extensive published literature and the key technique is almost mature, the aim of the paper is not to present a more excellent simulation method or build a more powerful model for the PMSM servo control, but rather to discuss how to demonstrate the fundamental and detail for the student.

2 Structure of Simulation Model and Education Application

The overall structure of the servo control system is shown in Fig.1, which has been discussed in the literature [1-3, 9]. In the simulation, many components are idealized based on some rational assumptions. The simulation model based on Fig.1 includes several subsystem models: PI controllers for position, speed and current, Park/Clarke and inverse Park/Clarke transform, SVPWM (Space Vector PWM), inverter, PMSM.

G. Shen and X. Huang (Eds.): CSIE 2011, Part I, CCIS 152, pp. 297–302, 2011.
© Springer-Verlag Berlin Heidelberg 2011

Because SVPWM has high precision requirements on the simulation step size. The simulation model is always time consuming, although this will be not a heavy burden with the performance improvement of the computer hardware and simulation software. The subsystems in the dash line box can be replaced by a PMSM model in dq coordinate system to get a simplified simulation model. The simplified model has many advantages, such as saving simulation time, easy to build and understand for the beginner.

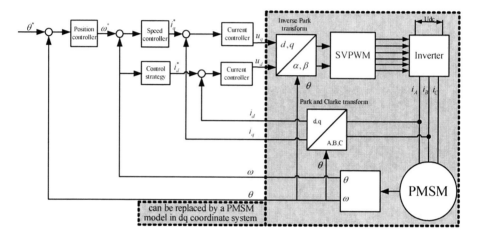

Fig. 1. Overall structure of the PMSM servo control system. θ^*, ω^*, i_d^*, i_q^* are the reference/command position, angular speed, d-axis current, q-axis current respectively. θ, ω, i_d, i_q are the actual position, angular speed, d-axis current, q-axis current respectively.

The servo control and simulation relate to many a curricula and education stage, as can be expressed in Table 1.

Table 1. The correlative curricula

Subsystem	Theory and technology	Curricula
Whole structure	Control theory and system	Control Theory and Application
PMSM model	PMSM modeling	Electrical Machinery
PMSM model, Clarke/Park transform	Vector control	Electronic Control Theory and Practice
Controller	Control theory	Control Theory and Application
SVPWM model	PWM technology	Power and Electronics
Inverter	Power and Electronics	Power and Electronics
Simulation model building	Computer simulation	Computer Simulation Technology
Code generation	Digital signal processor	DSP Principle and Application

The simplified model can be used to (1) understand the structure and basic principle of the PMSM servo control, (2) assess the effects of the controller parameters on the servo system, test the controller performance, (3) learn the modeling method of PMSM based on FOC (Field Oriented Control), and so on. Besides the above aspects, the unsimplified model can be used to demonstrate the principle of SVPWM, and the simulation results are more realistic. The simulation model can be utilized in almost all education stages, such as course design, classroom instruction and experiment.

3   Key Components and Techniques

3.1   PMSM Simulation Model

Extensive literature has presented the simulation model of PMSM. In almost all the literature, PMSM simulation model is derived from several equations. In dq coordinate system, the voltage equation is [1, 10]

$$\begin{cases} u_q = R_s i_q + L_q p i_q + \omega L_d i_d + \omega \psi_f \\ u_d = R_s i_d + L_d p i_d - \omega L_q i_q \end{cases} \tag{1}$$

where u_d and u_q are the d-axis voltage and q-axis voltage respectively, R_s is the stator phase resistance, L_d and L_q are the d-axis inductance and q-axis inductance respectively, ω is the electric angular speed, ψ_f is the flux induced by the rotator permanent magnet, and p is the differential operator.

The output voltages from d, q current controllers are fed to the PMSM model in the simplified model. The simplified model does not concern three-phase voltages, so the coordinate transform is needless. The PMSM model includes three inputs: load torque, d-axes voltage and q-axes voltage. In the unsimplified model, the PMSM model includes four inputs: load torque, three phase voltages.

The PMSM model can be found in many simulation software packages such as MATLAB/Simulink and Plecs, which facilitates the education. But it should be noticed that the coordinate systems are not consistent in different simulation software packages. For example, the model in MATLAB is not consistent with the model in Plecs. In order to observe the motor state, the PMSM model must be modified in some cases [4]. The instructor should choose proper software based on teaching aims.

3.2   SVPWM and Inverter Simulation Models

SVPWM is a regular sampling PWM in essence, and the modulation wave is implicit [11-13]. In order to intuitively demonstrate the essential difference between SVPWM and SPWM (Sinusoidal PWM), it is important to display the modulation waves and zero sequence component. Because the output voltage is series of pulses, the low pass filter should be utilized, as shown in Fig.2. The first order low pass filter is adequate, as given in [13]. Because of the principle of PWM (voltage-second balance) and the intrinsic switch property of the electronic device, the harmonics are inevitable [12].

The harmonic and voltage error are an important factor in the system performance assessment, because it can result in torque ripples. FFT (Fast Fourier Transform) is a powerful tool to analyze the spectra. FFT function can be found in almost all the simulation software.

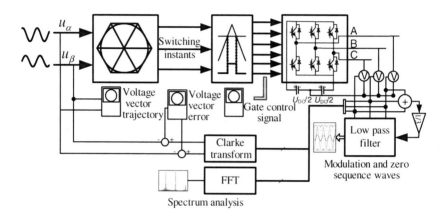

Fig. 2. SVPWM and inverter simulation model

How to generate the gate control signals based on the voltage vector from the current controllers is an important part in both computer simulation and physical implementation, but there are many differences under the two conditions.

The widely utilized SVPWM strategy with equal durations of the two zero voltage vectors can be realized by the software-determined method in DSPs (Digital Signal Processors) [13]. The timer and compare units may be used in DSP implementation. The switching time instants must be loaded to the according registers, and the gate control signals are generated automatically. In order to simplify the computation and programming, another three-phase coordinate system is always used to determine the sector in which the reference output voltage resides [5,13].

In the computer simulation, the computing procedure is simpler than in DSP implementation. The simulation software provides the functions to compute the phase angle and amplitude, so the sector can be gotten directly from the phase angle. There are several methods to generate the gate control signals based on the switching instants. And the triangle intersection method-an intuitive one discussed in extensive literature, is recommended here. Because this method is similar to the principle of timer/compare units in DSP, it can help the student understand and grasp the DSP implementation method after simulation.

3.3 PI Controller

The servo system includes four PI (Proportional-Integral) controllers: position, speed, d-axes and q-axes controllers. If the no-load EMF term is considered as constant, the two equations in Equ. (1) have cross coupling terms. PI controller can be utilized to decouple the two-axe voltage equations [3]. The accurate determination of the control parameters is difficult, and many computing methods have been discussed in plenty of literature. The integrator windup may give large transients when the controlled object saturates [14]. A PI controller with anti-windup (shown in Fig.3) based on back-calculation is detailedly discussed in [14] and widely used in PMSM FOC.

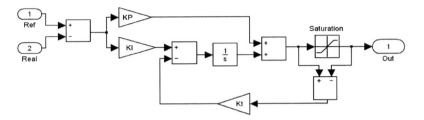

Fig. 3. Simulation model of PI controller with anti-windup

3.4 Simulation Environment

The simulation model can be built in almost every software package. But in the undergraduate education, the instructor should choose the simulation software that provides abundant control blocks and functions, even complex models. Plenty of literature has discussed methods to the control system and motor vector control in Psim, Pspice, MATLAB/Somulnk, Plecs and so on [4-8]. MATLAB/Simulink is an excellent software package and recommended here. Models of PMSM, SVPWM, Park/Clarke transform are provided in MATLAB/Simulink/SimPowerSystems. The Scope block and X-Y Graph block can be used to display the results intuitively. The results also can be saved to the workspace variable for the complex processing.

4   Simulation Application Level

The simulation is not the ultimate goal, but only a tool for student to grasp the knowledge on the servo control. The instructor should choose a proper application level according to the education requirement and the student state. As shown in Fig.4, the understanding becomes deeper and deeper from left to right.

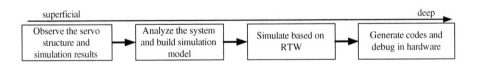

Fig. 4. Application level and procedure in education

MATLAB/Simulink/Target Support PackageTC1 and TC6 integrate the simulation and automatic code generation in a whole, which is the excellent material for education.

5 Conclusions

As a typical case in the undergraduate education, the PMSM servo control system including several subsystems: PMSM, controller, SVPWM and inverter relates to many a course. The paper only briefly introduces and discusses the keys to its application in education. The literature on the detailed procedure to build the simulation model is intensive and extensive.

References

1. Hao, S.-h., Tang, Z.-l., Hao, M.-h., Liu, J.: Vector Control of High Speed PMSM Based on Single-Pole Magnetic Encoder. Journal of Tianjin University 43, 411–416 (2010) (in Chinese)
2. Sun, Y.-w.: Development and Application of the Modern PM SM and AC-Servo System. Small & Special Electrical Machines (3), 71–73 (2010)
3. Wang, X.-p., Li, S.-y., Huang, X.-d.: Design and Simulation of PMSM Servo System. Science Technology and Engineering 9, 2907–2911 (2009) (in Chinese)
4. Xie, C.: Discuss on the PMSM model of Power System Blockset inMATLAB5.3. Electric Drive (3), 51–52 (2003) (in Chinese)
5. Jia, G., Zhao, H., Shao, H.: Simulation Research on PMSM Vector Control System Based on SVPWM. In: 1st International Conference on Electrical and Control Engineering, pp. 1936–1940. IEEE Press, New York (2010)
6. Liu, T., Tan, Y., Wu, G., Wang, S.: Simulation of PMSM vector control system based on Matlab/Simulink. In: International Conference on Measuring Technology and Mechatronics Automation, vol. 2, pp. 343–346. IEEE Computer Society, Los Alamitos (2009)
7. Wang, C., Ji, Y., Luan, H., Zhang, Z.: Simulation of PMSM Vector Control System Based on MATLAB/SIMULINK. Journal of Jilin University 27, 17–22 (2009) (in Chinese)
8. Fan, X.-m.: Simulation of SVPWM based on SIMULINK. Electric Drive Automation 131, 19–21 (2009) (in Chinese)
9. Li, X., Geng, L.: Development and Application of the Modern PMSM & AC-Servo System. Electrical Machinery Technology 5, 20–22 (2009) (in Chinese)
10. Wang, C., Xia, J., Yang, J., Sun, Y.: Modern Motor Control Technology. China Machine Press, Beijing (2006) (in Chinese)
11. Chen, G.: PWM inverse technology and application. China Electronic Press, Beijing (2007) (in Chinese)
12. Grahame Holmes, D., Lipo, T.A.: Pulse Width Modulation for Power Converters. IEEE Press, USA (2003)
13. Yu, Z.: Space-Vector PWM With TMS320C24x/F24x Using Hardware and Software Determined Switching Patterns. TI Instruments (1999)
14. Visioli, A.: Practical PID Control. Springer, Heidelberg (2006)

Shape Determination of the Rigid Body Located in Incompressible Flow

Jun-Ping Zhao

School of Science, Xi'an University of Architecture and Technology,
Xi'an 710055, P.R.China
jpzhao87@163.com

Abstract. The purpose of this paper is to investigate the shape determination of a rigid body located in incompressible fluid flow in two dimensions. This state problem is controlled by the Stokes equations. The derivative of the cost functional is given by an adjiont method. The level set method is successfully utilized as the minimization algorithm. Since the level set method is implemented in an Eulerian framework, the computational cost is moderate. Finally, a numerical example is presented to illustrate the effectiveness and validity of the proposed algorithm.

Keywords: Shape determination; Incompressible flow; Level set method; Stokes equations.

1 Introduction

The shape determination of the rigid body located in incompressible fluid flow, which is a branch of inverse problems, has been a challenging task for a long time. To solve such problems, the optimal control methods based on shape sensitivity analysis are mostly utilized and the applications are uncountable [1]–[7]. But these methods are implemented in a Lagrangian framework, remeshing process cannot be avoided in most cases, hence it is very time-consuming.

The level set method, first proposed by Osher and Sethian [6], has been recently introduced in the field of optimal shape control problems [5]. The main feature of this kind of method is to enable an accurate description of the boundaries on a fixed mesh. Therefore, it leads to fast numerical algorithms. The simplicity and flexibility of the level set method has significantly contributed to an increase in the development of new procedures for solving inverse problems, including shape determination or reconstruction problems [4]-[8].

In this paper, we will consider the shape determination of the body immersed in the flows governed by the Stokes equations. The level set method is used to avoid the difficulties associated with remeshing. An algorithm to determine the shape of unknown objects immersed in the stationary Stokes fluid flow is given.

This paper is organized as follows. In the next Section, we give the state problem and shape sensitivity analysis; Section 3 briefly recall the level set method and the numerical algorithm is presented; In section 4, an illustrative numerical benchmark example is given. Conclusions are given in the last section.

G. Shen and X. Huang (Eds.): CSIE 2011, Part I, CCIS 152, pp. 303–308, 2011.
© Springer-Verlag Berlin Heidelberg 2011

2 The State Problem

We will consider the following inverse problem: a rigid body Ω is located in an incompressible Stokes fluid, where Ω is the obstacle we want to determine. The fluid is flowing in a greater working domain D in which contains all admissible shape Ω. We will only consider the two-dimensional incompressible fluid flow that governed by the Stokes equations. Here we assuming that an open and bounded domain $D = \mathsf{D}/\overline{\Omega}$ with Lipschitz continuous boundary $\Gamma := \partial D = \partial \Omega \cup \partial \mathsf{D}$. We are looking for the velocity $\boldsymbol{u} = (u_1, u_2)$ and the pressure of the fluid p, which are defined in D D and satisfy the following stationary Stokes equations:

$$\begin{cases} -v\Delta \boldsymbol{u} + \nabla p = \boldsymbol{f}, & in\ D \\ \operatorname{div}\boldsymbol{u} = 0, & in\ D \\ \boldsymbol{u} = 0, & on\ \partial\Omega \\ \boldsymbol{u} = \boldsymbol{g}, & on\ \partial M \end{cases} \tag{1}$$

where v is the kinematic viscosity and $\boldsymbol{f}$ is the body force.

We will consider the difference between design and target velocities integrated in the design domain, which can be described by the following objective functional

$$\Im(D) = \int_D (\boldsymbol{u} - \boldsymbol{u}_d)^2 \mathrm{d}x, \tag{2}$$

i.e., to find the velocities $\boldsymbol{u}$ such that the functional (2) is minimized subject to the Stokes problem (1).

In order to use the level set method, some classical shape sensitivity analysis results are recalled here.

Let D be a regular open set in R^2, we consider domains of the type $D(\boldsymbol{h}) = (Id + \boldsymbol{h})(D) := \{x + \boldsymbol{h}(x), \text{such that } x \in D\}$. For small vector field $\boldsymbol{h}$, the open set is one-to-one perturbations of the initial domain D and $(Id + \boldsymbol{h})$ is a diffeomorphism in R^2. The shape derivative of $\Im(D)$ at D is defined as the Fréchet derivative in at 0 in the $\boldsymbol{h}$ direction:

$$\Im((Id + \boldsymbol{h})(D)) = \Im(D) + DJ(D)(\boldsymbol{h}) + o(\boldsymbol{h}) \tag{3}$$

where $\Im_d(D)$ is a continuous linear form on $W^{1,\infty}(\mathsf{R}^2, \mathsf{R}^2)$.

The directional derivative $D\Im(D)(h)$ depends only on the normal trace $\boldsymbol{h} \cdot \boldsymbol{n}$ on the boundary ∂D, i.e. let D be a smooth bounded open set and $\phi(x) \in W^{1,1}(\mathsf{R}^2)$, then the domain shape functional $\Im_d(D) = \int_D \phi(x)\mathrm{d}x$ is differentiable at D and

$$\mathsf{D}\mathfrak{I}_d(D)\boldsymbol{h} = \int_D div(\boldsymbol{h}(x)\phi(x))\mathrm{d}x = \int_{\partial D} \boldsymbol{h}(x)\cdot n(x)\phi(x)\mathrm{d}s, \qquad (4)$$

For any $\boldsymbol{h} \in W^{1,\infty}(\mathbb{R}^2, \mathbb{R}^2)$. By Green's formula we can deduce that: Let D be a smooth bounded open set and $\boldsymbol{h} \in W^{1,\infty}(\mathbb{R}^2, \mathbb{R}^2)$. Assume that the data $\boldsymbol{f}$ and the solution $\boldsymbol{u}$ of (1) are smooth enough, say $\boldsymbol{f} \in \mathbf{H}^1(D)$, $\boldsymbol{u} \in \mathbf{H}^2(D)$. Then the shape derivative of $\mathfrak{I}(D)$ is

$$\mathsf{D}\mathfrak{I}(D)h = \int_\Gamma [v(\frac{\partial \boldsymbol{u}}{\partial n}, \frac{\partial \boldsymbol{w}}{\partial n}) + \frac{1}{2}(\boldsymbol{u}-\boldsymbol{u}_d)^2](\boldsymbol{h}, n)\mathrm{d}s \qquad (5)$$

where $\boldsymbol{u}$, p is the solution of the state equations (1) and $\boldsymbol{w}$, q is the solution of the following adjiont equations

$$\begin{cases} -v\Delta \boldsymbol{w} + \nabla q = \boldsymbol{u}-\boldsymbol{u}_d, & in \ D \\ \mathrm{div}\boldsymbol{w} = 0, & in \ D \\ \boldsymbol{w} = 0. & on \ \Gamma \end{cases} \qquad (6)$$

3   Level Set Method

Considering the working domain $D \subset \mathbb{R}^2$ in which all admissible shapes Ω are included. Assuming there exists an implicit function $\phi(x)$, the so-called level set function, which satisfies

$$\begin{cases} \phi(x) > 0 & \forall x \in D \\ \phi(x) = 0, & \forall x \in \partial\Omega \\ \phi(x) < 0. \ \forall x \in D \setminus \overline{D} = \Omega \end{cases} \qquad (7)$$

The local unit normal and the curvature of the surface are given by $n = \dfrac{\nabla \phi}{|\nabla \phi|}$ and $\kappa = \nabla \cdot n = \mathrm{div}\left(\dfrac{\nabla \phi}{|\nabla \phi|}\right)$ respectively. The level set function $\phi(x)$ is used to represent the boundaries during the evolution.

The evolution of the level set function is governed by the Hamilton-Jacobi equation of the form

$$\frac{\partial \phi(x,t)}{\partial t} - V|\nabla \phi(x,t)| = 0 \qquad (8)$$

with initial value given by $\phi(\cdot,0) = \phi_0$. The crucial part of any level set method is an appropriate choice of the velocity V. As mentioned above, the shape derivative can be written as the following form

$$\mathcal{D}\mathfrak{I}(D)h = \int_\Gamma V h \cdot n ds \tag{9}$$

where

$$V = v(\frac{\partial u}{\partial n}, \frac{\partial w}{\partial n}) + \frac{1}{2}(u - u_d)^2 \tag{10}$$

The normal component can be used as the advection velocity in the Hamilton-Jacobi equation (8).

4 Numerical Example

We will use the following algorithm in the numerical example:

i) Initialization of the level-set function $\phi_0(x)$ as an initial guess of the unknown shape Ω_0;

ii) Iteration until the relative difference between two successive cost functional value $|\mathfrak{I}(D_{k+1}) - \mathfrak{I}(D_k)|$ is less than the prescribed error, for $k \geq 0$:

    a) Compute the state u_k and adjiont state w_k through two problems (1) and (6), then obtain the shape derivative of the cost functional by (5).

    b) Update the level set funvtion by solving the Hamilton-Jacobi equation (8).the new shape Ω_{k+1} is characterized by the zero-contour of the level-set function ϕ_{k+1}.

iii) Re-initialization the level set function as a distance function if needed.

We use a benchmark numerical example of two-dimensions shape determination problem to verify the promising features of our proposed algorithm. In the numerical example, the shape determination of the flow past a circular cylinder is considered. The same problem as previous treated in [8].

The analytical domain is shown in Fig.1. The analytical domain is 12.5D wide and 25D long and the central point of the circular cylinder is being put the circular cylinder in the position in 6.25D width and 6.25D length. The Reynolds number is 500.

The initial shape which was assumed to be a rectangle that enclosed the target shape and the streamline of the velocity fields are shown in Fig.2. The blue dot line denotes the exact shape. The final shape and the velocity fields are depicted in Fig.3. The surface plot of the level function corresponding to the final shape is given in Fig.4. It can be seen that we were able to closely match the target field and the shape although the initial shape is far from the target one.

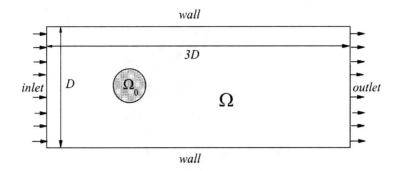

Fig. 1. Design domain

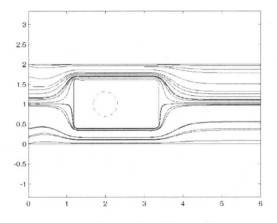

Fig. 2. The initial shape and the streamline of the velocity field

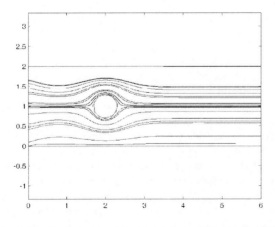

Fig. 3. The final shape and the streamline of the velocity fields

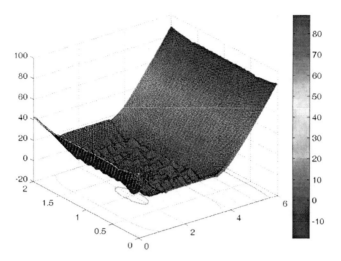

Fig. 4. The surface plot of the level set function

5 Conclusions

In this paper, a unified computation approach to the simulation of the flow and the shape determination was presented. This algorithm has at least the following advantages: The level set method in our formulation can be easily implemented and is computationally very efficient since it is an Eulerian shape capture method; It is insensitive to the initial shape, such that the level set function can be initialized with any distance functions with any shape that are more efficient to construct and easier to use in practice. The numerical example illustrated that the present algorithm is successful in accuracy, convergence speed and stabilization.

References

1. Modhammadi, B., Pironneau, O.: Applied shape optimization for fluids. Clarendon Press, Oxford (2001)
2. Ito, K., Kunish, K., Li, Z.: Level-set function approach to an inverse interface problem. Inverse Problem 17, 1225–1242 (2001)
3. Allaire, G., Jouve, F., Toader, A.M.: A level-set method for shape optimization. C. R. Acad. Sci. Paris, Ser.I 334, 1125–1130 (2001)
4. Allair, G., Jouve, F., Toader, A.M.: Structural optimization using sensitivitity analysis and a level-set method. Journal of Computational Physics 194, 393–393 (2004)
5. Wang, M.Y., Wang, X.M., Guo, D.M.: A level set method for structural topology optimization. Comp. Meth. Appl. Mech. Eng. 192, 227–246 (2003)
6. Osher, S., Sethian, J.A.: Fronts propagating with curvature-cependent speed: algotithms based on Hamilton-Jacobi formulations. J. Comp. Phys. 79, 12–49 (1988)
7. Sethian, J.A.: Level set methods and fast marching methods: evolving intetfaces in computational geometry, fluid mechanics, computer vision and materials science. Cambridge University Press, Cambridge (1999)
8. Burger, M.: A level set method for inverse problems. Inverse Problem 17, 1327–1355 (2001)

Oscillation Criteria for a Class of Neutral Hyperbolic Partial Differential Equations

Yu Bai and Ailing Shi

School of Science, Beijing University of Civil Engineering and Architecture,
Beijing, 100044, China
buceaby@163.com

Abstract. Oscillation theory of functional partial differential equations has wide applications in mechanics, physics and mathematical biology, economics, automatic control, communications theory etc. In this paper, we consider a class of neutral hyperbolic partial differential equations with continuous distributed deviating arguments and damped term. Some sufficient conditions for oscillation of all solutions with certain boundary value problems are obtained, which are two theorems by integrating directly.

Keywords: Hyperbolic partial differential equations, Oscillatory criteria, Distributed deviating arguments, Damped.

1 Introductions

In the last decades, the oscillatory behavior of solutions of partial differential equations is of both theoretical and practical interest. Some applicable examples can be found in [1]. Results on the oscillatory behavior of hyperbolic equations with deviating arguments can be referenced in [2, 3, 4, 5 and 6]. However, most of the literatures deal with equations not containing the damped term and containing distributed deviating arguments. In this paper, we deal with a class of neutral hyperbolic partial differential equations with continuous distributed deviating arguments and damped term of the form

$$\frac{\partial}{\partial t}[r(t)\frac{\partial}{\partial t}(u(x,t) + \sum_{i=1}^{m_1} c_i(t)u(x,\tau_i(t)))] + p(t)\frac{\partial}{\partial t}(u(x,t) + \sum_{i=1}^{m_1} c_i(t)u(x,\tau_i(t)))$$

$$+e(x,t)u(x,t) + \int_a^b q(x,t,\xi)f(u[x,g(t,\xi)])d\sigma(\xi) = a(t)\Delta u(x,t) + \int_a^b \sum_{j=1}^{m_2} b_j(t,\xi)\Delta u[x,h_j(t,\xi)]d\sigma(\xi),$$

$$(x,t) \in G = \Omega \times R_+. \tag{1}$$

And the boundary value conditions of

$$u(x,t) = 0, (x,t) \in \partial\Omega \times R_+. \tag{2}$$

Where Ω is a bounded domain in R^n $(n \geq 1)$ with a piecewise smooth boundary $\partial\Omega$, $R_+ = [0, +\infty)$, Δu is the Laplacian in R^n.

Throughout, we will assume that the following conditions (H) hold:

(H1) $c_i(t) \in C(R_+, R_+)$, $0 \leq \sum_{i=1}^{m_1} c_i(t) \leq 1$, $\tau_i(t) \in C(R_+, R)$, $\tau_i(t) \leq t$ are non-decreasing and $\lim_{t\to\infty} \tau_i(t) = +\infty$, $i = 1, 2, \cdots, m_1$;

G. Shen and X. Huang (Eds.): CSIE 2011, Part I, CCIS 152, pp. 309–315, 2011.
© Springer-Verlag Berlin Heidelberg 2011

(H2) $r(t) > 0, r'(t) \geq 0, p(t) \geq 0, a(t) \geq 0, t \in R_+$.

Denote $R(t) = e^{\int_{t_0}^{t} \frac{r'(s)+p(s)}{r(s)} ds}$, and assume $\int_{t_0}^{\infty} \frac{ds}{R(s)} = +\infty$;

(H3) $e(x,t) \in C(\overline{\Omega} \times R_+, R_+)$, $q(x,t,\xi) \in C(\overline{\Omega} \times R_+ \times [a,b], R_+)$, $f(u) \in C(R,R)$ is convex in R_+ , $uf(u) > 0$ and $f(u)/u \geq \lambda > 0$ for $u \neq 0$;

(H4) $b_j(t,\xi) \in C(R_+ \times [a,b], R_+)$. $h_j(t,\xi) \in C(R_+ \times [a,b], R)$. $h_j(t,\xi) \leq t$ for $\xi \in [a,b]$ $(j = 1,2,\cdots,m_2)$. $g(t,\xi) \in C(R_+ \times [a,b], R)$. $g(t,\xi) \leq t$ for $\xi \in [a,b]$. $g(t,\xi)$ and $h_j(t,\xi)$ are non-decreasing with respect to t and ξ respectively. And $\liminf_{t \to \infty, \xi \in [a,b]} g(t,\xi) = \infty, \liminf_{t \to \infty, \xi \in [a,b]} h_j(t,\xi) = \infty, (j = 1,2,\cdots,m_2)$;

(H5) $\sigma(\xi) \in ([a,b], R)$ is non-decreasing, and the integral of equation (1) is a Stieltjes one.

The objective of this paper is to derive some general oscillatory criteria of equation (1) and (2).

Definition 1. A function $u(x,t) \in C^2(G) \cap C^1(\overline{G})$ is called a solution of the problem (1) and (2), if it satisfies (1) in the domain G along with the corresponding boundary condition (2).

Definition 2. A solution $u(x,t)$ of the problem (1) and (2) is said to be oscillatory in the domain G, if for each positive number μ there exists a point $(x_1,t_1) \in \Omega \times [\mu,+\infty)$, such that $u(x_1,t_1) = 0$.

Definition 3. A function $U(t)$ is called eventually positive (negative) if there exists a number $t_1 \geq t_0$ such that $U(t) > 0 (< 0)$ holds for all $t_1 \geq t_0$.

2 Main Results

In this section we will give some oscillation criteria of (1) with the boundary conditions (2).

With each solution $u(x,t)$ of the problem (1) and (2), we associate a function $V(t)$ defined by

$$V(t) = \frac{\int_{\Omega} u(x,t)\Phi(x)dx}{\int_{\Omega} \Phi(x)dx}, t \geq 0. \tag{3}$$

Consider the Dirichlet problem in the domain Ω

$$\Delta u + \alpha u = 0, in(x,t) \in \Omega \times R_+, \tag{4}$$

$$u = 0, on(x,t) \in \partial\Omega \times R_+, \tag{5}$$

in which α is a constant. It is well known [7] that the smallest Eigen value α_1 of problem (4) and (5) is positive and the corresponding Eigen function $\Phi(x)$ is also positive for $x \in \Omega$ .Let

$$E(t) = \min_{x \in \Omega} e(x,t), Q(t,\xi) = \min_{x \in \Omega} q(x,t,\xi). \tag{6}$$

2.1 First Theorem

Theorem 1. Suppose that the conditions (H1)-(H5) hold, and
(H6) There exists a function $\gamma(t) \in C(R_+, R_+)$ satisfying $\gamma(t) \leq g(t,a)$,

$$\gamma(t) \leq h_j(t,a), (j = 1, 2 \cdots, m_2), \quad \gamma'(t) > 0 \text{ and } \lim_{t \to +\infty} \gamma(t) = +\infty \ .$$

hold. If there exists a function $\rho(t) \in C^1(R_+, (0, \infty))$ such that

$$\limsup_{t \to \infty} \int_0 [F(s)\rho(s) - \frac{\rho(s)r(\gamma(s))}{4\gamma'(s)}(\frac{\rho'(s)}{\rho(s)} - \frac{p(s)\rho(s)}{r(s)})]ds = +\infty. \tag{7}$$

where $\quad F(t) = [E(t) + \alpha_1 a(t)](1 - \sum_{i=1}^{m_1} c_i(t)) + \int_a^b \lambda Q(t,\xi)(1 - \sum_{i=1}^{m_1} c_i[g(t,\xi)])d\sigma(\xi)$

$$+ \alpha_1 \sum_{i=1}^{m_2} \int_a^b b_j(t,\xi)(1 - \sum_{i=1}^{m_1} c_i[h_j(t,\xi)])d\sigma(\xi). \tag{8}$$

Then every solution of (1) and (2) is oscillatory in G .

Proof. Suppose that the contrary that there is a non-oscillatory solution $u(x,t)$ to the problem (1) and (2). Without loss of generality, we assume that $u(x,t) > 0, (x,t) \in \Omega \times [t_0, \infty), (t_0 \geq 0)$. By the conditions (H1) and (H4), there exists a $\overline{t}_0 > t_0$ such that $g(t,\xi) \geq t_0$, $h_j(t,\xi) \geq t_0$, $(t,\xi) \in [\overline{t}_0, +\infty) \times [a,b]$, and $\tau_i(t) \geq t_0, t \geq \overline{t}_0$, then

$$u[x, g(t,\xi)] > 0, (x,t,\xi) \in \Omega \times [\overline{t}_0, +\infty) \times [a,b],$$

$$u[x, \tau_i(t)] > 0, (x,t) \in \Omega \times [\overline{t}_0, +\infty), i = 1, 2, \cdots, m_1,$$

and

$$u[x, h_j(t,\xi)] > 0, (x,t,\xi) \in \Omega \times [\overline{t}_0, +\infty) \times [a,b], j = 1, 2, \cdots, m_2.$$

Multiplying both sides of the equation (1) by $\Phi(x)$, and integrating with respect to x over the domain Ω , we have for $(x,t) \in G = \Omega \times R_+$,

$$\frac{d}{dt}[r(t)\frac{d}{dt}(\int_\Omega u(x,t)\Phi(x)dx + \sum_{i=1}^{m_1} c_i(t) \int_\Omega u(x,\tau_i(t))\Phi(x)dx)]$$

$$+ p(t)\frac{d}{dt}(\int_\Omega u(x,t)\Phi(x)dx + \sum_{i=1}^{m_1} c_i(t) \int_\Omega u(x,\tau_i(t))\Phi(x)dx)$$

$$+ \int_\Omega e(x,t)u(x,t)\Phi(x)dx + \int_\Omega \int_a^b q(x,t,\xi)f(u[x, g(t,\xi)])\Phi(x)d\sigma(\xi)dx$$

$$= a(t)\int_\Omega \Delta u(x,t)\Phi(x)dx + \int_\Omega \int_a^b \sum_{j=1}^{m_2} b_j(t,\xi)\Delta u[x, h_j(t,\xi)]\Phi(x)d\sigma(\xi)dx. \tag{9}$$

In view of (6), using Jensen's inequality and (H3) we have

$$\int_\Omega e(x,t)u(x,t)\Phi(x)dx \geq E(t)\int_\Omega u(x,t)\Phi(x)dx, t \geq \overline{t}_0. \tag{10}$$

And

$$\int_\Omega \int_a^b q(x,t,\xi)f(u[x, g(t,\xi)])\Phi(x)d\sigma(\xi)dx = \int_a^b \int_\Omega q(x,t,\xi)f(u[x, g(t,\xi)])\Phi(x)dxd\sigma(\xi)$$

$$\geq \int_a^b Q(t,\xi) \int_\Omega [f(u[x,g(t,\xi)])\Phi(x)dx]d\sigma(\xi)dx$$

$$\geq \int_a^b Q(t,\xi)[f(\frac{\int_\Omega u[x,g(t,\xi)]\Phi(x)dx}{\int_\Omega \Phi(x)dx}) \int_\Omega \Phi(x)dx]d\sigma(\xi)$$

$$\geq \int_a^b Q(t,\xi)[\lambda(\frac{\int_\Omega u[x,g(t,\xi)]\Phi(x)dx}{\int_\Omega \Phi(x)dx}) \int_\Omega \Phi(x)dx]d\sigma(\xi)$$

$$\geq \int_a^b \lambda Q(t,\xi)[V(g(t,\xi)) \int_\Omega \Phi(x)dx]d\sigma(\xi), t \geq \bar{t}_0. \tag{11}$$

Using Green's formula and (2), we have

$$\int_\Omega \Delta u(x,t)\Phi(x)dx = \int_{\partial\Omega} (\Phi(x)\frac{\partial u}{\partial n} - u\frac{\partial \Phi(x)}{\partial n})ds + \int_\Omega u(x,t)\Delta\Phi(x)dx$$

$$= -\alpha_1 \int_\Omega u(x,t)\Phi(x)dx, t \geq \bar{t}_0. \tag{12}$$

and

$$\int_\Omega \Delta u(x,h_j(t,\xi))\Phi(x)dx = -\alpha_1 \int_\Omega u(x,h_j(t,\xi))\Phi(x)dx, t \geq \bar{t}_0. \tag{13}$$

(9) and (10-13) yield for $t \geq \bar{t}_0$

$$\frac{d}{dt}[r(t)\frac{d}{dt}(V(t) + \sum_{i=1}^{m_1} c_i(t)V(\tau_i(t)))] + p(t)\frac{d}{dt}(V(t) + \sum_{i=1}^{m_1} c_i(t)V(\tau_i(t)))$$

$$+E(t)V(t) + \int_a^b \lambda Q(t,\xi)V(g(t,\xi))d\sigma(\xi) + \alpha_1[a(t)V(t) + \int_a^b \sum_{i=1}^{m_2} b_j(t,\xi)V[h_j(t,\xi)]d\sigma(\xi)] \leq 0. \tag{14}$$

Let

$$Z(t) = V(t) + \sum_{i=1}^{m_1} c_i(t)V(\tau_i(t)).$$

We have

$$[r(t)Z'(t)]' + p(t)Z'(t) + E(t)V(t) + \int_a^b \lambda Q(t,\xi)V(g(t,\xi))d\sigma(\xi)$$

$$+\alpha_1[a(t)V(t) + \int_a^b \sum_{i=1}^{m_2} b_j(t,\xi)V[h_j(t,\xi)]d\sigma(\xi)] \leq 0, t \geq \bar{t}_0. \tag{15}$$

It is easy to obtain $Z(t) > 0$ for $t \geq t_0$. Next we prove $Z'(t) > 0$ for $t \geq \bar{t}_0$.

In fact assume the contrary, there exists $T \geq \bar{t}_0$ such that $Z'(T) \leq 0$. From (15), (H3), (H4) and the assumptions we have

$$[r(t)Z'(t)]' + p(t)Z'(t) \leq 0, t \geq \bar{t}_0. \tag{16}$$

that is,

$$r(t)Z''(t) + [r'(t) + p(t)]Z'(t) \leq 0, t \geq \bar{t}_0. \tag{17}$$

From (H2) we have $R'(t) = R(t)\frac{r'(t) + p(t)}{r(t)}$, and $R(t) > 0, R'(t) \geq 0$ for $t \geq \bar{t}_0$. Thus we times $\frac{R(t)}{r(t)}$ on both sides of equation (16), and we have

$$R(t)Z''(t) + R'(t)Z'(t) = (R(t)Z'(t))' \leq 0, t \geq \bar{t}_0. \tag{18}$$

From (18) we have $R(t)Z'(t) \leq R(T)Z'(T) \leq 0, t \geq T$. Thus

$$\int_T^t Z'(s)ds \leq \int_T^t \frac{R(T)Z'(T)}{R(s)}ds, t \geq T,$$

that is

$$Z(t) \leq Z(T) + R(T)Z'(T)\int_T^t \frac{ds}{R(s)}, t \geq T.$$

From (H2) and $Z'(T) \leq 0$ we have $\lim_{t \to +\infty} Z(t) = -\infty$. This contradicts with $Z(t) > 0$ for $t \geq t_0$. Thus $Z'(t) > 0$ for $t \geq \overline{t}_0$.

Denote $t_1 = \overline{t}_0$, from (17) and (H2) we have $Z(t) > 0, Z'(t) > 0, Z''(t) \leq 0$ for $t \geq t_1$.
Since $Z(t) \geq V(t)$, $Z'(t) > 0$ and $\tau_i(t) \leq t(i = 1, 2, \cdots, m_1)$ for $t \geq t_1$, we have

$$V(t) = Z(t) - \sum_{i=1}^{m_1} c_i(t)V(\tau_i(t)) \geq (1 - \sum_{i=1}^{m_1} c_i(t))Z(t), t \geq t_1.$$

Thus from (15) we have

$$[r(t)Z'(t)]' + p(t)Z'(t) + E(t)(1 - \sum_{i=1}^{m_1} c_i(t))Z(t)$$

$$+ \int_a^b \lambda Q(t,\xi)(1 - \sum_{i=1}^{m_1} c_i[g(t,\xi)])Z[g(t,\xi)]d\sigma(\xi) + \alpha_1 a(t)(1 - \sum_{i=1}^{m_1} c_i(t))Z(t)$$

$$+ \alpha_1 \int_a^b \sum_{j=1}^{m_2} b_j(t,\xi)(1 - \sum_{i=1}^{m_1} c_i[h_j(t,\xi)])Z[h_j(t,\xi)]d\sigma(\xi) \quad \leq 0, t \geq t_1. \quad (19)$$

From (H4) and $Z'(t) > 0 (t \geq t_1)$, we have

$$Z[g(t,\xi)] \geq Z[g(t,a)] > 0, \xi \in [a,b].$$

$$Z[h_j(t,\xi)] \geq Z[h_j(t,a)] > 0, \xi \in [a,b], j = 1, 2, \cdots, m_2.$$

Then

$$[r(t)Z'(t)]' + p(t)Z'(t) + E(t)(1 - \sum_{i=1}^{m_1} c_i(t))Z(t)$$

$$+ Z[g(t,a)]\int_a^b \lambda Q(t,\xi)(1 - \sum_{i=1}^{m_1} c_i[g(t,\xi)])d\sigma(\xi) + \alpha_1 a(t)(1 - \sum_{i=1}^{m_1} c_i(t))Z(t)$$

$$+ \alpha_1 \sum_{j=1}^{m_2} Z[h_j(t,a)]\int_a^b b_j(t,\xi)(1 - \sum_{i=1}^{m_1} c_i[h_j(t,\xi)])d\sigma(\xi) \leq 0, t \geq t_1. \quad (20)$$

From (H4) and (H6) we have $\gamma(t) \leq g(t,a) \leq t$, $\gamma(t) \leq h_j(t,a) \leq t(j = 1, 2, \cdots, m_2)$, thus $Z(\gamma(t)) \leq Z[g(t,a)]$, $Z(\gamma(t)) \leq Z(t)$ and $Z(\gamma(t)) \leq Z[h_j(t,a)](j = 1, 2, \cdots, m_2)$ for $t \geq t_1$. Then

$$[r(t)Z'(t)]' + p(t)Z'(t) + [E(t)(1 - \sum_{i=1}^{m_1} c_i(t))$$

$$+ \int_a^b \lambda Q(t,\xi)(1 - \sum_{i=1}^{m_1} c_i[g(t,\xi)])d\sigma(\xi) + \alpha_1 a(t)(1 - \sum_{i=1}^{m_1} c_i(t))$$

$$+ \alpha_1 \sum_{i=1}^{m_2} \int_a^b b_j(t,\xi)(1 - \sum_{i=1}^{m_1} c_i[h_j(t,\xi)])d\sigma(\xi)]Z(\gamma(t)) \leq 0, t \geq t_1. \quad (21)$$

From (8), (21) changes to

$$[r(t)Z'(t)]' + p(t)Z'(t) + F(t)Z(\gamma(t)) \leq 0, t \geq t_1. \tag{22}$$

Let

$$W(t) = \frac{p(t)r(t)Z'(t)}{Z(\gamma(t))}, t \geq t_1. \tag{23}$$

It is obvious that $W(t) > 0 (t \geq t_1)$. From (16) and (H2) we have $[r(t)Z'(t)]' \leq 0, t \geq t_1$. While $\gamma(t) \leq t$, then $r(t)Z'(t) \leq r(\gamma(t))Z'(\gamma(t))$. Thus from (23) we have

$$W'(t) = \frac{p'(t)r(t)Z'(t)}{Z(\gamma(t))} + \frac{p(t)[r(t)Z'(t)]'}{Z(\gamma(t))} - \frac{p(t)r(t)Z'(t)Z'(\gamma(t))\gamma'(t)}{Z^2(\gamma(t))}$$

$$\leq \frac{p'(t)}{p(t)}W(t) - \frac{p(t)p(t)}{r(t)}W(t) - F(t)p(t) - \frac{\gamma'(t)}{p(t)r(\gamma(t))}W^2(t), t \geq t_1. \tag{24}$$

thus

$$W'(t) \leq -F(t)p(t) + \frac{p(t)r(\gamma(t))}{4\gamma'(t)}\left(\frac{p'(t)}{p(t)} - \frac{p(t)p(t)}{r(t)}\right)$$

$$-[\sqrt{\frac{\gamma'(t)}{p(t)r(\gamma(t))}}W(t) - \frac{1}{2}\sqrt{\frac{p(t)r(\gamma(t))}{\gamma'(t)}}\left(\frac{p'(t)}{p(t)} - \frac{p(t)p(t)}{r(t)}\right)]^2, t \geq t_1. \tag{25}$$

Then

$$W'(t) \leq -[F(t)p(t) - \frac{p(t)r(\gamma(t))}{4\gamma'(t)}\left(\frac{p'(t)}{p(t)} - \frac{p(t)p(t)}{r(t)}\right)] \tag{26}$$

Integrating (26) from t_1 to t we have

$$W(t) \leq W(t_1) - \int_{t_1}^t [F(s)p(s) - \frac{p(s)r(\gamma(s))}{4\gamma'(s)}\left(\frac{p'(s)}{p(s)} - \frac{p(s)p(s)}{r(s)}\right)]ds. \tag{27}$$

Letting $t \to +\infty$, we have in view of (7) that $W(t) \to -\infty$, which is a contradiction, since $W(t) > 0$. If $u(x,t) < 0, (x,t) \in \Omega \times [t_0, \infty), (t_0 \geq 0)$, then $-u(x,t)$ is a positive solution of (1) and (2), and the proof is similar. This completes the proof. ∎

2.2 Second Theorem

Because $r(t) > 0, p(t) \geq 0$, Theorem 1 can be simplified as the following theorem.

Theorem 2. Suppose that the conditions (H1)-(H6) hold. If there exists a function $p(t) \in C^1(R_+, (0, \infty))$ such that

$$\limsup_{t \to \infty} \int_{t_0}^t [F(s)p(s) - \frac{p'(s)r(\gamma(s))}{4\gamma'(s)}]ds = +\infty. \tag{28}$$

where $F(t)$ is defined as (8). Then every solution of (1) and (2) is oscillatory in G.

Proof. Suppose that the contrary that there is a non-oscillatory solution $u(x,t)$ to the problem (1) and (2). Without loss of generality, we assume that $u(x,t) > 0, (x,t) \in \Omega \times [t_0, \infty), (t_0 \geq 0)$. Then, proceeding as in the proof of Theorem 1, because from (H2) we have $r(t) > 0, p(t) \geq 0$, and $p(t) > 0, W(t) > 0$, (24) changes to the following, for $t \geq t_1$,

$$W'(t) \leq -F(t)\rho(t) + \frac{\rho'(t)}{\rho(t)}W(t) - \frac{\gamma'(t)}{\rho(t)r(\gamma(t))}W^2(t)$$

$$\leq -F(t)\rho(t) + \frac{\rho'(t)r(\gamma(t))}{4\gamma'(t)} - [\sqrt{\frac{\gamma'(t)}{\rho(t)r(\gamma(t))}}W(t) - \frac{1}{2}\sqrt{\frac{\rho'(t)r(\gamma(t))}{\gamma'(t)}}]^2. \qquad (29)$$

Then

$$W'(t) \leq -[F(t)\rho(t) - \frac{\rho'(t)r(\gamma(t))}{4\gamma'(t)}] \qquad (30)$$

Integrating (31) from t_1 to t we have

$$W(t) \leq W(t_1) - \int_{t_1} [F(s)\rho(s) - \frac{\rho'(s)r(\gamma(s))}{4\gamma'(s)}]ds \qquad (31)$$

Letting $t \to +\infty$, we have in view of (28) that $W(t) \to -\infty$, which is a contradiction, since $W(t) > 0$. If $u(x,t) < 0, (x,t) \in \Omega \times [t_0, \infty), (t_0 \geq 0)$, then $-u(x,t)$ is a positive solution of (1) and (2), and the proof is similar. This completes the proof. ∎

3 Conclusion

In this paper we consider a class of hyperbolic partial differential equations with continuous distributed deviating arguments and damped term, and obtain oscillation criteria of equation (1) and the boundary condition (2). Theorem 1 and Theorem 2 are given by integrating directly, which are given first.

Acknowledgments. This work is supported by Funding Project for Academic Human Resources Development in Institutions of Higher Learning under the Jurisdiction of Beijing Municipality (PHR201107123) and 2011 Science and Technology Research Project of Beijing Municipal Education Commission.

References

1. Wu, J.H.: Theory and Applications of Partial Functional Differential Equations. Springer, New York (1996)
2. Lalli, B.S., Yu, Y.H., Cui, B.T.: Oscillations of certain partial differential equations with deviating arguments. Bull. Austral. Math. Soc. (2), 73–380 (1992)
3. Lalli, B.S., Yu, Y.H., Cui, B.T.: Oscillations of hyperbolic equations with functional arguments. Appl. Math. Comput. (1), 97–110 (1993)
4. Wang, P.G., Yu, Y.H.: Oscillation of solutions for nonlinear second order neutral equations with deviating arguments. Math. Slovaca (1), 205–213 (2001)
5. Saker, S.H.: Oscillation criteria of hyperbolic equations with deviating arguments. Publ. Math. Debrecen (1-2), 165–185 (2003)
6. Lin, S.Z., Zhou, Z.X., Yu, Y.H.: Oscillation criteria for a class of hyperbolic equations with continous distributed deviating arguments. J. of Math. (PRC), 521–526 (2005)
7. Vladimirov, V.S.: Equations of Mathematical Physics, Nauka, Moscow (1981)

The Appraisal Model of Real Estate Project Based on PCA and BP Neural Network

Hui Zhao

School of management, Qingdao Technological University, Qingdao, China

Abstract. A appraisal model based on the integration of principal component analysis (PCA) and back propagation (BP) neural network is put forward for appraising the real estate project. Firstly, principal component analysis (PCA) is used to reduce the evaluation index dimensions. And then, back propagation (BP) neural network is used to appraise the real estate projects. In order to grasp this appraisal model better, finally, the paper provides a case to demonstrate the application of this model in appraising the real estate project. The case has shown that the model applied to appraise the real estate project is feasible and reliable.

Keywords: Real estate project; PCA; BP neural network.

1 Introduction

With the steady development of Chinese market economy, the investment of Real estate has become more active, and the competition of Real estate also become intensely. So a correct selection is the key to get success. Presently, it is an important study area of the Real estate that the way to appraise the feasibility of Real estate projects and the way to select the most appropriate project from many alternative projects.

Comprehensive appraisal methods of real estate project are mainly DELPHI, SAW, AHP, TOPSIS, DEA, fuzzy appraisal method, gray theory, expert system appraisal method, artificial neural network method. These methods have their advantages, but also have their own shortcomings. How to overcome the shortcomings of the above methods and take the advantages of theirs has becoming an important direction of current research.

To make the real estate project appraised more scientifically and reasonably, this paper presents the appraisal model integrated principal component analysis (PCA) and back propagation (BP) neural network. PCA is mainly used to reduce the appraisal dimensions of the Real estate project, which will facilitate the BP'S calculations. BP neural network is used to score the Real estate project.

2 Theoretical Basises

2.1 PCA

The PCA is a multivariate statistical method that selects a small number of components to account for the variance of original multi-response. In PCA, the original dataset of multiple quality characteristics are converted into PC which is a linear combination of

G. Shen and X. Huang (Eds.): CSIE 2011, Part I, CCIS 152, pp. 316–320, 2011.
© Springer-Verlag Berlin Heidelberg 2011

multi-responses obtained in a trial run. The procedure of PCA can be described as follows:

① The S/N ratios of each quality characteristics obtained form TM are normalized as

$$x_i^*(j) = \frac{x_i(j) - x(j)^-}{x(j)^+ - x(j)^-}$$

(1)

where $x_i^*(j)$ is the normalized S/N ratio for jth quality characteristic in ith experimental run, $x_i(j)$ is the S/N ratio for jth quality characteristic in ith experimental run, $x(j)^-$ is the minimum and $x(j)^+$ is the maximum of S/N ratios for jth quality characteristic in all experimental runs.

② The normalized multi-response array for m quality characteristics and n experimental runs can be represented by matrix x^* as

$$X^* = \begin{bmatrix} x_1^*(1) & x_1^*(2) & \cdots & \cdots & x_1^*(m) \\ x_2^*(1) & x_2^*(2) & \cdots & \cdots & x_2^*(m) \\ \cdots & \cdots & \cdots & \cdots & \cdots \\ \cdots & \cdots & \cdots & \cdots & \cdots \\ x_n^*(1) & x_n^*(2) & \cdots & \cdots & x_n^*(m) \end{bmatrix}$$

(2)

③ The correlation coefficient array (R_{jl}) of matrix X^* is evaluated as follows:

$$R_{jl} = \frac{\mathrm{cov}(x_i^*(j), x_i^*(l))}{\sigma x_i^*(j) \times \sigma x_i^*(l)}, \quad j=1,2,\dots,m; \quad l=1,2,\dots,m.$$

(3)

where $\mathrm{cov}(x_i^*(j), x_i^*(l))$ is the covariance of sequences $x_i^*(j)$ and $x_i^*(l)$; $\sigma x_i^*(l)$ is the standard deviation of sequence $x_i^*(l)$.

④ The eigenvalues and eigenvectors of matrix R_{jl} are calculated.

⑤ The PC are computed as follows:

$$p_i(k) = \sum_{j=1}^{m} x_i^*(j) \times v_k(j)$$

(4)

where $p_i(k)$ is the kth PC corresponding to ith experimental run, $v_k(j)$ is jth element of kth eigenvector.

⑥ The total principal component index (TPCI) corresponding to ith experimental run (p_i) is computed as follows:

$$p_i = \sum_{k=1}^{m} p_i(k) \times e(k) \tag{5}$$

$$e(k) = \frac{eig(k)}{\sum\limits_{k=1}^{m} eig(k)} \tag{6}$$

where $eig(k)$ is the kth eigenvalue.

⑦ The TPCI for each experimental run is used to find out the average factor effect at each level.

2.2 BP Neural Network

BP neural network is a network structure of three levels or over three levels. The adjacent neurons are entire link, that is, each neuron in the lower and upper level is all weight connection, but there is the non-connection between neurons. BP neural network takes the way of learning according to the teacher's teaching. When a double-learning mode is provided to the network, activation values of neurons will be spread from the input layer (then through the middle layer) to the output layer, and finally, the responses will be obtained in the output layer. After that, according to the direction of reducing the error between the expected output and the actual output, each connection weight will be amended from the output layer (then through the middle layer) to the input layer. A typical three-level structure of BP neural network is shown in figure1.

3   A Case Studies Applying the Model

The paper takes some real estate corporate in shandong province for example. The existing 12 real estate projects can be appraised. The goal is to select the most appropriate real estate project for the real estate corporate.

The indicators of appraising the real estate project are so many. Many scholars at home and abroad in this respect have made much research. There is no uniform standard at present. In this paper, based on the previous research, 14 indicators are selected, There are the net present value (x_1), the internal return rate(x_2), the payback period (x_3), the asset-liability ratio(x_4), the liquidity ratio(x_5), the financing risk(x_6), the tax policy change(x_7), the supply and demand risk(x_8), the regional environmental change(x_9), the project risks(x_{10}), the increasing production cost(x_{11}), the management capacity building(x_{12}), the corporate brand(x_{13}), the product innovation(x_{14}).

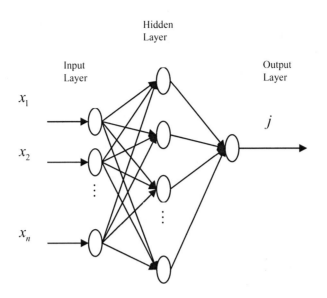

Fig. 1. A Typical Three-level Structure of BP Neural Network

3.1 Using PCA to Reducing Evaluation Index Dimensions

The sample data are processed by PCA(here software R being used). Finally the appraisal indicators becomes 5. Table 1 shows the five principal components' information.

Table 1. The five principal components' information

PC	1	2	3	4	5
Standard deviation	2.56031746	1.66853632	1.56807005	0.98864081	0.59809637
Contribution rate	0.2187796	0.2063154	0.1961076	0.1122825	0.07451314
Accumulated Contribution rate	0.2187796	0.425095	0.621203	0.733485	0.807998

3.2 BP'S Computing

Evaluation indicators of the real estate project become 5 after reduction by PCA. These five factors are the input layer. The output layer is one node for the comprehensive appraisal score.

The former 10 are the training group. The training accuracy is $\varepsilon=10^{-4}$. After 5000 times of learning, the learning result is shown in the table 2. From the table 2, it can be seen that BP is ideal for learning outcomes. Then after the training results completed, all the calibration data are input to produce the last comprehensive-appraisal score, which is shown in table 3.

From the table 3, It can be seen that, overall, the 6th real estate project has the highest desired output among 12 real estate projects, which should be selected for the real estate investment.

Table 2. Learning Result

Item code	1	2	3	4	5	6	7	8	9	10
Training results	0.863	0.6018	0.3418	0.4895	0.7174	0.9182	0.8083	0.6444	0.6886	0.8277
Desired output	0.863	0.6019	0.3410	0.4884	0.7173	0.9110	0.8183	0.6443	0.6887	0.8277

Table 3. Comprehensive-appraisal Score

Item code	1	2	3	4	5	6	7	8	9	10
Training results	0.863	0.6018	0.3418	0.4895	0.7174	0.9182	0.8083	0.6444	0.6886	0.8277
Desired output	0.863	0.6019	0.3410	0.4884	0.7173	0.9110	0.8183	0.6443	0.6887	0.8277

4 Summary

This paper presents a appraisal model based on PCA and BP neural network for appraising the real estate project. The model is primarily designed for the purpose, namely, to assist project clients in selecting the most appropriate real estate project. The appraisal model based on PCA and BP neual network realizes the advantages of both and makes up for their deficiencies, which make the appraisal model more scientific and reasonable for appraising the real estate project.

Reference

1. Wang, X.Q., Yu, G.: Study of construction project bidding based on the BP neural network improved by GA. China Civil Engineering Journal 40(7), 93–98 (2007)

Computer Aided Teaching in Experiments of Building Physics

Jian Yao

Faculty of Architectural, Civil Engineering and Environment,
Ningbo University, Ningbo, China
yaojian@nbu.edu.cn

Abstract. Experiments are commonly used method to help students learn building physics, however the drawback of this method is that it can only measure part of parameters and could not give an accurate evaluation. This paper proposes a computer aided tool in experiments to help students understand the principles of physics in the built environment and improve the design of a building. The results show that it has 7 advantages over conventional manual computation method, and the improved teaching quality in the experiment teaching of building physics evidences its significance.

Keywords: Computer simulation; Teaching; Building physics.

1 Introduction

The energy crises of the 1970s, complaints about sick buildings, thermal, visual and acoustical discomfort, and the move towards more sustainability in buildings have pushed building physics to the forefront of building innovation. The pressure to diminish energy use in buildings acted as a trigger to activate the implementation of building energy efficiency. In order to reduce building energy consumption in China, energy efficiency measures such as the use of high performance building materials, improved design strategies [1-3] are important and essential in achieving it. However, to identify the optimal energy efficiency measures requires a large amount of knowledge on building physics, which encompasses all the aspects of our living and working environment: acoustics, daylight admittance, traffic noise and the thermal behaviour of a building, and is the application of the principles of physics to the built environment. Therefore scientific knowledge that focuses on the analysis and control of the physical phenomena affecting buildings is a necessity for students in learning building design. As a eligible architect, one should know the natural laws relevant for the sustainability of a building, in other words for comfort, energy need and durability of a building, be able to explain the corresponding relations on drawings and constructions, and be able to judge design proposals, energy concepts and possibly improve them. Thus building physics is a significant course for students in architectural engineering technologies and should be taught with various technologies such as computer simulations [4], experiments [5], and theoretical calculations [6] etc. to improve the quality of teaching. However a computer technology and experiment

G. Shen and X. Huang (Eds.): CSIE 2011, Part I, CCIS 152, pp. 321–325, 2011.

combined method in teaching building physics has not been reported. As a result, this paper introduces a computer aided tool in experiments to help students understand the principles of physics in the built environment and improve the design of a building. The followings give a case study of indoor thermal environment tests to illustrate the effectiveness of the method.

2   A Case Study of PMV-PPD

Indoor thermal environment tests is important to help evaluate a person's thermal comfort feeling which is calculated by PMV (Predicted Mean Vote) index. PMV is used to define the standard of air control design ISO 7730 [7], and affected not only by indoor temperature but also humidity, air velocity, clothing insulation, persons' health and ages, the environment people adapting, etc. The thermal comfortable model based on Fanger's PMV can be written as a function of four environmental variables (air temperature: Ta, relative humidity:φ, mean radiant temperature: Tr and air velocity: V) and two individual parameters (metabolic rate: M and clothing index: Ir), as follows [8]:

$$
\begin{aligned}
PMV &= F(T_a, \phi, T_r, V, M, I_r) \\
&= (0.028 + 0.3033e^{-0.036M}) \times \{(M - W) - 3.05[5.733 \\
&\quad - 0.000699(M - W) - Pa] - 0.42[(M - W) - 58.15] \\
&\quad - 0.0173M(5.867 - Pa) - 0.0014M(34 - T_a) - 3.96 \\
&\quad \times 10^8 \times fcl[(T_{cl} + 273)^4 - (T_r + 273)^4] - fcl \times h_c(T_{cl} - T_a)\}
\end{aligned}
\tag{1}
$$

where:

$$
\begin{aligned}
T_{cl} &= 35.7 - 0.028(M - W) - 0.155I_r\{3.96 \times 10^{-8} \\
&\quad \times fcl[(T_{cl} + 273)^4 - (T_r + 273)^4] - fcl \times h_c(T_{cl} - T_a)\}
\end{aligned}
\tag{2}
$$

$$
h_c = \begin{cases}
2.38(T_{cl} - T_a)^{0.25}, for(T_{cl} + T_a)^{0.25} \geq 12.1\sqrt{V} \\
12.1\sqrt{V}, for(T_{cl} + T_a)^{0.25} \leq 12.1\sqrt{V}
\end{cases}
\tag{3}
$$

Where M is metabolism, W external work, Pa water vapor pressure, fcl ratio of clothed body surface area to nude body surface area, Tcl surface temperature of clothing, Icl thermal resistance of clothing (clo) and hc is convectional heat transfer coefficient. The term rate of mechanical work can be determined by W/M. PPD (Predicted Percentage of Dissatisfied) as a function of PMV is determined in equation 4.

$$
PPD = 100 - 95e^{-(0.03353PMV^4 + 0.2179PMV^2)}
\tag{4}
$$

Table 1 shows the relationship among PMV and PPD. It is clear that determining PMV and PPD indexes using manual computation method with limited field test data is a very difficult task for students. However without PMV-PPD indexes, indoor thermal conditions can not be evaluated accurately merely using indoor temperature

Table 1 Relationship between PMV, PPD and thermal sensation

PMV	Thermal sensation	PPD (%)
+3	Hot	100
+2	Warm	75
+1	Slightly warm	25
0	Neutral	5
-1	Slightly cool	25
-2	Cool	75
-3	Cold	100

or 2 to 3 parameters. Therefore we propose a computer aided tool and experiment combined method to accurately calculate the PMV-PPD indexes.

3 Computer Aided Teaching

In order to simplify the calculation for students, a computer program was developed with Visual Basic based on the above equations. Fig. 1 illustrates the friendly interface of the program which only need 3 parameters to be tested including ambient air temperature, air velocity and relative humidity. Other parameters such as metabolic rate can be selected according to different human activities.

The advantages of this tool is that it gives the PMV-PPD indexes accurately and fast in the results box as shown in Fig.1 and the input parameters for students to measure in experiments is only three, one third of required parameters in manual computations. In addition, this tool can also present the PMV-PPD results graphically (a dot on the curve represents the PMV-PPD values) which is significant for students to understand the indoor thermal environment conditions. The detailed 7 advantages, shown in table 2, include fast calculation speed, easy to use, friendly interface,

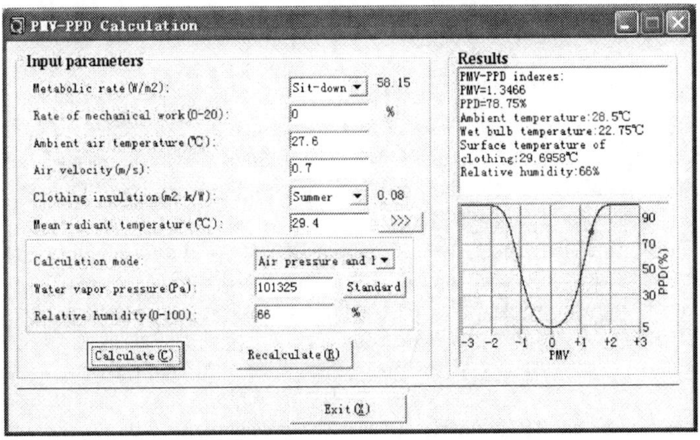

Fig. 1. The interface of the computer-aided tool for PMV-PPD

Table 2. Comparison of the computer aided tool and manual computation in PMV-PPD calculations

Performance	Computer aided tool	Manual computation
Calculation speed	fast	slow
Utility	easy	difficult
Interface	friendly	unfriendly
Calculation results	infallible	fallible
Understandability	easy	difficult
Parameters needed	few	all
Comparison with other tests	convenient	inconvenient

infallible in calculations, being easy to understand and use, few parameters needed and convenience in comparing with other tests. This method has been tested in the experiment teaching of building physics with an improved teaching quality.

4 Conclusions

In order to help students learn knowledges about building physics, a computer-aided tool was developed for simplifying the complex calculation of experiment results with accuracy. The results show that it has 7 advantages over conventional manual computation method, and the improved teaching quality in the experiment teaching of building physics evidences its significance. Therefore this tool has a great potential in application.

Acknowledgement

This work was sponsored by Teaching and Research Fund in Ningbo University.

References

1. Yan, Z., Yong, D., Jian, Y.: Preferable Rebuilding Energy Efficiency Measures of Existing Residential Building in Ningbo. Journal of Ningbo University (Natural science & engineering edition) 22, 285–287 (2009)
2. Yao, J., Xu, J.: Effects of different shading devices on building energy saving in hot summer and cold winter zone. In: 2010 International Conference on Mechanic Automation and Control Engineering, MACE 2010, Wuhan, China, pp. 5017–5020 (2010)
3. Yao, J., Yuan, Z.: Study on Residential Buildings with Energy Saving by 65% in Ningbo. Journal of Ningbo University (Natural science & engineering edition) 23, 84–87 (2010)
4. Schwarte, Borrmann, J., Reinhardt, H.W.: Computer aided teaching in civil engineering materials science at the University of Stuttgart. Materials and Structures 40, 441–448 (2007)

5. Xu, G.Y., Liu, C.H., Liu, P.B.: Application DeST Software of Building Thermal Humidity Environment Teaching Course. Journal of Architectural Education in Institutions of Higher Learning 1, 131–133 (2009)
6. Jun, M.L.: Exploration on Physics Experimental System and Inquiry Learning. Research and Exploration in Laboratory 9, 77–78 (2005)
7. Olesen, Parson: Introduction to Thermal Comfort Standards and to the Proposed New Vffersion of EN ISO 7730. Energy and Buildings 34, 537–548 (2002)
8. Fanger, P.O.: Thermal Comfort: Analysis and Applications in Environmental Engineering. McGraw-Hill, New York (1970)

The Application of AR Model and SVM in Rolling Bearings Condition Monitoring

Dan Zhang and Wentao Sui

School of Electrical & Electronic Engineering,
Shandong University of Technology, Zibo, Shandong, China
zhangdan_sdut@163.com

Abstract. A condition monitoring method for rolling element bearings based on auto-regressive (AR) model and support vector machine (SVM) is proposed. The AR model of the vibration signal of bearings is established. The auto-regressive parameters and the variances of remnant are used as the feature vectors. Then multi faults classifier is established by support vector machines to identify the condition of bearings. The experimental result shows that the proposed method is effective.

Keywords: auto-regressive model; support vector machine; rolling element bearing; condition monitoring.

1 Introduction

Bearings are widely used in automobile, engineering machinery, machine tools, electrical, chemical industry, the condition monitoring for the rolling element bearings can significantly reduce the risk of equipment downtime and production costs. In the field of engineering, Condition monitoring technology plays an important role in normal operation of equipment and production[1].

Condition monitoring consists of two main steps: feature extraction and decision making. Feature extraction is a process in which the signal space is mapped into the feature space, while the decision making is to classify the different characteristics of the process. Traditional Condition monitoring based on human experience, which are laborious and not accurate under complex conditions. With the development of artificial intelligence, the intelligent Condition monitoring of automatic Condition monitoring is developed. Artificial intelligence technologies, such as neural networks, fuzzy logic, support vector machines, automatic Condition monitoring technology have been used in many applications.

Since the Auto-Regressive model (AR model) is a time series analysis method, the model parameter contains important information about bearings operation condition. At the same time, AR model parameters are most sensitive to the condition changes of the bearings operation condition. Using AR model parameters as the feature vectors to analyze the change of state are very effective.

For the problem of pattern recognition, although artificial neural networks have strong classification ability to spatial patterns of multi-dimensional and nonlinear

G. Shen and X. Huang (Eds.): CSIE 2011, Part I, CCIS 152, pp. 326–331, 2011.

pattern recognition; it can not overcome its drawbacks. For example, the neural network structure selection and weight initial setup requires the help of experience, and network training is slow and easily falling into local minimum. Artificial neural network is based on empirical risk minimization principle. Only when the training samples approaches infinity, it converges to the true model, so this constraints its application in mechanical Condition monitoring. SVM (Support vector machine) effectively improved the traditional classification of the defect, such as the choice of neural network structure, local minimization problem, and overfitting problems. Support vector machine has been in the bearing Condition monitoring of mechanical components such good results obtained.

The condition monitoring method for rolling element bearings is proposed, which is based on and rolling bearing Condition monitoring. In this method, an AR model is established for vibration signals, and then the regression residual variance of the AR model is used as feature vectors. The feature vectors are input into support vector machine classifier to further determine the condition and fault type. Analysis of experimental signals verifies that the AR model and SVM can be applied to the bearings condition monitoring.

2   Multi-class SVM Classifier

2.1   Binary SVM Classification Algorithm

The two-dimensional input space is taken as an example to explain svm, which is shown in Fig.1. The solid circle and hollow circle represent two categories. The SVM will construct a separating hyperplane in that space, one which maximizes the margin between the two data sets. To calculate the margin, two parallel hyperplanes are constructed, one on each side of the separating hyperplane. A good separation is achieved by the hyperplane that has the largest distance to the neighboring datapoints of both classes, since in general the larger the margin the better the generalization error of the classifier.

In the linearly separable case, for finding the optimal hyperplane, one can solve the following constrained optimization problem [2]:

$$\min \frac{1}{2} \| \mathbf{w} \|^2$$

$$s.t \quad y_i(\mathbf{w} \cdot \mathbf{x_i} - b) \geq 1 \quad (i = 1, 2, ..., n) \tag{1}$$

To find an optimal hyperplane for a linearly not separable case is to solve the following constrained optimization problem:

$$\min \frac{1}{2} \| \mathbf{w} \|^2 + C \sum_{i=1}^{n} \xi_i$$

$$s.t \quad y_i(\mathbf{w} \cdot \mathbf{x_i} - b) \geq 1 - \xi_i \quad (i = 1, 2, ..., n) \tag{2}$$

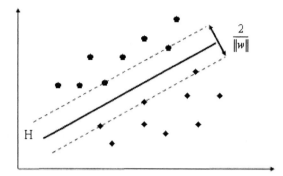

Fig. 1. Optimal separating plane

By introducing a set of Lagrange multipliers α_i, the problem becomes the one of finding the saddle point of the Lagrangian. Thus, the dual problem becomes

$$Q(\alpha) = \sum_i \alpha_i - \frac{1}{2}\sum_{i,j} \alpha_i \alpha_j y_i y_j (\mathbf{x_i} \cdot \mathbf{x_j})$$

$$s.t \quad \sum_i \alpha_i y_i = 0, \qquad \alpha_i \geq 0$$

(3)

SVMs map the input vector into a higher dimensional feature and thus can solve the nonlinear case. By choosing a nonlinear mapping function $\Phi(x)$, the SVM can construct an optimal hyperplane in this new feature space. $K(x,xi)$ is the innerproduct kernel performing the nonlinear mapping into feature space

$$K(x,x_i) = K(x_i,x) = \Phi(x) \cdot \Phi(x_i)$$

(4)

The only requirement on the kernel $K(x,xi)$ is to satisfy the Mercer's theorem.

After the optimization problem is solved, we can have the classifier of SVM as follows:

$$f(x) = \text{sgn}(\sum_i \alpha_i y_i K(x_i \cdot x) + b)$$

(5)

2.2   Multi-class SVM Classifier

SVM was originally designed for binary classification, so its extension for multi-class classification is still an on-going research issue. The popular methods which decompose multiclass problems into many binary class problems are "one-against-all" and "one-against-one" approaches [3].

The "one-against-all" approach shows somewhat less accuracy, but still demands heavy computing resources, especially for real time applications. The "one-against-one" approach demonstrates superior performance, so one-against-one method is used in this research.

k(k-1)/2 different binary classifiers are constructed and each one trains data from two different classes. In this application, there are 4 different classes relating to the 4 different conditions. In practice one-against-one method is one of the more suitable strategies for multi-classification problems. After training data from the ith and the jth classes, the following voting strategy is used: if a binary classifier says that a given sample x is associated to class j then the vote for the class j is incremented by one. Finally, sample x is predicted to be in the class with the largest vote, so this approach is referred as the max-wins strategy.

3 Condition Monitoring Method Based on AR Model

Assumed bearing vibration signal is $x(t)$, according to the vibration signal the $AR(p)$ is established

$$x(t) = \sum_{k=1}^{p} a_k x(t-k) + e(n) \qquad (6)$$

where a_k(k=1, 2, $\cdots$, n)and p are the autoregressive parameter and model order respectively. $e(t)$ is the residuals for the model, which is white noise sequence with zero mean and varianceσ^2. Since the regression parameters a_k reflects the inherent characteristics of rolling bearing vibration system, and the residual variance is closely related to output characteristics of rolling bearings, the a_k andσ^2 as feature vector $F=[a_1, a_2, a_3, \cdots, a_p, \sigma^2]$ is used to identify the state of rolling bearings.

The condition monitoring method for roller bearing vibration based on AR and SVM is as follows:

1) Four types of samples vibration data are collected, which correspond to normal state, inner race fault, outer race fault and ball fault.

2) The $AR(p)$ model is established according to AIC criterion (Akaike information criterion), the model includes regression coefficient a_k(k=1, 2, $\cdots$, n) and residual varianceσ^2。

3) The learning samples feature vector $F=[a_1, a_2, a_3, \cdots, a_p, \sigma^2]$ is obtained.

4) Input the training samples into the support vector machine, and multi-fault classifier is established.

5) Vibration signals were collected as a diagnostic signal, the vibration signal to establish AR model parameters and determine their own regression model residual variance, the feature vector is F=$[a_1, a_2, a_3, \cdots, a_p, \sigma^2]$.

6) Fault pattern recognition.

4 Experimental Demosntration

4.1 Experimental Setup and Vibration Data

The vibration acceleration data of bearings with four types of faults are obtained from the Case Western Reserve University. In the test instrument, the ball bearings are installed in a motor driven mechanical system, and are tested under four types of motor loads (0 hp, 1 hp, 2 hp, and 3 hp). An accelerometer is mounted on the motor housing at the drive-end of the motor acquiring the vibration signals from the bearing. The sampling frequency is 12000 Hz. Faults were introduced into the drive-end bearing of the motor using the Electric Discharge Machining (EDM) method [4].

The shaft rotating frequency is about 30 Hz; the characteristic frequency of bearing with outer race fault is 105 Hz; the characteristic frequency with inner race fault is 159 Hz.

The geometrical information of bearing and characteristic frequencies is shown in Table 1. In Table 1, the bearing characteristic frequencies, ball pass frequency of inner race (BPFI) and ball pass frequency of outer race (BPFO), are shown in Hz.

Table 1. Bearing specification and characteristic frequencies

Outer diameter	52 mm	BPFI	159Hz
Inner diameter	25 mm	BPFO	105Hz
Thickness	15 mm	Fault depth	0.28 mm
Pitch diameter	39 mm	fault diameter	0.18 mm

Four types of rolling bearing vibration signal of the 20 sets of data are collected, and condition types are: normal, inner ring fault, outer race fault, ball fault. Four time domain waveform are shown in Figure 2. The four categories of data are randomly divided into two groups, and sample of 10 sets of data is as training data, the rest of the data is as test data. So the number of training samples is 40, and the number of diagnostic samples is 40 too. The feature vectors are calculated by the aforementioned method, and the model's order of P is determined through AIC criterion.

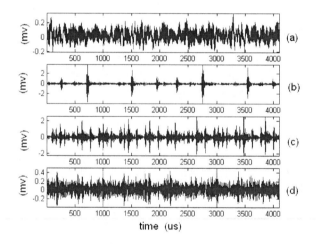

Fig. 2. The time-domain waveform of four states (a) normal (b) outer race fault (c) inner race fault (d) rolling element fault

After multi-fault classifier is set up, the test samples are numbered. The 40 samples to be diagnosed are input into four classifiers, the 4 classifier function value are calculated for test samples. For example, for which classifier output code is +1, then the sample belong to this category device bearing state.

4.2 Comparison with the Neural Network

In order to analyze the performance of the proposed method, BP neural network, RBF neural network were compared, using the same training samples and test samples. Both neural networks' structure was 3-layer with an input layer, hidden layer and output layer. The input nodes 32, the output nodes is 4, hidden layer of 10 nodes. BP neural network correct classification rate is 91%, and RBF neural network correct classification rate is 93%.

This correct classification rate of the proposed method is 95%, although with little difference between the two above-mentioned neural networks, the neural network is inadequate. The neural network methods need take a lot of historical data to train the network, a comprehensive Condition monitoring example of the training samples is necessary. However, the vibration of the scene retained fewer instances of failure, the fault set of orthogonality and completeness is difficult to guarantee, which is bound to affect the reliability of diagnostic results. In addition, the neural network convergence is slow and sometimes diverges.

5 Conclusion

In this paper, AR model was established according to the vibration signal of rolling element bearings. The regression parameters and residual variance of the AR model were treated as the feature vectors, and the support vector machine is used as a pattern recognition tool. By this method, the type of bearing faults can be determined.

Experimental results show that the proposed method for fault detection is effective, which provides a useful method for Condition monitoring of rolling bearings. Through experiments of performance comparison between support vector machine and neural network, it is showed that support vector machine fault recognition accuracy is superior to neural networks. In addition, the proposed method can effectively solve the small sample size problem. The proposed algorithm has some reference value to other types of Condition monitoring.

References

1. Sui, W., Lu, C.H., Zhang, D.: Bearing Condition monitoring Based on Feature Weighted FCM Cluster Analysis. In: 2008 International Conference on Computer Science and Software Engineering, pp. 518–521. IEEE Press, New York (2008)
2. Sui, W.-T., Zhang, D.: Rolling element bearings fault classification based on SVM and feature evaluation. In: 2009 International Conference on Machine Learning and Cybernetics, pp. 450–453. IEEE Press, New York (2009)
3. Llorca, D.F., et al.: A multi-class SVM classifier ensemble for automatic hand washing quality assessment. In: BMVC Proc. Brit. Mach. Vision Conference, Warwick, UK, p. 223 (2007)
4. Zhang, D., Sui, W.-T.: The optimal morlet wavelet and its application on mechanical fault detection. In: Proceedings of the 5th International Conference on Wireless Communications, Networking and Mobile Computing, pp. 1191–1194. IEEE Press, Piscataway (2009)

A Genetic Algorithm for the Flexible Job-Shop Scheduling Problem

Jin Feng Wang, Bi Qiang Du, and Hai Min Ding

Department of Mechanical Engineering,
North China Electric Power University,
Baoding, China
wjf266@163.com, du219@163.com, dinghaimin@yahoo.com

Abstract. Scheduling for the flexible job-shop problem (FJSP) is very important. However, it is quite difficult to achieve an optimal solution to the FJSP with traditional optimization approaches. This paper examines the development and application of a genetic algorithm (GA) to the FJSP. A algorithm is proposed based on a basic genetic algorithm, an improved chromosome representation is represented, different strategies for crossover and mutation operator are adopted. The algorithm is tested on instances of 7 jobs and 7 machines. The results obtained from the computational study have shown that the proposed algorithm is a viable and effective approach for the FJSP.

Keywords: FJSP, genetic algorithm, crossover, mutation.

1 Introduction

Scheduling of operations is one of the most critical issues in the planning and managing of manufacturing processes. To find the best schedule can be very easy or very difficult, depending on the shop environment, the process constraints and the performance indicator. One of the most difficult problems in this area is the JSP. The decision concerns how to sequence the operations on the machines, such as a given performance indicator is optimized. A typical performance indicator for JSP is the makespan, i.e., the time needed to complete all the jobs. The JSP is a well-known NP-hard problem[1].

Although an optimal solution algorithm for the classical JSP has not been developed, there is a trend in the research domain to solve a much more complex version of the problem. The problem is referred to as the FJSP. The FJSP is an extension of the classical JSP which allows an operation to be processed by any machine from a given set. It incorporates all of the difficulties and complexities of its predecessor JSP and is more complex than JSP because of the addition need to determine the assignment of operations to machines. The scheduling problem of a FJSP consists of a routing sub-problem, that is, assigning each operation to a machine out of a set of capable machines and the scheduling sub-problem, which consists of sequencing the assigned operations on all machines in order to obtain a feasible schedule minimizing a predefined objective function. The FJSP mainly presents two

G. Shen and X. Huang (Eds.): CSIE 2011, Part I, CCIS 152, pp. 332–339, 2011.

difficulties. The first one is to assign each operation to a machine, and the second one is to schedule these operations in order to make a predefined objective minimal [2].

In this paper, a practical approach based on a genetic algorithm is proposed for solving the FJSP. The proposed approach makes use of GA to assign operations on machines and to schedule operations on each machine. The considered objective is to minimize makespan (maximal completion time).

2 The FJSP

The flexible job-shop scheduling problem can be formulated as follows. Let $J = \{0,1,...,n,n+1\}$ denote the set of operations to be scheduled and $M = \{0,1,...,m\}$ the set of machines.

The operations 0 and $n+1$ are dummy, have no duration and represent the initial and final operations. The operations are interrelated by two kinds of constraints.

First, the precedence constraints, which force each operation j to be scheduled after all predecessor operations, P_j are completed.

Second, operation j can only be scheduled if the machine it requires is idle. Further, let d_j denote the (fixed) duration (processing time) of operation j. Let F_j represent the finish time of operation j. A schedule can be represented by a vector `of finish times $(F_1, F_m,...,F_n)$. Let $A(t)$ be the set of operations being processed at time t, and let $r_{j,m} = 1$ if operation j requires machine m to be processed and $r_{j,m} = 0$ otherwise[3].

The conceptual model of the FJSP can be described the following way:

$$\text{Minimize } F_{n+1}(C_{max})$$

subject to :

$$F_k \leqslant F_j - d_j, \; j = 1, \ldots, n + 1; k \in P_j$$
$$\sum_{j \in A(t)} r_{j,m} \leq 1, m \in M; \; t \geqslant 0$$

$$F_j \geq 0, j - 1,...,n + 1 \qquad (1)$$

The objective function minimizes the finish time of operation $n+1$ (the last operation), and therefore minimizes the makespan. The first constraints impose the precedence relations between operations. The second constraints state that one machine can only process one operation at a time. The last constraints force the finish times to be non-negative.

Except for the above 3 constraints, hypotheses considered are summarized as follows:

- All machines are available at time 0;
- All operations are released at time 0;
- Each operation can be processed without interruption on one of a set of available machines;

- Recirculation occurs when a job could visit a machine more than once;
- The order of operations for each job is predefined and cannot be modified.

3 Genetic Algorithm

GAs are adaptive methods, which may be used to solve search and optimization problems. They are based on the genetic process of biological organisms. Over many generations, natural populations evolve according to the principles of natural selection, i.e. survival of the fittest. Before a genetic algorithm can be run, a suitable encoding for the problem must be devised. A fitness function is also required, which assigns a figure of merit to each encoded solution. It is assumed that a potential solution to a problem may be represented as a set of parameters. These parameters are joined together to form a string of values. The individuals, during the reproductive phase, are selected from the population, producing offspring, which comprise the next generation. Parents are randomly selected from the population using a scheme, which favors fitter individuals. Having selected two parents, their chromosomes are recombined, typically using mechanisms of crossover and mutation. Mutation is usually applied to some individuals, to guarantee population diversity.

The general structure of the GA adopted in this paper is described as follows:

Step 1. Initialization: Construct an initial population of *pop_size* solutions.

Step 2. Genetic operators: Generate offspring by using crossover and mutation.

Step 3. Selection: Select pop_size solutions from the solutions in the current population and the new solutions generated in *Step 2* to form the next generation.

Step 4. Iteration: Repeat *Steps 2 - 3* until an optimum solution is found or the maximum number of generations, *max_gen*, is reached.

4 Scheduling Algorithm Based on GAs

The following takes the FJSP in Table 1. as a sample to illustrate the application of GAs. In Table 1, there are 2 jobs and 5 machines, where rows correspond to operations and columns correspond to machines. Each cell denotes the processing time of that operation on the corresponding machine. In the table, the "X" means that the machine cannot execute the corresponding operation.

Table 1. Processing time table of an instance of the FJSP

Jobs	Operation	Machines				
		M_1	M_2	M_3	M_4	M_5
1	O_{11}	5	3	5	3	X
1	O_{12}	10	X	5	6	3
2	O_{21}	5	7	3	X	X
2	O_{22}	X	8	5	2	X
2	O_{23}	10	X	6	7	8

4.1 Chromosome Representation

An improved chromosome representation is proposed to reduce the cost of decoding, due to its structure and encoding rule, it requires no repair mechanism. Our chromosome representation has two components: Machine Selection(MS) and Operation Sequence(OS)[4]. According to the FJSP in Table I. The chromosome representation for such problem is shown in Fig. 1.

Machine Selection(MS)					Operation Sequence(OS)				
2	4	3	3	3	1	1	2	2	2

Fig. 1. Chromosome Gene

● Machine Selection (MS) part

We use an array of integer values to represent Machine Selection. The length equals to L. Each integer value equals the index of the array of alternative machine set of each operation. For the problem in Table 1, one possible encoding of the Machine Selection is shown in Fig. 2.

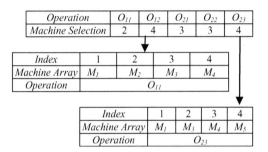

Fig. 2. Machine Selection

For instance, M_4 is selected to process operation O_{23} since the value in the array of alternative machine set is 3. The value could also equal 1, 2 and 4 since operation O_{23} can be processed on four machines M_1, M_3, M_4 or M_5, the valid values are 1, 2, 3 and 4. This demonstrates a FJSP with recirculation if more than one operation of the same job is processed on the same machine. For example, O_{11} and O_{12} both belong to J_1 and may be processed on the same machine M_1, M_3 or M_4. If only one machine could be selected for some operations, the value is 1 in the Machine Selection array. Therefore, the MS representation is flexible enough to encode the FJSP. It may easily use the same structure to represent FJSP. This property improves the search process by requiring less memory and ignoring unused data especially to the FJSP.

● Operation Sequence (OS) part

We use the operation-based representation, which defines all operations for a job with the same symbol and then interpret them according to the sequence of a given chromosome. The length equals to L too. The index i of job J_i appears in the Operation Sequence J_{io} times to represent its J_{io} ordered operations. It can avoid generating an infeasible schedule by replacing each operation corresponding to job index. For the instance in Table 1, one possible encoding of the Operation Sequence is shown in Fig. 3. J_1 has two operations O_{11} and O_{12}; J_2 have three operations. Reading the data from left to right and increasing operation index of each job, the Operation Sequence 2-2-1-2-1 depicted could be translated into a list of ordered operations: O_{21}-O_{21}-O_{22}-O_{11}-O_{23}-O_{12}.

Job	J_2	J_2	J_1	J_2	J_1
Operation Sequence	2	2	1	2	1
Operation	O_{21}	O_{22}	O_{11}	O_{23}	O_{12}

Fig. 3. Operation Sequence

4.2 Initializing Population

In this section, we mainly take into account both the processing time to assign each operation to the suitable machine. We define that a stage is the process of selecting a suitable machine for an operation. Thus this method records the sum of the processing time of each machine in the whole processing stage. Then the machine which has the minimum processing time in every stage is selected. In particular, the first job and next job are randomly selected. The implementation of initializing population is given in Fig. 4. We assume that the first selected job is J_1, and the next job is J_2. From Fig. 4, we easily see that the processing time on M_2 is the shortest in the alternative machine set of operation O_{11}. So the machine M_2 is selected to process the operation

Time	0	3	0	0	0	0	3	0	0	3	0	3	3	0	3	0	3	3	2	3	0	3	8	2	3
Operation	O_{11}					O_{12}					O_{21}					O_{22}					O_{23}				
Machine Array	M_1	M_2	M_3	M_4		M_1	M_3	M_4	M_5		M_1	M_2	M_3			M_2	M_3	M_4			M_1	M_3	M_4	M_5	
Processing time	5	3	5	3		10	5	6	3		5	7	3			8	5	2			10	6	7	8	
Added time	5	3	5	3		10	5	6	3		5	10	3			10	8	2			10	9	9	11	
Shortest time	3					3					3					2					5				
Selected machine	M_2					M_5					M_3					M_4					M_3				
Update time	0	3	0	0	0	0	3	0	0	3	0	3	3	0	3	0	3	3	2	3	0	3	8	2	3
MS	2	0	0	0	0	2	4	0	0	0	2	4	3	0	0	2	4	3	3	0	2	4	3	3	4

Fig. 4. The process of initializing population

O_{11} of job J_1, and set corresponding allele in MS to the index of M_2. Then the processing time is added to the corresponding position in time array. Finally, the selected machines of all operations may be M_2-M_5-M_3-M_4-M_3, and the corresponding MS representation is 2-4-3-3-4.

4.3 Selection

Selection is the basic operators of GA. In order to guarantee the astringency of GAs, the optimal individual in one population is retained to the next population directly, namely, the elite chromosomes must be retain. The criterion used to select the elite chromosomes can be chosen among three selection methods well known in the GA literature: binary tournament, n-size tournament and linear ranking. In this paper, the criterion of linear ranking is adopted which has to be repeated until the number of individuals equals the population size. In order to avoid local optima, The probability of selection is setted for the elite chromosomes, usually is 5%-20%.

4.4 Crossover and Mutation Operator

Chromosome representation has two components: MS and OS. The two components are initialized by the different rules. So the crossover and mutation operator of the two components is different. Generally, MS is generated based on OS. In this paper, We mainly discuss the crossover and mutation operator of MS.

The goal of the crossover is to obtain better chromosomes to improve the result by exchanging information contained in the current good ones. The crossover operation of MS is performed on two Machine Selection parts and generates two new Machine Selection parts each of which corresponds to a new allocation of operations to machines. We adopt two-point crossover. MS crossover operator only changes some alleles, while their location in each individual i.e., their preceding constraints are not changed.

Mutation introduces some extra variability into the population to enhance the diversity of population. Usually, mutation is applied with small probability. Large probability may destroy the good chromosome. MS mutation operator only changes the assignment property of the chromosomes. We select the shortest processing time from alternative machine set to balance the workload of the machines[5][6].

To illustrate the effectiveness and performance of algorithm, an instance of the FJSP(7×7) in Table 2 is selected to compute.

According to the FJSP in table 2, 100 chromosomes are setted. Selection probability is setted to be 10%, crossover probability is setted to be 80%, mutation probability is setted to be 3%, Initial temperature is setted to be 3, termination temperature is setted to be 0.01, decreasing rate is setted to be 0.9, iterations are 100. Finally, the corresponding Gantt chart is shown in Fig. 5.

Table 2. An instance of the FJSP(7×7)

Jobs	Operation	Machines						
		M_1	M_2	M_3	M_4	M_5	M_6	M_7
1	O_{11}	3	3	5	3	5	X	10
1	O_{12}	10	X	5	6	3	9	X
1	O_{13}	X	10	X	5	6	3	4
2	O_{21}	5	7	3	9	8	X	9
2	O_{22}	X	8	5	2	6	7	10
2	O_{23}	X	10	X	5	X	4	1
2	O_{24}	10	8	9	6	4	7	X
3	O_{31}	10	X	X	7	6	5	2
3	O_{32}	X	10	6	4	8	9	10
3	O_{33}	1	4	5	6	X	10	X
4	O_{41}	4	3	6	5	9	7	8
4	O_{42}	X	11	7	8	10	5	6
4	O_{43}	4	6	7	2	3	9	5
5	O_{51}	9	5	7	8	3	X	10
5	O_{52}	10	X	7	4	X	8	6
5	O_{53}	X	9	8	7	4	2	7
5	O_{54}	11	9	X	6	7	5	3
6	O_{61}	6	7	1	4	6	9	X
6	O_{62}	11	4	9	X	9	7	6
6	O_{63}	10	9	4	10	11	X	10
6	O_{64}	7	9	5	6	X	3	11
7	O_{71}	5	4	2	6	7	X	10
7	O_{72}	X	9	X	9	5	9	10
7	O_{73}	3	X	5	2	4	X	3

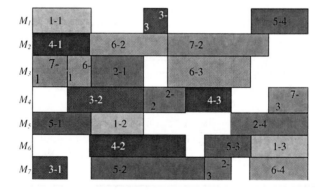

Fig. 5. Gantt chart

5 Conclusion

This paper proposed a GA for solving the flexible job-shop scheduling problem. An improved chromosome representation is designed based on machine selection and operation sequence. The selection, crossover and mutation operation are also given.

Finally, the Gantt chart is drawn based on 7 jobs and 7 machines. The computational result shows the GA can obtain better solution.

References

[1] Li, Y., Chen, Y.: A Genetic Algorithm for Job-Shop Scheduling. Journal of Software 5(3), 269–275 (2010)

[2] Xia, W., Wu, Z.: An effective hybrid optimization approach for multi-objective flexible job-shop scheduling problems. Computers & Industrial Engineering 48, 409–425 (2005)

[3] Liaw, C.-F.: A hybrid genetic algorithm for the open shop scheduling problem. European Journal of Operational Research 124, 28–42 (2000)

[4] Xi, W.-d., Qiao, B., Zhu, J.-y.: A genetic algorithm for flexible job shop scheduling based on two-substring gene coding method. Journal of Harb in Insitute of Technology 39(7), 1151–1153 (2007)

[5] Pezzella, F., Morganti, G., Ciaschetti, G.: A genetic algorithm for the Flexible Job-shop Scheduling Problem. Computers & Operations Research 35, 3202–3212 (2008)

[6] Zhang, G., Gao, L., Shi, Y.: An effective genetic algorithm for the flexible job-shop scheduling problem. Expert Systems with Applications (2010), doi:10.1016/j.eswa.2010.08

Research on Neural Network Controller for the System of Online Synchro Record and Simulation of Motion

Shizhu Feng, Bo Su, Ming Xu, Shuling Yang, Guoxuan Lu,
Qichang Yao, Wei Lan, and Ning Mao

China North Vehicle Research Institute
Huaishuling 4 courtyard, Fengtai district,
Beijing, China 100072
f_s_z@126.com

Abstract. Technology of online synch record and simulation of motion is a spiry integral technology of mechanics, electrics and hydraulics. Systematical study of it is carried out using a 6-DOF(Degree Of Freedom) synchronous on-line recorder and simulator. The algorithm of the 6-DOF synchronous on-line recorder and simulator is deduced. the adaptive neural network controller is designed accordingly. with the existing hydraulic servo driven 6-DOF simulator, a synchronous on-line recorder and simulator control system is set up, and the experiment proves the algorithm is correct and the controller's design is fully a success.

Keywords: neural network controller, synchro record and simulation, mobile robot, 6-DOF motion base.

1 Introduction

Technology of online synchro record and simulation of motion(SRSM) include two aspects, one is motion synchronous recording and replaying with video and audio signal presented. The other is synchronously imitating a remote moving object, such as vehicle, ship, aero plane, etc. with video and audio signal synchronously presented.

Technology of online SRSM can extensively applied in military aspects, safety detective, emergency disposal, aviation and aerospace, robot, remote control, medical treatment, vehicle experiment, game industry [1~6] and numerous other realms. For example, when the Technology of online SRSM is applied to the remote controlled battle vehicle(mobile robot), the operator can sit on the simulation motion base in the control room which is far from the dangerous battle area, not only can he hears the sound and sees the pictures of the arena, but also the high quality motion feeling of the remote controlled battle vehicle. And even can he judge if the vehicle is crossing a grain of rocks, this will doubtlessly be advantageous to grasp battle opportunity. SRSM can also be apply to other hazardous situation such as the disaster spot manipulation, the assistance to dispose the nuclear radiation, deep sea and underground application, astro-space works and remote control of the engineering vehicle operation, etc.

G. Shen and X. Huang (Eds.): CSIE 2011, Part I, CCIS 152, pp. 340–346, 2011.
© Springer-Verlag Berlin Heidelberg 2011

2 System Composing

Our system is illustrated in Fig.1 below. This system consists of six parts: a mobile robot, a 6-DOF (degrees of freedom) motion base (hydraulically driven), two sets of computer control systems, a vision and audition system and a hydraulic power source. The operator sitting on the motion base manipulates the on-site robot with operating handle according to the images based on data from the tele-robot. The motion base simulates the motions of the tele-robot, so that the operator feels as if he is sitting on the mobile robot. At the same time, the grasping force with which the robot grasps an object is fed back to the operating handle via force sensors. Consequently, the operator can also feel the magnitude of the working force and the stiffness or softness of the object being grasped. [1]

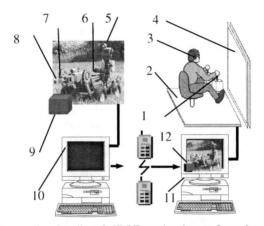

1-operating handle; 2-6DOF motion base; 3-earphone ; 4-3D scene; 5-3-eye camera; 6-accelerator sensor; 7-force, torque, displacement sensors; 8-hydraulic hand ; 9-object ; 10- slave control computer ; 11-master control computer; 12- object

Fig. 1. Tele-robotic system for a mobile robot using SRSM

In such a system, to produce the motion of the mobile robot, it is important to measure the motion of the mobile robot and control the movement of the 6-DOF motion base. This paper focuses on the measure of the motion of the mobile robot and analysis of electro-hydraulic servo system that control 6-DOF motion base, and investigates a intelligent control method for servo system of the motion base that simulating the motions of a mobile tele-robot.

3 Theory of Motion Base

The 6-DOF motion base used in the experiment consists of a seat, a connecting mechanism attached under the seat, and six hydraulic cylinders that can generate six motion elements: roll (±15°), pitch (±15°), yaw (±15°), surge (±130mm), sway (±130mm) and heave (±125mm). Two operating handle for manipulating the mobile robot are installed close to the armrests of the seat on the motion base. First the posture parameter received from remote area was calculated by a special designed algorithm, and give the extended displacement of each hydraulic cylinder as the reference. then controls the 6-DOF motion base to the position which present the posture of remote robot. The displacement of each cylinder, detected by the electromagnetism displacement sensors, is fed back, and compare with the reference, the difference is outputted to control the 6-DOF motion base to track the motion of the remote robot. The whole process constitutes a closed-loop system. [2], [3].

4 Control System Design

A new style PID controller [4] based on the neural network was developed, whose PID parameters could be modified online by RBF(Radian Base Function) neural network. the PID control provide the stable control and RBF network adjust the PID control parameters to ensure the broad band stability for system control

4.1 System Modeling

The plant in Fig.2, namely, the electro hydraulic servo valves and dissymmetric hydraulic cylinder can be modeled as the following transfer function (TF).

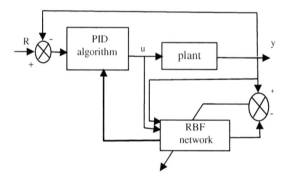

Fig. 2. Schematic diagram for RBF-PID control system

The TF of the displacement of cylinder to the servo valve's input current is as follow :

$$G_{hp}(s) = \frac{y(s)}{u(s)}$$

$$= \frac{8\times10^{-3}\times1647}{s(\dfrac{s^2}{2634129} + \dfrac{0.79s}{1632} + 1)} \cdot \frac{1.96\times10^{-3}}{(\dfrac{s^2}{462400} + \dfrac{1.4s}{680} + 1)} \tag{1}$$

4.2 Parameter Designing

Using Ziegler-Nichols method and numeric simulation, the PID parameter is determined. the sampling time is 10ms, the rising time is 0.05s, stable time is 0.15s, the stable error is converge to 0.

4.3 RBF-PID Control System

The RBF network is a feed-forward neural network with three layers, input layer, middle layer and output layer. Middle layer is also called hidden layer. Each hidden node evaluates a kernel function on the incoming input and the output is a simple weighted linear summation of the kernel function. RBF network has not only the global approaching feature but also the optimal approaching feature. and it has no problem of false local optimization [5][6][7]. The network used in this paper has 10-input, 8-hidden node and 3-output. The structure is illustrated in Fig.3.

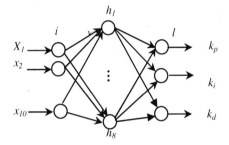

Fig. 3. Topological Structure of RBF Neural Network

The ten inputs of the RBF network are middle parameters of the control system. When the TF of Eq.(1) is transformed to a differential equation as Eq.(2), sampling time is t=0.01s.

$$A\left(z^{-1}\right) y(k) = B\left(z^{-1}\right) u(k-1) \tag{2}$$

where $A = \begin{bmatrix} 1 & -0.8042 & 0.06673 & 9.466 \times 10^{-6} & -4.513 \times 10^{-7} & -6.238 \times 10^{-10} \end{bmatrix}$

$B = \begin{bmatrix} 0.1958 & 0.06662 & 7.964 \times 10^{-5} & -2.815 \times 10^{-7} & -4.11 \times 10^{-10} \end{bmatrix}$

$y(k)$—output of the displacement of hydraulic cylinder at time k

$u(k)$—control input of control system at time k

So the input vector X of the RBF network is:

$X = [x_1, x_2, ..., x_{10}]^T$

Where: $x_i = A(1+i)$ $i=1,2,3...5$

$x_j = B(j-5)$ $j=6,7,...10$

The Gauss function used in RBF hidden layer is:

$$h_j = \exp\left(- \frac{\| X - c_j \|^2}{2b_j^2} \right) \qquad j=1,2,\ldots10$$

Where: c_j is the center of the h_j, it form a matrix $c_{ji}=[c_{j1}, c_{j2}, \ldots c_{j8}]^T$; b_j is the standard deviation of h_j. It forms a vector $b_j=[b_1, b_2 \ldots b_8]^T$. So the RBF network vector $H=[h_1,h_2,\ldots h_8]^T$

If the weight of the RBF is $W=[w_1, w_2, \ldots w_8]^T$, the output of middle layer is

$$y_m(k) = w_1 * h_1 + w_2 * h_2 + \ldots + w_8 * h_8 \tag{3}$$

The parameters of c_{ji}, b_j , w_j and h_j are first given some values, then modified using Gradient descent algorithm described as follow :

$$w_j(k)=w_j(k-1)+\eta(y(k)-y_m(k))*h_j+\alpha(w_j(k-1)-w_j(k-2)) \tag{4}$$

$$\Delta b_j = (y(k) - y_m(k))w_j h_j \frac{\| X - C_j \|^2}{b_j^3} \tag{5}$$

$$b_j(k)=b_j(k-1)+\eta\Delta b_j+\alpha(b_j(k-1)-b_j(k-2)) \tag{6}$$

$$\Delta c_{ji} = (y(k) - y_m(k))w_j \frac{x - c_{ji}}{b_j^2} \tag{7}$$

$$c_{ji}(k)=c_{ji}(k-1)+\eta\Delta c_{ji}+\alpha(c_{ji}(k-1)-c_{ji}(k-2)) \tag{8}$$

Where: the study rate η=0.2, factor of momentum α=0.05. The Jacobian information used is as Eq. (19).

$$\frac{\partial y(k)}{\partial u(k)} = \frac{\partial y_m(k)}{\partial u(k)} = \sum_{j=1}^{m} w_j h_j \frac{c_{ij} - u(k)}{b_j^2} \tag{9}$$

So the control algorithm for the RBF-PID control system is:

$$E(k) = R(k) - y(k) \tag{10}$$

$$u(k)=u(k-1)+k_p(E(k)-E(k-1))+k_i E(k)+k_d(E(k)-2*E(k-1)+E(k-2)) \tag{11}$$

Where: $R(k)$—is reference input of the control system.

$E(k)$—is control error.

The PID parameters are modified by following algorithm:

$$\Delta k_p = -\eta \frac{\partial J}{\partial k_p} = \eta E(k)\frac{\partial y(k)}{\partial u(k)}(E(k)-E(k-1)) \tag{12}$$

$$\Delta k_i = -\eta \frac{\partial J}{\partial k_i} = \eta E(k)\frac{\partial y(k)}{\partial u(k)}E(k) \tag{13}$$

$$\Delta k_d = -\eta \frac{\partial J}{\partial k_d} = \eta E(k)\frac{\partial y(k)}{\partial u(k)}(E(k)-2*E(k-1)+E(k-2)) \tag{14}$$

$$k_p = k_p + \Delta k_p,\ k_i = k_i + \Delta k_i,\ k_d = k_d + \Delta k_d \tag{15}$$

5   Experiment Result

Because of the difficulty of moving the mobile robot to various poses, a foursquare board with six acceleration sensors was used as a substitute for the mobile robot to conduct the experiment. The target values of the linear displacements are calculated by the special designed algorithm. Then input into the control system proposed herein. After processed by RBF-PID controller, the position of each hydraulic cylinder is controlled. The motion of the foursquare board was accomplished manually within 5 seconds. The experiment curves are shown in Fig.4. The results show that the design of the RBF-PID algorithm is good enough with the fast response and good transient property, and can fulfill the task in actual system.

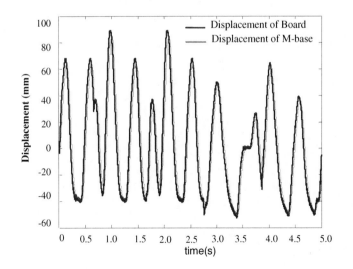

Fig. 4. The displacement of piston driver track the displacement of the Board

6 Conclusion

Technology of online synchro record and simulation of motion is a spiry integral technology of mechanics, ectrics and hydraulics. Systematical study of it is carried out using a 6-DOF(Degree Of Freedom)synchronous on-line recorder and simulator. The algorithm of the 6-DOF synchronous on-line recorder and simulator is deduced. a RBF-PID controller was developed to control the 6-DOF motion base that accomplishes the presence of realistic motions in the tele-robot system. The simulation results and experimental results proves the algorithm is correct, and indicate that the design of RBF-PID controller is a success. The whole research will provide a reference to the study of SRSM.

References

1. Zhao, D., Yamada, H., Muto, T., et al.: DOF Presentation of Realistic Motion in Operating a Construction Tele-Robot System. In: Proceedings of the 5th JFPS International Symposium on Fluid Power, vol. 2, pp. 507–512 (2002)
2. Zhao, D., Xia, Y., Yamada, H., et al.: Control Method for Realistic Motion in a Construction Tele-robotic System with 3-DOF Parallel Mechanism. Journal of Robotics and Mechatronics 15(4), 361–368 (2003)
3. Zhao, D., Xia, Y., Yamada, H., et al.: Presentation of Realistic Motion to the Operator in Operating a Tele-operated Construction Robot. Journal of Robotics and Mechatronics 14(2), 98–104 (2002)
4. Tao, Y.: New style PID control and application. Publishing House of Mechanical Industry, Beijing (2005)
5. Feng, S.: Bilateral Servo Control of the 6-DOF Parallel Electro-hydraulic Tele-Manipulator with Force-feedback. paper of PH.D of JiLin University, Changchun (2008)
6. Feng, S., Zhao, D., et al.: Research on p-f control for Construction Telerobot with Force Telepresence. Transaction of the Chinese Society for Agricultural Machinery 39, 120–124 (2008) (in Chinese)
7. Liu, J.: Advanced PID control and MATLAB simulation, 2nd edn. Publishing House of Electronics Industry, Beijing (2004)

Gait and Stability Analysis of a Quadruped Robot

Junming Wei, Zhiguo Shi, Qiao Zhang, Jun Tu, and Zhiliang Wang

School of Information Engineering,
University of Science and Technology Beijing,
Beijing, 10083 P.R. China
weijunming05@126.com, szg@ustb.edu.cn, abby20082008@163.com,
tujun2011@163.com, wzg@ustb.edu.cn

Abstract. In the multi-legged robot research, a challenging task is to manage its walking balance. This paper presents the gait and stability analysis of a simple quadruped robot. First, a quadruped robot which consists of 15 DOFs was built up. To analyze its walking balance, we specified the straight walking gait and the turning gait in every step. A practical obstacle avoidance experiment and further stimulations demonstrate that the proposed gaits can achieve the walking stability of the quadruped robot.

Keywords: quadruped robot, mechanism, stability, gait analysis, experiment.

1 Introduction

Mobile robots are being used among an increasingly wide range of tasks, such as technology, education, military, industry, healthcare, community services, etc. In the world, a variety of mobile robots are being studied and they can be classified as three types of locomotion mechanisms: wheeled, legged and the mixed Robot [1].

Currently, most existing mobile robots rely on wheels for locomotion. Wheeled platforms are the best solutions for traversing relatively even surfaces, but they have difficulties in dealing with obstacles. On the other hand, legged robots are more adaptable in rough terrain and very recommended to do a task passing through a stairway or some obstacles.

The rest of the paper is organized as follows:

Section 2 introduces research background. Section 3 presents system composition of the new quadruped robot. Section 4 analyses the robot gaits and walking stability. Experiments and conclusion are given in section 5 and section 6 respectively.

2 Related Work

In spite of the well known theoretical advantages of walking robots over wheeled robots to move on very irregular terrain, mechanism complexity increases when a robot has legs. Another challenge is the stability question. While wheeled mobile robots are inherently stable with wheels remaining on the ground, a legged robot must shift its center of gravity (CoG) as it walks in order to maintain stability.

G. Shen and X. Huang (Eds.): CSIE 2011, Part I, CCIS 152, pp. 347–354, 2011.
© Springer-Verlag Berlin Heidelberg 2011

When walking slowly, static stability theories are applied. Commonly, a quadruped animal is supported all the time by three feet on the ground, which form a triangle encompassing the center of mass of the body. This is the general criterion [2] that lays a foundation for legged robot research such as gait planning, motion and structure parameters selection, control method and so on. Apart from static stability, the stable dynamic locomotion control is also a common research topic for quadruped robots, which traditionally uses Zero Moment Point based and limit-cycle based methods [3].

Quadrupeds are characterized by a number of different periodic sequences of leg movements, which is called gait. Quadrupeds use two kinds of gaits, namely symmetrical gaits and asymmetrical gaits [4]. Gait selection criteria can be various according to different requirements and mechanism and mainly considers energy efficiency, stability, velocity, mobility, comfort and environmental impact [5]. The duty fact β presents the rate of standing period to the total period of one stride motion [6]. Changing the duty factor implies to the change of the gait. The transition from one gait to another is qutie related to speed and efficiency [7]. Morever, a real-time reasonable selection of walking pattern is necessary to maintain the best walking balance [8].

3   System Composition of the New Quadruped Robot

In this section, the system architecture of the robot would be described in three parts, each as a subsystem. The robot consists of 15 joints. Specifically, there are three joints on each leg, two on the head and one one the tail. The composition of the whole system and the papameter of the subsystem are shown in Figure 1 and Table 1.

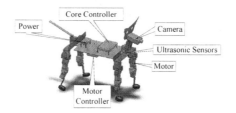

Fig. 1. The overall structure of the quadruped robot

Table 1. The parameter table of the quadruped robot

Component	Number of Motor	Weight (kg)	Size(m)
Head	2	0.18	0.2×0.15
Leg	3×4	0.36×4	0.24×0.05
Tail	1	0.12	0.15×0.02
Trunk		0.25	0.37×0.23
Control system		0.3	0.26×0.18
Whole body	15	2.29	0.37×0.23×0.3

3.1 Leg Design

Leg structure is the key component of the mechanical structure of the quadruped robot. Robot leg structure can be divided into two types, namely open chain structure and closed chain structure. We need a higher flexibility of the leg moving, so the open chain structure is our choice. In addition, considering the control, motion and mechanical durability, we had two schemes for leg design, as shown in Figure 2 and Figure 3. Initially, the first option was taken. While it has compact structure, realizes flexible moving and is easily controlled, high capability of Motor1 is required as its shaft needs to support the entire weight of the body. Comparing to Structure I, Structure II avoids this problem, which reduces the burden on the component. Based on discussions above, so we chose Leg Structure II in the end.

3.2 Head Design

A CCD camera is equipped on the head and the robot can use it to acquire video information of the surrounding environment. The head has 2 DOFs. One is used to swing up and down, the other serves for shaking head right and left, as shown in Figure 4. Motor1 controls the horizontal rotation of the camera and 150-degree level scanning can be achieved. Motor2 implements vertical movement and 120-degree vertical scanning can be realized.

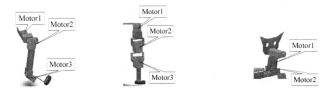

Fig. 2. Leg Structure I   **Fig. 3.** Leg Structure II   **Fig. 4.** Head Structure

4   Gait Planning and Stability

Gait planning is the key to achieve stable walking for the quadruped robot. For a walk without falling, the robot's center of gravity(CoG) needs to be actively shifted to an equilibrium position during walking. Thus, we need to consider how to manage the balance of quadruped robot during standing and walking.

Generally, three legs are needed to support the whole body. To this end, there exists an approach that the robot tries to adjust its CoG to be projected inside the triangle formed by supporting feet. While the triangle area is constantly alternating during the process of walking, the walking robot is stable as long as the vertical projection of its CoG is always in the alternating regions.

The center of gravity is denoted as O that coincides with the geometric center of the body projection plane. As shown in Figure 5(a), the vertical projection of four feet is expressed by the rectangle drawn by thin solid line. The area formed by the feet is 220mm × 370mm.

4.1 Straight Walking Gait

Taking   into   account   robot real-time control, gait stability   and minimal energy consumption, we use a simple gait for straight walking according to the criterion of stastic stability. This gait requires a leg in the swing phase and the remaining three legs in the support phase all the time. By taking turns in a certain order periodically,   the   quadruped robot   can   walk   in   a   straight   path.   To make a more clear description of the gait cycle, this moving process is divided into the following steps, as shown in Figure 5:

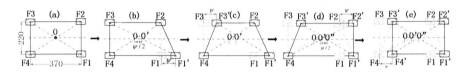

Fig. 5. The process of straight walking gait for the quadruped robot

(1) At the beginning, as shown in Figure 5(a), the quadruped robot is in its initial state, where each foot on the boundary line of the static stability area and the robot's CoG coincides with the geometric center of the rectangular formed by the projection of four feet on the ground. O denotes the robot's CoG and F1, F2, F3, F4 denotes the four legs of the robot.

(2) Figure 5(b) shows that F1 moves forward one step ψ . According to the criterion of static stability, the robot's center of gravity needs to move forward $\psi / 2$ so that it can be maintained in the triangular formed by the projection of F1, F2, F4 in the vertical direction. In this case, the robot is stable. F3 is in the swing phase and F1, F2, F4 are in the support phase.

(3) Figure 5(c) shows that F3 moves forward one step ψ . From Figure 5 (b), we know that, to keep the robot stable, only F3 can be moved, otherwise, it will become instability.

(4) In this gait cycle, another leg F2 moves forward one step ψ and the robot's CoG needs to move forward $\psi / 2$ so that it can be maintained in the triangular formed by the projection of F1, F2, F3 in the vertical direction, as shown in Figure 5(d), and the robot is stable.

(5) Figure 5(e) shows that F3 moves forward one step ψ . From Figure 5(d), we know only F4 exists out of the triangular stability region, so F4 is in the swing phase.

Now the pose of the robot returns to the initial state and the center of gravity O moved forward one step ψ to O', which means the robot move forward one step ψ . By repeating the leg order peridically, the quadruped robot can move forward stably.

4.2 Turning Gait

After discussing the straight walking gait, it is necessary to explore the turning gait as the quadruped robot may need to change directions while walking.

We studied the fixed-point turn (The turning radius is equal to zero.) of the quadruped robot in this paper. Planning this turning gait can help the robot to turn around in any direction, thereby enhancing the moving flexibility in the environment.

On the basis of the criterion of the statistic stability, the α - degeree stable turning in counter-clockwise direction of the quadruped robot is achieved, which is specified in Figure 6. Accordingly, the clockwise turning and turning in the greater angle can be achieved.

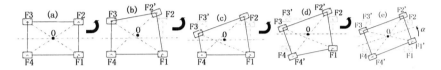

Fig. 6. The process of turning walking gait for the quadruped robot

5   Experiment and Stimulation

5.1   The Obstacle Avoidance Experiment in Indoor Environment

During the fixed-point turn, the turning radius is equal to zero theoretically. When taking into account the shape of the quadruped robot, there exists a safety radius - R_0 which can make sure the turning is implemented without collision. The expression of the safety radius is as follows:

$$R_0 = \varepsilon \sqrt{(\frac{a}{2})^2 + (\frac{b}{2})^2} = \frac{\varepsilon \sqrt{a^2 + b^2}}{2} \tag{1}$$

Where ε denotes the safety factor of the turning radius. It is related to the shape of obstacles and can prevent the robot from toughing the obstacles. Usually, it is equal to 1.2.

In this paper, the width of the quadruped robot a=220mm, the length of it b=370mm, so the safety radius R_0=271.3mm. The neck of the quadruped robot we developed is equipped with ultrasonic sensors which are used to avoid obstacles. Based on the value of the safety turning radius, the threshold value is set to 30cm. In the process of walking, the transition between the straight walking gait and turning gait occurs. The experiment using the quadruped robot is shown in Figure 7.

Fig. 7. The process of obstacle avoidance experiment for the quadruped robot

5.2 Gait Stimulation

We also use the virtual prototyping technology to study the gait planning of the quadruped robot. The specific process includes creating a model into ADAMS, as shown in Figure 8.

Fig. 8. Mechanical model of the quadruped robot

When the step $= \psi$, the gait cycle $T = 2s$, the trot gait simulation is conducted through the ADAMS / View. After processing by ADAMS / PostProcessor, the simulation results are shown in Figure 9.

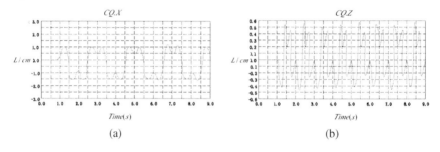

(a)   (b)

Fig. 9. Wave curve of center of gravity for the quadruped robot

In Figure 5-11(a), CQ.X is the displacement curve of the quadruped robot's CoG in the horizontal direction. As can be seen from the curve, the maximum volatility of CoG in the horizontal direction is 2.1cm and this displacement is almost equal in value and opposite in the direction during the entire cycle. While the CoG swings left and right in the horizontal direction during walking, it moves forward in one direction. If the rate of horizontal fluctuation is within 10%, the robot's gait is stable.

As shown in Figure 5-11(b), CQ.Z is the displacement curve of the quadruped robot's CoG in the vertical direction. The maximum volatility is 1.1cm and considering that the total height of the quadruped robot is 30cm, the vertical fluctuation rate is 3.67%, which shows that the fluctuation in the vertical direction is small while walking.

We change the step ψ of the quadruped robot and do similar simulations. As can be seen from the comparison of the results in Table 2, in the case of the same gait cycle, increasing the robot's step, which means to increase the robot's walking speed, leads that the horizontal and vertical fluctuations of the quadruped robot's CoG increase significantly and the robot dog's gait stability reduced.

Table 2. The gait stimulation results for the quadruped robot

ψ Step/mm	CQ.X/mm	CQ.Z/mm	Volatility (X)	Volatility (Z)
ψ =20	24	9.2	10.4%	3.07%
ψ =40	25	11	10.8%	3.67%
ψ =60	37	22	16.1%	7.33%

Note: $\Delta_x = \dfrac{Q.X}{L}$, $\Delta_z = \dfrac{Q.Z}{H}$, where L is the horizontal width of the quadruped robot, $L = 220$mm, H is the height of the quadruped robot, $H = 300$mm.

6 Conclusion

In this paper, we presented the gait and stability analysis of a quadruped mobile robot platform developed by our team. The center of gravity of alternating feet triangle formed in a quadruped robot's walking was identified to analyze its walking balance. We designed the straight walking gait and turning gait for the quadruped robot. The effectiveness of the proposed approach was illustrated by the experimental result of our quadruped robot. Stimulations were conducted to show that increasing the robot's walking speed will make the robot unstable. Future work includes how to enhance the walking speed and improve its adaptability on irregular terrains.

Acknowledgments. This work was supported by the National Natural Science Foundation of China (NO. 60903067).

References

1. Siegwart, R., Nourbakhsh, I.R.: Introduction to Autonomous Mobile Robots. The MIT Press, Cambridge (2004)
2. Pengfei, W., Lining, S.: The Stability Analysis for Quadruped Bionic Robot. In: 2006 IEEE/RSJ International Conference on Intelligent Robots and Systems, Beijing, China, pp. 5238–5242 (2006)
3. Christophe, M., Hiroshi, K., Kunikatsu, T.: Stable Dynamic Walking of a Quadruped via Phase Modulations against Small Disturbances. In: IEEE International Conference on Robotics and Automation Kobe International Conference Center Kobe, Japan, pp. 4201–4206 (2009)
4. Lianqing, Y., Yujin, W., Weijun, T.: Gait Analysis and Implementation of a Simple Quadruped Robot. In: 2nd International Conference on Industrial Mechatronics and Automation, Wuhan, China, pp. 431–434 (2010)
5. Silva, M.F., Machado, J.A.T., Lopes, A.M., Tar, J.K.: Gait Selection for Quadruped and Hexapod Walking Systems. In: IEEE International Conference on Computational Cybernetics, Vienna, Austria, pp. 217–222 (2004)

6. Inagaki, K., Kobayashi, H.: A Gait Transition for Quadruped Walking Machine. In: IEEE/RSJ International Conference on Intelligent Robots and Systems, Yokohama, Japan (1993)
7. Radkhah, K., Kurowski, S., von Stryk, O.: Design Considerations for a Biologically Inspired Compliant Four-legged Robot. In: IEEE International Conference on Robotics and Biomimetics, Guilin, China, pp. 19–23 (2009)
8. Byoung-Ho, K.: Centroid-based Analysis of Quadruped-Robot Walking Balance. Advanced Robotics, 1–6 (2009)

Assessment of the Survivability of Networked System Based on Improved TOPSIS

Chengli Zhao[1,2], Yanheng Liu[1], and Zhiheng Yu[3]

[1] Department of Computer Science and Technology, Jilin University,
Jilin Changchun, China
[2] Department of Information, Jinlin University of Finance and Economics,
Jilin Changchun, China
[3] Academy of Fineart, Northeast Normal University, Jinlin Changchun, China
zhaocl069@gmail.com, lyh_lb_lk@yahoo.com.cn, yuzh496@gmail.com

Abstract. Survivability has been one of the active fields in network security recently. In order to evaluate the survivability of networked system effectively, this paper proposes a method of combining improved TOPSIS and grey relation analysis for quantitative assessment. Firstly, it normalizes indicator matrix according to traditional TOPSIS method and determines the positive and negative ideal solutions. Secondly, it calculates relation degree of every critical service in terms of grey relation analysis, according to which it gets the optimal dependency degree. Then it evaluates the whole survivability of networked system depending on the survivable function. At last a case study is given to show the availability and effectiveness of the method.

Keywords: Network Security, Survivability, Improved TOPSIS, Grey Relation.

1 Introduction

Survivability has been a new field in network security. Survivability is the capability of a system to fulfill its mission, in a timely manner, in the presence of attacks, failures, or accidents [1]. Unlike traditional security measures, Survivability focuses on the delivery of essential services and preservation of essential assets, even when systems are penetrated and compromised.

Assessment of the survivability is to use all kinds of mathematics methods for qualitative and quantitative analysis of the survivability of networked system and then it evaluates the performance. The purpose of the assessment is to judge the capability of systems to maintain the services in unsafe environments.

1.1 Related Works about Assessment

There has been considerable work done on it. Zhang et al. analyzed the survivability using fuzzy method [2]. Jun explored the application of rough set in evaluating the survivability [3]. Gao et al. provided a framework for quantifying the '3R' of survivability [4]. Zhao et al. proposed a novel quantitative analysis method based on grey relation analysis to evaluate the actual network survivability [5]. Zhang et al.

G. Shen and X. Huang (Eds.): CSIE 2011, Part I, CCIS 152, pp. 355–360, 2011.

normalized interval number performance indicators and gave quantitative evaluations for the whole network storage system [6].

Different from above, this paper proposes a quantitative method of combining improved TOPSIS and grey relation to evaluate the survivability of networked system.

2   Grey Relation

Grey theory, proposed by Deng in 1982 [7], is an effective mathematical means to deal with system analysis characterized by incomplete information. Based on statistical analysis of many factors, grey relation is used to describe uncertain relations among elements of systems. The definition of grey relation is as follows.

$$\varsigma(k) = \frac{\min_i \min_k |x_0(k) - x_i(k)| + \rho \max_i \max_j |x_0(k) - x_i(k)|}{|x_0(k) - x_i(k)| + \rho \max_i \max_j |x_0(k) - x_i(k)|} . \tag{1}$$

Where $\min_i \min_k |x_0(k) - x_i(k)|$ is the minimum of the difference in two levels, and $\max_i \max_j |x_0(k) - x_i(k)|$ is the maximum of the difference in two levels. ρ is the distinguished coefficient, and $\rho \in [0,1]$, usually, $\rho = 0.5$.

3   TOPSIS

TOPSIS that is the abbreviation for The Technique for Order Preference by Similarity to Ideal Solution was used to compare many plans in terms of a number of indicators. Its main steps are: normalize the original evaluation matrix, construct the weighted normalized evaluation matrix based on weighted matrix, determine positive and negative ideal solutions, calculate the relative closeness to the ideal solution, and sort all the plans. While the method of traditional TOPSIS arises reverse order easily because of weighted normalized evaluation matrix [8, 9], this paper uses improved TOPSIS, and that is, ideal solutions don't depend on any weighted indicators.

There exists a certain degree of similarity between the input and operation of grey relation and the multiple criteria evaluation of TOPSIS. Thus, this paper is based on the concept of improved TOPSIS in combination with the application of grey relation in order to evaluate the survivability of the networked system.

4   The New Method

The method presented in this paper describes as follows.

4.1   Improved TOPSIS

V and V'. Supposing there are n critical services and m performance indicators, $A = (A_1, A_2, \ldots, A_j, \ldots, A_m)$, which is gotten by Statistic Log Database in the past, we can conclude that x_{ij} is the value of service S_i on indicator A_j, therefore original data metric V is gotten. Because of different dimensions, the original evaluation matrix V needs to be normalized into V' according equation (2).

$$
V = \begin{bmatrix} x_{11} & x_{12} & \cdots & x_{1j} & \cdots & x_{1m} \\ x_{21} & x_{22} & \cdots & x_{2j} & \cdots & x_{2m} \\ \vdots & \vdots & \vdots & \vdots & \vdots & \vdots \\ x_{i1} & x_{i2} & \cdots & x_{ij} & \cdots & x_{im} \\ \vdots & \vdots & \vdots & \vdots & \vdots & \vdots \\ x_{n1} & x_{n2} & \cdots & x_{nj} & \cdots & x_{nm} \end{bmatrix} \quad V' = \begin{bmatrix} x'_{11} & x'_{12} & \cdots & x'_{1j} & \cdots & x'_{1m} \\ x'_{21} & x'_{22} & \cdots & x'_{2j} & \cdots & x'_{2m} \\ \vdots & \vdots & \vdots & \vdots & \vdots & \vdots \\ x'_{i1} & x'_{i2} & \cdots & x'_{ij} & \cdots & x'_{im} \\ \vdots & \vdots & \vdots & \vdots & \vdots & \vdots \\ x'_{n1} & x'_{n2} & \cdots & x'_{nj} & \cdots & x'_{nm} \end{bmatrix}
$$

$$
x'_{ij} = x_{ij} / \sqrt{\sum_{k=1}^{n} x_{kj}^2}, i=1,2,\ldots,n, j=1,2,\ldots m \cdot \tag{2}
$$

The Positive and Negative Ideal Solutions. Equation (3) is the positive and negative ideal solutions according to V'. Where J^+ is the set of profit-oriented indicators and J^- is the set of cost-oriented indicators.

$$
p_j^+ = \begin{cases} \max(x'_{ij}), j \in J^+ \\ \min(x'_{ij}), j \in J^- \end{cases}, j=1,2,\ldots m \text{'} \quad p_j^- = \begin{cases} \min(x'_{ij}), j \in J^+ \\ \max(x'_{ij}), j \in J^- \end{cases}, j=1,2,\ldots m \cdot \tag{3}
$$

4.2 Calculate Grey Relation Degree

Relation Matrix. Supposing ς_{ij}^+ and ς_{ij}^- (i=1,2,…,n, j=1,2,…,m) is the relation coefficient of S_i and A_j to the positive and negative solution separately, we can get them from equation (4). Therefore, we can obtain relation matrix E^+ and E^-.

$$
\varsigma_{ij}^+ = \frac{\min_i \min_j |x'_{ij} - p_j^+| + \rho \max_i \max_j |x'_{ij} - p_j^+|}{|x'_{ij} - p_j^+| + \rho \max_i \max_j |x'_{ij} - p_j^+|}, \quad \varsigma_{ij}^- = \frac{\min_i \min_j |x'_{ij} - p_j^-| + \rho \max_i \max_j |x'_{ij} - p_j^-|}{|x'_{ij} - p_j^-| + \rho \max_i \max_j |x'_{ij} - p_j^-|} \cdot \tag{4}
$$

$$
E^+ = \begin{bmatrix} \varsigma_{11}^+ & \varsigma_{12}^+ & \cdots & \varsigma_{1j}^+ & \cdots & \varsigma_{1m}^+ \\ \varsigma_{21}^+ & \varsigma_{22}^+ & \cdots & \varsigma_{2j}^+ & \cdots & \varsigma_{2m}^+ \\ \vdots & \vdots & \vdots & \vdots & \vdots & \vdots \\ \varsigma_{i1}^+ & \varsigma_{i2}^+ & \cdots & \varsigma_{ij}^+ & \cdots & \varsigma_{im}^+ \\ \vdots & \vdots & \vdots & \vdots & \vdots & \vdots \\ \varsigma_{n1}^+ & \varsigma_{n2}^+ & \cdots & \varsigma_{nj}^+ & \cdots & \varsigma_{nm}^+ \end{bmatrix} \quad E^- = \begin{bmatrix} \varsigma_{11}^- & \varsigma_{12}^- & \cdots & \varsigma_{1j}^- & \cdots & \varsigma_{1m}^- \\ \varsigma_{21}^- & \varsigma_{22}^- & \cdots & \varsigma_{2j}^- & \cdots & \varsigma_{2m}^- \\ \vdots & \vdots & \vdots & \vdots & \vdots & \vdots \\ \varsigma_{i1}^- & \varsigma_{i2}^- & \cdots & \varsigma_{ij}^- & \cdots & \varsigma_{im}^- \\ \vdots & \vdots & \vdots & \vdots & \vdots & \vdots \\ \varsigma_{n1}^- & \varsigma_{n2}^- & \cdots & \varsigma_{nj}^- & \cdots & \varsigma_{nm}^- \end{bmatrix}
$$

Grey Relation Degree. Supposing that the weight of indicator j is w_j derived from Delphi, we can achieve the grey relation degree of S_i to the ideal solution described as equation (5).

$$\gamma(S_i, p^+) = \sum_{j=1}^{m} w_j \varsigma_{ij}^+ \cdot \gamma(S_i, p^-) = \sum_{j=1}^{m} w_j \varsigma_{ij}^- \cdot \tag{5}$$

4.3   The Whole Survivability of Networked System

The Optimal Dependency Degree. The bigger $\gamma(S_i, p^+)$ gets, the better S_i behaves. In turn, the bigger $\gamma(S_i, p^-)$ gets, the worse S_i behaves. Therefore, the optimal dependency degree of S_i can be defined as follows.

$$u_i = \frac{\gamma(S_i, p^+)}{\gamma(S_i, p^+) + \gamma(S_i, p^-)} \cdot \tag{6}$$

The Whole Survivability of Networked System. From the definition of survivability, we can know the critical service must be survivable, so the whole survivability of networked system can be defined as equation (7), where δ is threshold, usually, $\delta=0.3$, and w_i is gotten from Delphi.

$$\text{SURV}= \begin{cases} \sum_{i=1}^{n} w_i u_i, & \forall u_i \geq \delta , \sum_{i=1}^{n} w_i = 1 \\ 0, & \exists u_i < \delta \end{cases} \cdot \tag{7}$$

5   A Case Study

Supposing that there are three critical services: ftp, telnet and rpc in networked system, and weight is 0.5, 0.3, and 0.2 separately. The system mainly considers three factors: integrity, confidentiality, availability, which can be divided into seven performance indicators in detail as Table 1.

Table 1. Original Data

Critical services	Integrity		Confidentiality		Availability		
	data reuse rate	check intensity	accept access	deny access	channel throughput	channel utilization	channel delay
ftp	0.6	600	1	1	800	0.85	0.6
telnet	0.8	700	3	3	600	0.75	0.4
rpc	0.5	500	2	2	700	0.8	0.5

According to equation (2), normalized metrics V' is derived.

$$V' = \begin{bmatrix} 0.54 & 0.57 & 0.27 & 0.27 & 0.66 & 0.61 & 0.68 \\ 0.71 & 0.67 & 0.80 & 0.80 & 0.49 & 0.54 & 0.45 \\ 0.45 & 0.48 & 0.53 & 0.53 & 0.57 & 0.58 & 0.57 \end{bmatrix} V_1 = \begin{bmatrix} 0.55 & 600 & 1 & 1 & 700 & 0.65 & 0.8 \\ 0.7 & 700 & 3 & 3 & 500 & 0.6 & 0.5 \\ 0.5 & 500 & 2 & 2 & 500 & 0.7 & 0.65 \end{bmatrix}$$

According to equation (3), we can get P and N. And according to equation (4), correlation metrics E^+ and E^- are arrived.

$$P = (0.71, 0.67, 0.27, 0.27, 0.66, 0.61, 0.45), N = (0.45, 0.48, 0.80, 0.80, 0.49, 0.54, 0.68)$$

Derived from Delphi, W= (0.2,0.1,0.17,0.11,0.1,0.19,0.13), according to equation (5), the relation degree of each service is derived. In the same way, according to equation (6), the optimal dependency degree gets.

$$\gamma^+ = (0.84, 0.73, 0.63), \gamma^- = (0.66, 0.80, 0.72), u = (0.56, 0.48, 0.47)$$

At last, we get the whole survivability of the networked information system.

SURV=0.52

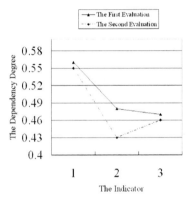

Fig. 1. The optimal dependency degree

At different time, we get another data again as V_1. In the same way, the optimal dependency degree is gotten. u_1 = (0.55, 0.43, 0.46) and SURV$_1$=0.50. Fig. 1 depicts the comparing of the two results. When Data reuse rate, channel throughput, and channel utilization decrease while Channel delay arises, the optimal dependency degree also decreases, the same as the survivability. The results of the experiment and the running system are in the agreement, which shows that the proposed method is feasible and effective.

6   Conclusions

This paper did some work on the assessment of the networked system, but there are a number of problems to be solved, such as how to make the weight of the indicators fair and reasonable, how to restore the damaged services etc.

Evaluating the survivability is one important aspect of networked system, based on which enhanced technology can be implemented. This paper presented a method of evaluating survivability by combining improved TOPSIS and grey relation and gave detailed steps. The case study showed the method was feasible and effective.

Acknowledgement. This work was supported in part by Jilin Province Science and Technology Development Plan under Grant No. 20100173; Jilin Province Philosophy and Social Science Plan under Grant No. 2008Bwx10.

References

1. Ellison, R.J., Fisher, D.A., Linger, R.C., et al.: Survivable Network Systems: an Emerging Discipline. Technical report, Carnegie Mellon University (1997)
2. Qiuyu, Z., Ning, S., Ning, C., Ye, L.: Evaluation for Security Situation of Networked Systems Based on Fuzzy Information Fusion. J. Com. Engi. 33(13), 182–184 (2007)
3. Jun, Y., Lei, W.: Research on Comprehensive Evaluation Method Based on Rough Set and AHP. J. App. Res. Comp. 27(7), 2484–2488 (2010)
4. Xianwei, G., Xuegang, L., Rongsheng, X.: Quantifying of 3R in Survivable Network Analysis. J. Com. Simu. 21(11), 125–128 (2004)
5. Guosheng, Z., Huiqiang, W., Jian, W.: Study on Situation Evaluation for Network Survivability Based on Grey Relation Analysis. J. Min. Syst. 27(10), 1861–1864 (2006)
6. Yi, Z., Shanshan, H.: Quantitative Assessment of Survivability of Network Storage Systems. J. Tsi. Univ. 49, S2, 2119–2125 (2009)
7. Julong, D.: Grey Forecast and Decision. Huazhong University of Science of Technology, Wuhan (1986)
8. Wei, C.: On the Problem and Elimination of Rank Reversal in the Application of TOPSIS Method. J. Ope. Mana. 14(3), 39–43 (2005)
9. Gensheng, Q., Shuimu, Z., Rihua, L.: Improvement of the TOPSIS for Multiple Criteria Decision Making. J. Nanc. Aero. 19(3), 1–4 (2005)

AIIS: An Efficient String Index on Inconsistent Data[*]

Qing Wang, Shouxu Jiang, Hongzhi Wang, and Hong Gao

School of Computer Science and Technology, Harbin Institute of Technology,
150001 Harbin, China
j4y.wangqing@gmail.com, {jsx,wangzh,honggao}@hit.edu.cn

Abstract. Inconsistency has become an important issue in many data-centric applications. Performing query on such data may result in wrong decisions. To obtain query results with high quality, it is necessary to process queries on inconsistent data. The significant limitations of current major methods include the low efficiency and the absence of effective data access mechanism. To process query on inconsistent data efficiently and effectively, in this paper, an index, AIIS (Adaptive Index for Inconsistent String), is presented for string attributes in inconsistent data. With effective graph decomposition and representative selection strategies, this index is an approximately balanced data structure. Extensive experimental results on both real and synthetic data sets demonstrate efficiency and effectiveness.

Keywords: Inconsistent data; String similarity; Graph decomposition.

1 Introduction

Many data-centric applications require integrating data from different sources, where different sources may represent the same real-world entity in different ways. Such cases are called inconsistency. It has increasingly become an important issue. When queries are performed on such data, it is likely to mislead the decision based on query results. To reduce the impact and obtain query result with quality assurance on inconsistent data, it is necessary to manage inconsistent data. The significant limitations of current major methods[1-3] include the low efficiency and absence of effective data access mechanism.

To accelerate the query processing on inconsistent database, it is natural to use indices. However, current indices cannot be applied on inconsistent string attributes.

[*] This research is partially supported by National Science Foundation of China (No. 61003046), the NSFC-RGC of China (No. 60831160525), National Grant of High Technology 863 Program of China (No. 2009AA01Z149), Key Program of the National Natural Science Foundation of China (No. 60933001), National Postdoctoral Foundation of China (No. 20090450126, No. 201003447), Doctoral Fund of Ministry of Education of China(No. 20102302120054), Postdoctoral Foundation of Heilongjiang Province (No. LBH-Z09109), Development Program for Outstanding Young Teachers in Harbin Institute of Technology (No. HITQNJS.2009.052).

G. Shen and X. Huang (Eds.): CSIE 2011, Part I, CCIS 152, pp. 361–367, 2011.

Variations in representation in different data sources are from typographical errors, abbreviated, incomplete, or lack of standard formatting convention, and their combinations. Furthermore, existing indices for strings such as inverted table [3], suffix array and signature files [4] are designed for accurate string matching and not suitable for query processing on inconsistent string attributes since they cannot handle variant and abbreviation on strings. The indices for approximate string matching [5] are not enough for inconsistent data since they only use edit distance as the measure of similarity without the consideration of the order of tokens and abbreviation in inconsistent string attributes.

To process the queries with string attributes efficiently on inconsistent data, in this paper, we present a novel index structure, AIIS (Adaptive Index for Inconsistent String). The basic idea of AIIS is to represent the relationships between attribute values as a graph, then decompose the graph into subgraphs with strong cohesion based on the diameter and the weight of edge, and lastly select one node as the representative. When performing a query on the index, some representatives with the large similarities with the query value are chosen and then the nodes with large similarity with the query value are returned.

This paper has following contributions:1)An index structure, AIIS, is presented for string attributes in inconsistent data; 2) We propose a graph model and present a graph decomposition method to keep the index approximately balanced. 3) Extensive experimental results show that our index can accelerate the query processing significantly.

The rest of the paper is organized as follows. Section 2 explains r the structure for AIIS. We describe the construction algorithms for AIIS in Section 3. Section 4 shows experimental results of the methods. Section 5 concludes the whole paper.

2   The Structure of AIIS

For an inconsistent relation R, AIIS is built on its attribute s with string type. All the values in $R[s]$ are represented as a weighted graph $G_{R[s]} = (V_{R[s]}, E_{R[s]}, w, \varepsilon)$, where w is the weight function and ε is the threshold. Each value v in $R[s]$ is represented as a node $n_v \in V_{R[s]}$. Each edge $e = (n_u, n_v)$ represents that in $R[s]$, u and v are similar. The weight function w: $V_{R[s]} \times V_{R[s]} \rightarrow [0,1]$ represents the similarity degree of two vertices. For two value u and v, an edge $e = (n_u, n_v) \in E_{R[s]}$, if and only if $w(n_u, n_v) \geq \varepsilon$.

AIIS on attribute s of a relation R is a set of binaries $\{(g_i, r_i) | \subseteq, r_i \in g_i\}$, where g_i is a subgraph of $G_{R[s]}$ and r_i is the representative of g_i. For the efficient search on representatives, a qgram-based secondary index [6] is built on them.

3   AIIS Construction

This section proposes the construction process of AIIS, and discusses the techniques in every step of AIIS construction. For the convenience of discussion, P denotes the given string similarity threshold, Q denotes the given diameter threshold and W denotes the given deleting edge weight threshold.

The index construction motivates three problems in every step. (1) How to evaluate the weight of edge. (2) How to decompose a graph. (3) How to select the representatives.

3.1 String Similarity

In the Step (1), the evaluation of the weight is crucial to the construction of graph G, it affects the edge set E. we propose a hybrid string similarity suitable for our problem.

For two strings S and T, the corresponding cardinal token numbers are n and m, respectively. Without loss of generality, it is supposed that $n \geq m$. Then the similarity between S and T is defined as

$$similatity(S, T) = \max_{i=1 \ldots P(n, m)} (V(S_i, T_i))$$ (1)

In formula (1), S_i is a permutation of a m-token sets combination of S, and T_i is a permutation of token sets of T. $P(n,m)$ is the number of permutation of m-token sets combination of S.

$$V(S_i, T_i) = \sum_{k=0}^{m} sim(s_k, t_k) / n$$ (2)

In formula (2), s_k is the k-th token of S_i. And t_k is the k-th token of T_i permutation.

For the similarity measure $sim(s_k, t_k)$ between tokens, we use existing method, Jaro-Winkler distance. This method emphasizes matches in the first few characters.

Overall, the idea of string similarity algorithm is that given two strings S and T, firstly they are converted to token multisets with each token as a word. For the similarity between S_i and T_i, the sum of the similarity between every token of S_i and the corresponding position token of T_i is computed, and then divide n as the similarity between S_i and T_i, the maximal similarities between all such S_i and T_i is returned as the similarity of S and T. The pseudo code of the algorithm is shown in Algorithm 1.

Observed from Algorithm1, the time complexity of the similarity between two strings is $P(n,m) \times m \times n$, which is inefficient. It is reasonable that the comparisons are performed only on the tokens with the same length or initial, based on the assumption that the length of token is below 10, so the time complexity is

$$\sum_{i=1}^{N} \sum_{j=i+1}^{N} P^2(n, m) \times m \times n \times (\frac{1}{10^m} + \frac{1}{26^m})$$

Algorithm 1: Similarity(string S , T)
```
1: Token1[]←S, Token2[]←T;//convert S and T to token substring.
2: m←Token1.size();n←Token2.size();
3: initialize all the elements of the array similar 0.
4: for(each Sᵢ is a permutation of a m-token sets combination of S)
5:     for k←1 to m
6:         similar[i] ←similar[i]+jaro-winkler(sₖ,tₖ)
7:     similar[i] ←similar[i]/n;
8: return max(similar[]);
```

3.2 Graph Decomposition

In *Step (2)*, we will discuss the method about graph decomposition in this section.

Existing graph decomposition algorithms include the methods based on Clique[2]. However, these methods may result in large storage space requirement and slow down the query processing. Thus it is not applicable for AIIS. Therefore, we propose a graph decomposition strategy based on diameter and the edge weight. The steps are as following.

It is supposed that the graph $G= (V, E)$ to be decomposed is connected. Otherwise, same operations are performed on each connected component in G. First of all, BFS is performed from a random node v until the nodes with the distance to v smaller than Q are all visited. Then V is decomposed to V_1 and V_2 with V_1 as the set of nodes met during the traversal and the rest nodes are in V_2. With V_1, an edge set $E_1 = \{e| (k, j), k, j \in V1\}$ is generated. Then the set of edges $E_2=\{e|(i, j), i \in V_1, j \in V_2\}$ is considered. For each $e \in E_2$, $w (e)> W$, j and e are added to V_1 and E_1, respectively. Above process is repeated until all the weight of deleting edge is below W. Then G is divided into one subgraph $G_1= (V_1, E_1)$ and one forest $G_2= (V_2, E_2)$. For G_2, we repeat the above process until the distance between every node of G_2 to v is below Q. The Pseudo-code is showed in Algorithm 2.

```
Algorithm 2: GraphDecomposition(int v)
1:  Q1 ← ∅; Q2 ← ∅;
2:  ENQUEUE(Q1,v);
3:  while Q1 ≠∅‖ Q2≠∅
4:      do for each y  DEQUEUE(Q1)
5:      for each z  Adj[y]&&visited[z]==false
6:          then visited[z] ←ture; Add(V1,z); ENQUEUE(Q2,z);
7:      if Q1==∅ Then distance←distance+1;
9:      If distance==Q
10:         Then for each node x of DEQUEUE(Q2)
11:             ENQUEUE(Q3,x);
12:             for each z  Adj[x]&&visited[z]==false&&weight[x][z]>=W
13:             ENQUEUE(Q2,v);
14:         Then for each node x of DEQUEUE(Q3)
15:             for each z  Adj[x]&&visited[z]==false
16:                 delete edge(x,z) and edge(z,x)  end if
17:     else
18:         Q1←Q2;Q2←∅
```

In *Step (3)*, we select a representative as the index entry from every subgraph. The focus of selecting graph representation is that the representative is close to every node of subgraph. Based on the above considerations and efficiency, the node that the corresponding degree is maximal is chosen as the representative.

Time Complexity

In graph decomposition processing, we just scan every node and every edge of the graph G once, so the time complexity is Θ $(|V|+|E|)$, the time complexity of representative selection is Θ $(|V|)$.

4 Experiments

In this section, we show experimental results to evaluate the efficiency and effectiveness of system both on the real-life data sets and synthetic data sets. Our experiments focused on four important aspects: *precision, recall, F* and *query processing time*.

Definition 1 (*precision and recall*). when we perform query on AIIS, we denote the returned query set as T, and denote the consistent query set as S, then

$$precision = \frac{S \cap T}{T} \qquad recall = \frac{S \cap T}{S}$$

Definition 2 (*F*). When we perform query on AIIS described in the above sections of paper, we perform N selection query, we record the number of query which the query result is empty but the consistent query result which is manual gained is not empty, or the intersection between query result and right result is empty as M, then $F = M / N$.

Firstly, we used three real-life data sets to test the *recall* and *precision*, In order to investigate various properties of a data set, we also perform experiments on the synthetically data set. The synthetically data set is generated with the number of tuple as parameter, denoted by N. Then we generate steps are omitted for lack of space.

The information of real data is shown in Table 1.

Table 1. The information of real data

The file name	N	Size
data1.txt	1000	14.4k
data2.txt	1000	14.8k
data3.txt	1000	15.1k

Table 2. The result on real data sets

N	Recall	precision
1000	1	0.9865
1000	1	1
1000	1	0.975

From our method, the query result is affected by six factors: N, P, Q, K, p, W. The default setting of the synthetic data is $N=8,000$, $P=0.8$, $Q=3$, $p=0.8$, $K=10$, $W=0.96$.

The experimental results on real data sets are shown in Table 2. From the Table 2, it is noted that *precision* is always above 97% and the *recall* reaches to 100%. Since $p=0.8$, we may obtain the result nodes with distance to the query string is above p. AIIS demonstrates efficiency and effectiveness on real data sets.

Then the impact of the six parameters on the effectiveness and scalability of AIIS is tested. Experimental results are shown in Fig. 3. to Fig.8. on the synthetically data.

From Fig.3, it is observed that the *recall* grows with P, this is because that when P increases, the similarity threshold between the representative and every node increases. With $K=10$, the probability of consistent answers occurring in the top K connected subgraph gets larger. It mean *recall* is rising. Obviously, F decreases for the same reason.

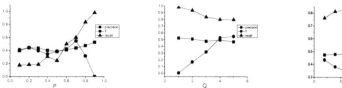

Fig. 3. The trend with change of *P*   **Fig. 4.** The trend with change of *Q*   **Fig. 5.** The trend with change of *K*

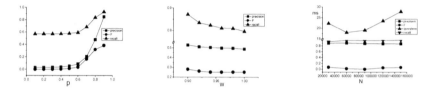

Fig. 6. The trend with change of *p*   **Fig. 7.** The trend with change of *W*   **Fig. 8.** The trend with change of *N*

It is observed from Fig.4. that with the increasing of Q, the similarities between the representative and some nodes in the corresponding subgraph get smaller. The selection of representatives cannot promise the similarity between the representative and every node in the subgraph is large enough. Therefore, we may not obtain correct result. Then F rises and *recall* declines. *Precision* only has connection with p, so it is stable.

From Fig.5, the *recall* increases with K and the probability of F decreases with K. It is because that the growing of K means more candidate subgraphs will be retrieved.

As observed from Fig.6, *precision, recall* and F all increase with p. When the similarity between query result and query string gets larger, the probability that a string is included in the consistent result gets larger, and then *precision* increases. Some strings in consistent answer may not be similar to the query string. Therefore, when p increases, the probability of getting right answer decreases, then F and *recall* increase.

Fig.7. tells us that *recall* get smaller with the increasing of W. The reason is as follows. With the increasing of W, the number of subgraphs becomes large and just top K candidate subgraphs are retrieved. Therefore, some query answer may be excluded. As a result, *recall* diminishes. From the result, F firstly increases to a certain degree then keeps constant. It is because when the number of subgraphs increases to a constant, with the increasing of the number of subgraphs, the similarity between the representative and the nodes gets larger and the probability of failing to return the correct results declines.

As observed from Fig.8, the *querytime* firstly decreases with N, then increases. This is because that when N is relatively small, the generation process of data sets is the same. Therefore, the number of subgraphs will be larger, so the time is very long.

When N grows, the threshold diameter is constant, although the number of subgraphs decreases, the average number of nodes of every subgraph will be relatively increased.

From Fig.8, when we do query on the 30000 to 150000, the *recall* will be always above 98%, *precision* is around 88% , because p=0.8. F can constantly be below 8%.

5 Conclusions

In this paper, we introduce an index, AIIS, to accelerate query processing on the inconsistent database. With this idea, we describe the technologies referred in the process of constructing the AIIS and how to evaluate queries efficiently with AIIS. Our experimental results on real and manual data demonstrate efficiency and extensibility

This paper do not consider join operation on inconsistent data, this is the next focus in my future work.

References

[1] Fuxman, A., Miller, R.J.: First-order query rewriting for inconsistent databases. J. Comput. Syst. Sci. 73(4), 610–635 (2007)
[2] Courcelle, B., Olariu, S.: Upper bounds to the clique width of graphs. Discrete Applied Mathematics 101, 77–114 (2000)
[3] Colby, E.R., Gai, W.: Summary report of the working group on electromagnetic structure-based acceleration concepts. In: 9th Workshop on Advanced Accelerator Concepts, pp. 47–56 (2001)
[4] Chen, Y., Shi, Y.: Signature Files and Signature File Construction. Encyclopedia of Database Technologies and Applications, 638–645 (2005)
[5] Papamichail, D.P., Papamichail, G.P.: Improved algorithms for approximate string matching. BMC Bioinformatics (BMCBI) 10(S-1) (2009)
[6] Li, C., Wang, B., Yang, X.: VGRAM: Improving Performance of Approximate Queries on String Collections Using Variable-Length Grams. In: VLDB 2007, pp. 303–314 (2007)

Research on the Analytical and Hierarchical Concept Framework of E-Business Model

Zhaoyang Sun, Jiafeng Jin, Yang Wen, and Rui Zheng

Commercial & Trade Department of NEU at Qinhuangdao,
Taishan Road. 143, 066004, Qinhuangdao, China
zhaoyangneuq@126.com

Abstract. E-business model innovation is one of the focus e-business research fields and no consensus of e-business model concept hinders the e-business model innovation research. After analyzing the current state of e-business model research, an analytical and hierarchical concept framework of e-business model is proposed, which includes classification, operating and implementation level. From the view of static, e-business model can be regarded as role model, scale model and model organism. From dynamic perspective, e-business model can be regarded as recipe, which guides entrepreneurs to innovate e-business model. This study lays necessary foundations for further research on method of e-business model innovation.

Keywords: e-business model; concept framework; role model; scale model; recipe model.

1 Introduction

One of the drivers to promote the rapid development of e-business is from the information technology companies providing IT infrastructure, like IBM, Microsoft, Oracle, etc. More importantly, the other driver is from companies using Internet and Web technology to create unprecedented business activities approach and to change the traditional power of business. Therefore e-business model innovation has become one of the principal means for network rookie and traditional enterprises to develop new market and create profits. The e-business model innovation is one of the focus e-business research fields[1].

Whether in industry or academia, the concept of e-business model is vague, with each researcher using it in different meaning according to certain context. This hinders the development of e-business model innovation. It is essential to integrate and clarify many different meanings of e-business model, clearing away the obstacles of e-business model innovation.

It is suitable to regard the e-business model as models for e-business model innovation[2]. Therefore, the paper analyzes the meaning of e-business models from the perspective of model, clarifies the concept of EBM, and proposes the analytical framework for the hierarchical e-business model, discussing the different meanings of e-business model as role model, scale model, model organism, recipes model, and that the relationship between the four models. The analytical framework for the concept of

G. Shen and X. Huang (Eds.): CSIE 2011, Part I, CCIS 152, pp. 368–373, 2011.

hierarchical e-business model provides necessary theoretical basis for e-business model innovation research.

We start reviewing of theories about e-business model, illustrating the current state and the challenge of e-business model research. We then propose the analytical and hierarchical concept framework of e-business model, laying an essential foundation for studying the approach of enterprise's e-business model innovation, which is the main body of this article. Finally, we draw our conclusions.

2 Challenges Facing e-Business Model Research

With the application of Internet technology, successful e-business models appeared. Scholars studied e-business model from different perspectives, classifying it into B2B, B2C, C2C, B2G, and etc.[3-7]. However, e-business model research still faces challenges as follows.

First of all, there is no consensus on the understanding of the connotation and extension of e-business models in academia and industry. This hinders the breadth and depth of e-business model research. In other words, lacking of a common analytical framework for e-business model hinders the mutual integration of e-business models research.

Second, it's obvious that too much emphasis were put on the classification of e-business model, attempting to describe the similarities and differences between business models, in order to classify a specific enterprise as a single class, or that specific company's business model is a combination of some atom business models, as Weil did. Such research can help classify an enterprise as an e-business model, but cannot explain the reason why this business model succeeds. Therefore, the connotation of e-business model need to include such content: "Why a certain e-business model could succeed?"

Third, it is the e-business field that is the most innovative areas, and the academia and the industry have been focused on e-business model innovation. Too much emphasis put on the classification of e-business model, is far meet the research and practice needs in the field of e-business model innovation.

In short, the key to e-business model research is lack of consensus of e-business models' connotation and an analytical framework in which ideas in certain context could be understood each other for academia and industry. The framework includes both the meaning of the existing level of classification, but also includes new connotation to answer the question, like 'why some e-business model can succeed?' This article, to meet the requirements above, proposes a concept framework of the hierarchical e-business model.

3 Analytical and Hierarchical Concept Framework of e-business Model

With reference to research in the field of management and biology, this article, from static and dynamic perspective, builds the hierarchical and analytical framework for e-business model, including three levels of the four meanings, as shown in Figure 1.

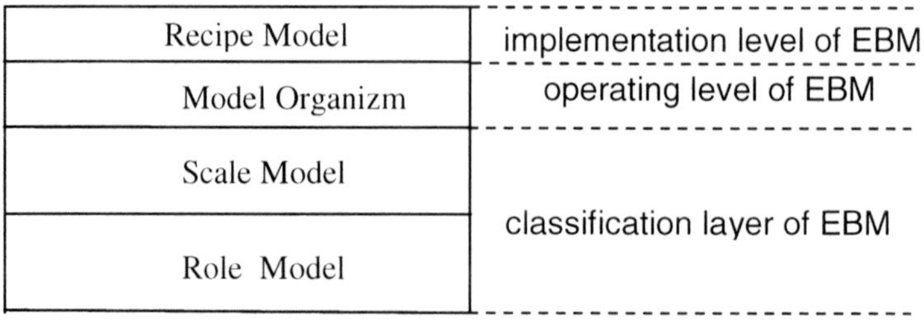

Recipe Model	implementation level of EBM
Model Organizm	operating level of EBM
Scale Model	classification layer of EBM
Role Model	

Fig. 1. Hierarchical and analytical framework for e-business model (EBM)

3.1 Static and Dynamic Perspective

Being regarded as results of behavior from the static view, e-business model is classified into three logical levels: role model, scale models and model organism. The static e-business model, in essence, is results of the analysis of certain enterprise or of a certain type of business, in certain period, from certain perspectives.

Viewing from the dynamic perspective, e-business model can be referred as recipe model, which provides a practical guidance for an entrepreneur innovating e-business model, just like a recipe provides a practical guidance for a cook innovating dinner.

3.2 Levels of Classification: Role Model and Scale Model

Actually, the static analysis perspective is to investigate an identified object, studying its behavioral characteristics. It is the classification of e-business model that is the most basic meaning of it. That is, to classify enterprises in the real world into different categories, according to its behavioral characteristics' differences and similarities.

Attention should be paid that the classification methods of e-business include two types: bottom-up inductive classification (taxonomy) and top-down interpretation of the classification (typology). Role Model and Scale Model are mainly used for classification, classifying the different enterprise models into different e-business models of categories. Role model is used for induction by the bottom-up classification, while scale model for the top-down interpretation of the classification. The role of the two is different, so does the meaning.

Take 'Amazon' for instance, when it was first established, we would find the nature between the company and any existing company has a number of different content. That is, the company should belong to a new category, although we are still not clear what the new category is on earth. So, at that moment, the meaning of "Amazon" model belongs to a role model, which means that we need to study the behavior of "Amazon", and find the behavioral characteristics of online bookstores.

But now, after more than 10 years later, "Amazon" is not an unknown species any more. On the contrary, the Amazon has become a known species in classification. It is classified into "online bookstore", belonging to "online mall". Therefore, one can describe the behavioral characteristics of the new species, such as "online bookstore" or "online mall". Then, scholars can also develop the interpretation of the "online bookstore", classifying "www.dangdang.com" as "online bookstore". Here, "online bookstore ", this brief term describes the behavioral characteristics of the new type, giving the significance of existence to the new type, defining the catalog of this type, laying a necessary foundation for further study of its internal mechanism. It is the top-down interpretation of the classification (typology) and this is scale model.

In short, the role model could throw the starting point of research on the real world enterprise. By further abstraction of role model and forming an ideal model, a new category is added to the existing scale models.

On the classification level, the e-business model takes on role model and scale model, which is of great significance for e-business model innovation. New models emerge so fast in the area of e-business industry that it cannot be classified with the existing scale model. Then, the role model plays a role of tag. Classification of e-business model is start point to understanding e-business model and is the basis of e-business model innovation.

3.3 Model Organism

After studying and abstracting the behavioral characteristics of enterprises, we have recognized the behavioral characteristics of any category. However, we still could not answer questions such as "why this model succeed?" Why a certain e-business model would succeed is not always obvious and self-evident. Take www.taobao.com for example, what are its critical factors for success? Which factors make the model work and must be combined in the model? What factors are just the occasional and not belonging to the e-business models in essence?

Classification can solve the unique characteristics of its own existence of these models. But it is insufficient as to explain questions above. With particular reference to the extensive literature in biology, we propose the next level meaning of e-business models: model organism. To study the model organism will help researchers get a better understand of the internal operation of this model, knowing the reason why the model should survive well, grasping a better knowledge of the internal mechanism of this model.

For e-business model researchers, it is the typical e-business enterprise that is their model. The case analysis of typical e-business business enterprise is exactly to analyze model organism. For instance, by analysis of TAOBAO as a model organism, we can find out its operating method, the linkages between its value activities, the similarities of behavioral characteristics to TAOBAO mode, and the characteristics which are only enjoyed by the specific enterprise of TAOBAO.

Model organism is further study of business model based on role model and scale model. The model organism is a direct study of role model, that is, the specific enterprises, such as TAOBAO. But the results of the study are applicable not only to TAOBAO, but also to a high level of scale models.

3.4 Recipe Model

The meaning of these two levels above is the analysis in the static level of the enterprise e-business models. The significance of analysis in the static level lies not only in understanding what the world is, more importantly, to guide the practice in the real world. In other words, after the classification and research on operation of enterprise e-business models, the results obtained need to guide the e-business model innovation in practice. On this level, the e-business models focused on the meaning of recipe model, including some certain principles, components, and certain operating procedures. Although the recipe is same, but dinner made according to recipe is very different in different kitchens and restaurants. Similarly, different entrepreneur, in different business situations, e-business model innovated according to same recipe are different.

To TAOBAO model, for example, and eBay model have some in common: both as a platform model for buyers and sellers, and the key to success is to quickly capture market scale. EBay is born in the United States, a developed country where the main motivation of people purchase on the network is to pursuit stimulating experience. So the dominant product of eBay is auction. But in China, a developing country, where the primary motivation of people buying online is pursuit product with low price and high quality, TAOBAO, if it directly copied the eBay platform model, including the auction, TAOBAO would not be successful than eBay. Similarly, eBay directly copied the success of their recipes in the United States, making dinner in China the same as in the U.S. But China is a different kitchen and restaurant. The implementation of eBay mode in China the same as the United States determined the failure of eBay. Also it proved that TAOBAO referred to eBay as the recipe, cooking a tasty dish: the "TAOBAO" in "the kitchen and restaurant of China", nearly perfectly meeting the needs of buyers and sellers in China. TAOBAO defeated eBay in the Chinese kitchen and restaurant.

Recipe model indicates that theory is not enough when creating a new e-business model. Local situations and conditions must be taken into account. In other words, guiding by the same recipe, the dishes can be good or bad. Only making a perfect combination of local actual situation and recipe model, the e-business model innovation may be successful

3.5 Hierarchy

In the analytical and hierarchical framework of e-business model, the relationship between these levels is of step by step progression: the lower level model is the cognitive basis of the top, and the upper model is an evolution and deepening of the lower. In the bottom of the framework is the classification which is the basis and starting point for e-business model innovation. The model organism in intermediate level, based on the classification level, investigates the internal operation mechanism of the specific e-business model by case study, and the results obtained not only applicable to specific enterprises, but also to this type of e-business model represented. On the implementation level, when applying the theory of the first two levels to e-business model innovation, attention must be paid that innovation is not equal to copy, but the process of making individual dishes in specific situation, according to the recipe.

4 Conclusions

This article analyzes the current state of e-business model research and proposes the analytical and hierarchical framework for e-business model including three levels and four models.

The main contribution of the paper is as follows: First, from the perspective of model, to clarify the meanings of e-business model as classification, model organism and implementation of recipe model. When e-business model is regarded as model, research of biology, economics and other fields of model approach can help increase awareness of e-business models, and be applied to e-business models innovation. Secondly, the classification meaning of e-business model is the starting point of e-business model innovation. Thirdly, model organism studies the reasons why e-business model successes and the research methods is case analysis for example enterprise. Finally, the recipe model gives a guide to e-business model innovation: although the recipe is same, the kitchen and the restaurant is different, the dishes made (e-business model innovation) are not the same.

Acknowledgements

We acknowledge support from the Hebei Education Department of Humanities and Social Sciences Projects Fund(SZ2010226). We thank all those who participated in our research.

References

1. Wang, Y.: Theories and research directions of electronic commerce. Bulletin of National Natural Science Foundation of China 4, 193–199 (2007) (in Chinese)
2. Baden-Fuller, C., Morgan, M.S.: Business models as models. Long Range Planning 43, 156–171 (2010)
3. Weill, P., Vitale, M.: From Place to Space: Migrating 10 atomic e-business models. Harvard Business School Press, Boston (2001)
4. Applegate, L.M.: Overview of E-business Models. Harvard Business School Press, Boston (2000)
5. Bambury, P.: A taxonomy of Internet commerce,
   http://firstmonday.org/htbin/cgiwrap/bin/ojs/index.php/fm/article/view/624/545
6. Timmers, P.: Business models for electronic markets. Electronic Markets Journal 8(2), 3–8 (1998)
7. Yi, Z., Sun, Z.-y., Liu, B.-d.: Typology of Talents in e-Business industry. In: 2010 International Conference on Management Science and Engineering, vol. 3, pp. 19–22. Engineering Technology Press, Wuhan (2010)

Application of Wavelet Component Selection and Orthogonal Signal Correction in the Multivariate Calibration by Near-Infrared Spectroscopy

Dan Peng, Junmin Ji, Xia Li, and Kaina Dong

College of Grain Oil and Food Science,
Henan University of Technology, 450052 Zhengzhou, China
{pengdantju,iecircuit}@gmail.com
lixia@126.com, kaina@163.com

Abstract. To improve the quality of input data of multivariate calibration model, a new hybrid preprocessing algorithm (WPT-GA-OSC) was proposed, which is the combination of wavelet packet transform (WPT), genetic algorithm (GA) and orthogonal signal correction (OSC) algorithm. At first, WPT algorithm is applied to split the raw spectra into different frequency components. Then, based on the root mean square error of prediction models, the genetic algorithm is employed to select the WPT components related to analyte as the input data of regression model. At last, to further improve the quality of input data, OSC algorithm is applied to each GA-filtered component to eliminate the information irrelevant to analyte information. To validate the WPT-GA-OSC algorithm, it was applied to develop the calibration model for oil concentration measurement of corn. Compared with the conventional preprocessing algorithm, the WPT-GA-OSC algorithm can take full advantages of multiscale property of near infrared (NIR) spectra, and also can significantly decrease the prediction error by up to 48.3%, indicating that it is a promising way for filtering the spectral data to develop the NIR calibration model.

Keywords: wavelet packet transform; near-infrared spectra; original extract concentration; genetic algorithm.

1 Introduction

Near-infrared (NIR) spectroscopy technique is promising for the fast and nondestructive analysis, including agriculture, food, biotechnology, medicine, etc[1]. However, the efficient use of NIR analysis is dependent on multivariate calibration and quality of spectral data[2]. Due to the multiscale property of NIR spectral, the signal residing in different frequency bands represents different sample-specific information or property-specific information, indicating that the importance of different frequency band is also different. This phenomenon makes the NIR-based analysis more complicate. Therefore, the interference information should be eliminated as much as possible. NIR dataset usually have lots of frequency variables including both the irrelevant variables and useful variables for multivariate calibration. Spectral interferences in some frequency band can lead to problems of quality of spectra[3]. For these aims, two kinds of methods named as preprocessing method and interval regression method

G. Shen and X. Huang (Eds.): CSIE 2011, Part I, CCIS 152, pp. 374–380, 2011.

have been developed. The preprocessing methods usually remove the interference information before multivariate calibration, such as the wavelet transform (WT)[4], net analyte signal (NAS)[5], orthogonal signal correction (OSC)[6], etc. The interval regression methods usually construct the calibration models using parts of spectra instead of global spectral, such as interval partial least squares (iPLS)[7], etc. As known to us, spectral interference contains noise and signal from other components, overlapping in time domain and frequency domain. Most of existing algorithms remove the spectral interference by explaining global spectral variance only in the time or frequency domain through isolation of localized effect. Thus, none of those algorithms can achieve appropriate result. To make progress in this field, both time domain and frequency domain have to be considered in the new algorithms, meaning that multiscale algorithms may be a potential way.

In this paper, a novel preprocessing algorithm, which takes the advantages of wavelet packet transform (WPT)[4], genetic algorithm (GA)[8], and OSC, is proposed and named as WPT-GA-OSC algorithm. The algorithm is composed of two parts: the GA-based WPT components selection algorithm and the WPT-based OSC algorithm. To validate the WPT-GA-OSC algorithm, a real NIR spectral dataset of corn were analyzed for oil concentration measurement, where significant improvement over spectral interference elimination can be observed.

2 Principle and Method

2.1 Wavelet Packet Transform

A wavelet function ψ^i can be obtained from the following recursive relationships[4]:

$$\psi^{2j}(t) = \sqrt{2}\sum_{k=-\infty}^{\infty} h(k)\psi^i(2t-k)\,,\ \psi^{2j+1}(t) = \sqrt{2}\sum_{k=-\infty}^{\infty} g(k)\psi^i(2t-k) \tag{1}$$

where the discrete filters $h(k)$ and $g(k)$ are the quadrature mirror filters associated with the scaling function and the mother wavelet function. The WPT contains a complete decomposition at every level. The recursive relations between the jth and the $(j+1)$th level components of signal $s(t)$ are

$$s_j^i(t) = s_{j+1}^{2i-1}(t) + s_{j+1}^{2i}(t) \tag{2}$$

$$s_{j+1}^{2i-1}(t) = H \cdot s_j^i(t),\ \ s_{j+1}^{2i}(t) = G \cdot s_j^i(t) \tag{3}$$

where H and G are the filtering-decimation operators of the discrete filters $h(k)$ and $g(k)$. After L levels decomposition, the original spectral signal $s(t)$ can be expressed as

$$s(t) = \sum_{i=0}^{2^L-1} s_{L,i}(t) \tag{4}$$

It should be noted that these (2^L) frequency components don't overlap where the analyte information resides. This is why it is possible to analyze the raw signal.

2.2 GA-Based WPT Component Selection Algorithm

In order to select the WPT components containing analyte information, GA algorithm is adopted here. This selection aims to investigate the contribution of each component to the calibration result. In other words, GA-based WPT component selection algorithm focuses on searching the appropriate components combination, which can give the best result. This processing can be summarized by the following steps:

Step1. Decomposition. Perform WPT decomposition on X_{raw} by the maximum L_{max} levels getting the $2^{L_{max}}$ frequency components $\left\{ x_{L_{max},i} \right\}$ according to (4).

Step2. Initialization. Generate a random population with size of N, where each chromosome is coded as a binary string with length of $2^{L_{max}}$. In a chromosome, the *i*th gene with value 1 means $x_{L_{max},i-1}$ is selected. The fitness function is defined as

$$F = (\sum_{i=1}^{a} 1 / RMSEC_i)^{-1} \tag{5}$$

where $RMSEC_i$ is the root mean square error of calibration set obtained by PLS model with i LVs. Then calculate the value of F for each chromosome.

Step3. Selection. The Roulette Wheel Selection is used for selection operation, and the probability of selection (p) of *i*th chromosome is given by

$$p_i = F_i / \sum_{j=1}^{N} F_j \tag{6}$$

The selection rate P_s controls this operation, meaning that the $N \times (1 - P_s)$ best chromosomes go directly to the next generation.

Step4. Crossover and mutation. The probability P_C and P_M control these operations. Both the crossover point and the mutation point are randomly selected.

Step5. If convergence criterion is achieved, the algorithm ends with the best chromosome (C_{op}) and the appropriate components are determined. Otherwise, the algorithm switches to *Step3*. The dataset (X_{GA}) of component selection is denoted as

$$X_{GA} = \left\{ x_{L_{max},i} \right\}, \text{ the ith gene in } C_{op} \text{ is } 1 \tag{7}$$

To correct the spectra of prediction set, X^* should be split into (2^L) frequency components. Then these components X_{GA}^* must be selected based on the C_{op}.

2.3 WPT-Based OSC Algorithm

To further remove the irrelevant information, OSC algorithm is employed to filter all the components in X_{GA}. The WPT-based OSC algorithm can be described as:

Step1. Perform an OSC calculation on each component in X_{GA}, getting a OSC-filtered matrix $x_{L_{max},i}^{OSC}$, a weight matrix $w_{L,i}$ and a loading matrix $p_{L,i}$.

Step2. After the OSC correction, sum all the OSC-filtered frequency components in X_{GA} to produce the finally corrected spectral matrix X_{GA}^{OSC} :

$$X_{GA}^{OSC} = \sum x_{L_{max},i}^{OSC} \tag{8}$$

To correct the prediction set X^{*}_{GA}, the weight matrix and loading matrix calculated in *step1* would be applied to the corresponding selected component for removal of unrelated information as

$$(x^{*})^{OSC}_{L_{max},i} = (x^{*})_{L_{max},i} - (x^{*})_{L_{max},i} w_{L_{max},i} (p^{T}_{L_{max},i} w_{L_{max},i})^{-1} p^{T}_{L_{max},i} \qquad (9)$$

Finally, the filtered prediction set can be produced by summation operation according to (8) as

$$(X^{*})^{OSC}_{GA} = \sum (x^{*})^{OSC}_{L_{max},i} \qquad (10)$$

3 Experiments

NIR spectra data were obtained from Cargill Inc., and can be downloaded from http://www.eigenvector.com/Data/Corn/ index.html. At Cargill, 80 corn samples were measured between 1100nm and 2498nm, operating at 2nm resolution (Fig. 1). The objective is to predict oil content of the samples. The oil contents of samples range from 3.088%~3.832%. For this study, these corn samples were split into a calibration set and a prediction set, each including 40 samples. All computation were performed in Matlab v2007a (MathWorks, USA) using the PLS Toolbox v5.2 (Eigenvector Technology). A leave-one-out cross-validation procedure is applied to the calibration set. The performances of multivariate models were evaluated by the correction coefficient (R), the RMSEC and the root mean square error of prediction (RMSEP).

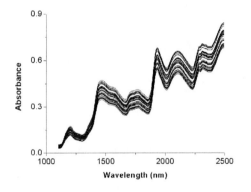

Fig. 1. The spectra of samples in calibration set

4 Results and Discussion

4.1 Wavelet Packet Component Selected by GA Algorithm

In the spectral matrix collected, each spectrum contains 700 wavelength points indicating the maximum decomposition level L is 9. Thus, each chromosome in GA should be coded as a binary string with length of 512. The values of P_S, P_C and P_M were set to 0.8, 0.8 and 0.1, respectively. Additionally, the population size (N) of chromosome is set to 50, maximum LVs is 15 and the maximum number of generations is 300. In the initialization step, a chromosome equaling to 2^{512}-1 was particularly added to the chromosome set. With these parameters, the results obtained by GA-based selection algorithm are shown in Fig. 2(a) and (b). It can be seen that the values of fitness function descend sharply and then tend to be flat when the number of generations is over 150, meaning that the convergence criterion can be achieved in 300 generations. However, the number of selected components was almost stable with small jitter, validating that only part of the spectra is correlated with the analyte.

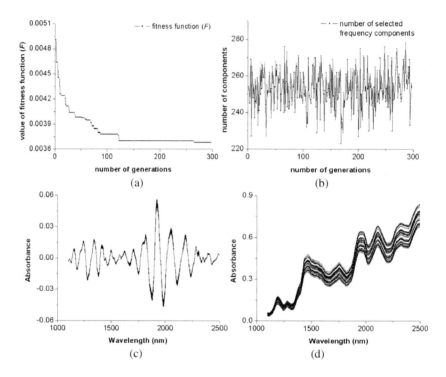

Fig. 2. (a) Value of fitness with number of generations, (b) Number of components selected ineach generation, (c) The sum of selected components, (d) The sum of deselected components

During GA-based search process, the minimum value of fitness is obtained in the 297th generation with 233 frequency components. Thus, the summation of these WPT components can be identified as the filtered spectra of GA selection process. The filtered spectra and the removed spectra are illustrated in Fig. 2(c) and 2(d). Through selection, the filtered spectral data show sharper change compared with the raw spectra in Fig. 1. Apparently from these two figures, the deselected spectra are similar to the raw spectra, indicating that the removed spectra contain most of spectral energy.

4.2 The Unrelated Information Eliminated by OSC Algorithm

From Fig. 2(b), small variation is present in the number of selected component, indicating that GA can't determine the usefulness of some components. To further eliminate noise in the spectra after selection, the OSC algorithm is employed. Due to the multiscale property of NIR spectroscopy, it is impossible to eliminate the interference by viewing the spectra as a whole. Thus, the OSC algorithm is applied to each selected wavelet component for interference elimination. The OSC-filtered spectra are illustrated in Fig. 3(a). It can be seen that the profile of Fig. 3(a) is much similar to that of Fig. 2(c) except the smoothness in some bands. This is can be explained by the fact that most of interested components are selected through the GAbased selection. The interference removed by OSC algorithm is shown in Fig. 3(b). Through computation, about 1.7% of spectral energy is removed after applying OSC algorithm, which may be the reason for small jitter in the number of selection process.

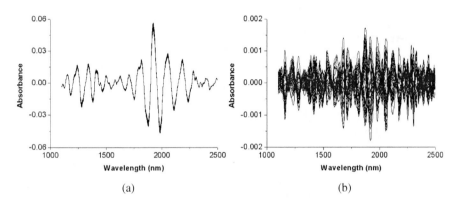

(a)   (b)

Fig. 3. (a)The WPT-GA-OSC-filtered spectra, (b)the interference removed by OSC

4.3 Prediction Results

After performing WPT-GA-OSC algorithm on the raw spectra, calibration models for oil concentration measurement were developed by PLS algorithm. In PLS model, number of latent variables is the key factor to determine the accuracy of model. Fig. 4 shows that the RMSEP curves of different models as a function of number of LVs

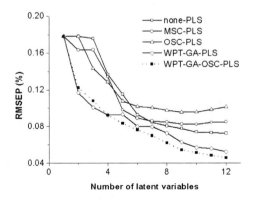

Fig. 4. Prediction results using different algorithms

developed by different algorithms. For the sake of comparison, the first twelve PLS latent variables are computed. It is can be observed that the RMSEP curves of WPT-GA algorithm and WPT-GA-OSC algorithm descend sharply and are lower than that those of other algorithms. With the increase of number of latent variables, the RMSEP curves tend to be fat with small jitter. When the number of LVs is beyond 9, the RMSEP curve of WPT-GA-OSC can reaches the minimum (0.042%). Moreover, with the number of LVs beyond 4, the precision of WPT-GA-OSC-based outperforms that of WPT-GA-based models by a considerable margin, showing the necessity of noise elimination using OSC. Compared with the model using conventional PLS, the WPTGA-OSC-based model can improve the RMSEP by up to 48.3%, indicating that the proposed algorithm has the ability to improve the quality of regression model.

5 Results and Discussion

In this paper, a new preprocessing method named as WPT-GA-OSC is proposed to develop the multivariate regression model. Then it was successfully applied to analyze for oil concentration measurement. Experimental results show that the WPT-GA-OSC algorithm can effectively improve the prediction ability of the calibration models, meaning that it is a suitable preprocessing algorithm for analysis using NIR spectra.

Acknowledgement

This work has been supported by the Doctoral Foundation Program of Henan University of Technology (No.2009BS008).

References

1. McGoVerin, G.M., Ho, L.C.H., Zeitler, J.A., Strachan, C.J., Gordon, K.C., Rades, T.: Quantification of binary polymorphic mixtures of ranitidine hydrochloride using NIR spectroscopy. Vib. Spectrosc. 41, 225–231 (2006)
2. Li, Y.K., Shao, X.G., Cai, W.S.: A consesus least squares support vector regression for analysis of near-infrared spectra of plant samples. Talanta 72, 217–222 (2007)
3. Seasholtz, M.B., Kowalsk, B.: The parsimony principle applied to multivariate calibration. Anal. Chim. Acta. 277, 165–177 (1993)
4. Galvão, R.K.H., Filho, H.A.D., Martins, M.N., Araújo, M.C.U., Pasquini, C.: Sub-optimal wavelet denoising of coaveraged spectra employing statistics from individual scans. Anal. Chim. Acta. 581, 159–167 (2007)
5. Liu, R., Chen, W.L., Xu, K.X.: Study of net analyte signal with near infrared spectra for quantitative. Anal. Spectrosc. Spectra. Anal. 24, 1042–1046 (2004)
6. Shen, Q., Jiang, J.H., Shen, G.L., Yu, R.Q.: Ridge estimated orthogonal signal correction for data preprocessing prior to PLS modeling: QSAR studies of cyclooxygenase-2 inhibitors. Chemometr. Intell. Lab. Syst. 82, 44–49 (2006)
7. Leardi, R., Norgaard, L.: Sequential application of backward interval partial least squares and genetic algorithms for the selection of relevant spectral regions. J. Chemometr. 18, 486–497 (2004)
8. Holland, J.H.: Adaptation in natural and artificial systems. University of Michigan, Ann Arbor (1975)

Efficient Entity Resolution Based on Sequence Rules[*]

Yakun Li , Hongzhi Wang, and Hong Gao

Harbin Institute of Technology, China
{liyakun,wangzh,honggao}@hit.edu.cn

Abstract. Entity resolution (ER) is to find the data objects referring to the same real-world entity. When ER is performed on relations, the crucial operator is record matching, which is to judge whether two tuples referring to the same real-world entity. Record matching is a longstanding issue. However, with massive and complex data in applications, current methods cannot satisfy the requirements. A Sequence-rule-based record matching (SeReMatching) is presented with the consideration of both the values of the attributes and their importance in record matching. And with the help of the Bloom Filter we changed, the algorithm greatly increases the checking speed and makes the complexity of entity resolution almost $O(n)$. And extensive experiments are performed to evaluate our methods.

Keywords: Entity resolution, Record matching , Bloom Filter.

1 Introduction

When an information system is created, even with good design and planning, there is no guarantee in all cases, the quality of the data can be stored to meet the requirements of users. Some factors such as input error, data sources merging and business environment changing over time will affect the data quality [11]. To overcome the harm dealt by data quality problem, it is necessary to process dirty data in information systems. Many techniques have been proposed [13~16]. Among them, entity resolution is important. It is useful in inconsistency and inaccuracy discovery as well as duplication detection.

Entity resolution (ER) is to find the data objects referring to the same real-world entity. When ER is performed on relations, the crucial operator is record matching, which is to judge whether two tuples referring to the same real-world entity. Record matching techniques are required in many applications. For example, when two companies are merged, it is necessary to combine their customer's records. While

[*] Supported by the This research is partially supported by National Science Foundation of China (No.61003046), the NSFC-RGC of China (No.60831160525), National Grant of High Technology 863 Program of China (No.2009AA01Z149), Key Program of the National Natural Science Foundation of China (No.60933001), National Postdoctoral Foundation of China (No.20090450126, No.201003447), Doctoral Fund of Ministry of Education of China(No.20102302120054), Postdoctoral Foundation of Heilongjiang Province (No.LBH-Z09109), Development Program for Outstanding Young Teachers in Harbin Institute of Technology (No. HITQNJS.2009.052).

G. Shen and X. Huang (Eds.): CSIE 2011, Part I, CCIS 152, pp. 381–388, 2011.
© Springer-Verlag Berlin Heidelberg 2011

some of the customers may in both of their databases but not all the same in all the attributes. A fragment of the dirty data in some data source is shown in Table 1. In this table, tuples 1, 3 and 6 refer to the same entity even though their representations are different. To deduplicate such data, it is necessary to perform record matching to find duplicated records.

Table 1. A Dirty Data Fragement

C#	Name	City	Zipcode	Phn	Reprsnt	others
1	Wal-Mart	BJ	90015	80103389	Sham	null
2	Carrefour	null	20016	80374832	Morgan	no
3	Wal-Mart	beijing	90015	010-80103389	Sham	any
4	walmart	Harbin	20040	70937485	Sham	^^
5	Carrefour	BeiJing	90015	83950321	Morgan	null
6	Mal-Mart	BJ	null	80103389	Sham	null

Record matching is a longstanding issue that has been studied for decades [1]. However, with massive and complex data in applications, current methods cannot satisfy the requirements. Existing methods can be classified into four kinds by their originally thoughts.

A common-used record matching method is to is choose the key attributes, combine them, order them, and check the neighborhood with the combined key[2,5,6,8]. The drawback of such kind of method is that it is difficult to gather similar tuples as neighborhoods each other with just a combined attribute. Let's consider an example. To perform the record matching on Table 1, a key is generated by extracting a few symbols from each attributes. The results of the tuples referring to the entity Wal-Mart in Beijing is shown in Table 2 and the column KEYs is the extracted key. Obviously, the keys of tuple 3 and 6 are not similar.

Table 2.

C#	Name	City	Zipcode	Phn	Reprsnt	others	KEYs
1	Wal-Mart	BJ	90015	80103389	Sham	null	WB9089SL
3	Wal-Mart	beijing	90015	010-80103389	Sham	any	Wb9089Sy
6	Mal-Mart	BJ	null	80103389	Sham	null	MBnu89SL

The basic idea of the second kind is to concatenate all attributes into a string, partition the string in to k-grams, and use the similarity of the k-gram set to determine whether two records referring to the same entity[7,9,10]. In practice, some attributes may be useless or even misleading, and it is costly to compare all the k-grams with each other. Example 1 illustrates this point.

Example 1: If record matching is performed on Table 1 by concatenating all the attributes, as can be seen, the empty properties are really misleading, and the attribute 'others' have a negative effect on the result. Form the concatenated attributes in Table 3, with null and noises, it is hardly to judge whether two records match.

Table 3.

C#	Strings
1	Wal-MartBJ9001580103389Shamnull
2	Carrefournull2001680374832Morganno
6	Mal-MartBJnull80103389Shamnull

Another way is use iterative block [12]. Blocks are iteratively processed until no block contains any more matching records in this algorithm. We present the Algorithm of Table 1 in the Table 5. We partition the tuples by the name and the zipcode. By the partition name T1 and T3 are in the same cluster, by the partition zipcode T1, T3 and T5 are the same, so we can say that T1, T3 and T5 are in the same cluster. As we can see, by the partition name, T2 and T5 are in the same cluster, so we add T2 to the cluster, then we have T1, T2, T3, T5 in the cluster. The result of Table 5 is presented in Table 6. In this way, many attributes can be used. However, when we want to use more attributes, the algorithm is costly and the precisions of results are often not satisfying.

Table 4.

Criterion	Partition by	$b_{,1}$	$b_{,2}$	$b_{,3}$	$b_{,4}$
SC_1	Name	T1,T3	T2,T5	T4	T6
SC_2	Zipcode	T1,T3,T5	T2	T4	T6

Table 5.

Clusters	c_1	$c_{,2}$	c_3
Tuples	T1, T2,T3 ,T5	T4	T6

In sum, existing methods have three shortcomings. The first is that all the tuples are compared with each other, which is inefficient. The second is that the methods do not take advantages of as many as attributes and generates results with low precision. The third is that all these methods are not suitable for massive data.

To overcome the drawbacks of current methods and perform entity resolution efficiently and effectively on massive data set, we consider not only the values of the attributes but also their importance in record matching. A ***Sequence-rule-based record matching*** (SeReMatching) is presented with the consideration of both of the two factors. We assign different attributes different weights, and according to their weights we partition them into different kinds. The recorder matching starts from the matching of the most important attribute A_1. If A_1 can't distinguish records effective, the second important attributes are used. Such process continues until the entity resolution is performed successfully on the entire data set. Our method gets advantages from two aspects. One is that its effectiveness is assured by accessing as many as useful attributes. The other is that all attributes are not used and the method is efficient.

2   The General Model for SeReMatching

In this section, the general model of SeReMatching is presented. We first define a general model for SeReMatching. Then we add the transformation and the similarity comparison into the basic model.

2.1   A General Model for SeReMatching

If we want to check the attributes in sequence, we have to make the sequence first. In fact we may want to check several attributes at the same step, so we can devide them into kinds, and give them different weights. Then we will check them in sequence by their kinds.

Example 2: We partition the attributes in example 1 into 4 kinds. After we partitioned the kinds, we will have a result like **Table 6**. First kind: name, phn; Second kind: zipcode; Third kind: reprsnt; Fourth kind: C#, city, others.

Table 6. The kind-partition result

	Attr1	Attr2	Attr3
Kind1(1)	Name	phn	
Kind2(0.5)	Zipcode		
Kind3(0.3)	Reprsnt		
Kind4(0)	C#	City	others

When we are convinced by the attributes in the former kinds if two tuples are the same or not, there is no need for us to check those left. The SeReMatching algorithm can be explained by the pseudo-code as following.

```
1:    input K
2:    for tuple T1 and T2 in the data source
3:        for kind i from 1 to n do
4:            for each attribute j in kind i from 1 to m do
5:                check(attribute j);
6:                If T1[attrij] ≈ T2[attrij] then
7:                    Sim(T1,T2) = Sim(T1,T2) + W(attrij);
8:                end if;
9:            end for;
10:           if Sim(T1,T2) >= K
11:               output(T1,T2);
12:               break;
13:           end if;
14:       end for;
15:   end for;
```

Fig. 1. General Model for SeReMatching Algorithm

2.2 Transformation

If we know the properties of the attributes, we can do some pre-work to make them more comparable, like:

Table 7.

C#	Name	City	Zipcode	Phn	Reprsnt	others
1	Wal-Mart	BJ	90015	80103389	Sham	null
3	Wal-Mart	beijing	90015	010-80103389	Sham	null

Before we check or at the start we begin to check, we can transform the phn of T[3] to "80103389" and then we begin to check. In fact, we can do the transformations while we are checking. Since we don't have to compare all the attributes, we can save the cost to do their transformations.

3 SeReMatching Algorithm Framework

In this section, we define the framework for SeReMatching. First, we introduce the Bloom filter into the record matching. Then we change the structure of the Bloom Filter to index the tuples. Finally the advanced SeReMatching will be presented.

3.1 An Introduction to Bloom Filter

Bloom Filter [3, 4] was first proposed by Bloom in 1970. It is composed of a vector v of m bits. We have k independent hash functions. The vector v can show the existence of an element. However, there is a certain probability that it will give a false result.

3.2 Change the Data Structure of Bloom Filter

We change the Bloom Filter into an array of link like the next figure. If an attribute is hashed into a number, we just add a node to the link containing the order number of the tuple. For example, if an attribute Name in tuple 22 is hashed into 3, Name in tuple 43 and tuple 55 are hashed into 0, our changed Bloom Filter will be,

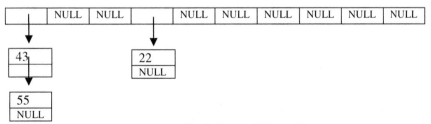

Fig. 2. Changed Bloom Filter

By this way, our comparison will all between the tuples which Bloom check's result are yes. It will improve the speed as much as enough.

3.3 Advanced SeReMatching Algorithm

By using the changed Bloom Filter, we actually index the tuples whose results of check in Bloom Filter will be the same, and skip all the other tuples. After we insert all the tuples into the changed Bloom Filter, a tuple just need to be checked once, and then we will get the link, and check the tuples in the link. We can define the model of *Advanced SeReMatching* as following.

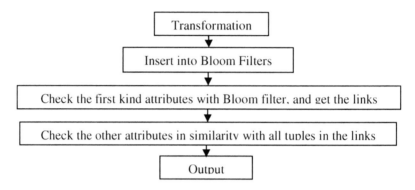

Fig. 3. Advanced SeReMatching with Bloom Filter Model

4 Disk-Based Advanced SeReMatching

To make the advanced SeReMatching can deal with the massive data sources, the disk-based algorithm will be introduced in this part. The main memory will be partitioned to minimize the number of hard disk blocks scheduling.

We divide the memory into 2 partitions to accommodate tuples and Bloom Filters as in the next figure. Our first block contain the current tuples and reserve a tuple's place for the to compare tuple.

We run the advanced SeReMatching in the memory. We start with the first tuple in the block 1 in memory. We check it with the changed Bloom filter in memory. Then

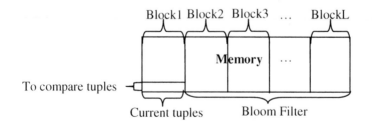

Fig. 4. Blocks distribution

we get the link of the tuples to be compared. If the number of the tuples is much larger than the filter size, we have to make several Bloom Filters for each attribute. And for the best, we may set the filter size of the Bloom Filters as the largest our main memory can afford.

Efficient: Suppose our data has $\underline{S}$ tuples, our memory can contain $\underline{L}$ disk blocks, a Bloom Filter occupies $\underline{L\text{-}1}$ blocks, and we have $\underline{Q}$ Bloom Filters, a block can contain $\underline{T}$ tuples, The probability of a tuple is a duplication is $\underline{P}$, the probability of the erroneous judgment of Bloom filter is $\underline{E}$, the number of disk scheduling $\underline{D_M}$ will be:

$$D_M = \frac{S}{T-1}\left[(L-1)Q + S(P+E)\right]$$

5 Experimental Evaluation

In this part, we will experiment the advanced SeReMatching with Bloom Filter in efficiency, precise, recall rate.

5.1 Efficiency, Precise and Recall Rate

We run our system based on *SeReMatching algorithm* to check 7 dirty data sources in the next table. The efficiency of our system is presented in **Figure 5.** The precise and recall rate of our checking is presented in **Figure 6.**

As we can see in the figure 5, if we twice the size of dirty data source, our checking time almost be twice as before. That evaluates that our checking complexity is smaller than O(nlog(n)). In fact, since the duplication is often little, our checking complexity is almost O(n).

Table 8

data NO	D1	D2	D3	D4	D5	D6	D7
Tuple num	8K	16K	32K	64K	128K	256K	512K
Cluster num	1K	2K	3K	4K	5K	6K	7K

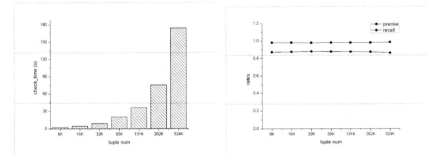

Fig. 5. Efficient   **Fig. 6.** Precise and recall

In the figure 6, precise and recall rate are always high enough and almost unchanged when the size of dirty data increase. That demonstrates our system is an effective system.

6 Conclusion

We have proposed a novel framework for ER, and with the changed Bloom Filter we improve the record matching speed significantly with high precise and recall rate. The experimental evaluation has proved that our method is an efficient and effective.

References

1. Fan, W., Gao, H., Jia, X., Li, J., Ma, S.: Dynamic constraints for record matching. The VLDB Journal, doi:10.1007/s00778-010-0206-6
2. Hernandez, M.A., Stolfo, S.J.: Real-World data is dirty: data cleansing and the merge/purge problem. Data Mining and Knowledge Discovery 2(1), 9–37 (1998)
3. Mullin, J.K.: A second look at Bloom filters. Communications of the ACM (1983)
4. Mitzenmacher, M.: Compressed bloom filters. IEEE/ACM Transactions on Networking, TON (2002)
5. Monge, A.E.: Matching Algorithms within a Duplicate Detection System. Bulletin of the Technical Committee (2000)
6. Rahm, E., Do, H.H.: Data Cleaning: Problems and Current Approaches, Bulletin of the Technical Committee (2000)
7. Hassanzadeh, O., Miller, R.J.: Creating probabilistic databases from duplicated data. The VLDB Journal 18, 1141–1166 (2009)
8. Hellerstein, J.M.: Quantitative Data Cleaning for Large Databases. White paper, United Nations Economic Commission for Europe (February 2008)
9. Hassanzadeh, O., Sadoghi, M., Miller, R.J.: Accuracy of approximate string joins using grams. In: Proc. of the International Workshop on Quality in Databases (QDB), Vienna, pp. 11–18 (2007)
10. Hassanzadeh, O.: Benchmarking Declarative Approximate Selection Predicates. Master's thesis, University of Toronto (February 2007)
11. Guo, Z., Zhou, A.: Research on Data Quality and Data Cleaning:a Survey. Journal of Software 13(11), 2076–2082 (2002)
12. Whang, S.E., Menestrina, D., Koutrika, G., Theobald, M., Garcia-Molina, H.: Entity Resolution with Iterative Blocking. In: SIGMOD 2009 Proceedings of the 35th SIGMOD International Conference on Management of Data (2009)
13. Dasu, T., Johnson, T.: Exploratory data mining and data cleaning. John Wiley, Chichester (2003)
14. Lup, L.W., Li, L.M., Wang, L.T.: Aknowledge-based approach for duplicate elimination in data cleaning. Information Systems 26(8), 585–606 (2001)
15. Waldvogel, M., Rinaldi, R.: Efficient topology-aware overlay network. ACM SIGCOMM Computer Communication Review 33(1) (January 2003)
16. Aebi, D., Perrochon, L.: Towards improving data quality. In: Proc. of the International Conference on Information Systems and Management of Data, pp. 273–281 (1993)

Modeling Energy-Aware Embedded Software Using Process Algebra

Yi Zhu

School of Computer Science and Technology, Xuzhou Normal University
No. 29 Shanghai Road, Tongshan New Borough Xuzhou, Jiang su, China
xzzhuyi@163.com

Abstract. With the progress of low-power research on embedded systems, the estimation and analysis of energy consumption of embedded systems becomes a hot topic. Process Algebra is a formal method fit for analyzing the functional properties of embedded software, but it can not analyze the energy consumption properties. This paper proposes a process algebra support for modeling and analyzing energy consumption of embedded software. Priced Timed Communicating Sequential Process (PTCSP) is proposed in this paper can handle it efficiently by extending price information on Timed Communicating Sequential Process (TCSP). In this paper, the power consumption of instructions in embedded systems is mapped into the price of PTCSP, the energy consumption of embedded software can be modeled and optimized by using PTCSP. This formal method improves the accuracy and efficiency of energy calculation, the calculation results can be used to quantitatively analyze and optimize the energy consumption of embedded systems.

Keywords: embedded software; energy consumption; price; process algebra.

1 Introduction

With the progress of low-power research on embedded systems, the estimation and analysis of energy consumption of embedded systems becomes a hot topic. Tiwari consider that if we only analyze the energy consumption at the aspect of system hardware, it can not meet the requirements of system-level energy analysis, so he proposed the concept of software energy consumption. Software energy consumption is the energy consumed by system components in the process of executing system instructions [1].

The methods based on energy consumption model are the main methods of current research, they can estimate and analyze software energy consumption in the beginning of system development, but these methods lack description ability, and can not meet the demands of modeling different kinds complex relationship in the system, so it restricts the utility of them. Process algebra is a formal method being used to solve the communication problems of concurrent systems, which can be used to describe and analyze concurrent, asynchronous, non-deterministic behaviors of real-time systems. Due to its sound semantics and extendibility, it is very suitable for energy consumption modeling and analysis of embedded systems. Communicating Sequential Process (CSP) is widely accepted as a kind of Process Algebra to model the behaviors

G. Shen and X. Huang (Eds.): CSIE 2011, Part I, CCIS 152, pp. 389–394, 2011.

of a concurrent system [2]. Timed CSP (TCSP) was proposed in 1986 which is extended with time information on CSP [3]. In this paper, TCSP will be extended with price semantics, which can be used to characterize the energy consumption properties of embedded systems.

The outline of the remainder of the paper is as follows: Section 2 presents the syntax of PTCSP; Section 3 presents the operational semantics of PTCSP; Section 4 illustrates how to apply PTCSP in modeling and analysis of embedded software; The related work are presented by Section 5, and Section 6 concludes.

2 Priced Timed Communicating Sequential Process

In this section, implementation of system task is mapped into process, and energy consumption is mapped into running cost, each instruction is mapped into every event of process, the dynamic power consumption used by a instruction is mapped into the price of an event, and the static power consumption is mapped into the price of WAIT, so the energy consumption characteristics of embedded systems is expressed as the cost characteristics of process.

Price semantics is not important if we only consider the logic among the entities of system, however, it may become very important if our goal is figuring out the minimum cost that the system needs. PTCSP is proposed on TCSP which extended with price semantics.

Definition 1: The language of PTCSP is defined by the following grammar rule:

$$P ::= STOP \mid SKIP \mid WAIT \ (t, p_s) \mid a \xrightarrow{(t, p_d)} P \mid P; Q \mid P \Box Q \mid$$
$$P \sqcap Q \mid P \ _A\|_B \ Q \mid P \| \| Q \mid f(P) \mid \mu X \cdot F(X)$$

In this rule, $\Sigma = \{a_1, a_2, \ldots \ldots a_n\}$ is the set of all synchronizations and a_i is drawn from set Σ, event set A range over the set of subsets of Σ; $\mathbf{P\Sigma}$ is the power set of Σ; $T = \{t_0, t_1, t_2 \ldots \ldots t_{n-1}\}$ is the set of delay times for all events, which implies that the implementation of event a_i needs to delay t_i time units; Function f is a function from Σ to Σ; $\Gamma = \{p_{d0}, p_{d1}, p_{d2} \ldots \ldots p_{dn-1}\}$ is the set of prices for all events, and $p_{di} \in \mathfrak{R}^+$. p_s is the price of WAIT, and $p_s \in \mathfrak{R}^+$. Δ is the set of process variables, and $X \in \Delta$.

The expression of definition is following:

STOP is a process which will never engage in external communication, it is a broken process.

SKIP is a process which does nothing except terminate, and is ready to terminate immediately.

WAIT (t, p_s) is a delayed from of Skip. it does nothing, but is ready to terminate successfully after t time units, and the price of *WAIT* is p_s. The semantics of *WAIT* is not same as its semantics in [4], it means IDLE in this paper.

The process $a \xrightarrow{(t, p_d)} P$ is initially prepared to engage in synchronization a. if this event occurs, it immediately begins to behave as P. The prefix operator $\to$ allows us to add communication events to a process description. The price of event a is p_d.

In the process $P;Q$, control is passed from process P to process Q if and when P performs the termination event $\sqrt{}$. This event is not visible to the environment, and occurs as soon as P is ready to perform it. The sequential composition operator transfers control upon termination.

$P \square Q$ is an external choice between process P and Q. If the environment is prepared to cooperate with P but not Q, then the choice is resolved in favor of P.

$P \sqcap Q$ is a internal choice between P and Q, the outcome of this choice is nondeterministic.

The relabeled process $f(P)$ has a similar control structure to P, with observable able events renamed according to function f.

In the hybrid parallel program $P \parallel_{A} Q$, components P and Q must synchronize upon events from set C, and on termination, and they interleave on all other events.

In an asynchronous parallel combination $P \parallel\parallel Q$, both subprograms evolve concurrently without interacting, though they must agree on termination. If both subprograms are capable of performing the same event a, then a degree of nondeterminism may be introduced.

$\mu X \cdot F(X) : X$ is a process variable, $A = \alpha X$, a recursively defined process must immediately unwind before it is able to perform any visible action.

3 Operational Semantics

Now we discuss the semantics of priced timed transition system for PTCSP, PTCSP must be calculated according to operational semantics, and we can calculate the cost of process by use of operational semantics. Firstly, we give the definition of transition and evolution of PTCSP, then we define a set of operational rules.

$P \xrightarrow{(t,a,p_d)} P'$ denotes that process P can perform event $a \in \Sigma$ and become P' by involving for length of time t. p_d is the price of event a, so the cost of event a is $p_d t$.

$P \xrightarrow{(t,p_s)} P'$ denotes P become P' by waiting for length of time t, p_s is the price of evolution, so the cost of evolution is $p_s t$.

Dead Lock

$$init(STOP) = \{\} \qquad \frac{-}{STOP \dashrightarrow_{(t,p_s)} STOP}$$

Successful Termination

$$init(SKIP) = \{\sqrt{}\} \qquad \frac{-}{SKIP \dashrightarrow_{(t,p_s)} SKIP}$$

Delay

$$init(WAIT\ d) = \{\} \qquad \frac{-}{WAIT\ d \dashrightarrow_{(t,p_s)} WAIT\ (d-t)} [t \le d]$$

Event Prefixing

$$init(a \xrightarrow{(t,p_d)} P) = \{a\} \qquad \frac{-}{(a \xrightarrow{(t,p_d)} P) \xrightarrow{(t,a,p_d)} P}$$

Sequential Composition

$$init(P;Q) = init\{P\} \setminus \{\surd\} \qquad \frac{P \xrightarrow{(t,a,p_d)} P'}{P;Q \xrightarrow{(t,a,p_d)} P';Q} [\surd \notin init(P)]$$

Choice

$$init(P \square Q) = init\{P\} \cup init\{Q\} \qquad \frac{P \xrightarrow{(t,a,p_d)} P'}{P \square Q \xrightarrow{(t,a,p_d)} P'}$$

$$init(P \sqcap Q) = \{\} \qquad \frac{-}{P \sqcap Q \xrightarrow{(0,\tau,p_d)} P}$$

Event Renaming

$$init(f(P)) = f(init(P)) \qquad \frac{P \xrightarrow{(t,a,p_d)} P'}{f(P) \xrightarrow{(t,f(a),p_d)} f(P')}$$

Parallel Combination

$$\frac{P \xrightarrow{(t,a,p_d)} P'}{P \,_A\|_B Q \xrightarrow{(t,a,p_d)} P' \,_A\|_B Q} [a \in A \setminus B \cup \{\tau\}]$$

$$\frac{P \xrightarrow{(t,a,p_d)} P' \quad Q \xrightarrow{(t,a,p_d)} Q'}{P \,_A\|_B Q \xrightarrow{(t,a,p_d)} P' \,_A\|_B Q'} [a \in A \cap B]$$

$$init(P \,\|\|\, Q) = init(P) \cup init(Q) \qquad \frac{P \xrightarrow{(t,a,p_d)} P'}{P \,\|\|\, Q \xrightarrow{(t,a,p_d)} P' \,\|\|\, Q}$$

4   Application in Embedded Software Energy Modeling

In this section, we will model a Traffic alert and Collision Avoidance System (TCAS) by PTCSP, and analyze its energy consumption characteristics. Figure 1 shows A simple UML sequence diagram, which describes a possible scenario of TCAS.

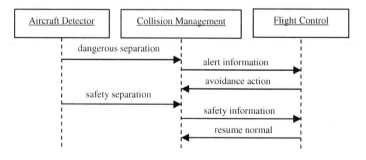

Fig. 1. A simple UML sequence diagram for the TCAS scenario

Before modeling TCAS with PTCSP, the energy used by each instruction must be acquired. Assuming Flight Control module can only take three different avoidance behaviors, such as climbing, descending and maintain. Table 1 shows the energy used by each instruction of TCAS.

Table 1. Execution time and power consumption of instructions

Instruction(Abbreviation)	Execution time	Power consumption
dangerous separation(ds)	3	6
alert information(ai)	4	9
climbing(cb)	8	18
maintain(mt)	8	13
descending(dc)	8	15
safety separation(ss)	4	8
safety information(si)	4	7
resume normal(rn)	3	9

Using data in table 1, energy of TCAS can be modeled with RCSP, and the TCAS is expressed as following:

$$AD \triangleq \mu X \bullet (ds \xrightarrow{(3,6)} ss \xrightarrow{(4,8)} X \sqcap SKIP)$$

$$CM \triangleq \mu X \bullet ((ds \xrightarrow{(3,6)} ai \xrightarrow{(4,9)} (cb \xrightarrow{(8,18)} ss \xrightarrow{(4,8)} si \xrightarrow{(4,7)} rn \xrightarrow{(3,9)} X$$
$$\square mt \xrightarrow{(8,13)} ss \xrightarrow{(4,8)} si \xrightarrow{(4,7)} rn \xrightarrow{(3,9)} X$$
$$\square dc \xrightarrow{(8,15)} ss \xrightarrow{(4,8)} si \xrightarrow{(4,7)} rn \xrightarrow{(3,9)} X))\square SKIP)$$

$$FC \triangleq \mu X \bullet ((ai \xrightarrow{(4,9)} (cb \xrightarrow{(8,18)} si \xrightarrow{(4,7)} rn \xrightarrow{(3,9)} X$$
$$\square mt \xrightarrow{(8,13)} si \xrightarrow{(4,7)} rn \xrightarrow{(3,9)} X \square dc \xrightarrow{(8,15)} si \xrightarrow{(4,7)} rn \xrightarrow{(3,9)} X))\square SKIP)$$

$$TCAS \triangleq AD \ _A\|_C \ CM \ _C\|_F \ FC$$

Where $A=\alpha AD=\{ds,ss\}$; $C=\alpha CM=\{ds,ai,cb,mt,dc,ss,si,rn\}$;
$F=\alpha FC=\{ai,cb,mt,dc,si,rn\}$.

By using a algorithm for calculating minimum cost reachability path, it can be re-solved that the minimal energy consumption path is $\langle ds, ai, mt, ss, si, rn \rangle$, and the minimal energy consumption is 245. This shows that taking avoidance behavior *mt* can meet the requirements of the system and consumes least accumulated energy.

5   Related Work

Current research lacks the methods to consider both functional requirements and non-functional requirements simultaneously. Priced timed Petri net is proposed in [5, 6], this is the development of Petri net for business process modeling, they defines a price for every transition, price represents the price of business process. Weighted timed automata is proposed in [7], and the priced timed automata is also proposed at the same time [8]. Priced timed Petri net and priced timed automata are two formal meth-ods which can model check whether the system meets functional and non-functional requirements as same as process algebra, however, they have not make in-depth analysis of energy consumption of embedded systems, especially they have not mapped dynamic and static power consumption into the definitions of the formal models as price information.

6 Conclusion

This paper proposes a process algebra support for modeling energy-aware embedded software. Based on studying the related work of TCSP, price semantics are extended on TCSP to give a feasible method to model and quantitatively analyze embedded software. The main work is: Firstly, this paper presents the syntax of PTCSP; Secondly, it presents the operational semantics of PTCSP; Finally, it illustrates how to apply PTCSP in modeling and analysis of TCAS. Furthermore, the problem about state space explosion of labeled transition system is out of consideration, so the future work is how to reduce state space based on current study.

Acknowledgments. This research is supported by the Natural Science Foundation for Colleges and Universities in Jiangsu Province of China under grant No.10KJB520019.

References

1. Tiwari, V., Malik, S., Wolfe, A.: Power analysis of embedded software: A first step towards software power minimization. IEEE Transactions on Very Large Scale Integration 2(4), 437–444 (1994)
2. Hoare, C.A.R.: Communicating Sequential Processes. Communications of the ACM 21(8), 666–677 (1978)
3. Reed, G.M., Roscoe, A.W.: A Timed Model for Communicating Sequential Processes. In: Kott, L. (ed.) ICALP 1986. LNCS, vol. 226, pp. 314–323. Springer, Heidelberg (1986)
4. Schneider, S.: An Operational Semantics for Timed CSP. Information and Computation 116, 193–213 (1995)
5. Liu, W.D., Song, J.X., Lin, C.: Modeling and analysis of grid computing application based price timed Petri net. Acta Electronica Sinica 33(8), 1416–1420 (2005) (in Chinese)
6. Liu, X.M., Li, S.X., Li, W.J., Pan, L.: A Time Petri Net Extended with Price Information. Journal of Software 18(1), 1–10 (2007) (in Chinese)
7. Alur, R., La Torre, S., Pappas, G.J.: Optimal paths in weighted timed automata. In: Morari, M., Thiele, L. (eds.) HSCC 2001. LNCS, vol. 2034, pp. 49–62. Springer, Heidelberg (2001)
8. Behrmann, G., Larsen, K., Rasmussen, J.: Optimal scheduling using priced timed automata. ACM SIGMETRICS Performance Evaluation Review 32(4), 34–40 (2005)

Internal Feedback Particle Swarm Optimization Control Method of the Integral Time-Delay Systems

Liu Qi, Guo Rongyan, and Jin Yutao

Department of Physics and Electronic Engineering,
Zhoukou Normal University, Henan, China
{liuqi,guorongyan,jinyutao}@zknu.edu.cn

Abstract. The traditional PID controller has structural flaws in the integral process control, a kind of internal feedback particle swarm optimization PID control method is put forward in this paper, which solves the problem of controlling the integral process. The integral time-delay systems in superheated steam temperature system is difficult to be controlled, but by using the method brought in this paper, the simulation results of the steam flow temperature control system have non-overshoot, short adjusting time, which shows the rationality and validity of the PID control based on internal feedback PSO.

Keywords: integral time-delay systems; internal feedback; particle swarm; superheated steam temperature system; PID; generalized stable processes.

1 Introduction

Superheated stem temperature of power plant has the highest temperature in steam-water channel of boiler, and the temperature of superheater is close to the limiting temperature of metal materials. If the temperature of superheated steam is too high, strength of the metal materials and service life of steam pipeline will decrease, also excessive thermal expansion in steam turbine will be caused, as a result metal of the high-pressure part will be damaged, but if the temperature of it is too low, the thermal efficiency of the equipments will be reduced, and when the steam temperature changes greatly, fatigue in piping material and related components will be caused, in consequence the steam turbine rotor and differential expansion will change, when serious, turbine vibration will occur, which is dangerous to production safety. The over-heat steam temperature system has some features, such as large delay, large inertia, integration, time-varying and so on, and the control quality directly affect safety and economy of the electric power production[1].

PID control is an important method in the industrial process control[2], and almost 90% of the controllers in industry are PID controllers[3]. As PID controller has the virtue of simple structure, strong robustness, simplicity of operation and some other advantages, it has been widely used in chemical industry, metallurgy, machinery, thermal engineering, light industry and many other control systems. The PID control for superheated steam temperature is difficult to reach perfect control effect in variable condition and the condition of large disturbance, and for the objection with time delay properties, controller output can not get optimum in the case of noise and load

G. Shen and X. Huang (Eds.): CSIE 2011, Part I, CCIS 152, pp. 395–400, 2011.

disturbance by the PID controller simply based on feedback information, and in this condition the feedback quantity can not reflect the change of object model and disturbance. Most power plants adjust the superheated steam temperature by manpower in variable condition, as a result the level of production automation is low.

Particle swarm optimization algorithm is a global optimization algorithm based on swarm intelligence, which originates from the research of birds predation, superiorities of it are having good robustness, simplicity of operation and higher calculation accuracy, which has been successfully used in solving many optimization problem[4]. In this paper, a PID control algorithm optimized by PSO is put forward. In contrast, as for neural network, a large sample data has to be trained repeatedly, and there is a problem of numerical ill-condition; as for genetic algorithm, several steps such as copy, cross and alter have to be done, as a result the evolution velocity is slow, and the performance greatly depends on the parameters. Through simulation of the superheated steam temperature, the result is fast and non-overshoot, which shows that the algorithm put forward in this paper has great effectiveness and superiority.

2   PID Control Based on Internal Feedback PSO

2.1   Mathematical Model of Superheated Steam Temperature System

Superheated steam temperature system is a multiple input and single output object. There are several influence factors for temperature changes, such as steam flow rate, the heat of flue gas, water flow rate. When the boiler load is disturbed, change of the steam flow will make the steam flow velocity change almost at the same time along different points of the entire superheater pipeline, thus if the convective heat transfer coefficient of the superheater changes, the steam temperature of each points of the superheater changes almost the same time. Therefore the steam temperature responses fast, which has properties of time-delay, inertial and integration. Suppose both τ and T are small, the dynamic characteristics of steam flow which is influenced by the change of steam flow is showed as (1).

$$G(s) = \frac{K}{s(Ts+1)} e^{-\tau s}$$

(1)

As the integration process in equation (1) is difficult to control, some self-turning method[5-8] of integration process has large overshoot and long adjusting time. Because there are structural defects in the integration process, it is difficult to be controlled by traditional PID controller[9].

2.2   Control Structure of Internal Feedback

The dynamic characteristics of steam flow is a system model with a first order lag integrator, according to the integrator process in this model, a double feedback circuit is put forward by Sung and Lee[9], for this algorithm, a control structure of internal feedback is introduced, shown as fig.1, the proportional controller K_l in the internal feedback circuit can change the integrate process into generalized stable processes, and the external feedback circuit of PID controller can be designed by the expectation performance index.

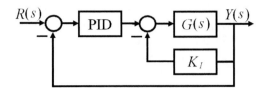

Fig. 1. The diagram for integrating Process

By adding the proportional controller K_I in the internal feedback circuit, the close-loop transfer function is shown as equation (2).

$$G_0(s) = \frac{G(s)}{1 + K_I G(s)} = \frac{Ke^{-\tau s}}{Ts^2 + s + KK_I e^{-\tau s}} \tag{2}$$

Use Taylor series to expanse, it can obtain:

$$e^{-\tau s} \cong 1 - \tau s + 0.5\tau^2 s^2 \tag{3}$$

Combine equation (3) with $e^{-\tau s}$ in the denominator of (2), the model of second order delay is shown as equation (4).

$$G_0(s) \cong \frac{Ke^{-\tau s}}{(T + 0.5KK_I\tau^2)s^2 + (1 - KK_I\tau)s + KK_I} \tag{4}$$

According to louts criterion, to achieve stability of the system, the following equation should be meet.

$$K_I < \frac{1}{K\tau} \tag{5}$$

The gain of proportion controller which can greatly suppress disturbance is brought forward by Sung and Lee.

$$K_I = \frac{0.2}{K\tau} \tag{6}$$

Combine equation (6) with (4), the generalized stable processes can be obtained, shown as (7).

$$G_0(s) \cong \frac{e^{-\tau s}}{\frac{T + 0.1\tau}{K}s^2 + \frac{0.8}{K}s + \frac{0.2}{K\tau}} \tag{7}$$

2.3 Particle Swarm Optimization

Parameter optimization is a main problem of PID control, which can get best control quality through searching global minimum and improving convergence rate.

Basic principle of optimization algorithm of PSO is shown as follows[4]: Suppose there are m particles in D-dimensional space, and its coordinate is $x_i=(x_{i1},x_{i2},...,x_{iD})$, which has a fitness related with optimization object function $f(x)$ (usually this is called as fitness of particles), and velocity of each particle is $v_i=(v_{i1},v_{i2},...,v_{iD})$. Assume that the best location passed by particle i is $p_i=(p_{i1},p_{i2},...,p_{iD})$, denoted as p_{best}; and the best location passed by all the particles is $g_i=(g_{i1},g_{i2},...,g_{iD})$, denoted as g_{best}. For particle i of the tth generation, according to equation (8), velocity and location of the jth dimension of the $(t+1)^{th}$ generation can be obtained.

$$v_{ij}(t+1) = v_{ij}(t) + r_1 c_1 (p_{ij} - x_{ij}(t)) + r_2 c_2 (g_{ij} - x_{ij}(t))$$
$$x_{ij}(t+1) = x_{ij}(t) + v_{ij}(t+1)$$
(8)

In the above equation, r_1 and r_2 are random numbers from [0, 1], c_1 and c_2 are acceleration constants, furthermore both of c_1 and c_2 are positive. The maximum speed of particle is limited by V_{max}. Later on, Shi and Eberhart [10] added factor w as an inertia weight, at this time equation (8) can be changed to (9), and this is called as basic PSO algorithm.

$$v_{ij}(t+1) = w v_{ij}(t) + r_1 c_1 (p_{ij} - x_{ij}(t)) + r_2 c_2 (g_{ij} - x_{ij}(t))$$
$$x_{ij}(t+1) = x_{ij}(t) + v_{ij}(t+1)$$
(9)

2.4 PID Control

A proportional-integral-differential controller is a generic control loop feedback mechanism, which is using linear superposition of proportion, integration, and differentiation of deviation to reach the control purpose. The transfer function is shown as below:

$$G_c(s) = K_p + \frac{K_i}{s} + K_d s$$
(10)

Take parameters K_p, K_i and K_d of PID as particles of PSO, and then use PSO algorithm to find the parameter optimization $\theta=[K_p, K_i, K_d]$, with a goal of reaching some objective performance of the control system, such as small overshoot, short adjusting time and so on. The system structure of PID control based on internal feedback PSO is shown as below:

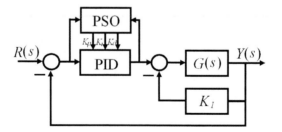

Fig. 2. PID control based on internal feedback PSO

3 Simulation

The change of steam flow makes a fast reaction of the steam temperature, generally the gain is $K=1\sim3$, delay is $\tau=10\sim20s$, and time constant is $T=30\sim60s$, in this paper, it is deemed that $K=2$, $\tau=10s$ and $T=50s$, as a result the dynamic characteristics of steam flow is shown as equation (11).

$$G(s) = \frac{2}{50s^2 + s} e^{-10s} \tag{11}$$

After adding the proportional controller K_I into the internal feedback circuit, according to the gain of K_I, the generalized stable processes can be obtained, shown as equation (12), and the unit step response curve is shown as curve 1 in figure 3.

$$G_0(s) \cong \frac{e^{-10s}}{25.5s^2 + 0.4s + 0.01} \tag{12}$$

Through the method of PID control based on PSO, and according to the optimization object function ISE to control the object in equation (12), and the unit step response curve is shown as curve 2 in figure 3

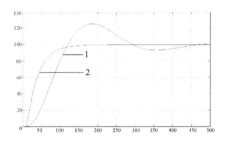

Fig. 3. Comparison of internal feedback result

Seen form the simulation result, the method of PID control based on internal feedback PSO has advantages such as: non-overshoot and short adjusting time, also the performance has greatly changed, and ISE is small.

4 Conclusion

Particle swarm optimization is one of the representative methods of swarm intelligence, which provides a new and effective solution for the optimization of nonlinear and nondifferentiable minimization, multi-peak value and some other problems. According to the defects of integral process in traditional PID controller, a method of PID control based on internal feedback PSO is put forward in this paper, which has solved the problem that the integral process is hard to control. In the example of superheated steam temperature, the method put forward in this paper has got satisfying result, and shows good effectiveness and rationality.

Acknowledgments. The research of this paper has sponsored by the natural science foundation of Henan province Educational Committee in China. (Project Number: 2008B510027, 2011B510021).

References

1. Han, P., Wang, G.Y., Wang, D.F.: On the application of predictive function control in steam temperature system of thermal power plant. IEEE Proc. -Control Theory 148(6), 135–138 (2004)
2. Abido, M.A.: Particle swarm optimization formultimachine power system stabilizer design. Power Engineering Society Summer Meeting (3), 1346–1349 (2001)
3. Bennett, S.: The Past of PID controllers. Annual Reviews in Control 25, 43–53 (2001)
4. Kennedy, J., Eberhart, R.: Particle Swarm Optimization. In: Proc. IEEE Int. Conf. on Neural Networks, pp. 1942–1948. IEEE Press, Perth (1995)
5. Kwak, H.J., Sung, S.W., Lee, I.B.: On-line Process identification and autotuning for integrating Processes. Industrial Engineering Chemistry Research 36(12), 5329–5338 (1997)
6. Luyben, W.L.: Tuning Proportional-Integral-Derivative Controllers for Integrator/Deadtime Processes. Industrial Engineering Chemistry Research 35(10), 3480–3483 (1996)
7. Wang, L., Cluett, W.R., Tuning, PID.: controllers for integrating processes. IEE Proceedings-Control Theory & Applications 144(5), 385–392 (1997)
8. Song, S.H., Cai, W.J., Wang, Y.G.: Auto-tuning of cascade control systems. ISA Transaction 42(1), 63–72 (2003)
9. Sung, S.W., Lee, I.: Limitations and countermeasures of PID controllers. Industrial & Engineering Chemistry Research 35(8), 2596–2610 (1996)
10. Yuhui, S., Eberhart, R.: A modified particle swarm optimizer. In: Proc. IEEE Int. Conf. on Evolutionary Computation, pp. 303–308. IEEE Press, Anchorage (1997)

Reaserch on Aerodynamic Characteristics of the High-Speed Train under Side Wind

Huan Wang[1], Xin-zhe Zhang[1], Wei-hong Peng[2], and Li-na Ma[1]

[1] School of Electric Power Engineering,
China University of Mining and Technology, Xuzhou, Jiangsu 221116, China
[2] School of Mechanics & Civil Engineering, China University of Mining and Technology,
Xuzhou, Jiangsu 221116, China

Abstract. Based on the RNG $k - \varepsilon$ turbulence model, numerical simulation was carried out for aerodynamic characteristics of German ICE high-speed railway train under different wind direction angles and different wind angles of attack. In order to verify the accuracy of numerical simulation, the experimental platform of CUMT for the flow field visualization was used to check the result under the same conditions. Further more, the interaction among wind angles of direction, wind angles of attack and pressure coefficient, lift coefficient, overturning moment coefficient were discussed in this paper. The calculation results show that, with the increasing of wind angle of direction and wind angle of attack, the aerodynamic forces and overturning moment of the train increased gradually, which is unfavorable for high-speed railway train.

Keywords: high-speed railway train; side wind conditions; aerodynamic characteristics; overturning moment.

1   Introduction

High-speed railway is an important symbol of modernization, and the running speed refers to the traveling speed rather than testing speed. More consistent worldwide view is that the maximum speed of 200km/h or more, operation speed faster than 150km/h is considered as high-speed[1]. At present, the construction of high-speed railway of the world is accelerating, and the train's speed increases a lot. For instanse, Japan has built four Shinkansen: the Toukaidou line, the Sanyo line, the Joetsu line and the Northeast line. With the use of electric multiple unit, the highest speed has reached 220 ~ 275km/h; France has built four high-speed railways: the Southeast line, Atlantic line, the Northern line and the Paris ring. The TGV train has reached the highest speed of 270~300km/h in business, meanwhile, the test speed has topped 574.8km/h[2]. China is also gradually accelerating the building of high-speed railways. But with the increasing speed of high-speed train, the security issues of running trains are more and more important. Especially under the strong side wind, the aerodynamic characteristics of train will be worse, not only increase the train air resistance, lift, lateral force rapidly, but also affect the lateral stability of the train. Seriously, the train may be capsized in case of inclement. For some special environment, such as huge bridge, viaduct,

G. Shen and X. Huang (Eds.): CSIE 2011, Part I, CCIS 152, pp. 401–409, 2011.

embankment, the flow field of the train changes a lot, and the aerodynamic force increased significantly.

At present, there are real vehicle experiment, train model experiment, numerical simulation and other methods to research the train aerodynamics. For the first and second experiment methods, the experiment conditions are very strict, and the costs are relatively expensive.

Based on the flow field show experimental platform of China University of Mining and Technology, both the train model experiment method and numerical simulation experiment method were used to study the German ICE high-speed railway train. The aerodynamic characteristics of the train under side wind, and the effect of different wind angles of direction and different wind angles of attack to the running high-speed railway train were studied.

2   Numerical Simulation Basic Equations and Turbulence Model

Time-averaged continuity equations (mass equations)

$$\frac{\partial u}{\partial x} + \frac{\partial v}{\partial y} + \frac{\partial w}{\partial z} = 0 \tag{1}$$

Time-averaged momentum equations

$$\rho\left(u\frac{\partial u}{\partial x} + v\frac{\partial u}{\partial y} + w\frac{\partial u}{\partial z}\right) = -\frac{\partial p}{\partial x} + \mu\left(\frac{\partial^2 u}{\partial x^2} + \frac{\partial^2 u}{\partial y^2} + \frac{\partial^2 u}{\partial z^2}\right) - \rho\left(\frac{\partial \overline{u'u'}}{\partial x} + \frac{\partial \overline{u'v'}}{\partial y} + \frac{\partial \overline{u'w'}}{\partial z}\right)$$

$$\rho\left(u\frac{\partial v}{\partial x} + v\frac{\partial v}{\partial y} + w\frac{\partial v}{\partial z}\right) = -\frac{\partial p}{\partial y} + \mu\left(\frac{\partial^2 v}{\partial x^2} + \frac{\partial^2 v}{\partial y^2} + \frac{\partial^2 v}{\partial z^2}\right) - \rho\left(\frac{\partial \overline{u'v'}}{\partial x} + \frac{\partial \overline{v'v'}}{\partial y} + \frac{\partial \overline{v'w'}}{\partial z}\right) \tag{2}$$

$$\rho\left(u\frac{\partial w}{\partial x} + v\frac{\partial w}{\partial y} + w\frac{\partial w}{\partial z}\right) = -\frac{\partial p}{\partial z} + \mu\left(\frac{\partial^2 w}{\partial x^2} + \frac{\partial^2 w}{\partial y^2} + \frac{\partial^2 w}{\partial z^2}\right) - \rho\left(\frac{\partial \overline{u'w'}}{\partial x} + \frac{\partial \overline{w'v'}}{\partial y} + \frac{\partial \overline{w'w'}}{\partial z}\right)$$

Where ρ refers to the air density; u, v, w are the three components of direction of the air velocity v along the x, y, z axes; t is the time variable, p is the static pressure, μ is the aerodynamic viscosity coefficient.

For steady incompressible flow, the transport equations of RNG $k-\varepsilon$ turbulence model are as follows:

$$\rho\left(u\frac{\partial k}{\partial x} + v\frac{\partial k}{\partial y} + w\frac{\partial k}{\partial z}\right) = \frac{\partial}{\partial x}\left(\alpha_k \mu_{ef}\frac{\partial k}{\partial x}\right) + \frac{\partial}{\partial y}\left(\alpha_k \mu_{ef}\frac{\partial k}{\partial y}\right) + \frac{\partial}{\partial z}\left(\alpha_k \mu_{ef}\frac{\partial k}{\partial z}\right)\rho + S_k \tag{3}$$

$$\rho\left(u\frac{\partial \varepsilon}{\partial x} + v\frac{\partial \varepsilon}{\partial y} + w\frac{\partial \varepsilon}{\partial z}\right) = \frac{\partial}{\partial x}\left(\alpha_\varepsilon \mu_{ef}\frac{\partial \varepsilon}{\partial x}\right) + \frac{\partial}{\partial y}\left(\alpha_\varepsilon \mu_{ef}\frac{\partial \varepsilon}{\partial y}\right) + \frac{\partial}{\partial z}\left(\alpha_\varepsilon \mu_{ef}\frac{\partial \varepsilon}{\partial z}\right) + S_\varepsilon - R \tag{4}$$

Where, $S_k = G_k - \rho\varepsilon$, $S_\varepsilon = C_{1\varepsilon}\frac{\varepsilon}{k}G_k - C_{1\varepsilon}\rho\frac{\varepsilon^2}{k}$, $R_\varepsilon = \frac{C_\mu \rho \eta^3 \left(1-\eta/\eta_0\right)}{1+\beta\eta^3}\frac{\varepsilon^2}{k}$, $G_k = \mu_t S^2$,

$\eta = Sk/\varepsilon$, $S = \sqrt{2S_{ij}S_{ij}}$, $S_{ij} = \frac{1}{2}\left(\frac{\partial u_j}{\partial x_i} + \frac{\partial u_i}{\partial x_j}\right)$, $\mu_{ef} = \mu + \mu_t$, α_k , α_ε are the inverse effective Prandtl numbers of k, ε, G_k is the generated items of turbulent kinetic energy caused by the average velocity gradient; R_ε is the effect of average strain rate to ε, μ_{ef} is the effective viscosity coefficient.

3   The Analysis of Numerical Simulation and Train Model Experiment Results

Based on the experimental platform of the flow field visualization, the prototype of train model experiment is the German ICE train. And according to the ratio of 1:72 an experimental model of the train was built to conduct the model experiment. The shape of the real train is very complex, the slenderness ratio is very large[4] , the characteristics of train's bottom and outside surface are variational, and the geometry of railway also is relatively complex. Therefore, according to the similarity principle in engineering fluid mechanics, the geometric model of the train was simplified properly [5~7].

The inlet wind is Vector sum. Under different wind angles, the same vehicular speed and same environmental wind speed will not get the same synthetic speed, so the aerodynamic force of vehicle is not only effected by the vehicular speed, environmental wind speed, but also by the environmental wind angle. The principle of resultant wind is displayed in Fig. 1. Assuming that the train speed is V, the direction is from right to left, environmental wind speed is W, the direction is from the top to down, and the angle between the axis of the train and the wind is α. According to the relative motion principle, the train is assumed to be stationary relative to the ground, and the air in front of the train is flowing at a speed of V from left to right. Compose the air's speed in front of the train and environmental wind speed, the resultant velocity is U. And the angle between it and the air speed in front of the train is β(slip angle).

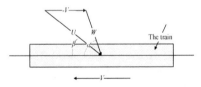

Fig. 1. The figure of velocity vector synthesis

According to the original train, the size of which is 20.20m* 3.07m* 3.98m in volume and the scale is 1:72. The size of the model experimental space is: 40cm* 40cm*40cm in volume, and the size of the train model is: 28cm*4.2cm*5.5cm in volume. The train operating conditions are assumed as follows: train speed is 150km/h, wind angle of attack is 10°, environmental wind speed is 4m/s, and the train runs on an ordinary bridge. The train model experiment was conducted with the use of the flow field show experimental platform, and the flow field is shown in Fig. 2 (a). Under the same conditions, the aerodynamic characteristics of the train were studied by numerical simulation method. The surface of the bridge and the train were designated no-slip boundary, the boundary layer technology was applied to making grid in FLUENT and the total number of grid is 91050. Based on the RNG $k - \varepsilon$ turbulence model numerical simulation calculation, the stream function distribution is shown in Fig. 2 (b).

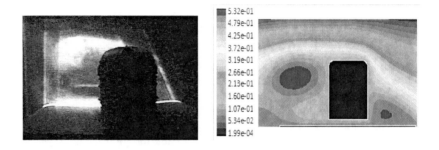

Fig. 2 (a) Experimental original photo   **Fig. 2 (b)** The picture of stream function

The Fig. 2 (a) shows that a distinct vortex is existent of the train and the bottom gap which is caused by the wheel height produces the boundary layer in the leeward side. As can be seen from Fig. 2 (b), under the same conditions, the phenomenon of the numerical simulation is similar with the train model experiment. And it shows that the calculation model and the calculation method used in this paper are reasonable.

4   Aerodynamic Characteristics of the Train

While studying the aerodynamic characteristics of the train with numerical simulation method, the typical embankment road condition of Qing-Zang Railway was selected. The height of embankment is 4m. According to the References [9,10], six experimental conditions were selected. The wind angle of direction were 0°, 18°, 36°, 54°, 72° and 90°; the wind angle of attack selected were 0°, 10° , 20° 30°, 40° and 50°(wind angle of attack more than 50° is rare in actual working conditions).

4.1   Aerodynamic Characteristics of Train Under Different Wind Angles of Direction

Actually, when the high-speed train is running, the environmental wind direction is random at any possible angles. So it is necessary to study the Aerodynamic characteristics of train under different wind angles of direction. Take train speed for 250km/h, environmental wind speed for 20.4m/s, the aerodynamic characteristics of the train was studied under different wind angles of direction, calculation conditions are shown in Table 1. Because of the limited number of words, this paper only gives the results of pressure and stream function when the wind angle of direction is 0°, 36° and 90°. And the corresponding figures are shown in Fig. 3, Fig. 4 and Fig. 5. The relationships between different wind angles of direction and pressure coefficient, lift coefficient, overturning moment coefficient are shown in Fig. 6.

Table 1. Calculation conditions

Working condition	1	2	3	4	5	6
Wind angle of direction(°)	0	18	36	54	72	90
Slip angle(°)	0	4.05	7.94	11.44	14.35	16.35

Fig. 3 (a) The picture of stream function when wind angle of direction is 0°

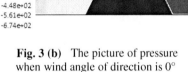

Fig. 3 (b) The picture of pressure when wind angle of direction is 0°

Fig. 4 (a) The picture of stream function when wind angle of direction is 36°

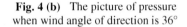

Fig. 4 (b) The picture of pressure when wind angle of direction is 36°

Fig. 5 (a) The picture of stream function when wind angle of direction is 90°

Fig. 5 (b) The picture of pressure when wind angle of direction is 90°

As can be seen From Fig. 3 (b), Fig. 4 (b) and Fig. 5 (b): the pressure of the windward side is positive, and it is negative on the leeward side of the train. Thus, the lateral force of the train is relatively large, which is an important factor to cause the vehicles overturn.

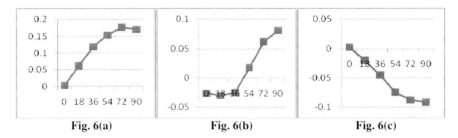

Fig. 6(a)   **Fig. 6(b)**   **Fig. 6(c)**

Fig. 6. The relationship between different wind angles of direction and pressure coefficient(a), lift coefficient(b), overturning moment coefficient(c)

It can be seen from Fig. 6: with the increasing of wind angle of direction, the pressure coefficient of train increases. When the wind angle of direction is larger than 54°, the change rate of pressure coefficient is decreasing. When wind angle of direction is 72°, the pressure coefficient comes to its maximum value 0.176, after that, it keeps steady. As for the lift coefficient, when the wind angle of direction is small, the lift of the body is negative. With the angle increases, the lift coefficient is becoming positive gradually. In short, when the wind angle of direction gradually increases, the pressure, lift, overturning moment of the train gradually increased, when wind angle of direction is greater than 72°, the pressure and t overturning moment keep steady.

4.2 Aerodynamic Characteristics of Train under Different Wind Angles of Attack

In addition to the impact of wind angle of direction, different wind angles of attack on the train which will bring some influences to the actual operating train. So the aerodynamic characteristics of the train were studied under different wind angles of attack under the same embankment road condition. Suppose the train speed is 250km/h, environmental wind speed is 16m/s. Due to the limited words, this paper gives the pictures of pressure and stream function when the wind angle of attack is 0°, 30°and 50°, the results are as shown in Fig. 7, Fig. 8 and Fig. 9. The relationship between different wind angles of attack and pressure coefficient, lift coefficient, overturning moment coefficient are shown in Fig. 10.

Table 2. Calculation conditions

Working condition	1	2	3	4	5	6
Wind angle of attack(°)	0	10	20	30	40	50

As from Fig. 7 (b), Fig. 8 (b) and Fig. 9 (b): the pressure of the top and bottom of the train are negative, and pointing to the contrary directions. The air on the top of train can be expanded freely, thus, the negative pressure is larger. While the air at the bottom of train is limited by the ground, the negative pressure is lesser. Accordingly, the train can get a large lift under the huge environmental wind, which is another important factor of overturning.

Fig. 7 (a) The picture of stream function
when wind angle of attack is 0°

Fig. 7 (b) The picture of pressure
when wind angle of attack is 0°

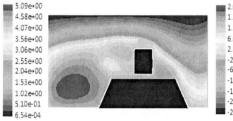
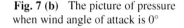

Fig. 8 (a) The picture of stream function
when wind angle of attack is 30°

Fig. 8 (b) The picture of pressure
when wind angle of attack is 30°

Fig. 9 (a) The picture of stream function
when wind angle of attack is 50°

Fig. 9 (b) The picture of pressure
when wind angle of attack is 50°

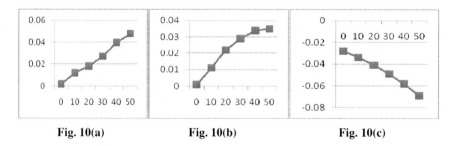

Fig. 10(a)   **Fig. 10(b)**   **Fig. 10(c)**

Fig. 10. The relationship between different wind angles of attack and pressure coefficient(a), lift
coefficient(b), overturning moment coefficient(c)

It can be seen from Fig. 10: when the wind angle of attack is from 0° to 50°, with the wind angle of attack increases, the pressure coefficient approximate linear growth; As for the lift coefficient, with the wind angle of attack increases, the lift coefficient of train increases, when wind angle of attack is greater than 40°, the growth rate of lift coefficient decreases; With the increases of wind angle of attack, the overturning moment coefficient of train increases, and the growth rate of overturning coefficient keep increasing. Therefore, when the wind angle of attack gradually increases, the pressure, lift, overturning moment of the train gradually increases, and also the growth rate of overturning coefficient keeps increasing, which is unfavorable for the running high-speed railway train.

5   Conclusions

Through the comparison of train model experiment and numerical simulation analysis, the calculation model and the calculation method used in this paper are reasonable.

Wind angle of direction and wind angle of attack will cause varying degrees of lateral force and lift force, and these two forces are the important factors that lead to the overturning of the train.

With the increases of wind angle of direction and wind angle of attack, the pressure coefficient, lift coefficient and overturning moment coefficient of the train are increasing gradually. And they are disadvantageous and needing for further work.

Acknowledgement

This research is sponsored by the "National Science Foundation for Young Scientists of China" (50909093) and the "National Student Research Training Program" (091029010).

References

1. Wang, Q.C.: High-speed Railway Civil Engineering. Southwest Jiaotong University Press, Chengdu (1999)
2. Xie, X.L.: Speed of 574.8 km/h - French high-speed train create new world record. Railway knowledge 5, 32–37 (2007)
3. Zhu, Z.W., Chen, Z.Q.: Aerodynamic characteristics of single and double-deck vehicle passing the railway bridges in cross-wind. Journal of Central South University of Technology 32, 410–413 (2001)
4. Khier*, W., Breuer, M., Durst, F.: Flow structure around trains under side wind conditions: a Numerical study. Computers & Fluids 29, 179–195 (2000)
5. Coleman, S.A., Baker, C.J.: High sided road vehicles in crosswinds. Wind Engineering and Industrial Aerodynamics 36, 1383–1392 (1990)
6. Anderssonl, E., Haggstrom, J., Sima, M.: Assessment of train-overturning risk due to strong cross-winds. Rail and Rapid Transit, Proc. Instn. Mech. Engrs. 218, 213–223 (2004)
7. Suzuki, M., Tanemoto, K., Maeda, T.: Aerodynamic characteristics of train/vehicles under cross winds. Wind Engineering and Industrial Aerodynamics 91, 209–218 (2003)

8. Bettle, J., Holloway, A.G.L., Venart, J.E.S.: A computational study of the aerodynamic forces acting on a tractor-trailer vehicle on a bridge in cross- wind. Wind Engineering and Industrial Aerodynamics 91, 573–592 (2003)
9. Wei, Y.G., Yang, H., Han, X.L.: Study on Critical Wind Speed for Vehicle Turnover along Qing-Zang Railway. China Safety Science Journal 16, 14–17 (2006)
10. Huang, Q.: Study on general technical specifications of locomotive and car of Qing-Zang railway (Golmud-Lhasa Section). Chinese Railways 3, 41–46 (2002)

Design of Multimedia Computer Room Based on Virtual Desktop Infrastructure

Xueqing Liu[1], Wenwen Sheng[1], and Jing Wang[2]

[1] School of Information Science & Technology, Rizhao Polytechnic College
[2] College Office, Rizhao Polytechnic College
Rizhao, 276826, P.R. China
rzxxgc@163.com

Abstract. The reform of teaching in colleges and universities not only requires more for multimedia computer room day by day, but also leads to various sorts of conflicts. Along with continuous development of "cloud computing" and virtual technology, the application of virtual desktop infrastructure (VDI) based on cloud computing provides an effective way which is characterized by lower cost, more reliable data security and more convenient desktop management for construction and management of multimedia computer room in colleges and universities.

Keywords: virtual desktop infrastructure, cloud computing, computer room.

1 Introduction

Multimedia computer room consists of public computer room and specialized computer room in colleges and universities and serves as the important practice place for students to study computer and related courses. Today, we carry out the reform of higher education, especially; we advocate such teaching methods as "task-driven", "project-oriented" and "integrated teaching", so more courses shall be taught in computer room and even more computer rooms in colleges and universities shall be open to students after classes. As students frequently make use of them and a computer room shall often satisfy different needs of students in computer practice, bottlenecks in management and maintenance arise as follows:

1. In terms of management, operation and maintenance of computer centre, the scattered deployment of servers reduces the efficiency of maintenance and management of computer center. In addition, it is very complex and burdensome for administrators of computer center to maintain 300-400 PCs and servers which are scattered in classrooms.

2. In terms of teaching continuity, "system recovery card" and shielding I/O hardware are set up on each PC to protect data security of single-point PC, prevent students from installing software randomly and protect the teaching environment which is formally deployed by administrators, but in the meantime, system recovery card imposes restrictions on copy and save of teachers and students' courseware, homework and so on. However, we don't have a better way to protect servers at present; especially, once severs in multimedia computer room break down suddenly, classes

G. Shen and X. Huang (Eds.): CSIE 2011, Part I, CCIS 152, pp. 410–414, 2011.
© Springer-Verlag Berlin Heidelberg 2011

have to break off, so the persons concerned in colleges and universities are also very concerned about continuity of teaching software.

3. In terms of advanced teaching, especially for students majoring in information management, information-based education software, such as software development and database, actually studied by them have laagered behind for at least 2 years than mainstream software in the society and market, and even some teaching software can't be acquired in colleges and universities so that they can't meet the social needs and have much employment pressure after graduation. The main reason is that purchasing cycle lasts for a period of more than a year, some software are hard to be deployed and can't be deployed precisely and quickly and hardware and network environment are required; therefore, the persons concerned in colleges and universities are also very concerned how to accelerate the application and deployment of new technology and mainstream software.

4. In terms of hardware security and responsibility system, the persons concerned in multimedia computer room shall not only protect application and software, but also shall protect hardware security to safeguard teaching environment. However, PC hardware still loses and systems break down, so it is necessary to monitor students when they practice computers to guarantee hardware security.

5. In terms of funds, funds are all allocated from the state treasury instead of profit-making unit, so performance of hardware in multimedia computer room is general and especially, many PCs with retarded performance shall be eliminated. As a matter of the fact, the mode of repeated purchasing and elimination belongs to a serious wasting of resources. It is an issue for the persons concerned in colleges and universities to consider how to reduce funding in computer center under the premise of guaranteeing teaching environment.

2   Solution to Management of Multimedia Computer Room

Administrators of training room shall confront and solve these issues that how to avoid these problems, or how to quickly recover the normal teaching environment in labs after problems arise and how to integrate the existing software and hardware resource to serve students and teachers; in addition, these issues call higher request on scientific and efficient management of labs. Therefore, colleges and universities have made all sorts of attempts:

2.1   Strengthening Management

Colleges and universities try to find a more scientific management proposal which can save more cost. Although formulating strict management regulations, setting up original card, shielding U flash disk, restricting limits of authority and restricting web surfing have alleviated the problems set forth above to a certain extent, they have caused inconvenience to teaching.

2.2   Diskless Computer

Although non-disk system is easy to be maintained, it runs slowly and can't make full use of hardware resources of diskless computer. Particularly, common PCs are now configured with more performance, so it is unwise to achieve centralized management by wasting resources and reducing speed.

In a word, strengthening management of multimedia computer room can only alleviate contradictory to a certain extent and can't thoroughly solve contradictory because contradictory shall be solved from the root cause. With development of computer virtualization and emerging of VDI, we try to place all virtual desktop computers in data center for trusteeship and centralized management; in addition, users can acquire the experience of using the complete PC. It can be said that VDI brings about a new revolution in management and construction of multimedia computer room.

3   Introduction to VDI

VDI refers to virtualized desktop of computer to use desktop safely and flexibly. As it is a server-based computational model which uses traditional thin client, users can acquire the user experience in conformity with traditional PC in local area networks or remote access via thin client or similar device. In short, VDI refers to the technology which can be used to support enterprises to achieve remote dynamic access of desktop system and centralized trusteeship of data center. In an obvious analogy, today, we can access our mail systems or net disk on the Internet anywhere anytime via any device; and in the future, we can access our personal desktop system on the Internet anywhere anytime via any device.

VDI changes users' desktop application system so that users feel like returning to the era of mainframe computer and users can remain their desktop operating system and application program, but actually, these cases refer to virtual computer operated based on server. By virtue of VDI, users can use thin client with low cost instead of traditional PC terminal.

4   Benefits Gained from VDI

4.1   More Flexible Access and Use

The whole process from the birth to promotion of IT goes along with a pair of contradictory: use and IT management. At the era of large-scale machine, use and management are performed in the computer room, although users are hard to use, it alleviates work load of administrator; with emerging of PC, users don't have to work in computer room and are easy to use IT, but administrators have to face complex management because the management is decentralized with decentralization of PC; even though management can be completed via network with appearance of network, the success rate is lower and management capacity is limited. And today, network access isn't bottleneck any more because the pair of contradictory is solved with VDI: users can remotely access desktop system and acquire the experience in conformity with PC and administrators can complete all management easily in data center. Therefore, VDI actually separates use from system management. The direct benefit gained from the point is that users are allowed to access desktop anywhere anytime via any device, so we can access our desktops via any one device which meets requirements. In this way, staff can't have to work overtime in the companies and can access the company desktop via device at home at home to continue to work and assure the data security.

4.2 Wider and Simple Terminal Equipment Support

As a mode of cloud computing, all computations are placed on the servers, the request for terminal equipment greatly reduces with no need for traditional desktop and note-book computers; as Wikipedia mentions, thin client goes back to our vision and smart phone, notebook, PC to be scrapped and TV can become available equipment which is the soul of cloud computing. Driven by virtual desktop, IT in enterprises will be-come more flexible and is easy to be used like television networks in the future. As computation is performed in computation centre, client witnesses lower pressure, simpler client can be widely applied, and terminal equipment can be widely selected and can meet different application needs.

4.3 Sharp Reduction in Cost of Purchasing and Maintaining Terminal Equipment

Simplifying IT architecture can reduce the cost of purchasing terminal equipment. Let's take thin client as an example, the cost of purchasing thin client is about RMB 2,000 and the price of PC is about RMB 4,000 at present, so each client can save RMB 2,000 to be invested in physical servers. As per compression ratio of 1:1 (all people use virtual desktops at the same time), servers with amount of RMB 100,000 can load 50 virtual desktops and capitalized cost of hardware remain equal. However, the general compression ratio won't be 1:1 and above all, scrap cycle of thin client generally lasts for 6-8 years, twice of PC, so the phase II terminal investment directly decreases. Moreover, the existing PC system can greatly extend service cycle and can be transferred to common terminal if peripheral equipment is available to indirectly reduce the number of e-wastes.

4.4 Centralized Management, Unified Configuration and Safe Use

As the computation, all desktop management and configuration are performed in data center, administrators can perform unified configuration and management for all desktops and application in data center, such as system upgrade, application and in-stallation to avoid management difficulty and high cost caused by terminal distribu-tion. Particularly, it is very suitable for large-scale application places (frequently changing operating system) with volatile demand including computer rooms in colleges and universities and teaching centre. As what is transferred is only the final operating image and all data and computation are performed in data center, confidential data and information aren't required to be transferred via Internet to in-crease the security. What is more, these data aren't allowed to be downloaded to client via configuration to assure that users can't take away and spread confidential information.

4.5 Power Consumption Reduction, Energy Conservation and Emission Reduction

The traditional PC needs the power of above 200W, but thin client needs the power of about 25W, so the power can be saved one-tenth. In the meantime, computation pressure of server can lead to increase in power consumption to a certain extent, but it can be ignored compared to substantial quantity of clients. Therefore, electric charge can be decreased by about 90% annually. Power consumption reduction means the reduction of carbon emission and meets the requirements of low carbon era; meanwhile, the advantages of VDI are typical and are of scale effect, more terminals, more prominent benefits and advantages.

5 Conclusion

To sum up, the application of VDI can greatly simplify the complex management of multimedia computer room in colleges and universities, and meantime, as for different needs of computer room, can strengthen security and management, reduce cost and achieve flexible functions of multimedia computer room in colleges and universities. Consequently, we can foresee that with development and improvement of VDI, hardware cost constantly lowers, traditional multimedia computer room will gradually adopt VDI-based solution and VDI enjoys wider prospect.

References

1. Dong, X., et al.: Research of the Virtual Desktop Infrastructure. China Information Times (April 2010)
2. Yan, L., et al.: Research and Application of the Virtual Desktop Infrastructure. Electric Power Information Technology (August 2010)
3. Liu, J.: Analysis of VDI's Technology and Prospect. Computer Programming Skills & Maintenance (June 2010)
4. Shen, Y.: Application of Virtual Desktop Infrastructure in Colleges and Universities. Time Education (August 2010)

User Session Data based Web Applications Test with Cluster Analysis

Jin-hua Li and Dan-dan Xing

College of Information Engineering, Qingdao University,
Ningxia Road 308, 266071 Qingdao, China
lijh@qdu.edu.cn, qingdaoxdd@163.com

Abstract. The special features of heterogeneous components, frequent user interactions and the system dynamics cause new problems of testing web applications. With a little modification of the server configuration, log files that contain user interactions with a web application can be collected and used for the test purpose. The great issues of user session based software testing are how to effectively select an appropriate set of test data generated from such log files. The paper describes a method of using cluster techniques to partition user session data and to generate test cases for web applications. The key problems of object data types and dissimilarity definition for the special data of user sessions are elaborated. An algorithm of generating test cases from user session data is presented. The experiment with a real web application demonstrated the method's effectiveness in the code coverage and in the data reduction.

Keywords: user session, web application, cluster analysis, software test.

1 Introduction

The increasing deployment of web applications has produced a significant growth of the demand on tools and methodologies for systematic testing and validation. Broadly defined, a web application consists of a set of web pages and other components including web server, application server, network, HTTP, and a browser. A web page can be either static, in which case the content is fixed, or dynamic, the content of which may depend on the user inputs. Users of all over the world interact with the application server via a browser through the Internet. User input to a web application consists of both navigational requests and data provided often through forms, which eventually affect the state of the underlying code on the server. The input field names and their values, called name-value pairs, become part of the request parsed by scripts or the application server. A database is often queried in response to a request, resulting sometimes in dynamically generated HTML code (i.e., a new web page), which is presented to the user.

Although testing of web applications shares the same objectives of 'traditional' application testing, in most cases, traditional testing theories and methods cannot be directly used, because of the peculiarities and complexities of web applications. These include the heterogeneous components, frequent interactions of users with the application concurrently, and the system dynamics. For example, a web application is

G. Shen and X. Huang (Eds.): CSIE 2011, Part I, CCIS 152, pp. 415–421, 2011.

usually written in multi-programming language with the client in HTML and JavaScript, the application logics in PHP and the database in SQL.

To test a web application, man usually selects the test data as a scenario of user interaction with the application, namely a sequence of actions on the application. Designing and selecting effective large of test data, and setting up a test environment simulating the real operational one is a tough work of web application testing. To solve such issues, user session based techniques are recently adopted in the research field of web applications testing [1, 2, 3]. User session data which represent client interactions with application are recorded in web server log files. The data can be easily collected, reconstructed of HTTP requests as test cases and sent back to web applications. Usually a log file consists of millions of entries recording user behaviors with a web application. The key questions to be addressed for user session based testing approaches involve whether they can be cost-effective and what is a trade-off between costs and benefits.

This paper proposes a novel method of generating and selecting test cases from web log files. User session data are partitioned into equivalent groups with clustering analysis. Clustered data in each group are similar of covering the application code. Representatives of each group are selected as test cases for testing web application. The paper is structured as follows. Section 2 gives an overview of the background. Section 3 describes the method of testing data generation from a large amount of user session data with clustering analysis in details. Section 4 presents the design and results of our empirical study. Section 5 summarizes and discusses future work.

2 Background

2.1 User Session Based Web Applications Testing

A web server records each user actions with a web application in log files. A user session represents a serial of interactions with a web application from an individual user. The user session data consist of sequences of client requests made by users. Each sequence reports the static or dynamic pages the user visited together with the inputted data, as well as the data resulting from the elaboration of requests the user made. To transform a user session into a test case, each logged request of the user session is changed into an HTTP request which consists of a URL and name-value pairs. Each HTTP request is transformed into a test case using some strategy and then sent to the web server.

The main advantage of this approach is the possibility of generating test cases without analyzing the internal structure of the web application. In addition, generating test cases utilizing user session data is less dependent on the heterogeneous and fast changing technologies used by web applications. Empirical studies compared effectiveness of white box techniques and user session ones [3, 4].

However, the effectiveness of user session testing techniques depends on the set of user session data collected. There must be a tradeoff between test suite size and testing capacity. Key issues with respect to user session based web application testing are thus the selection and reduction methods of test case suites.

2.2 Cluster Analysis

Clustering analysis is the process of grouping the data into classes or clusters with no or little prior knowledge, so that objects within a cluster have high similarity in comparison to one another but are very dissimilar to objects in other clusters [5]. Similarity or dissimilarity is assessed based on the attributes describing the objects. The dissimilarity of objects with n attributes is measured using a dissimilarity metric, such as n-dimensional Minkowski distance or Euclidean distance.

Object attributes are very crucial to the effectiveness of clustering analysis. Elegant selection of attributes can greatly decrease the workload and simplify the subsequent design process. Ideal attributes should be useful in distinguishing objects belonging to different clusters, immune to noise, easy to extract and interpret.

A great number of clustering algorithms exist in the literature [6]. The comparative studies [6,7] show clearly that 1) no clustering algorithm can be universally used to solve all problems and that 2) attributes selection, extract and normalization are as important as clustering algorithms. Consequently, the aim of the current paper is not to find out the best clustering method of selecting user session data for testing web application. Instead, the paper investigates whether clustering methods are suitable for dividing user session set into equivalent groups of test data.

3 Constructing Test Suite from Log Files with Cluster Analysis

3.1 Concepts and Definitions

Definition 1: Client request is a HTTP request of resources on the server. The format of a client request r can be written as URL [name-value]*, where star * means that the name-value occurs zero or more times.

Definition 2: A basic request for a web application is the request type and resource location without associated data. Basic request of a client request is actually the name of the requiring method or function implemented in a web programming language in the URL, e.g. a method name with postfix .php in the paper.

Definition 3: User session is defined as a sequence of client requests on a server. Let r be a client request, the user session is written as $<r_1, r_2, ..., r_m>$, meaning that a user sends a serial of requests $r_1, r_2, ..., r_m$ one by one. Usually, a user session expresses the interaction with the application within a certain time range.

Definition 4: A test suite is defined as a set of user sessions with the response status code.

3.2 Data Type and Dissimilarity Measures

The attribute of user session data is a composite structure of ordered client requests. Each client request is a binary tuple: the first element is a string (basic request), the second is a group of name-value pairs (user inputs). The number of user inputs in any two client requests is not necessarily equal. The client request cannot be simply assigned with a single data type of binary, discrete or continuous.

Since the attribute values are used for comparison of any two objects, the absolute values are not obligatory. The sufficient and necessary condition when comparing any two user session data is that they difference can be quantified. Two client requests are equal if and only if they have the same basic request, the same parameters and the same values. We give the following definition.

Definition 5: Difference measure $d(r1, r2)$ of two client requests $r1$ and $r2$ is defined as the number of their different attributes / maximum of attributes in $r1$ and $r2$, wherein the basic request, each parameter name and the corresponding value are regarded as an independent attribute of a client request.

Now we can define the dissimilarity of two user sessions $us1$ and $us2$ $dist(us1, us2)$. Each client request is regarded as an attribute of the user session object. Considering that the number of client requests in user sessions may not be the same, we use the piecewise function to compute dissimilarity function.

Definition 6: For two user sessions $us1 = < r_1, r_2, ..., r_i >$ and $us2 = < r_1, r_2 ..., r_m >$ ($1 \leq i \leq m$), the dissimilarity is

$$dist(us_1, us_2) = \begin{cases} \sqrt{d(r_{11}, r_{21})^2 + ... + d(r_{1i}, r_{2i})^2}, & if \ i = m \\ \sqrt{d(r_{11}, r_{21})^2 + ... + d(r_{1j}, r_{2j})^2 + (m-i)^2}, & if \ i \neq m \ and \ j = \min(m, i) \end{cases} \tag{1}$$

3.3 Clustering User Session Data

We adopted k-medoids algorithm for clustering user session data as follows.

```
Algorithm KCUserSession (user session set, n, k)
// Input: a set of n user sessions { us₁,us₂,...,usₙ },
// the number of clusters k.
// Output: a set of k clusters.
Begin
(1) Arbitrarily choose k user sessions z₁,z₂,...,z_k as the
initial cluster centers from the user session set;
(2) Assign each user session us_i, i=1,...,n to cluster
C_j, j=1,...,k, iff
dist(us_j,z_i) < dist(us_m,z_i), m=1,...,k and m ≠ j
(3) Chose new cluster centers z'₁,z'₂,...,z'_k as follows
for each z'_ij ∈ C_i,i=1,...,k, j=1,...,n, and z'_ij ≠ z_i select such
z'_ij with the least cost, where
```

$$cost(i) = \frac{1}{n_i} \sum_{us_j \in C_i} dist(us_j, z'_{ij}), i = 1, ..., k \tag{2}$$

```
(4) If z'_i = z_i, i=1,...,k then terminate. Otherwise continue
from step (2).
End.
```

4   Experiments

Experiments are made to investigate the following research issues:

1) Can user session data be effectively and efficiently partitioned with clustering techniques? This issue is related with the k-medoids algorithm, the definition of dissimilarity, and the used data types.

2) Can the selected user sessions generated with the clustering algorithm serve as effective test data for web applications? To answer this question, we selected several metrics of testing coverage in the experiment.

The test target in our experiment is ifanr.com, a Chinese online community of Hi-tech super-fans. PHP is the main programming language. Before clustering techniques are applied, the log file data needs to be preprocessed. The data fields retained in log files were: IP address, time stamp, basic request, and name-value pairs if they exist. We used the log file recorded in October 2010. After the preprocessing, the original log file in size of 304MB was reduced to 26MB. Table 1 shows the metrics of the user session data.

Table 1. Metrics of the user session data

Metrics	Values
Total number of client requests	112,418
Total number of user sessions	8,107
Number of basic requests	901
Largest user session in number of client requests	73
Smallest user session in number of client requests	1
Average user session in number of client requests	14
Number of unique parameter-values	2,415

Metrics collection. Three metrics of validating test data effectiveness were chosen for the experiment: function coverage, block coverage and statement coverage. Besides, metrics related to cluster techniques and user sessions were also collected.

The open-source tool Spike PHPCoverage [8] is used to collect and report these metrics of each test execution. Each client request in the user session is built as a HTTP request and sent to infanr.com sequentially by Send HTTP Tool [9], an open source tool which automatically sends HTTP requests to the web server.

Generation of test suites. In order to compare the effect of cluster sizes on the testing data selection, we chose three values of k for the k-medoids clustering algorithm described above: 106, 71 and 53. A certain number of user sessions were randomly selected from each of the resulting clusters with the different k values so that the total number of test data is equal. In the study, 212 test data are selected for the k-medoids algorithm, where one user session was removed randomly from the test suite with k= 71 after the second procedure.

In the experiment, each test data generation algorithm was executed five times and the results were average of the runs. Table 2 summarizes the characteristics of the clustering analysis.

Table 2. Characteristics of the clustered user session data

Characteristics	K=106	K=71	K=53
Random selected test data from each cluster	2	3	4
Total number of client requests	3,439	3,842	4,102
Number of unique requests	23.30	23.41	23.30
Largest user session in number of requests	72.28	68.87	66.97
Smallest user session in number of requests	1.15	1.32	1.65
Average user session in number of requests	16.22	18.12	20.29
Number of unique parameter-values	219.55	204.66	199.59

A test suite were generated from each cluster of user sessions and then sent to ifanr.com with HTTP Send Tool. Table 3 displays the statistical data collected in the test execution.

Table 3. Code coverage of the test suites

	with language functions			without language functions		
	K=106	K=71	K=53	K=106	K=71	K=53
Function coverage	92.43%	90.81%	89.17%	98.37%	96.24%	92.47%
Block coverage	86.33%	84.74%	81.91%	92.33%	90.52%	87.98%
Statement coverage	78.43%	74.69%	71.36%	84.43%	80.82%	77.46%

Analysis of code coverage. With the determined number of test cases, none of the test suites cover all of the functions, blocks and statements in ifanr.com. By analyzing the source code, we found that some functions deal with multi-languages such as ru.php for Russian or es.php for Spanish, and they were not executed. If the language related functions are not taken into consideration, the measurements of the function coverage, block coverage and statement coverage increase accordingly.

The table indicates that the k-medoids algorithm really partitions the user sessions into similar groups. The coverage ratios in the larger cluster with k=53 are lower than the smaller cluster with k=106 or k=71. Although the number of randomly selected data in clusters with k=53 are two times of the data in clusters with k=106, their coverage ratios are not correspondingly doubled and halved. The tendency is clear that the large a cluster is, the smaller the data in the cluster can cover the program code. But we have not found the boundary values of the cluster size in the current experiment.

5 Conclusion and Future Work

The paper reports our work of testing web application based on user session data with clustering techniques. Less than 3% of the real user sessions are selected as test data with our algorithm. The experiment shows the usefulness of data normalization and the cluster analysis based test data generating method. The k-medoids algorithm divides the user session set into equivalent groups of test data that cover the web application code. Different cluster sizes produce different coverage ratios. The experiment showed that the large the number of clusters is, the more code will be covered and the more faults in the application will be possible discovered.

In the future, we will validate our method with the approach of seeding faults, by which specially devised faults are randomly seeded in an application and then tried to detect them with test data. Other scalable cluster techniques such as BIBCH, CLA-RANS and DBSCAN [5] will be studied and experimented in order to find more effective and efficient partitioning methods of user session data.

Acknowledgments. Thank Alex Zhang for providing the server log files and for setting up the experiment environment.

References

1. DiLucca, G.A., Fasolino, A.R.: Testing Web-based applications: The state of the art and future trends. Information and Software Technology 48, 1172–1186 (2006)
2. Elbaum, S., Rothermel, G., Karre, S., Fisher II, M.: Leveraging user session data to support web applications testing. IEEE Transactions on Software Engineering 31(3), 187–202 (2005)
3. Wang, W.H., Sampath, S., Lei, Y., Kacker, R.: An Interaction-Based Test Sequence Generation Approach for Testing Web Applications. In: 11th IEEE High Assurance Systems Engineering Symposium, Nanjing, China, pp. 2009–2018 (2008)
4. Sprenkle, S., Gibson, E., Sampath, S., Pollock, L.: A Case Study of Automatically Creating Test Suites from Web Application Field Data. In: Workshop on Testing, Analysis, and Verification of Web Services and Applications, Portland, Maine, pp. 1–9 (2006)
5. Gan, G., Ma, C., Wu, J.: Data Clustering: Theory, Algorithms, and Applications. SIAM-ASA, Philadelphia (2007)
6. Xu, R., Wunsch II, D.: Survey of clustering algorithms. IEEE Transactions on Neural Networks 16(3), 645–678 (2005)
7. Budayan, C., Dikmen, I., Talat, B.M.: Comparing the performance of traditional cluster analysis, self-organizing maps and fuzzy C-means method for strategic grouping. Expert Systems with Applications 36, 11772–11781 (2009)
8. Spike PHPCoverage, http://gcov.php.net
9. Send HTTP Tool, http://soft-net.net/SendHTTPTool.aspx

Wavelet Packet Transform and Support Vector Machine Based Discrimination of Roller Bearings Fault

Yun-Jie Xu and Shu-Dong Xiu

School of Engineering, Zhejiang Agricultural & Forestry University,
Lin'an, China
xyj9000@163.com

Abstract. Fault diagnosis of roller bearings is very complex, so it is difficult to use the mathematical model to describe their faults. The fault diagnosis methods of ball bearing based on Wavelet packet transform with entropy features and support vector machine (SVM) are proposed in this paper. Wavelet packets have greater decor relation properties than standard wavelets in that they induce a finer partitioning of the frequency domain of the process generating the data. A two cycles of ball bearing fault current data is processed through wavelet packet transform to obtain wavelet coefficients and then Energy eigenvector of frequency domain are extracted by using Shannon entropy principle. Subsequently, the extracted Energy eigenvector of frequency domain are applied as inputs to SVM for roller bearings from internal fault. Fault state of ball bearing is identified by using radial basis function genetic-support vector machine. The results of the proposed new technique were found to be reliable, fast and accurate in identifying the fault condition.

Keywords: roller bearings; wavelet packet transform; fault diagnosis; support vector machine.

1 Introduction

Roller bearings are frequently applied components in the vast majority of rotating machines. Their running quality influences the working performance of equipment. Noise is the biggest obstacle that makes the incipient fault diagnosis results of roller bearings uncorrected; the diagnosis for roller bearings of wood-wool working device is a complicated non-linear system, whose developmental changes have dual trends of increase and fluctuation, so it is difficult to use the mathematical model to describe their faults [1].

Support vector machine (SVM) based on statistical learning theory is used in many applications of machine learning because of its good generalization capabilities. SVM classifies better than artificial neural network (ANN) because of the principle of risk minimization. In ANN, traditional empirical risk minimization (ERM) is used on training data set to minimize the error. But in SVM, structural risk minimization (SRM) is used to minimize an upper bound on the expected risk [2, 3, 4]. These parameters of SVM mainly include the penalty constant C, and the parameters in kernel function, and they affect the performance of SVM.

G. Shen and X. Huang (Eds.): CSIE 2011, Part I, CCIS 152, pp. 422–428, 2011.
© Springer-Verlag Berlin Heidelberg 2011

Wavelet analysis possesses excellent characteristic of time-frequency localization and is suitable for analyzing the time-varying or transient signals. However, genetic-support vector machine (GSVM) is successful in recognizing non-linear system and classifying pattern. Genetic-support vector machine (GSVM) intelligence diagnostic model has been established with the above principle, and it has been used in rolling bearing's failure diagnosis. According to the vibration signal features of frequency-domain, energy eigenvector was established by means of wavelet packet. Then recognition of fault pattern of rolling bearing was presented using Genetic-support vector machine (GSVM). Therefore, in this study, The high frequency demodulation analysis was used to abstract the characteristic of signals, The signals were decomposed into eight frequency bands and the information in the high band was used as a characteristic vector, an intelligent diagnostic method based on genetic-support vector machine (GSVM) approach is presented for fault diagnosis of roller bearings in the wood-wool production device. The test results show that this GSVM model is effective to detect failure of roller bearings in the wood-wool production device. The experimental result shows that the system can not only detect the fault of bearing but also can recognize fault pattern correctly.

2 Principle of Wavelet Packet Transform and Feature Extraction

The structure of wavelet packet transform (WPT) is similar to discrete wavelet transform (DWT). Both have the framework of multi-resolution analysis (MRA). The main difference in the two techniques is the WPT can simultaneously break up detail and approximation versions, but DWT only breaks up an approximation version. Therefore, the WPT have the same frequency bandwidths in each resolution and DWT does not have this property. The mode of decomposition does not increase or lose the information within the original signals. Therefore, the signal with great quantity of middle and high frequency signals can offer superior time-frequency analysis. The WPT suits signal processing especially no stationary signals because the same frequency bandwidths can provide good resolution regardless of high and low frequencies. The principle of WPT can be described as follows[9].

$$W^n j,k(t) = 2^{j/2} W^n (2^j t - k) \tag{1}$$

Where the integers j, k -index scale and translation operations. The index n is an operation modulation parameter (or) oscillating parameter. The first wavelet packet functions are scaling and mother wavelet functions:

$$W^0 0,0(t) = \phi(t) \tag{2}$$

$$W^1 0,0(t) = \psi(t) \tag{3}$$

The equation (2) and (3) represents scaling and mother wavelet functions respectively.

Where $n=2, 3\ldots$ the function can be defined by following recursive relation ship:

$$W^{2n}0,0(t) = \sqrt{2}\sum_{k} h(k)W1,k(2t-k) \tag{4}$$

$$W^{2n+1}0,0(t) = \sqrt{2}\sum_{k} g(k)W1,k(2t-k) \tag{5}$$

Where $h(k)$ and $g(k)$ are the quadrature mirror filter (QMF) associated with the predefined scaling function and mother wavelet function. The wavelet packet coefficients, $W^{n}j,k$ are computed by the inner product $<f(t), W^{n}j,k>$ where defined as

$$W^{n}j,k \leq f(t)W^{n}j,k \geq \int f(t)W^{n}j,k(t)d_{t} \tag{6}$$

The framework of WPT algorithm broken up to three resolution levels is shown in the Figure.1 In this present study, the transformer fault cases will be broken up to third resolution. WPT framework is broken up to third resolution levels $j=3$, as a result, three resolutions will produces 8 subspaces ($2^{j} =2^{3} =8$) and wavelet frequency intervals of each subspace can be computed by

$$((n-1)2^{-j-1}f_{s}, n2^{-j-1}f_{s}), n = 0,1,2,\cdots 7$$

Where f_{s} is the sampling frequency. In this study $f_{s} =10KHz$. $X(n)$ is the original signal with the frequency [$0.2^{-1}f_{s}$]. The frequency interval of 1st and last node in the 3rd resolution is given by [0-625Hz] and [4375-5000 KHz] as given in Table.1 respectively. Width of each frequency band 625Hz.

3   Fault Diagnosis for Roller Bearings Based on Genetic Classifier

3.1   Support Vector Machine

The main aim of an SVM classifier is obtaining a function f(x) which is use to determine the decision hyper plane. Margin is the distance from the hyper plane to the closest point for both classes of data points.

Given a training data set $\{(x_{i}, y_{i})\}_{i}^{n}$, where $x_{i} \in R^{n}$ denotes the input vector, $y_{i} \in R$ denotes the corresponding output value and n denotes the number of training data set. The regression function is defined as:

$$f(x) = w \cdot \varphi(x) + b \tag{10}$$

where w denotes the weight vector and b denotes the bias term.

The coefficients w and b can thus be gained by minimizing the regularized risk function.

$$R(C) = C\frac{1}{n}\sum_{i=1}^{n} L_{\varepsilon}(y) + \frac{1}{2}\|w\|^{2} \tag{11}$$

$$L_\varepsilon(y) = \begin{cases} |f(x)-y|-\varepsilon & |f(x)-y| \geq \varepsilon \\ 0 & |f(x)-y| < \varepsilon \end{cases}$$

where C denotes a cost function measuring the empirical risk. $\|w\|^2/2$ denotes the Euclidean norm. The ε-insensitive loss function is employed to stabilize estimation.

The Lagrange multipliers a_i and a_i^* are introduced, which satisfy the equalities $a_i \cdot a_i^* = 0$, $a_i \geq 0$, $a_i^* \geq 0$. This constrained optimization problem is solved using the following Lagrange form:

Maximize

$$-\sum_{i=1}^{n} y_i(a_i - a_i^*) + \varepsilon \sum_{i=1}^{n}(a_i + a_i^*) + \frac{1}{2}\sum_{i,j}^{n} (a_j - a_j^*)(a_i - a_i^*)k(x_i,x_j) \qquad (12)$$

Subject to

$$\sum_{i=1}^{n}(a_i - a_i^*) = 0 \quad a_i, a_i^* \in [0,C]$$

where $K(x_i,x_j) = \varphi(x_i)\varphi(x_j)$ is positive definite kernel function. The kernel function can have different forms, and at present, Gaussian function is the most widely used.

Hence, the regression function is:

$$f(x) = \sum_{i=1}^{n}(a_i - a_i^*)k(x_i,x) + b \qquad (13)$$

3.2 Optimum Classification by Using GSVM Algorithm

Genetic algorithms are inspired by theory of evolution. The problems are solved by the process results in genetic algorithm. The generalization ability of the SVM is controlled by the three parameters C, σ (σ is the width of Gaussian function) and ε. Inappropriate parameters in SVM lead to over-fitting. To construct the SVM model efficiently, SVM's parameters C, σ and ε must be set carefully. So the proposed GA-SVM model dynamically optimizes the values of SVM's parameters C, σ and ε, where genetic algorithm is used to search for better combinations of the parameters in SVM. As shown in Fig.1, the framework of optimizing the SVM's parameters with genetic algorithm is presented; Outline of the basic genetic algorithm can be summarized below:

Step 1. Code SVM's parameters

The training parameters C, σ are represented by a chromosome composed of binary numbers.

Step 2. Initialize a population of chromosomes

The fitness values of chromosomes are calculated. If the fitness value of a chromosome is the more suitable, it has more chances for reproduce.

Step 3. Calculate the fitness function of chromosomes

Selection, crossover and mutation are operated in GSVM. It is selected two parent chromosomes from a population according to their fitness. Chromosomes are randomly selected and replaced each other for crossover operations. The bit inversion method is used for mutation operator.

Step 4. Genetic algorithm operators: selection, crossover, and mutation operation

In this study, the election of the training parameters in genetic algorithm operators. Selection is performed to reproduce excellent chromosomes according to their fitness. Crossover is performed randomly to exchange genes between two chromosomes using scattered crossover. The bit inversion method is used for mutation operator. A new population in the next generation is formed by the operations. The evolutionary process proceeds until stop conditions are satisfied.

3.3 Fault Diagnosis for Roller Bearings Based on Genetic-SVM Classifier

The accurate diagnosis of rolling beating was studied. The high frequency demodulation analysis was used to abstract the characteristic of signals[7]. The signals were decomposed into eight frequency bands and the information in the high band was used as a characteristic vector. GSVM were used to realize the map between the feature and diagnosis. Based on the characteristics of different fault types of roller bearings, three SVM's are developed to identify the four states, including normal, ball fault, outer ring fault, inner ring fault, which is shown in Fig.2. With all training samples of the four states, GSVM1 is trained to separate normal state from fault states. With samples of fault states, GSVM2 is trained to separate discharge from thermal heating.

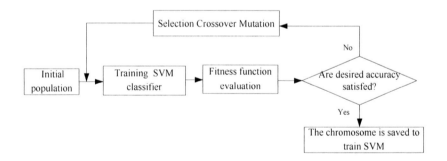

Fig. 1. The framework of optimizing the SVM's parameters with genetic algorithm

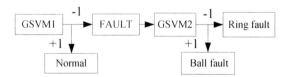

Fig. 2. Fault diagnosis for gearbox based on genetic-SVM classifier

4   Experimental Results

The training data are shown in Tab.1, and testing data are shown in Tab.2. The kernel function parameter and soft margin constant C penalty parameter of support vector machine classifier are selected by GA. The test results show that this GSVM model is effective to detect failure of roller bearings in the wood-wool production device.

Table 1. The training data

Frequency band /Hz								Actual state
Node (3,0)	Node (3,1)	Node (3,2)	Node (3,3)	Node (3,4)	Node (3,5)	Node (3,6)	Node (3,7)	
0~ 625	625~ 1250	1250~ 1875	1875~ 2500	2500~ 3125	3125~ 3750	3750~ 4375	4375~ 5000	
0.129	0.128	0.036	0.057	0.149	0.089	0.147	0.034	Normal
0.089	0.176	0.104	0.082	0.113	0.103	0.066	0.078	Normal
0.146	0.086	0.132	0.104	0.076	0.032	0.025	0.103	Normal
0.206	0.307	0.108	0.109	0.676	0.973	0.894	0.579	Ball fault
0.182	0.201	0.304	0.065	0.772	0.865	0.973	0.672	Ball fault
0.086	0.083	0.205	0.243	0.676	0.587	0.764	0.724	Ball fault
0.495	0.956	0.578	0.496	0.102	0.147	0.189	0.176	Ring fault
0.962	0.473	0.115	0.097	0.1425	0.062	0.227	0.364	Ring fault
0.526	0.544	0.676	0.378	0.104	0.112	0.201	0.077	Ring fault

Table 2. The testing data

Frequency band /Hz								Actual state	Diagnostic results
0~ 625	625~ 1250	1250~ 1875	1875~ 2500	2500~ 3125	3125~ 3750	3750~ 4375	4375~ 5000		
0.138	0.179	0.088	0.214	0.043	0.090	0.085	0.060	Normal	Normal
0.259	0.200	0.049	0.005	0.022	0.007	0.089	0.230	Ball fault	Ball fault
0.151	0.248	0.082	0.036	0.032	0.033	0.038	0.152	Ring fault	Ring fault

5   Conclusion

When there are incipient faults of roller bearings, very weak fault feature signals are often inundated with vibration signals and noise, the de-noising of the vibration signal is a main approach of diagnosing incipient fault of roller bearings. In this paper, an intelligent diagnostic method based on genetic-support vector machine approach is presented for fault diagnosis of roller bearings. The GSVM selects kernel function parameter and soft margin constant C penalty parameter of support vector machine classifier. The test results show that this GSVM model is effective to detect failure of roller bearings in the wood-wool production device.

References

1. Gong, h.-c.: Fault identification in gearbox based on Elman neural network. Lifting the Transport Machinery 5, 70–73 (2009)
2. Zhang, Y., Liu, X.-D., Xie, F.-D., Li, K.-Q.: Fault classifier of rotating machinery based on weighted support vector data description. Expert Systems with Applications 36(4), 7928–7932 (2009)
3. Yélamos, I., Escudero, G., Graells, M., Puigjaner, L.: Performance assessment of a novel fault diagnosis system based on support vector machines. Computers & Chemical Engineering. Expert Systems with Applications 33(1), 244–255 (2009)
4. Ekici, S.: Classification of power system disturbances using support vector machines. Expert Systems with Applications 36(6), 9859–9868 (2009)
5. Zhu, Y.-s., Zhang, Y.-y.: The study on some problems of support vector classifier. Computer Engineering and Applications 11(13), 36–38 (2003)
6. Cen, X.-h., Xiong, X.-y.: Fault diagnosis of ball bearing based on wavelet and radial bas is function neural networks. Mechanical Engineering & Automation 134(1), 13–15 (2006)
7. Wang, G.-f., Wang, Z.-l.: Accurate diagnosis of roller bearings based on wavelet packet and RBF neural networks. Journal of University of Science and Technology Beijing 26(2), 184–187 (2004)
8. Pentersen, J.C.: Asphalt oxidation-an overview including a new model for oxidation proposing that physicochemical factors dominate the oxidation kinetics. Fuel Sci. and Technol. 11(1), 57–87 (1993)
9. Wu, J.-D., Liu, C.-H.: An expert system for fault diagnosis in internal combustion engines using WPT and NN. Expert Systems with Applications 36(3), 4278–4286 (2009)

Video Vehicle Inspection Combined with Fiber Grating Pressure Sensor for Vehicle Heavy Identification

Tian Xia[1] and Mingmin Yao[2]

[1] Wuhan Charges Management Centre of Urban Road&Bridge,
Wuhan, 430000, China
[2] Wuhan University of Technology,
Wuhan, 430000, China

Abstract. This paper describes a vehicle heavy identification method, which use of both video vehicle inspection and fiber grating pressure sensor. In this method, firstly, video vehicle inspection system is used to find the target vehicle in the area which fiber grating sensors been buried in. Then the stress testing systems is driven by the recognition results. If there is vehicle in the area, we collect data from fiber grating pressure sensor, analyze the wavelength variation curves, and calculate the weight of the target, which decide what to do at the next step. This method can reduce the fiber grating sensor data collection frequency and effectively avoid false detection of fiber grating sensors.

Keywords: video vehicle inspection; fiber grating pressure sensor; Vehicle Heavy Identification.

1 Introduction

With the city's prosperity and development, pressure on urban traffic is increasing. The control of heavy vehicle traffic can effectively reduce the generation of urban roads disease to decrease the road running costs, and alleviate the severe traffic environment in cities., Artificial control used at the early period not only had a large economic cost ,but also worked inefficiently. The vehicles heavy automatic identification system has being widely used currently.

In most of the vehicle heavy identification system, people usually use pressure sensors for original data collection. In this paper, we choose the fiber grating pressure sensor, because of its better ability to adapt to environment and more powerful data transfer capability. However, in practice, fiber grating pressure sensor is not perfect. In some application environments, for example, when be used on bridges or overpasses, due to the self-vibration of roads or other environment factors, the data from

G. Shen and X. Huang (Eds.): CSIE 2011, Part I, CCIS 152, pp. 429–435, 2011.

fiber grating pressure sensors maybe exists serious distortion, which cause false detection results. Taking the above factors into account, we propose a vehicle heavy identification method combined with the video vehicle inspection and the fiber optic grating sensor. This method collect data from fiber grating pressure sensors only when there do have targets in the monitoring areas, effectively avoiding false alarms caused by external environment.

Then, we will discuss in detail the implementation of the system from two aspects: the implementation of video vehicle inspection, and the implementation fiber Bragg Grating sensor data acquisition and processing.

2   Video Vehicle Inspection

2.1   Introduction to the Principles of Video Vehicle Inspection

The main purpose of video vehicle inspection is to identify the target vehicle in the monitor area. The identification process can be divided into image acquisition and image detection in two parts.

In this video vehicle inspection system, we collect image data by a two channels video capture card and two cameras. In the pilot project, our application environment is a two-way six-lane bridge, each camera is responsible for the image data collection for three lanes with the same direction.

In the image detection part, we choose a kind of difference method[1] for the detection of the image data. We will get each real-time image frame and background image difference to find out the target.

2.2   Background Image Reconstruction

We also use a kind of difference method to reconstruct the background image[2]. Firstly, get a set of image sequences V_n by the video capture card. In this process, the default values of the collected intervals of image sequence and the number n of frames of image sequence can be changed according to actual situation. Then, get the adjacent two images of image sequence difference to obtain a difference image sequence D_{n-1}, $D_i = D_{i+1} - D_i (i=1,2,...n-1)$. At the next step, we deal with D_{n-1} by a binarization method and remove noise in the binary difference image sequence by Median filter. For every pixel at the same location in the difference image sequence, find the longest difference image sequence, in which the images are continuous and have a zero value at the pixel. Choose the image in the middle D_i ($0<i<=n$) of the longest difference image sequence, set the pixel in background image by the value if the corresponding pixel in V_i. At the end, we set all the pixels in background image, so we finish the background image reconstruction.

Program flow chart of background image reconstruction shown in Figure 1:

Fig. 1. Program flow chart of background image reconstruction

2.3 Target Identification

The steps of target identification algorithm are as follows: getting the current image; subtracting the background image from current image to get the difference image; obtaining binary image; counting the number of pixels which have the non-zero value, if the number is greater than a threshold value, update the background image and check the current image again; if not, we think there has a target when the number of non-zero pixels in a monitoring area is greater than a threshold value, otherwise, the result is no target.

In order to improve the real time response feature of results, we use multi-threading technology. One thread is for collecting the images, and the other one is used to handle images. The two threads are running at the same time. Compared to a single thread for sequentially dealing with image capture and image detection, multi-threaded approach makes our system has better real-time feature, provides more reaction time for driving sensor. Especially when the system is running in multi-core computer, this advantage reflects the more pronounced. In the pilot project, we set the detection frequency is 100 ms/frame, that is to say, we collect an image per 100ms. According to the final experimental test results, image processing thread can complete the processing of the current image within 100ms. Of course, testing frequency can also adjust depending on the actual application environment. For the environment of pilot project, because we want to base on test results to drive the fiber grating sensors, 100 ms/frame is a reasonable value. It's not too fast to cause detection lag behind acquisition, and not too slow to missing a target.

There are some details need our in-depth discussion. When the test results show a target vehicle in monitoring area, should we drive the sensor immediately? Seemingly yes, but, actually we also need to take the condition that the same car staying in the area into account, because this condition may cause dealing with a same target many times, which can reduce the efficiency of the system. To solve this problem, we hope that the system deal with the target when it get into the area, and do nothing when the target leave or stay in the area. Then, the real problem is how to recognize the status of the target. We can find the answer from the following table 1:

Table 1. The current target's state table

	Previous frame	Current frame	Final state
results of each frame Y:exist target N: not exist target)	Y	Y	staying
	Y	N	leaving
	N	Y	coming
	N	N	

When both of the frames get Y, we consider they have the same target, but, does there have the probability that they are two different targets? If yes, the target in current frame must get into the area in 100ms after the target in previous frame leaving. To analyze this problem, we assume that the vehicle speed is 108km / h, video image sampling frequency is 100ms/frame. During 100ms, the target can move 3m, that is to say, the answer is yes just when the distance between two targets less than 3m. But, in the real environment, keeping 3m distance under the speed of 108km/h is impossible. So, the answer is no.

When the two frame get N, does there have the probability that we miss a target? If yes, the target must get into and leave the area in 100ms. We just assume a limit state: the width of the area is zero, so if we do missing a target, the target must move a distance at least equal to the length of itself in 100ms. According to our analysis of the above, at the speed of 108km/h, the length of the target has to shorter than 3m. But, actually, most of the cars' lengths are longer than 3m. So the answer is no, too. Specific program flow chart is shown in Figure 2.

3   Fiber Grating Sensor Processing Module

When the server get the result of Video vehicle inspection system, it drives the fiber grating sensor to collect data, and then calculate the target's weight based on this data [3]. The next step of the server is depended on the target's weight.

Fiber grating pressure sensors are embedded in the monitoring area in advance, the pressure on sensors will change when a target passing by the monitoring area. And this change causes the wavelength's change of reflected light. We can use equation (1) to calculate the current target's weight:

$$Weight = (max(\nabla\lambda) - min(\nabla\lambda)) * T \tag{1}$$

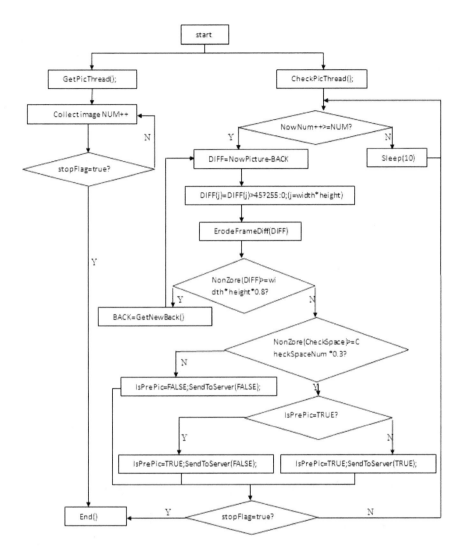

Fig. 2. Image detection module's flowchart

In this equation, weight means the weight of the current car; $\nabla\lambda$ stands for the data we get from the sensor during the time target staying in the area; T is the corresponding weight of a unit transformation of the wavelength, which is decided by the load test in advance.

Of course, in fact, not only the passing of car can lead to the change of the reflected light's wavelength[4], but also the shaking of roads or another factors can lead to it. After the sensors sending us the data, if we consider the data causing by cars without taking the other reasons into account, there must be lots of wrong results, which will seriously affect the actual application results[5]. In this system, we distinguish the situation by the video vehicle inspection, and collect and deal with data just when there a target exists in the area by fiber grating sensor processing module. The combined of these two modules can improve the accuracy of the system to a large extent. The program flow chart of fiber grating sensor processing module is shown in Figure 3.

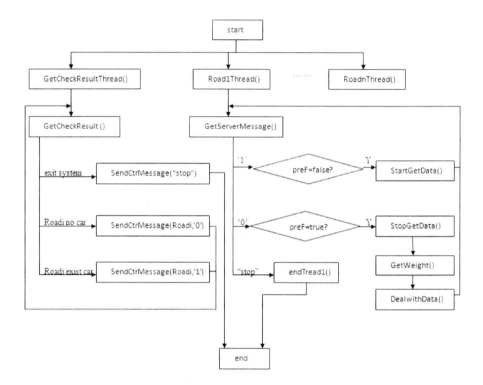

Fig. 3. Fiber grating sensor processing module's program flow chart

4   Conclusion

At present, the method provided in this paper has been tested in a bridge health monitoring system, and the experimental result is very good to some extent. That is to say, this method is useful. The high-quality basis data can make the system work better for the next step.

References

1. Wang, B., Jia, K.: Synthetic Algorithm of Vehicle Flow Detection Based on Video Analysis. Journal of Transport Information and Safety 28(1) (2010)
2. Luo, D., Yu, Z., et al.: Application of edge-based background difference in traffic volume extraction. OPTO-Electronic Engineering 34(11) (2007)

3. Li, T.-x., Li, C., Meng, L.: The Sensing Principle and Structure of Fiber Bragg Grating Sensor. Infrared Technology 32(7) (2010)
4. Zhou, Q., Ning, T.: Research in demodulation methods of FBG sensor. Optical Communication Technology 34(8) (2010)
5. Melle, S.M., Liu, K., Measures, R.M.: A passive wavelength demodulation system for guided wave Bragg grating sensors. IEEE Photon. Technol. Lett. 23(12), 1424–1428 (2003)

Crowd Evacuating Process Model with Cellular Automata Based on Safety Training

Shi Xi Tang and Ke Ming Tang

YanCheng Teachers University Information Science & Technology College,
YanCheng, JiangSu, China
tsxlyh@163.com, tkmchina@126.com

Abstract. To solve the problem that the crowd evacuating process model with cellular automata is quite different from the reality crowd evacuating process, the crowd evacuating process model with cellular automata based on safety training is addressed. The crowd evacuating process based on safety training is simulated and predicted, and the result is very close to the reality. Using the vertical way to place the shelves gets both a higher escaping rate and a larger shelf area that the total area is up to $216m^2$, and the average death number is 4.2 by safety training when the fire level being 2.

Keywords: Cellular Automata; Fire; Crowd Evacuation; Safety Training.

1 Introduction

In recent years, Manny types of natural disasters and man-made events from the United States 911 events to China WenChuan earthquake occurred; it strengthened the study of crowd emergency evacuating process. The key of emergency evacuation modeling is crowd evacuation modeling; its essence is the pedestrian flow model implementation in a specific environment. A model that can describe the evacuation accurately is needed to simulate hundreds of thousands of human activities on the computer. Cellular automata as a mathematical model framework which time, space, states are discrete has strong ability to simulate various physical systems and natural phenomena by constructing the dynamic evolution system through the interaction between elements. A series results about pedestrian evacuation simulation based on cellular automata have been gained, which are two floors field model proposed by C. Bur stedde and Kirchner[1], discrete social force model proposed by L. Z. Yang[2], and dynamic parameters model proposed by Hao Yue[3]. These cellular automata models can simulate the macro evacuation characteristics, which are jamming and clogging, faster-is-slower [1-4].

All evacuation models have a common problem that we try to build complex real-life evacuation model by using cellular automata assumed to be random, without any training, and having the crowd with a variety of complex psychological. All these are the most complex phenomenon of life which is possible to achieve by using the fourth cellular automata model at the edge of chaos. But the various results are studied based on elementary cellular automaton mode, which are the theoretical reasons that can not completely describe the objects' portraits. The crowd evacuating process model with

G. Shen and X. Huang (Eds.): CSIE 2011, Part I, CCIS 152, pp. 436–441, 2011.

cellular automata based on safety training (**EPMCAST**) is raised in this paper to study the evacuating process by using elementary cellular automata, and the simulating and predicting results are more realistic than other models.

2   EPMCAST Model

Cellular automata is a time and space discrete power system, each cell distributed in the regular grid takes in the finite discrete state following the same effect, updating synchronously according to the local rules. A large number of cellular constitute the evolution of dynamic system by simple interacting. Cellular automaton consists of the basic cell, cellular space, neighborhood and rules. Cellular automata can be considered as a cellular space and a transformation function in the space, which can be expressed by a four-tuple [5]:

$$A= (d, S, N, f)$$

Dimension of cellular automaton is d, S is the finite and discrete status set of cellular, N is a combination of cellular in neighborhood space, f is the rule of change, is a conversion function. Unlike the general dynamic model, cellular automata are not strictly defined by the physical equation or function, but by a series of rules constructed with model. Models to meet all of these rules can be counted as a cellular automaton model. Therefore, the cellular automata model is a general term for the kind of models, or a methodological framework characterized by discrete time, space and states. Each variable takes only a finite number of states, and the rules changing the state are local in time and space. We need to construct cellular automaton according to the actual research questions for there is no fixed mathematical formula.

2.1   Selecting Cell for EPMCAST

The grid of cellular automata includes the grid number, grid size and its boundary conditions. The number and size of the grid based on simulation of the needs. The two-dimensional grid structure is usually triangular, square and hexagonal [6].

Cellular automata adjacent space is named neighborhood, two-dimensional cellular neighborhood types are Moore-type, extended type and Margolus Moore type. EPMCAST considers not only the spread of fire, but also the evacuation. The impact of safety training including the command role of training staff to assure a reasonable direction, to ensure an orderly evacuation, and to ensure the protecting of fire and smoke in the evacuating process, so that minimize the victims. We use the quadrilateral grid-type structure and the eight direction neighborhood of Moore-type and extended Moore-type as the cellular model in EPMCAST. The eight direction neighborhood of Moore-type is used to determine the direction of the direction of fire spread and evacuation, and the extended Moore-type is used to select the reasonable direction for evacuation.

2.2   Replacement Model for Fire Spreading

The fire spreading state of cellular A_{ij} is among 0 (not burning), 1 (not burning), 2 (just burn), 3 (burning) and 4 (off). The main factors affecting the fire spread include the role of thermal radiation, the characteristics of buildings, the role of large fire retardant elements, and the environmental impact. The probability of Cellular (i, j) fire occurrence is

$$Q_{ij} = W_{ij} \cdot A_{ij} \cdot L_{ij} \cdot H_{ij}$$

W_{ij} is the wind load effects, A_{ij} is the impact indicators of building structure, L_{ij} is the impact indicators for the fire load, H_{ij} is the collapsed factor coefficients by considering the fire performance requirements and the risk factor coefficients of building, and their values see [7,8]. Replacement of fire spreading is complied by taking larger adjacent cellular Q_{ij}.

2.3   The Solution of Preference Matrix for EPMCAST

The probability of movement of crowd in different directions in the cellular space (i.e. building) is signed with preference matrix M as shown in Figure 1. Preference matrix element values are determined with the velocity v and the direction standard deviation σ [9]. Two-dimensional cellular M_{ii} is composed of two one-dimensional cellular, representing horizontal and vertical movements respectively. Horizontal one-dimensional cellular neighborhood I is expressed as $\{-1, 0, 1\}$, the probability the cellular moving toward neighborhood is p_i (p_{-1}, p_0, p_1), the probability of vertical cellular automata is q_i (q_{-1}, q_0, q_1), which values are determined by the cellular current moving velocity v and the direction standard deviation σ.

$M_{-1,-1}$	$M_{-1,0}$	$M_{-1,1}$
$M_{0,-1}$	$M_{0,0}$	$M_{0,1}$
$M_{1,-1}$	$M_{1,0}$	$M_{1,1}$

Fig. 1. The preference matrix M in different direction in cellular space

$M_{ij}=q_i \times p_j$

And

$q_i : q_{-1}=\sigma_t^2/2 \qquad q_0= 1 -\sigma_t^2 \qquad q_1=\sigma_t^2/2$
σ_t is the standard deviation of the vertical direction
$p_j : p_{-1}= (\sigma_h^2+v^2-v)/2 \quad p_0= 1 - (\sigma_h^2+v^2) \quad p_1= (\sigma_h^2+v^2+v)/2$
σ_h is the standard deviation of horizontal direction
Standard direction deviation σ is determined by the current cellular moving velocity, the effective value interval of σ is $[\sigma_l, \sigma_k]$, computing as
$\sigma_l^2= [|v| -1/2]^2/4 \qquad \sigma_k^2= 1 -v^2$

Cellular choose the target cell location in the next time according to the preference matrix, cell states are updated paralleling. If the target cellular locations are occupied in the current time, time the current cellular does not move during the next moment. If the target cell is not occupied, A lot of cellular may choose the same target element cellular location next time according to the preference matrix, which may result in conflict, and this is solved by calculating the relative movement probability of each cellular to determine which cell movement, which cell does not move.

2.4 Obtaining the Relative Movement Probability of Cellular of EPMCAST

When more than one cellular compete in the same grid at the same time, only one cellular left, the others continue to find the best location in accordance with the current obtained moving direction, the probability coming in position (0, 0) by the surrounding cellular is

$$p(i, j) = \frac{k_{i,j} \bullet M_{i,j}}{M_{1,-1} + M_{1,0} + M_{0,-1} + M_{0,1} + M_{-1,1} + M_{-1,1} + M_{-1,0} + M_{-1,1}}$$

k_{ij} is training factor of moving cellular (i , j), the evacuation crowd do not panic and do not crowded, knowing the fire exits location and the expanding trend of fire and smoking due to staff training, and its function is

$$k_{ij} = d_{smoke-m} \bullet \min_{l}(\sqrt{(i_p - i_l)^2 + (j_p - j_l)^2} \bullet \sqrt{(i_m - i_l)^2 + (j_m - j_l)^2})$$

(i_p, j_p) is the current cellular location, (i_l, j_l) is the possible export position, (i_m, j_m) is the last person position of current from the potential export positions, dsmoke is the of degree of fire and smoking in position (i_m, j_m). The person position in the grid is relocated after each crowd's time step is updated. This procedure is continued until all crowd are evacuated out of the building or burned up.

3   Implementation of EPMCAST

We take fire evacuation of Times Mall of Yancheng City, Jiangsu Province as the actual background, and resulting in the best way to place shelves with maximum shelf space and minimum fire casualties. The intermediate fire is often took place in Yancheng. Power supply room is the most vulnerable to fire in Times Mall. The safety export numbers must be greater than two according to state regulations. There are two security exports in Times Mall, one is the elevator, and the other is the stairs, but the former can not be used when fire broke, so the latter is considered. We suppose shelves and cashier are making in metal, and non-combustible. The fire

Table 1. Different shelve placing style

the shelve No.	shelve placing style	the total area (m^2)
1	horizontal	14 * 16 = 224
2	horizontal	14 * 14 = 196
3	vertical	24 * 8 = 192
4	vertical	24 * 9 = 216
5	vertical	26 * 9 = 234
6	dispersed	18 * 7 = 126

equipments are failure in use for power failure when the fire occurs in power supply room. The fire is put out by fire brigade after all crowd escaped. We design six different shelve placing style by considering the various situations that may occur during fire escaping, considering the purpose for profit of shopping mall, according to architectural principles and fire escape means in public places as shown in table 1.

A two-dimensional global object array is constructed. Each object is assigned with a status obtained by scanning the array, status 0 means empty space, status 1 means crowd, status 2 means fire, status 3 means barrier. The bigger the number of fire level, the lighter the fire, and a serious fire is happened when we select 1. The bigger the number, the litter the number of crowd, a maximum crowd number is reached when we select 1.

The escaping person chooses the best path to escape based on knowledge of escape training according to the actual situation when the fire continued to spread. The crowding phenomenon is appeared when there is too much escaping crowd in one region, and the whole escape velocity is slow down, so the escaping person selects the path by judging the situation of all exports. The evacuation is completed in 86 seconds, the total number of crowd is 422 before the fire, the number of escaped crowd is 421, and the number of crowd killed in the fire is 1.

4   Analyzing the Simulation Results of EPMCAST

The escaping rate is different with the different shelf placing style, the simulation results by placing the same way for 5 times is shown in Table 2. The number of crowd in escaping is up to the limit, and the crowds in the Mall are in a random distribution.

Table 2. The evacuation simulation result of Yancheng Times Mall with cellular automata based on safety training for fire A/B/C

the shelve No.	the total area (m^2)	The death number of the first simulating	The death number of the second simulating	The death number of the third simulating	The death number of the fourth simulating	The death number of the fifth simulating	The average death number
1	224	81/9/1	55/3/2	67/7/2	51/8/2	78/9/3	66. 4/7. 2/2
2	196	67/11/2	73/9/3	77/11/2	84/11/3	71/15/2	74. 4/11. 4/2. 4
3	192	60/6/1	71/2/2	75/3/3	70/7/2	65/4/1	68. 2/4. 4/1. 8
4	216	74/2/2	64/3/1	71/6/2	55/5/1	72/5/2	67. 2/4. 2/1. 6
5	234	72/7/2	69/3/3	64/5/1	82/5/2	61/5/2	69. 6/5/2
6	126	48/1/1	44/1/1	55/3/0	48/1/1	47/2/0	48. 4/1. 6/0. 6

We recommend the fourth shelf placing style for Yancheng Times Mall which is not easy to fire to get higher escape rate and a larger shelf area when the number of escape crowd reaches the upper. For the dry climate areas, we recommend the sixth shelf placing style to get highest escape rate and to achieve 0 casualties for fires less than C.

5 Conclusion

We design the crowd evacuating process model with cellular automata based on safety training by using the evacuation strategies based on safety training. The simulation results show that the crowd evacuating process model with cellular automata based on safety training can simulate the emergency evacuation behavior of supermarket shopping center, and the simulation results are very close to reality. This simulation method is intuitive, flexibility and scalability, and provides good ideas for the emergency management research. We will expand this method to study the more complex evacuation situation in future.

References

1. Burstedde, C., Klauck, K., Schadschneider, A., Zittartz, J.: Simulation of pedestrian dynamics using a two dimensional cellular automaton. Physical A (S0378-4371) 295(3), 507–525 (2001)
2. Yang, L.Z., Fang, W.F., Huang, R., Deng, Z.H.: Occupant evacuation model based on cellular automata in fire. Chinese Science Bulletin 47, 1484–1488 (2002)
3. Yue, H., Hao, H.R., Chen, X.M., Shao, C.F.: Simulation of pedestrian flow on square lattice based on cellular automata model. Physica A (S0378-4371) 384(2), 567–588 (2007)
4. Kirchner, A., Nishinari, K., Scha dschneider, A.: Friction effects and clogging in a cellular automaton model for pedestrian dynamics. Physica l Revies E 67(056122), 2–9 (2003)
5. Kai, N., Michael, S.: A cellular automaton model for freeway traffic. J. Phys. I 2(12), 2221–2229 (1992)
6. Talia, D.: Parallel Cellular Environments to Enable Scientists to Solve Complex Problems (1999), http://www.cscfac.uk/euresco99/presentations/Talia.ppt
7. Ohgai, A., Gohna, Y., Watanabe, K.: Cellular automata modeling of fire spread in built - up areas - A tool to aid community-based planning for disaster mitigation. Computers, Environment and Urban Systems 31(4), 441–460 (2007)
8. Meng, X., Yang, L.-z., Li, J.: Based on cellular automata model for urban areas the probability of fire spread. China Safety Science Journal 18(2), 28–33 (2008)
9. Zhao, S.-y., Su, G.-j., He, Y., Xu, X.-h.: Research of Emergency Evacuation System Simulation Based on Cellular Automata. Journal of Chinese Computer Systems 28(12), 2220–2224 (2007)

An Optimal and Safe Path Planning for Mobile Robot in Home Environment

Yinghua Xue[*] and Tianbing Xu

School of Computer and Information Engineering,
Shandong University of Finance,
Jinan, 250014, China
yhua_xue@yahoo.cn, xutianbing@163.com

Abstract. In order to obtain a safer path in home environment, a modified particle swarm optimization algorithm is first introduced in the paper to get an initial global optimized path. Then an improved A* algorithm is proposed to avoid obstacles based on dynamic danger degree map. The local layer can get multi-mode information of obstacles, and create dynamic danger degree map of the environment. Finally, the head-for-goal strategy is designed to help the mobile robot arrive at the destination with lowest cost. Experiments demonstrate the feasibility and safety of the proposed system.

Keywords: Mobile robot; Path Planning; Particle Swarm Optimization; A* Algorithm.

1 Introduction

Path planning can be classified into two classes: global path planning in a totally known environment and local path planning in a partly or totally unknown environment. The global path planning methods include C-space methods [1], genetic algorithm methods [2], fuzzy logic algorithm methods, and neural networks approaches [3], etc. The local methods include artificial potential field methods, and rolling path planning, etc [4-6].

Recently, particle swarm optimization (PSO) is widely used in robot path planning. PSO is an evolutionary computation technique developed by Dr. Kennedy and Dr. Eberhart in 1995, inspired by the social behavior of bird flocking or fish schooling [7]. Compared with other evolution technology such as GA, PSO has many advantages, such as fewer control parameters, and fast convergence [8,9]. PSO has been successfully applied in many areas: function optimization, artificial neural network training, fuzzy system control, and other areas where GA can be applied.

The indoor environment is partly unknown, so the conventional path planning methods can not meet the safety and real-time requirements in indoor environment. In this paper, we use layered path panning method. The static path planning uses modified PSO to generate an initial optimal path according to the global environment. The

---

[*] Yinghua Xue is a lecture in Shandong University of Finance, her research interests include: robot path planning, intelligent object management.

dynamic path planner adopts method based on behavior, which can correct the static path according to dynamic information.

2 Global Path Planning

Suppose the dimension of the searching space is m, the number of the particles is n. In Fig. 1, we draw m equidistant vertical dashed lines $y_1, y_2 \ldots \ldots y_j \ldots \ldots y_m$, and each particle is located on each line. In iteration, the y values (columns) of all the path points are invariable while the x values (rows) of particles are adjusted to change position upon vertical dashed lines.

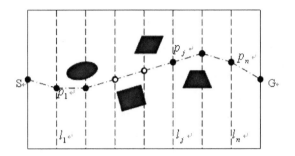

Fig. 1. Model of PSO path planning

The length L_P and the danger degree D_P of the collision-free path can be expressed as follows:

$$L_P = l_{Sp1} + \sum_{j=1}^{m-1} l_{p_j p_{j+1}} + l_{p_d G} = \sum_{j=0}^{m} l_{p_j p_{j+1}} \tag{1}$$

$$D_P = d_S + \sum_{j=1}^{m} d_{p_j} + d_G = \sum_{j=0}^{m+1} d_{p_j} , \tag{2}$$

where the start point S is defined as p_0 and the goal point G is defined as p_{m+1}. $l_{p_j p_{j+1}}$ is the distance between the path point p_j and p_{j+1}, and d_{p_j} is the danger degree of the path point p_j.

The i th particle's fitness value is defined as

$$F_i = w_l L_{Pi} + w_d D_{Pi} = w_l \sum_{j=0}^{m} l_{ij,i(j+1)} + w_d \sum_{j=0}^{m+1} d_{ij} , \tag{3}$$

where w_l and w_d are positive parameters called weighted factor of the length and the danger degree of the path, respectively. $l_{ij.i(j+1)}$ is the distance between the j th dimension and the $j+1$ th dimension of the i th particle, and d_{ij} is used to express the danger degree of the j th dimension of the i th particle.

The algorithmic flow in PSO starts with a population of particles whose positions, that represent the potential solutions for the studied problem, and velocities are randomly initialized in the search space. The search for optimal solution is performed by updating the particle velocities and positions in each iteration [10]. The conventional evolutionary equations of PSO are:

$$V_i(t+1) = \omega * V_i(t) + c_1 * rand() * (P_i - X_i(t)) + c_2 * rand * (P_g - X_i(t)) \quad (4)$$

$$X_i(t+1) = X_i(t) + V_i(t+1) \quad (5)$$

where V, X and P are the velocity vector, the position vector, and the individual best previous position of the i th particle, respectively. P_g is the global best position found by the whole particle swarm, $c1$ and $c2$ are positive constant parameters called acceleration coefficients. $rand()$ is a random function with the scope [0,1], and ω is inertia weight.

3   Local Path Planning

The local path planning includes three behaviors: global path tracing, obstacle avoiding, and head-for-goal [11, 12]. The weighted A* algorithm based on dynamic danger degree map is used for obstacle avoiding.

3.1   Global Path Tracing

If there are no dynamic obstacles in the indoor environment, the static path planned by modified PSO is an optimal path. The robot just needs to trace this static path. The static path we got in Section 2 is $\{S, p_1, p_2, \ldots\ldots p_m, p_G\}$, and $p_j(j = 1,2,\ldots\ldots m)$ is used as sub goals in the paper. The method is simple and easy to realize; the robot can arrive at the sub goals rapidly, and can meet the real-time requirement of autonomous robot navigation.

3.2   Obstacle Avoiding

A weighted A* algorithm is adopted in the paper based on the dynamic danger degree map. The evaluation function is shown as follows:

$$f_w(n) = w_g g(n) + w_h h(n) \quad (6)$$

From Equation (6), we can conclude that the evaluation function $f_w(n)$ is the weighted sum of practical dissipation $g(n)$ and heuristic function $h(n)$, where the weighted factor w_g and w_h can be changed during the search process, and $n(n = 1,2,......8)$ is the index of grids which are adjacent to the robot. $g(n)$ is the practical cost from the current grid to grid n, and $h(n)$ is the evaluation cost from the current node to the destination which indicates the heuristic information during the searching process.

In order to reduce the danger degree of the path during obstacle avoiding, we add danger degree information to $g(n)$. We use $g(n) = w_l l_n + w_d d_n$, where l_n is the length of the path from the current node to node n, d_n is the danger degree of the node n, w_l and w_d are the weighted factors.

The Euclidean distance between node n and the destination is used as $h(n)$, that is:

$$h(n) = \sqrt{(x_n - x_G)^2 + (y_n - y_G)^2} \qquad (7)$$

where (x_n, y_n) are the coordinate values of node n, and (x_G, y_G) are the coordinate values of the destination. Then the final evaluation function is:

$$f_w(n) = w_g(w_l l_n + w_d d_n) + w_h\sqrt{(x_n - x_G)^2 + (y_n - y_G)^2} \qquad (8)$$

From Equation (8), we can conclude that when the danger degree of a node is smaller, and the distance to the robot and the destination is shorter, the heuristic function will be smaller, and then this node will be selected more easily.

3.3 Head for Goal

When the robot avoids obstacles, he will usually deviate from the initial static path. Generally speaking, when the robot deviates from the static path slightly, the robot should move to the initial path, and trace the static path continuously; but if the robot already deviates from the initial path greatly, the robot should re-plan the remaining path instead of looking for the static path due to tracing the initial path may cost more than re-planning the path. We take into account different circumstances, and make the head-for-goal strategy.

4 Experiment and Analyses

Fig. 2 is the global simulation result. Fig. 2(a) shows the path obtained by conventional PSO algorithm. Fig. 2(b) is the path obtained using our method. We can conclude that the path obtained by modified PSO is a little longer than conventional PSO, but the danger degree of the path is much lower than conventional PSO. Anther advantage of the modified PSO is that the time consumption is less than half of the conventional PSO, so the convergence speed is greatly improved.

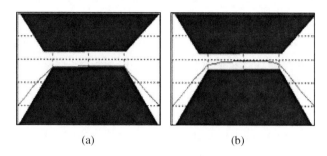

(a)   (b)

Fig. 2. Global path planning

Fig. 3 shows the simulation result of local path planning. The dynamic obstacle moves from the right bottom to the left top. If the robot don't avoid obstacle, he will collide the obstacle at time 10.

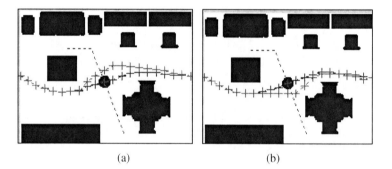

(a)   (b)

Fig. 3. Local path planning

Fig. 3(a) shows the dynamic path when the robot finds the static path after avoiding. Fig. 3(b) is the dynamic path obtained when the robot select to re-plan the remaining path after avoiding. We can conclude that: the optimal dynamic path can be obtained when different head-for-goal strategy is used. Furthermore, the length of the dynamic path is a little longer than the static path, but the danger degree of the dynamic path is lower, due to the dynamic obstacle avoiding algorithm pay more attention to safety.

5 Conclusions

Safety is an important problem in robot path planning. A new kind of layered path planning method is proposed in the paper for the indoor environment. The proposed method adds danger degree evaluation to the path aiming to overcome the disadvantages of conventional methods such as only pursuing the shortest path while ignoring the safety. The experiments demonstrate the feasibility of the proposed method.

References

[1] Henrich, D., Wurll, C., Worn, H.: Online Path Planning with Optimal C-space Discretization. In: Proceedings of the IEEE/RSJ International Conference on Intelligent Robots and Systems, vol. 3, pp. 147–1484. IEEE Press, NJ (1998)

[2] Gao, M., Xu, J., Tian, J., Wu, H.: Path Planning for Mobile Robot Based on Chaos Genetic Algorithm. In: Fourth International Conference on Natural Computation, vol. 4, pp. 409–413. IEEE Press, Jinan (2008)

[3] Yang, S., Luo, C.: A Neural Network Approach to Complete Coverage Path Planning. IEEE Trans. Syst. Man Cybern, Part B. 34(1), 718–724 (2004)

[4] Xi, Y.G., Zhang, C.G.: Rolling Path Planning of Mobile Robot in a Kind of Dynamic Uncertain Environment. Acta Automatica Sinica 28(2), 161–174 (2002)

[5] Mora, M.C., Tornero, J.: Path Planning and Trajectory Generation using Multi-rate Predictive Artificial Potential Fields. In: Proceedings of the IEEE/RSJ International Conference on Intelligent Robots and Systems, pp. 2990–2995. IEEE Press, Nice (2008)

[6] Willms, A., Yang, S.: An Efficient Dynamic System for Real-Time Robot-Path Planning. IEEE Trans. Syst. Man Cybern. 36(4), 755–766 (2006)

[7] Kennedy, J., Eberhart, R.: Particle Swarm Optimization. In: Proceedings of the IEEE International Conference on Neural Networks IEEE Service Center, IV, pp. 1942–1948. IEEE Press, Perth (1995)

[8] Shi, Y., Eberhart, R.: A Modified Particle Swarm Optimizer. In: IEEE World Congress on Computational Intelligence, pp. 69–73. IEEE Press, Anchorage (1998)

[9] Jiao, B., Lian, Z., Gu, X.: A dynamic inertia weight particle swarm optimization algorithm. Chaos, Solutions and Fractals 37(3), 698–705 (2008)

[10] Eberhart, R., Shi, Y.: Particle Swarm Optimization: Developments, Applications and Resources. In: Proceedings of the 2001 Congress on Evolutionary Computation, pp. 81–86. IEEE Press, Soul (2001)

[11] Tompkins, P., Stentz, A., Wettergreen, D.: Mission-Level Path Planning and Re-planning for Rover Exploration. Robotics and Autonomous Systems 54(2), 174–183 (2006)

[12] Piao, S.H., Hong, B.R.: A Path Planning Approach to Mobile Robot under Dynamic Environment. Robot 25(1), 18–21 (2003)

Information Flow Control of Vendor-Managed Inventory Based on Internet of Things

Xiaohui Liu[1,2] and Youwang Sun[1]

[1] School of Transportation Engineering, Tongji University,
Caoan Road 4800, Shanghai, 201804, China
[2] School of Economics and Management, Shanghai Second Polytechnic University,
Jinhai Road, 2360, Shanghai, 201209, China
Xiaohui Liu, 18xhliu@tongji.edu.cn

Abstract. Reducing inventory levels is a major supply chain management challenge. With the development of information technology new cooperative supply chain contracts emerge such as Vendor-Managed Inventory (VMI). This research aims to look at the literature of information management of VMI and the Internet of Things, then analyzes information flow model of VMI The paper is carried out to make analysis of information flow control of VMI based on the environment of Internet of Things.

Keywords: Vendor-Managed Inventory; Information Flow Control; Supply Chain Management; Internet of Things.

1 Introduction

The concept of VMI has received much research attention and evidence has shown that VMI can improve supply chain performance by decreasing inventory costs for the supplier and buyer and improving customer service levels, such as reduced order cycle times and higher fill rates. [1] VMI is a collaborative commerce initiative where suppliers are authorized to manage the buyer's inventory of stock-keeping units. It integrates operations between suppliers and buyers through information sharing and business process reengineering. [2] A number of research papers have studied information flow control through VMI or similar programs.

Automation of information services could make members of the supply chain perceive, predict and respond timely to changing market conditions and accelerate the transfer of critical information among its members, which is necessary to improve the controllability, flexibility, performance and capabilities of abnormal events of supply chain. It is critical to control information flow in VMI supply chain. In addition to information sharing structure and information flow control, it is equally important to define information flow in supply chain (parameters design). Description of the information flow process by information parameters and optimization of the process can help us identify and reduce information distortion and information transmission delay because of the unreasonable process of supply chain business. This paper will

G. Shen and X. Huang (Eds.): CSIE 2011, Part I, CCIS 152, pp. 448–454, 2011.

use United Modeling Language (UML) to model information flow of VMI supply chain.

The Internet of Things (IoT) is an emerging global Internet-based information architecture facilitating the exchange of goods and services in global supply chain networks. From a technical point of view, the architecture is based on data communication tools, primarily RFID-tagged items (Radio-Frequency Identification). The IoT has the purpose of providing an IT-infrastructure facilitating the exchange of "things" in a secure and reliable manner. [3] This paper aims to study information flow control of VMI supply chain based on Internet of Things.

2 Literature Review

In this section, we review the literature on information management of VMI and the Internet of Things. The literature review provides the theoretical foundation for this research.

There is a rich body of literature on the value of information sharing in supply chains, for example, Cachon and Fisher (2000) [4], Chen et al. (2000) [5], Gavirneni and Kapuscrinski (1999) [6] and Lee et al. (1997) [7] concluded that the bullwhip effect could be minimized through information sharing. And Cachon and Zipkin (1999) et al found that policies such as VMI can decrease the bullwhip effect, thereby improving supply chain efficiency, such as by lowering inventory levels and reducing cycle time. [8] Yuliang and Dresner (2008) analyze the benefits realized for manufacturers and retailers under information sharing, continuous replenishment programs (CRP) or vendor managed inventory (VMI) and compare the distribution of benefits between manufacturers and retailers. Their analysis shows that IS, CRP, and VMI bring varying benefits in terms of inventory cost savings to firms, and that the benefits are not consistently distributed between retailers and manufacturers. And their findings also point out the managerial implications on how managers decide the product sets and replenishment frequency for improved benefit realization under CRP and VMI. [9]

The IoT-idea is not new[1]. The term of IoT was firstly used by Kevin Ashton in a presentation in 1998. [10] It only recently becomes relevant to the practical world, main because of the progress made in hardware development in the last decade. Figure 1 shows the technology roadmap of the IoT. [11] The IoT is an emerging global Internet-based information architecture facilitating the exchange of goods and services in global supply chain networks. The IoT could provide an IT-infrastructure facilitating the exchanges of "things" based on an Electronic Product Code (EPC) by carrying RFID tags with a unique EPC. The information of "things" could be available through linking and cross-linking with the help of an Object Naming Service (ONS). Based on Domain Name System (DNS), the ONS can be considered as subset of the DNS and will also inherit all of the well-documented DNS weaknesses [12].

---

[1] Early mentors of the IoT and similar concepts include Gershenfeld (1999), Ferguson (2000), Kindberg at al. (2002), Schoenberger et al. (2002) and Wright et al. (2004).

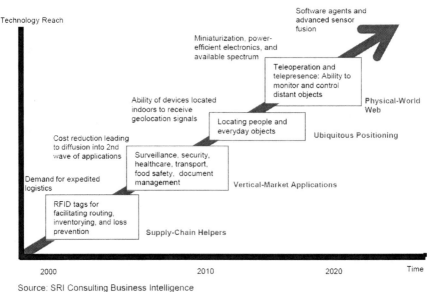

Source: SRI Consulting Business Intelligence

Fig. 1. The technology roadmap of Internet of Things [11]

3   Information Flow Model of Vendor-Managed Inventory

A great deal of evidence has shown that VMI approach can improve supply chain performance by decreasing inventory-related costs and increasing customer service. In VMI supply chain, the supplier (vendor) is responsible for the replenishment of its partners, as summarized conceptually in Fig. 2[13]. The information shared by

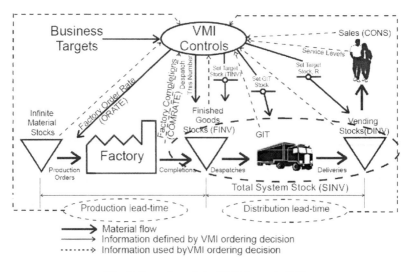

Fig. 2. Overview of the VMI Scenario [13]

members of the supply chain includes sales data and forecasts, order status, production and distribution arrangements and capacity, performance indicators, etc.

UML is a model standard describing process and it can be used to: ① easily describe information sharing structures of specific supply chain environment; ② make the reference way of model built easy to share with other members by direct reference or converted into XML (eXtensible Markup Language). According to the semantics of activity-object flow graph of UML, the information to send is described as Action, the information flow as Object flow. As analyzed in Fig. 3, there exists two-way information flow between partners in VMI supply chains and needs extensive collaboration. So information sharing can not apply the simple linear structure (sequential structure). For example, if the state in Fig. 3 is more than one replenishment order, it is suitable to adopt the whole channel structure (reciprocal structure) for the replenishment orders; and for the order sending, information sharing is still a linear structure. Identified on Fig. 3 in the 1, 2, 3 to describe the information flow are as follows:

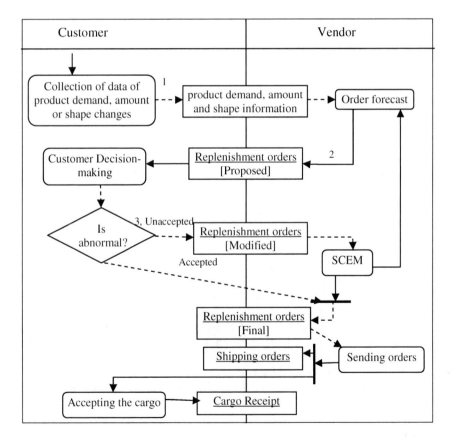

Fig. 3. Modeling VMI with UML Activity Diagram [14]

1. SendUsage
Event: Predetermined time events, such as 24:00 on Friday
Sender: Customers
Receiver: Supplier
Data_ object: the Amount of week (or month, quarter, etc.)
Data_template: EDI # format numbe
Req_action: Proposed (suggested) Order
Mode: Batch
2. ProposeOrder
Event: the Amount received
Condition: Inventory levels $<$ Reorder point (ROP)
Sender: Supplier (vendor)
Receiver: Customer
Data_ object: the Proposed Replenishment Orders
Data_template: EDI # format number
Req_action: Order confirmation (Y or N)
Mode: Batch
3. RejectOrder
Event: Recommended Order received
Condition: Order Fulfillment Rate $<$ 95%
Sender: Customer
Receiver: Supplier (vendor)
Data_ object: the Modified Replenishment Orders
Data_template: EDI # format number
Req_action: Generating Shipping Notice
Mode: Batch or Real-time[14]

4   Information Flow Control of VMI Based on Internet of Things

4.1 Information Transparency in VMI Supply Chain

From the above information flow control mode and Fig. 3, the traditional VMI still has a lot to improve. First, the batch mode may result in the delay of the shared information and cause that fluctuation in demand could not be promptly reflected in forecast prediction, which results in wrong or abnormal forecast. So the anomaly caused by inaccurate information flows should be reduced and real-time information is necessary. At this point, EDI appears to lack flexibility because of its batch processing and data exchange turns to the data template based on XML format. Second, the information shared in VMI supply chain is asymmetric. Most of the information flow is from the customer to the supplier while the supplier's information flow is opaque. Suppliers should provide some scene analysis, such as displaying the effect of modified information flow, analog forecasting and replenishment strategies etc. in order to increase transparency of information.

4.2 Information Flow Control of VMI Based on Internet of Things

From the above discussion, in most cases information is exchanged in batch mode in VMI supply chain because the need of information has a well defined structure.

Therefore a linear sharing structure is mainly adopted rather than Hub (center) sharing structure.

The IoT is an emerging Internet-based information architecture facilitating the exchange of goods and services in global supply chain networks. The basic idea of the IoT is that virtually very physical thing in this world can also become a computer that is connected to the Internet.

In VMI supply chain network, information flow is large and complex, usually in state of a high degree of uncertainty and multi-directional links between members. In this case, real-time information sharing is required so as to monitor the status of supply chain and exceptions in the supply chain broadcast. In order to increase transparency, visibility, availability and improving level of coordination of the supply chain, hub (center) type of information-sharing structure should be used. Integrating promising information technologies such as RFID can help improve the effectiveness and convenience of information flow in VMI supply chain. The Internet of Things based on RFID provides an information sharing platform among all participants of the construction chain using web technology and RFID-enabled PDA[15]. On this basis, the architecture of information flow control of VMI based on Internet of Things is shown on Figure 4.

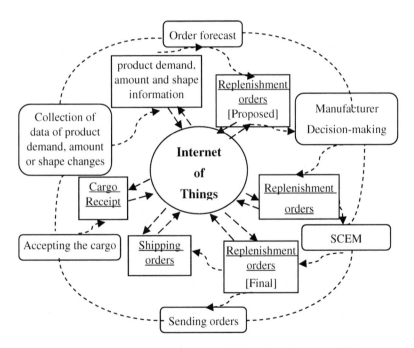

Fig. 4. Information Flow Control of VMI Based on Internet of Things

5 Conclusion

The information flow control in VMI supply chain and the Internet of Things are both focus of research in present-day society. This paper is carried out to make analysis of information flow control of VMI based on the environment of Internet of Things. This analysis aims to provide a new vision to research logistics and supply chain management.

Acknowledgment

This work is supported by the Joint Research Scheme of National Science Foundation of China and Research Grants Council of Hong Kong (Grant No. 70731160015 and N_HKUST 612/6) and Educational Highland funds by Shanghai Municipal Education Commission.

References

1. Waller, M., Johnson, M.E., Davis, T.: Vendor-Managed Inventory in the Retail Supply Chain. Journal of Business Logistics 20(1), 183–203 (1999)
2. Yao, Y., Evers, P.T., Dresner, M.E.: Supply Chain Integration in Vender-Managed Inventory. Decision Support Systems 43, 663–674 (2007)
3. Weber, R.H.: Internet of Things — New Security and Privacy Changes. Computer Law & Security Review 26, 23–30 (2010)
4. Cachon, G., Fisher, M.: Supply Chain Inventory Management and the Value of Shared Information. Management Science 46(8), 1032–1048 (2000)
5. Chen, F., Drezner, Z., Ryan, J.K., Simchi-Levi, D.: Quantifying the Bullwhip effect in a simple supply chain: the Impact of Forecasting, Lead times, and Information. Management Science 46(3), 436–443 (2000)
6. Gavirneni, S., Kapuscinski, R.: Value of Information in Capacitated Supply Chain. Management Science 45(1), 16–24 (1999)
7. Lee, H.L., Padmanabhan, V., Whang, S.: Information Distortion in a Supply Chain: the Bullwhip effect. Management Science 43(4), 546–559 (1997)
8. Cachon, G., Zipkin, P.H.: Competitive and Cooperative Inventory Policies in a Two-stage Supply Chain. Management Science 45(7), 936–953 (1999)
9. Yao, Y., Dresner, M.: The inventory value of information sharing, continuous replenishment, and vendor-managed inventory. Transportation Research Part E: Logistics and Transportation Review 44(3), 361–378 (2008)
10. Santucci, G.: From Internet of Data to Internet of Things. Paper for the International Conference on Future Trends of the Internet,
    ftp://ftp.cordis.europa.eu/pub/fp7/ict/docs/enet/20090128-speech-iot-conference-lux_en.pdf
11. SRI Consulting Business Intelligence/National Intelligence Council: Disruptive Technologies Global Trands 2025. In: SRI Consulting Business Intelligence, Appendix F-2 (2010)
12. Weber, R.H.: Internet of Things – New security and privacy challenges. Computer Law & Security Review 26(1), 23–30 (2010)
13. Disney, S.M., Towill, D.R.: The effect of vendor managed inventory (VMI) dynamics on the Bullwhip Effect in supply chains. International Journal of Production Economic 85(2), 199–215 (2003)
14. Peng, J.: Study on Information Share and Application Integrating in Supply Chain. Master Thesis of Chongqing Jiaotong University, pp. 23–25 (2007)
15. Wang, L.-C., Lin, Y.-C., Lin, P.H.: Dynamic mobile RFID-based supply chain control and management system in construction. Advanced Engineering Informatics 21, 377–390 (2007)

Power System Unit Commitment Based on Quantum Genetic Algorithm

Xin Ma

School of Management and Economics, North China University of Water
Conservancy and Electric Power,Zhengzhou, Henan Province, 450011 China
maxin72@163.com

Abstract. Unit commitment problem is traditional mixed variables programming which is difficult to find the optimal solution in mathematics. A quantum
genetic algorithm to solve unit commitment problems presented in this paper.
The proposed algorithm can solve problems for which the objective function is
non-linear, non-convex, non-differentiable, stochastic, or even discontinuous.
Quantum genetic algorithm guarantees global convergence and only needs values of objective function and barrier functions consisted by constraint condition
while discards the information of their derivative. Simulations are executed on
systems of 10-units in 24 hour intervals and the results verify the effectiveness
of the proposed algorithm.

Keywords: Power system scheduling, unit commitment, mixed integer program, quantum genetic algorithm.

1 Introduction

Power unit commitment problem is an important optimization problem in the power
production. A reasonable unit commitment would greatly reduce operating costs of
power system, unit commitment problem is a constrained large scale nonlinear mixed
integer programming problem, a lot of optimization methods has made to solve the
problem, such as the dynamic programming [1], priority method [2], Lagrangian
relaxation [3], particle swarm optimal algorithms [4] and genetic algorithms [5] and
so on. However, these algorithms all have defects in one way or another. So there is
much room for improvement to solve the unit commitment problem. On the basis of
the biological evolution, the quantum genetic algorithm is applied to unit commitment
problem and the simulation shows that the method has a good result.

2 Unit Commitment Problem Formulation

In this paper the following standard notations will be used. Additional symbols will
be introduced when necessary. i: index for the number of units(i=1,2,...,G) . j: index
for time (j=1,2,...,T) . Ξ : total operating cost. P_{ij}: power generated by unit i at time j,
in MW. P_{Dj}: system demand at time j, in MW. P_{Rj}: system spinning reserve requirement at time j, in MW. P_i^{max}: maximum generation level of unit i at time j, in MW.

G. Shen and X. Huang (Eds.): CSIE 2011, Part I, CCIS 152, pp. 455–461, 2011.
© Springer-Verlag Berlin Heidelberg 2011

P_i^{min}: minimum generation level of unit i at time j, in MW. T: time horizon of commitment, in hours. Φ_{ij}: zero-one decision variable indicating whether unit i is up or down in time period j. T_i^{md}: the minimum number of periods unit i must remain off after it has been turned off, in hours. T_i^{mu}: the minimum number of periods unit i must remain on after it has been turned on, in hours. T_i^{cs}: cold start-up time of unit i, in hours. t_{ij} : state variable indicating the length of time that unit i has been up or down in time period j, in hours. T : time horizon of commitment, in hours. C_i^{cs}: cold start-up cost of unit i, in \$. C_i^{hs}: hot start-up cost of unit i, in \$. $C_i(P_{ij})$: fuel cost of unit i for generating power P_{ij} at time j, usually represented as quadratic function, in \$.a_i,b_i,c_i: fuel factors. S_{ij}: start up cost of unit i, in \$.

Unit commitment problem can be expressed as mixed integer nonlinear programming model in mathematical to meet the different constraints. The goal is the minimum total operating cost in a scheduling cycle and the operating costs including generation costs and start-up costs. Objective function is described as below.

$$Min\Xi = \sum_{j=1}^{K} \sum_{i=1}^{G} [C_i(P_{ij})\phi_{ij} + S_{ij}\phi_{ij}(1 - \phi_{i(j-1)})] \tag{1}$$

Power balance constraints:

$$\sum_{i=1}^{G} P_{ij}\phi_{ij} - P_{Dj} = 0 \qquad j = 1,2,\cdots,T \tag{2}$$

Spinning reserve constraints:

$$\sum_{i=1}^{G} P_i^{max}\phi_{ij} \geq P_{Dj} + P_{Rj} \tag{3}$$

Up and down generation constraints of unit:

$$P_i^{min} \leq P_{ij} \leq P_i^{max} \tag{4}$$

Cost function:

$$C_i(P_{ij}) = a_i + b_i P_{ij} + c_i P_{ij}^2 \tag{5}$$

The minimum turned on or turn off constraints:

$$\begin{cases} t_{ij} \geq T_i^{mu} & t_{ij} > 0 \\ -t_{ij} \geq T_i^{md} & t_{ij} > 0 \end{cases} \tag{6}$$

Start up cost constraints:

$$S_{ij} = \begin{cases} C_i^{hs} & T_i^{md} < -t_{ij} \leq T_i^{md} + T_i^{cs} \\ C_i^{cs} & -t_{ij} > T_i^{md} + T_i^{cs} \end{cases} \tag{7}$$

3 Solution Methodology

The algorithm coding mechanism of quantum probability vector from the genetic algorithm through the crossover and quantum computing at the same time from the update strategy in order to improve the ability of the quantum effective global search algorithm [6,7].

3.1 Quantum Bit

This is because the smallest unit of information stored in a two-state quantum computer is called a quantum bit or qubit. A quantum bit can represent not only the basic state "0"and" 1 "[8], but also in any superposition state of the two, that "0" state and "1" state existences together with a certain probability. If the two basic states of quantum bits represented by symbol | 0> and | 1> , then the superposition state of a quantum bit described in the two-dimensional Hilbert space shown in Figure 1.

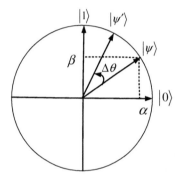

Fig. 1. Basic quantum bit under the superposition state in the two-dimensional Hilbert space

The state of a quantum bit can be described as:

$$|\psi\rangle = |0\rangle + |1\rangle \tag{8}$$

Normalization of the state to unity guarantees that:

$$|\alpha|^2 + |\beta|^2 = 1 \tag{9}$$

Where $|\alpha|^2$ or $|\beta|^2$ gives the probability that the quantum bit will be found in "0" or "1" state, respectively. Each q chromosome with length m (m quantum bits) is represented as following:

$$q = \begin{bmatrix} \alpha_1 & \alpha_2 & \cdots & \alpha_m \\ \beta_1 & \beta_2 & \cdots & \beta_m \end{bmatrix} \tag{10}$$

Where, the following condition should be satisfied:

$$|\alpha_i|^2 + |\beta_i|^2 = 1 \quad (i = 1, 2, \cdots, m) \tag{11}$$

3.2 Quantum Rotation Gate

In the quantum genetic algorithm, the design of quantum gates is a key step. According to the normalization condition, the quantum gates must be reversible unitary matrices. Each quantum bit is updated using the quantum rotation gate as follows:

$$U(\Delta\theta_i) = \begin{bmatrix} \cos(\Delta\theta_i) & -\sin(\Delta\theta_i) \\ \sin(\Delta\theta_i) & \cos(\Delta\theta_i) \end{bmatrix} \tag{12}$$

The update quantum bit as follows:

$$\begin{bmatrix} \alpha' \\ \beta' \end{bmatrix} = U(\Delta\theta_i) \times \begin{bmatrix} \alpha \\ \beta \end{bmatrix} \tag{13}$$

The characteristics of algorithm are decided by the value and direction of quantum rotation angle $\Delta\theta_i$, and the search strategies listed in Table 1.

Table 1. Look up table for $\Delta\theta_i$, the rotation angle is constant in this table

x_i	b_i	$f(x) \geq f(b)$	$\Delta\theta_i$
0	0	False	θ_1
0	0	True	θ_2
0	1	False	θ_3
0	1	True	θ_4
1	0	False	θ_5
1	0	True	θ_6
1	1	False	θ_7
1	1	True	θ_8

The rotation angle is constant in Table 1, and the rotation angle of quantum bit gate decided by the following formulation:

$$\theta = k \times f(\alpha_i, \beta_i) \tag{14}$$

k is a coefficient relation with the convergence speed. The value of θ can not be too large nor too small in order to keep the convergence of algorithm. If the value of θ is small will make the grid of searching is too narrow and the optimal solution can not be find in the limited iterative times for the slow searching speed. It is usually as premature. Since the value of $f(\alpha_i, \beta_i)$ selected as ± 1, so mainly through the change of

k value to control the convergence speed, k is defined as the variables related with algebra of evolution in the literature [9].

$$k = 10 \times \exp(-t / \max t) \tag{15}$$

Where, t is the algebra of evolution and max t is the largest iteration of evolution. The α_1 and β_1 are the probability amplitude for the optimal solution found, α_2 and β_2 is the probability amplitude for the current solution, d_1 and d_2 are all larger than 0 at the same time, it means that the current solution and the optimal solution found are both in the first or the third quadrant.

Table 2. Look up table for $f(\alpha_i, \beta_i)$ function

| $d_1 > 0$ | $d_2 > 0$ | \multicolumn{2}{c}{$f(\alpha_i, \beta_i)$} ||
		$|\xi_1| \geq |\xi_2|$	$|\xi_1| < |\xi_2|$
True	True	+1	-1
True	False	+1	+1
False	True	-1	-1
False	False	-1	+1

$$d_1 = \alpha_1 \times \beta_1 \tag{16}$$

$$d_2 = \alpha_2 \times \beta_2 \tag{17}$$

$$\xi_1 = \tan^{-1}(\beta_1 / \alpha_1) \tag{18}$$

$$\xi_2 = \tan^{-1}(\beta_2 / \alpha_2) \tag{19}$$

3.3 The Steps for Quantum Genetic Algorithm

```
Procedure of Quantum genetic algorithm
Begin
   Initialize P(t);
   Generate R(t)by observing P(t-1);
   Evaluate R(t) and store the best solution among R(t);
   While(not termination condition)do
      T=t+1;
      Generate R(t) by observing P(t-1);
      Evaluate R(t)and store the best solution among
R(t);
      Update P(t) using Quantum gates;
   End While
End Begin.
```

4 Simulation

There are 10 conventional thermal power generators and the operation period is 24h. The units parameters, load and other data, see [10]. The population of chromosomes and quantum chromosomes is set at value of 100 and 80, respectively, and the maximum number of generations is 200, the rotation angle is selected on the basis of Table 1. Optimized output of 10-unit system is show as Table 3.

Table 3. Optimized solution of 10-unit system with the proposed method. The output distribution of each unit is shown at the left position in each column and the reserve of each unit is shown at the brackets.

Time	Power and reserve (MW)						
	Unit1	Unit 2	Unit3	Unit4	Unit5	Unit6	Unit7~10
1	455(0)	245(60)	0(0)	0(0)	0(0)	0(0)	0(0)
2	455(0)	295(70)	0(0)	0(0)	0(0)	0(0)	0(0)
3	455(0)	395(60)	0(0)	0(0)	0(0)	0(0)	0(0)
4	455(0)	455(0)	0(0)	0(0)	43(91)	0(0)	0(0)
5	455(0)	455(0)	0(0)	0(0)	60(103)	0(0)	0(0)
6	455(0)	455(0)	0(0)	128(0)	49(110)	0(0)	0(0)
7	455(0)	455(0)	0(0)	128(0)	46(110)	0(0)	0(0)
8	455(0)	455(0)	0(0)	128(0)	40(121)	0(0)	0(0)
9	455(0)	455(0)	128(0)	128(0)	32(125)	0(0)	0(0)
10	455(0)	455(0)	128(0)	128(0)	162(0)	61(17)	0(0)
11	455(0)	455(0)	128(0)	128(0)	162(0)	80	0(0)
12	455(0)	455(0)	128(0)	128(0)	162(0)	80	0(0)
13	455(0)	455(0)	128(0)	128(0)	27(135)	0(0)	0(0)
14	455(0)	455(0)	128(0)	128(0)	31(126)	0(0)	0(0)
15	455(0)	455(0)	128(0)	128(0)	30(120)	0(0)	0(0)
16	455(0)	455(0)	0(0)	0(0)	57(105)	0(0)	0(0)
17	455(0)	455(0)	0(0)	0(0)	59(100)	0(0)	0(0)
18	455(0)	455(0)	0(0)	0(0)	50(110)	0(0)	0(0)
19	455(0)	455(0)	0(0)	0(0)	42(115)	0(0)	0(0)
20	455(0)	455(0)	0(0)	0(0)	25(135)	0(0)	0(0)
21	455(0)	455(0)	0(0)	0(0)	31(130)	0(0)	0(0)
22	455(0)	455(0)	0(0)	0(0)	50(110)	0(0)	0(0)
23	455(0)	455(10)	0(0)	0(0)	0(0)	0(0)	0(0)
24	455(0)	340(70)	0(0)	0(0)	0(0)	0(0)	0(0)

Table 4. Comparison of the optimized solutions of 10-unit system by different algorithms

The solution	Quantum GA	GA
The best solution($)	109510	109873
The worst solution($)	109322	109610
Average($)	109457	109723

Table 4 lists the optimal total solutions (costs) of genetic algorithm and the quantum genetic algorithm which presented in this paper. From the table, the optimal solution of quantum genetic algorithm is better than the result of genetic algorithm and the simulation result also shows the robustness of the new algorithm and practical.

5 Conclusion

Power system unit commitment problem is an important part of power system optimization operation, the units are determined to turn on or turn off during a scheduling cycle (24h) under the various constraints in order to obtain the least total operation cost of power system. But unit commitment problem is traditional mixed variables programming which is difficult to find the optimal solution. The quantum genetic algorithm to solve unit commitment problems presented in this paper. The simulation results verify the effectiveness and robustness of the proposed algorithm.

References

1. Wang, C.: Dimension-reduced semi-analytical dynamic programming approach for solving unit commitment problem. Transactions of China Electro-technical Society 21, 110–116 (2006)
2. Pokharel, B.K.: Profit based unit commitment in competitive markets. International Journal on Power System Technology 2, 1728–1733 (2004)
3. Fredondo, N.J.: Short-term hydro-thermal coordination by Lagrangian relaxation: solution of the dual problem. IEEE Trans. on Power Systems 14, 89–95 (1999)
4. Hu, J.-s.: A hybrid particle swarm optimization method for unit commitment problem. In: Proceedings of the CSEE, vol. 24, pp. 25–29 (2004)
5. Cheng, C.P.: Unit commitment by Lagrangian relaxation and genetic algorithm. IEEE Trans. on Power System 15, 707–714 (2000)
6. Han, K.-H.: Quantum-inspired evolutionary algorithm for a class of combinatorial optimization. IEEE Transactions on Evolutionary Computation 6, 580–593 (2002)
7. Han, K.-H.: Quantum-inspired evolutionary algorithms with a new termination criterion, the gate, and two-phase scheme. IEEE Transactions on Evolutionary Computation 8, 156–169 (2004)
8. Ge, X.-z.: An new quantum genetic algorithm and its application. Journal of Electric. 32, 476–479 (2004)
9. Ge, X.-z.: An improved quantum inspired genetic algorithm and its application to time frequence atom decomposition. Dynamics of continues. Discrete and Impulsive Systems 14, 764–771 (2007)
10. Kazarlis, S.A.: A genetic algorithm solution to the unit commitment problem. IEEE Transactions on Power Systems 11, 83–92 (1996)

Motion Planning for Intelligent Security Robot with Limited Sensory Information

Wei Liu, JianHua Su, and ZhiCai Ou

Institute of Automation Chinese Academy of Sciences
95 Zhongguancun East Road, 100190, Beijing, China
{wei.liu,jianhua.su,zhicai.ou}@ia.ac.cn

Abstract. Plenty of motion planning methods have been proposed and achieved good performance in static environments. However, motion planning for obstacle avoidance in dynamic and changeable environment is still a challenging task, especially when the tracked object moves freely. This paper presents a practical fuzzy logic based motion planning method for the mobile intelligent security robot with limited sensory information. Vision sensor is used for object tracking, and sonar sensors are used for obstacle avoidance. Fuzzy logic together with three modules: the environment construction module, the reactive planning module, and the action control module are used for obstacle avoidance and navigation. Experimental results show the efficiency and the reliability of this method in the dynamic and uncontrolled environments.

Keywords: Obstacle avoidance, Sonar sensors, Fuzzy Logic, Navigation.

1 Introduction

For mobile robots' safe navigation, fast and efficient motion planning method is required. This paper proposes a motion planning approach for the mobile robot's obstacle avoidance while tracking the moving object. Nowadays, obstacle avoidance methods are mainly divided into global motion planning methods and local ones.

Global motion planning methods are designed for static or perceived environment, and a collision-free path is calculated from the initial position to the goal. For example, the Artificial Potential Fields (APF) [1] considered that obstacles assert repulsive forces and the goal asserts attractive forces on the vehicle, and proposed an approach on real time obstacle avoidance. Based on the occupancy grid method, Borenstein et al. developed a Vector Field Histogram (VFH) [2] approach which used a two-dimensional Cartesian histogram grid as a world model and the motion direction are computed from the world model information.

Local planning methods are more effective than the global ones, because they are usually based on sensory information and show superiority in unknown or dynamic environment. Castro et al. proposed a behavior-based method [3] which made category of the behaviors, and the environmental structures could be built up through categorizing the behaviors. Fukayama et al. [4] proposed a method in which sub-skills called behaviors composed the robot's task. This approach employed perceptual sequencing method for appropriate behavior activation. A fuzzy behavior-based system

G. Shen and X. Huang (Eds.): CSIE 2011, Part I, CCIS 152, pp. 462–467, 2011.

[5] was applied to a three-link manipulator by Dassanayake and it was conducted for three kinds of behaviors and they could perform tasks of reaching the target and avoiding an obstacle. Igor [6] introduced a reactive motion control method which took into account of preference function and divided the world model into three parts, then made different actions correspondingly.

This paper presents a practical fuzzy logic based motion planning method for the mobile intelligent security robot with limited sensory information. Fuzzy logic together with three modules is used for obstacle avoidance and navigation.

The rest of this paper is organized as follows: Section 2 is the analysis of the robot's behavior. Section 3 is the analysis of robot tracking using the camera fixed on the top of the robot. Section 4 illustrates the building up of the fuzzy control and shows the corresponding behaviors. Section 5 gives the conclusions.

2   Robot Behavior Definition

The proposed method is based on the reactive method with three modules: the environment construction module, the reactive planning module, and the action control module. The architecture of the navigation system is illustrated in Fig.1. The solid rectangle in the Reactive planning module denotes the motion planning part composed of four layers. The high level layers can subsume the roles of lower levels, and lower layers continue to work when high layers are added.

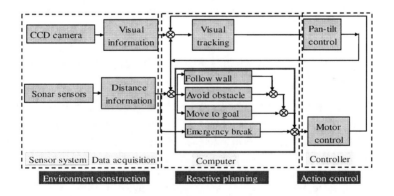

Fig. 1. The architecture of the robot navigation system

3   Object Tracking

We present an algorithm to track the object for the mobile robot which can move freely with the maximum velocity of one meter per second.

Suppose θ_{oc} denotes the angular misalignments of the object relative to the center of camera, then the position of the object relative to the robot can be denoted as $\theta_{oc} + \theta_{cr}$, where θ_{cr} denotes the angle between the camera and the robot. θ_{oc} is controlled to tend to zero, so the position of the object is denoted as θ_{cr} which can be obtained through the robot base. So the precise position of the object can be figured out.

4 Motion Planning

The sonar sensors all have sensitive thresholds, which means when the distance of the obstacle is in the range of the sensitive threshold, the sensor will return an alert. With the detection result of sensors, a state vector is built up to complete the planning. It can also be considered as the membership function of the response of the seven sensors. It has 128 situations, and this is just one special case for example in Table 1.

Table 1. The membership functions of the response.

Number / Response	1	2	3	4	5	6	7
Detected	1	1	1	0	0	0	0

If the robot encounters local minimum (e.g., inside a U-shaped obstacle), investigations of the follow wall behavior could be performed. The quantification that encounters a wall is judged by the equation as below:

$$Q:\left\{(\rho > \rho_{near}) \bigcap (l = 0 \bigcap r = 0) \bigcup (\theta > \pi/2) \bigcup (\theta < -\pi/2)\right\}. \tag{1}$$

where ρ denotes the distance between robot and the nearest obstacle, ρ_{near} denotes the sensitive threshold of the sensor, θ denotes the angle between the robot instant moving direction and the object, and l, r denote the left and right value in the vector mentioned in Table 1.

If there exists little space for the robot to move through, the architecture converts to the avoid obstacle behavior. The quantification is denoted as:

$$Q:\left\{(\rho > \rho_{near}) \bigcap \left(\bigcup_{i=|\theta - \alpha_i| < 60} obs\_dist_i < \rho_{near}\right)\right\}. \tag{2}$$

where obs_dist_i denotes the detected distance of the ith sensor, α_i denotes the angle in the direction of ith sensor. We utilize the triangle membership function illustrated in Fig.2 to build the fuzzy logic decision. The membership matrix of the turning angle is illustrated in Table 2, and the fuzzy logic control is illustrated in Table 3.

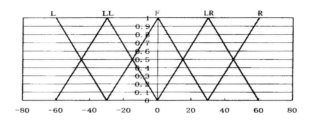

Fig. 2. The membership functions of the turning angle

Table 2. The membership functions of the turning angle

Direction Number	L	LL	F	LR	R
1	0.6	0.4	0	0	0
2	0.4	0.6	0	0	0
3	0	0.6	0.4	0	0
4	0	0	1	0	0
5	0	0	0.4	0.6	0
6	0	0	0	0.6	0.4
7	0	0	0	0.4	0.6

The relationship matrix R between the response and the direction can be obtained through the multiply of S and A :

$$R = S \circ A. \tag{3}$$

The multiply we utilized is the operator zedeh. Suppose $S = (s_{ij})_{n \times m}$ and $A = (a_{jk})_{m \times t}$, then $R = (r_{ik})_{n \times t}$ and r_{ik} can be calculated as:

$$r_{ik} = \bigcup_{i=t}^{n}(s_{ij} \cap a_{jk}), 1 \leq i \leq n, 1 \leq k \leq t. \tag{4}$$

where $\cup$ denotes (max), $\cup$ denotes (min). n denotes the number of the elements in the response set, t denotes the number of the elements in the direction set, and m denotes the number of sensors.

The Fuzzy logic control decision is shown in Table 3. The direction that the robot moves is determined by the maximum membership. From Table 3, we can deduce that the robot should move right as there are obstacles detected on the left side.

Table 3. Fuzzy logic control decision

Direction Response	L	LL	F	LR	R
Detected	0.6	0.6	0.4	0	0

Another behavior is to move to goal. If there is enough space to go through, the robot can go straight to the goal, and here, the camera plays an important role. The behavior can be activated in the situation below:

$$Q : \left\{ (\rho > \rho_{near}) \cap \left(\bigcap_{i=|\theta-\alpha_i|<60} obs\_dist_i > \rho_{near} \right) \right\}. \tag{5}$$

We get the desired motion control matrix as the form of a line combination of three angles as below, in which cam_ang refers to the position of the object, $best\_ang$ refers to the fuzzy logical output, and $penalty$ refers to the function of the distance between robot and the nearest obstacle, and it is inversely proportional to the distance, if the distance is too near, it becomes smaller or even negative to reduce the parallel velocity and rotational velocity, and a,b,c are all proportional factors. The overall output is as follows:

$$F = a \cdot cam\_ang + b \cdot best\_ang + c \cdot penalty. \tag{6}$$

$$Q : \left\{ (\rho > \rho_{near}) \cup isobjectlost \right\}. \tag{7}$$

where $isobjectlost$ denotes the object is lost. In this situation, the robot should stop immediately.

5   Experimental Results

The robot utilized has a base diameter $d = 40cm$. The seven sensors were distributed in a circle and the degree between two adjacent sensors is $15°$, and all of the sensors had a sensitive measure distance from $0.6m - 2m$. Supposing three successive sensors with obstacles undetected can assure the size of space the robot could go through, the sensitive threshold of the sensor can be calculated as $R = d / 30° = 0.75m$. As it satisfies the sensitive range of the sensor ($0.6m - 2m$), so three successive sensors can be considered as the safe space for robot's moving. As mentioned above, the threshold angle we choose is 30 degrees.

The experiment environment was in an office area with three boxes surrounded and the experimental results are shown in Fig.3. The picture a showed the avoid obstacle behavior, because the robot made a left turn and avoid the right box; the picture b showed the follow wall behavior, we should pay attention to the two boxes because they had just formed a U-circle situation which was the perfect local minimum state, and our robot made a right turn and avoid the left boxes; the picture c illustrated the move to goal behavior; the picture d showed the emergency break situation was activated because when the robot is near the goal, it stopped behind the goal.

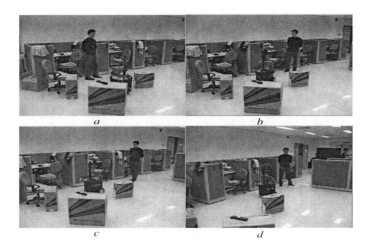

Fig. 3. The different behaviors in navigation. a, the avoid obstacle behavior; b, the follow wall behavior; c, the move to goal behavior; d, the emergency break behavior

6 Conclusions

Artificial Potential Field (APF) is a general method for fast moving robot, and the algorithm we use in this article is based on the APF method and attempt to make some development in the mobile robot navigation. It is proved to be efficient and in some degrees, it contains many creative methods to solve the long living problem and just using some simple calculations.

References

1. Borenstein, J., Koren, Y.: Real-time Obstacle Avoidance for Fast Mobile Robots. IEEE Trans. Syst. Man Cybern. 19, 1179–1187 (1989)
2. Borenstein, J., Koren, Y.: Histogramic In-Motion Mapping for Mobile Robot Obstacle Avoidance. IEEE Trans. Robot. Autom. 7, 535–539 (1991)
3. Castro, D., Nunes, U., Ruano, A.: Obstacle Avoidance in Local Navigation. In: IEEE Mediterranean Conference on Control and Automation MED (2002)
4. Fukayama, A., Ida, M., Katai, O.: Behavior-Based Fuzzy Control System for a Mobile Robot with Environment Recognition by Sensory-motor coordination. In: Proceedings of IEEE International Conference on Fuzzy Systems, pp. 105–110 (1999)
5. Dassanayake, P., Watanabe, K., Kiguchi, K., Izumi, K.: Fuzzy Behavior-Based Motion Planning for the PUMA Robot. In: Proceedings of IEEE Intel. Conf. on Intelligent Robots and Systems, pp. 1912–1917 (2000)
6. Igor, E.P., Uwe, M.N.: Reactive Motion Control for an Omni-Directional Mobile Robot. In: Proceedings of the Third European Control Conference, pp. 5–8 (1995)
7. Brooks, R.A.: A Robust Layered Control System for a Mobile Robot. IEEE J. Robot. Autom. 2, 14–23 (1986)

Performance Analysis of Six-Phase Induction Machine Based on Trapezoidal Phase Current Waveform

Li Wenxing, Lian Liming, and Niu Lianbo

Electromechnical Engineering College, Xinxiang University,
Henan, 451003, China

Abstract. With the characteristic which the control of the multiphase machine is more complex compared with three-phase ac machine, a novel control method is proposed in this paper, namely six-phase motor trapezoidal wave phase current control. By using the trapezoidal phase current waveform, the stator winding is separated into the field winding and the torque winding. The function which is about the field and torque control in directed and separated mode can be realized without the complex Park transformation. The paper carries on the theoretical analysis, the computation of the air gap magnetomotive force (MMF), the electromagnetism torque and MMF decoupling parameter k. And these results are validated by the experiment. It is shown from the theoretical analysis computation and experiment result that it is possible for the control strategy proposed in this paper and it is also of some advantages not only in the control method but also for motor control performance.

Keywords: six-phase induction machine; Trapezoidal wave phase current; Air gap flux linkage; Electromagnetism torque.

1 Introduction

Because of the inherent shortcoming of the DC drive system, The AC drive system has developed quickly these years. VVVF speed control and vector control are the most widely used in the AC drive system at present. [1-2] With the rapid development of the power electronics and control theory, Some big power and good reliability drive systems are needed in aerospace and submarine, which makes more and more researchers study multi-phase motor and its drive system.

However, the control of the multiphase machine is more complex than three-phase ac machine. The character and development of six-phase induction machine control is introduced and summarized, and a novel control method is proposed in this paper, namely six-phase motor trapezoidal wave phase current control.

2 Six-Phase Current Waveform Configuration

A six-phase current configuration as shown in Fig. 1. The current waveforms produce a rectangular flux density in the air gap. The field and torque current components, I_F and I_T, can be controlled separately like in a dc machine.

G. Shen and X. Huang (Eds.): CSIE 2011, Part I, CCIS 152, pp. 468–474, 2011.

The phase current waveforms are assumed to be supplied by six full-bridge converters, one converter per phase. With these current waveforms two separate rotating stator MMFs are generated, namely a field rotating MMF and a torque rotating MMF.

Consider phase a as an example. Fig. 2 shows the composition of the waveform, whereby time 0 - t_3 and time t_3 - t_6 show field and torque components respectively. The other phase current waveforms follow the same pattern of phase a, but with a certain phase displacement. The function of the field current component is to produce a magnetic field inside the motor. Normally, the average amplitude of the flux density distribution in the air gap is fixed, so that the amplitude of the field current component is fixed. At rated field current this will ensure that the average flux density in the iron is at the knee of the BH magnetization curve.

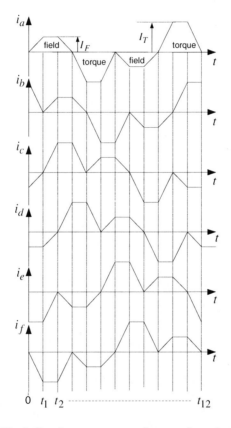

Fig. 1. Six-phase current waveform configuration

3   Magnetomotive Force Analysis

F_f is the field MMF due to the three-phase field currents, i_a, i_c and i_d. F_t is the torque MMF due to the three-phase torque currents, i_b, i_e and i_f.

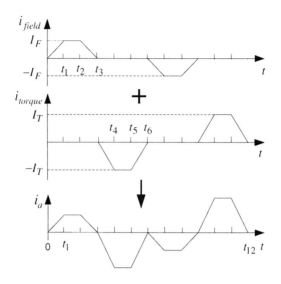

Fig. 2. Composition of phase a current

From this the resultant amplitude of the field MMF, F_f, for time interval $0-t_1$ can be calculated as,

$$\begin{aligned}
F_f &= N_a i_a - N_c i_c - N_d i_d \\
&= N_s i_a - N_s i_c - N_s i_d \\
&= N_s (i_a - i_c) - N_s (-I_F) \\
&= 2 N_s I_F
\end{aligned} \tag{1}$$

For the stator torque currents during time $t = 0 - t_1$, as shown in Figure 1, the amplitude of the torque MMF, F_t, can be expressed as,

$$F_t = N_b i_b - N_e i_e - N_f i_f = 2 N_s I_T \tag{2}$$

With seven (of the fourteen) rotor phases active for this machine, the amplitude of the rotor MMF, F_r, can be expressed as,

$$F_r = 7 I_r N_r \tag{3}$$

From figure 3 we can find the special current waveform configuration produces perpendicular field and torque magnetic fields. The rotor current field intensity, is opposite to the torque current field intensity which means that it is possible that these field intensities in the air gap can cancel each other.

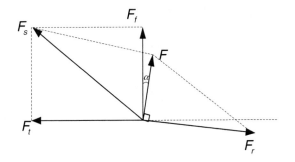

Fig. 3. Magnetomotive force composition diagram

From Figure 3 it follows that:

$$F^2 = F_s^2 - F_r^2$$
$$= F_f^2 + F_t^2 - F_r^2$$

(4)

By ignoring the stator and rotor core reluctances, the air flux density can be expressed as,

$$B = \mu_0 \frac{F}{2l_g}$$
$$= \mu_0 \frac{\sqrt{(2N_s I_F)^2 + (2N_s I_T)^2 - (7N_r I_r)^2}}{2 l_g}$$

(5)

4 Torque Analysis

With a constant flux density, B, the Electromotive Force voltage is induced in the rotor phase windings. The amplitude of this induced rotor voltage can be calculated, as for brush dc motors, as

$$E_r = 2N_r BL\omega_{sl} r_g$$

(6)

The induced rotor phase current is given by

$$I_r = \frac{E_r}{R_r}$$

(7)

For the specific motor with seven rotor phases active and using the Lorentz force, the electromagnetic torque law is given by

$$T = 7N_r BLr_g I_r$$

(8)

5 Calculation of Parameters k

For correct operation F_t must be controlled in such a way that it is equal in amplitude but opposite in direction to F_r which means that $2N_s I_T = 7N_r I_r$, thus

$$I_T = \frac{m_r N_r I_r}{4N_s} \qquad (9)$$

From eqn (7) and (9), the important relationship between I_T and ω_{sl} is obtained namely,

$$k = \frac{\omega_{sl}}{I_T} = \frac{I_r}{I_T} \frac{R_r}{2N_r BLr_g} = \frac{2N_s R_r}{m_r N_r^2 BLr_g} \qquad (10)$$

Form eqn (10) it is clear that the control gain k is dependent on two variables namely r_{eq}, which is temperature sensitive, and B, which is dependent on the field current I_F. The field current can be controlled to keep B at the desired value, but r_{eq} can easily vary by 40% due to temperature changes. This will cause that a wrong k-value is used in the control system, which will disturb the MMF balance and torque output of the motor. Using the design data of the six-phase induction machine (Table1) and with $B = 0.47$ T, k of eqn (10) is calculated as $k = 7.08$ (rad/s)/A.

To k as a parameter,the relationship between torque by torque current is as follows:

$$T = \frac{m_r N_r^2 u_0^2 L^2 r_g^2 \left(F_f^2 + F_t^2 - F_r^2\right) k}{2l_g^2} I_T \qquad (11)$$

Table 1. Design data of six-phase induction machine

Number of phases	6
Number of poles	2
Number of stator slots	36
Number of slots per pole per phase	3
Number of turns in series per stator phase	249
Stator phase resistance (Ω)	9.6
Stack outer diameter (mm)	165
Stack length (mm)	128
Air gap radius (mm)	49
Number of rotor slots	28
Number of rotor phase	14
Number of turns in series per rotor phase	28
Rotor phase resistance (Ω)	0.43

6   Experimental Results

Using the experimental evaluation of the proposed drive system with a six-phase induction machine [4]. In order to measure the induced voltage and flux density, a special wound rotor is designed and built. Two rotor phases are connected to slip rings for the purpose of measurement. Apply the torque sensors, torque can be directly measured. Change the parameter K, the relationship between torque current and flux density B, output torque T are shown in Figure 4-5.

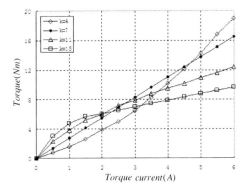

Fig. 4. The relationship between torque current and torque with different k values

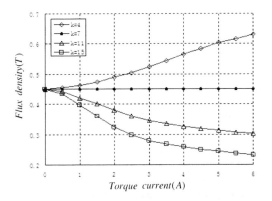

Fig. 5 The relationship between torque current and flux density with different k values

Figure 4 shows that, when k = 7, a linear relationship between electromagnetic torque and torque current ,which shows the magnetic force and torque magnetic force is completely decoupled, Similarly, Figure 5 can also receive similar explanation.

To the step input of the torque current, electromagnetic torque response is shown in Figure 6. Obviously, the six-phase motor is controled with trapezoidal wave phase current, electromagnetic torque response is faster.

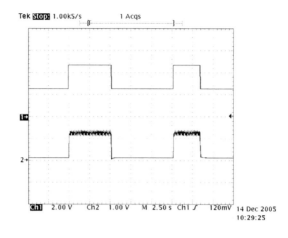

Fig. 6. Electromagnetic torque response (ch1 –electromagnetic torque; ch2 – step input current)

7 Conclusions

Simulate the control strategy of the DC motor, achieving six-phase induction motor decoupling control. By using the trapezoidal phase current waveform, the stator winding is separated into the field winding and the torque winding. The function which is about the field and torque control in directed and separated mode can be realized without the complex Park transformation.

Relationship between electromagnetic torque and torque current is linear. As the actual existence of the rotor winding resistance, there is a certain bias in electromagnetic torque obtained.

To the step input of the torque current, electromagnetic torque response is faster.

References

1. Boss, B.K.: Modern power electronics and ac drives. Prentice-Hall, Englewood Cliffs (2002)
2. Vas, P.: Vector control of AC machines. Oxford Science Publication (1990)
3. Novotny, D.W., Lipo, T.A.: Vector control and dynamics of AC drives. Oxford University Press, Oxford (1997)
4. Ai, Y., Kamper, M.J., Wang, Y.: Investigation of airgap density and torque performance of six-phase induction motor with special phase current waveform. In: Proc. 8th Conf. 2005 ICEMS, P.R.China, pp. 99–104 (September 2005)
5. Lyra, R.O.C., Lipo, T.A.: Torque density improvement in a six-phase induction motor with third harmonic current injection. IEEE Trans. IAS. 38(5), 1351–1360 (2002)

Optimization on H.264 Motion Estimation Algorithm in Real-Time Video

Qin Huanchang[1], Zhu Yunfeng[1,*], Huang Yong[2], Qin Min[1],
Pan Dasheng[1], Xie Dongqing[3], and Jing Xinxing[4]

[1] Department of Physics and Electronics Information Engineering,
Baise University, Baise, China
[2] Office of Scientific Research Administration, Baise University, Baise, China
[3] School of Computer Science & Educational Software,
Guangzhou University, Guangzhou, China
[4] School of Information and Communication, Guilin University of Electronic Technology,
Guilin, China

Abstract. This paper presents the UMHexagonS algorithm, reflected in two aspects: In the search process of this algorithm has added the adaptive threshold value and played a role ahead of deadline in the search process, saving the search time; Its has turned into five steps search and increased the step rectangle search, reducing the search time. The results show that the proposed method can not only guarantee the coding effect of UMHexagonS algorithm, improve the speed of motion estimation, but also saving the coding time, and improve the overall coding rate. Simulation results show that the H.264 encoder, using the proposed rate control algorithm, achieves a visual quality improvement up to 0.388 dB, meets better with target bit rates and produces more flat bit-rate curve than that using the H.264 previous rate control method.

Keywords: real-time video; H.264; UMHexagonS algorithm.

1 Introduction

Rate control plays an important role in H.264. Many existing rate control algorithms are based on a quadratic rate-quantizer(R-D) model. Lee et al. proposed a scalable rate control algorithm which can be simultaneously applied at frame layer, object layer and macroblock layer. The mean absolute difference (MAD) parameter and overhead have been introduced into the quadratic R-D model to accurately estimate the target bit rate. Li et al. proposed the rate control algorithm, adopted by the Joint Video Team(JVT) for H.264/AVC, which employs a linear MAD predict model to solve dilemma between rate control and RDO. The concept of basic unit introduced by Li is to obtain a good tradeoff between the bit fluctuation and the coding efficiency. The basic unit can be a macroblock (MB), a slice, or a frame[1-4]. As the motion estimation part of the computation process of the coding is in the largest proportion, therefore it also increased the H. 264 encoder computation, limiting further

---

* Corresponding author.

G. Shen and X. Huang (Eds.): CSIE 2011, Part I, CCIS 152, pp. 475–481, 2011.
© Springer-Verlag Berlin Heidelberg 2011

promote the H.264 standard. In this paper research the motion estimation algorithm and discuss focusing on the UMHexagonS search algorithm, and propose the improved algorithm based on this algorithm.

2 Umhexagons Algorithm

In the existing block-matching algorithm, the whole search method has the highest search accuracy, but there exists shortcomings of a long search time and a large quantity of computing, and it is difficult to meet the real-time requirements. In order to reduce search time, it has proposed a number of search methods, such as three steps (TSS), diamond search (DS) and so on. This classic fast search algorithm simplifies the calculation, but it is actually take sacrifices the image quality as the price, and reduce the prediction accuracy, the corresponding code rate is higher. In the practical application mostly using a variety of search algorithms combined approach, UM-HexagonS (non-symmetrical cross-shaped multi-level hexagonal grid search algorithm) combines a variety of search modes, and use the hierarchical motion vector search, in a large extent improve the effectiveness and robustness of prediction [5].

As shown in fig. 1, UMHexagonS algorithm includes the following four steps: (1) the initial search point prediction; (2) non-symmetrical cross search; (3) non-symmetric multi-hexagonal grid search; (4) extended hexagon search. The following steps will make a brief introduction.

In UMHexagonS algorithm, estimate the initial motion vector block by using four forecasting models obtained. The four forecasts were the vector forecast value, upper vector forecast, the relevant piece of vector forecast and corresponding reference block vector forecast. As shown in fig. 1, the algorithm second step carries on a standard search for the shape and vertical search range of W/2 of the non-symmetrical cross search, where W is the scope of search window. Search step is 2 and take the search location with the minimum cost function value as the starting point for step. In the third step, first carry on a 5×5 full search, which is within the scope of search 5x5 each point and taking the smallest cost function value of the search center point as the next step. Then using non-symmetrical hexagonal grid search strategy and it starts from the center and gradually throughout the search window in the non-symmetric hexagon search, until the search window boundary. Finally, set the smallest cost point of the function value as the next search center. The fourth step uses a expanded hexagon and a small diamond search pattern cycles hexagon search, until there has a minimum point of the cost function value at the center of hexagons, and then carry out a small diamond, these four location has the smallest cost function value points, which as the current block motion vector position [6].

As UMHexagonS algorithm has good coding results, so this paper will research the algorithm based on dissect foundation, and carry on a certain optimized work to this algorithm. Flow chart of UMHexagonS algorithm encoding as shown in Fig. 1.

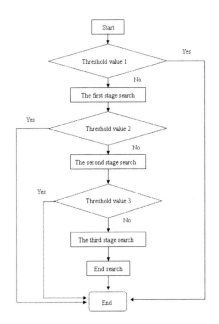

Fig. 1. Flow chart of UMHexagonS algorithm encoding

3 Technical Introduction of Rate Control

Inconsistent bandwidth video stream transmitted over the network, in order to take full advantage of available network resources, and ensure that users get the best visual quality, need to introduce a rate control mechanism. Over-rate video encoder output will lead to unimaginable business congestion and lead to network congestion. On the other hand, the video encoder output bit rate reduction without control, will result in unnecessary quality degradation and the inefficient use of existing bandwidth. Need to adopt rate control to adjust and control the output bit rate video source to obtain the quality and bandwidth utilization in the best equilibrium [7].

Video coding rate control is an important part of the algorithm, it is intended to ensure the video encoder bit-rate limitations in certain conditions, to achieve a rational allocation of coding bits. Whether for the storage media or real-time transmission applications, need to control the use of rate control the output bit rate encoder so limited within a certain range. The rate control algorithm is to study how to implement the encoder rate distortion theory, to achieve the bit rate and image quality at the best balance between the objectives.

Since the requirements of video applications and for different purposes, whether the requirements of the output rate constant, rate control can be divided into CBR (constant bit rate) and VBR (variable bite rate) two, that is, constant bit rate and variable rate control rate control the bit rate.

As each frame of video encoding is not used as the frame coding complexity are not the same, so each frame encoded bits generated there is not a small difference: in the video frame house, the activity level of each macro block different bit allocation of each macro block should also be different. Accordingly, the rate control algorithm can be divided into the frame layer rate control and the macro block layer rate control. In general, the frame layer rate control algorithm is the encoder must be, if at the same time using the macro block layer rate control algorithm can achieve higher control accuracy.

Frame layer rate control is mainly allocated for each video frame rate target, some of the ways in early, there is no full account of distortion and inter frame correlation [7], and a simple formula to obtain the target rate , there are some methods based on search rate - distortion strategy to achieve target frame bits, some of these methods will have a greater delay, and some complexity is high, it only applies to off-line and high-complexity encoding device. For example, in [8] the algorithm requires many different quantization parameter to encode a frame, and the literature coding algorithm is required before the GOP should be carried out for each motion compensation and pre-analysis. Compared with these methods, H.263 rate control algorithms TMN8 taking into account the relevance of the frame and frame distortion measure, and the algorithm complexity is low, this approach also applies to other uses to the B frames encoder, such as MPEG-2 and so on.

Macroblock layer rate control focused mainly on each frame for the macroblock quantization step choose the right on this issue, the first people to use different quantization step of encoding the same macro block, and then select the encoding effect quantization step, but this approach, large, not suitable for real time applications. Later, people began to establish the mathematical model for the encoder, the available number of bits, the buffer occupancy to select the quantization step, but these simple model-based approach in general can not accurately rate goals, and because they allow a larger buffer delay (number of stream buffers in the code to accumulate), in the case of low bit rate may lead to frequent skipping or a waste of channel bandwidth [9].

3.1   The Basic Principles of Rate Control

Control system, in order to obtain a certain performance index, the appropriate location in the system need to introduce some additional devices, so that the original system deficiencies are corrected, "the introduction of an additional device called the calibration device" from the control theory point of view, the correction control system can be divided into feedforward and feedback correction of a correction or series, "In general, the series than the feedback correction correction simple and easy to transform the signal, but the poor stability of the correction work series" in the actual control system, it is also widely used feedback correction device "rate control is no exception, often used in the system by adding feedback control device, the characteristics of the system changes to meet the performance indicators given" rate control in the rate of performance indicators! buffer delay ! buffer status "Figure of a schematic diagram for the rate control".

3.2   The Rate Distortion Theory

As the transmission bandwidth and storage space constraints, video applications have a higher compression ratio requirements. Lossless compression can provide can not meet the actual demand for video applications, but if we can accept some degree of distortion, high compression ratio is not difficult to obtain. Human visual system is not sensitive to high frequency signal changes, some high-frequency loss of information does not reduce the subjective video quality, mainstream video coding algorithm is used to quantify the physiological approach vision video signal to eliminate redundancy, access to more than lossless compression compression ratio but will not bring a significant reduction in video quality.

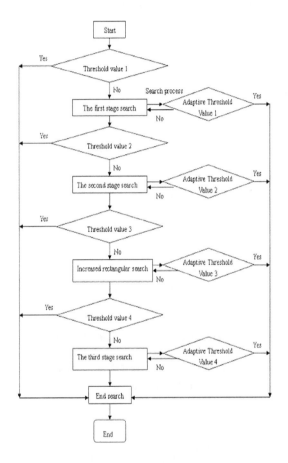

Fig. 2. Search flow chart of the improved algorithm

In this paper we improve the algorithm from two aspects:

The first aspect is after achieve the desired results, early end the search, this step we will search through every link, Adaptive threshold setting, And in the course of each search will compare value with the threshold, If the conditions are met, then the search ahead of deadline, this will greatly save the search time.

The second aspect is through the search range and methodology changes to reduce the search time, because the level of activity than the vertical image direction of activity to be a little more, and the first two phases of the search is very fast, so we will not get the first two stages where the desired results, add a large horizontal rectangle search step.

This paper proposed the improved algorithm search process shown in Fig. 2.

4   Experimental Results and Analysis

The experimental environment is: Windows XP operating system, visual C++2008 software, JM14.0 official version of H.264 encoding, and evaluation used in YUV player. The main part of the validation of the three algorithms from JM14.0: Fast full search, multi-level non-symmetrical cross hexagon search algorithm, EPZS algorithm and this "only improve the motion estimation of non-symmetrical cross search algorithm for multi-layered hexagonal" .We compared and analyzed through The validation of the coding sequence of time, motion estimation time and PSNR as the goal. As shown in table 1.

Table 1 is 4:2:0 QCIF test sequences, Time is the total time of encoding, ME is the time of motion estimation, UMHexagonS (1) is only conducted the motion estimation algorithm optimization. We can see that after motion estimation improvement, significantly improved the speed of motion estimation in encoding time has greatly improved.

After the improvement of transformation and quantization, improving the motion estimation than the effect of light is more advantageous in effect, in the following has analysis for the results, test each sequence, the results as shown in Table 2.

The table is fully optimized algorithm after the end of the test data, there has a good effect on the improvement in the time from the data. In the JM algorithm, UMHexagonS algorithm is already have a very good results, while improving the algorithm after the algorithm than the original UMHexagonS nearly 20 percent improvement. Of course, this algorithm has a larger impact on the PSNR.

Table 1. The schedule of the algorithm code

Sequence	Y(dB)	U(dB)	V(dB)	Bandwidth(kb/s)
Paris	39.70	42.15	42.31	668.35
Tempete	34.07	37.11	38.84	643.31
Mobile	31.94	34.85	34.64	668.31
Goldfish	40.59	43.46	43.46	668.36

Table 2. Total improved results

MV resolution	1/4 pel
Hadamard	ON
RD optimization	ON
Search Range	±32(QCIF,CIF), ± 64 (HDTV)
Restrict Search Range	2
Reference Frames	1
Symbol Mode	CABAC
GOP structure	IBBPBB or IPPP
IntraPeriod	10 or 0

Acknowledgment

The work is supported by the Natural Science project of Guangxi province Education Department of China under Grant Nos. 201012MS191 and the Joint Science project of Guangzhou University & Baise University under Grant Nos. GBK2010002.

References

1. Vetro, Sun, H., Wang, Y.: MPEG-4 rate control for multiple video objects. IEEE Trans. Circuit Syst. Video Technology 9, 186–199 (1999)
2. Ribas-Corbera, J., Lei, S.: Rate control in DCT video coding for low-delay communications. IEEE Trans. Circuit Syst. Video Technology 9, 172–185 (1999)
3. MPEG-2 Test Model 5, Doc. ISO/IEC JTC1/SC29 WG11/93-400 (April 1993)
4. Li, Z.G., Xiao, L., Zhu, C., Feng, P.: A Novel Rate Control Scheme for Video Over the Internet. In: Proceedings ICASSP 2002, Florida, USA, May 13-17, pp. 2065–2068 (2002)
5. Chen, C.-T.: Linear system theory and design. Rinehart and Winston, New York (1984)
6. Joint Video Team (JVT) of ISO/IEC MPEG and ITU-T VCEG Document JVT-B118R2, 2002-03-25
7. Wiegand, T., Girod, B.: Parameter Selection in Lagrangian Hybrid Video Coder Control. In: ICIP (2001)
8. Luo, J., Ahmad, I., Liang, Y., Swaminathan, V.: Motion Estimation for Content Adaptive Video Compression. IEEE Transactions On Circuits And Systems For Video Technology 18(7) (July 2008)
9. Zhang, S., Yang, F., Wang, L.: An improved classification rate of the fast motion estimation algorithm. Computer Applications 28(5) (May 2008)

Using FPGA Circuits for Implementing and Evaluating Image Processing Algorithms

Enrique Guzman, Ivan Garcia, and Manuel Manzano

Universidad Tecnológica de la Mixteca,
Carretera a Acatlima, Km. 2.5. México
{guzman,ivan,manzano}@mixteco.utm.mx
www.utm.mx

Abstract. The scientific and academic interest for image processing and analysis on autonomous systems for solving problems associated to the artificial vision, such as objects recognition, trajectory planning of robots, etc., has grown in the last years. On the other hand, the reconfigurable logic has attractive features to implement applications of artificial vision on embedded systems. In this context, this paper aims to show the design and implementation of an integral environment for implementing and evaluating algorithms for digital images processing and analysis inside a FPGA.

Keywords: Image processing and analysis, embedded systems, FPGA.

1 Introduction

The development of applications on Field Programmable Gate Array (FPGA) is a highly laborious and specialized activity performed by electronic and computer engineers using hardware description languages and vendor-specific tool flows and device interfaces. In this area, the implementing and evaluating digital image analysis algorithms with high-speed processing on FPGA technologies has rapidly become a computational paradigm of prime interest of the research community focused in the real-time image processing. These interests center on the development of techniques to implement these systems on FPGAs, where inherent advantages in cost, power, size, performance and versatility are highly attractive as compared to traditional microprocessor and ASIC technologies. Furthermore, the reconfigurable logic allows the modeling of parallel architectures that generate high processing speeds and the use of design paradigms based on software methodologies.

Some works that have relation with the development of tools focused to digital image processing using FPGA are summarized in the following. Crookes et al. presented the design of an FPGA-based Image Processing Coprocessor (IPC) with a core instruction set based on the operations of Image Algebra [1]. Also, the presented system includes a high level programming environment for the IPC, which integrates a generator which generates optimized architectures for specific user-defined operations. The SnoopP, a real-time, non-intrusive, on-chip software profiler tool for soft core processors on a reconfigurable platform is introduced by Lesley Shannon and

G. Shen and X. Huang (Eds.): CSIE 2011, Part I, CCIS 152, pp. 482–487, 2011.

Paul Chow in [2]. SnoopP is an essential tool for hardware/software co-design on a reconfigurable platform which provides a clock cycle accurate profile of the real time performance of a software program running on a soft-core processor instantiated on an FPGA. It allows the user to quickly obtain accurate profiling information that may greatly influence the partitioning of the design. In [3], Medany describes the architecture of a hardware remote laboratory based on using FPGA development boards for hardware of digital electronics circuit design. A GUI has been design using Visual Basic by which the user can easily test the designed remotely by applying forces to the design input and read the corresponding output. Seunghun Jin et al, in [4], proposes a dedicated hardware architecture FPGA-based which can assist both the mobile terminal and the remote robot by taking complete charge of the vision related tasks and thus decreasing the computational burden still to be performed. Each image processing module in the proposed architecture is based on the virtual camera configuration which enables the various connections among the processing units within the system. In [5], Jie Li et al. present a general-purpose, multi-task, and reconfigurable platform for video and image processing. The authors propose a system by using the powerful parallel processing architecture in the FPGA to achieve a software implementation to provide a real-time, low cost, high performance, and scalable hardware platform.

In this paper we present a tool focused in the implementing and evaluating image processing algorithms on FPGAs, the FPGA Tool. The remaining sections of this paper are organized as follows. Section 2 describes the design and implementation of the proposed system. The experimental results are presented in Section 3; edge detection algorithms on reconfigurable logic are evaluated. Finally, the Section 4 contains the conclusions of this paper.

2   The FPGA Tool

The basic architecture of FPGA Tool is divided into two layers and it is composed by four modules (see Fig. 1). The physical layer establishes the configuration of embedded system used to process, analyze, and retrieve information stored in a memory system. The layer is composed by the following modules:

- *The FPGA's specific application architecture modeling:* This module follows a descendent methodology for designing and modeling a basic structure of specific application architecture, called Hardware Applications Manager (HAM).
- *Embedded systems construction:* Using the SPIES method, an embedded system is constructed using the FPGA's HAM modeling. The HAM modeling and the embedded system are designed to allow to add new peripheral to the system and to facilitate the integration of new algorithms to the architecture.
- *The Integration method:* This module provides the capability for integrating new algorithms for processing and/or analyzing to HAM architecture and enables its evaluation. The module incorporates an integration method that establishes the activities sequence to specify, integrate and evaluate the performance of a new algorithm.

The logical layer allows to select the image that will be processed, to send it to embedded system and enables visualization of images processed inside the images processor. The layer is composed by the following module:

- *User interface design:* All the processing work inside the FPGA is showed by the user interface separating the algorithms parameters from processed images.

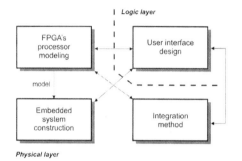

Fig. 1. Modules of FPGA Tool

To make possible the implementation of the image processing tool it was used a FPGA Spartan 3E-500 from Xilinx Company. This FPGA is used to store the image processing algorithms modeled by user. Fig. 2 shows the block diagram of the proposed tool and describes each component.

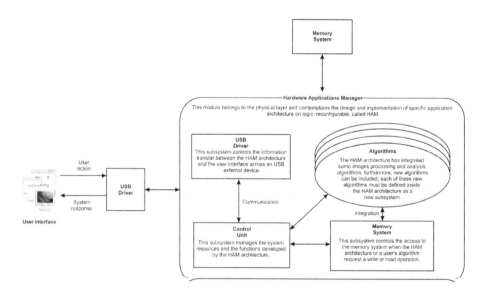

Fig. 2. Architecture of FPGA Tool

In the design of this module the top-down methodology was used and its modeling follow the structural description using VHDL language; the HAM modeling does not consider to the FPGA architecture where it will be implemented, due to this fact the HAM modeling is portable, it can be implemented in any technology FPGA whose design tool supports the VHDL standard. In the HAM architecture implementation, the board Nexys 2 and Xilinx ISE Foundation 8.2i EDA tools was used. The Nexys 2 board was designed by Digital Inc. Company and it is based on Xilinx FPGA Spartan 3E-500. The Xilinx ISE Foundation is an integrated software environment used in the digital systems design.

FPGA tool was developed concurrently with the hardware and other components of the product in the Product Development phase of the SPIES method [6]. Development processes specification belongs to engineering process field of TSP [7] and process areas from Level 2 of CMMI-DEV v1.2 [8]. Engineering process field is usually related to requirement development, technical solutions, etc. Therefore, SPIES provides concrete technical development specification for embedded applications that includes templates and guidelines. In addition, besides software processes, hardware related processes are emphasized here. Using SPIES and the HAM architecture as central element, an embedded system focused to digital image processing and analysis is constructed; it represent the second module of our tool, called Embedded systems construction. In this context, the FPGA tool' interface was developed using the VY method proposed in [9]. The VY method modifies the traditional way of GUI development for embedded applications by adding a simulator. The simulator was designed to simulate the graphic functions and processing algorithms into the HAM architecture; in addition a graphic interface which is implemented by Graphical Device Interface on PC was developed. The logic part of GUI includes focusing, state transaction, and user functions. The simulator was implemented on the FPGA including image processing algorithms. The second important feature of the simulator is the mechanism of the message-driven process. The processes are always waiting for selection of processing algorithms from the user, and when received, the image is stored in memory.

The integration method module on physical layer establishes a sequence of procedures that enables the implementation and performance evaluation of an algorithm over the FPGA. With the integration of this module into the system, a tool for design is obtained for pre visualizing the results of use an algorithm before its final application. Thus, the development cycle for image processing software is considerably reduced.

3 Experimental Results

This section shows how to integrate a new algorithm to the proposed tool; also, the results of its evaluation using the user interface are presented. Two edge detection algorithms, using Sobel and Roberts operator, are integrated to the tool. The edge detection is a technique that provides an indication of the physical extent of objects within the image based on changes or discontinuities in an image amplitude attribute such as luminance or tri-stimulus value [10]. The integration of these algorithms to the proposed tool it is done by means of the integration method exhibited in Fig. 1 and presented as follows:

Phase 1. Algorithm analysis and specification. The specifications to consider for the algorithms integration are the following ones:

- Two edge detection algorithms will be evaluated.
- Grayscale images will be processed.
- The processing results are 3 new images with the same number of elements as original: horizontal and vertical differencing gradients and edge image.
- The memory system space used to store the original image is 0x000000-0x00FFFF and the obtained results will be stored from loc. 0x010000.
- Parameters to consider in the edge algorithms: used operator, Sobel o Roberts and the threshold.

Phase 2. Integrated conceptual design. In this phase, the conceptual design of the algorithms, inside of the HAM architecture and its corresponding GUI are developed. Also, with the information spilled in the specifications the communications protocol packages are formed. The following steps are performed:

- Conceptual design of the edge detection algorithms.
- Conceptual design of the edge detection algorithms user interface.
- Packages definition: send image package, implement algorithm package and results package.

Phase 3. Parallel implementation. Based on conceptual design, defined in the Phase 2, in this phase the modeling of the edge detection algorithms and its adaptation to the user's interface are implemented. The edge detection algorithms interface is developed and adapted to the user's interface following the VY method; the edge detection algorithms interface is a Single Document Interface (SDI) application contained in the user's interface and accessible across its principal menu.

Phase 4. Component integration. When the user's interface has been modified and adapted for the visualization of the edge detection results in a new SDI application and a new version of the HAM architecture, which includes to the edge detection algorithms, has been programmed in the FPGA, both components are integrated to evaluate the new version of the FPGA Tool.

Phase 5. Edge detection algorithms evaluation. Fig. 3 shows the results obtained when our FPGA Tool applied the edge algorithms on 8 bits/pixel grayscale Lena image with size 256x256. The results showed in this figure coincide with the theory; therefore, the incorporation of the edge algorithms to our tool has been successful.

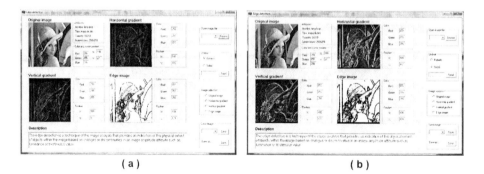

(a)   (b)

Fig. 3. Edge detection algorithms interface, (a) Roberts operator and (b) Sobel operator

4 Conclusions

The main goal of our tool is to make more agile the design, modeling and evaluation of an algorithm inside the FPGA and visualize the obtained results before that the implementation occurs. The proposed tool in this paper has been used to evaluate diverse algorithms of images processing and analysis showing a high efficiency.

The FPGA tool was divided in four modules. The first module designs a specific application architecture using a hardware description language. Another module uses the designed architecture for designing a hardware system using the SPIES development method. A third module develops a GUI to interact with the embedded system and show the obtained results for processing images with an algorithm inside a FPGA. A last module enables the user to implement and integrate images processing/analysis algorithms through the developed tool. We believe that the FPGA tool can be used for academic and research interests with a high level of success.

References

1. Benkrid, K., Crookes, D., Smith, J., Benkrid, A.: High Level Programming for Real Time FPGA Based Video Processing. In: IEEE International Conference on Acoustics, Speech and Signal Processing, pp. 3227–3230. IEEE Press, Istanbul (2000)
2. Shannon, L., Chow, P.: Using Reconfigurability to Achieve Real-Time Profiling for Hardware/Software Codesign. In: International Symposium on Field Programmable Gate Arrays, pp. 190–199. ACM, California (2004)
3. El Medany, W.: FPGA Remote Laboratory for Hardware E-Learning Course. In: International Conference on Computational Technologies in Electrical and Electronics Engineering, pp. 106–109. IEEE Press, Novosibirsk (2008)
4. Seunghun, J., Dongkyun, K., Xuan, D., Jae, W.: FPGA-based Image Processing System for Remote Robot Control. In: International Conference on Robotics and Biomimetics, pp. 120–124. IEEE Press, Guilin (2009)
5. Li, J., He, H., Man, H., Desai, S.: A General-Purpose FPGA-Based Reconfigurable Platform for Video and Image Processing. In: Yu, W., He, H., Zhang, N. (eds.) ISNN 2009. LNCS, vol. 5553, pp. 299–309. Springer, Heidelberg (2009)
6. Garcia, I., Pacheco, C., Herrera, A.: Defining a Software Process Improvement-based Methodology for Embedded Systems Development. In: Electronics, Robotics, Automotive Mechanics Conference, pp. 120–125. IEEE Press, México (2010)
7. Humphrey, W.: Introduction to Team Software Process. Addison-Wesley, Reading (2000)
8. CMMI Product Team. CMMI for Development (CMMI-DEV, V1.2). CMU/SEI-2006 TR-008, Software Engineering Institute, Carnegie Mellon University (2006)
9. Yang, L., Choi, Y., Seo, C., Yang, T., Kim, M.: Design of VY: A Mini Visual IDE for the Development of GUI in Embedded Devices. In: Fifth International Conference on Software Engineering Research, Management and Applications, pp. 625–632. IEEE Press, Montreal-Canada (2007)
10. Pratt, W.K.: Digital Image Processing. John Wiley & Sons, New York (2001)

Research on the Reliable Video Multicast Based on Wireless Ad Hoc Networks

Zhanwei Chen and Wenhuan Wu

Department of Computer Science, Zhoukou Nomal University,
Zhoukou 466001, China
chenzhanwei@zknu.edu.cn, wuwenhuan15@163.com

Abstract. A new method for the reliable video multicast communication is presented by the study of the communicating technique based on wireless ad hoc networks. In the method, the network layer adopts the on-demand multicast routing protocol, and the application layer combines the Forward Error Correction with Automatic Repeat Request to effectively control errors, so it can provide the reliable data transmission of the wireless video multicast with almost no affecting the system performance. The simulation results show the effectiveness of the method.

Keywords: Ad hoc; reliable video multicast; error control; ODMRP.

1 Introduction

The meaning of the reliability of video multicast is to ensure that the data packet can be correctly sent to the group members by the sender, thus, it is necessary to control errors. In addition, for the network availability, we have to provide relevant mechanisms to avoid network congestion. Therefore, reliable video multicast includes technology of video multicast, error control and congestion control. The author has descried the technology and its realization of multicast of video in reference [1]. Congestion control is usually researched as a separate problem, so the study of reliability of video multicast is limited to the error control in this paper.

2 Reliable Video Multicast Technique

2.1 The Error Control of Multicast Video

The error control of the application of multicast video includes two aspects: error detection and error recovery. The former is to discover loss, while the latter is to retransmit the loss. In each aspect, two questions should be made clear▯ how and by whom to detect error and how and by whom to recover error.

(1) Error Detection

The implementation patterns of error detection is that when the receiver found the sequence number of received data packet is not continuous, it is believed to be the packet loss. The time for detecting the packet loss in this pattern is relatively short,

G. Shen and X. Huang (Eds.): CSIE 2011, Part I, CCIS 152, pp. 488–493, 2011.

unless there is continuous or explosive packet loss, so it is unpredictable for the next data packet. To judge the expected data packet is lost or not we should set a random timer.

The receiver is responsible for detection, when the timer times out or receives the sequence number of packet is not continuous, the receiver is sure that something wrong occurred and sends NAK(Negative Acknowledgement). Based on the receiver's strategy, the sender has no status change, and is in a good performance in the maximum throughput.

(2) Error Recovery

The cost for the transmission of the video multicast is generally higher, because the retransmitting data packets have been correctly received last time by most of recervers. Another approach is to multicast within a certain range according to the scale of error occurred (percentage). Who completes retransmission may be the sender, a recipient or a special representative. The sender is responsible for a kind of recovery which is called centralized recovery. The other is known as distributed recovery. Distributed recovery is further divided into local recovery and global recovery. The former retransmit in the local group with the packet loss, the latter can retransmit with any correctly received point. With the combination of error detection and error recovery, the mechanism of controlling error can be achieved in the application layer.

2.2   Video Multicast Reliability

Error control is a combination of ARQ (Automatic Repeat request) and FEC (Forward Error Correction).ARQ ensures the reliability of data transmission by sending feedback-including ACK(Positive Acknowledgement)and NAK(Negative Acknowledgement).when receives the package, the recipient will send ACK to confirm; when detects packet loss, it will send NAK to require retransmission.

Through sending redundancy check data in advance, FEC can ensure error control-a proactive mechanism. As long as the receiver receives sufficient number of packets, reconstruction of data is possible. For example, h packets and k parity packets encoded into n packets ($n = k + h$), if any k packets are received, then the original data packets can be rebuilt. Common are the Reed-Solomon Erasure (FEC encoding and decoding modes are shown in Figure 1). In short, because FEC reduces data loss by sending redundancy check data, the time delay is reduced and the handling of feedback is simple. However, due to not using feedback information, the reliability can not be ensured. In addition, when network traffic conditions are better, redundant data is a waste of bandwidth.

Hybrid error control is a combination of these two ways. FEC reduces the data error rate, but does not have data retransmission mechanism, when the network connection quality is below a certain threshold, FEC can not provide full reliability, so ARQ is added into FEC to accomplish data retransmission. On the other hand, though the reliability of ARQ is better, more delay is needed when resend the loss data. Data retransmission of ARQ can decrease by inducting FEC and check codes. Through integrating FEC and ARQ, the number of retransmissions is reduced, bandwidth utilization is improved and the error control become more robust and have good extensibility.

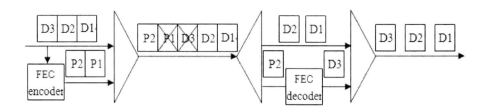

Fig. 1. FEC encoding and decoding modes

3 ODMRP Protocol in Ad Hoc network

ODMRP is a multicast routing protocol using on-demand routing technique. This technique effectively reduces the load of protocol control packets of network channel, improves channel utilization. On-demand multicast routing protocol is very suitable for multi-hop wireless Ad hoc network, so the development and improvement ODMRP is be of great importance for large-scale application of Ad hoc networks.

3.1 ODMRP Routing Mechanism

In ODMRP, group membership and multicast routes are established by the source node and updated as needed. When a multicast source has data to send, it broadcast a member advertising package called JOIN QUERY to the entire network to update information and routing. Figure 2 shows a example about forwarding process of JOIN REPLY. Node S1 and S2 are multicast sources, nodes R1, R2, and R3 are multicast recipients.R2 and R3 send their JOIN REPLIES to S1 and S2 through I2. R1 sends its JOIN REPLY to S1 through I1, to S2 through I2. When the recipients send their JOIN REPLIES to hop neighbor nodes, intermediate node I1 is set as transmit group status and establishes its own JOIN REPLY because ID of the next node in the JOIN RE-PLY that R1 received is in line with its own ID.

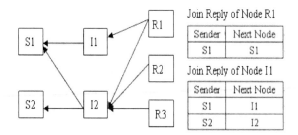

Fig. 2. Forwarding process of JOIN REPLY

3.2 Reliability analysis of ODMRP

Reliable transmission of JOIN REPLIES is significant in establishing and updating multicast routing and distributing group. Therefore, if it is sent incorrectly, JOIN

REPLIES can not implement effective multicast routing through ODMRP. In figure 2, once I1 and I2 received JOIN REPLY from R1, they will build and send forwards their own JOIN REPLY to the next hop. Sending their own JOIN REPLY, the nodes I1 and I2 may overlap with each other. I1 and I2 will maintain properly for the characteristics of CSMA when they are in the receiving range. However, if I1 and I2 are out of their receiving range, they will not recognize the hidden terminal condition and then R1 can not receive passive confirmation of overlap. Thus, a node may not receive its upstream neighbors' passive confirmation because of the hidden terminal conflicts. The node can not receive the passive confirmation even though it remove the hidden terminal conflicts. The node will retransmit information when it can not be received in any cases overtime.

If the packet can not be confirmed after sending a certain number of transmissions, the node believes the routing is invalid. At this time, the most likely reason is that one of the nodes has failed or was removed, so the routing must be changed. Therefore, the node broadcasts a message to some neighbors in order to declare that the following node of some sources can not reach. After receiving this packet, each neighbor node will create and unicast JOIN REPLY to its next hop if there is a route to the multicast source; If there is no route, its simple broadcasting package will present to show the next hop is unreachable. In both cases, the node sets its FG_FLAG. In the actual implementation, the redundant path can build the alternative path until a more effective routing was established in the next updating phases. FG_FLAG of each neighbor can create more redundancy, but most of these settings will be invalidated because the only necessary forwarding group nodes will be updated in the next JOIN REPLY's sending stage.

4   Reliable Video Multicast Protocol Based on Ad Hoc

The reliable communication of Ad hoc networks is guaranteed by network protocols. Multicast fault-tolerant technology is applied to the network layer and application layer of network protocols. Since the main function of network layer is routing, the research and implementation of fault-tolerant routing is the core problem. And application Layer is focus on the combined application of FEC and ARQ.

4.1   The Realization of FEC and ARQ on Application Layer

As an independent layer, FEC layer, which is under the ARQ layer, receives data from the ARQ layer, and cuts them into original data units, then generates parity data based on these data and multicasts the final data packages(FEC blocks) to the group receivers.

If the packages received are too few to rebuild data, Receiver will discards the parity data received, and requests the sender to retransmit. FEC is transparent to ARQ, ARQ protocol only see a significant reduction in transmission error. This transparency can improve the performance of ARQ. In addition, FEC-based erasure codes can be used in FEC layer to ensure the reliable transmission of data in real time.

4.2 The Reliable Video Multicast Data Distribution Protocol

In the Ad hoc network, when a source node needs to send information, it has to firstly establish a routing to the destination node in multicast working group. It launches a route discovery process, and sets up a path to the destination node. ARQ layer generates data, and then passes them to FEC layer. FEC layer cuts them into original data units, and generates parity data based on these data units using FEC coding, then multicasts the final data packages(FEC blocks) to the group receivers. FEC coding is very effective, even if a few of packets is lost because of the wireless link, the receiver can still be able to recover data, which can guarantee the accuracy of the received information.

Even so, if there is still a number of receivers can not rebuild data because the packages they received is small,they can discard the check data received and send NAK to the sender for retransmission. The missing data will be sent in next FEC block using unicast ARQ retransmission mechanism. When the packet loss rate is not high, this approach ensures that most of the receiver can receive data correctly without retransmission.

5   Simulation Experiments of Protocol Module

The establishment of complete protocol simulation model consists of several parts of modules, including the routing module and error control module in the application layer. The purpose of this simulation is to compare the performance of error control, so error control module in application layer is simulated. In the experiment, we choose a typical simple data transmission and the most simple multicast which consists of three nodes in Ad hoc network. Using strong interference on part of the network to verify the error control performance of the algorithm when these nodes receiving packages. Performance parameters are described in Table 1.

Modeling steps:

(1) Defines the package structure. Create a new package format, edit the package properties, set the destination address.
(2) Defines the link model.
(3) Establish the node processing model. Node records the end to end delay of package.
(4) Establish network model.

Table 1. Performance parameters

Parameters(symbol)	value
Network coverage(L×L)	100m×100m
Network nodes(n)	3
Node movement speed(v)	1m/s
Wireless transmission range of node(r)	200m
Simulation time(t)	300s

From the simulation results, we can found that when packet loss rate of partial channel is high, protocol error control mechanism can improve the packet delivery rate, fully guarantee reliable transmission of data. By comparison, the error control algorithm for application layer has played an effective role in error control. When there is a strong interference in the channel, it can still maintain high delivery ratio of data packet. The method has good performance on the fault-tolerant and its delay is kept in the relatively stable range.

6 Conclusion

The method of reliable video multicast presented in this paper can ensure the reliability of video data transmission in terms of error control. It can be used in remote education, video conferencing, teaching and experiments, and provide a certain reference value for distributed management, coordinated computing and distributed software.

The video multicast protocols are related to its application fields, and in the wireless environment the mobile nodes are different in mobile speed, energy, processor performance, storage capacity etc. and the wireless network are also different in bandwidth and reliability. Therefore, the fault tolerant algorithms and protocols of the mobile multicast also need more in-depth research.

Acknowledgment

This paper is supported by the Scientific and Technological Project of the Educational Department of Henan Province in China(Grant No. 2011B520042).

References

1. Lee, S.J., Su, W., Gerla, M.: On-Demand Multicast Routing Protocol in Multihop Wireless Mobile Networks. Mobile Networks and Applications 7(6), 1298–1302 (2002)
2. Mao, S., Lin, S., Wang, Y., et al.: Multipath Video transport over Ad Hoc Networks. IEEE Wireless Communications 12(4), 42–49 (2005)
3. Wei, W., Zakhor, A.: Mulipath unicast and multicast video communication over wireless Ad Hoc networks. In: Proceedings of BROADNETS, pp. 496–505. IEEE Press, New York (2004)
4. Chee-Onn, C., Hiroshi, I.: Multiple tree multicast Ad Hocon-demand distance vector(MT-MAODV)routing protocol forvideo multicast over mobile Ad Hoc networks. IEICE Transactions on Communications, 428–436 (2008)
5. Yeo, C.K., Lee, B.S., Er, M.H.: A survey of application level multicast techniques. Computer Communications 27(15), 1547–1568 (2004)
6. Chen, Z., Li, Q.: Research and Realization of video Multicast in the Wireless LAN. Journal of Harbin University of Science and Technology 14(6), 33–37 (2009) (in Chinese)

Leveraging Tradeoff on Resource Utilization and Application Performance in Virtualized Systems

Ritai Yu, Congfeng Jiang, Xianghua Xu, Hui Cheng, and Jian Wan

Grid and Service Computing Technology Lab,
Hangzhou Dianzi University Hangzhou 310037, China
{yrt,cjiang,xhxu,wanjian}@hdu.edu.cn
chenghui2050@gmail.com

Abstract. In virtualized systems, such as large data centers and cloud computing environments, resources are shared across multiple virtual machines, which results in contentions and conflicting under heavily loaded or consolidated situations. In order to accommodate as many as computing and service capabilities while still delivering performance guarantees, resource utilization and application performance should be tradeoffed such that fewer resources will be utilized for a specific performance requirement. To achieve this goal, in this paper we propose an adaptive resource allocation for tradeoff between resource utilization and upper level application's performance such as response time and throughput. This approach does not require a highly accurate performance model in a virtualized system where workloads usually change frequently with time in some intervals. Experiments on a Xen based virtualized environment are conducted and evaluated. The results show that the proposed approach utilizes less CPU resources to achieve the same performance goals compared to the fixed over-provisioning of resources.

Keywords: virtualization; thin provisioning; resource allocation; performance feedback.

1 Introduction

Virtualization has become a rapidly growing solution for modern computing systems, especially in large scale data centers and the emerging cloud computing infrastructures. In virtualized environments, consolidated servers run components and services continuously, such as Web and e-commerce applications sharing the same physical resources. In this kind of consolidated system, resources are shared across multiple virtual machines and instances, which results in the contentions and conflicting under heavily loaded or consolidated situations. In order to maximize the resource revenue and to accommodate as many as service instances while still delivering performance guarantees, resource utilization of a dedicated virtual machines should be minimized and the saved resources are restored into a resource pool for future use, either for new coming requests or new service instances, or just for energy saving purpose. Therefore, resource utilization and application performance should be tradeoffed such that fewer resources will be utilized for a specific performance requirement of individual virtual machines (VMs).

G. Shen and X. Huang (Eds.): CSIE 2011, Part I, CCIS 152, pp. 494–499, 2011.

In order to allocate CPU, memory, and disk I/O resource properly and to provide adequate application performance guarantees efficiently, the following challenges must be addressed, such as automation, adaptation and system scalability. All these challenges make it impossible to directly apply traditional resource allocation techniques to the virtualization environment without modification. And these challenges then become the problem how to tradeoff between the resource utilization and applications performance. For example, how to meet the Service Level Agreements (SLAs) requirements, how to maximize resource revenue and to minimize resource consumption, etc [1].

In our approach, the virtual machine monitor (VMM) is responsible for allocating resources such as CPU slices, memory capacities, and disk and network I/O bandwidth. In runtime, resource allocation decisions are automated based on the performance feedback of dedicated VMs. In our approach, once the allocation is made, the resulted specific performance can be measured using application-specific performance metrics such as response time and/or throughput, to aid for the next allocation decision, i.e., the next cycle of resource allocation. Since the resource allocation decision is made only based on the estimation that the expected allocation can provide performance improvement when resource demand is increasing, it does not require much highly accurate knowledge about the relationship between application performance and resource allocation.

The remainder of this paper is organized as follows: In section 2, we review some related work. In section 3, we propose the allocation model and describe its mechanism for resource allocation. In section 4, we evaluate the algorithm in experiments, and make performance analysis. Finally we conclude our contribution in section 5.

2   Related Work

In a virtualized environment, physical resources are multiplexed and applications and operating systems are sand-boxed. Thus, the data center administrators and the VMM have little or even no knowledge about them, which makes application or VM aware models unusable. Therefore, the resource competition and conflicting by VMs can compromise the accuracy of isolated application models. Thus, researchers use performance modeling techniques for workload characterization [2,3,4,5]. For instance, Kundu et al [2] demonstrated that conventional linear regression fail to adequately model virtualized applications and proposed an artificial neural network (ANN) model combined with a custom training process to predict virtualized application performance.

While the above architecture-specific and performance-counters based models have the potential to provide more precise predictions for a single application, they are difficult to train and hard to use. These application and domain-specific approaches are only suitable for a specific model of the application or the deployment platform and hard to apply to applications running inside multiple VMs running on a shared hardware. Moreover, some of the above techniques is only suitable for the CPU-intensive applications and can only model the CPU resource consumption alone. In contrast, we outline the CPU, memory, and I/O resource as main resource and this simple coarse-grained view of a virtualized system's resources can provide adequate control accuracy.

VMware proposed a memory ballooning method [6] provides a way of controlling the memory allocation to a VM. However, the ballooning algorithm does not know about the upper application goals or multiple tiers, and only uses the memory pressure as seen by the operating system. In this paper, we consider a virtualized platform with identical servers and the resource allocator controls the services sharing among one or multiple VM instances and ensures that requests to the services are dispatched to appropriate undertaking servers. We assume that precise sharing of hardware resources among VM instances, such as CPU slices, RAM space, and disk space can be obtained via VMM mitigating and arbitrary sharing.

Some facilities have been developed to profile and monitor the VM instances such as the XenMon [7], xenoprof[8]. There are also some implementations for monitoring and profiling VMs, such as *xentop*, *xentrace*, *xenstat*, these are Xen version of the original Linux command. In the context of security, the behavior of VMs can also be discovered via a combination of introspection and configuration variation [9, 10].

3 Resource Allocation Based on VM Performance Feedback

In this paper, we argue that the ultimate goal of resource allocation in virtualized environment is to provide predefined desirable performance guarantees with minimal resource utilization including CPU cycles, memory capacities, disk or network band width, and energy. To achieve this goal, we first develop a two-level resource allocation framework, as illustrated in Fig.1.

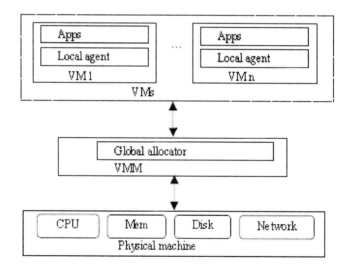

Fig. 1. The two-level resource allocation framework

Our resource allocation framework consists of two key parts, i.e., the local allocator agent within individual VM and the global allocator within the VMM. The local allocator agent consists of coarse grained workload characterization and estimation module that automatically determines the amount of resources necessary to achieve individual application performance requirements. The global allocator detects resource bottlenecks on the shared physical servers and properly allocates resources of multiple types to individual VMs and their applications. In contending cases, the global allocator can provide service differentiation by prioritizing allocation among different VMs. Based on this two level allocator framework, tradeoff between resource utilization and performance guarantees are accomplished.

In our approach, the resource demand only is satisfied when the allocation can make the system performance better, for example, to make the resource available earlier, or to make the workload finished earlier. Here we use a simple performance feedback approach to regulate the amount of resource allocation. For example, if the performance is improved after the previous allocation of the resource, the next allocation amount will be added with a specific amount. It is same when we need to reduce the resource allocation to a specific VM and restore the resources to the resource pool.

The pseudo codes of the allocation amount adaptation are listed as follows:

Amount adaptation for resource allocation
```
for every VM
for every kind of resource
  if resource allocation is increasing
      if the performance is improving
         increase allocation amount
  else
      if the performance is not changing
      decrease allocation amount
```

4 Experiments and Performance Analysis

In order to evaluate our proposed approach, we conducted experiments with a combination of random and sequential workloads sharing the same physical devices. To identify the beneficial of our approach, the investigated workloads include RUBiS [11], an FTP application and a customized prime number computation program. All these applications contain CPU, memory and disk IO requests which can be split into various components such as data access, index access, log writing, etc.

All the experiments were conducted on two physical servers, one is the server and the other is the client. We developed a program to capture the performance parameters and to examine the behavior of several benchmark applications in a virtualized environment. In our implementation, the testing clients connected to the VMs via a LAN cable. The allocator collected application performance statistics within the hosted Dom0 and from the client. The memory allocated to the VM is 600MB, 500MB, and 400MB respectively. To implement the allocator's allocation decision, we use Xen's credit-based CPU scheduler which allows each domain (or VM) to be assigned a cap. We used the cap to specify a CPU slice sharing for each VM to provide better performance isolation among applications running in different VMs. In this section, we present the performance results from these experiments that demonstrate the effectiveness of the thin provisioning approach. All the experiment results are listed in the followings tables.

Table 1. Average throughput of experiments (req/s)

Statistics	600MB	500MB	400MB
up ramp	42	40	37
runtime session	40	39	40
down ramp	25	40	43
overall	40	40	40

Table 2. Average time of experiments(ms)

Statistics	600MB	500MB	400MB
up ramp	5519	5836	6331
runtime session	5895	6022	5915
down ramp	9121	5936	5686
overall	5982	5991	5939

The first goal of our allocator is to detect and mitigate resource bottlenecks in multiple resources and across multiple application tiers. And from the results we can see that for different types of bottlenecks and applications, our allocation approach can automatically identify resource bottlenecks and allocate the proper amount of resources to each VM such that all the VMs can meet their performance targets if possible. This occurs and for bottlenecks across multiple tiers of an application. When we mix all the applications simultaneously, the performance degrades with respond to the resource contention, but the degradation is acceptable. For example, in the prime number computation application, the execution time reduced as the CPU contention was decreased, almost proportionately.

5 Conclusion

In data centers, virtualization provides the opportunity of carving individual physical servers into multiple virtual containers that can be run and managed separately. A key challenge is the simultaneous on-demand provisioning of shared resources to virtual containers and the management of their capacities to meet service quality targets at the least cost. Making resource allocations in such environments is an active area of research. We have shown an example environment for tradeoffing between the resource allocation and application performance. Our work is very helpful in enabling users to generate realistic impressions of real workloads for their research. And we believe that the proposed scheme and techniques are useful for resource allocation among multiple VMs in virtualization environments.

Acknowledgements

The funding supports of this work by Natural Science Fund of China (No. 61003077,60873023 and 60973029), State Key Development Program of Basic Research of China (No. 2007CB310906), Technology Research and Development Program of Zhejiang Province, China (No. 2009C31033, 2009C31046), Natural Science Fund of Zhejiang Province (No.Y1090940, Y1101092, Y1101104), and Research Fund of Department of Education of Zhejiang Province (No. GK100800010) are greatly appreciated.

References

1. Carrera, D., Steinder, M., Whalley, I., Torres, J., Ayguade, E.: Utility based placement of dynamic web applications with fairness goals. In: Proceedings of 2008 IEEE Network Operations and Management Symposium (NOMS 2008), pp. 9–16 (2008)
2. Kundu, S., Rangaswami, R., Dutta, K., Zhao, M.: Application Performance Modeling in a Virtualized Environment. In: Proceedings of 2010 IEEE 16th International Symposium on High Performance Computer Architecture (HPCA 2010), pp. 1–10 (January 2010)
3. Wood, T., Cherkasova, L., Ozonat, K., Shenoy, P.: Profiling and modeling resource usage of virtualized applications. In: Proceedings of the 9th ACM/IFIP/USENIX International Conference on Middleware (Middleware 2008) (2008)
4. Padala, P., Shin, K.G., Zhu, X., Uysal, M., Wang, Z., Singhal, S., Merchant, A., Salem, K.: Adaptive control of virtualized resources in utility computing environments. In: Proceedings of the 2nd ACM SIGOPS/EuroSys European Conference on Computer Systems (EuorSys 2007), pp. 289–302 (2007)
5. Stewart, C., Kelly, T., Zhang, A., Shen, K.: A dollar from15 cents: Cross-platform management for internet services. In: Proceedings of the USENIX Annual Techinal Conference (USENIX ATC 2008), pp.199–212 (2008)
6. Waldspurger, C.: Memory resource management in VMware ESX server. In: Proceedings of Symposium on Operating Systems Design and Implementation, OSDI 2002 (2002)
7. Gupta, D., Gardner, R., Cherkasova, L.: XenMon: QoS Monitoring and Performance Profiling Tool. Technical Report HPL-2005-187, Hewlett-Packard Labs (2005), http://www.hpl.hp.com/techreports/2005/HPL-2005-187.html
8. Xenoprof - System-wide profiler for Xen VM, http://xenoprof.sourceforge.net/
9. Jones, S. T., Arpaci-Dusseau, A. C., Arpaci-Dusseau, R. H.: Antfarm: Tracking Processes in a Virtual Machine Environment. In: Proc. of the USENIX Annual Technical Conference (USENIX ATC 2006) (June 2006)
10. Jones, S.T., Arpaci-Dusseau, A.C., Arpaci-Dusseau, R.H.: Geiger: Monitoring the Buffer Cache in a Virtual Machine Environment. In: Proceedings of Architectural Support for Programming Languages and Operating Systems, ASPLO 2006 (October 2006)
11. Amza, C., Ch, A., Cox, A., Elnikety, S., Gil, R., Rajamani, K., Cecchet, E., Marguerite, J.: Specification and implementation of dynamic Web site benchmarks. In: Proceedings of IEEE 5th Annual Workshop on Workload Characterization, IISWC 2002 (2002)

Author Index